Artificial Intelligence for Advanced Problem Solving Techniques

Dimitris Vrakas
Aristotle University, Greece

Ioannis PL. Vlahavas
Aristotle University, Greece

T0325011

Information Science
REFERENCE

INFORMATION SCIENCE REFERENCE

Hershey · New York

Acquisitions Editor:	Kristin Klinger
Development Editor:	Kristin M. Roth
Assistant Development Editor:	Meg Stocking
Editorial Assistant:	Deborah Yahnke
Senior Managing Editor:	Jennifer Neidig
Managing Editor:	Sara Reed
Copy Editor:	Jeannie Porter
Typesetter:	Michael Brehm
Cover Design:	Lisa Tosheff
Printed at:	Yurchak Printing Inc.

Published in the United States of America by
Information Science Reference (an imprint of IGI Global)
701 E. Chocolate Avenue, Suite 200
Hershey PA 17033
Tel: 717-533-8845
Fax: 717-533-8661
E-mail: cust@igi-global.com
Web site: http://www.igi-global.com

and in the United Kingdom by
Information Science Reference (an imprint of IGI Global)
3 Henrietta Street
Covent Garden
London WC2E 8LU
Tel: 44 20 7240 0856
Fax: 44 20 7379 0609
Web site: http://www.eurospanonline.com

Library of Congress Cataloging-in-Publication Data

Artificial intelligence for advanced problem solving techniques / Dimitris Vrakas and Ioannis PL. Vlahavas, editors.
        p. cm.
  Summary: "This book offers scholars and practitioners cutting-edge research on algorithms and techniques such as search, domain independent heuristics, scheduling, constraint satisfaction, optimization, configuration, and planning, and highlights the relationship between the search categories and the various ways a specific application can be modeled and solved using advanced problem solving techniques"--Provided by publisher.
  Includes bibliographical references and index.
  ISBN-13: 978-1-59904-705-8 (hardcover)
  ISBN-13: 978-1-59904-707-2 (ebook)
  1. Artificial intelligence--Data processing. I. Vrakas, Dimitris, 1977- II. Vlahavas, Ioannis.
  Q336.A77 2008
  006.3'33--dc22
                    2007032031

British Cataloguing in Publication Data
A Cataloguing in Publication record for this book is available from the British Library.

All work contributed to this book set is original material. The views expressed in this book are those of the authors, but not necessarily of the publisher.

Table of Contents

Preface xi

Acknowledgment xvii

Section I
Automated Planning

Chapter I
Multi-Vehicle Missions: Architecture and Algorithms for Distributed Online Planning /
Johan Baltié, Eric Bensana, Patrick Fabiani, Jean-Loup Farges, Stéphane Millet,
Philippe Morignot, Bruno Patin, Gérald Petitjean, Gauthier Pitois, and Jean-Clair Poncet 1

Chapter II
Extending Classical Planning for Time: Research Trends in Optimal and Suboptimal
Temporal Planning / *Antonio Garrido and Eva Onaindia* 23

Section II
Constraint Satisfaction and Scheduling

Chapter III
Principles of Constraint Processing / *Roman Barták* 63

Chapter IV
Stratified Constraint Satisfaction Networks in Synergetic Multi-Agent
Simulations of Language Evolution / *Alexander Mehler* 107

Chapter V
Soft-Constrained Linear Programming Support Vector Regression for Nonlinear
Black-Box Systems Identification / *Zhao Lu and Jing Sun* 137

Section III
Machine Learning

Chapter VI
Reinforcement Learning and Automated Planning: A Survey /
Ioannis Partalas, Dimitris Vrakas, and Ioannis Vlahavas 148

Chapter VII
Induction as a Search Procedure / *Stasinos Konstantopoulos, Rui Camacho,*
Nuno A. Fonseca, and Vítor Santos Costa 166

Chapter VIII
Single- and Multi-Order Neurons for Recursive Unsupervised Learning /
Kiruthika Ramanathan and Sheng Uei Guan 217

Section IV
Optimization

Chapter IX
Optimising Object Classification: Uncertain Reasoning-Based Analysis Using CaRBS
Systematic Search Algorithms / *Malcolm J. Beynon* 234

Chapter X
Application of Fuzzy Optimization in Forecasting and Planning of Construction Industry /
P. Vasant, N. Barsoum, C. Kahraman, and G. M. Dimirovski 254

Chapter XI
Rank Improvement Optimization Using PROMETHEE and Trigonometric
Differential Evolution / *Malcolm J. Beynon* 266

Section V
Genetic Algorithms and Programming

Chapter XII
Parallelizing Genetic Algorithms: A Case Study / *Iker Gondra* 284

Chapter XIII
Using Genetic Programming to Extract Knowledge from Artificial Neural Networks /
Daniel Rivero, Miguel Varela, and Javier Pereira 308

Compilation of References 328

About the Contributors 359

Index 366

Detailed Table of Contents

Preface xi

Acknowledgment xvii

Section I
Automated Planning

Chapter I

Multi-Vehicle Missions: Architecture and Algorithms for Distributed Online Planning /
Johan Baltié, Eric Bensana, Patrick Fabiani, Jean-Loup Farges, Stéphane Millet,
Philippe Morignot, Bruno Patin, Gérald Petitjean, Gauthier Pitois, and Jean-Clair Poncet 1

This chapter deals with the issues associated with the autonomy of vehicle fleets, as well as some of the dimensions provided by an artificial intelligence (AI) solution. This presentation is developed using the example of a suppression of enemy air defense mission carried out by a group of Unmanned Combat Air Vehicles (UCAV). The environment of the mission management system (MMS) includes the theatre of operations, vehicle subsystems, and the MMS of other UCAV. An MMS architecture, organized around a database including reactive and deliberative layers, is described in detail. The deliberative layer includes a distributed mission planner developed using constraint programming and an agent framework. Experimental results demonstrate that the MMS is able, in a bounded time, to carry out missions, to activate the contingent behaviors, to decide whether to plan or not.

Chapter II

Extending Classical Planning for Time: Research Trends in Optimal and Suboptimal
Temporal Planning / *Antonio Garrido and Eva Onaindia* 23

This chapter focuses on complex features such as explicit management of time and temporal plans, more expressive models of actions to better describe real-world problems, and presents a review of the most successful techniques for temporal planning. They first start with the optimal planning-graph-based approach, they do a thorough review of the general methods, algorithms, and planners, and finish with heuristic state-based approaches, both optimal and suboptimal. Second, they discuss the inclusion of time features into a partial order causal link (POCL) approach. In such an approach, they analyse the possibility of mixing planning with constraint satisfaction problems (CSPs), formulating the planning problem as a CSP and leaving the temporal features to a CSP solver. The ultimate objective here is to come up with an advanced, combined model of planning and scheduling. Third, they outline some techniques used in hybrid approaches that combine different techniques. Finally, they provide a synthesis of many well-known temporal planners and present their main techniques.

Section II
Constraint Satisfaction and Scheduling

Chapter III
Principles of Constraint Processing / *Roman Barták*.. 63

This chapter gives an introduction to mainstream constraint satisfaction techniques available in existing constraint solvers and answers the question "How does constraint satisfaction work?" The focus of the chapter is on techniques of constraint propagation, depth-first search, and their integration. It explains backtracking, its drawbacks, and how to remove these drawbacks by methods such as backjumping and backmarking. The focus is then on consistency techniques; the chapter explains methods such as arc and path consistency and introduces consistencies of higher level. It also presents how consistency techniques are integrated with depth-first search algorithms in a look-ahead concept and what value and variable ordering heuristics are available there. Finally, techniques for optimization with constraints are presented.

Chapter IV
Stratified Constraint Satisfaction Networks in Synergetic Multi-Agent
Simulations of Language Evolution / *Alexander Mehler* 107

This chapter describes a simulation model of language evolution which integrates synergetic linguistics with multi-agent modelling. On one hand, this enables the utilization of knowledge about the distribution of the parameter values of system variables as a touch stone of simulation validity. On the other hand, it accounts for synergetic interdependencies of microscopic system variables and macroscopic order parameters.

Chapter V
Soft-Constrained Linear Programming Support Vector Regression for Nonlinear
Black-Box Systems Identification / *Zhao Lu and Jing Sun* 137

This chapter is concerned with support vector regression and its application to nonlinear black-box system identification. As an innovative sparse kernel modeling method, support vector regression (SVR) has been regarded as the state-of-the-art technique for regression and approximation. In the support vector regression, Vapnik developed the ε-insensitive loss function as a trade-off between the robust loss function of Huber and one that enables sparsity within the support vectors. The use of support vector kernel expansion provides a potential avenue to represent nonlinear dynamical systems and underpin advanced analysis. However, in the standard quadratic programming support vector regression (QP-SVR), its implementation is more computationally expensive and enough model sparsity can not be guaranteed.

In an attempt to surmount these drawbacks, this chapter focuses on the application of soft-constrained linear programming support vector regression (LP-SVR) in nonlinear black-box systems identification, and the simulation results demonstrate that the LP-SVR is superior to QP-SVR in model sparsity and computational efficiency.

Section III
Machine Learning

Chapter VI

Reinforcement Learning and Automated Planning: A Survey /
Ioannis Partalas, Dimitris Vrakas, and Ioannis Vlahavas 148

This chapter presents a detailed survey on Artificial Intelligent approaches that combine Reinforcement Learning and Automated Planning. There is a close relationship between those two areas as they both deal with the process of guiding an agent, situated in a dynamic environment, in order to achieve a set of predefined goals. Therefore, it is straightforward to integrate learning and planning in a single guiding mechanism and there have been many approaches in this direction during the past years. The approaches are organized and presented according to various characteristics, such as the used planning mechanism or the reinforcement learning algorithm.

Chapter VII

Induction as a Search Procedure / *Stasinos Konstantopoulos, Rui Camacho,
Nuno A. Fonseca, and Vítor Santos Costa* 166

This chapter introduces inductive logic programming (ILP) from the perspective of search algorithms in Computer Science. It first briefly considers the Version Spaces approach to induction and then focuses on Inductive Logic Programming: from its formal definition and main techniques and strategies, to priors used to restrict the search space and optimized sequential, parallel, and stochastic algorithms. The authors hope that this presentation of the theory and applications of inductive logic programming will help the reader understand the theoretical underpinnings of ILP and also provide a helpful overview of the state-of-the-art in the domain.

Chapter VIII

Single- and Multi-Order Neurons for Recursive Unsupervised Learning /
*Kiruthika Ramanathan
and Sheng Uei Guan* 217

This chapter presents a recursive approach to unsupervised learning. The algorithm proposed, while similar to ensemble clustering, does not need to execute several clustering algorithms and find consensus between them. On the contrary, grouping is done between two subsets of data at one time, thereby saving training time. Also, only two kinds of clustering algorithms are used in creating the recursive clustering ensemble, as opposed to the multitude of clusterers required by ensemble clusterers. In this chapter, a recursive clusterer is proposed for both single and multi-order neural networks. Empirical results show as much as 50% improvement in clustering accuracy when compared to benchmark clustering algorithms.

Section IV
Optimization

Chapter IX

Optimising Object Classification: Uncertain Reasoning-Based Analysis Using CaRBS
Systematic Search Algorithms / *Malcolm J. Beynon* 234

This chapter investigates the effectiveness of a number of objective functions used in conjunction with a novel technique to optimize the classification of objects based on a number of characteristic values, which may or not be missing. The Classification and Ranking Belief Simplex (CaRBS) technique is based on Dempster-Shafer theory and hence operates in the presence of ignorance. The objective functions considered minimize the level of ambiguity and/or ignorance in the classification of companies to being either failed or not-failed. Further results are found when an incomplete version of the original data set is considered. The findings in this chapter demonstrate how techniques such as CaRBS, which operate in an uncertain reasoning based environment, offer a novel approach to object classification problem solving.

Chapter X

Application of Fuzzy Optimization in Forecasting and Planning of Construction Industry /
P. Vasant, N. Barsoum, C. Kahraman, and G. M. Dimirovski 254

This chapter proposes a new method to obtain an optimal solution using a satisfactory approach in an uncertain environment. The optimal solution is obtained by using possibilistic linear programming approach and intelligent computing by MATLAB. The optimal solution for profit function, index quality, and worker satisfaction index in the construction industry is considered. Decision maker and implementer tabulate the final possibilistic and realistic outcome for objective functions with respect to the level of satisfaction and vagueness for forecasting and planning. When the decision maker finds the optimum parameters with acceptable degree of satisfaction, the decision maker can apply the confidence of gaining much profit in terms of helping the public with high quality and least cost products. The proposed fuzzy membership function allows the implementer to find a better arrangement for the equipments in the production line to fulfill the wanted products in an optimum way.

Chapter XI

Rank Improvement Optimization Using PROMETHEE and Trigonometric
Differential Evolution / *Malcolm J. Beynon* 266

This chapter investigates the modeling of the ability to improve the rank position of an alternative in relation to those of its competitors. PROMETHEE is one such technique for ranking alternatives based on their criteria values. In conjunction with the evolutionary algorithm Trigonometric Differential Evolution, the minimum changes necessary to the criteria values of an alternative are investigated, for it to achieve an improved rank position. This investigation is compounded with a comparison of the differing effects of two considered objective functions that measure the previously mentioned minimization. Two data sets are considered, the first concerns the ranking of environmental projects and the second the ranking of brands of a food product. The notion of modeling preference ranks of alternatives and the subsequent improvement of alternative's rank positions is the realism of a stakeholders' appreciation of their alternative in relation to their competitors.

Section V
Genetic Algorithms and Programming

Chapter XII

Parallelizing Genetic Algorithms: A Case Study / *Iker Gondra* 284

This chapter introduces the major steps, operators, theoretical foundations, and problems of genetic algorithms (GA). A parallel GA is an extension of the classical GA that takes advantage of a GA's inherent parallelism to improve its time performance and reduce the likelihood of premature convergence. An overview of different models for parallelizing GAs is presented along with a discussion of their main advantages and disadvantages. A case study: A parallel GA for finding Ramsey Numbers is then presented. According to Ramsey Theory, a sufficiently large system (no matter how random) will always contain highly organized subsystems. The role of Ramsey numbers is to quantify some of these existential theorems. Finding Ramsey numbers has proven to be a very difficult task that has led researchers to experiment with different methods of accomplishing this task. The objective of the case study is both to illustrate the typical process of GA development and to verify the superior performance of parallel GAs in solving some of the problems (e.g., premature convergence) of traditional GAs.

Chapter XIII

Using Genetic Programming to Extract Knowledge from Artificial Neural Networks /
Daniel Rivero, Miguel Varela, and Javier Pereira 308

This chapter describes a technique that makes it possible to extract the knowledge held by previously trained artificial neural networks. This makes it possible for them to be used in a number of areas (such as medicine) where it is necessary to know how they work, as well as having a network that functions. This chapter explains how to carry out this process to extract knowledge, defined as rules. Special emphasis is placed on extracting knowledge from recurrent neural networks, in particular when applied in predicting time series.

Compilation of References 328

About the Contributors 359

Index 366

Preface

Problem Solving is a complex mental activity that occurs when an agent (biological, robotic, or software) does not know how to proceed from a given state to a desired goal state. The nature of human problem solving has been studied by psychologists over the past hundred years and it has also been a subject of research in Artificial Intelligence (AI) from the early 1960s with the General Problem Solver (GPS). Artificial Intelligence is concerned with two major topics in Problem Solving: representation of the problem and automatically extracting a solution to it. Automated Problem Solving is the area of Artificial Intelligence that is mainly concerned with the development of software systems for which, given a formal representation of a problem, they find a solution.

These systems usually explore a search space, utilizing search algorithms in order to reach one or more goal states. These search problems are divided in five main categories: (a) Automated Planning, (b) Constraint Satisfaction and Scheduling, (c) Machine Learning, (d) Optimization, and (e) Genetic Algorithms and Genetic Programming.

The fist category, namely planning, refers to problems where the solution is a sequence of actions that if applied to the initial state will eventually lead to a new state that satisfies the goals. Examples of this category includes robot control problems, navigation problems (e.g., path planning), logistics, and so forth.

The second category is constraint satisfaction and scheduling and is concerned with problems where the goal is to assign values to a set of variables in a way that a set of constraints is met, while optimizing a certain cost function. There are numerous examples of problems of this category such as workers' shifts, timetabling, resource allocation, and so forth.

Machine learning, which is the third category, is concerned with problems in which an artificial agent must learn. The major focus of machine learning is to extract information from data automatically by computational and statistical methods. The applications of machine learning mainly concern data analysis tasks in decision support systems. Data mining is the application of machine learning in large data bases.

The fourth category is optimization problems, where there is a function that measures the appropriateness of each state and the goal of the problem is to find a state that either maximizes or minimizes this function. In contrast to the other categories, no information concerning the goal state is included in the problem representation. A representative example of this category is the Travelling Salesman Person (TSP) problem.

The last category includes genetic algorithms and genetic programming. Genetic algorithms are a particular class of evolutionary algorithms that use techniques inspired by evolutionary biology such as inheritance, mutation, selection, and crossover in order to solve optimization and search problems. Genetic programming is an area of genetic algorithms which is concerned with the automatic creation of computer programs that perform a specific user-defined task.

This edited volume, entitled *Artificial Intelligence for Advanced Problem Solving Techniques*, consists of 13 chapters, bringing together a number of modern approaches on the area of Automated or Advanced Problem Solving. The book presents in detail a number of state-of-the-art algorithms and systems mainly for solving search problems. Apart from the thorough analysis and implementation details, the authors of each chapter of the book also provide extensive background information about their subjects and present and comment on similar approaches done in the past.

INTENDED AUDIENCE

The book will be ideal for researchers in search algorithms since it will contain state-of-the-art approaches in this area. It will also be useful for researchers in other areas of Artificial Intelligence as it could assist them in finding ideas and ways for applying the results of their work in other areas related to their interests. Furthermore, the book could be used by postgraduate students in courses related to Artificial Intelligence such as Advanced Problem Solving, Planning, Scheduling, Optimization, and Constraint Satisfaction as a reference book.

Artificial Intelligence for Advanced Problem Solving is an ideal source of knowledge for individuals who want to enhance their knowledge on issues relating to problem solving and artificial intelligence. More specifically, the book is intended to aid:

1. Researchers in planning, constraint satisfaction, scheduling, optimization, machine learning, and genetic algorithms since it contains state-of-the-art approaches in building efficient search systems. These approaches are presented in detail, providing information about the techniques and methodologies followed, and are accompanied by thorough discussions of the current trends and future directions.
2. Researchers in other areas of Artificial Intelligence and Informatics, as it can assist them in finding ideas and ways for applying the results of their work in other areas related to their interests. Apart from the research innovations in the area of planning, the book presents issues related to other areas that remain open and are worth further investigation.
3. Postgraduate students and teachers in general courses such as Artificial Intelligence and in specialized courses such as planning, scheduling, and optimization or machine learning as a reference book. The chapters of the book were carefully selected so as to cover the most important applications of AI. The authors of each chapter are experts in the specific subject and are highly appreciated in the academic community. Concerning the content of the book, each chapter contains extensive introductory material and a comparative survey with similar past approaches; therefore, the reader will be informed about general issues and state of the art approaches.
4. Practitioners and the general community interested in Artificial Intelligence and its applications. The general computer science community will also benefit from *Artificial Intelligence for Advanced Problem Solving*, since the topics covered by the book are active research fields with quite promising futures that are based on the basic principles of Informatics.

ORGANIZATION OF THE BOOK

The Intelligent Techniques for Planning is divided into five major sections:

I: Automated Planning
II: Constraint Satisfaction and Scheduling
III: Machine Learning
IV: Optimization
V: Genetic Algorithms and Programming

Section I deals with Automated Planning systems and the algorithms they use in order to solve a large variety of problems. This section is further divided into two chapters:

Chapter I contributed to by Johan Baltié, Eric Bensana, Patrick Fabiani, Jean-Loup Farges, Stéphane Millet, Philippe Morignot, Bruno Patin, Gérald Petitjean, Gauthier Pitois, and Jean-Clair Poncet, deals with the issues associated with the autonomy of vehicle fleets, as well as some of the dimensions provided by an Artificial Intelligence (AI) solution. This presentation is developed using the example of a suppression of enemy air defense mission carried out by a group of Unmanned Combat Air Vehicles (UCAV). The environment of the Mission Management System (MMS) includes the theatre of operations, vehicle subsystems and the MMS of other UCAV. An MMS architecture, organized around a database, including reactive and deliberative layers, is described in detail. The deliberative layer includes a distributed mission planner developed using constraint programming and an agent framework. Experimental results demonstrate that the MMS is able, in a bounded time, to carry out missions, to activate the contingent behaviors, to decide whether to plan or not.

Chapter II by Antonio Garrido and Eva Onaindia focuses on complex features such as explicit management of time and temporal plans, more expressive models of actions to better describe real-world problems, and presents a review of the most successful techniques for temporal planning. The authors first start with the optimal planning-graph-based approach, they do a thorough review of the general methods, algorithms, and planners, and they finish with heuristic state-based approaches, both optimal and suboptimal. Second, they discuss the inclusion of time features into a Partial Order Causal Link (POCL) approach. In such an approach, they analyse the possibility of mixing planning with Constraint Satisfaction Problems (CSPs), formulating the planning problem as a CSP, and leaving the temporal features to a CSP solver. The ultimate objective here is to come up with an advanced, combined model of planning and scheduling. Third, they outline some techniques used in hybrid approaches that combine different techniques. Finally, they provide a synthesis of many well-known temporal planners and present their main techniques.

Section II gives an introduction to Constraints and presents several real world applications. The section contains three chapters:

Chapter III by Roman Barták gives an introduction to mainstream constraint satisfaction techniques available in existing constraint solvers and answers the question "How does constraint satisfaction work?" The focus of the chapter is on techniques of constraint propagation, depth-first search, and their integration. It explains backtracking, its drawbacks, and how to remove these drawbacks by methods such as backjumping and backmarking. Then, the focus is on consistency techniques; it explains methods such as arc and path consistency and introduces consistencies of higher level. It also presents how consistency techniques are integrated with depth-first search algorithms in a look-ahead concept and what value and variable ordering heuristics are available there. Finally, techniques for optimization with constraints are presented.

Chapter IV by Alexander Mehler describes a simulation model of language evolution which integrates synergetic linguistics with multi-agent modelling. On one hand, this enables the utilization of knowledge about the distribution of the parameter values of system variables as a touch stone of simulation validity. On the other hand, it accounts for synergetic interdependencies of microscopic system variables and macroscopic order parameters. This approach goes beyond the classical setting of synergetic linguistics by grounding processes of self-regulation and self-organization in mechanisms of (dialogically aligned) language learning. Consequently, the simulation model includes four layers: (i) the level of single information processing agents which are (ii) dialogically aligned in communication processes enslaved (iii) by the social system in which the agents participate and whose countless communication events shape (iv) the corresponding language system. In summary, the chapter is basically conceptual. It outlines a simulation model which bridges between different levels of language modelling kept apart in contemporary simulation models. This model relates to artificial cognition systems in the sense that it may be implemented to endow an artificial agent community in order to perform distributed processes of meaning constitution.

Chapter V by Zhao Lu and Jing Sun is concerned with Support Vector Regression and its application to nonlinear black-box system identification. As an innovative sparse kernel modeling method, support vector regression (SVR) has been regarded as the state-of-the-art technique for regression and approximation. In the support vector regression, Vapnik developed the ε-insensitive loss function as a trade-off between the robust loss function of Huber and one that enables sparsity within the support vectors. The use of support vector kernel expansion provides a potential avenue to represent nonlinear dynamical systems and underpin advanced analysis. However, in the standard quadratic programming support vector regression (QP-SVR), its implementation is more computationally expensive and enough model sparsity can not be guaranteed. In an attempt to surmount these drawbacks, this chapter focuses on the application of soft-constrained linear programming support vector regression (LP-SVR) in nonlinear black-box systems identification, and the simulation results demonstrates that the LP-SVR is superior to QP-SVR in model sparsity and computational efficiency.

Section III consists of three chapters and deals with algorithms and techniques used in machine learning applications:

Chapter VI by Ioannis Partalas, Dimitris Vrakas and Ioannis Vlahavas presents a detailed survey on Artificial Intelligent approaches that combine Reinforcement Learning and Automated Planning. There is a close relationship between those two areas as they both deal with the process of guiding an agent, situated in a dynamic environment, in order to achieve a set of predefined goals. Therefore, it is straightforward to integrate learning and planning, in a single guiding mechanism, and there have been many approaches in this direction during the past years. The approaches are organized and presented according to various characteristics, as the used planning mechanism or the reinforcement learning algorithm.

Chapter VII by Stasinos Konstantopoulos, Rui Camacho, Nuno A. Fonseca, and Vítor Santos Costa introduces Inductive Logic Programming (ILP) from the perspective of search algorithms in computer science. It first briefly considers the version spaces approach to induction, and then focuses on inductive logic programming: from its formal definition and main techniques and strategies, to priors used to restrict the search space and optimized sequential, parallel, and stochastic algorithms. The authors hope that this presentation of the theory and applications of Inductive Logic Programming will help the reader understand the theoretical underpinnings of ILP, and also provide a helpful overview of the state-of-the-art in the domain.

Chapter VIII by Kiruthika Ramanathan and Sheng Uei Guan presents a recursive approach to unsupervised learning. The algorithm proposed, while similar to ensemble clustering, does not need to execute several clustering algorithms and find consensus between them. On the contrary, grouping is done between two subsets of data at one time, thereby saving training time. Also, only two kinds of clustering algorithms are used in creating the recursive clustering ensemble, as opposed to the multitude of clusterers required by ensemble clusterers. In this chapter, a recursive clusterer is proposed for both single and multi-order neural networks. Empirical results show as much as 50% improvement in clustering accuracy when compared to benchmark clustering algorithms.

Section IV discusses several applications of optimization problems. There are three chapters in this section:

Chapter XI by Malcom Beynon investigates the effectiveness of a number of objective functions used in conjunction with a novel technique to optimize the classification of objects based on a number of characteristic values, which may or not be missing. The Classification and Ranking Belief Simplex (CaRBS) technique is based on Dempster-Shafer theory and, hence, operates in the presence of ignorance. The objective functions considered minimize the level of ambiguity and/or ignorance in the classification of companies to being either failed or not-failed. Further results are found when an incomplete version of the original data set is considered. The findings in this chapter demonstrate how techniques such as CaRBS, which operate in an uncertain reasoning based environment, offer a novel approach to object classification problem solving.

Chapter X by P. Vasant, N. Barsoum, C. Kahraman, and G.M. Dimirovski proposes a new method to obtain optimal solution using satisfactory approach in uncertain environment. The optimal solution is obtained by using possibilistic linear programming approach and intelligent computing by MATLAB. The optimal solution for profit function, index quality and worker satisfaction index in construction industry, is considered. Decision maker and implementer tabulate the final possibilistic and realistic outcome for objective functions respect to level of satisfaction and vagueness for forecasting and planning. When the decision maker finds the optimum parameters with acceptable degree of satisfaction, the decision maker can apply the confidence of gaining much profit in terms of helping the public with high quality and least cost products. The proposed fuzzy membership function allows the implementer to find a better arrangement for the equipment in the production line to fulfill the wanted products in an optimum way.

Chapter XI by Malcom Beynon investigates the modeling of the ability to improve the rank position of an alternative in relation to those of its competitors. PROMETHEE is one such technique for ranking alternatives based on their criteria values. In conjunction with the evolutionary algorithm Trigonometric Differential Evolution, the minimum changes necessary to the criteria values of an alternative are investigated for it to achieve an improved rank position. This investigation is compounded with a comparison of the differing effects of two considered objective functions that measure the previously mentioned minimization. Two data sets are considered, the first concerns the ranking of environmental projects, and the second the ranking of brands of a food product. The notion of modeling preference ranks of alternatives and the subsequent improvement of alternative's rank positions is the realism of a stakeholders' appreciation of their alternative in relation to their competitors.

Section V deals with evolutionary algorithms and more specifically genetic algorithms and genetic programming. The section consists of two chapters:

Chapter XII by Iker Gondra introduces the major steps, operators, theoretical foundations, and problems of Genetic Algorithms. A parallel GA is an extension of the classical GA that takes advantage of a GA's inherent parallelism to improve its time performance and reduce the likelihood of premature convergence. An overview of different models for parallelizing GAs is presented along with a discussion of their main advantages and disadvantages. A case study, "A parallel GA for Finding Ramsey Numbers," is then presented. According to Ramsey Theory, a sufficiently large system (no matter how random) will always contain highly organized subsystems. The role of Ramsey numbers is to quantify some of these existential theorems. Finding Ramsey numbers has proven to be a very difficult task that has led researchers to experiment with different methods of accomplishing this task. The objective of the case study is both to illustrate the typical process of GA development and to verify the superior performance of parallel GAs in solving some of the problems (e.g., premature convergence) of traditional GAs.

Chapter XIII by Daniel Rivero, Miguel Varela, and Javier Pereira describes a technique that makes it possible to extract the knowledge held by previously trained artificial neural networks. This makes it possible for them to be used in a number of areas (such as medicine) where it is necessary to know how they work, as well as having a network that functions. This chapter explains how to carry out this process to extract knowledge, defined as rules. Special emphasis is placed on extracting knowledge from recurrent neural networks, in particular when applied to predicting time series.

CONCLUSION

The book deals with Automated Problem Solving, an area of Artificial Intelligence that is mainly concerned with the development of software systems that solve search problems. Solving search problems is a key factor in any intelligent agent, biological or artificial, since it enables it to make decisions and to reason about its actions. This book presents a collection of 13 chapters that present various methods, techniques, and ideas in order to effectively tackle this kind of problem. Furthermore, it describes systems that adopt these ideas and present real world applications.

Artificial Intelligence for Advanced Problem Solving Techniques has a dual role; apart from the scientific impact of the book, it also aims to provide the user with knowledge about the principles of Artificial Intelligence and about innovative methodologies that utilize the effort spent by researchers in various different fields in order to build effective problem-solving systems. All of the authors are highly appreciated researchers and teachers and they have worked very hard in writing the chapters of this book. We hope that *Artificial Intelligence for Advanced Problem Solving Techniques* will fulfill the expectations of the readers.

Dimitris Vrakas and Ioannis Vlahavas
Thessaloniki, Greece
June 2007

Acknowledgment

The editors wish to thank all the people involved in the collation and review process of the book, without whose support the project could not have been satisfactorily completed. Special thanks go to the staff at IGI Global, whose contributions throughout the process of editing the book have been of great importance. The authors would also like to thank the administration of the department of Informatics at the Aristotle University of Thessaloniki for providing them with the necessary equipment in order to carry out this project. Moreover, the editors would like to thank the other members of the Logic Programming and Intelligent Systems Group (http://lpis.csd.auth.gr) for their constructive comments on the book.

Special thanks goes also to the people that served as reviewers for the chapters submitted to *Artificial Intelligence for Advanced Problem Solving Techniques*.

List of Reviewers:

- José Luis Rojo-Álvarez University Rey Juan Carlos, Madrid, Spain
- Roman Barták, Charles University, Czech Republic
- Nick Bassiliades, Aristotle University of Thessaloniki, Greece
- Malcolm Beynon, Cardiff University, U.K.
- Maarten van Emden, University of Victoria, Canada
- Jean-Loup Farges, ONERA, France
- Fernando Fernández, Universidad Carlos III de Madrid, Spain
- Antonio Garrido, Universidad Politécnica de Valencia, Spain
- Iker Gondra, St. Francis Xavier University, Nova Scotia, Canada
- Michael A. Goodrich, Brigham Young University, U.S.A.
- Patrik Haslum, National ICT, Australia
- Te-Ming Huang, Microsoft adCenter Labs
- Sonja Petrovic-Lazarevic, Monash University, Melbourne, Australia
- Carlos Linares López, Universidad Carlos III de Madrid, Spain
- Nikola S. Nikolov, University of Limerick, Ireland
- Jan Ramon, Katholieke Universiteit Leuven, Belgium
- Hava Siegelmann, University of Massachusetts Amherst, U.S.A.
- Kostas Stergiou, University of the Aegean, Greece
- P. Vasant, Universiti Teknologi Petronas, Tronoh, Malaysia
- Oscar Sapena Vercher, Polytechnic University of Valencia, Spain
- Vincent Vidal, Université d'Artois, France
- Kursat Yenilmez, Eskisehir Osmangazi University, Turkey

Section I
Automated Planning

Chapter I
Multi–Vehicle Missions:
Architecture and Algorithms for Distributed Online Planning

Johan Baltié
Sophis Technology, France

Eric Bensana
ONERA, France

Patrick Fabiani
ONERA, France

Jean-Loup Farges
ONERA, France

Stéphane Millet
Dassault Aviation, France

Philippe Morignot
Axlog Ingénierie, France

Bruno Patin
Dassault Aviation, France

Gérald Petitjean
EURODECISION, France

Gauthier Pitois
Axlog Ingénierie, France

Jean-Clair Poncet
Sophis Technology, France

ABSTRACT

This chapter deals with the issues associated with the autonomy of vehicle fleets, as well as some of the dimensions provided by an artificial intelligence (AI) solution. This presentation is developed using the example of a suppression of enemy air defense mission carried out by a group of unmanned combat air vehicles (UCAV). The environment of the mission management system (MMS) includes the theatre of operations, vehicle subsystems, and the MMS of other UCAV. An MMS architecture, organized around a database including reactive and deliberative layers, is described in detail. The deliberative layer includes a distributed mission planner developed using constraint programming and an agent framework. Experimental results demonstrate that the MMS is able, in a bounded time, to carry out missions, to activate the contingent behaviors, to decide whether to plan or not. Some research directions remain open in this application domain of AI.

INTRODUCTION

The autonomy of vehicle fleets is a major artificial intelligence (AI) challenge. Indeed, the behavior of each agent associated to each vehicle of the fleet has to be specified not only in terms of actions on the environment but also in terms of flexible group decision making. Three AI topics may be useful to achieve this objective:

- Agent architectures can help in designing the architecture of the software of each vehicle
- A multi-agent approach can address the problem of interactions between vehicles
- Automated planning can provide the basis of vehicle intelligence

The purpose of this chapter is to present the problems associated with the autonomy of vehicle fleets together with some solutions via the example of a suppression of enemy air defense (SEAD) mission carried out by a group of unmanned combat air vehicles (UCAV). The first section of the chapter is devoted to the presentation of the example problem.

The problems linked to architectural choices are addressed in the second section. Indeed, autonomous vehicles are a specific kind of agent: they have to be very reactive in order to move at high speed and they have to be intelligent in order to aim at the right goal. Research conducted in the AI and robotic domains give some architectural answers to these challenges.

The capability of an agent to plan for itself and for other agents is also a key component of agent intelligence. In the third section, the planning problems arising in multi-vehicle management and their distribution across the agents are presented. The methods used for treating those problems are detailed.

The fourth section gives some experimental results obtained on the example problem. The behavior of the planning module is illustrated and the complete multi-vehicle mission management system (MMS) is tested with a simulation tool. Finally some conclusions are presented along with directions for future research.

EXAMPLE PROBLEM

The example problem proposed in this chapter is the development of a MMS for a group of UCAV. The environment of the group includes a safe area and a dangerous area, no flying zones, a command and control (C2) center, the terrain, some threats, and some targets. This environment is dynamic: threats and targets may be discovered during the course of the mission. The dynamic flight constraints of the UCAV are considered. Moreover, some subsystems interact with the MMS. The functions of those subsystems are location, flight management, communication, self-defense, sensor management, and weapon management. A mission plan is defined before take-off, and the aims of the MMS are to follow the mission plan, to ensure safety, to ensure survivability, and to ensure the success of the mission. Some requirements are deduced from those aims: the plan must be applied, disruptive events must be detected and analyzed, reactive actions must be carried out and, if needed, the mission plan must be recomputed online.

The example problem is more complex than the sum of every single agent mission management problem. The set of actions that can be performed by a group of UCAV is larger than the one for a single UCAV. For instance, the group can split: some UCAV fly to a convenient place to perform detection, identification, and localization of targets and other UCAV fly to another place to perform the strike itself. After the action the group can merge. Military pilots in SEAD missions apply this type of action rules.

Mission Description

The considered mission is an air to ground mission which can combine SEAD, suppression of targets (STRIKE), and battle damage assessment (BDA) operations. Take-off, landing, and refuelling are not considered. The considered UCAV is a subsonic stealth aircraft with an internal weapon bay. Figure 1 illustrates a typical mission.

The mission can be split in a sequence of phases:

- **Domestics in:** transit to forward edge of battle area (FEBA)
- **FEBA crossing:** cross the FEBA. This area can be very protected.
- **Tactics in:** transit from FEBA to target area

- **Attack:** localize, identify, acquire, destroy the mission targets
- **Tactics out:** transit from target area to FEBA
- **FEBA crossing:** cross the FEBA. This area can be very protected.
- **Domestics out:** transit from FEBA to end of mission point

All of these phases can be described in term of constraints. For example, which equipment is usable, or in which condition a piece of equipment can be used to fire on a target.

UCAV System Description

Figure 2 illustrates the UCAV system and the exchanges between the different system modules.

Figure 1. Illustration of a typical mission; the environment includes surface to air missiles (SAM), a main operating base (MOB), and an airborne warning and control system (AWACS)

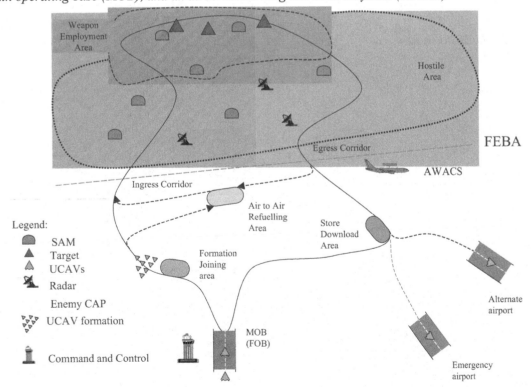

- The navigation module is responsible for applying the navigation plans. A navigation plan is a sequence of waypoints.
- The localization module is responsible for computing the current position of the UCAV from different sources (global positioning system, or GPS, inertial, numeric terrain).
- The sensor module is responsible for managing the onboard sensors (synthetic aperture radar, or SAR, electro optical).
- The weapon module is responsible for managing the onboard weapons.
- The communication module is responsible for managing the datalinks:
  - **Intra formation datalink** (short distance, bidirectional, stealth)
  - **Low bandwidth datalink** (long distance, bidirectional)
  - **High bandwidth datalink** (long distance, images upload)
- The self-defence function is responsible for managing the following pieces of equipment:

- **Missile approach warner**, in charge of detecting incoming missiles
- **Radar warning receiver**, in charge of detection and identifying ground to air threats
- **Active electronic counter-measure**, in charge of jamming ground to air threats
- The tactical situation module is in charge of elaborating tracks on ground to air threats with data coming from internal Radar Warning Receiver or other aircraft.
- The MMS is in charge of managing the overall mission at two levels: vehicle and group levels. At vehicle level, it is responsible for:
  - Elaborating the current vehicle mission status and tactical situation with the information pushed by all the other modules,
  - Executing the current mission plan,
  - Executing emergency actions when

Figure 2. The UCAV system

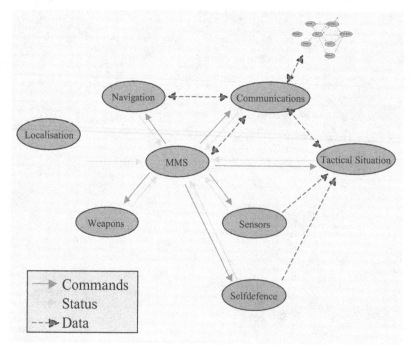

needed (reaction to threats, for example).

- At group level (all the UCAV participating in the mission), it is responsible for:
  o Elaborating the group mission status and tactical situation and
  o Creating a new mission plan from the old one, the current status, and tactical situation when the old one is no longer applicable.

ARCHITECTURAL CHOICES

Existing architectures for autonomous vehicles may be purely reactive or may have a deliberative layer. Those architectures may integrate mission management systems.

Pure Reactive Architectures

The idea beyond this kind of architecture is that mobile agents do not need online problem solving algorithms and can rely solely on modules quickly processing signals and logical conditions. The modules may then be organized in an undetermined number of asynchronous layers, the lowest layer being in direct connection with sensors and actuators and each layer being controlled and parameterized by the next upper layer. Brooks (1986) has formalized a reactive architecture: the subsumption architecture where each layer is generalized by the next upper layer. The wiring of the interconnection between modules is predefined and the actuation of a module is either internal or made by the reception of a message from another module. Exchanges between layers are performed using special kind of generic functions: inhibitor and suppressor. An inhibitor inhibits output messages and a suppressor suppresses the usual input message and provides a replacement.

A reactive architecture can be built using the model that flexible planning and scheduling with contingencies is performed on the ground and

that vehicle autonomy is ensured by a conditional executive, a resource manager and a model-based mode identification and reconfiguration system. Washington, Golden, Bresina, Smith, Anderson, and Smith (1999) derive this reactive vehicle architecture from the Remote Agent (Muscettola, Nayak, Pell, & Williams, 1998) reactive and deliberative architecture. The plan commands are sent to the vehicle real time control system, with results coming back via state monitors into the mode identification and reconfiguration system. This system infers the state of the system from the monitored information and updates the state for the conditional executive. If commands fail or schedule constraints are violated, the conditional executive tries to recover using contingency plans. Reactive architectures are not able to support problem solving but react quickly to events. They are proposed for planetary exploration missions.

Another approach is based on formalisms close to the decision trees: universal plan (Schoppers, 1995) or teleo-reactive trees (Benson, 1995). The instantaneous behavior of the agent is defined through a tree of tests. The tested variables may be given by sensors or internal values. Each test leads to two other tests (if-yes and if-not) and leaves of the tree are quick atomic actions. The tree is permanently tested from root to leaves by a looping procedure. Modal logic can be integrated in this formalism in order to take into account the temporal extent of actions and differences between the agent's expectation and reality (Schoppers, 1995). Trees can also modify themselves by learning (Benson, 1995). The advantage of this approach is to allow a fluid behavior of the vehicle. However, even if it is theoretically possible, the integration of deliberative features in this approach seems practically difficult.

Reactive and Deliberative Architectures

Deliberative architectures are fully based on problem solving and usually react slowly. They are not used for vehicle mission management.

Practical intelligence of a vehicle consists in a mix of reactive and deliberative behaviors. The architecture includes two layers: the reactive layer that interacts with the environment using sensors and actuators and the deliberative layer that includes reasoning modules. For instance, the Entropy Reduction Engine architecture of Bresina and Drummond (1990) includes a reactor that provides reactive behavior in an environment. In this architecture, the deliberative layer provides plans with the help of two modules: the projector and the reductor:

1.   The projector explores possible futures and provides advice about appropriate behaviors to the reactor.
2.   The reductor reasons about behavioral constraints and provides search control advice to the projector.

Gat (1992) proposed a third layer that supervises the modules of the reactive and deliberative layers. This third layer activates the modules, receiving their termination messages. It has to react quickly taking into account the reasons of a module execution failure. This supervision layer may be implemented in a flexible way as a Petri net player playing Petri nets described in a hierarchical way (Verfaille and Fabiani, 2000). Application of that type of architecture has been proposed for planetary exploration rovers.

One important requirement for architectures having both reactive and deliberative layers, is the independence of the two layers in terms of execution of modules. Indeed, even with high environmental pressure, the architecture must avoid stopping the execution of a reactive module to start a deliberative module. For this reason, reactive and deliberative layers may each present an independent supervision functionality (Hayes-Roth, Pfleger, Lalanda, & Morignot, 1995). For instance, an independent controller for each layer (deliberative, reactive) dictates which behavior (cognitive behavior at the cognitive layer, physi-

cal behavior at the physical layer) to activate now, given information present on a common structure of each layer. One of these cognitive behaviors may be "planning," in our case. One of these reactive behaviors may be, "take an evasive maneuver," in our case. This architecture has been demonstrated on a mobile robot performing secretarial tasks in a laboratory.

Then comes the discussion: what is a plan? Investigators have first considered a plan as a simplified program (in the sense of a program in a programming language), for example, a sequence of programming instructions. Executing the plan means executing the instructions. That is the view of a pure computer scientist. Other authors have considered plans as a communication medium (Agre & Chapman, 1987): a plan is considered as data in a formal language that provides information to other agents about the intentions (short term, long term) of the agent. For other authors, plans are considered as intended behaviors (Hayes-Roth et al., 1995) capturing the idea that an action in a plan is not a simple one-shot action but a more continuous and meaningful activity of the agent named behavior. Hence, the sequence of action descriptions in the plan corresponds, when executed, to a sequence of behaviors, not of actions.

We follow this latter approach, with the notable difference that behaviors, in our architecture, always unfold in the same order. Hence there is no need for a declarative approach for expressing (encoding) behaviors (at the reactive layer and at the deliberative layer). In other words, the logical unfolding of behaviors (at the reactive and at the deliberative layers) is simply hard-wired through a simple sequential graph.

An intermediate layer, between the reactive and deliberative layers, is proposed by Alami, Chatila, Fleury, Ghallab, and Ingrand (1998). In the resulting architecture, the deliberative layer includes a planning module and a supervision module that activates one plan in function of a stack of agent's intentions. The reactive layer is reduced to modules controlling sensors and actuators. The intermediate layer is called the execution control layer. It chooses and parameterizes the adequate module of the reactive layer with respect to the tasks of the plan given by the deliberative layer. It also elaborates, from the information returned by the reactive layer, execution reports. Finally, it transmits the reports to the supervision module of the decisional layer.

The Remote Agent architecture (Muscettola et al., 1998) integrates not only a deliberative layer and an execution control layer but also a model-based mode identification and reconfiguration. The deliberative layer includes a mission manager that formulates short-term planning problems for a planner and scheduler on the basis of a long-range mission profile. The executive achieves robustness in plan execution by exploiting the plan flexibility, for example, by being able to choose execution time within specified windows or being able to select different task decompositions for a high-level activity. The mode identification tracks the most likely vehicle states by identifying states whose models are consistent with sensed values and commands sent. The mode reconfiguration uses the vehicle model to find a command sequence that establishes or restores desired functionality.

Level of Detail in the Plan

Architectures with an advanced execution control layer raise the issue of plan abstraction and contingencies. Indeed, the more flexibility is given to the execution control layer, the less precise is the planned action and the more unpredictable are its effects. The basic formalism for abstraction of action is the Hierarchical Task Network (HTN). This formalism states that elementary actions are derived from abstract actions that are the purpose of the plan. This decomposition is made through non-elementary actions called methods. A method includes an identifier, arguments and a list of pairs (conditions–list of actions, elementary

action or method). Activating a method means to choose a pair whose conditions are compatible with the current state and to activate the actions of its list. It is possible to specify if the actions have to be activated in sequence or if the actions may be activated in parallel. This formalism decomposes the most abstract action in an "and/or" tree. Bresina and Washington (2001) use such decompositions in their Contingent Rover Language to provide a flexible plan to a conditional utility-based executive.

Architecture for the Example Problem

The vehicle architecture for the example problem is already defined. In that architecture a part of the reactive layer is outside the scope of the mission management problem. However the mission management system is subject to time pressure and cannot include only a deliberative layer. The design principles for the example problem are:

1. Online planning shall be activated only when the current plan is invalidated by the current situation.
2. The reactive layer shall not only execute the plan but also handle emergency situations.
3. Sensor inaccuracy is managed through planning of behavioral procedures for inaccuracy reduction.

Figure 3 presents the mission management system architecture for the example problem. It includes reactive and deliberative layers. This architecture is organized using an underlying database that stores information about the vehicle, the other vehicles, the mission, and the environment.

The reactive layer includes the following modules: "observe and compare," "pre-empt," and "act."

The "observe and compare" module receives the messages from the platform, marshals them into structured data, updates the database information, and performs tests about the short-term situation. It tests the possible disruptive events such as unexpected exposure to a threat, presence in a No Fly Zone (NFZ), loss of communication, and failure of other vehicle subsystems using some simple threshold-based functions applied on limited time horizon and geographical range. It includes a function of inhibitor, in the sense of Brooks (1986), of the messages in direction to "pre-empt."

The "pre-empt" module is activated once a threshold has been passed over. According to the nature and to the emergency level of this event, it determines candidate contingent behaviors and selects the one that has to be applied in the system to secure aircraft situation as soon as possible. This could necessitate to quickly check the overall UCAV situation and, if necessary, to compute some parameters to determine the contingent behavior and activate it. Finally, "Preempt" determines the sequence of unit actions generated by the behavior. Four behaviors may be activated by the module:

- The behavior for new radar threat detection implements updates of the radar list and radar locations, active electronic counter measure

under specified conditions, maneuver for avoidance or information gathering under other specified conditions.

- The behavior for approaching missile detection implements unconditional use of active electronic counter measures, chaff and flare decoy, and evasive maneuvers.

- The behavior for loss of communication between neighboring vehicles consists in commanding the altitude of the vehicles to different predetermined flight levels in order to ensure the absence of collision between them. The secured altitude slots are attributed to each aircraft at plan generation time, ensuring their uniqueness for each aircraft of a formation.

- The behavior for NFZ violation avoidance is implemented in two parts. First, a modification of the current trajectory is computed, attempting to avoid incoming NFZ, going round it by the shortest way. If this fails or if the situation evaluation reports that the aircraft suddenly appears to be inside a NFZ, the solution consists in a fast trajectory computing that will attempt to exit the NFZ by crossing the closest frontier point.

Figure 3. The mission management system architecture

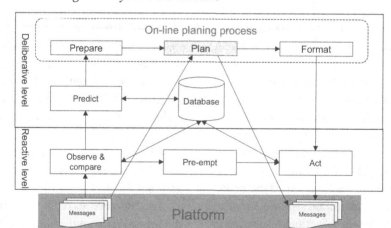

All behaviors have a date parameter, a time-out, and a homing waypoint parameter. They are updated each time the "preempt" component is activated. This update can be null according to the current aircraft situation, meaning that the system can return to nominal plan execution. Otherwise, the contingency ends once its associated timeout has been passed out or when homing point is reached. All behaviors, except loss of communication, have a Boolean parameter indicating whether the global path can be modified. Finally, the behavior for new radar threat detection has an additional parameter indicating the origin waypoint.

Four types of information represent the behaviors:

- The warning processing information indicates what should be done in terms of knowledge management.
- The system management information indicates what should be done in terms of auto-protection actions.
- The flight plan modification information indicates what should be done in terms of navigation actions.
- The end of contingency information indicates conditions for terminating the behavior.

The "act" module carries out the unit actions of the plan or of the "pre-empt" module and determines whether an action is correctly performed or not. Hence, the module analyzes the status of the subsystems stored in the database. When actions of the plan and from "pre-empt" are conflicting, it always gives the priority to preemption actions in order to ensure platform safety. This mechanism corresponds to a suppressor function in the sense of Brooks. Finally the module sends messages to the platform subsystems.

The deliberative layer includes the following modules: "predict," "prepare," "plan," and "format."

The "predict" module assesses the feasibility of the on going plan and decides whether to compute a new plan or not. Probabilities of UCAV survival and of target killing are updated and compared to a threshold. The possibilities of fulfilling time constraints at some waypoints and of having enough fuel to finish the mission are checked. It should be noted that the "predict" component faces a dilemma. On the one hand, deciding to re plan all the time leads the agent to an erratic behavior, always starting the beginning of new unrelated plans, and therefore not leading to any goal at all (too often replanning). On the other hand, deciding to plan too infrequently leads the agent to follow unusable plans, since the behavior of the agent does not adapt to what actually happens in the environment (too infrequent replanning). The solution we propose for this "predict" component is a medium term on the previous spectrum, by using variables representing states of the agent. When the mean of these variables is above some threshold, then the replanning decision is taken (and replanning occurs). This solution is not satisfactory in principle, since it does not solve the problem of the continuity of the behavior of the agent over successive replanning activities. But at least it provides a practical and simple (but not elegant) solution, even if these variables and thresholds need careful tuning for a realistic replanning frequency to be adopted. Moreover, the occurrence of a replanning request while replanning has to be managed. This management is performed using priorities on replanning reasons. If the priority of the reason of the present replanning request is lower than the one of the on going replanning, the request is ignored. Otherwise, the on going replanning activity is stopped and the replanning is started with a context including the present request.

The "prepare" module gathers and generates data for the "plan" module. The data includes:

- Participating vehicles.
- Available resources for each vehicle.

- Environment including threats, targets, and NFZ.
- A graph including possible paths for acquisition, attack, and return to base. This graph is built in two steps. An initial graph is deduced from the initial mission plan by associating mission waypoints to graph nodes and transitions between these waypoints to graph edges. Nodes and edges are tagged according to their strategic properties for acquisition, shooting, and so forth. The second step is done each time the component is activated. It consists in the generation of different alternative paths for each strategic action, including Return To Base. These paths are generated using a potential field based algorithm in which threats and NFZ are associated to repulsing potential while targets and base airport are associated with attractive potentials. Motion planning is fully explained in the next section.
- Time intervals at waypoints.

The "format" module refines the macro actions of the plan into sequences of unit actions. For instance the macro action "launch bomb 1 on target 101 at time t" is refined in the sequence of unit actions: "select resource type bomb 1 at time t-d" then "initialize selected resource with target 101 features at time t-e" then "ask to C2 go/no go at time t-f" then "if C2 answer is go fire bomb 1 at time t-g."

The "plan" module directly receives some messages and is also able to send directly other messages. This feature of the architecture allows multi-UCAV distributed planning.

The MMS is activated every 0.1 seconds. For most of the cycles only three modules are activated: "observe and compare," "predict," and "act." For those cycles, the result of the analysis of messages from the platform by "observe and compare" and "predict" indicates that no preemptive behavior has to be activated and no new plan has to be

computed. The "act" module continues carrying on actions of the current plan.

For cycles where "observe and compare" indicates that a pre-emptive behavior has to be activated, the "preempt" module is additionally activated. This module may remain activated for several consecutive cycles until the behavior is finished. Meanwhile the "act" module applies the actions issued from the behavior. For instance, if the disruptive event is the detection of a missile launch, the module remains activated until the end of the escape maneuver.

For cycles during which "predict" indicates that a new plan has to be computed, the "prepare" module is additionally activated. In the same cycle, the "plan" module is activated in the background. Several cycles afterwards, the "plan" module provides a plan and activates the "format" module just for a single cycle.

Special attention is given to the way the computation time constraints are taken into account: different priorities are assigned to the input messages, only a bounded number of messages are processed each cycle and long processing is performed over several cycles or in a separate thread. The conjunction of those techniques ensures that a computation time bound for a time cycle of the mission management system can be predetermined.

PLANNING

Specifying the Mission and the Planning Problem

A specific grammar can be used to specify the mission of a multi-vehicle system (Brumitt & Stentz, 1998). The basic elements of the grammar are the vehicles, the goals, and the motions of combination of vehicles towards combination of goals. Those elements can be combined using "or," "and," and "and then" operators. The specification given by the user is translated in an expression allowing planning. The basic elements of this expression can be treated as:

- A shortest path problem
- A traveling salesman problem
- A path selection problem
- A multiple traveling salesman problem

However most of the time missions have to be specified through formats that are specific to the application. For the example problem, the following information has to be given to the planner each time a new plan is requested:

- The date for the plan to start, because problems are not stationary. For instance, the FEBA shall be crossed only in specific time windows.
- The UCAV to be considered. Indeed the vehicles are basic elements of mission specification. However additional information must also be provided. For instance, the UCAV predicted state in terms of geometry and resources at the date for the plan to start. Moreover, because a permanent communication network cannot be established and because enemies may destroy the UCAV, three classes of vehicles are to be distinguished: (i) the UCAV involved in the communication cluster in which the planning is carried on, (ii) the UCAV not involved in the communication cluster but presenting a plan assumption, and (iii) the UCAV not involved in the communication cluster and assumed out of order.
- The goals to be considered. Indeed goals are basic elements of the mission specification. Goals are described through action prototypes for target destruction. A prototype includes the resources to be used by the UCAV at specified places in the space and at specified times in order to have a specified probability of destroying the target. Figure

4 gives an example of an action prototype as a xml text. This prototype specifies that the target 1168 is a SAM site at a given latitude, longitude, and altitude. The target can be attacked either by delivering one bomb of type 1 with a UCAV with global positioning system capability or by delivering three bombs of type 1 with one or several UCAV. In the first case , the probability of destruction is 0.95. In the second case it is 0.80. Moreover the attack can be conducted either through node 1072 and edge 1069 with a heading of 270 degrees or through node 1074 and edge 1070 with a heading of 0 degrees.

- The navigation data including relevant characteristics of the environment. This includes a graph and the description of the airspace parts threatened by the different threats.

Motion Planning

Planning for multi-vehicle missions obviously includes motion planning for each vehicle of the fleet. The result of this motion planning is a sequence of "go to" actions to different points in the space. Different requirements for the path can be found in the literature (Allo, Guettier, Legendre, Poncet, & Strady-Lecubin, 2002; Kuwata, 2003; Szczerba, Galkowski, Glickstein, & Ternullo, 2000):

- The angle between two successive legs at each point of the path must be below a given value.
- The angle between two successive legs at each point of the path must be feasible through a sequence of three circle arcs that do not conflict with forbidden area.
- The distance between two consecutive points must be larger than a value that depends on the distance to the origin and on the distance to destination.
- The distance between two consecutive points must be large enough not to have any

Figure 4. Action prototype

```
<target id="1168" type="SAM_SITE" lat="45.241111" lon="8.810983" alt="0.">
    <mode bomb1="1" bomb2="0" pr="95" gps="1"></mode>
    <mode bomb1="3" bomb2="0" pr="80" gps="0"></mode>
    <node id="1072" type="weapon" axis="270.000000" edge="1069"></node>
    <node id="1074" type="weapon" axis="0.000000" edge="1070"></node>
</target>
```

interference from the sequence of circle arcs at the upstream point with the sequence at the downstream point.

- The length of the path must be below a given value.
- The heading of the last leg is given.
- The total combustible consumption must be lower than the combustible available at the beginning of the plan.

Two kinds of approaches for motion planning exist: the covering of the space by cells (Szczerba et al., 2000) and the construction of a graph (Allo et al., 2002; Fabiani et al., 2005; Kuwata, 2003). If the space is covered by cells, the solution of the problem can be provided by an A* algorithm. For each cell a local cost and an optimal cost to go under relaxing assumptions are computed. The A* algorithm uses the optimal cost to go as a heuristic function. If a graph is built, it can be done either by the Voronoi method (Fabiani et al., 2005) or by the visibility method (Kuwata, 2003). Then the path on the graph is found either by a Dijkstra (1959) algorithm, a modified Dijkstra algorithm (Kuwata, 2003), or constraint programming (Allo et al., 2002; Strady-Lecubin & Poncet, 2003).

For the example problem, the graph given to the planning module is complemented by the visibility method in order to provide paths around the threatened areas. Each node j of the graph presents a set of upstream edges (In_j) and a set of downstream edges (Out_j). Then the motion-planning component of the problem is formulated using constraint programming. Some variables are associated to UCAV and nodes; the fact that the UCAV i passes by the node j ($P_{i,j}$), the arrival time of the vehicle at the node, the altitude, speed, fuel, mass, logarithm of survival probability, and the fuel spent for the heading change at the node. Other variables are associated to vehicles and edges; the fact that the UCAV i flies the edge k ($U_{i,k}$), the flight time, altitude variation, fuel consumption, logarithm of conditional survival probability, and exposure time to the different threats of the UCAV on the edge. Constraints describe navigation possibilities. They include:

- A vehicle mass definition constraint,
- Constraints ensuring consistency between passing at a node and flying edges,
- Constraints modeling the feasibility of the heading change at a node and its consequence on the speed and consumption,
- Constraints associated to the initial state of each vehicle,
- Constraints ensuring consistency between the values of variables at the upstream node, the downstream node, and on the edge when a vehicle flies the edge, and
- Constraints associated to the terminal nodes of the graph.

For instance, consistency between passing at node and flying edges is given by:

$$\text{If } In_j \neq \varnothing, \sum_{k \in In_j} U_{i,k} = P_{i,j} \qquad (1)$$

$$\text{If } Out_j \neq \varnothing, \sum_{k \in Out_j} U_{i,k} = P_{i,j} \qquad (2)$$

If the heading change from edge k to edge l at not j is not possible:

$$U_{i,k} + U_{i,l} \leq 1 \qquad (3)$$

Otherwise:

$$U_{i,k} + U_{i,l} = 2 \Rightarrow CS_{SC} \qquad (4)$$

Where CS_{SC} is a set of constraints on speed and consumption of UCAV i at node j.

For the node *jinit(i)* where the UCAV i is at the date the plan begins:

$$P_{i,jinit(i)} = 1 \qquad (5)$$

For each edge k:

$$U_{i,k} = 1 \Rightarrow CS_{UD} \qquad (6)$$

Where CS_{UD} is a set of constraints between upstream and downstream nodes of edge k on arrival time, altitude, speed, fuel, logarithm of survival probability involving flight time, altitude variation, fuel consumption, logarithm of conditional survival probability, and exposure time on the edge k.

Finally the path ends in a node without downstream links:

$$\sum_{j\,/\,Out_j = \varnothing} P_{i,j} = 1 \qquad (7)$$

The constraint satisfaction problem derived includes linear, nonlinear, disjunctive, and conditional constraints. The variable domains are finite.

Consistent Group Motion

Multi-vehicle missions may also imply a consistent group motion: vehicles must remain close one to the other but must not collide. To take into account this kind of requirement, flocking has been adapted and implemented on fleets of actual robots by Hayes and Dormiani-Tabatabaei (2002). Moreover Olfati-Saber and Murray (2003) studied the adaptation of flocking algorithms in case of communication constraints and obstacle avoidance. Usually, flocking is not used at the deliberative layer but at the reactive layer. However, the use of a flocking criterion in a Dynamic Programming successive approximation scheme allows the computation of coordinated motion for two unmanned vehicles (Corre, 2003). For missions where vehicles move in an encumbered environment, the absence of collision and deadlock is ensured through planning. In Alami, Ingrand, and Qutub (1997), the edges of a navigation graph are resources to be shared among the mobile robots. The planning is then performed incrementally in a decentralized way: each time a robot receives a new goal, it builds a new plan compatible with the activities of its current plan and with the resource usage of the activities of the plans of the other robots. In other missions, the absence of collision is not handled by planning but is treated locally in a reactive way, for instance by stopping the robot with lower priority (Brumitt & Stentz, 1998).

A different kind of consistent group motion can be found with exploration missions: the vehicles must share the area to be explored. In the work of Walkers, Kudenko, and Strens (2004), agents are in charge of mapping a two dimensional area. Each agent builds heuristically a value function for each cell of the space. The path is obtained by selecting the neighboring cell with the best value. Several ways of computing the value are proposed. The computation of the value may take into account, when the communication between agents is possible, the path planned and the area already explored by other agents.

For the example problem, consistent group motion is not handled by the planner. The planner may produce a plan where some UCAV fly on the same edge at the same time. In that case the reactive layer gathers those UCAV in a formation and specific flying rules are applied.

Performing Tasks

In a group of vehicles, the vehicles may have different capabilities of action and observation. In that context, one vehicle may perform an action for another one and the exchange of information between vehicles may be explicitly planned. Some actions using resources of the sub-systems of the vehicle are in the plan besides the "go to" actions. Tavares and Campos (2004) give an example of such a situation: two helicopters have to travel a given path as quickly as possible but there is, somewhere on the path, one threat that can be perfectly observed and destroyed only by one of them. The plan is obtained using a team Partially Observed Makov Decision Process where the path is divided in steps and each agent has, in addition to original actions and observations, communication actions and observations. However, solving the simple problem exactly, where the path is already given, is not tractable and the heuristics used are sometimes not optimal.

Multi-vehicle mission planning may also include task selection and assignment. Several approaches for task assignment exist:

- Using rules on the state of the vehicles such as assigning the task to the nearest vehicle with the capability to perform it (Beard, McLain, Goodrich, & Anderson, 2002).
- Making requests to compute the cost of a path to a task destination or of a visit of several task locations for vehicles and using the results of the requests for optimizing the decision (Brumitt & Stentz, 1998).
- Computing for each vehicle the travel time associated to permutations of combinations of feasible, in terms of resources and tasks, selecting a limited number of permutations for each vehicle. Finally optimizing a criterion based on time of achievement of the last task, the permutation travel time and the total waiting time. This optimization selects one permutation per vehicle and set

the instants of task achievement (Kuwata, 2003). This approach is based on the use of libraries of linear programming with mixed variables.

Finally, vehicles assigned to the same task may have to be synchronized. Kuwata (2003) proposes to solve synchronization and assignment in a single problem. Another solution consists in generating, for each vehicle, a set of good paths to the point it has to perform the task and then to find among those sets the best feasible instant for task achievement (Beard et al., 2002). The assignment or synchronization is performed by computing, for each vehicle, a set of initial paths and selecting one path in each set. Then the selected path is refined in a last step by optimizing, taking into account the given synchronization instants (Beard et al., 2002; Kuwata, 2003).

The example problem involves different aspects: selection of goals, selection of an action mode for each goal, assignment of vehicles and their resources to each selected action mode, and scheduling attacks. Constraint programming and integer programming are powerful approaches for integrating those different aspects. Indeed, this approach is efficient even for planning problems expressed in a propositional representation (van Beek & Chen, 1999; Vossen, Ball, Lotem, & Nau, 1999). Moreover, the use of constraint programming allows a formulation consistent with the one for motion planning. For additional details about the encoding of a planning problem as a constraint programming formulation, see the chapter entitled Extending Classical Planning for Time: Research Trends in Optimal and Suboptimal Temporal Planning in this book. Variables indicating quantities of different resources (bombs, missiles, and so forth) of the UCAV when passing the node are associated to vehicles and nodes. For nodes j attached to the attack of a target, additional variables are the participation of the UCAV to the attack ($I_{i,j}$) and the quantities of different resource k used by the UCAV at the node ($Q_{k,i,j}$). Finally variables are associated to goal achievement. For each target, the variables are:

- The fact that the target o is attacked (A_o),
- The fact that it is attacked at a given node ($A_{o,j}$),
- The fact that it is attacked at a given node in a given mode ($A_{o,j,m}$),
- The attack time,
- The gross efficiency of the attack (Eff_o),
- The gross efficiency of the attack at a given node ($Eff_{o,j}$),
- The logarithm of the efficiency discounted by survival probability of participant UCAV.

Constraints describe conditions for goal achievement. The constraints associated to goal achievement include constraints associated to the attack of the targets and constraints defining some global criteria such as global efficiency (Eff) and global survivability. An important aspect is the link between the motion planning part of the model and the goal achievement part of the model. This link is ensured by constraints of the type:

$$I_{i,j} \leq P_{i,j} \tag{8}$$

$$I_{i,j} \leq \sum_k Q_{k,i,j} \tag{9}$$

$$Q_{k,i,j} \leq K_{k,i} I_{i,j} \tag{10}$$

$$\sum_i Q_{k,i,j} \geq R_{k,m} A_{o,j,m} \tag{11}$$

$$\sum_m A_{o,j,m} = A_{o,j} \tag{12}$$

$$\sum_j A_{o,j} = A_o \tag{13}$$

Equations (8) and (9) indicate that preconditions for an UCAV to participate to an attack at a node are to pass by that node and to have some resource to use at that node. Equation (10) bounds the resources usage by zero if the UCAV does not participate and by the available quantity, $K_{k,i}$, otherwise. Equation (11) indicates that the

precondition for the group to attack a target in a given mode is to have at least the resource amount requested for that mode, $R_{k,m}$. Equations (12) and (13) indicate that a single mode and a single node are selected for the attack of the target. Similar equations ensure the link between attack times and passage times at points.

A simplified equation for efficiency of the attack of target o at node j is:

$$Eff_{o,j} = \sum_m p_{o,m} A_{o,j,m} \tag{14}$$

where $p_{o,m}$ is the probability of destruction of the target o when attacked in mode m. This probability is directly taken from the action prototype. Then the efficiency of the attack of target o is given by:

$$Eff_o = \sum_j Eff_{o,j} \tag{15}$$

Finally the global efficiency is defined as the sum of the probability of destruction of the different targets:

$$Eff = \sum_o Eff_o \tag{16}$$

The modeling of the example problem using a constraint programming approach entails the definition of a large number of variables. But the graph of variables and constraints associated to a multi-vehicle mission presents a star structure: the variables associated to goal achievement are connected by constraints to the variables associated to the different vehicles but there is no direct constraint between the variables of two vehicles. This structure allows the decomposition of the initial problem into a problem associated to each vehicle and a goal achievement problem. The decomposition of the initial problem has the advantage of permitting the use of the computing resources of all vehicles and it corresponds to the approaches of Brumitt and Stentz (1998),

Beard et al. (2002), and Kuwata (2003). Several techniques are available to perform the distributed search of a solution. Among those techniques, it is possible to make the distinction between methods that start by solving the goal achievement problem and then making requests to motion planning solvers (Brumitt & Stentz, 1998) and methods that start by creating several proposals with the motion planning solvers (Beard et al., 2002; Kuwata, 2003). For the example problem, it seems that the first method would be blind starting the search mainly for setting attack time variables and performance evaluation variables. Thus the problem is solved with a three step technique where: (1) sets of solutions are searched for the problems associated to each vehicle, (2) a coordination problem, including the goal achievement problem and the selection of one solution per set, is solved, and (3) the solution is refined for each vehicle.

Important technical points are the assumptions made at step 1 to compute feasible paths between the points associated to goal achievement and the assumptions made for the representation of the different schedule on the same path with their impact on fuel consumption and threat exposure. It has been decided to compute feasible paths with a simplified consumption model and to provide the impact of the timing on other variables by linear relations.

Implementation

Implementation of distributed planning algorithms for multi-vehicle missions is often performed using custom software built without off-the-shelf packages. However, Kuwata (2003) uses CPLEX as a mixed variable linear programming engine for solving the assignment problem.

For the example problem the implementation relies on JADE (Bellifemine, Poggi, & Rimassa, 1999), a FIPA agent compliant framework. This framework allows implementing the three steps

of the distributed planning algorithm as two behaviors of the planner agent. The first behavior is activated by the "to prepare" module, sends a request for proposals to the different UCAV, waits for the reception of the proposals and solves the coordination problem. The second behavior is activated by a request for proposals. It computes and sends the set of solutions, waits for the selected solution, and refines it. The CHOCO (Laburthe, 2000) tree searching constraint solver is used for enumerating the set of solutions, solving the coordination problem and refining the selected solution. For additional information about constraint satisfaction techniques used by current constraint solvers, see the chapter entitled Principles of Constraint Processing in this book.

Computation Time Constraints

The control of the time to find a plan may also be an important implementation issue for some multi-vehicle online mission planning. One approach to avoid performing long plan computation on line is to provide a policy, computed off-line, that for each possible state gives almost immediately an action. In that case the performance is grounded on the introduction of expert knowledge or on dynamic programming or on reinforcement learning (Harmon & Harmon, 1996). However, the drawbacks of this approach are the limitation of the amount of memory for policy storage, the time taken off-line to compute the policy and the difficulty of assessing the quality of the learned policy.

Another approach for controlling the computation time is to plan with different levels of detail, either in time or in state space. For instance the receding horizon approach, used by Kuwata and How (2004) for UAV, consists in computing at each sample time a very detailed plan from the end of the current sample time to the end of a short-term horizon. The computation takes into account a rough plan evaluation from the end of this horizon to the end of the planning problem. Damiani, Verfaillie, and Charmeau (2004) propose for observation satellites an approach with a planning horizon not defined a priori. Indeed, breadth first tree search algorithms, like forward dynamic programming, can be interrupted at anytime and a rough evaluation can be added to the criterion of the leaves of the last fully developed level. For a classical planning domain, the propositions describing the state are classified in different classes of abstraction (Knoblock, 1991). The planning is performed starting with the most abstract class of propositions and then treating progressively less abstract classes. This approach may reduce computation time, but leads sometime to degraded performances (Smith & Peot, 1992). Zilberstein (1993) proposes algorithms that progressively improve the solution and studies the problem of splitting a given computation time in a sequence of such algorithms using their performance profiles. Zilberstein and Russel (1993) demonstrate the practical application of computation time splitting on a sequence made of an image analyzer feeding a path planner. At each less abstract level, the terrain description is refined by using a grid with twice number of discrete values in each dimension.

For some missions with ground vehicles and stationary environment it could be possible to stop the vehicles while the plan is computed. For the example problem this is not possible. The plan has to be ready at the time at which it should begin. The time spent by the solver to solve the sub-problems is controlled by the selection of variables to be assigned, by the selection of values for those variables, and by interruption of the tree search. For instance, an obvious solution of the coordination problem is to attack no targets. The selection of variables and values for the solver is performed in order to find this obvious solution first and then to improve it. Moreover before beginning to plan, the remaining time is split and assigned to each step of the solution.

EXPERIMENTAL RESULTS

Experimental results are given in the context of SEAD and STRIKE scenarios.

Behavior of the Planning Module

In order to assess the performance of the planning function, tests are conducted on a single Sun Blade 1500 computer. The planning module is requested to provide a plan for four UCAV with four targets on a graph with 50 nodes and 57 edges. The searches for a set of solutions by each vehicle correspond to a constraint satisfaction problem of about 300 variables and 500 constraints. This step leads to the generation of 46 solutions for the first UCAV after 1.0 seconds, 46 solutions for the second UCAV after 1.6 seconds, 46 solutions for the third UCAV after 1.7 seconds, and 138 solutions for the fourth UCAV in 2.4 seconds. It is interesting to note that the number of solutions found in the first step corresponds to the size of the domains of four of the variables of the second step. The second step of the method induces an optimization problem with about 1500 variables and 4200 constraints. The first constraint propagation made by CHOCO reduces the number of free variables to about 920. The following figure illustrates the anytime behavior of the second step of the planning method. A solution with no target attacked is found in about 1.0 seconds. Then as solution time increases, the efficiency of the solution, as defined by equation (16), is improved and more targets are attacked. Finally, the third step conducts to optimization problems of about 300 variables and 200 constraints for each UCAV. The refinement of the solution is given in 0.05 seconds for the first UCAV, 0.09 seconds for the second UCAV, 0.14 seconds for the third UCAV and 0.24 seconds for the fourth UCAV. Note that the solution times for the first and third step of the method are over-estimated because the tests are conducted using a single computer. Finally, it can be observed that if optimality is not required the computation time for the coordination step can be reduced to few seconds.

FULL SIMULATION RESULTS

Those results demonstrate the capacity of a fleet of vehicles integrating a distributed planning module within a reactive and deliberative architecture. The mission management system is able to carry on nominal missions as specified, to activate the contingent behaviors on disruptive events, to decide whether or not to plan and, if necessary, to plan and to run in a bounded time. Moreover, datalink requirements for the functions of the mission management system and performance of distributed planning are assessed.

The MMS is evaluated on different scenarios, starting from a very simple situation, one aircraft, one target, and moving on to more complex situations with multiple aircraft, threats, and targets. The following figure illustrates the nominal simplest scenario. The white line is the navigation of the aircraft. The red area is the FEBA, the green ones no-fly-zones, and the yellow one is a threat detection range. The MMS is able to execute this mission correctly and in time.

On this scenario, events are injected:

- **Discovery of a new threat on the path of the UCAV:** The reaction of the UCAV is first a modification of the flight path, induced by the reactive layer, in order to localize the threat. Then the deliberative layer plans online the mission in order to respect its timings. The new plan is applied and executed successfully. It is correct with respect to mission goals.
- **C2 sends new threat data when a jammer is available:** The reaction of the UCAV is no reaction at all as it considers it will be able to cross it using its jammer for self-defense.
- **C2 sends new threat data when a jammer isn't available:** The reaction of the UCAV is replanning in order to maximize survivability. The new plan is applied and executed successfully. It is correct with respect to mission goals. The new flight path goes around the new threat.
- **C2 sends data about two new threats while a jammer is available:** The reaction of the UCAV is replanning in order to maximize survivability. The new plan is applied and executed successfully. It is correct with respect to mission goals.

Figure 6. The nominal simplest scenario

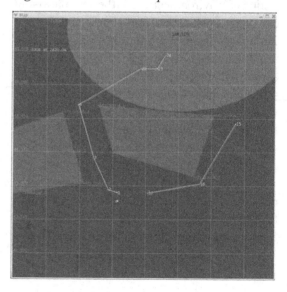

Figure 5. Performance profile for the second step of the planning algorithm. The efficiency is the sum of the destruction probabilities, expressed in %, of the targets attacked.

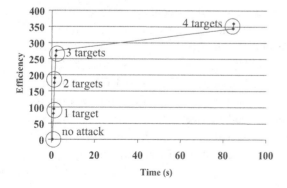

During a test with two aircraft, the nominal scenario is executed correctly and in time. Events are also injected in this scenario.

- **Loss of a sensor on the UCAV responsible for target acquisition:** The reaction of the group is mission replanning, the acquisition task is reallocated to the other UCAV. The new plan is applied and executed correctly.

- **C2 sends new threat data when a jammer is available:** The reaction of the group is no reaction at all as it considers it will be able to go through it using its jammer for self-defense.

- **C2 sends new threat data when a jammer isn't available:** The reaction of the group is replanning in order to maximize survivability. The new plan is applied and executed successfully. It is correct with respect to mission goals. The new flight path goes around the new threat.

- **C2 sends new mission target: the reaction of the group is replanning in order to be able to treat all mission targets.** The new plan is applied and executed successfully. It is correct with respect to the new mission goals. Each UCAV is responsible for a target.

The conjunction of those experimental results demonstrates the feasibility of the proposed mission management system.

CONCLUSION

The proposed architecture and distributed planning method for multi-vehicle missions contribute to the increase of vehicle intelligence and autonomy. Indeed, with the integration of online planning, disruptive events in absence of human intervention do not lead necessarily to aborting the mission. However, it is important to note that

Figure 7. Illustration of change of trajectory resulting from a new plan

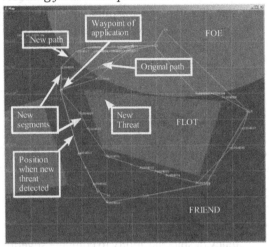

the architecture proposed for the example problem addresses a specific class of multi-vehicle missions. For this class the plan exists at the beginning of the mission and provides actions up to the end of the mission. In a context where there is a large uncertainty about the ending conditions of the mission or where there are systematically a large difference between the situation expected at planning time and the actual situation, other architectures based on a more systematic activation of the planning module are more suited.

Some research directions remain for this application domain of AI:

- Study of the link between the geometry and the actions.
- Study of the method for taking into account uncertainty about the state of the vehicles and the environment as distance from current date increases. Indeed, in the real world sensing is not perfect and actions may have uncertain outcomes not only in terms of rewards, as considered in the example, but also in terms of future state. The solution provided through the architecture proposed for the example is to compute a plan for the

current context using a deterministic model and to recompute it when the context changes significantly from the initial hypothesis. A more proactive solution could be obtained by using for instance probabilistic planning as proposed by Teichteil-Königsbuch and Fabiani (2006) for the mission of a search and rescue rotorcraft. The extension of this approach to multi-vehicle missions is a very promising research direction.

- Study of the efficiency of other distributed methods.
- Study of mixed initiative planning for fleets with manned and unmanned vehicles.
- Study of the sustainability of mission consistency despite the ability to compute several new plans during the mission.

ACKNOWLEDGMENT

The French "Délégation générale de l'armement," a part of the ministry of defense, has funded this work from 2003 to 2006 in the scope of the ARTEMIS project, thanks to this institution. The authors acknowledge the ARTEMIS partners for their contribution, thanks to Jean-Francois Gabard and Catherine Tessier. Finally, the authors thank Richard Washington for correcting many English mistakes.

REFERENCES

Agre, P.E., & Chapman, D. (1987). Pengi: An implementation of a theory of activity. In *Proceedings of the Sixth National Conference on Artificial intelligence* (pp. 268-272).

Alami, R., Chatila, R., Fleury, S., Ghallab, M., & Ingrand, F. (1998). An architecture for autonomy. *International Journal of Robotic Research, 17*(4), 315-337.

Alami, R., Ingrand, F., & Qutub, S. (1997). Planning coordination and execution in multirobots environement. In *Proceedings of the 8th International Conference on Advanced Robotics* (pp. 525-530).

Allo, B., Guettier, C., Legendre, V., Poncet, J.C., & Strady-Lecubin, N. (2002). Constraint model-based planning and scheduling with multiple resources and complex collaboration schema. In *Proceedings of the 6th International Conference on Artificial intelligence Planning and Scheduling* (pp. 284-293).

Beard, R.W., McLain, T.W., Goodrich, M.A., & Anderson, E.P. (2002). Coordinated target assignment and intercept for unmanned air vehicles. *Institute of Electrical and Electronics Engineers Transactions on Robotics and Automation, 18*(6), 911-922.

Bellifemine, F., Poggi, A., & Rimassa, G. (1999). JADE–A FIPA-compliant agent framework. In *Proceedings of the Fourth International Conference on the Practical Application of Intelligent Agents and Multi-Agent Technology* (pp. 97-108).

Benson, S.S. (1995). *Learning action models for reactive autonomous agents.* Stanford: Stanford University.

Bresina, J.L., & Drummond, M. (1990). Integrating planning and reaction. A preliminary report. In *Proceedings of the American Association of Artificial intelligence Spring Symposium on Planning in Uncertain, Unpredictable or Changing Environments* (pp. 24-28).

Bresina, J.L., & Washington, R. (2001). Robustness via run-time adaptation of contingent plans. In *Proceedings of the American Association of Artificial intelligence Spring Symposium on Robust Autonomy* (pp. 24-30).

Brooks, R. (1986). A robust layered control system for a mobile robot. *Institute of Electrical and*

Electronics Engineers Journal of Robotics and Automation, 2(1), 14-23.

Brumitt, B.L., & Stentz, A. (1998). GRAMMPS: A generalized mission planner for multiple mobile robots in unstructured environements. In *Proceedings of the Institute of Electrical and Electronics Engineers International Conference on Robotics and Automation* (vol. 3, pp. 2396-2401).

Corre, J. (2003). *Planification distribuée sous contrainte de communication.* Master of Science dissertation, ESIGELEC, UFR des sciences de Rouen, Rouen, France.

Damiani, S., Verfaillie, G., & Charmeau, M.C. (2004). An anytime planning approach for the management of an Earth watching satellite. In *4th International Workshop on Planning and Scheduling for Space* (pp. 54-63). Darmstadt, Germany.

Dijkstra, E.W. (1959). A note on two problems in connection with graphs. *Numerische Mathematik, 1,* 269-271.

Fabiani, P., Smith, P., Schulte, A., Ertl, C., Peeling, E., Lock, Z., et al. (2004). *Overview of candidate methods for the «autonomy for UAVs» design challenge problem.* Group for Aeronautical Research and Technology in EURope, Flight Mechanics Action Group 14 Report.

Gat, E. (1992). Integrating planning and reacting in a heterogeneous asynchronous architecture for controlling real-world mobile robots. In *Proceedings of the National Conference on Artificial intelligence* (pp. 809-815).

Harmon, M.E., & Harmon, S.S. (1996). Reinforcement learning: A tutorial. Retrieved on August 14, 2007, from http://iridia.ulb.ac.be/~fvandenb/qlearning/rltutorial.pdf

Hayes, A.T., & Dormiani-Tabatabaei, P. (2002). Self-organized flocking with agent failure: Offline optimization and demonstration with real robots. In *Proceedings of the Institute of Electrical*

and *Electronics Engineers International Conference on Robotics and Automation* (p. 4).

Hayes-Roth, B. (1993). *An architecture for adaptive intelligent systems.* Stanford University: Knowledge Systems Laboratory.

Hayes-Roth, B., Pfleger, K., Lalanda, P., & Morignot, P. (1995). A domain-specific software architecture for adaptive intelligent systems. *Institute of Electrical and Electronics Engineers Transactions on Software Engineering, 21*(4), 288-301.

Knoblock, C.A. (1991). *Automatically generation abstractions for problem solving.* Unpublished doctoral dissertation, Carnegie Mellon University, School of Computer Science.

Kuwata, Y. (2003). *Real-time trajectory design for unmanned aerial vehicles using receding horizon control.* Master of Science dissertation, Massachusetts Institute of Technology.

Kuwata, Y., & How, J.P. (2004). *Three dimentional receding horizon control for UAVs.* Paper presented at the American Institute of Aeronautics and Astronautics Guidance, Navigation, and Control Conference and Exhibit.

Laburthe, F. (2000). CHOCO: Implementing a CP kernel. In *Proceedings of the Workshop on Techniques for Implementing Constraint Programming Systems,* Singapour (pp. 71-85).

Muscettola, N., Nayak, P.P., Pell, B., & Williams, B.C. (1998). Remote agent: To boldly go where no AI system has gone before. *Artificial intelligence, 103*(1/2), 5-47.

Olfati-Saber, R., & Murray, R.M. (2003). Flocking with obstacle avoidance: Cooperation with limited information in mobile networks. In *Proceedings of the 42nd Institute of Electrical and Electronics Engineers Conference on Decision and Control* (pp. 2022-2028). Retrieved on August 14, 2007, from http://www.cds.caltech.edu/~olfati/papers/cdc03/cdc03b_ros_rmm.pdf

Schoppers, M. (1995). The use of dynamics in an intelligent controller for a space faring rescue robot. *Artificial intelligence, 73*(1/2), 175-230.

Smith, D.E., & Peot, M.A. (1992). A critical look at Knoblock's hierarchy mechanism. In *1st International Conference on Artificial intelligence Planning Systems* (pp. 307-308).

Strady-Lécubin, N., & Poncet, J.C. (2003). Mission management system high level architecture, report 4.3. MISURE/TR/4-4.3/AX/01, EUCLID RTP 15.5.

Szczerba, R.J., Galkowski, P., Glickstein, I.S., & Ternullo, N. (2000). Robust algorithm for real-time route planning. *Institute of Electrical and Electronics Engineers Transactions on Aerospace and Electronics Systems, 36*(3), 869-878.

Tavares, A.I., & Campos, M.F.M. (2004). Balancing coordination and synchronization cost in cooperative situated multi-agent systems with imperfect communication. In *Proceedings of the 16th European Conference on Artificial intelligence* (pp. 68-73).

Teichteil-Königsbuch, F., & Fabiani, P. (2006). Autonomous search and rescue rotorcraft mission stochastic planning with generic DBNs. In M. Bramer (Ed.), *International federation for information processing* (p. 217), *Artificial intelligence in theory and practice* (pp. 483-492). Boston, MA: Springer.

van Beek, P., & Chen, X. (1999). CPlan: A constraint programming approach to planning. In *Proceedings of American Association for Artificial intelligence* (pp. 585-590).

Verfaillie, G., & Fabiani P. (2000). Planification dans l'incertain, planification en ligne. Presentation at Rencontres Nationales des Jeunes Chercheurs en Intelligence Artificielle.

Vossen, T., Ball, M., Lotem, A., & Nau, D. (1999). On the use of integer programming models in AI planning. In *Proceedings of the 16th International Joint Conference on Artificial intelligence* (pp. 304-309).

Walkers, T., Kudenko, D., & Strens, M. (2004). Algorithms for distributed exploration. In *Proceedings of the 16th European Conference on Artificial intelligence* (pp. 84-88).

Washington, R., Golden, K., Bresina, J., Smith, D.E., Anderson, C., & Smith, T. (1999). Autonomous rovers for Mars exploration. In *Proceedings of the Institute of Electrical and Electronics Engineers Aerospace Conference* (Vol. 1, pp. 237-251).

Zilberstein, S. (1993). *Operational rationality through compilation of anytime algorithms.* Unpublished doctoral dissertation, Computer Science Division, University of California at Berkeley.

Zilberstein, S., & Russel, S.J. (1993). Anytime sensing, planning and action: A practical model for robot control. In *Proceedings of the 13th International Joint Conference on Artificial intelligence,* Chambery, France (pp. 1402-1407).

Chapter II
Extending Classical Planning for Time:
Research Trends in Optimal and Suboptimal Temporal Planning

Antonio Garrido
Universidad Politécnica de Valencia, Spain

Eva Onaindia
Universidad Politécnica de Valencia, Spain

ABSTRACT

The recent advances in artificial intelligence (AI) automated planning algorithms have allowed tackling with more realistic problems that involve complex features such as explicit management of time and temporal plans (durative actions and temporal constraints), more expressive models of actions to better describe real-world problems (conservative models of actions vs. nonconservative models), utilisation of heuristic techniques to improve performance (strategies to calculate estimations and guide the search), and so forth. In this chapter we focus on these features and present a review of the most successful techniques for temporal planning. First, we start with the optimal planning-graph-based approach, we do a thorough review of the general methods, algorithms, and planners, and we finish with heuristic state-based approaches, both optimal and suboptimal. Second, we discuss the inclusion of time features into a Partial Order Causal Link (POCL) approach. In such an approach, we analyse the possibility of mixing planning with Constraint Satisfaction Problems (CSPs), formulating the planning problem as a CSP and leaving the temporal features to a CSP solver. The ultimate objective here is to come up with an advanced, combined model of planning and scheduling. Third, we outline some techniques used in hybrid approaches that combine different techniques. Finally, we provide a synthesis of many well-known temporal planners and present their main techniques.

INTRODUCTION

Artificial intelligence (AI) planning algorithms have shown an impressive speedup in the last decade (Ghallab, Nau, & Traverso, 2004; Long & Fox, 2002; Weld, 1999). Modern planners now easily subsume classical planning features and are able to deal with more realistic features such as an explicit management of temporal and metric capabilities, powerful expressive domain definition languages, heuristic estimations to improve the quality of the plans, multi-criteria optimisation, explicit management of metric resources, and so forth. The purpose of this chapter is to analyse the most relevant algorithmic approaches and planning systems that handle temporal capabilities in planning within the field of AI. But, before doing this, we first present some essential background on classical planning.

Background on Classical Planning

This section is aimed at providing the reader with a general overview on the problem of planning in AI by introducing the most basic concepts and representations. A more detailed and exhaustive overview can be found in Ghallab et al. (2004) and Russell and Norvig (2003). Planning, as it has been explored within the field of AI, is the task of coming up with a set of actions whose execution will lead from a particular initial state to a state in which a goal condition is satisfied. Broadly speaking, planning decides *which* actions to apply, whereas scheduling decides *when* and *how* execute such actions. Therefore, *classical planning* research has been almost exclusively concerned with the logical structure of the relationship between the actions in a plan, rather than with the metric temporal structure. That is, planning has been concerned with the orderings of actions—typically in a total order—in such a way that the logical executability of the plan is guaranteed (Long & Fox, 2003b).

The basic representation language in classical planning is the STRIPS language (Fikes & Nilsson, 1971): a problem is represented by a set of action schemas, or operators, an initial state, and a goal condition. A *state* is a conjunction of positive literals that represent the properties values of the problem objects. Literals in first-order state descriptions must be ground and function-free. A *goal* is a partially specified state, represented as a conjunction of positive ground literals. Literals in a goal state denote the desired values of the objects properties in the final state. An *operator* is specified in terms of its preconditions and positive and negative effects. A finite collection of action instances can be constructed from the operators by instantiating the variables in the operators in all possible ways (subject to type constraints). Therefore, an action is specified in terms of their logical preconditions, which must hold in the state of application, and the effects that ensue when it is executed. An action is *applicable* in any state that satisfies its preconditions; otherwise, the action has no effect. Starting in a state S, the result of executing an applicable action a is a state S' that is the same as S except that any positive literal in the effects of a is added to S' and any negative literal is removed from S'.

In classical planning, preconditions are evaluated in a state under the closed-world assumption, meaning that any conditions that are not mentioned in a state are assumed *false*. A common form for describing effects relies on the well-known STRIPS assumption: every literal not mentioned in the effect remains unchanged. In this way, the STRIPS assumption provides a simple solution to the frame problem.

Classical planning makes a number of simplifying assumptions: (i) the world state is fully observable, actions always have expected effects, and, consequently, the states that result from the application of actions are totally predictable; (ii) actions have instantaneous effects and time is relative; and (iii) actions can be directly executed in the environment and the task of planning is to devise a plan that achieves the goal condition before any part of the plan is executed (off-line planning). Under these assumptions, a plan is a totally or partially ordered collection of actions which, when executed in the initial state, produces a state that satisfies the goal conditions.

In general terms, the most relevant algorithmic approaches to classical planning are: the state-space search, the plan-space search, and the graph-plan search (Weld, 1999). State-space search can operate in a forward direction (progression) or a backward direction (regression). Effective heuristics can be derived by assuming subgoal independency or by various relaxations of the planning problem (Hoffmann & Nebel, 2001). Plan-space search takes place in a space of partial plans without committing to a totally ordered sequence of actions (partial-order planning). In this type of search, the algorithms usually work backwards from the goal, adding actions to the plan to achieve each subgoal (Weld, 1994). Plan-graph search constructs incrementally a data structure, called planning graph, consisting of alternating layers of positive literals (also known as propositions) and actions (see the section in this chapter on actions). Planning graphs are very useful to extract informative heuristics for state-space and partial-order planners and can be used directly in the Graphplan algorithm (Blum & Furst, 1997). These three algorithmic approaches have been extended and adequately exploited to address the new issues that arise in the management of temporal domains in planning. The remainder of this chapter is devoted to this topic and focuses on the extension of classical planning to deal with time and actions with duration, that is, temporal planning.

Temporal Planning Motivation

In real problems, the motivation for dealing with durative actions is clear: actions usually have widely different durations (Garrido, Fox, & Long, 2002; Smith & Weld, 1999). For instance, in a lo-gistics domain we cannot assume that two actions *fly(plane1,cityA,cityB)* and *fly(plane2,cityA,cityC)* have the same duration, because the average speed of the planes or the distance between the cities can be significantly different. Discarding the assumption that actions have the same duration leads to a more complex planning problem: not only does the planner need to find the appropriate set of actions to achieve the goals, that is, the plan, but also the appropriate execution time when the actions need to be executed, which highly increases the size of the search space. In other words, planning has to include some scheduling reasoning to allocate actions in time. Additionally, in temporal planning, the plan optimality is not only assumed in terms of the number of actions but in terms of the plan makespan (completion time): a plan with fewer actions can be longer than other which turns out shorter *w.r.t.* the overall duration of the plan. Consequently, an important issue in temporal planning is to guarantee the plan that minimises the global duration, that is, the plan with optimal makespan.

Although some planners have tried to directly include durations into the classical model of actions,[1] also known as the *conservative* model (Smith & Weld, 1999) because it maintains the same structure of the classical actions, the result is a modest extension where two actions cannot overlap in *any way* if they have conflicting preconditions or effects. This makes it possible to produce reasonable plans in some planning domains, but there exist other domains that require a richer model of actions (also known as *nonconservative*, with more types of conditions and effects) in which better quality (shorter makespan) plans can be found (Fox & Long, 2003). Therefore, in order to obtain more realistic and better quality plans, it becomes necessary to achieve a more accurate exploitation of action concurrency, thus taking advantage of the true overlapping possibilities of durative actions. Finding optimal temporal plans in a nonconservative model of actions is a hard task which becomes intractable in many problems. Consequently, the application of efficient heuristics to find good suboptimal plans is becoming more and more important in temporal planning.

A nice introductory paper about the role that time can play in the planning problem can be found in (Long & Fox, 2003b). In that work, the authors examine temporal planning in terms of the following four issues: (i) the choice of temporal ontology, (ii) causality, (iii) the management of concurrency, and (iv) continuous change. In this chapter, however, we describe the main techniques for temporal planning, particularly those used in most well-known planners, and address the main issues of their application to an expressive (nonconservative) model of actions. We present both optimal and suboptimal (also called satisficing) temporal planning under four perspectives: (i) planning-graph-based, (ii) POCL-based, (iii) heuristic-based, and (iv) hybrid-based. We also provide a series of algorithms with the general scheme of each technique that should be applicable to most systems in each approach. Hence, the algorithms do not intend to provide many specific technical details, but to show the readers the potential of each technique and give them a general feeling of their pros and cons. This way, the main contributions of the chapter are:

- An introduction of how to model durative actions in planning. We compare the conservative model of actions with several nonconservative models, including PDDL2.1 (Fox & Long, 2003), explaining the expressiveness supported by each model.
- An analysis of how to deal with durative actions under a planning graph approach, how several variations of temporal planning graphs can be generated, and a discussion of the possibilities for using planning graphs as a basis for heuristic estimations to be used in heuristic state-based planners. We also sketch the main ideas of well-known planners such as TGP, Sapa, and TP4.

- An explanation of how to extend POCL planning to include and handle time, and how to use an interval (and time points) representation as a flexible way to encode durative actions together with complex constraints. We also present three general solving methods for temporal POCL planning: (i) use special temporal networks to reason on temporal information; (ii) combine POCL and CSP techniques to reason on time; and (iii) formulate the temporal problem as a constraint programming model and solve it with a CSP solver. The chapter also provides major ideas about common systems such as HSTS, IxTeT, VHPOP, CPT, and others.
- An explanation of hybrid approaches that combine different techniques together with a concise description of the planners LPG and SGPlan.
- A synthesis of the main techniques used in well-known, optimal and suboptimal, temporal planners with good performance in any of the last three International Planning Competitions and publicly available.
- An indication of future directions for research on temporal planning from different perspectives, including more efficiency, expressiveness, and addressing integrated architectures for planning and scheduling.

This chapter is organised as follows. The next section introduces the model of durative actions, providing a comparison between a conservative and nonconservative model of actions. We then analyse the main techniques and algorithms for coping with temporal planning by using a planning graph approach and then present heuristic approaches that use admissible and nonadmissible estimations to guide the planning process. The following section reviews and proposes techniques and formulations for temporal planning under a POCL+CSP planning approach and in the next section this is done under a hybrid approach. A brief synthesis about the main techniques that use temporal planners that showed good performance in any of the last three International Planning Competitions is presented and finally, the conclusions and a discussion of future directions of research are presented in the final section.

MODELING DURATIVE ACTIONS FOR TEMPORAL PLANNING

A planning problem is modelled as the tuple $\langle I, G, A \rangle$, where I and G represent the initial state and the problem goals, respectively, as two sets of propositions, and A represents the set of ground durative actions. Traditionally, actions are modelled in planning with preconditions and effects. In a conservative model of actions, preconditions need to be maintained throughout the whole execution of the action, whereas the effects are asserted in the end of the action. This implies that preconditions are *protected* within the execution of the action, avoiding the simultaneous execution of a second action that deletes any of the preconditions of the first action. This involves an easier planning task because two actions that interact negatively (one deletes the proposition that the other requires/asserts) cannot overlap, which discards an important part of the search space. Although this helps simplify the solving process, it imposes a serious limitation in its applicability to realistic problems. In many problems, the preconditions do not necessarily need to be maintained throughout the whole execution of the action, but only during a portion of such an execution. Hence, it becomes necessary to distinguish invariant from non-invariant conditions depending on whether they can be affected or not during the interval of execution. Moreover, there might be effects to be asserted at several points during the execution of the action, and not only when it ends.

Conservative vs. a Nonconservative Model of Actions

We motivate the extension of a conservative model of actions to a nonconservative model with the following example of the classical logistics domain. Let us consider the action *fly(plane1,cityA,cityB)*. This action requires the proposition *at(plane1,cityA)* to be true before executing the action, and asserts the propositions {¬*at(plane1,cityA),at(plane1,cityB)*} at the end of the action. This means that the location of *plane1* is inaccessible until the end of the action, preventing concurrent actions (for instance, those that require *plane1* not to be in the *cityA*) from being executed in parallel with *fly(plane1,cityA,cityB)*, which may exclude many valid plans. In a nonconservative model of actions with more types of conditions, this situation can be avoided by simply asserting ¬*at(plane1,cityA)* as an effect when the action starts, and *at(plane1,cityB)* when it ends. In addition, if we want to know that *plane1* is *flying* during the action *fly*, it would be enough to assert the proposition *flying(plane1)* as an initial effect and ¬*flying(plane1)* as a final effect. In the conservative model, the action equivalent to this *fly* action would not be able to represent the fact of being *flying* due to the inability to express the proposition *flying(plane1)* and ¬*flying(plane1)* as an initial and final effect, respectively. This would prevent this model from working with more realistic actions which require this proposition, such as a possible *refuel-during-flight* action.

All in all, a nonconservative model provides actions with more types of conditions and effects, which allows a more precise modeling of the state transitions undergone by different propositions within the durative interval of the action. This allows to improve the quality of the plan and make it more realistic by giving rise to more sophisticated opportunities for concurrent actions. However, this also involves a more complex planning task because two actions that interact negatively could not start together but they could still overlap and, consequently, the search space increases.

Probably the most currently used nonconservative model of actions is the one proposed in level 3 of PDDL2.1 (Fox & Long, 2003), which subsumes the conservative model. Level 3 of PDDL2.1 provides a more permissive model of actions by requiring more conditions and asserting effects at the start/end of the action, as shown in the following definition.

Definition 1 (PDDL2.1 durative action): A durative action *a*, which is executed throughout

Figure 1. Definition of three durative actions for the transportation zenotravel domain, which involves transporting people around in planes. In addition to the duration attached to each action, the action fly consumes fuel (numeric planning) at different quantities according to the distance between the cities.

```
(:durative-action board
  :parameters (?p -person ?a -aircraft ?c -city)
  :duration (= ?duration (boarding-time))
  :condition (and (at start (at ?p ?c))
           (over all (at ?a ?c)))
  :effect (and (at start (not (at ?p ?c)))
         (at end (in ?p ?a))))

(:durative-action debark
  :parameters (?p -person ?a -aircraft ?c -city)
  :duration (= ?duration (debarking-time))
  :condition (and (at start (in ?p ?a))
           (over all (at ?a ?c)))
  :effect (and (at start (not (in ?p ?a)))
         (at end (at ?p ?c))))

(:durative-action fly
  :parameters (?a -aircraft ?c1 ?c2 -city)
  :duration (= ?duration (/ (distance ?c1 ?c2) (slow-speed ?a)))
  :condition (and (at start (at ?a ?c1))
           (at start (>= (fuel ?a)
                (* (distance ?c1 ?c2) (slow-burn ?a)))))
  :effect (and (at start (not (at ?a ?c1)))
         (at end (at ?a ?c2))
         (at end (decrease (fuel ?a)
              (* (distance ?c1 ?c2) (slow-burn ?a))))))
```

the interval $[S(a)..E(a)]$ is defined by the following elements:

- Conditions. There exist three types of conditions: (i) $SCond(a)$, with the conditions required at the start of the action ($S(a)$), (ii) $Inv(a)$, with the invariant conditions required over the execution of the action ($[S(a)..E(a)]$), and (iii) $ECond(a)$, with the conditions to be satisfied at the end of the action ($E(a)$).
- Duration, as a positive value represented by $dur(a) \in R^+$.
- Effects. There exist two types of effects: (i) $SEff(a)$, with the effects (both positive and negative) to be asserted at the start of the action ($S(a)$), and (ii) $EEff(a)$, with the effects (both positive and negative) to be asserted at the end of the action ($E(a)$).

Figure 1 shows an example of three durative actions (*board*, *debark* and *fly*) modelled in PDDL2.1 for a simple logistics domain called *zenotravel*. For instance, the action *board* requires the person *p* to be in the city *c* only at the beginning of the action, whereas the aircraft *a* needs to be in the same city during the whole execution of the action. On the other hand, *board* deletes the fact of the person being in the city at the beginning of the action and asserts the fact of being in the aircraft at the end. The effects of the action *fly* are similar: at the beginning of the action the aircraft leaves the origin city *c1* and, at the end, it reaches the destination city *c2*, also decreasing the fuel level of the aircraft. The use of the fluent *(fuel ?a)* as a numeric variable is part of the functionality included in planning with numeric (or metric) variables, that is strongly related to temporal planning (Do & Kambhampati, 2001; Fox & Long, 2003; Garrido & Long, 2004; Haslum & Geffner, 2001). Although numeric planning exceeds the scope of this chapter, currently many heuristic temporal planners also include capabilities for dealing with numeric variables under a multi-criteria optimisation point of view.

The success of level 3 of PDDL2.1 comes from its use as a standard Planning Domain Definition Language in the International Planning Competition (IPC[2]) celebrated in 2002. Since then, PDDL2.1 has evolved into PDDL2.2 (Edelkamp & Hoffmann, 2004) and PDDL3 (Gerevini & Long, 2005) but the nonconservative model of actions remains exactly the same. However, PDDL2.1 is not the only nonconservative model of durative actions that we can find in the literature, nor it is the most expressive.

Other Nonconservative Models of Actions

Despite the success of PDDL2.1 for modeling durative actions, it still presents an important limitation: both conditions and effects are attached to the extreme points of the actions (although invariant conditions are not strictly attached to the extreme points, they always need to persist from one extreme to the other). On the contrary, in other temporal planners such as ZENO (Penberthy & Weld, 1994), Sapa (Do & Kambhampati, 2003), or VHPOP (Younes & Simmons, 2003), conditions and effects can be temporally quantified within the interval of execution of the action.

Hence, conditions may be required either to be instantaneously true at the starting/ending time point of the action, or required from the start of the action and remained true for some duration within the execution of the action. Analogously, effects can be asserted at arbitrary intermediate points within the execution of the action and can be either instantaneously true or maintained for some duration. This model is more general and allows to reason about deadline goals, temporal windows, and exogenous events (facts that will become true or false at time points that are known to the planner in advance, regardless the actions in the plan) (Edelkamp & Hoffmann, 2004; Smith & Weld, 1999).

Following this line of extending the nonconservative model of actions we can go beyond and come up with a more elaborate model of actions (Garrido, Onaindía & Arangu, 2006). Figure 2 shows an example of this type of actions. First of all, the duration of the actions does not need to be a fixed value, but it can vary within a certain range $S(a)..E(a)$. Second, conditions are required in any interval of time that can be placed totally, partially or even out the execution of the action (obviously, if the bounds of the interval are equal the condition is required instantaneously). This

Figure 2. Example of actions fly and debark under a more elaborate model of conditions and effects

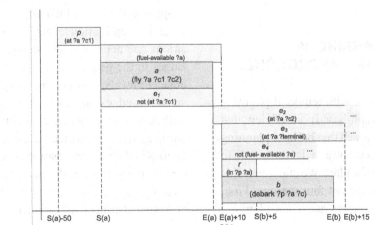

is interesting since it allows to model conditions that do not fall within the execution of the actions, that is, real preconditions to be satisfied some time before the actions start. For instance, now action *fly* requires condition *p* (the aircraft to be in the origin city) since 50 time units before starting, and to have fuel until 10 units after ending. Third, effects can also be generated at any time (within or outside the execution of the action) and persist throughout some time. This way, the effects may persist until an action deletes them or be *implicitly* deleted. For instance, the effect e_1 of *fly* is generated when *fly* starts and persists until it ends, whereas e_2, e_3 and e_4 have an infinite persistence. Additionally, both e_3 and e_4 are generated 10 time units after the action finishes because it is necessary the aircraft traverses the airport segments to arrive at the terminal, and after this the action *debark* starts. As can be seen, this model subsumes the conservative model of actions and provides a very general model for nonconservative actions capable of representing a wide range of real-world features. Although encoding such a general model turns out a bit difficult in some planers, it can be easily formulated via constraint programming, as presented in a later section.

In the rest of the chapter, we will use the nonconservative model of actions as proposed in level 3 of PDDL2.1 as it is the most widely used in temporal planners; otherwise, we will state explicitly when other model of actions is used.

TEMPORAL PLANNING IN PLANNING GRAPH APPROACHES

In this section we cope with temporal planning from the planning-graph-based point of view, that is, we present an approach that builds a planning graph and uses such a graph as a data structure to perform the search of a plan. We start with this approach mainly because of four reasons. First, although POCL approaches are *older*, planning graph techniques have led to a renewed interest in planning and its extensions for dealing with more realistic capabilities, neoclassical planning (Ghallab et al., 2004). Second, planning graphs can be generalised to deal with durative actions (both in a conservative and a nonconservative model) (Garrido et al., 2002; Smith & Weld, 1999). Third, planning graph techniques provide nice theoretical properties that allow us to deal with optimal temporal planning (Blum & Furst, 1997; Garrido et al., 2002; Smith & Weld, 1999). Four, planning graphs are widely used as a basis for calculating heuristic estimations in many state-based planners and even in POCL planners, both of which are discussed in later sections.

Planning Graphs in Planning

In this section, we introduce the basic formulation about planning graphs and their derivatives, such as propagation of mutual exclusion relations, relaxed plans, and heuristic estimations that can be extracted from them, which are necessary in most approaches presented in this chapter.

Introduction

A planning graph is a polynomial size structure that encodes both the static part (propositions and actions) and the dynamic part (ordering relations) of a planning problem. Particularly, a planning graph is a digraph which alternates proposition levels ($P_{[t]}$) and action levels ($A_{[t]}$), with the propositions and actions, respectively, of each level t. Edges in the graph are allowed to connect only adjacent levels; that is, preconditions are represented as edges that connect propositions in $P_{[t]}$ with actions in $A_{[t]}$, whereas effects (both positive and negative) are represented as edges that connect actions in $A_{[t]}$ with propositions in $P_{[t+1]}$. Basically, a planning graph builds incrementally, starting from $P_{[0]}=I$, and continues until all the goals in G are satisfied in any $P_{[t]}$. This termination condition makes the time taken to build the planning graph polynomial in the length of the problem size and the number of levels (time steps).

A planning graph keeps an implicit notion of time by means of its levels: actions are executed in levels $A_{[t]}$, $A_{[t+1]}$, $A_{[t+2]}$ and so on, while propositions are generated in the levels $P_{[t+1]}$, $P_{[t+2]}$, $P_{[t+3]}$... due to the execution of the actions. These levels provide very useful information as an optimistic measure of reachability. That is, if an action is not present in level $A_{[t]}$, it is known for certain that such an action is not reachable in t steps, and the same situation holds for propositions. Consequently, if $P_{[t]}$ is the earliest proposition level in which all propositions in G are present, a valid plan will require, at least, t steps. As can be noted this information is very valuable to find lower (optimistic) bounds of the plan's length.

Mutual Exclusion (Mutex) Relations

In general, a planning graph is too permissive in terms of the actions and propositions that are present in an action or proposition level, respectively. Particularly, having two actions in the same level $A_{[t]}$ does not mean that both actions can be executed concurrently in the real world because they can interact negatively. For instance, actions *fly(plane1,cityA,cityB)* and *fly(plane1,cityA,cityC)* are mutually exclusive (mutex) in any level since *plane1* cannot fly simultaneously to different cities. The same happens with propositions *at(plane1,cityA)* and *at(plane1,cityB)*, since *plane1* cannot be in both cities at the same time.

Planning graphs can be extended to include information about mutual exclusion relations between action-action and proposition-proposition in the form of binary constraints. Two actions (propositions) are mutex in a level if no valid plan can contain them simultaneously, that is, they cannot coexist in the real world. More formally, two actions are mutex if: (i) the effects of an action delete the effects or conditions of the other action, or (ii) the conditions of the two actions are mutex.

On the other hand, two propositions are mutex if all the ways (actions) to generate a proposition are mutex with all the ways to generate the other. A planning graph that propagates this information about mutex is more informed and provides a more precise estimation for lower bounds. For instance, if two actions (propositions) are present in level $A_{[t]}$ ($P_{[t]}$) but they are pairwise mutex they cannot be reachable together, and they can only be satisfied simultaneously in a level $t'>t$ in which they are not pairwise mutex, which enhances the estimations. Obviously, calculating a planning graph taking mutex relations into consideration entails a higher computational cost. On the contrary, a planning graph that ignores the negative effects of the actions can be generated easier and faster since there are no negative interactions between actions no calculus on mutexes needs to be done. Such a graph is called a *relaxed planning graph* and becomes very useful to calculate heuristic estimations in a fast way (Bonet & Geffner, 2001; Hoffmann & Nebel, 2001).

Planning Graphs as a Basis for Heuristic Estimations

As seen previously, planning graphs provide a compact structure that allows us to calculate heuristic estimations in the form of reachability analysis which can help guide the search during a state-based planning process. In order to calculate these estimations we can use either a relaxed or nonrelaxed planning graph. Obviously there exists a tradeoff between the cost of generating it (the former is faster) and the quality of the estimations (the latter is more exact). In both cases, the underlying idea is to build a planning graph from each state to the goal G. This way, the value $h(g)$ represents the earliest level in the planning graph in which goal g is present. Since G usually includes many goals, a family of powerful estimations for $h(G)$ is used (Bonet & Geffner, 1999), which include, among other:

- h_{sum}, which estimates the total cost as the sum of all the individual costs of each goal: $h_{sum}(G) = \sum_{g \in G} h(g)$.
- h_{max}, which estimates the total cost as the max of all the individual costs of each goal: $h_{max}(G) = \max_{g \in G} h(g)$.
- h_{max2}, which estimates the total cost as the max level in which each pair of goals is present and not pairwise mutex: $h_{max2}(G) = \max_{\{g1,g2\} \in G} h(g_1 \wedge g_2)$.[3]

Clearly, the first heuristic is nonadmissible because it does not consider that one action may generate more than one goal, while the second and third heuristics are admissible. In any case, planning graphs can be used as a basic structure to detect interactions between actions/propositions and to extract heuristic estimations.

Planning for Classical Planning: Graphplan

The original structure of planning graphs is ideal for classical planning, where all actions have the same instantaneous duration (levels are equidistant) and plans can have actions in parallel (actions can be executed in the same level). Graphplan is a well-known planning-graph-based planner that exploits that structure by working in two stages: first it builds a (nonrelaxed) planning graph and second it uses such a graph as the basis to perform a backward search (known as *extraction stage*) based on IDA* (Blum & Furst, 1997; Korf, 1985). Graphplan extends the generation of the planning graph by including additional reasoning on mutex between actions/propositions with the general meaning of keeping exclusivity between them. The reasoning and propagation of mutex throughout the planning graph is one of the main contributions of Graphplan because it helps produce very informed planning graphs, which also reduces the search space for the second stage. Actually, Graphplan builds the planning graph until reaching a level in which any pair of

goals in G is not mutex, thus avoiding fruitless search steps where there exist at least two goals that cannot be simultaneously satisfied. Graphplan has very nice properties for planning: soundness, completeness and optimality. Soundness and completeness appear as a consequence of the way the planning graph is generated and the completeness of the search. On the other hand, optimality is guaranteed in terms of planning steps (levels) but not in terms of actions because several actions can be executed concurrently in the same level. Therefore, Graphplan proposes a promising approach for including new capabilities, such as durative actions of temporal planning.

Pure Planning Graph Approaches

Graphplan's success motivated the use of planning-graph-based techniques and their application to temporal planning. TGP is the first temporal planner that generalises the planning graph representation to deal with time instead of pure graph levels and uses such a graph as a data-structure to perform the search of a plan (Smith & Weld, 1999). Although TGP uses a conservative model of durative actions, it introduces some key points to deal with actions that can have different duration under a planning graph approach, which are:

- Use a temporal planning graph rather than a planning graph where levels are labelled with time stamps (time is modelled by R^+ and their chronological order). Actually, TGP uses a more compact representation of the planning graph by means of a bilevel planning graph, with action and proposition nodes, that reduces the space costs. In this compact representation, actions and propositions are annotated by their earliest possible start times.
- Extend reasoning on mutex by classifying mutex into conditional mutex, which involve time bounds, and eternal mutex, which hold throughout the entire planning

graph. Moreover, the inclusion of durative actions in a planning graph requires a new (more complex) type of proposition-action mutex that better connect action-action to proposition-proposition mutexes.

- Build the temporal planning graph by incrementally adding new actions and propositions, while it also propagates more sophisticated information about mutexes. The main difficulty here is that actions $\{a_i\}$ in level $A_{[t]}$ generate their effects in proposition level $P_{[t+dur(a_i)]}$ instead of in level $P_{[t+1]}$, that is, the levels in the temporal planning graph are not equidistant and they depend on the duration of the actions generated.

- Extract a plan in the search stage by finding a flow of actions through the temporal planning graph. Again, the main difficulty here relies on the layout of the levels in the planning graph that are not equidistant. Actually, managing durative actions in a planning graph approach unbalances the original symmetry of a planning graph because actions can be executed throughout several levels in the graph.

- Graphplan's properties remain in a temporal setting and optimality is guaranteed in terms of plan makespan. Plans can contain actions in parallel and the degree of parallelism is now higher than in classical planning because two actions can overlap in many different ways, which unfortunately makes the search more complex.

- Manage time explicitly in a temporal planning graph allows to handle other temporal aspects, such as: (i) unconditional exogenous events (i.e., facts that allow to represent a kind of temporal constraints in the form of time windows, such as *((at 8 (available sunlight)) (at 17 (not (available sunlight))))*. (ii) goals with deadlines, (i.e., goals that are temporally constrained, such as having *(at(plane1,cityA) before 18)*, (iii) maximal

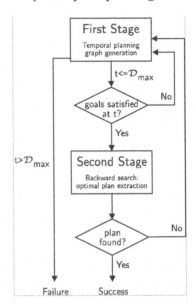

Figure 3. Typical scheme of a pure planning graph approach for temporal planning

duration of the plan allowed by the user ($D_{max} \leq 150$); and others.

The first and second points are not specific features for temporal planning. After all, the use of a bilevel planning graph can also be adopted in classical planning as an efficient implementation of the planning graph, like in STAN (Fox & Long, 1999), and similarly happens with the conditional/eternal classification of mutexes. Note, however, that using a bilevel graph becomes much more useful in temporal planning because the number of levels grows much larger (see an example in Figure 4). Additionally, removing the calculus of eternal mutexes, which always hold, from each level of the temporal planning graph speeds up its generation, particularly when there exist many levels.

The typical scheme of a pure temporal planner based on planning graphs is depicted in Figure 3. Similarly to Graphplan, the scheme consists of two stages that interleave: (i) the temporal planning graph generation, and (ii) the backward search that extracts an optimal plan. In the first

Figure 4. Fragment of the temporal planning graph generated for a problem of the zenotravel domain to transport person1 from cityA to cityB, that is, G = {at(person1, cityB)}

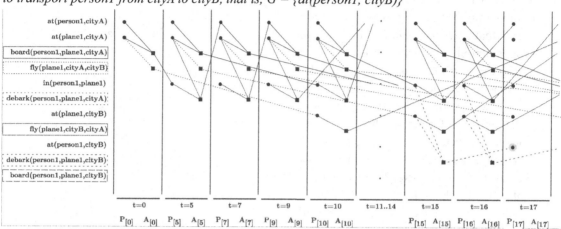

stage, the temporal planning graph is built up incrementally, as shown in Algorithm 1. Here, actions that can start (because their conditions are present and not mutex in $P_{[t]}$) are inserted into $A_{[t]}$, and their positive effects in the corresponding level $P_{[t+dur(a)]}$. According to the expressiveness supported by the planner, the calculus of mutexes in $A_{[t]}$ and $P_{[t]}$ may vary. Particularly TGP, which handles a conservative model of actions, calculates the following mutexes: proposition-proposition (PP), proposition-action (PA), and action-action (AA) mutexes. Intuitively, PP, PA, and AA mutexes represent the impossibility of having two propositions, a proposition and an action, and two actions simultaneously true in the same level, respectively. An example of the temporal planning graph generated for a problem of the *zenotravel* domain (see Figure 1) is shown in Figure 4. As can be seen, the number of levels in a temporal planning graph is higher than in its corresponding classical planning graph, and these levels do not need to be consecutive now because they are generated according to the duration of the actions. For instance, in level *t*=5 only actions with duration 2 and 5 can start, so only the levels *t* =7 and *t* =10 are generated.

Later, the level *t*=9 is generated from level *t*=7, which indicates that temporal levels can be generated from different previous levels and not always in a chronological order (though they are processed in Algorithm 1 in chronological order). The huge number and dispersion among the levels in a temporal planning graph influences negatively on the efficiency of the graph, and it is one of the reasons for TGP to dispense with this multilevel graph and build a bilevel planning graph (Smith & Weld, 1999).

We assume that the durations for actions *board*, *debark*, and *fly* are 5, 2, and 10, respectively. For simplicity, we avoid displaying all the levels *t*=11..14. Note that a nontemporal planning graph, where all actions have the same duration, would have only three levels. Small circles (squares) represent propositions (actions).

The second stage performs the extraction of an optimal plan through the temporal graph, as

Algorithm 1. General temporal planning graph generation.

```
1:  P_[0] ← I
2:  t ← 0
3:  while (G is not pairwise mutex in P_[t]) ∧ (t ≤ D_max) do
4:      for all a ∈ A | a can start in P_[t] do
5:          update A_[t] with a
6:          update P_[t+dur(a)] with positive effects of a
7:      calculate mutexes in A_[t] and P_[t]
8:      t ← next level in the temporal planning graph
```

Algorithm 2. General search stage for extracting an optimal temporal plan.

```
1:   t ← final value of t provided by Algorithm 1
2:   GTS_{[t]} ← G
3:   Plan ← ∅
4:   while t ≥ 0 do
5:       if t = 0 then
6:           if GTS_{[t]} ⊆ I then
7:               return success with Plan
8:           else
9:               backtrack
10:      else
11:          while GTS_{[t]} ≠ ∅ do
12:              extract p from GTS_{[t]}
13:              select a ∈ A_{[t']} that supports p | t ≥ t'+ dur(a) {if ¬∃a then backtrack}
14:              if a is not mutex in Plan then
15:                  update Plan_{[t']} with a
16:                  update GTS with conditions of a
17:              else
18:                  go to step 13 and select another action a
19:      t ← previous level in the temporal planning graph
```

shown in Algorithm 2. Basically, it extracts a plan, as a flow of actions, backwards from the top-level goals by satisfying all the subgoals in each level t (stored in $GTS_{[t]}$, which is initialised with the goals in G). This backward search finishes when all the goals to satisfy in $GTS_{[0]}$ are in I. Otherwise, if the search space is exceeded and no plan is found, an extension of the planning graph is required and the whole process goes back again to the first stage (see Figure 3 for the interleaved interaction).

Extension for a Nonconservative Model of Actions

TPSYS is a temporal planner which combines the ideas of Graphplan and TGP to deal with durative actions. Although initially TPSYS only managed the same conservative model of actions of TGP, it was extended to deal with the nonconservative model of actions of PDDL2.1 (Garrido et al., 2002). At first glance, the extension of a planning-graph-based planner to deal with nonconservative actions seems easy. However, it implies some changes in the previous algorithms for generating the temporal graph and in the way the plan search is performed:

- The reasoning on mutex is now complicated by the semantics of a more expressive model of actions. The strong mutex of the conservative model of actions must be modified to allow durative actions to be applied in parallel, even in cases in which they refer to the same propositions. Instead of simply defining two actions as mutex, now there exist four types of action-action mutex situations (see Figure 5). Type 1 (start-start) and type 2 (end-end) represent the mutex in which actions cannot start or end, respectively, at the same time. Type 3 (end-start) represents the mutex in which two actions cannot end and start at the same time, that is, the actions cannot meet. Finally, type 4 (during-during) represents the mutex in which an action cannot start or end during the execution of the other. Obviously, these types of mutex can be easily generalised for other more expressive nonconservative models of actions.

- A preprocessing stage before the generation of the planning graph to calculate the eternal (static) mutex shows beneficial for the global performance of the algorithm. Since there exist many mutexes that only depend on the definition of the actions, there is no reason to postpone their calculus to the planning graph generation stage, speeding such a stage.

- The generation of the temporal planning graph involves some subtle details. First, it needs to propagate the four types of mutex indicated above. Second, the condition for an action *a* to start in a given level *t* (see step 4 of Algorithm 1) needs to consider *SCond(a)*, *Inv(a)*, and *ECond(a)*, and the same happens with the termination criterion of the algorithm that must guarantee that *ECond(a)* are satisfied for any a_i useful in a plan (step 3 of Algorithm 1). Third, the effects of action *a* are inserted in the corresponding levels according to *SEff(a)* and *EEff(a)* (step 6 of Algorithm 1).

- The search stage requires some changes because now actions allow different ways to support goals (*SEff* and *EEff*). Additionally, planning an action implies to satisfy the start, invariant, and end conditions (*SCond*, *Inv* and *ECond*). This breaks the right to left *directionality* of Algorithm 2, and may make the search move forward and backward through the temporal planning graph.

An alternative way to encode temporality in a classical planning graph when dealing with a nonconservative model of actions is used in the planner LPGP (Long & Fox, 2003a). LPGP uses a compact representation of the planning graph

similarly to the planner TGP, but it associates the duration to the states and not to the actions: the planning graph represents the logical structure of the plan, with temporal constraints being managed separately by means of a linear constraint solver to ensure that temporal durations are correctly respected. This can be seen as a *less intrusive* way of dealing with time in a planning graph approach because time is only stored in proposition levels, while the underlying Graphplan behaviour remains unchanged.

In LPGP, each durative action is split into three actions: two instantaneous start/end actions, and one more for the invariant part. The advantage of this alternative is that the graph extension and mutex reasoning are like in Graphplan, and it only needs to be extended to propagate the information about the actions that manage the invariant part. However, the main disadvantage of this alternative is the increment in the number of actions (in a factor of three per each durative action) and the necessary changes in the more complex search (now as a linear programming algorithm) to keep the link among these three actions to model the duration of the original action. Additionally, LPGP is optimal *w.r.t.* the number of levels of actions (steps), but not *w.r.t.,* the makespan as other optimal temporal planners. Broadly speaking, LPGP minimises the number of state changes in the plan but this might not coincide with the optimal makespan plan. Hence, LPGP can return a plan with one action with a makespan longer than a plan with more actions. To conclude, the increase in the number of actions and the subtle detail about the plan optimality have made this approach uncommon.

HEURISTIC STATE-BASED APPROACHES

Heuristic planning has traditionally used several techniques to extract valuable information in an attempt to guide the search towards the plan in an

Figure 5. Four types of mutex that appear in a nonconservative model like PDDL2.1

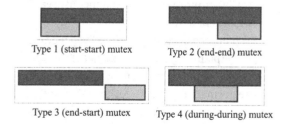

Type 1 (start-start) mutex   Type 2 (end-end) mutex

Type 3 (end-start) mutex   Type 4 (during-during) mutex

efficient way. As we have introduced in a previous section, planning graphs can be easily used to extract estimations that help reduce the search space. Although these heuristics were initially designed for classical planning, they were rapidly applied to optimal and parallel temporal planning with interesting results (Do & Kambhampati, 2001; Haslum & Geffner, 2001).

Most common heuristic approaches for temporal planning are state-based, where states are usually associated with a time instant (also known as *time stamped state* (Do & Kambhampati, 2001, 2003). A time stamped state describes the state of the world and the state of the planner's search at that particular time. Analogously, it is common to have propositions and actions associated with time instants as well. Therefore, the basic idea of the heuristic is to estimate the temporal distance from a given state to a state that satisfies all the problem goals in G. This can be easily achieved by generating a temporal planning graph from each state to the first state that satisfies G, and using the distance (*w.r.t.* makespan) to assess each state and control the search process. Unfortunately, building a complete temporal planning graph from each state becomes expensive, so the heuristics are derived from a relaxed temporal planning graph, where the relaxation relies now on ignoring both the negative effects of the durative actions and all possible temporal constraints.

Algorithm 3 shows a general scheme for generating such a relaxed planning graph from a given state S (that is initially I). In that algorithm we really use a bi-level planning graph (contrary to the one presented in Figure 4 and similar to the one that TGP generates), where all propositions and actions are stored in the structures $P_{[]}$ and $A_{[]}$, respectively. This simple algorithm provides very useful information because:

- It performs a reachability analysis, generating all the propositions and actions that may be useful in the planning resolution, starting from the state S.
- It estimates a lower bound, as an admissible estimation, of the temporal distance from S to the goal. Similarly, the algorithm can also estimate an upper bound for propositions and actions (in steps 7-8, both the lower and upper bounds for actions and propositions can be updated in $A_{[]}$ and $P_{[]}$, respectively). Moreover, these estimations can be extended for considering not only time but also other cost measures, such as resource consumption, cost of the actions, plan benefit, or any combination of them, which becomes very helpful for planning with numeric variables.
- It allows to know whether G is not satisfied because some goal has not been achieved

Algorithm 3. General scheme for generating a relaxed planning graph that calculates heuristic estimations where both actions and propositions are associated with the time they first appear in the graph. Instead of managing an explicit multi-level planning graph, we use a bi-level structure formed by $P_{[]}$ and $A_{[]}$ which encapsulate all the proposition and action levels, respectively.

```
1:   P'_[] ← ∅
2:   P_[] ← state S {the first state in the problem is I}
3:   A_[] ← ∅
4:   while P_[]' ≠ P_[] do
5:       P_[]' ← P_[]
6:       for all a ∈ A | (a can start in P_[]') ∧ (a ∉ A_[]) do
7:           update A_[] with ⟨a,t⟩ where t is the latest time of the conditions of a
8:           update P_[] with ⟨p,t⟩ ∀p ∈ positive effects of a, and t the time when a generates p
9:   if G is not satisfied in P_[] then
10:      return failure
```

during the generation of the graph. Intuitively, if a goal is not generated, or if the goal is generated after a given deadline (temporal constraint), the problem is unsolvable and no planning is necessary.

After calculating the heuristic estimations in the relaxed planning graph, a forward chaining planner can use these estimations to control its search. According to the admissibility of the heuristic, the search can be admissible or not. Sapa uses this strategy to handle durative actions (in a rich nonconservative model of actions as presented) together with metric resources and deadline goals (Do & Kambhampati, 2001, 2003). Sapa calculates several admissible heuristics that minimise the makespan, the slack, and so forth, and also investigates nonadmissible heuristics based on a relaxed plan built from the relaxed temporal planning graph. A relaxed plan is usually a partially ordered set of actions in which both the problem goals and action conditions hold. It is called relaxed because neither negative interactions nor mutex relationships between actions are considered. Like relaxed planning graphs, relaxed plans are very helpful as they can better estimate the makespan of the plan; although they represent very optimistic plans, they encapsulate real plans after all, which may even be used as a *skeleton* of the final plan. Generating a relaxed plan is an easy task, as shown in Algorithm 4, as it just consists of selecting actions from the relaxed temporal planning graph in a nondeterministic

way to support goals. Since negative effects are not considered, a relaxed plan can be always found in polynomial time with no backtracking.

Sapa uses nonadmissible heuristic estimations calculated from relaxed plans to minimise the number of actions, the sum of the durations of the actions in the relaxed plan, and so forth, as a kind of suboptimal search. This is, instead of optimising the makespan, which becomes very expensive in most problems, it focuses on suboptimal solutions, which shows beneficial in the scalability of the planner. Actually, when dealing with suboptimal planning, many problems that are nonaffordable in an optimal way can be easily solved with a reasonable plan quality.

The heuristics calculated on relaxed planning graphs are very useful in forward chaining planners despite having to build a relaxed planning graph from each visited state to the goals. Fortunately, these heuristics can be adapted for backward chaining planners with minimal modifications by simply building a relaxed planning graph, starting from the initial state I, and estimating the temporal distance to each individual proposition in the graph. Later in the regressive search, the temporal distance from each state to the initial state can be estimated in terms of the distance of the propositions that belong to that state. Note that for estimating the distance from each state to I we do not need to recalculate a planning graph from each state. For instance, given a regressed state $S=\{p_1, p_2... p_n\}$ we can estimate the distance from S to I in several ways, such as

Algorithm 4. Generation of a relaxed plan from a relaxed temporal planning graph that starts in a given state S.

```
1:    GTS ← G
2:    Plan ← IS {IS is a fictitious action that asserts propositions in state S}
3:    while GTS ≠ ∅ do
4:        extract p from GTS
5:        if p is not supported in Plan then
6:            select non-deterministically a that supports p in the relaxed temporal planning graph
7:            update Plan with a
8:            update GTS with conditions of a
```

the sum of the individual distances to each p_i, the max distance to all p_i, and so forth, as presented. Formally, the function $h(S)$ that estimates the cost (temporal distance to I) of state S is characterised by the equation:

$$h(S) = \begin{cases} 0 & \text{if } S \subseteq I \\ \min_{S' \in \mathrm{Re}\,gression(S)} h(S') + \delta(S,S') & \text{otherwise} \end{cases} \quad (1)$$

where *Regression(S)* contains all possible states resulting from regressing S, that it, all the successor states of S working in a backward way, and $\delta(S,S')$ is the increase in the temporal distance between the two states. Again, according to the admissibility of the heuristic $h(S)$, the planner can guarantee an optimal solution or not.

TP4 is an optimal temporal planner that uses an admissible heuristic $h^*(S)$ that is defined as the least time in which a plan can achieve S (Haslum, 2006; Haslum & Geffner, 2001). Although TP4 does not calculate $h^*(S)$ by generating a real relaxed planning graph, it uses an equivalent relaxation and approximates its value by considering some inequalities on the lower bounds of $h^*(S)$ which are derived automatically from the problem representation. Hence, the underlying idea is to store the estimations in a table which is later used to assess the states and speed up its backward chaining search.

An interesting result of the heuristic approaches used in planning is that they are flexible enough to be used not only in temporal planning, but also in numeric planning in both forward and backward chaining planners. This way, planners can cope with metric resource constraints and multicriteria optimisation, such as minimising the expression *((0.5*(plan_makespan)) + (0.01*(fuel plane1)))*. For instance, Sapa and TP4 cope with time and resources in a joint way by means of adjusting the heuristic values to account for resource consumption constraints under suboptimal and optimal approaches.

TEMPORAL PLANNING IN POCL APPROACHES

POCL planning approaches represent a natural and very appropriate way to include and handle time in a planning framework. This approach brings several facilities when extending the classical POCL algorithm to incorporate time because: (i) POCL is independent of the assumption that actions must be instantaneous or have the same duration, (ii) the partial order and the subgoal preserving mechanism allow POCL approaches to define actions of arbitrary duration as long as the conditions under which actions interfere are well defined (Smith, Frank, & Jonsson, 2000), and (iii) the great advantage of POCL-based frameworks is that they offer a high degree of execution flexibility in comparison to other temporal planning systems, thanks to the application of the least-commitment principle.

Most POCL temporal planners share a common representational framework based on an interval representation for actions and propositions. The idea of using an interval representation of time was first introduced and popularised by Allen (1983). The propositions that describe the world state and the actions hold over intervals of time and the constraints between intervals describe the relationships between actions and propositions (precondition and effect relationships) or between actions. Intervals are usually defined by pairs of timepoints, corresponding to the beginning and ending points of the interval, and constraints are then translated into simple equality and inequality constraints between end points.

Table 1 shows the general temporal relations between intervals, and the corresponding translation in terms of their endpoints, which are used by the planner HSTS (Muscettola, 1994). HSTS uses an object-oriented constraint specification language based on Allen's temporal interval logic and domains are specified using a qualitative

Table 1. HSTS temporal relations (Penix et al., 1998). Lowercase and uppercase letters in the temporal relations represent the minimum and maximum distance between the endpoints, respectively.

Temporal Relation	Endpoint Relation
I1 before [d D] I2	$d \leq I2.start - I1.end \leq D$
I1 starts_before [d D] I2	$d \leq I2.start - I1.start \leq D$
I1 ends_before [d D] I2	$d \leq I2.end - I1.end \leq D$
I1 starts_before end [d D] I2	$d \leq I2.end - I1.start \leq D$
I1 contains [[a A][b B]] I2	$a \leq I2.start - I1.start \leq A$ $b \leq I1.end - I2.end \leq B$
I1 parallels [[a A][b B]] I2	$a \leq I2.start - I1.start \leq A$ $b \leq I2.end - I1.end \leq B$

temporal interval logic with quantitative duration constraints (Penix, Pecheur, & Havelund, 1998). Note that all temporal relations have the corresponding inverse relation; for instance, the inverse relation of *I1 before [d D] I2* would be *I2 after [d D] I1*. Most of POCL temporal planners use this type of interval representation (or a similar one) as it permits to express all possible temporal relationships between the start and end points of two intervals.

The interval representation is very flexible and offers a richer expressiveness than the nonconservative model of PDDL2.1. It allows us to specify that a condition is only needed during some part of the action execution or that one action must be executed while another is being executed, or that one action must be executed *t* time units after the

end of another action. In this sense, the interval representation is closer to the more sophisticated model of actions presented. This rich expressiveness was already exploited by ZENO (Penberthy & Weld, 1994), a least-commitment planner which supports a rich class of metric-temporal features, including reasoning about deadline goals, continuous change and exogenous events.

Figure 6 shows an example on the utilisation of temporal relations between intervals encoded as their endpoints. Under the interval representation, actions, and propositions are temporally extended to denote they take place over an interval. For instance, *fly(?a,?c1,?c2,t1,t2)* indicates that the action will take place over the interval [*t1,t2*] and *at(?a,?c2,t3,t6)* is the effect of the *fly* action to denote that aircraft *?a* will stay over *?c2* from time *t3* to time *t6*. The *debark* operation needs the aircraft to stay over *?c2* throughout the interval *I3*, and action *debark* can only be initiated after 10 time units have elapsed since the aircraft arrival. Notice that the temporal relation *t2 before [0 0] t3* is equivalent to the temporal relation *I1 meets I2* in the Allen's basic interval relationships, and the two temporal relations between *t3-t4* and *t6-t5* comprise the temporal relation *I2 contains [[0 ∞)[0 ∞)]I3*.

Timepoints used in temporally qualified expressions will be eventually instantiated to a particular time over the timeline and, consequently, the final plan will be formed by a set of temporal occurrences of actions. Since POCL temporal planning also makes use of a least-commitment

Figure 6. Example on the utilisation of temporal relations between different intervals. This problem is taken from the more general example shown in Figure 2.

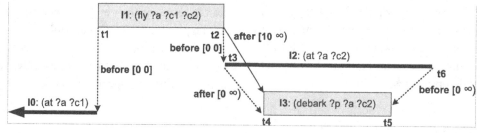

strategy, accurate times for timepoints are left unbound until the plan constraints determine their values. Timepoints might also be allocated to a time interval (rather than a fixed time) in case of the constraints in the problem do not provide enough information to assign a particular time value. For instance, in a final plan, start and end times for an action *fly(plane1,cityA,cityB,t1,t2)* might be *t1*=17 and *t2*=[25,28], which indicates that the exact departure time is known but the arrival time is expected between 8 and 11 time units after departure.

The interval representation is general and expressive enough to represent any temporal condition or particular time constraints on goals, actions or events. There exist other temporal planners that support even more expressive languages. IxTeT (Ghallab & Laruelle, 1994), for instance, includes timed preconditions, access to time points within the interval of a durative action, and some other features at the cost of increased complexity. IxTeT seeks a compromise between efficiency and expressiveness for handling concurrency and interfering actions, external events, and goals situated in time (Ghallab et al., 2004).

The difficulty of POCL temporal planning is that the algorithms for detecting and resolving threats become very complicated because the representation and handling of the time constraints between actions is more complex. We can distinguish three general solving methods to accomplish POCL temporal planning, which will be detailed in the following sections:

1   Extend the classical POCL algorithm to deal with time constraints between actions and propositions.
2   Cooperation between a POCL planner and a CSP solver: compute a plan as a CSP within a POCL framework.
3   Use of a formulation of temporal planning based on constraint programming and incorporate a reasoning mechanism to manage causal links, orderings, and threats.

We can view these three approaches as an evolving integration of planning and scheduling techniques. The first approach relies on separating the temporal aspects from the causal dependencies in a plan, and using a specialised data structure to handle each of the two aspects. The underlying principle of the second approach is to use a POCL algorithm and solve each node in the plan space as a CSP. Finally, the third approach presents the most integrated view as it translates a POCL planning problem into a CSP and applies CSP techniques for its resolution.

Extending the Classical POCL Algorithm

Formalisms that fall into this category attempt to incorporate temporal reasoning in a POCL planner by separating the temporal aspects of a plan from the procedural aspects of the plan construction. The algorithm for POCL temporal planning is very similar to the standard POP procedure: the planner works backwards from the goals, adding new actions to the plan, which in turn introduce new subgoals. However, the flaw resolution mechanism is now more complex because of the high number of constraints, which makes the representation and maintenance of the time constraints more complicated.

The underlying idea of the first planners that tackled with temporal planning as an extension of the classical POCL algorithm was to use a temporal network to represent all the temporal information in the plan, and then apply different types of graph algorithms to maintain the network consistency. This separation of the temporal aspects from the pure planning aspects was first introduced by some nonlinear planners such as FORBIN (Dean, Firby & Miller, 1988), O-PLAN2 (Drabble & Kirby, 1991), and TRIPTIC (Rutten & Hertzberg, 1993). Particularly, these planners use a Time Map Manager (TMM), Dean and McDermott (1987), to deal with the temporal information. One of the motivations to start research on systems for time map management was the idea to use them for implementing planners. TRIPTIC, for instance, is built as a classical (nontemporal) planner on top of a time map management system.

A time map is a database containing temporally qualified *tokens* that are true over some interval. The key issue in these planning systems is the distribution of the work between the two components, where all temporal information is treated by the TMM and the planner has only to deal with dependencies. Thus, the planner is simplified in that some of the work it classically does is here transmitted to the temporal level. The TMM uses a mechanism of persistence clipping for detecting and handling conflicts. Although TMMs were very popular in other contexts, their application to planning was not very successful. The main reason was, perhaps, that the interplay between a TMM and a nonlinear planner is a nontrivial task, imposing constraints and requirements on the functionalities of both of them.

There were also other similar ideas to incorporate temporal reasoning in a nonlinear planner like Allen's proposal described in (1991). Allen presented a nonlinear planning algorithm that works in two stages: the plan generator, which creates a particular plan, and the assumption verifier, which takes a suggested plan and validates the persistence assumptions. A plan is generated as a set of actions, a set of assumptions about the persistence of each true proposition over some time period, and the set of predictions that justify the goal and persistence assumptions. During the stage of verifying assumptions, the algorithm can extend or shorten intervals in order to fulfill the persistence assumptions. If the verification fails, then an inconsistency has been found, in which case the algorithm retracts an assumption and invokes the plan generator again in order to replan. This system represented an advance in the development of general representations for reasoning about actions as specialized inference

processes on a temporal logic. However, the system had several limitations and its contribution did not much influence the state-of-the-art in temporal planning.

Cooperation Between POCL Planning and CSP Solving

A common framework that appears in many POCL temporal planners like DEVISER (Vere, 1983), ZENO (Penberthy, 1993; Penberthy & Weld, 1994), HSTS (Muscettola, 1994), IxTeT (Ghallab & Laruelle, 1994), or RAX (Jonsson et al., 2000) is that they all use an interval representation and rely on constraint satisfaction techniques to represent and manage the relationships between intervals. This is referred as *Constraint-Based Interval* (CBI) approaches (Smith et al., 2000).

Let us consider again the example shown in Figure 6, where intervals are represented by their end points and constraints are translated into equality/inequality relations between these end points. Planners that use this interval representation maintain a constraint network to represent the temporal relations and keep track of the constraints in a plan. Unlike the planners cited earlier in this chapter, this approach offers a unified view of the temporal planning system, where the constraint network provides a single uniform mechanism for doing temporal reasoning and handling the planning conflicts. In this case, the constraint network is a compact representation of all aspects that define a plan.

The most common constraint network for CBI approaches is the Simple Temporal Network (STN) (Dechter, Meiri, & Pearl, 1991). This is a temporal constraint network without disjunctions, that is, where there exists at most one interval constraint between each pair of time points, that supports unary or binary metric constraints between time points. According to the example in Figure 6, we have:

- The temporal relation between *t3* and *t4* is represented as *I3.start-I2.end* $\in$ [0 ∞) or equivalently $0 \leq$ *I3.start-I2.end* $\leq \infty$.

- A duration constraint to denote that the *debark* action takes between *x* and *y* time units is represented as *I3.end-I3.start* $\in$ [*x*,*y*] or equivalently $x \leq$ *I3.end-I3.start* $\leq y$.

- A temporal constraint to denote that the *fly* action starts between *x* and *y* time units *w.r.t.* the time clock (*T0* is a reference point to represent time zero) is represented as *I1.start* $\in$ [*x*,*y*] or equivalently $x \leq$ *I1.start-T0* $\leq y$.

Figure 6 represents a temporal constraint network where intervals are used to represent both propositions and actions. Although each interval is placed on a definite portion of the timeline in the final plan, the appropriate start and end times for each interval may be undetermined for a while during planning. Therefore, intervals can be viewed as *floating tokens* over the timeline (Jonsson et al., 2000) as a result of the least-commitment strategy in POCL planning.

A STN can be represented using a completely connected distance graph (*d-graph*) where each edge is labelled by the shortest temporal distance between two time points. In a POCL temporal framework each plan generated during the search process is represented as a STN. The advantage of a STN is that it allows for rapid response to temporal queries as there exist well-known algorithms such as arc-consistency that can be applied for inference and constraint checking in the network. Planners like VHPOP (Younes & Simmons, 2003) or IxTeT (Ghallab & Laruelle, 1994) use a STN to record temporal constraints. A d-graph can be easily represented by means of a matrix representation where values denote the distance between two time points (Younes & Simmons, 2003).

There has been a long history of partial order planners which are often referred to as performing constraint posting. In these approaches, constraint satisfaction techniques are added as an adjunct to the planning process, but the planning process itself is not formulated as a CSP (Van Beek & Chen, 1999). Adding durative actions and the corresponding temporal constraints does not change the basic POCL algorithm because all the branching alternatives to support causal links and to solve both the mutexes and threats are considered. Therefore, the properties of soundness and completeness (Penberthy & Weld, 1992) are also maintained for a POCL temporal planner. The main differences appear at the time of adding a causal link or solving an unsafe link due to the temporal constraints that are necessary to establish for each flaw repair. Algorithm 5 outlines the general scheme of a POCL temporal planner; the branching is generated in step 9, where a plan is created for each possible resolver. Note that step 4 is to verify the consistency of the STN,

Algorithm 5. General sketch of a POCL temporal algorithm

```
1:   Plan_list ← ∅
2:   repeat
3:       select non-deterministically and extract Plan ∈ Plan_list
4:       if Constraints(Plan) are consistent then
5:           Pending ← open_conditions(Plan) ∪ threats(Plan)
6:           if Pending = ∅ then
7:               return success with Plan
8:           select and extract Φ ∈ Pending
9:           Resolvers ← {Plan_r} ∀ r | r is a resolver for Φ, Plan_r = Create_plan(Plan,Φ,r) {see Algorithm 6}
10:          if Resolvers ≠ ∅ then
11:              Plan_list ← Plan_list ∪ Resolvers
12:  until Plan_list = ∅
13:  return failure {no plan}
```

Algorithm 6. Temporal relations for flaw repairing: function Create_plan (Π, Φ, r).

1: **if** $\Phi \in open\_conditions(Plan)$ **then**

2:     let the flaw $\Phi = \langle p, r_{sp}, r_{ep} \rangle$ {p is required from time r_{sp} to r_{ep}}

3:     **if** the resolver r is an existing proposition **then**

4:        let $r = \langle q, t_{sq}, t_{eq} \rangle \mid q = p$

5:        set constraints between t_{sq} and r_{sp} in Plan {$r_{sp} \geq t_{sq}$ or r_{sp} after $[0 \infty)$ t_{sq}}

6:        set constraints between t_{eq} and r_{ep} in Plan {$r_{ep} \leq t_{eq}$ or r_{ep} before $[0 \infty)$ t_{eq}}

7:     **if** the resolver r is a new action **then**

8:        let $r = \langle a, t_{sa}, t_{ea} \rangle \mid q \in$ effects of $a \wedge q = p$

9:        set constraints between t_{sa}, t_{ea} and timepoints of {conditions of a + positive effects of a + negative effects of a} in Plan according to the domain temporal specification

10:        set constraints between t_{sq} and r_{sp} in Plan {$r_{sp} \geq t_{sq}$ or r_{sp} after $[0 \infty)$ t_{sq}}

11:        set constraints between t_{eq} and r_{ep} in Plan {$r_{ep} \leq t_{eq}$ or r_{ep} before $[0 \infty)$ t_{eq}}

12: **if** $\Phi \in threats(Plan)$ **then**

13:     let a_k be the action that threatens the causal link $a_i \xrightarrow{\ p\ } a_j \mid \langle p, t_{sp}, t_{ep} \rangle$ with $p \in$ negative effects of a_k

14:     **if** r is promotion of a_k **then**

15:        set constraints between t_{sp} and t_{sq} in Plan {$t_{sp} \leq t_{sq}$ or t_{sp} before $[0 \infty)$ t_{sq}, deleting time point before generation start time point}

16:     **if** r is demotion of a_k **then**

17:        set constraints between t_{sp} and r_{ep} in Plan {$r_{ep} \leq t_{sp}$ or t_{sp} after $[0 \infty)$ r_{ep}, deleting time point after required end time point}

---

which represents a plan; if the plan turns out to be inconsistent then the algorithm proceeds by selecting a new plan.

Algorithm 6 shows the routine *Create_plans*, which is an overview of the necessary temporal relations between the elements involved in the flaw repair. Constraints to manage threats are now added between time points instead of adding ordering constraints between actions. The two resolution methods for threats ensure that the deleting time point either precedes the generation start time point or goes after the required end time point.

Algorithms 5 and 6 show the basic procedure and temporal constraints to encode causal links and resolution of threats in any temporal POCL, although different adaptations of these two components can be found in other approaches. For instance, the work presented in (Refanidis, 2005) builds a heuristic POCL temporal planner by exploiting the information obtained from a temporal planning graph. This graph, which is a simplified version of the one in TGP, helps obtain estimates for open conditions during the plan construction phase and additional disjunctive constraints, based on both permanent and temporary mutex relations. This allows to obtain alternative ways to resolve threats other than promotion or demotion. Another difference in (Refanidis, 2005) with respect to the basic POCL algorithm is that threats in the plan are solved by posting disjunctive constraints, instead of creating a separate plan node for each possible solution. The advantage of having disjunctions is that it overcomes the problem of having numerous plan nodes with the same set of open conditions and actions, but with different orderings. On the other hand, disjunctive constraints demand stronger propagation rules to exploit pruning possibilities. Overall, this work shows the benefits of combining different planning techniques to improve performance of temporal POCL planning.

The combination of the interval representation and dynamic constraint satisfaction techniques provide a powerful and expressive framework for the construction of POCL temporal planners. The main drawback of these systems is the low performance they show in comparison to other modern temporal planners, due to the high branching and poor pruning rules. Therefore, the application of heuristics to prune the search space becomes a necessity in POCL planners. The most common way to come up with heuristics is to extract information from planning graphs such as distance based heuristics, disjunctive constraint handling (Refanidis, 2005), or the information provided by a reachability analysis.

RePOP (Nguyen, Kambhampati, & Nigenda, 2002) shows that distance based heuristics are very useful for POCL planners, particularly in their application to the flaw selection mechanisms. VHPOP (Younes & Simmons, 2003) estimates the remaining planning effort for an open condition by counting the total number of open conditions that would arise while resolving the open condition. This heuristic turns out to be more discriminating than an ordering criterion based on heuristic cost. IxTeT (Ghallab & Laruelle, 1994; Laborie & Ghallab, 1995) also uses heuristic techniques to guide flaw selection: for each possible resolver r, IxTeT calculates the amount of change (commitment) that would result from applying r to the current plan by considering not only the number of necessary actions to solve an open condition but also to what degree the current variable domains would be reduced and possible action orderings restricted. TPSYS (Garrido & Onaindía, 2003) combines the application of least-commitment and heuristic search in a temporal setting. TPSYS guides the search process by using a relaxed plan as a starting point where actions are only definitively allocated in the final plan when they are applicable and no mutex. TPSYS uses different heuristics to select the lowest cost plan and to set the allocation priority of each action.

Most POCL planners use non-dmissible heuristics because the main objective is to reduce the search space as much as possible in order to obtain efficient resolution methods. TPSYS, for instance, achieves impressive speedups with respect to Graphplan backward search and obtains suboptimal but good-quality solutions. Also, the quality of the plans, in terms of number of steps, generated by VHPOP is generally very high. In general, although the POCL framework easily admits the utilisation of admissible heuristics, most POCL planners leave optimality considerations aside for efficiency reasons.

POCL planners are traditionally aimed at solving problems requiring a much richer expressiveness for time and actions and, therefore, they have been extensively used in real applications. O-Plan (Currie & Tate, 1991; Drabble & Tate, 1994), a Web-based AI planning agent (Tate, Dalton & Levine, 2000), has been applied in evacuation operations, crisis action planning, air campaign planning, and logistics. SIPE-2 (Wilkins, 1988), a system for interactive planning and execution, has been used to integrate planning for military air campaigns (Lee & Wilkins, 1996), response to marine oil spills (Agosta & Wilkins, 1996), or production line scheduling. Other planners, such as ASPEN (Chien et al., 2000), have been applied for automating space mission operations. The successful performance of these planners on real applications is also due to the use of specific domain knowledge in planning, in what is being called knowledge-based planning (Wilkins & desJardins, 2001).

We can conclude by saying that POCL planning offers nice formal and theoretical properties as well as optimality guarantees but there is still an important performance gap that separates POCL planners from modern efficient planners (Vidal & Geffner, 2006). On the other hand, we could argue that POCL planning is more concerned with expressiveness for modeling realistic applications rather than efficiency of the search algorithms, which brings about a lack of serious comparisons with other planning techniques. This is partly the reason why these planners have not been extensively tested on the suite of classical benchmark problems. Recently, there are a few approaches that attempt to overcome this performance gap and undertake the challenge of extending temporal POCL planning with powerful reasoning mechanisms, as presented in the next section.

CONSTRAINT PROGRAMMING FORMULATION FOR TEMPORAL POCL PLANNING

In this section, we contemplate the formulation of temporal POCL planning problems using constraint programming. The idea is to model a temporal planning problem as a CSP, with all its variables and constraints, and solve it by applying CSP techniques. Although the idea of transforming and solving a planning problem as a CSP has already been applied to nontemporal planning in several works, such as LC-DESCARTES (Joslin & Pollack, 1996), these approaches tend to combine both planning and dynamic CSP techniques to solve the problem. On the contrary, here we focus on a more general formulation by means of constraint programming that has the ability to solve a temporal planning problem by reasoning about supports, mutex relations, and causal links in a very elaborate model of actions (see Figure 2 for an example). This formulation is based on the original model proposed by CPT, an optimal temporal POCL planner (Vidal & Geffner, 2004, 2006), and extended with more expressive and complex temporal constraints such as quantitative temporal constraints, persistences, deadlines, temporal windows, and so forth, as presented in (Garrido & Onaindía, 2006). A nice advantage is that once the constraint programming model is formulated it can be solved by any CSP solver.

Solving Temporal POCL Planning as Constraint Programming

There exist three key steps to solve temporal POCL planning as constraint programming: (i) formulate the variables that represent the actions, propositions and their constraints, (ii) formulate the branching situations, and (iii) formulate the pruning mechanisms to avoid parts of the search space. Hence, the objective is to be able to find a temporal plan by only using constraint satisfaction techniques and to come up with efficient, powerful, and sound pruning rules.

Step 1: Formulation of variables, domains, and constraints

In general, POCL planning can be formulated as constraint programming by translating the actions and their relations (causal links, support constraints, threats, and mutexes) into a constraint model. Additionally, this constraint model can also be extended to a more elaborate model of actions with the following general capabilities: (i) duration in actions can change within an interval, (ii) conditions and effects can be required/generated at any time, and (iii) support for extra constraints, such as persistences, precedences, quantitative temporal constraints, temporal windows, deadlines, and so forth.

Variables are basically used to define actions in the problem (A) and the conditions required by actions, along with the actions that support them and the time when these conditions occur (time is modelled by R^+). The model also includes two fictitious actions, IS and GS; IS supports the propositions of the initial state, whereas GS represents any state that requires the problem goals. These variables, the domains and their description are shown in Table 2. Since the duration of an action is variable, it becomes necessary to define variables for both the start and end time of each action ($S(a),E(a)$). The variables that encapsulate a causal link are $Sup(p,a)$ and $Time(p,a)$. Additionally, the variable $Persist(p,a)$ allows to model persistences (to simulate different states in propositions) in a very flexible way, based on the action that supports p, and the action a for which p is supported. Therefore, the persistence may depend on two factors: (i) the action that generates p, and (ii) the action that requires p. Note that a value $Persist(p,a)=\infty$ represents the infinite persistence used in traditional planning (once an effect is generated it only disappears when it is explicitly deleted by an action). On the other hand, the variables $Req_{start}(p,a)$, $Req_{end}(p,a)$ provide a high expressiveness for dealing with conditions, allowing representation of any type of conditions (punctual or over intervals). In this formulation, it is important to note that any variable associated with an action a that is not yet in the plan ($InPlan(a)=0$) is considered *conditional* (Vidal & Geffner, 2006), because they are only

Table 2. Formulation of variables and their domains

Variable	Domain	Description
$S(a)$, $E(a)$	$[0, \infty)$	Start and end time of action a. Clearly, $S(IS)=E(IS)=0$ and $S(GS)=E(GS)$
$dur(a)$	$[dur_{min}(a), dur_{max}(a)]$	Duration of action a within two positive bounds. Clearly, $dur(IS)=dur(GS)= 0$
$Sup(p,a)$	$\{b_i\} \mid b_i \in A$ supports p for a	Symbolic variable with the supporter b_i for (pre)condition p of a
$Time(p,a)$	$[0, \infty)$	Time when the causal link $Sup(p,a)$ happens, that is, the time in which the action b_i selected as a value for variable $Sup(p,a)$ generates p
$Persist(p,a)$	$[0, \infty)$	Persistence of condition p for a
$Req_{start}(p,a)$, $Req_{end}(p,a)$	$[0, \infty)$	Interval $[Req_{start}(p,a),Req_{end}(p,a)]$ in which action a requires p
$InPlan(a)$	$[0, 1]$	Binary variable that indicates the presence of a in the plan. Clearly, $InPlan(IS)= InPlan(GS)=1$ (*true*)

Table 3. Formulation of basic planning constraints

Constraint	Description
$S(a) + dur(a) = E(a)$	Binds the start and end of a
$E(IS) \leq S(a)$	Binds any action a to start after IS
$E(a) \leq S(GS)$	Binds any action a to end before GS
$Time(p,a) \leq Req_{start}(p,a)$	Forces to support condition p for action a before it is required (causal link)
if $Sup(p,a) = b_i$ **then** $Time(p,a)$ = time when b_i supports p	Time for the supporting constraint defined by the causal link $Sup(p,a)$. This constraint is only applicable if $InPlan(a)=InPlan(b_i)=1$

meaningful when $InPlan(a)=1$, that is, when they are part of the plan. Hence, when $InPlan(a)=1$, all variables and constraints that action a involves need to be activated, and deactivated otherwise. Intuitively, these variables allow modelling of those actions from the problem that take part in the plan, which action supports each condition (causal links), and when. The objective of the CSP is to reason among the actions of the problem and propagate the necessary information to provide a feasible assignment of values to the variables. On the other hand, the basic planning constraints simply create the relations between the variables and assign their values. Constraints are defined for each variable that involves action a or condition p for a. These constraints[4] and their description are shown in Table 3.

Finally, Table 4 shows the formulation of other complex constraints. The expressiveness of constraint programming facilitates the formulation of complex constraints that represent sophisticated combinations of variables and operators. Furthermore, this formulation also allows to model numeric variables to express the use of metric resources in the plan, by including the necessary numeric variables in the conditions and effects of the actions, as presented in (Garrido et al., 2006).

An example with the variables and constraints for the two actions of Figure 2 is shown in Table 5. In this table we can see the variables that involve the two actions and how they are related to each other.

For simplicity, only the variables, domains, and constraints for these two actions are represented,

Table 4. Formulation of additional complex constraints

Constraint	Description
Var_1 comp-op $Var_2 + x, x \in R$	Precedence and quantitative temporal constraints, which can involve propositions, actions and propositions-actions. This constraint is very flexible and can represent any combination of $Var_1, Var_2 \in \{Time(p,a), Req_{start}(p,a), Req_{end}(p,a), S(a), E(a)\}$ and comp-op $\in \{<, \leq, =, \geq, >, \neq\}$, such as $S(IS) + 200 < E(GS)$ that restricts the plan makespan
$Req_{end}(p,a) \leq Persist(p,a)$	Persistence constraints: states that the upper bound of the interval of a condition requirement never exceeds the value for the persistence of such a condition
$Var_1 \leq x, x \in R$	Deadlines, which can involve the start/end times of actions or propositions, where $Var_1 \in \{S(a), E(a), Time(p,a)\}$
$min(tw(p)) \leq Req_{start}(p, a) \leq Req_{end}(p,a) \leq max(tw(p))$ $min(tw(a)) \leq S(a) \leq E(a) \leq max(tw(a))$	Temporal windows, which encode external constraints that propositions and actions must hold, where $tw(p)$ and $tw(a)$ are the temporal windows for p and a, respectively
$Expression(Var_1, Var_2 ... Var_n)$	Other customised derived constraints, which encode more complex constraints among several variables of the problem

Table 5. Fragment for the constraint programming formulation generated for the actions fly and debark shown in Figure 2

Variables	Constraints
$S(fly), E(fly) \in [0, \infty)$	$S(fly) + dur(fly) = E(fly)$
$dur(fly) \in [dur_{min}(fly), dur_{max}(fly)]$	$S(IS) \leq S(fly)$
$Sup(p,fly) \in \{...\}$	$E(fly) \leq S(GS)$
$Sup(q,fly) \in \{...\}$	$Time(p,fly) \leq Req_{start}(p,fly)$
$Time(p,fly) \in [0, \infty)$	$Time(q,fly) \leq Req_{start}(q,fly)$
$Time(q,fly) \in [0, \infty)$	
$Persist(e_1,...) = E(fly) - S(fly)$	
$Req_{start}(p,fly) = S(fly) - 50; Req_{end}(p,fly) = S(fly)$	
$Req_{start}(q,fly) = S(fly); Req_{end}(q,fly) = E(fly) + 10$	
$InPlan(fly) \in [0, 1]$	
$S(debark), E(debark) \in [0, \infty)$	$S(debark) + dur(debark) = E(debark)$
$dur(debark) \in [dur_{min}(debark), dur_{max}(debark)]$	$S(IS) \leq S(debark)$
$Sup(e_3, debark) \in \{fly\}$	$E(debark) \leq S(GS)$
$Sup(r, debark) \in \{...\}$	$Time(e_3, debark) \leq Req_{start}(e_3, debark)$
$Time(e_3, debark) = E(fly) + 10$	$Time(r, debark) \leq Req_{start}(r, debark)$
$Time(r, debark) \in [...]$	
$Req_{start}(e_3, debark) = S(debark); Req_{end}(e_3, debark) = E(debark) + 15$	
$Req_{start}(r, debark) = S(debark); Req_{end}(r, debark) = S(debark) + 5$	
$InPlan(debark) \in [0, 1]$	

Table 6. Formulation of branching situations

Constraint	Description
$Sup(p,a)=b_i \wedge Sup(p,a) \neq b_j \mid \forall\, b_i, b_j\ (b_i \neq b_j)$ that supports p for a	Several possibilities to support p, one for each b_i (while $\mid Sup(p,a) \mid > 1$)
$\forall\, b_i, b_j$ with effect-interference (mutex) $time(b_i, p) \leftarrow$ time when b_i generates p $time(b_j, \neg p) \leftarrow$ time when b_j deletes p $time(b_i, p) \neq time(b_j, \neg p)$	To solve the mutex: b_i and b_j cannot modify (generate and delete, respectively) p at the same time
$\forall\, b_i$ that threats causal link $Sup(p,a)$ $time(b_i, \neg p) \leftarrow$ time when b_i deletes p $(time(b_i, \neg p) < Time(p,a)) \vee$ $(Req_{end}(p,a) < time(b_i, \neg p))$	To solve the threat: promotion or demotion

but the complete model needs to consider all the actions in the problem. Values that include other actions of the problem, or need other actions to be calculated, are indicated with the symbol '...'. For instance, $Sup(p,fly)$ will contain all the actions of the problem that support proposition p, and $Time(r,debark)$ will contain the time instants when actions of the problem support r.

Step 2: Formulation of branching situations
Analogously to classical POCL planning, branching is used to represent the expansion of different partial solutions, which appear when supporting a condition or when solving a mutex/threat between actions. Particularly, in the former case a partial plan is created for each possible alternative (action b_i) to support the condition. In the latter case, a distinct constraint is posted to solve the mutex, thus preventing two actions from modifying the same proposition simultaneously (effects interference). Note, however, that this operation does not prevent the actions from partially overlapping.[5] In order to solve the threat, two disjunctive partial plans are created (one for solving the conflict by promotion and another for demotion). All these situations are shown in Table 6.

Step 3: Formulation of pruning mechanisms
In most implementations, the success of POCL planning relies on the heuristics used to reduce the search space. A constraint programming solving process can adopt a similar solution:

use heuristic estimations, extracted from the problem definition, as lower and upper bounds to improve the performance. The underlying idea is to use estimations similar to the ones used by the heuristic approaches to approximate the cost (makespan) of achieving a set of propositions (subgoals) from an initial state. The heuristic estimations can be calculated in different ways: (i) using a relaxed planning graph (see Algorithm 3), (ii) using a relaxed plan (see Algorithm 4), or (iii) using approximated equations (see equation (1)). In particular, a simple heuristic calculated through a relaxed planning graph can estimate the distance between each pair of actions b_i, b_j as the distance between the time when they first appear in such a graph, namely $\delta(b_i, b_j)$. This way, any constraint in the form $S(b_i)+dur(b_i) \leq S(b_j)$ becomes $S(b_i)+dur(b_i)+\delta(b_i, b_j) \leq S(b_j)$, where $\delta(b_i, b_j)$ represents a lower bound to reduce the search space. For instance, the initial bound defined in Table 3 $S(IS)=E(IS) \leq S(a)$ now becomes $S(IS)+\delta(IS,a) \leq S(a)$ which approximates significantly better the start time of action a. As can be noted, this type of estimation is useful for both mutex and threat resolution. Like in any planning approach, a wide range of heuristics is applicable and the properties of each heuristic estimations affect the optimality of the solving process; if the heuristic is admissible the final plan will be optimal. In a sound and complete constraint programming approach, it is easy to compute optimal makespan plans: given an initial bound for variable $S(GS)$, such a bound may be increased until a plan is found or can be decreased until no plan is found (Vidal & Geffner, 2006).

Additionally, the heuristic estimations can also be used in the branching point that appears when supporting a causal link *Sup(p,a)*. In this case, the heuristic will provide an ordering criterion for the applications of the actions $\{b_i\}$ that support such a causal link. For instance, the heuristic estimation may determine to select first the action b_i with minimum value $\delta(b_i,a)$, that is, the most constrained first, or just the opposite if we want to maximise the slack. It is obvious that these heuristic estimations are very valuable in a wide variety of problems with many variables and constraints. For instance, the use of this type of heuristics allows CPT to be faster than other optimal temporal planners and competitive *w.r.t.* other parallel planners (Vidal & Geffner, 2006).

The application of heuristic strategies as pruning mechanisms provides two clear advantages: (i) the overall solving process is highly improved because the bounds allow to discard some partial plans, and reduce the search space considerably, and (ii) the calculus of the heuristics does not have a negative impact on the solving process as it can be computed in a preprocessing stage before starting the problem resolution, that is, the heuristic calculus is independent of the solving process itself.

Discussion

The constraint programming formulation presented in this section shows these advantages:

- The formulation shares the advantages of other CSP-like approaches, including the expressiveness of the modeling language. The constraint formulation allows us the declaration of a very elaborate type of actions and constraints, from basic causal links used in classical planning to very complex constraints, such as variable persistences,

customised derived constraints among variables, and so forth:

- The formulation is a purely declarative representation of the planning domain+problem and is independent of any algorithm (CSP solver). Consequently, the constraint model can be given to any systematic or local-search-based solver.

- The whole formulation can be automatically derived from the planning domain+problem definition, without the necessity of specific hand-coded domain knowledge.

- The formulation inherits the theoretical properties of a POCL framework, such as soundness, completeness and optimality. Basically, soundness and completeness are guaranteed by the definition of the model itself and the completeness of the CSP solver that performs a complete exploration of the domain of each variable. Optimality is easy by using a bound, which can be iteratively incremented/decremented, for variable *S(GS)* as commented above. However, this way of proceeding slightly depends on the precision supported by the CSP solver. Let us consider a sequential plan[6] with two actions *a* and *b* of fixed duration 1, such that $Req_{end}(p,a)=E(a)=1$ and $time(b,\neg p)=S(b)$, that is, *p* is required by *a* until its ending, and *b* deletes *p* when it starts. If the promotion rule to solve the mutex (see Table 6) imposes the constraint $Req_{end}(p,a)<time(b,\neg p)$, that is, that action *a* must be planned before *b*, $S(a)=0$, $E(a)=1$, $S(b)=1.1$ is part of an (optimal) plan. However, $S(b)=1.01$ also forms a better plan, and the same happens when $S(b)=1.001$. Consequently, the constraint $Req_{end}(p,a)<time(b,\neg p)$ actually becomes $Req_{end}(p,a)+\varepsilon \leq time(b,\neg p)$, where ε represents the minimal granularity managed by the solver.[7] This means that all the '<' or '>' constraints are internally managed by the solver like '≤' or '≥', respectively, plus the corresponding ε. Therefore, optimality is possible but taking into consideration the solver's precision.

- This formulation can also be used as a tool for plan validation to check whether the temporal constraints of the problem are feasible or not (Garrido et al., 2006). In this case, the constraint programming formulation only includes the actions that are present in a plan, and the task of the CSP solver is to validate the feasibility of the model and, consequently, of the plan.

HYBRID APPROACHES

The complexity of temporal planning and the difficulty of finding an approach that clearly outperforms the others in all situations has increased the interest in developing hybrid approaches that combine several strategies for planning. Moreover, the difficulty in guaranteeing an optimal temporal plan has changed the interest in planning to finding suboptimal solutions rather than optimal ones. Although there exist dozens of (suboptimal) hybrid temporal planners, in this section we focus on two of which have shown a top performance in the last international planning competitions, LPG and SGPlan (Chen, Wah, & Hsu, 2006; Gerevini, Saetti, & Serina, 2003), which combine many of the techniques presented in the previous sections.

LPG combines the use of planning graphs, heuristics (for time and resources) that also use POCL features, and incremental search based on stochastic local search. First, it uses a temporal action graph (*TA-graph*) that represents a partial plan, where both action and proposition nodes are marked with temporal values estimating the earliest time when the corresponding action terminates, or the earliest time when the proposition becomes true, respectively. This representation is similar to the one proposed in TGP, which can be calculated similarly through Algorithm 3. Some of the heuristics are estimated from the information in this action graph, but LPG also uses relaxed partial plans and notions of threats and open (unsupported) conditions of POCL frameworks.

The behaviour of LPG is to start from an initial partial plan encoded as an action graph, detect conflicts in such a plan, and incrementally solve them, as shown in Algorithm 7. Conflicts can either be unsupported conditions or mutex relations between actions, and the process of solving them consists of two steps: (i) generating a neighbourhood of action graphs, and (ii) evaluating and searching the most adequate graph in a local way. Given a conflict σ, the neighbourhood of a temporal action graph *TA* is $N(\sigma, TA)$, which contains new action graphs resulting from the modification to the current *TA* graph by removing the action that imposes the conflict

Algorithm 7. General scheme of the local search performed in LPG.

```
1:   TA ← initial partial plan
2:   max_steps ← maximal number of steps allowed for the search
3:   while (∃ conflicts in TA) ∧ (max_steps ≥ 0) do
4:       if TA is a solution plan then
5:           return success with TA
6:       else if max_steps =0 then
7:           return failure
8:       else
9:           select conflict σ to be solved in TA
10:          calculate N(σ,TA) as the neighbourhood of TA for σ
11:          TA ← select non-deterministically an action graph (partial plan) from N(σ,TA)
12:          max_steps ← max_steps − 1
```

(for unsupported conditions or mutex relations) or including actions that solve the conflict (for unsupported conditions). For instance, Figure 7 shows an example of the neighbourhood $N(\sigma,TA)$ when σ represents an unsupported condition. In $N(\sigma,TA)$ there exist new *TA* graphs where the unsupported condition is supported by different actions *a1*, *a2*, and so on, and where the conflicting action is removed. As indicated in Algorithm 7, the new current *TA* graph is chosen nondeterministically from $N(\sigma,TA)$ according to its heuristic cost, and the process repeats again. LPG bases its nondeterministic selection on several prioritised decisions. First, if there exists a graph in $N(\sigma,TA)$ with a better heuristic cost than *TA*, such a graph is selected. Second, the graph with the best cost in $N(\sigma,TA)$ is selected with a priority *p*. Third, a random graph in $N(\sigma,TA)$ is selected with a priority $1-p$. Obviously, the selected *TA* graph can have more conflicts, since solving each conflict σ may create new conflicts. This is the reason why the process is only repeated until a maximal number of steps is exceeded. The selection of the new *TA* graph is key in LPG that bases such a selection on heuristic estimations, which are part of its great success. These estimations include several parameters (Gerevini et al., 2003):

$$h(a)=\alpha\cdot Execution\_cost(a)+\beta\cdot Temporal\_cost(a)+\gamma\cdot Search\_cost(a) \qquad (2)$$

This heuristic is calculated separately estimating the cost of inserting an action node a $(h(a)^i)$ or removing it $(h(a)^r)$ in the *TA* graph. Hence, the cost of a *TA* graph includes three estimations: i) the increase of the plan execution cost due to action *a*, ii) the end time of each action *a* (to estimate the plan makespan), and iii) the increase of the number of search steps required to find a valid plan after inserting/removing *a*. That is, unlike other temporal planners that only consider estimations based on the temporality of the plan, LPG also includes in the estimations the search cost that involves reaching a solution, considering either

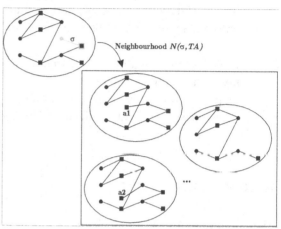

Figure 7. Example of the resulting neighbourhood N(σ,TA) in LPG calculated for a conflict σ (unsupported condition)

inserting or removing the action in the current *TA* graph. In addition to this, all these terms are associated with coefficients that help normalise the results and weight their importance in the solving process. Furthermore, the values for the coefficients change dynamically according to the plan metrics and the search process. This allows LPG to give more priority to reducing the search cost, rather than optimising the quality of the plan, in the first steps of the search (Gerevini et al., 2003).

LPG is very efficient, but the quality of its solutions is highly unpredictable because of the nondeterministic behaviour. Fortunately, a solution can be used as feedback for building a new initial plan, after removing some actions to artificially create some conflicts (unsupported conditions), and starting the algorithm again to refine the current solution and find a better quality plan. Now, the original plan cost (makespan in the particular case of temporal planning) is used as an upper bound to help prune and improve the search. Although this does not provide optimal plans, it incrementally helps improve their quality.

SGPlan goes a step beyond in the union of different techniques by combining different planners in the resolution of a problem (Chen,

Hsu, & Wah, 2004; Chen et al., 2006). SGPlan decomposes an initial problem into a collection of subproblems, which are solved independently by a basic planner (see Algorithm 8); the underlying idea is that smaller subproblems require less time to be solved. After this decomposition, thus partitioning an original problem with *n* goals into *n* subproblems with one goal each, a heuristic process fixes an ordering to solve these subproblems. Depending on the basic planner used to solve each subproblem, the resulting subplan can be locally optimal, which is not a guarantee for finding a globally optimal plan.

The fact of merging the subplans calculated separately into a consistent global plan may turn some global constraints invalid. For instance, in a nonconservative model of actions some mutexes (see Figure 5) between actions of different subplans can appear when they are grouped to compose the final solution. Consequently, the subproblems may need to be solved multiple times in order to fix the violated global constraints (Chen et al., 2006). This process is carried out by heuristically updating the penalty value of such constraints to guide the search until finding a solution or a limit (time or number of steps) is exceeded, as depicted in Algorithm 8.

All in all, the subgoal partitioning of SGPlan turns out very effective and fast for solving large planning problems, particularly temporal problems where the search space grows significantly, since each partitioned subproblem involves a substantially smaller search space than that of the

original problem. The main problem, as in LPG, is that the quality of the solutions may be unpredictable and not very good. After all, the original problem is split and solved independently, which, though fast, in some cases may not be beneficial for finding a good global solution.

TEMPORAL PLANNERS IN THE INTERNATIONAL PLANNING COMPETITIONS

In this section we present a brief synthesis of the state-of-the-art temporal planners and the principal algorithmic techniques they use. Although there exist many temporal planners in recent literature, our selection does not intend to be exhaustive since we have just focused on those that have shown a distinguished performance in temporal domains in any of the last three International Planning Competitions (IPC–2002, IPC–2004, and IPC–2006) and are publicly available.

Table 7 depicts the selected planners and includes the expressiveness supported by their action models (conservative vs. nonconservative) and performance. The planners are organised in two blocks: first the optimal planners and second the suboptimal planners. In temporal optimal planning, the most representative planners are CPT (with the recent version CPT2 that participated in IPC–2006) and TP4 & HSP$^*_a$ (Haslum, 2006). CPT's ideas and constraint programming formulation have been presented and significantly

Algorithm 8. General scheme of the search performed in SGPlan.

```
1:   Plan ← ∅
2:   decompose the original problem into subgoals {g₁,g₂,... gₙ} and fix a solving ordering
3:   repeat
4:       for all subgoal gᵢ do
5:           invoke a basic planner to find an independent subplan Sub_planᵢ that solves gᵢ
6:           update Plan with Sub_planᵢ
7:       update heuristic evaluation of the global constraints that are violated
8:   until (a plan is found) ∨ (a limit is exceeded)
```

Table 7. Brief synthesis of the temporal planners that showed a distinguished performance in any of the last three IPCs for temporal domains. The first block of planners is for optimal behaviour, whereas the second one is for suboptimal behaviour. "C" and "NC" stand for a Conservative and Nonconservative model of actions, respectively.

Planner	Main features used	Expressiveness	Performance
CPT	POCL and constraint programming satisfaction	C	Medium
TP4 & HSP$^*_a$	automatic extraction of admissible heuristic to inform search	C	Low
LPG & LPG-td	hybrid: non-deterministic local search and heuristic estimations	NC	High
Mips	hybrid: heuristic search and automatic domain compilation techniques	NC	Medium-High
Sapa	heuristic search with estimations based on relaxed temporal planning graphs	NC	Medium
SGPlan	hybrid: problem partitioning and heuristic search	NC	High
VHPOP	POCL and distance based heuristics plus reachability analysis	NC	Medium

extended. On the other hand, both TP4 & HSP$^*_a$ share the same strategy and extract admissible heuristic estimations that are used during the search; their only difference is that HSP$^*_a$ computes a more accurate heuristic and records information discovered in the search, which obviously requires more computation time. However, in general, they show little difference in performance.

In suboptimal planning, there are three outstanding planners: SGPlan (including its recent version SGPlan5 (Hsu, Wah, Huang, & Chen, 2006)), LPG/LPG-td and the recent version of Mips, called Mips-XXL (Edelkamp, Jabbar, & Nazih, 2006). Although Mips-XXL can also be used for optimal planning by using a branch and bound procedure, its best performance is offered in the non-optimal modality. The common feature is that all three planners use hybrid approaches that combine several techniques, such as planning graphs to calculate heuristics, model checking to precompile information about the planning domain (Edelkamp, 2002), or partial order and planning decomposition techniques. Sapa is a heuristic temporal planner that uses heuristic estimations similarly to TP4, whereas VHPOP

(Younes & Simmons, 2003) exploits versatile heuristics under a partial order planner.

Regarding the expressiveness supported by their model of durative actions, CPT, TP4, and HSP$^*_a$ use a conservative model, being less expressive than the other suboptimal planners that support a nonconservative model. However, it is important to highlight that both CPT and VHPOP can be more easily augmented to deal with more expressive features because they use constraint programming and/or POCL features. Particularly, as presented in another section of this chapter, CPT's constraint programming formulation can be modified to support a high expressiveness. Finally, performance of suboptimal planners is obviously superior to optimal planners. In optimal planning CPT performs quite well and, in suboptimal planning SGPlan and LPG show very efficient.

The main conclusions we can extract from Table 7 are twofold: (i) optimal planning is a very difficult approach, which just a few planners can deal with efficiently, and focuses on optimality issues instead of expressiveness, and (ii) suboptimal planning attracts more planners because it provides more practical results, that is, good quality plans in a reasonable execution time, that generally combine several techniques under a hybrid approach. Optimal planners use POCL features together with admissible heuristics, which are usually extracted from variations of planning graphs. This demonstrates that POCL reasoning is very valuable in a temporal planning setting. Recent suboptimal planners do not use a particular technique, but combine many of them, traditionally heuristic search, POCL features, and their own techniques.

CONCLUSION

AI planning has experienced a great advance in the last years, giving rise to very efficient algorithms capable to tackle with problems that were unsolvable some years ago. The advances in planning algorithms have led to an increasing interest in extending the basic capabilities of planners to deal with, among others, time, that is, duration in the actions and temporal constraints. Dealing with time in temporal planning is not as simple as *stretching* the actions to represent their duration, but a more elaborate (nonconservative) model of actions, with more types of conditions and effects, becomes necessary. A nonconservative model of actions exploits more opportunities to overlap actions, thus generally producing better quality plans in terms of makespan, which usually entails a more complex solving process. The nonconservative model of actions most widely accepted is the level 3 of PDDL2.1, although there exists more expressive approaches that allow to model real-world problems in greater detail.

Broadly speaking, temporal planning is not an easy task as it tends to be significantly more difficult than classical planning. After all, the problem of planning for durative actions subsumes classical planning and also includes other features of scheduling problems, which entails larger search spaces and increases the complexity of the process, particularly when searching

for optimal plans. This is the main reason for designing alternative heuristic techniques that focus on suboptimal planning in order to provide a reasonable tradeoff between plan quality and algorithms efficiency.

In this chapter, we have thoroughly reviewed the most important techniques for temporal planning, introducing the main issues to cope with temporality in plans and the most common solutions used by the planners. We have opted for presenting temporal planning approaches from different perspectives: (i) a (pure) planning-graph-based approach, (ii) a heuristic approach, (iii) a POCL-based approach, and (iv) a hybrid approach. Although some POCL approaches are prior to planning graphs, we have introduced first the latter approach as they have brought up a renewed interest and allowed to push forward the research on temporal planning. Most heuristic, modern POCL, and hybrid approaches benefit from many heuristic estimations calculated through planning graphs. Temporal planning techniques under a planning graph approach use a structure that alternates propositions and actions, which is later used as the search space. Hence, the main features these techniques provide are:

- An extensive calculus of mutual exclusion relations (mutex) between propositions, actions, and propositions/actions. This mutex information helps avoid important parts of the search space by discarding invalid situations for feasible plans.
- Algorithms to generate a temporal planning graph as a generalisation of a classical planning graph that explicitly includes time in its levels. This way, graph levels are indexed with time stamps to know when propositions and actions first appear in a plan. An additional advantage of temporal planning graphs is that they can be quickly generated in a relaxed way, and can be used to calculate heuristic estimations that are used in other approaches, such as heuristic or POCL.

- Algorithms to perform a search through the temporal planning graph, for both conservative and nonconservative models of actions. The chronological backtracking of Graphplan search can be applied to nonconservative models with some modifications. Additionally, calculating relaxed plans for cost estimations is a straightforward task when using relaxed planning graphs.
- Nice theoretical properties that allow us to deal with optimal temporal planning, that is, plans with optimal makespan under a sound and complete approach.

Planning graphs provide valuable foundations for designing other approaches, such as heuristic and hybrid approaches. Basically, the planning graph structures and their algorithms are adapted to be used to extract heuristic estimations for state-based planners or as an important decision point to split the original problem into smaller subproblems, and select which subproblem, and in which order, needs to be solved. Additionally, the heuristic estimations can be easily extended to include resource metrics and allow multicriteria optimisation, under suboptimal and optimal frameworks.

Temporal POCL techniques mostly rely on the least-commitment principle and a powerful representation to deal with durative actions. In general, temporal POCL techniques address the planning problem by means of: (i) extending its basic behaviour to include temporal constraints, (ii) relying on POCL+CSP techniques, or (iii) formulating the problem as a CSP and leaving a traditional CSP to solve it. The main features provided by POCL techniques are:

- A natural and very appropriate way to include time in a planning framework; the typical POCL mechanisms as partial order or subgoal preserving allowing for a natural extension to temporal planning.

- A very rich and expressive representation model that is also very well suited for integrating planning and scheduling (time+metric resource consumption) capabilities.
- A very flexible interval representation that allows us to express any temporal constraint between actions or actions and propositions in terms of the interval endpoints.
- A high degree of execution flexibility thanks to the application of the least-commitment principle which allows us to postpone not only the typical decisions in classical planning but also the allocation of actions and propositions in time.
- The incorporation of other resolution methods, such as CSP techniques, into a POCL framework. This allows us to benefit from the resolution power of other methods as well as improve the performance of temporal POCL planners.

Finally, it is important to note that planning graph, heuristic, and POCL approaches are not disjoint nor opposite ways to cope with temporal planning. On the contrary, they can be successfully combined to form hybrid approaches for complex real-world problems where a rich expressiveness is required (provided by POCL and constraint satisfaction techniques) and very efficient heuristics (provided by planning graph techniques and resource use estimations) need to be included to improve the solving process. Although this combination is not easy nor intuitive, it is a promising direction that may bring fruitful contributions and open new lines of research.

FUTURE DIRECTIONS

Temporal planning is currently a hot topic of research. However, the research works are not only focused on temporal planning itself, but on its combination with other capabilities. Particularly, research on temporal planning has given rise to planning with numeric capabilities to manage metric resources, multicriteria optimisation, situations with uncertainty, and so forth, under a more general approach for solving real-world problems. This has led to three main lines in research: (i) improving the efficiency of algorithms for (temporal) planning, (ii) increasing the expressiveness and the number of supported capabilities (more realistic planning), and (iii) integrating efficient algorithms for realistic planning.

From the efficiency point of view, the objective is to improve algorithms performance by working with models of limited expressiveness, thus allowing us to mainly focus on the algorithmic aspects and new developments for the resolution methods. From the expressiveness point of view, the challenge is to come up with representational models that allow us to specify more features and express (soft+hard) constraints of real-world problems. From the integrated point of view, the problem arises out in the combination of the two previous perspectives: how to obtain an expressive and efficient temporal planning model. Although transforming a temporal planning problem (with complex constraints) into a CSP and then solving the overall problem with CSP techniques that use reachability heuristics seems promising, the challenge is to see to what extent CSP methods can efficiently solve large size problems. Probably, the answer lies in the recent works that leave planners and schedulers to deal with their own functionalities; planners focus on planning, while schedulers focus on time and resource allocation, that is, systems with a true integrated architecture for planning and scheduling, where each component plays a similar role in the solving process.

ACKNOWLEDGMENT

We would like to thank the anonymous referees for helping improve this chapter. This work has been partially supported by the Spanish government project MCyT TIN2005-08945-C06-06 (FEDER) and by the Valencian government project GV06/096.

REFERENCES

Agosta, J.M., & Wilkins, D.E. (1996). Using SIPE-2 to plan emergency response to marine oil spills. *IEEE Expert, 11*(6), 6-8.

Allen, J. (1983). Maintaining knowledge about temporal intervals. *Communications of the ACM, 26*(11), 832-843.

Allen, J. (1991). Planning as temporal reasoning. In J. Allen, R. Fikes & E. Sandewall (Eds.), *Proceedings of the KR'91: Principles of Knowledge Representation and Reasoning* (pp. 3-14). Morgan Kaufmann.

Blum, A.L., & Furst, M.L. (1997). Fast planning through planning graph analysis. *Artificial Intelligence, 90,* 281-300.

Bonet, B., & Geffner, H. (1999). Planning as heuristic search: New results. In S. Biundo & M. Fox (Eds.), *Proceedings of the European Conference on Planning (ECP-99)* (pp. 360-372). Springer.

Bonet, B., & Geffner, H. (2001). Planning as heuristic search. *Artificial Intelligence, 129,* 5-33.

Chen, Y., Hsu, C.W., & Wah, B.W. (2004). SGPlan: Subgoal partitioning and resolution in planning. In *Proceedings of the International Conference on Automated Planning and Scheduling (ICAPS-2004) – International Planning Competition* (pp. 30-32).

Chen, Y.X., Wah, B.W., & Hsu, C.W. (2006). Temporal planning using subgoal partitioning and resolution in SGPlan. *Journal of Artificial Intelligence Research, 26,* 323-369.

Chien, S., Rabideau, G., Knight, R., Sherwood, R., Engelhardt, B., Mutz, D., et al. (2000). AS-

PEN—automating space mission operations using automated planning and scheduling. In *Proceedings of the SpaceOps 2000* (pp. 1-10).

Currie, K., & Tate, A. (1991). O-plan: The open planning architecture. *Artificial Intelligence, 52*(1), 49-86.

Dean, T.L., Firby, R.J., & Miller, D. (1988). Hierarchical planning involving deadlines, travel time and resources. *Computational Intelligence, 4,* 381-398.

Dean, T.L., & McDermott, D.V. (1987). Temporal data base management. *Artificial Intelligence, 32,* 1-55.

Dechter, R., Meiri, I., & Pearl, J. (1991). Temporal constraint networks. *Artificial Intelligence, 49,* 61-95.

Do, M.B., & Kambhampati, S. (2001). Sapa: A domain-independent heuristic metric temporal planner. In A. Cesta & D. Borrajo (Eds.), *Proceedings of the European Conference on Planning (ECP-2001)* (pp. 109-120).

Do, M.B., & Kambhampati, S. (2003). SAPA: A multi-objective metric temporal planner. *Journal of Artificial Intelligence Research, 20,* 155-194.

Drabble, B., & Kirby, R. (1991). Associating AI planner entities with an underlying time point network. In *European Workshop on Planning (EWSP'91)* (LNCS 522, pp. 27-38). Springer-Verlag.

Drabble, B., & Tate, A. (1994). The use of optimistic and pessimistic resource profiles to inform search in an activity based planner. In *Proceedings of the 2nd Conference on Artificial Intelligence Planning Systems (AIPS-94)* (pp. 243-248).

Edelkamp, S. (2002). Mixed propositional and numeric planning in the model checking integrated planning system. In M. Fox & A. Coddington (Eds.), *Proceedings of the Workshop on Planning for Temporal Domains (AIPS-2002)* (pp. 47-55).

Edelkamp, S., & Hoffmann, J. (2004). PDDL2.2: The language for the classical part of IPC-4. In *Proceedings of the International Conference on Automated Planning and Scheduling (ICAPS-2004) – International Planning Competition* (pp. 2-6).

Edelkamp, S., Jabbar, S., & Nazih, M. (2006). Large-scale optimal PDDL3 planning with MIPS-XXL. In *Proceedings of the International Conference on Automated Planning and Scheduling (ICAPS-2006) – International Planning Competition* (pp. 28-30).

Fikes, R.E., & Nilsson, N.J. (1971). STRIPS: A new approach to the application of theorem proving to problem solving. *Artificial Intelligence, 2,* 189-208.

Fox, M., & Long, D. (1999). Efficient implementation of the plan graph in STAN. *Journal of Artificial Intelligence Research, 10,* 87-115.

Fox, M., & Long, D. (2003). PDDL2.1: An extension to PDDL for expressing temporal planning domains. *Journal of Artificial Intelligence Research, 20,* 61-124.

Garrido, A., Fox, M., & Long, D. (2002). A temporal planning system for durative actions of PDDL2.1. In F. Van Harmelen (Ed.), *Proceedings of the European Conference on AI (ECAI-2002)* (pp. 586-590). Amsterdam: IOS Press.

Garrido, A., & Long, D. (2004). Planning with numeric variables in multiobjective planning. In L. Saitta (Ed.), *Proceedings of the European Conference on AI (ECAI-2004)* (pp. 662-666). Amsterdam: IOS Press.

Garrido, A., & Onaindía, E. (2003). On the application of least-commitment and heuristic search in temporal planning. In *Proceedings of the International Joint Conference on AI (IJCAI-2003)* (pp. 942-947). Acapulco, Mexico: Morgan Kaufmann.

Garrido, A., & Onaindía, E. (2006). Interleaving planning and scheduling: A collaborative approach. In *Proceedings of the ICAPS Workshop on Constraint Satisfaction Techniques for Planning and Scheduling Problems* (pp. 31-38).

Garrido, A., Onaindía, E., & Arangu, M. (2006). Using constraint programming to model complex plans in an antegrated approach for planning and scheduling. In *Proceedings of the 25th UK Planning and Scheduling SIG Workshop* (pp. 137-144).

Gerevini, A., & Long, D. (2005). *Plan constraints and preferences in PDDL3* (Tech. Rep.). Italy: University of Brescia.

Gerevini, A., Saetti, A., & Serina, I. (2003). Planning through stochastic local search and temporal action graphs in LPG. *Journal of Artificial Intelligence Research, 20,* 239-290.

Ghallab, M., & Laruelle, H. (1994). Representation and control in IxTeT, a temporal planner. In *Proceedings of the 2nd International Conference on AI Planning Systems* (pp. 61-67). Hammond.

Ghallab, M., Nau, D., & Traverso, P. (2004). *Automated planning. Theory and practice.* Morgan Kaufmann.

Haslum, P. (2006). Improving heuristics through relaxed search–an analysis of TP4 and HSP$^*_a$ in the 2004 planning competition. *Journal of Artificial Intelligence Research, 25,* 233-267.

Haslum, P., & Geffner, H. (2001). Heuristic planning with time and resources. In A. Cesta & D. Borrajo (Eds.), *Proceedings of the European Conference on Planning (ECP-2001)* (pp. 121-132).

Hoffmann, J., & Nebel, B. (2001). The FF planning system: Fast plan generation through heuristic search. *Journal of Artificial Intelligence Research, 14,* 253-302.

Hsu, C-W., Wah, B.W., Huang, R., & Chen, Y. (2006). New features in SGPlan for handling preferences and constraints in PDDL3.0. In *Proceedings of the International Conference on Automated Planning and Scheduling (ICAPS2006) – International Planning Competition* (pp. 39-41).

Jonsson, A., Morris, P., Muscettola, N., Rajan, K., & Smith, B. (2000). Planning in interplanetary space: Theory and practice. In *Proceedings of the 5th International Conference on AI Planning Systems (AIPS-2000)* (pp. 177-186). AAAI Press.

Joslin, D., & Pollack, M.E. (1996). Is "early commitment" in plan generation ever a good idea? In *Proceedings of the 13th Nat. Conference on AI (AAAI-96)* (pp. 177-186).

Korf, R. (1985). Depth-first iterative-deepening: an optimal admissible tree search. *Artificial Intelligence, 27*(1), 97-109.

Laborie, P., & Ghallab, M. (1995). Planning with sharable resource constraints. In *Proceedings of the International Joint Conference on AI (IJCAI-95)* (pp. 1643-1647). Morgan Kaufmann.

Lee, T.J., & Wilkins, D.E. (1996). Using SIPE-2 to integrate planning for military air campaigns. *IEEE Expert, 11*(6), 11-12.

Long, D., & Fox, M. (2001). Encoding temporal planning domains and validating temporal plans. In *Proceedings of the 20th UK Planning and Scheduling SIG Workshop* (pp. 167-180).

Long, D., & Fox, M. (2002). Progress in AI planning research and applications. *UPGRADE, The European Online Magazine for the IT Professional, 3*(5), 10-24.

Long, D., & Fox, M. (2003a). Exploiting a graphplan framework in temporal planning. In *Proceedings of the International Conference on Automated Planning and Scheduling (ICAPS-2003)* (pp. 51-62).

Long, D., & Fox, M. (2003b). Time in planning. In *Handbook of temporal reasoning in AI. Foundations of Artificial Intelligence*, vol. 1 (pp. 497-537). Elsevier Science.

Muscettola, N. (1994). HSTS: Integrating planning and scheduling. In M. Zweben & M.S. Fox (Eds.), *Intelligent Scheduling* (Vol 1, pp. 169-212). San Mateo, CA: Morgan Kaufmann.

Nguyen, X., Kambhampati, S., & Nigenda, R.S. (2002). Planning graph as the basis for deriving heuristics for plan synthesis by state space and CSP search. *Artificial Intelligence, 135*, 73-123.

Penberthy, J. (1993). Planning with continuous change. Technical Report Ph.D. dissertation 93-12-01, University of Washington, Department of Computer Science and Engineering.

Penberthy, J., & Weld, D.S. (1992). UCPOP: A sound, complete, partial-order planner for ADL. In *Proceedings of the International Conference on Principles of Knowledge Representation and Reasoning* (pp. 103-114). Los Altos, CA: Kaufmann.

Penberthy, J., & Weld, D. (1994). Temporal planning with continuous change. In *Proceedings of the 12th National Conference on AI* (pp. 1010-1015).

Penix, J., Pecheur, C., & Havelund, K. (1998). Using model checking to validate AI planner domain models. In *Proceedings of the 23rd Annual Software Engineering Workshop* (pp. 356-364). NASA Goddard.

Refanidis, I. (2005). Stratified heuristic POCL temporal planning based on planning graphs and constraint programming. In *Proceedings of the ICAPS-2005 Workshop on Constraint Programming for Planning and Scheduling* (pp. 66-73).

Russell, S., & Norvig, P. (2003). *Artificial intelligence: A modern approach*. Prentice Hall.

Rutten, E., & Hertzberg, J. (1993). Temporal planner=nonlinear planner+time map manager. *AI Communications, 6*(1), 18-26.

Smith, D.E., Frank, J., & Jonsson, A.K. (2000). Bridging the gap between planning and sched-uling. *Knowledge Engineering Review, 15*(1), 47-83.

Smith, D.E., & Weld, D.S. (1999). Temporal planning with mutual exclusion reasoning. In *Proceedings of the 16th International Joint Conference on AI (IJCAI-99)* (pp. 326-337), Stockholm, Sweden.

Tate, A., Dalton, J., & Levine, J. (2000). O-plan: A Web-based AI planning agent. In *Intelligent Systems Demonstrator, Proc. Nat. Conf. on Artificial Intelligence (AAAI 00)* (pp. 1131-1132).

Van Beek, P., & Chen, X. (1999). CPlan: A constraint programming approach to planning. In *Proc. Nat. Conf. on Artificial Intelligence (AAAI-99)* (pp. 585-590).

Vere, S. (1983). Planning in time: Windows and durations for activities and goals. *IEEE Transactions on Pattern Analysis and Machine Intelligence, 5*, 246-267.

Vidal, V., & Geffner, H. (2004). Branching and pruning: An optimal temporal POCL planner based on constraint programming. In *Proc. Nat. Conf. on Artificial Intelligence (AAAI-04)* (pp. 570-577).

Vidal, V., & Geffner, H. (2006). Branching and pruning: An optimal temporal POCL planner based on constraint programming. *Artificial Intelligence, 170*, 298-335.

Weld, D. (1994). An introduction to least commitment planning. *AI Magazine, 15*(4), 93-123.

Weld, D.S. (1999). Recent advances in AI planning. *AI Magazine, 20*(2), 93-123.

Wilkins, D. (1988). *Practical planning: Extending the classical AI planning paradigm*. San Mateo, CA: Morgan Kaufmann.

Wilkins, D.E., & desJardins, M. (2001). A call for knowledge-based planning. *AI Magazine, 22*(1), 99-115.

Younes, H.L.S., & Simmons, R.G. (2003). VH-POP: Versatile heuristic partial order planner. *Journal of Artificial Intelligence Research, 20,* 405-430.

ENDNOTES

[1]   In the classical model of actions, the preconditions must hold throughout the whole execution of the action and the effects are only guaranteed to hold at the end of the action.

[2]   More information about IPC can be found at http://www.icaps-conference.org/

[3]   This estimation requires a non-relaxed planning graph, that is, propagation of mutex information. Although h_{max2} can be generalised to any h_{maxk}, its calculation for $k>2$ turns out very expensive and hardly used.

[4]   CPT also includes other redundant constraints that, although are not necessary for soundness or completeness, help improve the performance by pruning values and detecting inconsistencies earlier (Vidal & Geffner, 2006).

[5]   This way of solving the mutex relations is more permissive than in a conservative model of actions, where the actions cannot overlap and must be sequentially executed.

[6]   We thank the anonymous referee for addressing this example, simply but very effectively.

[7]   The use of an $\epsilon > 0$ also appears in PDDL2.1 plan validation (Long & Fox, 2001) in order to specify the minimal precision with which evaluate the quality of the plans. Although changes in this value can change the makespan of the same optimal plan, this seems to be more a philosophical than a meaningful question in the constraint formulation.

Section II
Constraint Satisfaction and Scheduling

Chapter III
Principles of Constraint Processing

Roman Barták
Charles University in Prague, Czech Republic

ABSTRACT

Solving combinatorial optimization problems such as planning, scheduling, design, or configuration is a nontrivial task being attacked by many solving techniques. Constraint satisfaction, that emerged from Artificial Intelligence (AI) research and nowadays integrates techniques from areas such as operations research and discrete mathematics, provides a natural modeling framework for description of such problems supported by general solving technology. Though it is a mature area now, surprisingly many researchers outside the constraint satisfaction problem (CSP) community do not use the full potential of constraint satisfaction and frequently confuse constraint satisfaction and simple enumeration. This chapter gives an introduction to mainstream constraint satisfaction techniques available in existing constraint solvers and answers the question "How does constraint satisfaction work?" The focus of the chapter is on techniques of constraint propagation, depth-first search, and their integration. It explains backtracking, its drawbacks, and how to remove these drawbacks by methods such as backjumping and backmarking. Then, the focus is on consistency techniques; the chapter explains methods such as arc and path consistency and introduces consistencies of higher level. It also presents how consistency techniques are integrated with depth-first search algorithms in a look-ahead concept and what value and variable ordering heuristics are available there. Finally, techniques for optimization with constraints are presented.

INTRODUCTION: WHAT IS CONSTRAINT PROGRAMMING, WHAT ARE ITS ORIGINS AND WHY IS IT USEFUL?

Constraint programming is an emerging software technology for declarative description and effective solving of combinatorial optimization problems in areas such as planning and scheduling. It represents one of the most exciting developments in programming languages of the last decade and, not surprisingly, it has recently been identified by the Association for Computing Machinery as one of the strategic directions in computer research. Not only it is based on a strong theoretical foundation but it is attracting widespread commercial interest as well, in particular, in areas of modelling heterogeneous optimisation and satisfaction problems.

What Is a Constraint?

A constraint is simply a relation among several unknowns (or variables), each taking a value in a given domain. A constraint thus restricts possible values that the variables can take; it represents some partial information about the variables of interest. For instance, "the circle is inside the square" relates to objects without precisely specifying their positions, that is, their coordinates. Now, one may move the square or the circle and still be able to maintain the relation between these two objects. Also, one may want to add another object, say a triangle, and to introduce another constraint, say "the square is to the left of the triangle." From the user (human) point of view, the description of object relations remains transparent.

Constraints arise naturally in most areas of human endeavour. The three angles of a triangle sum to 180 degrees, the sum of the currents floating into a node must equal zero, the position of the scroller in the window scrollbar must reflect the visible part of the underlying document.

These are some examples of constraints which appear in the real world. Constraints can also be heterogeneous and so they can bind unknowns from different domains, for example the length (number) with the word (string). Thus, constraints are a natural medium for people to express problems in many fields.

We all use constraints to guide reasoning as a key part of everyday common sense. "I can be there from five to six o'clock." This is a typical constraint we use to plan our time. Naturally, we do not solve one constraint only but a collection of constraints that are rarely independent. This complicates the problem a bit, so, usually, we have to give and take.

What Is a Constraint Satisfaction Problem and Its Solution?

A *Constraint Satisfaction Problem* (CSP) consists of:

- a finite set of *variables* $X=\{x_1,...,x_n\}$,
- for each variable x_i, a set D_i of possible values (its *domain*), and
- a finite set of *constraints* restricting the values that the variables can simultaneously take.

Although the domains can be infinite (for example, real numbers), frequently only *finite domains* are assumed. This chapter covers techniques working with finite domains which have received the most attention in constraint programming. Hence we are speaking about solving combinatorial problems. Note that values need not be a set of consecutive integers (although often they are). They need not even be numeric.

The *constraint* is any relation between the subset of variables. This relation can be defined in an extensional way, as a set of compatible (or incompatible) tuples of values, or in an intentional way, as a logical or arithmetical formula. We will present the constraint satisfaction algorithms usually using the extensional formulation which is more general, though the intentional representation is more common when modelling problems as CSPs.

A *solution to a CSP* is an assignment of a value to every variable, in such a way that the value is from the domain of the variable and every constraint is satisfied. We may want to find:

- just one solution, with no preference as to which one,
- all solutions,
- an optimal, or at least a good solution, given some objective function defined in terms of some or all of the variables; in this case we speak about *constrained optimisation problem* (COP).

One may notice that a CSP is a generalisation of well known SAT problems, where only binary domains (true, false) are used for variables and the constraints are in the form of a disjunction of literals (positive or negative variables). Hence it is easy to see that the decision problem whether there exists a solution to a CSP is NP-complete.

The *reasons* for choosing to represent and solve a problem as a CSP rather than, say, as a mathematical programming problem are twofold:

- First, the representation as a CSP is often much closer to the original problem: the variables of the CSP directly correspond to problem entities, and the constraints can be expressed without having to be translated into linear inequalities. This makes the formulation simpler, the solution easier to understand, and the choice of good heuristics to guide the solution strategy more straightforward.
- Second, although CSP algorithms are essentially simple, they can sometimes find solutions more quickly than if integer programming methods are used.

A Bit of History

Constraints have emerged as a research area that combines researchers from a number of fields, including Artificial Intelligence, Programming Languages, Symbolic Computing, Computational Logic, and Operations Research. Constraint networks and constraint satisfaction problems have been studied in Artificial Intelligence starting from the seventies (Montanari, 1974; Waltz, 1975). Systematic use of constraints in programming has started in the 1980s when unification in logic programming was identified as a particular type of a constraint (Gallaire, 1985; Jaffar & Lassez, 1987).

Constraint satisfaction originates from Artificial Intelligence where the problems such as interactive drawing editors (Borning, 1981) or scene labelling were studied (Waltz, 1975). The scene labelling problem is probably the first constraint satisfaction problem that was formalised. The goal is to recognise objects in the scene by interpreting lines in the drawings. It requires the lines (or edges) to be labelled, that is, to be categorised into few types, namely convex (+), concave (-), and occluding lines (<). In some advanced systems, the shadow border is recognised as well. Figure 1 shows the original drawing (left) and the drawing where (some) edges are labelled by their types (right).

There are a lot of alternatives as so how to label the scene (exactly 3^n, where n is the number of edges) but only few of them have any 3D meaning. Naturally, we are looking for those labellings that are physically feasible. This physical feasibility

Figure 1. The goal of scene labelling is to assign a type to each line in the drawing

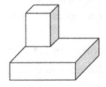 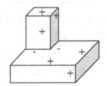

Figure 2. The three possible labellings of edges connected in an "arrow" type of junction

can be achieved (for some type of objects) by restricting the possible combinations of labels at junctions of edges. This reduces the problem a lot because there are only a very limited number of legal labels for junctions (see Figure 2 showing the only three legal labellings of the edges in the "arrow" type of junction).

To solve this combinatorial problem one needs to find legal labels for edges satisfying the constraints at junctions. In terms of constraint satisfaction, the edges correspond to variables and the junctions represent the constraints. The constraints restrict the possible combinations of labels to those that are physically feasible.

Some Examples

There are a lot of problems that can be naturally modelled and solved using constraint programming. Among them, N-queens, the graph (map) colouring, and crypto-arithmetic have a privileged position. Recently, Sudoku problems became a great example showing how constraint programming can beat other solving techniques.

N-Queens

The N-queens problem is a well known puzzle among computer scientists. Given any integer N, the problem is to place N queens on squares in an N*N chessboard satisfying the constraint that no two queens threaten each other (a queen threatens any other queen on the same row, column, and diagonal).

A typical way to model this problem is to assume that each queen is in a different row and to assign a variable R_i (with the domain $\{1,..., N\}$) to the queen in the i-th row indicating the position of the queen in the column. Now, its is easy to express "no-threatening" constraints between each couple R_i and R_j of queens:

$$i \neq j \Rightarrow (R_i \neq R_j \land | \text{i-j} | \neq | R_i - R_j |)$$

Graph (Map) Colouring

Another problem which is frequently used to demonstrate the potential of constraint programming and to explain the concepts of constraint satisfaction is the graph colouring problem. Given a graph (a map) and a number of colours, the problem is to assign colours to the nodes (to the areas in the map) satisfying the constraint that no adjacent nodes (areas) have the same colour assigned to them.

This problem is modelled naturally by annotating each node of the graph with a variable (with the domain corresponding to the set of colours) and introducing a nonequality constraint between each two variables for adjacent nodes (Figure 3).

Crypto-Arithmetic

Our next example of using constraint satisfaction techniques is a crypto-arithmetic problem. In fact, it is a group of similar problems. Given a mathematical expression where letters are used instead of numbers, the problem is to assign digits to those letters satisfying the constraint that different letters should have different digits assigned and

Figure 3. Graph colouring problem and its formulation using a constraint graph

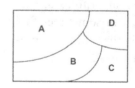

the mathematical formula holds. Here is a typical example of the crypto-arithmetic problem:

SEND + MORE = MONEY

The problem can be modelled by identifying each letter with a variable (with the domain $\{0,\ldots,9\}$), by direct rewriting the formulae to an equivalent arithmetic constraint:

$$
\begin{aligned}
& 1000*S + 100*E + 10*N + D \\
+ \ & 1000*M + 100*O + 10*R + E \\
= \ & 10000*M + 1000*O + 100*N + 10*E + Y
\end{aligned}
$$

and by adding auxiliary constraints $S \neq 0$ and $M \neq 0$. Moreover, inequality constraints between all pairs of variables should be used.

Sudoku

Our last example is a popular Sudoku puzzle. The task is to fill digits $1,\ldots,9$ to cells of 9×9 matrix in such a way that no digit appears two or more times in each row, column, and 3×3 sub-grids (see Figure 4).

There is a straightforward model of this problem with a variable for each cell (domain $\{1,\ldots,9\}$) and with inequality constraints between

Figure 4. A Sudoku problem, the dark digits are prefilled, the gray digits need to be found

9	6	3	1	7	4	2	5	8
1	7	8	3	2	5	6	4	9
2	5	4	6	8	9	7	3	1
8	2	1	4	3	7	5	9	6
4	9	6	8	5	2	3	1	7
7	3	5	9	6	1	8	2	4
5	8	9	7	1	3	4	6	2
3	1	7	2	4	6	9	8	5
6	4	2	5	9	8	1	7	3

the variables of the same row, same column, and same subgrid.

Practical Applications

Of course, constraint programming is not popular because of solving puzzles but because of its potential to model and solve real-life problems naturally and efficiently. CP has been successfully applied in numerous domains. Recent applications include computer graphics (to express geometric coherence in the case of scene analysis), natural language processing (construction of efficient parsers), database systems (to ensure and/or restore consistency of the data), operations research problems (like optimisation problems), molecular biology (DNA sequencing), business applications (option trading), electrical engineering (to locate faults), circuit design (to compute layouts), and so forth. The most successful application area is probably scheduling where CP techniques are used to allocate activities to limited resources and time.

The number of companies exploiting constraint technology increases each year. Here is a list of some of the well-known names among them: British Airways, SAS, Swissair, French railway authority SNCF, Hong Kong International Terminals, Michelin, Dassault, Ericsson, CISCO, and so forth.

Also, there are a lot of companies providing solutions based on constraints like PeopleSoft, i2 Technologies, SAP, or companies providing constraint-based tools like ILOG, IF Computer, Cosytec, SICS, or PrologIA.

SYSTEMATIC SEARCH: HOW TO SOLVE CONSTRAINT SATISFACTION PROBLEMS BY SEARCH?

Many algorithms for solving CSPs search systematically through the possible assignments of values to variables. Such algorithms are guaranteed to find a solution, if one exists, or to prove that the problem is insolvable. Thus the systematic search algorithms are sound and complete. The main disadvantage of these algorithms is that they may take a very long time to do so.

There are two main classes of systematic search algorithms:

- the algorithms that explore the *space of complete assignments*, that is, the assignments of all variables, until they find a complete assignment that satisfies all the constraints, and
- the algorithms that *extend a partial consistent assignment to a complete assignment* that satisfies all the constraints.

In this section we present the basic representatives of both classes. Although these algorithms look simple, it is important to understand their principles because they make the foundation of other algorithms that exploit more sophisticated techniques like constraint propagation or local search.

Generate and Test (GT)

The generate-and-test method is a typical representative of algorithms that explore the space of complete assignments. First, the GT algorithm generates some complete assignment of variables and, then, it tests whether this assignment satisfies all the constraints. If the test fails, that is, there exists any unsatisfied constraint then the algorithm tries another complete assignment. The algorithm stops as soon as a complete assignment satisfying all the constraints is found, in which case this is a solution of the problem, or all complete assignments are explored, that is, the solution does not exist

The GT algorithm explores systematically the space of complete assignments, that is, it explores each possible combination of the variable assignments. The number of combinations considered by

Algorithm 1. Generate and test

```
procedure GT(Variables, Constraints)
  for each Assignment of Variables do % generator
    if consistent(Assignment, Constraints) then
      return Assignment
  end for
  return fail
end GT

procedure consistent(Assignment, Constraints) % test
  for each C in Constraints do
    if C is not satisfied by Assignment then
      return fail
  end for
  return true
end consistent
```

this method is equal to the size of the Cartesian product of all the variable domains.

The above algorithm schema is parameterised by the procedure for generation of complete assignments of variables. The pure form of the GT algorithm uses a trivial generator that returns all complete assignments in some specified or-

Algorithm 2. Pure generator of complete assignments for GT

```
procedure generate_first(Variables)
  for each V in Variables do
    assign the first value in D_V to V
  end for
end generate_first

procedure generate_next(Assignment)
  find first X in Assignment such that
    all following variables Vs are instantiated by
    the last value from their respective domains
  if X is instantiated by the last value then
    return fail
  assign next value in D_X to X
  for each Y in Vs do
    assign the first value in D_Y to Y
  end for
end generate_next
```

```
Example:

Domains: D_X=[1,2,3], D_Y=[a,b,c], D_Z=[5,6]
First assignment: X/1, Y/a, Z/5
Other assignments are generated in the following order:
X/1,Y/a,Z/6
X/1,Y/b,Z/5
X/1,Y/b,Z/6
...
X/3,Y/c,Z/6
```

der. This generator assumes that the variables and the values in domains are ordered in some sense. The first complete assignment is generated by assigning the first value from the domain to each variable. The next complete assignment is derived from the given assignment by finding such a variable X that all following variables (in a given order) are instantiated by the last value from their respective domains (let Vs be the set of such variables). Then, the generator assigns the next value from the domain D_x to the variable X, the first value from respective domains to each variable in Vs and the rest of the variables hold their values. If such a variable X does not exist, that is, all variables are instantiated by the last values in their respective domains, then the algorithm returns *fail* indicating that there is no other assignment.

Disadvantages

The pure generate-and-test approach is not very efficient because it generates many wrong assignments of values to variables which are rejected in the testing phase. In addition, the generator leaves out the conflicting assignments and it generates other assignments independently of the conflict (a blind generator). There are two ways how to improve the pure GT approach:

- The generator of assignments is smart, that is, it generates the next complete assignment in such a way that the conflict found by the test phase is minimised. This is a basic idea of stochastic algorithms based on local search (the local search techniques are not covered by this chapter).
- The generator is merged with the tester, that is, the validity of a constraint is tested as soon as the constrained variables are instantiated. This method is used by the backtracking approach, which is explained in the next section.

Backtracking (BT)

The most common algorithm for performing systematic search is backtracking. The backtracking algorithm incrementally attempts to extend a partial assignment, which specifies consistent values for some of the variables, toward a complete assignment, by repeatedly choosing a value for another variable consistent with the values in the current partial assignment.

Backtracking can be seen as a merge of the generate phase and the test phase from the GT approach. In the BT method, the variables are instantiated sequentially and as soon as all the variables relevant to a constraint are instantiated, the validity of the constraint is checked. If a partial assignment violates any of the constraints, backtracking is performed to the most recently instantiated variable that still has alternative values available. Clearly, whenever a partial assignment violates a constraint, backtracking is able to eliminate a subspace from the Cartesian product of all variable domains. Consequently, backtracking is strictly better than generate-and-

Algorithm 3. Chronological backtracking

```
procedure BT(Variables, Constraints)
  BT-1(Variables,{},Constraints)
end BT

procedure BT-1(Unlabelled, Labelled, Constraints)
if Unlabelled = {} then return Labelled
pick first X from Unlabelled
for each value V from Dx do
  if consistent({X/V}+Labelled, Constraints) then
    R ← BT-1(Unlabelled-{X}, {X/V}+Labelled, Constraints)
    if R ≠ fail then return R
  end if
end for
return fail % backtrack to previous variable
end BT-1

procedure consistent(Labelled, Constraints)
for each C in Constraints do
  if all variables from C are Labelled then
    if C is not satisfied by Labelled then
      return fail
end for
return true
end consistent
```

test, however, its running complexity for most nontrivial problems is still exponential.

The basic form of backtracking algorithm is called *chronological backtracking*. If this algorithm discovers an inconsistency then it always backtracks to the last decision, hence chronologically.

Again, the above algorithm schema for chronological backtracking can be parameterised. It is possible to plug in various procedures for choosing the unlabelled variable (variable ordering) and for choosing the value for this variable (value ordering). It is also possible to use a more sophisticated consistency test that discovers inconsistencies earlier than the above procedure or it is possible to jump back further to recover from the detected inconsistency. We will discuss all these possibilities later.

Disadvantages

There are three major drawbacks of the standard (chronological) backtracking scheme:

- The first drawback is *thrashing,* that is, a repeated failure due to the same reason. Thrashing occurs because the standard backtracking algorithm does not identify the real reason of the conflict, that is, the conflicting variable. Therefore, searching in different parts of the space of partial assignments keeps failing for the same reason. Thrashing can be avoided by *backjumping,* sometimes called *intelligent backtracking,* that is, by a scheme on which backtracking is done directly to the variable that caused the failure.
- The other drawback of backtracking is performing *redundant work*. Even if the conflicting values of variables are identified during the intelligent backtracking, they are not remembered for immediate detection of the same conflict in a subsequent computation. The methods to resolve this problem are

called *backchecking* or *backmarking*. Both algorithms are useful methods for reducing the number of compatibility checks. There is also a backtracking based method that eliminates both of the above drawbacks of backtracking. This method is traditionally called *dependency-directed backtracking* and is used in truth maintenance systems. It should be noted that using advanced techniques adds overhead to the algorithm that has to be balanced with the overall advantage of using them.

- Finally, the basic backtracking algorithm still *detects the conflict too late* as it is not able to detect the conflict before the conflict really occurs, that is, after assigning the values to all the variables of the violated constraint. This drawback can be avoided by applying consistency techniques to detect (*forward check*) the possible conflicts early.

Backjumping (BJ)

In the above analysis of disadvantages of chronological backtracking we identified the thrashing problem, that is, a problem with a repeated failure due to the same reason. We also outlined the method to avoid thrashing, called backjumping (Gaschnig, 1979).

The control of backjumping (BJ) is exactly the same as backtracking (BT), except when backtracking takes place. Both algorithms pick one variable at a time and look for a value for this variable making sure that the new assignment is compatible with the values committed to so far. However, if BJ finds an inconsistency, it analyses the situation in order to identify the source of the inconsistency. The BJ algorithm uses the violated constraints as a guide to find out the conflicting variable. If all the values in the domain are explored, then the BJ algorithm backtracks to the most recent conflicting variable. This is the main difference from the BT algorithm that backtracks to the immediate past variable.

Figure 5 shows the advantage of backjumping over chronological backtracking. It displays a board situation in the typical 8-queens problem. We have allocated the first five queens to respective columns (each queen is in a different row) and now we are looking for a consistent column position for the sixth queen. Unfortunately, each position is inconsistent with the assignment of the first five queens so we have to backtrack. The chronological backtracking backtracks to Queen 5 and it finds another column for this queen (column H). However, it is still impossible to place Queen 6 because, in fact, Queen 5 did not cause the conflict and hence change of its position cannot resolve the conflict.

The backjumping algorithm is smarter in discovering the real conflict. For each position it finds the set of conflicting queens, that is, the already placed queens that are incompatible with the given position. The numbers in row 6 indicate the assigned queens that the corresponding squares are incompatible with. At this stage one can realise that changing the position of Queen 5 will not resolve the conflict because all positions

for Queen 6 are still in conflict. The closest queen that can resolve the conflict is Queen 4 because then there is a chance that column D can be used for Queen 6.

The question is how to identify the most recent conflicting variable in general for *n*-ary constraints. Figure 6 sketches the situation when a value is being assigned to the seventh variable. There are two possible values, A and B, and there exist two violated constraints for each value. Constraint C_1 connects the variables 2, 3, 5, and 7, constraint C_2 connects the variables 1, 3, and 7, and similarly constraints C_3 and C_4. Symbols "X" and "O" indicate the variables participating in the constraints. To repair the conflict in a constraint without skipping any solution, one needs to change the value of the variable closest to the currently instantiated variable, for example, the fifth variable in constraint C_1. These variables are marked "O" in the figure. Note that if we jump farther, we may skip some solutions. If we want to remove a conflict for a given value, we need to repair all conflicting constraints for this value. Hence we need to select the farther among the

Figure 5. The board situation for 8-queens problem, the numbers indicate conflicting queens for given positions

	A	B	C	D	E	F	G	H
1	Q							
2			Q					
3					Q			
4		Q						
5				Q				
6	1	3,4	2,5	4,5	3,5	1	2	3
7								
8								

Figure 6. Example of finding the conflicting level by analyzing the violated constraints

level	Violated constraints			
	C_1	C_2	C_3	C_4
1		X		
2	X		X	-O-
3	X	--O--		
4			O	
5	O			
6				
7	X	X	X	X
value	A		B	

conflicting variables for each constraint, which is the third variable for value A and the second variable for value B. These variables are marked "-O-" in the figure. Finally, we want at least one value to be released from the conflict so among the conflicting variables for each value, we select the closest to the current variable (recall, that we should not skip any solution, hence we should not jump farther). This variable is marked "--O--" in the figure. There is a direct consequence of the above method, namely, if there exists a consistent value for the variable then the algorithm jumps to the previous level upon backtracking.

The following pseudo-code (Algorithm 4) describes the backjumping algorithm. It assumes that variables are indexed in the order in which they are instantiated. In particular the set of already instantiated variables (Labelled) consists of triples X/V/L, where X is a variable, V is its value, and L is its order number. Then we can use min/max operations to compute the conflicting level to which one should jump upon backtracking. Notice also how the jump operation is realised in the recursive code via comparison of the current level with the level to which we are jumping (R ≠ fail(Level)).

There also exist less expensive methods of finding conflicting level, for example *graph-based backjumping* that jumps to the most recent variable that constrains the current variable (the fifth variable in the above example). However, graph-based backjumping behaves in the same way as chronological backtracking if each variable is constrained by every other variable (like in the N-Queens problem). On the other hand, *conflict-directed backjumping* (Prosser, 1993) maintains information about conflicts for each variable and it passes this information to the variable to which we are jumping. Hence, the algorithm can jump not only from the dead-end leaf nodes in the search tree, but it can also jump from the internal nodes which further decreases the number of search nodes to be explored to find the solution (and hence increases efficiency).

Algorithm 4. Backjumping

```
procedure BJ(Variables, Constraints)
 BJ-1(Variables,{},Constraints,0)
end BJ


procedure BJ-1(Unlabelled, Labelled, Constraints, Previou-
sLevel)
if Unlabelled = {} then return Labelled
pick the first X from Unlabelled
Level ← PreviousLevel+1
Jump ← 0
for each value V from D_X do
 C ← consistent({X/V/Level}+Labelled, Constraints, Level)
 if C = fail(J) then
 Jump ← max {Jump, J}
 else
 Jump ← PreviousLevel
 R ← BJ-1(Unlabelled-{X},{X/V/Level}+Labelled, Con-
straints, Level)
 if R ≠ fail(Level) then return R
        % success or backtrack to past level
 end if
end for
return fail(Jump) % backtrack to the conflicting variable
end BJ-1


procedure consistent(Labelled, Constraints, Level)
J ← Level
NoConflict ← true
for each C in Constraints do
 if all variables from C are Labelled then
 if C is not satisfied by Labelled then
 NoConflict ← false
 J ← min {{J}+ max{L | X in C & X/V/L in Labelled & L <
Level}}
 end if
 end for
if NoConflict then return true
else return fail(J)
end consistent
```

Backmarking (BM)

In the above analysis of disadvantages of chronological backtracking, we identified the problem with redundant work, that is, even if the conflicting values of variables are identified during the intelligent backtracking, they are not remembered for immediate detection of the same conflict in a subsequent computation. We mentioned two methods to resolve this problem, namely backchecking (BC) and backmarking (BM).

Both backchecking and its descendent backmarking are useful algorithms for reducing the number of compatibility checks. If the back-

Figure 7. The backmarking algorithm remembers found conflicts so the constraint checks are not repeated in subsequent search branches

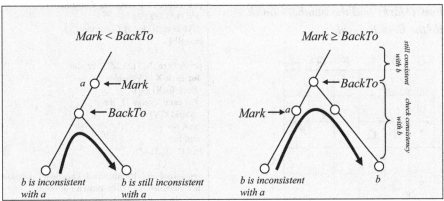

checking method finds that some assignment Y/b is incompatible with any recent assignment X/a then it remembers this incompatibility. As long as X/a is still committed to, Y/b will not be considered again.

Backmarking (Haralick & Elliot, 1980) is an improvement over backchecking that avoids some redundant constraint checks as well as some redundant discoveries of inconsistencies. It reduces the number of compatibility checks by remembering for every assignment the incompatible recent assignments. Furthermore, it avoids repeating the compatibility checks which have already been performed and which have succeeded.

To simplify the description of the backmarking algorithm we assume working with binary CSPs. Note, that this is not a restriction because each CSP can be converted to an equivalent binary CSP (Bacchus & van Beek 1998; Rossi, Dahr, & Petrie, 1990; Stergiou & Walsh, 1999). The idea of backmarking is as follows. When trying to extend a search path by choosing a value for some variable X, the backmarking method marks the farthest level, *Mark*, in the search tree at which an inconsistency is detected for each value of X. If no inconsistency is detected for the value, its *Mark* is set to the level above the level of variable X. In addition, the algorithm also remembers the

highest level, *BackTo*, to which search has backed up since the last time X was considered. Now, when backmarking next considers value V for X, the *Mark* and *BackTo* levels can be compared. There are two cases (see Figure 7):

- *Mark* < *BackTo*. If the level at which V failed before is above the level to which we have backtracked, we know, without further constraint checking, that V will fail again. The value it failed against is still there.
- *Mark* ≥ *BackTo*. If since V last failed we have backed up to or above the level at which V encountered a failure, we have to check V. However, we can start checking values against V at level *BackTo* because the values above that level are unchanged since we last successfully tested them against V and we know (from the previous consistency check) that they are consistent with V.

Figure 8 demonstrates how the values of the global variables (arrays) *Mark* and *BackTo* are computed. We use the 8-Queens problem again and the board shows the same situation as in the backjumping example. Note, that computing value *Mark* is identical to finding the conflicting level in backjumping. The board situation shows

Figure 8. The board situation for 8-queens problem, the numbers indicate conflicting queens for given positions (Mark) and the numbers on the right indicate the BackTo level

	A	B	C	D	E	F	G	H	*BackTo*
1	Q								1
2	1	1	Q						1
3	1	2	1	2	Q				1
4	1	Q							1
5	1	4	2	Q					1
6	1	3	2	4	3	1	2	3	5
7									1
8									1

the values of *Mark* (the number at each square) and *BackTo* at the state when all the values for Queen 6 have been rejected, and the algorithm backtracks to Queen 5 (therefore *BackTo*(6) = 5). If and when all the values of Queen 5 are rejected, both *BackTo*(5) and *BackTo*(6) will be changed to 4.

The following pseudo-code (Algorithm 5) describes the backmarking algorithm.

Further Reading

A nice survey on depth-first search techniques is Dechter and Frost (1998); also Dechter's (2003) work contains very well written chapters on search techniques in constraint satisfaction. Backjumping has been introduced by Gaschnig (1979); Dechter (1990) described the graph-based variant of backjumping that was followed by conflict-directed backjumping by Prosser (1993). These techniques together with some no-good recording are known under the umbrella term *intelligent backtracking* in the logic programming community. The further improvement of

Algorithm 5. Backmarking

```
procedure BM(Variables, Constraints)
 INITIALIZE(Variables)
 BM-1(Variables,{},Constraints,1)
end BM

procedure INITIALIZE(Variables)
 for each X in Variables do
  BackTo(X) ← 1
  for each V from D_x do
   Mark(X,V) ← 1
  end for
 end for
end INITIALIZE

procedure BM-1(Unlabelled, Labelled, Constraints, Level)
 if Unlabelled = {} then return Labelled
 pick the first X from Unlabelled % now, the order is fixed
 for each value V from D_x do
  if Mark(V,X) ≥ BackTo(X) then
   if consistent(X/V, Labelled, Constraints, Level) then
    R ← BM-1(Unlabelled-{X}, Labelled+{X/V/Level}, Constraints, Level+1)
    if R ≠ fail then return R % success
   end if
  end if
 end for
 BackTo(X) ← Level-1
 for each Y in Unlabelled do
  BackTo(Y) ← min {Level-1, BackTo(Y)}
 end for
 return fail % backtrack to the recent variable
end BM-1

procedure consistent(X/V, Labelled, Constraints, Level)
 for each Y/VY/LY in Labelled such that LY ≥ BackTo(X) do
 % in the increasing order of LY
  if X/V is not compatible with Y/VY using Constraints then
   Mark(X,V) ← LY
   return fail
  end if
 end for
 Mark(X,V) ← Level-1
 return true
end consistent
```

backjumping with a dynamic variable reordering called *dynamic backtracking* was proposed in Ginsberg (1993). Backmarking is described in Haralick and Elliot (1980).

In addition to complete depth-first search techniques, there also exist many incomplete techniques like depth-bounded search (Beldiceanu, Bourreau, Chan, & Rivreau, 1997), credit search (Cheadle, Harvey, Sadler, Schimpf, Shen, &

Wallace, 2003), or iterative broadening (Ginsberg & Harvey, 1990).

Recently, the techniques for recovery from a failure of the value ordering heuristic (see below) called *discrepancy search* became popular thanks to good practical efficiency. These techniques include algorithms such as limited discrepancy search (Harvey & Ginsberg, 1995), improved limited discrepancy search (Korf, 1996), discrepancy-bounded depth first search (Beck & Perron, 2000), interleaved depth-first search (Meseguer, 1997), and depth-bounded discrepancy search (Walsh, 1997). A survey can be found in (Harvey, 1995) and (Barták, 2004).

CONSISTENCY TECHNIQUES: CAN CONSTRAINTS BE USED MORE ACTIVELY DURING CONSTRAINT SATISFACTION?

The search algorithms presented in the previous section use constraints only passively, that is, to validate feasibility of the partial assignment. Now, we will look at how the constraints can actively contribute to solving the problem via maintaining their consistency. Consistency techniques were first introduced for improving the efficiency of picture recognition programs by researchers in artificial intelligence (Montanari, 1974; Waltz, 1975). Picture recognition involves labelling all the lines in the picture in a consistent way. The number of possible combinations can be huge, while only very few are consistent. Consistency techniques effectively rule out many inconsistent assignments at a very early stage, and thus cut short the search for a feasible assignment. These techniques have since proved to be effective on a wide variety of hard search problems.

Notice that consistency techniques are deterministic, as opposed to the search techniques which are nondeterministic. Thus the deterministic computation is performed as soon as possible and nondeterministic computation during search

Example 1.

Let $A < B$ be a constraint between variable A with the domain $D_A = \{3,\ldots, 7\}$ and variable B with the domain $D_B = \{1,\ldots, 5\}$. Clearly, for some values in D_A there does not exist a consistent value in D_B satisfying the constraint $A < B$ and vice versa. Such values can be removed from the domains without lost of any solution, that is, such domain reduction is safe. We get reduced domains $D_A = \{3,4\}$ and $D_B = \{4,5\}$.
Note, that this reduction does not remove all inconsistent pairs necessarily, for example $A = 4$, $B = 4$ is still in the domains, but for each value of A from D_A it is possible to find a consistent value of B and vice versa.

is used only when there is no more propagation to do. Nevertheless, the consistency techniques are rarely used alone to solve a constraint satisfaction problem completely (but they could).

In the remaining text, we will assume only unary and binary constraints. This is not a restriction because any CSP can be converted to a binary CSP, where all constraints are binary (Bacchus & van Beek 1998; Rossi et al., 1990; Stergiou & Walsh, 1999), that can be represented as a constraint network with nodes corresponding to variables and arcs describing binary constraints. A unary constraint can be represented by a cyclic arc. Moreover, the presented techniques, such as arc consistency, can also be generalised to constraints of higher arity.

In binary CSPs, various consistency techniques for constraint graphs were introduced to prune the search space. The consistency-enforcing algorithm makes any partial solution of a small sub-network extensible to some surrounding network. Thus, the potential inconsistency is detected as soon as possible.

Node Consistency (NC)

The simplest consistency technique is referred to as node consistency (NC).

Definition: *The node representing variable V in a constraint network is* node consistent *if and only if for every value A in the current domain*

Algorithm 6. Node consistency

```
procedure NC(G)
 for each variable V in nodes(G) do
  for each value A in the domain D_V do
   if unary constraint on V is inconsistent with A then
    delete A from D_V
   end for
  end for
end NC
```

Algorithm 7. REVISE

```
procedure REVISE(V_i,V_j)
 DELETED ← false
 for each A in D_i do
  if there is no such B in D_j such that (A,B) is consistent, that
  is, (A,B) satisfies all the constraints on V_i, V_j then
   delete A from D_i
   DELETED ← true
  end if
 end for
 return DELETED
end REVISE
```

D_V *of V, each unary constraint on V is satisfied. A CSP is node consistent if and only if all variables are node consistent, that is, for each variable all values in its domain satisfy the constraints on that variable.*

If the domain D_V of variable V contains a value A that does not satisfy the unary constraint on V, then the instantiation of V to A will always result in an immediate failure. Thus, the node inconsistency can be eliminated by simply removing those values from the domain D_V of each variable V that do not satisfy a unary constraint on V (Algorithm 6). Hence unary constraints can be eliminated from the problem description because they are represented via domains of variables.

Arc Consistency (AC)

If the constraint graph is node consistent then unary constraints can be removed because they all are satisfied. As we are working with a binary CSP, there remains to ensure consistency of binary constraints. In the constraint network, a binary constraint corresponds to an arc; therefore this type of consistency is called arc consistency (AC).

Definition: *An arc (V_i,V_j) is arc consistent if and only if for every value A in the current domain of V_i which satisfies the constraints on V_i there is some value B in the domain of V_j such that $V_i = A$ and $V_j = B$ is permitted by the binary constraint between V_i and V_j. Note, that the concept of arc*

consistency is directional, that is, if an arc (V_i,V_j) is consistent, then it does not automatically mean that (V_j,V_i) is also consistent. A CSP is arc consistent if and only if every arc (V_i,V_j) in its constraint network is arc consistent.

Clearly, an arc (V_i,V_j) can be made consistent by simply deleting those values from the domain of V_i for which there does not exist a corresponding value in the domain of D_j such that the binary constraint between V_i and V_j is satisfied (note, that deleting of such values does not eliminate any solution of the original CSP). The following algorithm REVISE does precisely that. Its worst-case time complexity is $O(d^2)$, where d is the size of the domain (for each value of V_i, we are looking for a compatible value of V_j).

To make every arc of the constraint graph consistent, that is, to make the corresponding CSP arc consistent, it is not sufficient to execute REVISE for each arc just once. Once REVISE reduces the domain of some variable V_i, then each previously revised arc (V_j,V_i) has to be revised

Algorithm 8. Arc consistency—1

```
procedure AC-1(G)
 Q ← {(V_i,V_j) in arcs(G), i≠j}
 repeat
  CHANGED ← false
  for each arc (V_i,V_j) in Q do
   CHANGED ← REVISE(V_i,V_j) or CHANGED
  end for
 until not(CHANGED)
end AC-1
```

Figure 9. All the arcs going to the node with a modified domain should be revised with the exception of the arc reverse to the arc that caused the deletion (AC-3)

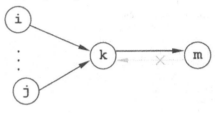

Algorithm 9. Arc consistency—3

```
procedure AC-3(G)
  Q ← {(Vᵢ,Vⱼ) in arcs(G), i≠j}
  while not empty Q do
    select and delete any arc (V_k,V_m) from Q
    if REVISE(V_k,V_m) then
      Q ← Q union {(Vᵢ,V_k) such that (Vᵢ,V_k) in arcs(G), i≠k, i≠m}
    end if
  end while
end AC-3
```

again, because some of the members of the domain of V_j may no longer be compatible with any remaining members of the revised domain of V_i. The easiest way to establish arc consistency is to apply the REVISE procedure to all arcs repeatedly until domain of any variable changes. The following algorithm, known as **AC-1**, does exactly this (Mackworth, 1977a).

The AC-1 algorithm is not very efficient because the deletion of a single value in some iteration forces all the arcs to be revised again in the next iteration. So there could be as many as nd iterations, where n is the number of variables and d is the size of domains. Each iteration revises e arcs and hence the worst-case time complexity of AC-1 is $O(end^3)$. Clearly, the only arcs affected by the reduction of the domain of V_k are the arcs (V_i,V_k), so it is not necessary to re-revise all arcs. Also, if we revise the arc (V_k,V_m) and the domain of V_k is reduced, it is not necessary to re-revise the arc (V_m,V_k) because none of the elements deleted from the domain of V_k provided support for any value in the current domain of V_m (see Figure 9).

The following variation of arc consistency algorithm, called AC-3 (Mackworth, 1977a), removes this drawback of AC-1 and performs re-revision only for those arcs that are possibly affected by a previous revision. Actually, this idea has been first introduced in AC-2 (Mackworth, 1977a), but we omit description of AC-2 because AC-3 is simpler and performs better.

Notice that when AC-3 reintroduces some arc into the queue, it is because a value is removed from the domain of some constrained variable. Consequently, the revision of a single arc is performed at most $O(d)$ times, where d is the domain size. If there are e arcs then the worst-case time complexity of AC-3 is $O(ed^3)$. Still, there is some hidden inefficiency of AC-3. When the algorithm AC-3 revises the arc for the second time it retests many pairs of values which are already known (from the previous iteration) to be consistent or inconsistent respectively and which are not affected by the reduction of the domain. The idea behind AC-3 is based on the notion of *support*; a value is supported if there exists a compatible value in the domain of every other variable. When a value A is removed from the domain of variable X, it is not always necessary to examine all the binary constraints $C_{Y,X}$. Precisely, we can ignore those values in D_Y which do not rely on A for support (in other words, those values in D_Y that are compatible with some other value in D_X other than A). Figure 10 shows these dependencies between the pairs of values (the compatible values are connected via an edge). If we remove value a from the domain of variable V_2 (because it has no

Figure 10. Microstructure of the constraint network with edges connecting compatible values

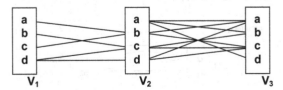

Algorithm 10. INITIALIZE

```
procedure INITIALIZE(G)
Q ← {}
S ← {} % initialize each element in the structure S_{x,v}
for each arc (V_i,V_j) in arcs(G) do
  for each a in D_i do
    total ← 0
    for each b in D_j do
      if (a,b) is consistent according to the constraint C_{ij} then
        total ← total + 1
        S_{j,b} ← S_{j,b} union {<i,a>}
      end if
    end for
    counter[(i,j),a] ← total
    if counter[(i,j),a] = 0 then
      delete a from D_i
      Q ← Q union {<i,a>}
    end if
  end for
end for
return Q
end INITIALIZE
```

Algorithm 11. Arc consistency—4

```
procedure AC-4(G)
Q ← INITIALIZE(G)
while not empty Q do
  select and delete any pair <j,b> from Q
  for each <i,a> from S_{j,b} do
    counter[(i,j),a] ← counter[(i,j),a] - 1
    if counter[(i,j),a] = 0 & „a" is still in D_i then
      delete „a" from D_i
      Q ← Q union {<i,a>}
    end if
  end for
end while
end AC-4
```

support in V_1), we do not need to check values a, b, c from the domain of V_3 because they all have other supports in the domain of V_2. However, we have to remove value d from the domain of V_3 because it lost the only support in V_2.

Checking pairs of values again and again is a source of potential inefficiency. Therefore the algorithm AC-4 (Mohr & Henderson, 1986) was introduced to refine handling of arcs (constraints). The algorithm works with individual pairs of values using support sets for each value. First, the algorithm AC-4 initialises its internal structures which are used to remember pairs of consistent (inconsistent) values of incidental variables (nodes)—structure $S_{i,a}$ representing the set of supports. This initialisation also counts "supporting" values from the domain of incidental variable—structure $counter_{(i,j),a}$—and it removes

those values which have no support. Once the value is removed from the domain, the algorithm adds the pair <Variable, Value> to the list Q for re-revision of affected values of corresponding variables. Clearly, the time complexity of the initialisation is $O(ed^2)$, where e is the number of arcs and d is the size of domains.

Figure 11 shows how the data structures look after initialisation.

After the initialisation, the algorithm AC-4 performs re-revision only for those pairs of values of incidental variables that are affected by the previous revision. Hence, each pair of values is checked at most once and so the worst-case time complexity of AC-4 is $O(ed^2)$, which is the optimal time complexity. However, the space complexity of AC-4 is also $O(ed^2)$ to keep the required data structures. Hence, the best-case time complexity of AC-4 is close to its worst-case time complexity because this time is needed to build the data structures.

Directional Arc Consistency (DAC)

In the above definition of arc consistency we mentioned a directional nature of arc consistency (for arc). Nevertheless, the arc consistency for a CSP is not directional as each arc is assumed in both directions in the AC-x algorithms. Although the node and arc consistency algorithms seem easy, they are still stronger than necessary for some problems, for example, for enabling back-

Figure 11. A counter and a set of supports after initialisation in AC-4

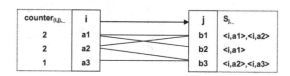

counter_{(i,j),_}	i		j	S_{j,_}
2	a1		b1	<i,a1>,<i,a2>
2	a2		b2	<i,a1>
1	a3		b3	<i,a2>,<i,a3>

Algorithm 12. Directional arc consistency

```
procedure DAC(G)
  for j = |nodes(G)| to 1 by -1 do
    for each arc (Vi,Vj) in arcs(G) such that i<j do
      REVISE(Vi,Vj)
    end for
  end for
end DAC
```

track-free search in CSPs which constraints form trees. Therefore, a simpler concept was proposed to achieve some form of consistency, namely, directional arc consistency (DAC).

Definition: *A CSP is directionally arc consistent under an ordering of variables if and only if every arc (V_i, V_j) in its constraint graph such that $i < j$ according to the ordering is arc consistent.*

Notice the difference between AC and DAC; in AC we check every arc (V_i, V_j) while in DAC only the arcs (V_i, V_j) where $i < j$ are considered. Consequently, arc consistency is stronger than directional arc consistency, that is, an arc consistent CSP is also directionally arc consistent but not vice versa (a directionally arc consistent CSP is not necessarily arc consistent). The DAC algorithm for achieving directional arc consistency is easier and faster than AC-x algorithms, because each arc is examined exactly once in DAC. Hence, the time complexity of DAC is $O(ed^2)$, where e is the number of arcs and d is the size of domains.

The DAC procedure potentially removes fewer redundant values than the algorithms already mentioned which achieve AC. However, DAC requires less computation than the procedures AC-1 to AC-3, and less space than procedure AC-4. The choice of achieving AC or DAC is domain dependent. In principle, more values can be removed through constraint propagation in more tightly constraint problems. Thus AC tends to be worth achieving in more tightly constrained problems.

The directional arc consistency is sufficient for backtrack-free solving of CSPs which constraints form trees. In this case, it is possible to order the nodes (variables) starting from the tree root and concluding at tree leaves. If the graph (tree) is made directionally arc-consistent using this order then it is possible to find the solution by assigning values to variables in the same order. Directional arc consistency guarantees that for each value of the root (parent) we will find consistent values in the children nodes and so on until the values of the leaves. Consequently, no backtracking is necessary to find a complete consistent assignment.

From DAC to AC

Notice that a CSP is arc-consistent if, for any given ordering < of the variables, this CSP is directionally arc-consistent under both < and its reverse.

Figure 12. DAC does not achieve AC even if it is applied in both directions

If DAC is applied to the following graph using the variable ordering X, Y, Z, the domains of respective variables do not change.

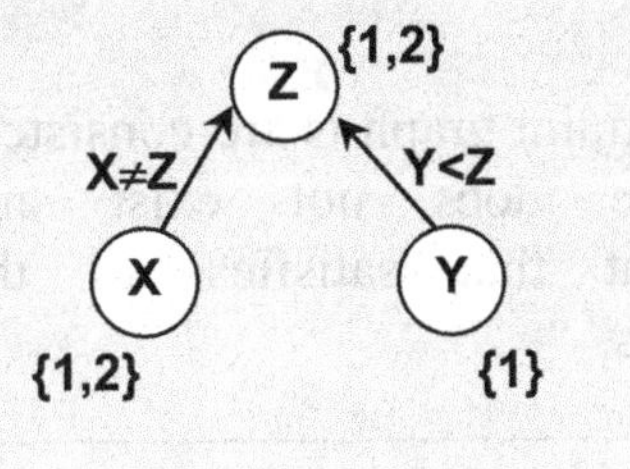

Now, if DAC is applied using the reverse order Z, Y, X, the domain of variable Z changes only but the resulting graph is still not arc-consistent (value 2 in D_X is inconsistent with Z).

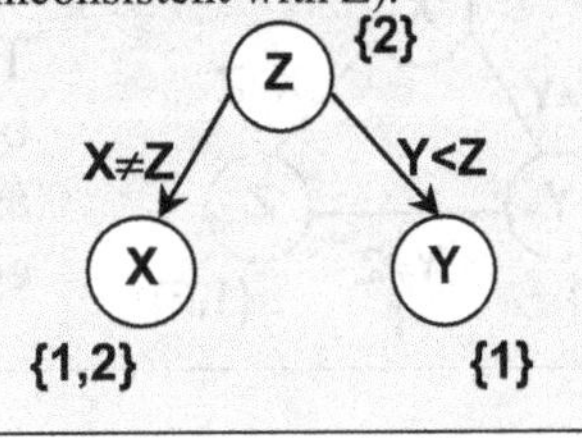

Figure 13. A microstructure of the tree-structured constraint graph where DAC is applied in the order from the root to leaves

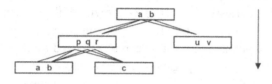

Therefore, it is tempting to believe (wrongly) that arc consistency could be achieved by running DAC in both directions for any given <. Figure 12 shows that this belief is a fallacy.

Nevertheless, in some cases it is possible to achieve arc consistency by running the DAC algorithm in both directions for a particular ordering of variables. In particular, if DAC is applied to a tree graph using the ordering starting from the root and concluding at leaves and, subsequently, DAC is applied in the opposite direction, then we achieve full arc consistency. In the above example, if we apply DAC under the ordering Z, Y, X (or Z, X, Y) and, subsequently, in the opposite direction, we will get an arc-consistent graph.

Figure 14. A micro-structure of tree-structured constraint graph where DAC is applied in the order from leaves to the root

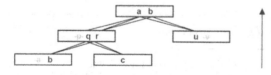

Proposition: *If DAC is applied to a tree graph using the ordering starting from the root and concluding at leaves and, subsequently, the DAC is applied in the opposite direction, then we achieve full arc consistency.*

Proof: *If the first run of DAC is finished then all values in any parent node are consistent with some assignment of child nodes. In other words, for each value of the parent node there exists at least one support (consistent value) in each child node. Figure 13 shows a tree structured graph, where edges connect compatible pairs of values.*

Now, if the second run of DAC is performed in the opposite direction (Figure 14) and some value is removed from a node then this value is not a support of any value of the parent node (this is the reason why this value is removed, it has no support in the parent node and, consequently, it is not a support of any value from the parent node). Consequently, removing a value from some node does not evoke losing support of any value of the parent node.

The conclusion is that each value in some node is consistent with any value in each children node (the first run) and with any value in the parent node (the second run) and, therefore the graph is arc consistent.

Is Arc Consistency Sufficient?

Achieving arc consistency removes many inconsistencies from the constraint graph but is any

Figure 15. An arc consistent problem which has no solution

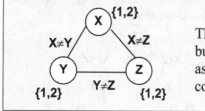

This constraint graph is arc-consistent but there does not exist any assignment that satisfies all the constraints.

(complete) instantiation of variables from the current (reduced) domains a solution to the CSP? Or can we at least prove that the solution exists?

If the domain size of each variable becomes one, then the CSP has exactly one solution which is obtained by assigning to each variable the only possible value in its domain (this holds for AC and DAC as well). If any domain becomes empty, then the CSP has no solution. Otherwise, the answer to above questions is no in general. Figure 15 shows such an example where the constraint graph is arc consistent, domains are not empty but there is still no solution satisfying all constraints.

A CSP after achieving arc consistency:

1. domain size for each variable becomes one $\Rightarrow$ exactly one solution exists
2. any domain becomes empty $\Rightarrow$ no solution exists
3. otherwise $\Rightarrow$ not known whether a solution exists

Path Consistency (PC)

Given that arc consistency is not enough to eliminate the need for search, is there another stronger degree of consistency that may eliminate the need for search? The above example shows that if one extends the consistency test to two or more arcs, more inconsistent values can be removed. This is the main idea of path consistency.

Definition: *A path $(V_0, V_1, ..., V_m)$ in the constraint graph for a CSP is path consistent if and only if for every pair of values x in D_0 and y in D_m that satisfies all the constraints on V_0 and V_m there exists a value for each of the variables $V_1, ..., V_{m-1}$ such that every binary constraint on the adjacent variables V_i, V_{i+1} in the path is satisfied. A CSP is path consistent if and only if every path in its graph is path consistent.*

Note carefully that the definition of path consistency for path $(V_0, V_1, ..., V_m)$ does not require values

Figure 16. Path consistency assumes only the constraints between adjacent nodes in the path

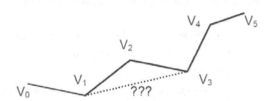

$x_0, x_1, ..., x_m$ to satisfy all the constraints between variables $V_0, V_1, ..., V_m$. In particular, variables V_1 and V_3 are not adjacent in the path $(V_0, V_1, ..., V_m)$, so their values x_1 and x_3 need not satisfy the constraint between V_1 and V_3 (Figure 16).

Naturally, a path consistent CSP is arc consistent as well because an arc is equivalent to the path of length 1. In fact, to make the arc (V_i, V_j) arc-consistent one can make the path (V_i, V_j, V_i) path-consistent. Consequently, path consistency implies arc consistency. However, the reverse implication does not hold, that is, arc consistency does not imply path consistency as Figure 15 shows (if we make the graph path consistent, we can discover that the problem has no solution). Therefore, path consistency is stronger than arc consistency.

There is an important proposition about path consistency that simplifies maintaining path consistency. In 1974, Montanari pointed out that if every path of length two is path consistent then the graph is path consistent as well. Consequently, we can check only the paths of length two to achieve full path consistency.

Proposition: *A CSP is path consistent if and only if all paths of length two are path consistent.*

Proof: *Path consistency for paths of length two is just a special case of full path consistency so the implication* path-consistent $\Rightarrow$ path-consistent *for paths of length two (1) is trivially true.*

The other implication path-consistent ⟸ path-consistent for paths of length two *(2) can be proved using the induction on the length of the path:*

1. **Base Step:** *When the length of the path is two then the above implication (2) holds (trivial).*

2. **Induction Step:** *Assume that the implication (2) is true for all paths with the length between two and some integer* m. *Pick any two variables V_0 and V_{m+1} and assume that x_0 in D_0 and x_{m+1} in D_{m+1} are two values that satisfy all the constraints on V_0 and V_{m+1}. Now pick any* m *variables $V_1,..., V_m$. There must exist some value x_m in D_m such that all the constraints on the $\{V_0, V_m\}$ and $\{V_m, V_{m+1}\}$ are satisfied (according to the base step). Finally, there must exists a value for each of the variables $V_1,..., V_{m-1}$ such that every binary constraint on the adjacent edges in the path $(V_0, V_1,..., V_m)$ is satisfied (according to the base step; we can assume that x_m satisfies all unary constraints on V_m). Consequently, every binary constraint on the adjacent edges in the path $(V_0, V_1,..., V_{m+1})$ is also satisfied and the path $(V_0, V_1,..., V_{m+1})$ is path-consistent.*

Algorithms which achieve path consistency remove not only inconsistent values from the domains but also inconsistent pairs of values from the constraints (remind that we are work-

Figure 17. From consistent paths of length two to consistent paths of any length

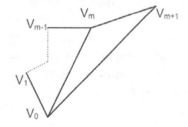

Figure 18. A matrix representation of binary and unary constraints

The binary constraint A > B+1 on variables A and B with domains $D_A = \{3,4,5\}$ and $D_B = \{1,2,3\}$ is represented by the following {0,1}-matrix:

A \ B	1	2	3
3	1	0	0
4	1	1	0
5	1	1	1

The domain of variable A, $D_A = \{3,4,5\}$, and the unary constraint A > 3 can also be represented by the {0,1}-matrix:

A \ A	3	4	5
3	0	0	0
4	0	1	0
5	0	0	1

Note, that we need to know the exact order of variables in the binary constraint as well as the order of values in respective domains.

ing with binary CSPs). The binary constraint is represented here by a {0,1}-matrix where value 1 represents a legal, consistent pair of values and value 0 represents an illegal, inconsistent pair of values. For uniformity, both the domain and the unary constraint of variable X is also represented using the {0,1}-matrix. In fact, the unary constraint on X is represented in the form of a binary constraint on (X, X).

Now, using the matrix representation, it is easier to compose constraints. This *constraint composition* is a kernel of the path consistency algorithms because to achieve path consistency of path (X, Y, Z) we can compose the constraint on (X, Y) with the constraint on (Y, Z) and make an intersection of this composition with the constraint on (X, Z). In fact, the composition of

Figure 19. Composition of constraints

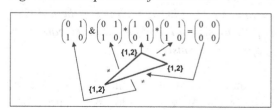

two constraints is equivalent to multiplication of {0,1}-matrices using binary operations AND, OR instead of *, + and the intersection of the matrices corresponds to performing AND operation on respective elements of the matrices (Figure 19). Therefore we use * to mark the composition operation and & to mark the intersection. More formally, let $C_{X,Y}$ be a {0,1}-matrix representing the constraint on X and Y. Then we can make the path (X, Y, Z) path consistent by the following assignment:

$$C_{X,Z} \leftarrow C_{X,Z} \& (C_{X,Y} * C_{Y,Y} * C_{Y,Z})$$

The time complexity of the composition operation is $O(d^3)$, where d is the size of domains. Naturally, the composition operation has to be performed for all pairs (X, Z) and for all intermediary nodes Y. Similarly to arc consistency, to make every path of the constraint graph consistent, that is, to make the corresponding CSP path consistent, it is not sufficient to execute this composition operation for each path (X,Y,Z) just once. Once a domain of a variable/constraint is reduced then it is possible that some previously revised path has to be revised again, because some pairs of values become incompatible due to the missing value of the intermediary node. The easiest way to establish path consistency is to apply the composition operations to all paths

repeatedly until the domain of any variable/constraint changes. The following naive algorithm PC-1 does exactly this (Mackworth, 1977a). Its worst-case time complexity is $O(n^5 d^5)$, where n is the number of variables and d is the size of domains. There are $O(n^3)$ cycles in each iteration and the maximal number of iterations is $O(n^2 d^2)$, if only a single pair of values is removed in each iteration.

The basic idea of PC-1 is as follows: for every variable V_k, pick every constraint $C_{i,j}$ from the current set of constraints Y^k and attempt to reduce it by means of relations composition using $C_{i,k}$, $C_{k,k}$ and $C_{k,j}$. After this is done for all variables, the set of constraints is examined to see if any constraint in it has changed. The whole process is repeated as long as some constraints have been changed. Note that $Y^k(i,j)$ represents the constraint $C_{i,j}$ in the set Y^k and that Y^k is only used to build Y^{k+1}.

Like AC-1, PC-1 is very inefficient because even a small change in one constraint will cause the whole set of constraints to be re-examined. Moreover, PC-1 is also very memory consuming as many arrays Y^k are stored. Therefore improved algorithm PC-2 (Mackworth, 1977a) was introduced in which only relevant constraints are re-examined.

Similarly to AC algorithms we first introduce a procedure for path revision that restricts a constraint $C_{i,j}$ using $C_{i,k}$ and $C_{k,j}$. The procedure returns

Algorithm 13. Path consistency-1

```
procedure PC-1(Vars, Constraints)
n ← |Vars|
Y(n) ← Constraints  % we use the {0,1}-matrix representation
% Y(k)(i,j) represents a matrix for constraint Ci,j in k-th step
repeat
 Y(0) ← Y(n)
 for k=1 to n do
 for i=1 to n do
 for j=1 to n do
 Y(k)(i,j) ← Y(k-1)(i,j) & Y(k-1)(i,k)* Y(k-1)(k,k)* Y(k-1)(k,j)
until Y(n)=Y(0)
Constraints ← Y(n)
end PC-1
```

Algorithm 14. REVISE PATH

```
procedure REVISE_PATH((i,k,j), C)
Temp ← C_{ij} & (C_{ik} * C_{kk} * C_{kj})
if (Temp = C_{ij}) then return FALSE
else
 C_{ij} ← Temp
 return TRUE
end if
end REVISE_PATH
```

TRUE, if the constraint domain is changed, and FALSE otherwise.

Note, that we do not need revise the path in both directions if $C_{i,j} = C^T_{j,i}$, that is, if only one $\{0,1\}$-matrix is used to represent the constraints $C_{i,j}$ and $C_{j,i}$ (C^T is the transposition of the matrix C, that is, rows and columns are interchanged). This is because the following deduction holds:

$$(C_{i,j} \,\&\, C_{i,k} * C_{k,k} * C_{k,j})^T =$$

$$C^T_{i,j} \,\&\, (C_{i,k} * C_{k,k} * C_{k,j})^T -$$

$$C^T_{i,j} \,\&\, C^T_{k,j} * C^T_{k,k} * C^T_{i,k} =$$

$$C_{j,i} \,\&\, C_{j,k} * C_{k,k} * C_{k,i}$$

Now, we can use some ordering of variables and examine only paths (i,k,j) such that $i \leq j$. Note, that there is no condition about k and, therefore, we do not restrict ourselves to some form of directional path consistency.

Finally, if the constraint $C_{i,j}$ is reduced in REVISE_PATH, we want to re-examine only the relevant paths. Because of above discussion about variable ordering there are two cases when the constraint $C_{i,j}$ is reduced, namely $i < j$ and $i = j$:

- If $i < j$ then all paths which contain (i,j) or (j,i) are relevant with the exception of (i,i,j) and (i,j,j) because $C_{i,j}$ will not be restricted by these paths as a result of itself being reduced.

Algorithm 15. RELATED PATHS

```
procedure RELATED_PATHS((i,k,j))
if (i<j) then
  return {(i,j,p) | i ≤ p ≤ n & p ≠ j} U
    {(p,i,j) | 1 ≤ p ≤ j & p ≠ i} U
    {(j,i,p) | j < p ≤ n} U
    {(p,j,i) | 1 ≤ p < i}
else %, that is, i=j
  return {(p,i,r) | 1 ≤ p ≤ r ≤ n} - {(i,i,i),(k,i,k)}
end if
end RELATED_PATHS
```

Algorithm 16. Path consistency—2

```
procedure PC-2(Vars, Constraints)
n ← |Vars|
Q ← {(i,k,j) | 1 ≤ i ≤ j ≤ n & i ≠ k & k ≠ j}
while Q ≠ {} do
  select and delete any path (i,k,j) from Q
  if REVISE_PATH((i,k,j),Constraints) then
    Q ← Q union RELATED_PATHS((i,k,j))
end while
end PC-2
```

- If $i = j$, that is, the restricted path was (i,k,i), then all paths with i in it need to be re-examined, with the exception of (i,i,i) and (k,i,k). This is because neither $C_{i,i}$ nor $C_{k,k}$ will be further restricted (it was the variable V_k which has caused $C_{i,i}$ to be reduced).

The following algorithm RELATED_PATHS returns paths relevant to a given path (i,k,j). Note that n is equal to the number of variables in the CSP (and the numbering of variables starts in 1).

Now, it is easy to write the PC-2 algorithm whose structure is very similar to the AC-3 algorithm. The algorithm starts with the queue of all paths to be revised and as soon as a constraint is reduced, the relevant paths are added to the queue. As we mentioned above, the algorithm assumes the ordering $<$ among the variables to further decrease the number of checked paths. Remember that this is because the reduction $C_{i,k} * C_{k,k} * C_{k,j}$ is equivalent to the reduction $C_{j,k} * C_{k,k} * C_{k,i}$.

The PC-2 algorithm is far away efficient than the PC-1 algorithm and it has also smaller memory consumption than PC-1. Its worst-case time complexity is $O(n^3 d^5)$, where n is the number of variables and d is the size of domains. Similarly to AC-3, the path is reintroduced into the queue only if a pair of values is removed from the constraint, which is at most $O(d^2)$ times, and there are $O(n^3)$ paths in the graph.

Figure 20. Directional path consistency is weaker than path consistency

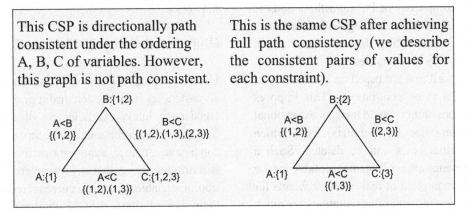

Directional Path Consistency (DPC)

Similar to weakening arc consistency to directional arc consistency we can weaken path consistency to directional path consistency. The reason for doing this is also the same as in DAC. Sometimes, it is sufficient to achieve directional path consistency which is computationally less expensive than achieving full path consistency.

Definition: *A CSP is directionally path consistent under an ordering of variables if and only if for every two variables V_i and V_j each path (V_i, V_k, V_j) in its constraint graph such that $k > i$ and $k > j$ according to the ordering is path consistent.*

Algorithm 16. Directional path consistency

```
procedure DPC(Vars, Constraints)
n ← |Vars|
Q ← {(i,j) | i<j & Cij in Constraints}
for k = n to 1 by -1 do
  for i = 1 to k-1 do
   for j = i to k do
   if (i,k) in Q & (j,k) in Q then
    Cij ← Cij & (Cik * Ckk * Ckj)
    Q ← Q union {(i,j)}
   end if
   end for
  end for
end for
end DPC
```

Again, notice the difference between PC and DPC. In PC we check every path (V_i, V_k, V_j) while in DPC only the paths (V_i, V_k, V_j) where $k > i$ and $k > j$ are considered. Consequently, path consistency is stronger than directional path consistency; however, it is less expensive to achieve directional path consistency. Figure 20 shows that path consistency is strictly stronger than directional path consistency, that is, PC removes more inconsistent values than DPC. It also shows that DPC can be even weaker than AC. However, DPC is at least as strong as DAC because if the path (V_i, V_k, V_j), where $i < k$, is path-consistent then also the arc (V_i, V_k) is arc-consistent.

Similarly to DAC, the algorithm for achieving directional path consistency is easier and more efficient than the PC algorithms. Again, the algorithm DPC goes through the variables in the descending order (according to the ordering <) and each path is examined exactly once. Its time complexity is $O(n^3 d^3)$.

Why Not Path Consistency?

Path consistency removes more inconsistencies from the constraint graph than arc consistency but it has also many disadvantages. Here are the three main reasons why path consistency algorithms are rarely implemented in commercial CSP-solving systems for solving general problems:

- The cost/performance ratio between the time complexity of PC algorithms and the simplification factor brings path consistency far less interesting than the same ration brought by arc consistency.

- PC algorithms are based on elimination of pairs of value assignments. This imposes that constraints should have an extensional representation ({0,1}-matrix) from which individual pairs can be deleted. Such a representation is often unacceptable for the implementation of real-world problems for which intentional representations are much more concise and efficient.

- Finally, enforcing path consistency has the major drawback of bringing some modifications to the connectivity of the constraint graph by adding some arcs to this graph (that is, if a path consistency for (V_i, V_k, V_j) is enforced and there is no constraint between V_i and V_j then a new constraint between these two variables appears).

Due to above mentioned drawbacks, path consistency is rarely used to solve general CSPs. Nevertheless, the ideas of path consistency are applied to special subproblems such as temporal networks.

Path Consistency Still Not Sufficient?

Enforcing path consistency removes more inconsistencies from the constraint graph than arc consistency but is it sufficient to solve any CSP? The answer is unfortunately the same as for arc consistency, that is, achieving path consistency still implies neither that any (complete) instantiation of variables from the current (reduced) domains is a solution to the CSP nor that the solution exists. Figure 21 shows such an example where the constraint graph is path consistent, domains are not empty but there is still no solution satisfying all constraints.

A CSP after achieving path consistency:

- domain size for each variable becomes one $\Rightarrow$ exactly one solution exists
- any domain becomes empty $\Rightarrow$ no solution exists
- otherwise $\Rightarrow$ not known whether a solution exists

Figure 21. A path consistent problem which has no solution

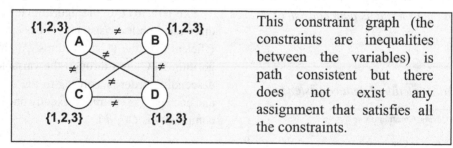

This constraint graph (the constraints are inequalities between the variables) is path consistent but there does not exist any assignment that satisfies all the constraints.

Figure 22. A 2-consistent problem that is not 1-consistent

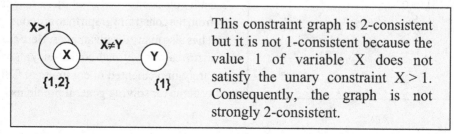

This constraint graph is 2-consistent but it is not 1-consistent because the value 1 of variable X does not satisfy the unary constraint $X > 1$. Consequently, the graph is not strongly 2-consistent.

K-Consistency

Because path consistency is still not sufficient to solve the CSP in general, there remains a question whether there exists any consistency technique that can solve the CSP completely without any search. Let us first define a general notion of consistency that covers node, arc, and path consistencies.

Definition: *A constraint graph is* K-consistent *if the following is true: Choose values of any K-1 different variables that satisfy all the constraints among these variables and choose any K-th variable. There exists a value for this K-th variable that satisfies all the constraints among these K variables. A constraint graph is* strongly K-consistent *if it is J-consistent for all J ≤ K.*

Clearly, a strongly K-consistent graph is K-consistent as well. However, the reverse implication does not hold in general as Figure 22 shows.

K-consistency is a general notion of consistency that covers all above mentioned consistencies. In particular:

- Node consistency is equivalent to strong 1-consistency,
- Arc consistency is equivalent to strong 2-consistency, and

- Path consistency is equivalent to strong 3-consistency.

Algorithms exist for making a constraint graph strongly K-consistent for K >2 but in practice they are rarely used because of efficiency issues. Although these algorithms remove more inconsistent values than any arc consistency algorithm they do not eliminate the need for search in general.

Clearly, if a constraint graph containing N nodes is strongly N-consistent, then a solution to the CSP can be found without any search. But the worst-case time complexity of the algorithm for obtaining N-consistency in an N-node constraint graph is exponential. If the graph is (strongly) K-consistent for K < N then, in general, backtracking (search) cannot be avoided, that is, there still exist inconsistent values (Figure 23).

N-ary and Global Constraints

So far we assumed that the constraints are binary, which is not a real restriction because any CSP can be converted to a binary CSP (Bacchus & van Beek 1998; Rossi et al., 1990; Stergiou & Walsh, 1999). We presented several higher-level consistency techniques that improve domain filtering but they are rarely used in practice due to their time and space complexity. So the question is if we can achieve a stronger pruning without

Figure 23. A strongly K-consistent problem, where K is smaller than the number of nodes, which has no solution

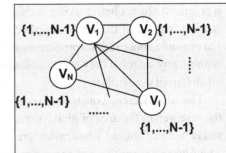

This constraint graph with inequality constraints between each pair of variables is strongly K-consistent for each K < N, where N is the number of nodes (variables). However, there does not exist any assignment that satisfies all the constraints.

Figure 24. An arc consistent CSP where some inconsistent values can still be removed

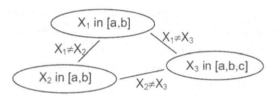

the deficiency of the higher-order consistency techniques. One of the possible ways is to handle n-ary constraints directly instead of decomposing them into a set of binary constraints.

The notion of arc consistency can be naturally extended to n-ary constraints—we obtain a so-called *generalised arc consistency* (GAC). The constraint is generalised arc consistent if and only if for any value in the domain of any constrained variable there exist values in the domains of the other constrained variables such that the value tuple satisfies the constraint. The above presented arc consistency algorithms can be naturally extended to n-ary constraints so they achieve generalised arc consistency. Nevertheless, we can do more. Van Hentenrych, Deville, and Teng (1992) already showed that the REVISE procedure can be implemented in a more efficient way if we assume semantics of the constraint. In particular, they presented more efficient consistency techniques for functional, anti-functional, and monotonic (binary) constraints. We can also use the semantics of the constraint for n-ary constraints that are frequently called *global constraints*. They got their name from global reasoning over a subset

of simpler constraints. In other words, the set of simpler constraints is encapsulated into a single global constraint that achieves either stronger pruning than (G)AC or the same pruning as (G)AC but in a more efficient way.

Assume the constraint satisfaction problem from Figure 24. This problem is arc consistent because all pairs of values are locally consistent. However, a more global view can discover that values a and b cannot be assigned to X_3 because they will be used both for X_1 and X_2. So if we do some global reasoning over this problem, we should be able to discover such inconsistency. Régin (1994) proposed an efficient filtering algorithm (the REVISE procedure) for this constraint which is called *all-different*. The basic idea of Régin's filtering algorithm is to represent the constraint as a bipartite graph with variables on one side and values on the other side—a so called *value graph* (Figure 25). The edges connect the variables with the values in their domains.

The filtering algorithm for the all-different constraint is then realised via computing a maximal matching in the value graph. Maximal matching is a subset of disjoint edges which is maximal. It corresponds to a solution of the all-different constraint. If an edge is not part of any maximal matching then this edge is removed from the graph because the corresponding value cannot be assigned to a given variable in any solution. This is the case of edges (X_3,a) and (X_3,b) in the above value graph. The advantage of Régin's (1994) algorithm is maintaining global consistency (GAC) over the set of variables while keeping the time efficiency close to local propagation. Therefore it is almost always better to use such global constraints instead of the set of simple constraints. For example, most Sudoku problems can be solved without any search if they are modelled using the all-different constraints.

The all-different constraint de-facto started the research in the area of global constraints and today tens of global constraints are available. The filtering algorithms of these constraints use

Figure 25. A value graph modelling the all-different constraint from Figure 24

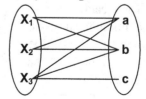

techniques from the graph theory such as network flows which are behind the global cardinality constraint (Régin, 1996) or automata theory which is used in the regular (Pesant, 2004) and grammar constraints (Quimper & Walsh, 2006; Sellmann, 2006). Many global constraints have been proposed to model particular problems, for example in the area of scheduling (Baptiste, Le Pape, & Nuijten, 2001). In general, global constraints represent a way how specialised solving techniques can be used within the constraint satisfaction framework.

Further Reading

Consistency techniques make the core of constraint satisfaction technology. The basic arc consistency and path consistency algorithms (AC-1, AC-2, AC-3, PC-1, PC-2) are described by Mackworth (1977a), their complexity study is descibed by Mackworth and Freuder (1985). Algorithm AC-4 with the optimal worst-case time complexity has been proposed by Mohr and Henderson (1986). Its improvement called AC-6 that decreases memory consumption and improves average time complexity was proposed by Bessiere (1994). This algorithm has been further improved to AC-7 by Bessiere, Freuder, and Régin (1999) by exploiting bi-directionality of constraints. AC-5 is a general schema for AC algorithms that can collapse to both AC-3 and AC-4. It is described by Van Hentenryck, Deville, and Teng (1992) and it covers special filtering techniques for functional (=), anti-functional (≠), and monotonic (<) constraints. Recently, optimal versions of AC-3 algorithms have been independently proposed, namely AC-3.1 (Zhang & Yap, 2001) and AC-2001 (Bessiere & Régin, 2001).

Mohr and Henderson (1986) proposed an improved algorithm for path consistency PC-3 based on the same idea as AC-4. However, this algorithm is not sound—a correction called PC-4 is described by Han and Lee (1988). Algorithm PC-5 using the ideas of AC-6 is described by

Singh (1995). Restricted path consistency that is a half way between AC and PC is described by Berlandier (1995).

The k-consistency scheme has been proposed by Freuder (1978) and further generalised into (i,j)-consistency by Freuder (1985). There also exist other consistency techniques going beyond the k-consistency scheme like inverse consistencies (Verfaillie, Martinez, & Bessiere, 1999), neighbourhood inverse consistencies (Freuder & Elfe, 1996), or singleton consistencies (Debruyne & Bessiere, 1997; Prosser, Stergiou, & Walsh, 2000).

Mackworth (1977b) extended definitions and consistency algorithms also to nonbinary constraints. Some papers use hyper arc consistency or domain consistency for n-ary constraints, but the most common name is *generalised arc consistency* (GAC). Many specialised filtering algorithms have been proposed for n-ary constraints, where the number of variables is not fixed. Such constraints are called *global constraints*. The element constraint has been proposed by Van Hentenryck and Carillon (1988), the well known all-different constraint has been proposed by Régin (1994), who also proposed its generalisation called global cardinality constraint (1996). The regular constraint has been proposed by Pesant (2004), but the ideas already appeared in the works of Barták (2002b). Beldiceanu, Carlsson, and Rampon (2005) proposed a way to classify global constraints based on graph invariants.

In some applications, such as scheduling, even arc consistency is too costly. This is usually the case when the domains are large. For such problems, a weaker notion of consistency called *bound consistency* (or arc-B-consistency) has been proposed by Lhome (1993). This consistency requires only the bounds of the domain to have a support in the domains of the other constrained variables which dramatically increases efficiency of constraint checks. Filtering algorithms for some global constraints have been altered to make the constraints bound consistent, for example Puget

(1998) described a bound consistent version of the all-different constraint.

A more thorough description of consistency techniques useful for teaching purposes is described by Dechter (2003). A deep theoretical study of all presented algorithms can be found in Tsang (1993). The recent consistency techniques are covered by a dedicated chapter in a handbook by Rossi, Van Beek, & Walsh (2006).

CONSTRAINT PROGAGATION: CAN WE COMBINE DEPTH-FIRST SEARCH AND CONSISTENCY TECHNIQUES?

In the previous sections, we presented two rather different schemes for solving a CSP: systematic search with chronological backtracking as its representative and consistency techniques. The systematic search was developed for general applications and it does not use constraints to improve the efficiency (backjumping and backmarking are two improvements that try to exploit constraints to reduce the search space). On the other hand, the consistency techniques reduce the search space using constraints until the solution is found. Neither systematic search nor consistency techniques prove themselves to be effective enough to solve the CSP completely. Therefore a third possible schema was introduced that embeds a consistency algorithm inside a search algorithm. Such schemas are usually called *look-ahead strategies* and they are based on the idea of reducing the search space through constraint propagation.

As a skeleton we use a simple backtracking algorithm that incrementally instantiates variables and extends a partial assignment, which specifies consistent values for some of the variables, toward a complete assignment, by repeatedly choosing a value for another variable. In order to reduce the search space, some consistency technique is applied to the constraint graph after assigning a value to the variable. Depending on the strength

Algorithm 17. Arc consistency for backtracking

```
procedure AC-BT(cv)
Q ← {(V_i,V_cv) in arcs(G), i < cv};
consistent ← true;
while not Q empty & consistent do
  select and delete any arc (V_k,V_m) from Q;
  consistent ← not REVISE(V_k,V_m)
end while
return consistent
end AC-BT
```

Figure 26. A search tree for solving a 4-queens problem using chronological backtracking

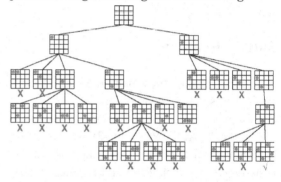

of the consistency technique we get various constraint satisfaction algorithms.

Backtracking, Once More

Even simple backtracking (BT) performs some kind of consistency check and it can be seen as a combination of pure generate-and-test and a fraction of arc consistency. The BT algorithm checks arc consistency among already instantiated variables, that is, the algorithm checks the validity of constraints considering the partial assignment. Because the domains of instantiated variables contain just one value, it is enough to check only those constraints/arcs containing the last instantiated variable. If any domain is reduced, then the corresponding constraint is not consistent and the algorithm backtracks to a new instantiation.

The following procedure AC-BT is called each time a new value is assigned to some variable V_{cv}

(cv is the consecutive number of the variable in the order of instantiating variables).

The BT algorithm detects inconsistency as soon as it appears, and, therefore, it is by far more efficient than the simple generate-and-test approach. But it must still perform too much search because it waits until the inconsistency really appears.

Figure 26 shows the search tree for the 4-queens problems solved using the backtracking algorithm. Each node describes a partial allocation of queens (dots).

As we demonstrated with the backjumping and backmarking strategies, the BT algorithm can be easily extended to backtrack to the conflicting variable and, thus, to incorporate some form of look-back scheme or intelligent backtracking. Nevertheless, this adds some additional expenses to the algorithm and it seems that preventing possible future conflicts is more reasonable than recovering from them.

Forward Checking

Forward checking is the easiest way to prevent future conflicts. Instead of checking consistency between the instantiated variables, it performs arc consistency between the pairs of a not-yet instantiated variable and an instantiated variable. Therefore, it maintains the invariance that for every un-instantiated variable all values in its current domain are compatible with the values of already instantiated variables.

The forward checking algorithm is realised in the following way. When a value is assigned to the current variable, any value in the domain of a "future" variable which conflicts with this assignment is (temporarily) removed from the domain. Notice, that we check only the constraints/arcs between the future variables and the currently instantiated variable. The reason is that the satisfaction of other constraints between the future variable and the already instantiated

Algorithm 18. Arc consistency for forward checking

```
procedure AC-FC(cv)
Q ← {(V_i,V_cv) in arcs(G), i > cv};
consistent ← true;
while not Q empty & consistent do
  select and delete any arc (V_k,V_m) from Q;
  if REVISE(V_k,V_m) then
    consistent ← not empty D_k
  end if
end while
return consistent
end AC-FC
```

Figure 27. A search tree for solving a 4-queens problem using forward checking (the crossed fields represent the pruned values)

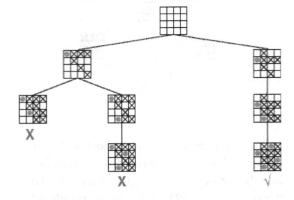

variables does not change. If the domain of a future variable becomes empty, then it is known immediately that the current partial assignment is inconsistent. Consequently, the forward checking algorithm allows branches of the search tree that will lead to a failure to be pruned earlier than with chronological backtracking. Note also that whenever a new variable is considered, all its remaining values are guaranteed to be consistent with the past variables, so checking the assignment against the past assignments is no longer necessary. Clearly, the domains of future variables must be restored upon backtracking.

Notice, that in the AC-BT algorithm we use the procedure REVISE as a consistency test and in the AC-FC algorithm we have to test the emptiness

Algorithm 19. Directional arc consistency for partial look ahead

```
procedure DAC-LA(cv)
  for i = cv+1 to n do
    for each arc (V_i,V_j) in arcs(G) such that i > j & j ≥ cv do
      if REVISE(V_i,V_j) then
        if empty D_i then return fail
    end for
  end for
  return true
end DAC-LA
```

Figure 28. A search tree for solving a 4-queens problem using partial look ahead (the crossed fields represent the pruned values)

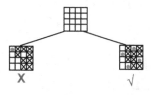

X √

of the domain explicitly. This is because the procedure REVISE is applied to domains containing exactly one value in AC-BT. Consequently, if the domain is reduced (REVISE returns True) then the domain becomes empty. In AC-FC, the reduction of the domain does not mean necessarily that the domain is empty (because the domain of a future variable can contain more than one value) so we have to test emptiness explicitly. Figure 27 shows that a search tree is much smaller in comparison with backtracking for the 4-queens problem (the crossed fields represent the positions forbidden via forward checking).

Forward checking detects inconsistency earlier than chronological backtracking and thus it reduces the search tree and (hopefully) the overall amount of work done. But it should be noted that forward checking does more work when an instantiated variable is added to the current partial assignment. Nevertheless, forward checking is still almost always a better choice than simple backtracking.

Partial Look Ahead

The more computational effort is spent on the problem reduction, the more inconsistencies can be removed. Consequently, less searching is necessary to find the solution. Forward checking performs only the checks of constraints between the current variable and the future variables. Now, we can extend this consistency checking to even later variables that do not have a direct connection with the already instantiated variables, using directional arc consistency. This algorithm is called DAC-look ahead or partial look ahead.

Recall that directional arc consistency requires some total ordering of the variables. For simplicity reasons, we will use the reverse ordering of variables from the backtracking skeleton. In practice, this is not necessary and any different orderings can be used. However, in such a case, the consistency of current variable with previously assigned variables has to be checked as well.

Notice, that we check directional arc consistency only between the future variables and between the future variables and the current variable. The reason is that the constraints between the future and past variables are not influenced by assigning a value to the current variable and therefore it is not necessary to re-check these constraints.

Partial Look Ahead checks more constraints than Forward Checking and, thus, it can find more inconsistencies than FC as Figure 28 shows.

Full Look Ahead

We showed that using directional arc consistency can remove more values from the domains of future variables than forward checking and hence to prune the search space. Clearly, if one performs full arc consistency then the domains of future variables can be pruned even more and more possible future conflicts are prevented. This approach is called (Full) Look Ahead or Maintaining Arc Consistency (MAC).

Algorithm 20. Arc consistency—3 for full look ahead

```
procedure AC3-LA(cv)
  Q ← {(Vᵢ,V_cv) in arcs(G),i > cv};
  consistent <- true;
  while not Q empty & consistent do
    select and delete any arc (V_k,V_m) from Q;
    if REVISE(V_k,V_m) then
      Q ← Q union {(Vᵢ,V_k) | (Vᵢ,V_k) in arcs(G), i ≠ k, i ≠ m, i > cv}
      consistent ← not empty D_k
    end if
  end while
  return consistent
end AC3-LA
```

Similarly to partial look ahead, in full look ahead we check the constraints between the future variables and between the future variables and the current variable. However, now the constraints are checked in both directions so even more inconsistencies can be detected. Again, whenever a new variable is considered, all its remaining values are guaranteed to be consistent with the past variables, so checking the instantiated variable against the past assignments is not necessary. Also, it is not necessary to check the constraints between the future and past variables because of the same reason as with partial look ahead.

The full look ahead procedure can use arbitrary arc consistency algorithm. In the following procedure (Algorithm 20) we use the AC-3 algorithm. Notice that we start checking arc consistency with the queue containing the arcs from the future variables to the current variable only. This is because only these arcs/constraints are influenced by assigning a value to the current variable.

Figure 29. A search tree for solving a 4-queens problem using full look ahead (the crossed fields represent the pruned values)

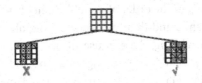

The advantage of full look ahead is that it allows branches of the search tree that will lead to a failure to be pruned earlier than with forward checking and with partial look ahead. However, it should be noted again that full look ahead does even more work when an instantiated variable is added to the current partial assignment than forward checking and partial look ahead. Again, Figure 29 shows a search tree when the full look ahead technique is used to prune the search space in the 4-queens problem.

Comparison of Propagation Techniques

The constraint propagation methods can be easily compared by exploring which constraints are being checked when a value is assigned to the current variable V_{cv}. Figure 30 shows which constraints are checked when the above described propagation techniques are applied. The graph represents a constraint network with nodes corresponding to variables and arcs describing the binary constraints. It is assumed that variables on left are already instantiated while variables on right are not yet instantiated. Note that in partial look ahead the same arcs are checked as in full look ahead. However, in partial look ahead each arc is checked exactly once and in one direction only.

Figure 30. A constraint graph with marked arcs that are checked by various propagation techniques

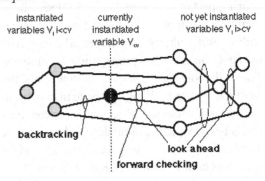

More constraint propagation at each search node will result in the search tree containing fewer nodes, but the overall cost may be higher, as the processing at each node will be more expensive. In one extreme, obtaining strong N-consistency for the original problem would completely eliminate the need for search, but as mentioned before, this is usually more expensive than simple backtracking. Actually, in some cases even the full look ahead may be more expensive than simple backtracking. That is the reason why forward checking and simple backtracking are still used in applications.

Further Reading

Backtracking algorithms have been used in artificial intelligence and combinatorial optimization before the advent of constraint programming. The backtracking algorithm was informally described by Golomb and Baumert (1965), but a nonrecursive formulation of Bitnerm and Reingold (1975) is used more frequently. The forward checking algorithm was originally introduced by McGregor (1979) for binary constraints and extended to n-ary constraints by Van Hentenryck (1989) and Bessiere, Meseguer, Freuder, and Larrosa (2002). The partial look ahead is due to Haralick and Elliot (1980). Gaschnig (1974) suggested maintaining arc consistency during search and gave the first explicit algorithm containing this idea under the name full look ahead. Sabin and Freuder (1994) gave the name MAC (maintaining arc consistency) to the very same idea and they showed that favouring partial look ahead over full look ahead (Haralick & Elliot, 1980) is dead because larger and more difficult problems are much better solved by applying stronger propagation techniques. The full look ahead, MAC, is nowadays the most widely used solving approach in constraint satisfaction packages. Recently, nondeterminism is being exploited in randomised versions of backtracking search using for example random restarts (Gomes, Selman, & Kautz, 1998).

SEARCH ORDERS AND SEARCH REDUCTION: CAN WE FURTHER IMPROVE EFFICIENCY OF SOLVING ALGORITHMS?

In the previous section we presented several search algorithms for constraint satisfaction. These search algorithms require the ordering in which the variables are to be considered for instantiation and the ordering in which the values are assigned to the variable on backtracking. Note that decisions about these orderings could affect the efficiency of the constraint satisfaction algorithm dramatically. For example, if the right value is chosen for each variable during search then the problem is solved completely without backtracking (provided that a solution exists). Of course, this is a hypothetical case but in many cases we can choose an ordering which can reduce the number of backtracks required in search. In the look-ahead algorithms, the ordering of variables could affect the amount of search space pruned.

Both topics of the search orders and the reduction of the search space are discussed in this section.

Variable Ordering

The search algorithms require information about which variables should be chosen for instantiation. Because all variables need to be instantiated at the end, it may seem that the order of variables during search is not important. However, experiments have shown that the ordering of variables can have substantial impact on the complexity of backtrack search. The reason is that the different order of variables leads to a different shape of the search tree and clearly, a smaller search tree is an advantage. The order of variables can be decided in advance and then we are speaking about the *static ordering*. This is useful, for example, in chronological backtracking where no additional information is obtained during search. However, look-ahead algorithms prune the search space

Figure 31. Computing the width of a (constraint) graph

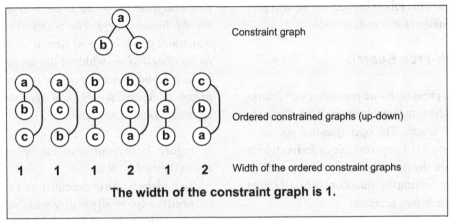

depending on the partial assignment of variables and hence it may be useful to use a different ordering of variables in different branches. Then we are speaking about the *dynamic variable ordering* (DVO).

The most common variable ordering heuristic is based on a so called FAIL-FIRST principle, which says:

To succeed, try first where you are most likely to fail.

This principle may seem strange but it has a rational background. As we mentioned, at the end all variables must be instantiated. So if instantiation of some variable is not possible (for the current partial assignment) then it is better to discover it early during search because it will save exploring many search branches that do not lead to a solution.

The question now is, how to realise the fail-first principle in practice. Assume that we have no information about which values participate in the solution, that is, any value is equally likely to participate in the solution. Hence, the more values are in the domain of the variable, the more likely one of them can be assigned to the variable. According to the fail-first principle, the variables with the smallest domain should be instantiated

first, because the chance of failure is highest for them. This heuristic is sometimes called *min-domain ordering*.

Another view of the fail-first principle takes in account the constraints related to a given variable. Assume that we have two variables, one participating in a single constraint while the second variable participating in five constraints. There is a higher chance to consistently instantiate the first variable than the second variable. Again, according to the fail-first principle, it is better to instantiate first the variables participating in the largest number of constraints. This approach is sometimes called the *most-constrained heuristic* and it is frequently combined with the min-domain ordering in the following way. The variables are ordered according to the min-domain principle and the variables with equally large domains are ordered using the most-constrained heuristic. This heuristic was first used by Brélaz (1979) for solving the graph colouring problems.

The most-constrained heuristic is sometimes used in a restricted way in chronological backtracking when the variable with the largest number of constraints with the past variables is chosen first. For instance, during solving a graph colouring problem, it is reasonable to assign a colour to the vertex which has common arcs with already coloured vertices so the conflict is detected as soon as possible. This is an example of static variable ordering and in the following section we will give some explanation for this heuristic.

Backtrack-Free Search

In the above paragraphs we presented variable orderings which can noticeably improve the efficiency of backtrack search. The open question is:

Does there exist any variable ordering which can eliminate the need for backtracking at all?

Before answering this question we first define what backtrack-free search is.

Definition: *A search in a CSP is* backtrack-free *if in a depth-first search under an ordering of its variables, for every variable that is to be instantiated, one can always find a value which is compatible with all assignments committed to so far.*

If the ordering of variables is backtrack-free then we know that for each variable there exists a value compatible with the assignment of foregoing variables in the search and, therefore, no backtrack to change a value of foregoing variable is necessary. The following definitions and theorem show how to establish such backtrack-free ordering for strongly K-consistent constraint graphs.

Definition: *An* ordered constraint graph *is a constraint graph whose vertices have been ordered linearly. The* width of the vertex *in an ordered constraint graph is the number of constraint arcs that lead from the vertex to the previous vertices (in the linear order). The* width of the ordered constraint graph *is the maximum width of any of its vertices and the* width of the constraint graph *is the minimum width of all the orderings of that graph. In general the width of a constraint graph depends upon its structure.*

Figure 31 demonstrates the meaning of the above defined notions.

To find the width of the constraint graph we do not need to explore all possible variable orderings. The procedure (Algorithm 21) by Freuder (1982) finds a sequence of variables (vertices) which has the minimal width of the graph. In other words, the width of the ordered constraint graph defined by the returned ordering is the width of the constraint graph. The input to the procedure is a general graph and the output is a sequence of vertices which has the minimal width.

Proposition: *If a constraint graph is strongly K-consistent, and $K > w$, where w is the width of the constraint graph, then there exists a search order that is backtrack free*

Proof: *The proof of the above proposition is straightforward. There exists an ordering of the graph such that the number of constraint arcs leading from any vertex of the graph to the previous vertices is at most w. Now if the variables are instantiated using this ordering, then whenever a new variable is instantiated, a value for this variable is consistent with all the previous assignments because:*

1. *this value is to be consistent with the assignments of at most w other variables, and*
2. *the graph is strongly $(w+1)$-consistent.*

Interestingly, all tree structured constraint graphs have width 1, so it is possible to find at least one ordering that can be used to solve the

Algorithm 21. Minimum width ordering

```
procedure Min-Width-Ordering((V,E))
Q ← {};
while not V empty do
  N ← the node in V joined by the least number of edges in E;
    % in case of a tie, make arbitrary choice
  V ← V - {N};
  Remove all the edges from E which join V to other nodes in
V;
  Q ← N:Q % put N as a head of the sequence Q
end while
return Q;
end Min-Width-Ordering
```

constraint graph without backtracking provided that the constraint graph is arc consistent.

Value Ordering

The role of value ordering, that is the order in which values are considered during search, is clear—if a value belonging to the solution is always selected then no backtracks are necessary. However, it should be also said that if all solutions are required or if there is no solution then the value ordering is indifferent. Assume that we are looking for one solution. How should we choose which value to try first? If there is a value that belongs to the solution then this value should be tried first. If no value will lead to a solution then every value for the variable should be considered and the order does not matter. Analogically to variable ordering, we can call the above principle SUCCEED-FIRST.

Again, the question is how to realise this principle in practice. Clearly, it is hard to expect that a correct value is always known so we need some heuristic that estimates which values belong to the solution. Typical value ordering heuristics are based on maximizing the number of available options. For example, each value has a different number of supports (AC-4 computes these numbers). The value with a larger number of supports has higher chances to belong to the solution and hence such value should be tried first. There exist other general heuristics that are estimating the number of solutions by relaxing the problem (for example by removing the constraints to obtain a tree-structured CSP) and solving fast the relaxed problem. However, these heuristics are usually computationally expensive and, hence, rarely used in practice. Usually, problem-dependent value ordering heuristics are applied.

Further Reading

Variable ordering heuristics studied in literature can be classified into two categories: heuristics that are based primarily on the domain sizes and heuristics that are based on the structure of the CSP. Golomb and Baumert (1965) were the first the propose a dynamic ordering heuristic based on the choosing the variables with the smallest domain that is called a *min-domain heuristic* or simply a *dom heuristic*. Haralick and Elliot (1980) formulated the *fail-first principle* and showed that the dom heuristic is effective in combination with forward checking. Some generalisations of the dom heuristic have been proposed lately. Brélaz (1979) proposed to combine the dom heuristic with the number of constraints per variable which is called *dom+deg heuristic*. The idea is to choose the variable with the smallest domain and to break ties by choosing the variable with the highest degree (with the largest number of constraints). Bessiere and Régin (1996) proposed another generalisation called *dom/deg heuristic*. This heuristic chooses the variable with the smallest ratio domain size/degree.

Structure-guided variable ordering heuristics use information about the structure of the graphical representation of the CSP. Freuder (1982) was the first to propose a structure-guided variable heuristic based on the width of the constraint graph. Namely he showed that there exists a backtrack-free static variable ordering heuristic if the level of k-consistency is greater than the width of the constraint graph. Dechter and Pearl (1988) proposed a variable ordering heuristic which first instantiates variables which cut cycles in the constraint graph (a so called cutset). Sabin and Freuder (1997) then used this heuristic together with maintaining arc consistency. A general idea behind the structure-guided variable ordering heuristics is similar to the divide-and-conquer principle used in algorithm design. The variables whose instantiation will decompose the constraint graph into disjoint sub-graphs should be instantiated first. A variable ordering heuristic based on such a recursive decomposition of the constraint graph has been proposed by Freuder and Quinn (1985). Structure-guided variable ordering heuristics are not used as frequently nowadays because they are either static or nearly static and moreover, they can break down in the presence of global constraints, which are common in practice.

Generally applicable value ordering heuristics are based on estimating either the number of solutions or the probability of a solution when a given value is used. Dechter and Pearl (1988) approximated the number of solutions by solving a tree relaxation of the problem which was obtained by removing the constraints until the constraint graph representing the CSP was a tree (counting all solutions to a tree-structured CSP is polynomial so the number of solutions can be computed exactly). Ginsberg, Frank, Halpin, and Torrance (1990) proposed to select first the value that maximizes the product of the remaining domain sizes after assigning this value to a variable. This is sometimes called a *promise heuristic*. Frost and Dechter (1995) proposed choosing the value that maximizes the sum of the remaining domains which is called a *min-conflicts heuristic*. Geelen (1992) noted that the product differentiates much better than summation. He also showed the maximizing the product is similar to maximizing the probability that we are branching into a sub-problem that contains a solution.

CONSTRAINED OPTIMISATION: HOW TO FIND AN OPTIMAL SOLUTION SATISFYING THE CONSTRAINTS?

Until now we have presented the constraint satisfaction algorithms for finding one or all solutions satisfying all the constraints, that is, all solutions were considered equally good. However, in many real-life applications, we do not want to find any solution but a good solution. The quality of solution is usually measured by some application dependent function called an *objective function*. The goal is to find such an assignment that satisfies all the constraints and minimises or maximises

the objective function. Such problems are called *Constrained Optimisation Problems (COP)*.

Definition: *A constrained optimisation problem (COP) consists of a standard CSP and an objective function f which maps every solution (a complete assignment of variables satisfying all the constraints) to a numerical value. The task is to find such a solution that is optimal regarding the objective function, that is, it minimises or maximises the objective function.*

In order to find the optimal solution, we potentially need to explore all the solutions of the CSP and to compare their values using the objective function. Therefore techniques for finding or generating all solutions are more relevant to the COP than techniques for finding a single solution.

Branch and Bound

Perhaps the most widely used technique for solving optimisation problems including a COP is branch-and-bound (B&B) which is a well known method both in artificial intelligence and operations research. This method uses a heuristic to prune the search space. This heuristic, which we will call h, is a function that maps assignments (even partial) to a numeric value that is an estimate of the objective function. More precisely, h applied to some partial assignment is an estimate of the best value of the objective function applied to all solutions (complete assignments) that arise by extending this partial assignment. Naturally, the efficiency of the branch-and-bound method is highly dependent on availability of a good heuristic. In such a case, the B&B algorithm can prune the search sub-trees where the optimal solution does not occur. Note, that there are two possibilities when the subtree can be pruned:

- there is no solution in the sub-tree at all,
- all solutions in the sub-tree are sub-optimal (they are not optimal).

Algorithm 22. Branch & bound

```
procedure BB(Variables, Constraints)
  Bound ← infinity; % looking for minimum of function f
  Best ← nil;    % best solution found so far
  BB-1(Variables,{},Constraints)
  return Best
end BB

procedure BB-1(Unlabelled, Labelled, Constraints)
  if Unlabelled = {} then
    if f(Labelled) < Bound then
      Bound ← f(Labelled); % set new upper bound
      Best ← Labelled;    % remember new best solution
    end if
  else
    pick the first X from Unlabelled
    for each value V from D_X do
      if consistent({X/V}+Labelled, Constraints)
        & h({X/V}+Labelled) < Bound then
        BB-1(Unlabelled-{X}, {X/V}+Labelled, Constraints)
      end if
    end for
end BB-1
```

Algorithm 23. Branch & bound with acceptability bound

```
procedure BB-2(Unlabelled, Labelled, Constraints)
  if Unlabelled = {} then
    if f(Labelled) < Bound then
      Bound ← f(Labelled); % set new upper bound
      Best ← Labelled;   % remember new best solution
      if f(Labelled) ≤ Acceptability_Bound then
        return Best
    end if
  end if
  else
    ... % this part is identical to the BB-1 procedure
end BB-2
```

Of course, the closer the heuristic is to the objective function, the more and larger subtrees can be pruned. On the other hand, we need an admissible heuristic ensuring that no subtree, where the optimal solution settles, is pruned. This admissibility can be achieved easily if, in case of the minimisation problem, the heuristic is an underestimate of the objective function, that is, the value of the heuristic function is not higher than the value of the objective function. In case of the maximisation problems, we require the heuristic to be an overestimate of the objective function. In both cases, we can guarantee soundness and completeness of the branch-and-bound algorithm.

Unfortunately, it is not easy to find an admissible and efficient heuristic and, sometimes, such heuristic is not available. In such a case, it is up to the user to choose:

• a more efficient heuristic with the risk of pruning a subtree with an optimal solution (consequently, suboptimal solution is obtained), or

• an admissible but less efficient heuristic with a longer time of computation.

There exist several modifications of the branch-and-bound method; we will present here the depth-first branch-and-bound algorithm that is derived from the backtracking algorithm for solving a CSP. The algorithm uses two global variables for storing the current upper bound (we are minimising the objective function) and the best solution found so far. It behaves like the chronological backtracking algorithm except that as soon as a value is assigned to the variable, the value of the heuristic function is computed. If this value exceeds the bound, then the subtree under the current partial assignment is pruned immediately. Initially, the bound is set to (plus) infinity and during computation it records the value of the objective function for the best solution found so far.

The efficiency of B&B is determined by two factors:

• the above discussed quality of the heuristic function and
• whether a good bound is found early.

Notice that we set (plus) infinity as the initial bound in the algorithm. However, if the user knows the value of optimum or its approximation (an upper bound in case of minimisation) then he or she can set the initial bound to a "better" value closer to optimum. Consequently, the algorithm can prune more sub-trees sooner and it is much more efficient.

Observations of real-life problems show also that the "last step" to optimum, that is, improving a good solution even more, is usually the most computationally expensive part of the solving process. Fortunately, in many applications, users are satisfied with a solution that is close to optimum if this solution is found early. The branch-and-bound algorithm can be modified to find sub-optimal solutions by using the second "acceptability" bound that describes the upper bound of the acceptable solution. The only modification of the above B&B algorithm to use the acceptability bound is in the part where a complete assignment is found. If the algorithm finds a solution that is better than the acceptability bound then this solution is accepted, that is, it can be returned immediately to the user even if it is not proved to be optimal.

Further Reading

There are two basic approaches to solve optimisation problems: the most common search algorithm for constraint optimisation is branch-and-bound, while the most common inference algorithm is dynamic programming. The idea of *branch-and-bound* can be traced back the work of Fulkerson, Dantzig, and Johnson (1954) on solving linear programming problems. Van Hentenryck (1989) proposed a constraint-based version of branch-and-bound. Freuder (1992) also studied how to extend backtracking algorithms for optimization. The *Russian Doll Search* (Verfaillie, Lamaitre, & Schiex, 1996) algorithm is another elegant search algorithm for optimization problems. The idea is to run *n* successive branch-and-bound searches, where *n* is the number of variables, each search involving a single additional variable with added relevant constraints. The optimal cost of sub-problems can be added to the lower bound as a contribution to future variables which recalls the principles of dynamic programming.

Dynamic programming was developed by Bellman (1957) as an inference algorithm for optimization problems. *Bucket Elimination* (Dechter, 1997) is a basic inference algorithm for solving constraint satisfaction problems that can be adapted also to constrained optimization problems. The serious drawback of bucket elimination, which is exponential space requirement unless the problem is sparse, can be overcome by using mini-bucket elimination (Dechter & Rish, 2003).

The recent research focuses on improving the bound of the objective function which is realised via techniques of constraint propagation. The cost which substitutes the objective function has been introduced into global constraints. For example Régin (1999) proposed a global cardinality constraint with costs and Van Hoeve (2004) studied soft all-different constraints. Scheduling global constraints with costs is described by Baptiste, Le Pape, and Nuijten (2001).

Solving optimisation problems shares the same principles as solving over-constrained problems, that is, the problems where it is not possible to satisfy all the constraints (then usually the task is to maximize the number of satisfied constraints). Currently, these problems are studied under the umbrella of *soft constraints*. There exists several unifying frameworks for soft constraints; the *semi-ring-based formalism* by Bistarelli, Montanari, and Rossi (1997) is probably the most developed among them. Barták (2002a) surveys the existing formalisms for soft constraints.

CONCLUSION: WHERE TO GO NEXT?

The goal of this chapter was to give readers a compact background of mainstream constraint satisfaction techniques in an easy to understand form which will hopefully help the readers in further studies of the subject. The chapter content was strongly motivated by surveys (Jaffar & Maher,

1996; Kumar, 1992) and tutorials (Barták, 1998; Smith, 1995). The ambition was not to provide exhaustive and detailed material where everything is covered. We just slightly touched active research areas like global constraints and soft constraints and we did not cover at all areas such as the local search techniques that are successfully applied to very large problems (Van Hentenryck & Michel, 2005), or the practically important area of modelling problems with constraints (Barták, 2005; Marriott & Stuckey, 1998). Fortunately, there are already many good books on constraint satisfaction that will help the reader to fill these gaps (Apt, 2003; Dechter, 2003; Frühwirth & Abdennadher, 2003). There are also useful online sources informing about the recent developments, such as Constraints Archive (2007) or ACP Web site (2007). To simplify selection of relevant materials we accompanied each main section of the chapter by a sub-section *Further Reading* that provides initial references to papers covering in more details the presented techniques.

Let us finish this chapter by a short note on how to use the presented techniques in practice. The readers interested in using the constraint satisfaction technology to solve their own problems are not requested to implement the presented techniques from scratch. There are constraint satisfaction libraries available for many programming languages, both free and commercial. Constraints emerged as a generalisation of unification in logic programming so they are naturally integrated into logic programming systems like ECLiPSe (eclipse.crosscoreop.com, open source) or SICStus Prolog (www.sics.se/sicstus, commercial). Nevertheless, constraint satisfaction packages are also available for other languages such as C++ or Java, for example the Gecode environment (www.gecode.org, open source) or the ILOG CP library (www.ilog.com/products/cp/, commercial). Users may also find complete development environments supporting constraints such as the Mozart system based on the Oz programming language (www.mozart-oz.org, free).

The message of this chapter is that constraint satisfaction is not simple enumeration, but a more sophisticated technology for solving combinatorial optimization problems that can naturally accommodate special solving techniques under the unifying umbrella of a CSP.

ACKNOWLEDGMENTS

The author is supported by the Czech Science Foundation under the contract no. 201/07/0205. The author would like to thank the reviewers for careful reading of the chapter draft and for proposing valuable extensions and corrections.

REFERENCES

Apt, K.R. (2003). *Principles of constraint programming*. Cambridge University Press.

Association for Constraint Programming. (2007). Retrieved August 17, 2007, from http://slash.math.unipd.it/acp/

Bacchus, F., & van Beek, P. (1998). On the conversion between non-binary and binary constraint satisfaction problems. In *Proceedings of the National Conference on Artificial Intelligence (AAAI-98)* (pp. 311-318). Madison, WI: AAAI Press.

Baptiste, P., Le Pape, C., & Nuijten, W. (2001). *Constraint-based scheduling: Applying constraints to scheduling problems*. Dordrecht: Kluwer Academic Publishers.

Barták, R. (1998). *Online guide to constraint programming*. Retrieved August 17, 2007, from http://kti.mff.cuni.cz/~bartak/constraints

Barták, R. (2002a). Modelling soft constraints: A survey. *Neural Network World, 12*(5), 421-431.

Barták, R. (2002b). Modelling resource transitions in constraint-based scheduling. In W.I. Grosky & F. Plášil (Eds.), *Proceedings of SOFSEM 2002:*

Theory and Practice of Informatics (LNCS 2540, pp. 186-194). Springer Verlag.

Barták, R. (2004). Incomplete depth-first search techniques: A short survey. In *Proceedings of CPDC 2004,* Gliwice, Poland (pp. 7-14).

Barták, R. (2005). Effective modeling with constraints. In *Applications of declarative programming and knowledge management* (LNAI 3392, pp. 149-165). Springer Verlag.

Beck, J.C., & Perron, L. (2000). Discrepancy-bounded depth first search. In *Proceedings of CP-AI-OR* (pp. 7-17).

Beldiceanu, N., Bourreau, E., Chan, P., & Rivreau, D. (1997). Partial search strategy in CHIP. In *Proceedings of 2nd International Conference on Metaheuristics-MIC97.*

Beldiceanu, N., Carlsson, M., & Rampon, J.X. (2005). *Global constraint catalogue* (Tech. Rep. No. T2005-06, SICS).

Bellman, R.E. (1957). *Dynamic programming.* Princeton University Press.

Berlandier, P. (1995). Improving domain filtering using restricted path consistency. In *Proceedings of the IEEE CAIA-95* (pp. 32-37). Los Angeles, CA.

Bessiere, C. (1994). Arc-consistency and arc-consistency again. *Artificial Intelligence, 65,* 179-190.

Bessiere, C., Freuder, E.C., & Régin, J.-R. (1999). Using constraint metaknowledge to reduce arc consistency computation. *Artificial Intelligence, 107,* 125-148.

Bessiere, C., Meseguer, P., Freuder, E.C., & Larrosa, J. (2002). On forward checking for non-binary constraint satisfaction. *Artificial Intelligence, 141,* 205-224.

Bessiere, C., & Régin, J.-Ch. (1996). MAC and combined heuristics: Two reasons for forsake FC (and CBJ?) on hard problems. In *Proceedings of the Second International Conference on Principles and Practice of Constraint programming (CP)* (LNCS 1118, pp. 61-75). Springer Verlag.

Bessiere, C. & Régin, J.-Ch. (2001). Refining the basic constraint propagation algorithm. In *Proceedings of IJCAI-01* (pp. 309-315).

Bistarelli, S., Montanari, U., & Rossi, F. (1997). Semiring-based constraint satisfaction and optimization. *Journal of the ACM, 44*(2), 165-201.

Bitnerm, J.R., & Reingold, E.M. (1975). Backtracking programming techniques. *Communications of the ACM, 18*(11), 651-656.

Borning, A. (1981). The programming language aspects of ThingLab, a constraint-oriented simulation laboratory. *ACM Transactions on Programming Languages and Systems, 3*(4), 252-387.

Brélaz, D. (1979). New methods to color the vertices of a graph. *Communications of the ACM, 22,* 251-256.

Cheadle, A.M., Harvey, W., Sadler, A.J., Schimpf, J., Shen K., & Wallace, M.G. (2003). ECLiPSe: An introduction (Tech. Rep. No. IC-Parc-03-1). Imperial College London.

Constraints archive. (2007). Retrieved August 17, 2007, from http://4c.ucc.ie/web/archive/

Debruyne, R., & Bessiere, C. (1997). Some practicable filtering techniques for the constraint satisfaction problem. In *Proceedings of the 15th IJCAI* (pp. 412-417).

Dechter, R. (1990). Enhancement schemes for constraint processing: Backjumping, learning, and cutset decomposition. *Artificial Intelligence, 41,* 273-312.

Dechter, R. (1997). Bucket elimination: A unifying framework for processing hard and soft constraint. *Constraints: An International Journal, 2,* 51-55.

Dechter, R. (2003). *Constraint processing.* Morgan Kaufmann.

Dechter, R., & Frost, D. (1998). Backtracking algorithms for constraint satisfaction problems; a survey. Retrieved December 5, 2007, from citeseer.ist.psu.edu/dechter98backtracking.html

Dechter, R., & Pearl, J. (1988). Network-based heuristics for constraint satisfaction problems. *Artificial Intelligence, 34,* 1-38.

Dechter, R., & Rish, I. (2003). Mini-buckets: A general scheme for approximating inference. *Journal of the ACM, 50*(2), 107-153.

Freuder, E.C. (1978). Synthesising constraint expressions. *Communications of the ACM, 21*(11), 958-966.

Freuder, E.C. (1982). A sufficient condition for backtrack-free search. *Journal of the ACM, 29,* 24-32.

Freuder, E.C. (1985). A sufficient condition for backtrack-bounded search. *Journal of the ACM, 32*(4), 755-761.

Freuder, E.C. (1992). Partial constraint satisfaction. *Artificial Intelligence, 50,* 510-530.

Freuder, E.C., & Elfe, C.D. (1996). Neighborhood inverse consistency preprocessing. In *Proceedings of the AAAI National Conference* (pp. 202-208). AAAI Press.

Freuder, E.C., & Quinn, M.J. (1985). Taking advantage of stable sets of variables in constraint satisfaction problems. In *Proceedings of the Ninth International Joint Conference on Artificial Intelligenc* (pp. 1076-1078).

Frost, D., & Dechter, R. (1995). Look-ahead value ordering for constraint satisfaction problems. In *Proceedings of the Fourteenth International Joint Conference on Artificial Intelligence* (pp. 572-578).

Frühwirth, T., & Abdennadher, S. (2003). *Essentials of constraint programming.* Springer.

Fulkerson, D.R., Dantzig, G.B., & Johnson, S.M. (1954). Solution of a large scale travelling salesman problem. *Operations Research, 2,* 393-410.

Gallaire, H. (1985). Logic programming: Further developments. In *IEEE Symposium on Logic Programming* (pp. 88-96), Boston, MA. IEEE.

Gaschnig, J. (1974). A constraint satisfaction method for inference making. In *Proceedings of the 12th Annual Allerton Conference on Cirucit and System Theory* (pp. 866-874).

Gaschnig, J. (1979). Performance measurement and analysis of certain search algorithms. CMU-CS-79-124, Carnegie-Mellon University.

Geelen, P.A. (1992). Dual viewpoint heuristics for binary constraint satisfaction problems. In *Proceedings of the Tenth European Conference on Artificial Intelligence* (pp. 31-35).

Ginsberg, M.L. (1993). Dynamic backtracking. *Journal of Artificial Intelligence Research, 1,* 25-46.

Ginsberg, M.L., Frank, M., Halpin, M.P., & Torrance, M.C. (1990). Search lessons learned from crossword puzzles. In *Proceedings of the Eighth National Conference on Artificial Intelligence (AAAI)* (pp. 210-215). AAAI Press.

Ginsberg, M.L., & Harvey, W.D. (1990). Iterative broadening. In *Proceedings of Eighth National Conference on Artificial Intelligence (AAAI-90)* (pp. 216-220). AAAI Press.

Golomb, S., & Baumert, L. (1965). Backtrack programming. *Journal of the ACM, 12,* 516-524.

Gomes, C., Selman, B., & Kautz, H. (1998). Boosting combinatorial search through randomization. In *Proceedings of National Conference on Artificial Intelligence (AAAI)* (pp. 432-327). AAAI Press.

Han, C., & Lee, C. (1988). Comments on Mohr and Henderson's path consistency algorithm. *Artificial Intelligence, 36,* 125-130.

Haralick, R.M., & Elliot, G.L. (1980). Increasing tree search efficiency for constraint satisfaction problems. *Artificial Intelligence, 14,* 263-314.

Harvey, W.D. (1995). Nonsystematic backtracking search (Ph.D. thesis, Stanford University).

Harvey, W.D., & Ginsberg, M.L. (1995). Limited discrepancy search. In *Proceedings of the 14th International Joint Conference on Artificial Intelligence* (pp. 607-613).

Jaffar, J., & Lassez, J.L. (1987). Constraint logic programming. In *Proceedings of the ACM Symposium on Principles of Programming Languages* (pp. 111-119). ACM.

Jaffar, J., & Maher, M.J. (1996). Constraint logic programming—a survey. *Journal of Logic Programming, 19/20,* 503-581.

Korf, R.E. (1996). Improved limited discrepancy search. In *Proceedings of National Conference on Artificial Intelligence (AAAI-96)* (pp. 286-291). AAAI Press.

Kumar, V. (1992). Algorithms for constraint satisfaction problems: A survey. *AI Magazine,* 13(1), 32-44.

Lhomme, O. (1993). Consistency techniques for numeric CSPs. In *Proceedings of the 13th International Joint Conference on Artificial Intelligence* (pp. 232-238).

Mackworth, A.K. (1977a). Consistency in networks of relations. *Artificial Intelligence, 8,* 99-118.

Mackworth, A.K. (1977b). On reading sketch maps. In *Proceedings IJCAI 1977* (pp. 598-606).

Mackworth, A.K., & Freuder, E.C. (1985). The complexity of some polynomial network consistency algorithms for constraint satisfaction problems. *Artificial Intelligence, 25,* 65-74.

Marriott, K., & Stuckey, P.J. (1998). *Programming with constraints: An introduction.* The MIT Press.

McGregor, J.J. (1979). Relational consistency algorithms and their application in finding subgraph and graph isomorphisms. *Information Science, 19*(3), 229-250.

Meseguer, P. (1997). Interleaved depth-first search. In *Proceedings of 15th International Joint Conference on Artificial Intelligence* (pp. 1382-1387).

Mohr, R., & Henderson, T.C. (1986). Arc and path consistency revised. *Artificial Intelligence, 28,* 225-233.

Montanari, U. (1974). Networks of constraints fundamental properties and applications to picture processing. *Information Sciences, 7,* 95-132.

Pesant, G. (2004). A regular language membership constraint for finite sequences of variables. In *Proceedings of the Tenth International Conference on Principles and Practice of Constraint Programming (CP)* (LNCS 3258, pp. 183-195). Springer Verlag.

Prosser, P. (1993). Hybrid algorithms for constraint satisfaction problems. *Computational Intelligence, 9*(3), 268-299.

Prosser, P., Stergiou, K., & Walsh, T. (2000). Singleton consistencies. In *Proceedings, Principles and Practice of Constraint Programming (CP2000)* (LNCS 1894, pp. 353-368). Springer Verlag.

Puget, J. (1998). A fast algorithm for the bound consistency of Alldiff constraints. In *National Conference on Artificial Intelligence (AAAI)* (pp. 359-366). AAAI Press.

Quimper, C.-G., & Walsh, T. (2006). Global grammar constraints. In *12th International Conference on Principles and Practices of Constraint Programming (CP-2006)* (LNCS 4204, pp. 751-755). Springer Verlag.

Régin, J.-C. (1994). A filtering algorithm for constraints of difference in CSPs. In *Proceedings of the National Conference on Artificial Intelligence (AAAI-94)* (pp. 362-367). AAAI Press.

Régin, J.-C. (1996). Generalized arc consistency for global cardinality constraint. In *Proceedings of National Conference on Artificial Intelligence (AAAI-96)* (pp. 209-215). AAAI Press.

Régin, J.-C. (1999). Arc consistency for global cardinality constraints with costs. In *Proceedings of the Fifth International Conference on Principles and Practice of Constraint Programming (CP)* (LNCS 1713, pp. 390-404). Springer Verlag.

Rossi, F., Dahr V., & Petrie, C. (1990). On the equivalence of constraint satisfaction problems. In *Proceedings of the European Conference on Artificial Intelligence (ECAI-90)* (pp. 550-556). Stockholm. MCC (Tech. Rep. No. ACT-AI-222-89).

Rossi, F., Van Beek, P., & Walsh, T. (2006). *Handbook of constraint programming.* Elsevier.

Sabin, D., & Freuder, E.C. (1994). Contradicting conventional wisdom in constraint satisfaction. In *Proceedings of ECAI* (pp. 125-129).

Sabin, D., & Freuder, E.C. (1997). Understanding and improving the MAC algorithm. In *Proceedings of the Third International Conference on Principles and Practice of Constraint Programming* (LNCS 1330, pp. 167-181). Springer Verlag.

Sellmann, M. (2006). The theory of grammar constraints. In *Proceedings of 12th International Conference on Principles and Practice of Constraint Programming (CP2006)* (LNCS 4204, pp. 530-544). Springer Verlag.

Singh, M. (1995). Path consistency revised. In *Proceedings of the 7th IEEE International Conference on Tolls with Artificial Intelligence* (pp. 318-325).

Smith, B.M. (1995). A tutorial on constraint programming (Tech. Rep. No. 95.14). University of Leeds.

Stergiou, K., & Walsh, T. (1999). Encodings of non-binary constraint satisfaction problems. In *Proceedings of the National Conference on Artificial Intelligence (AAAI-99)*, Orlando, FL (pp. 163-168). AAAI Press.

Tsang, E. (1993). *Foundations of constraint satisfaction.* Academic Press.

Van Hentenryck, P. (1989). *Constraint satisfaction in logic programming.* The MIT Press.

Van Hentenryck, P., & Carillon, J.-P. (1988). Generality vs. specificity: An experience with AI and OR techniques. In *National Conference on Artificial Intelligence (AAAI)* (pp. 660-664). AAAI Press.

Van Hentenryck, P., Deville, Y., & Teng, C.-M. (1992). A generic arc-consistency algorithm and its specializations. *Artificial Intelligence, 57,* 291-321.

Van Hentenryck, P., & Michel, L. (2005). *Constraint-based local search.* The MIT Press.

Van Hoeve, W.-J. (2004). A hyper-arc consistency algorithm for the soft all different constraint. In *Proceedings of the Tenth International Conference on Principles and Practice of Constraint Programming (CP)* (LNCS 3258, pp. 679-689). Springer Verlag.

Verfaillie, G., Lemaitre, M., & Schiex, T. (1996). Russian doll search for solving constraint optimization problems. In *Proceedings of AAAI National Conference* (pp. 181-187). AAAI Press.

Verfaillie, G., Martinez, D., & Bessiere, C. (1999). A generic customizable framework for inverse local consistency. In *Proceedings of the AAAI National Conference* (pp. 169-174). AAAI Press.

Walsh, T. (1997). Depth-bounded discrepancy search. In *Proceedings of 15th International*

Joint Conference on Artificial Intelligence (pp. 1388-1393).

Waltz, D.L. (1975). Understanding line drawings of scenes with shadows. In *Psychology of Computer Vision*. New York: McGraw-Hill.

Zhang, Y., & Yap, R. (2001). Making AC-3 an optimal algorithm. In *Proceedings of IJCAI-01* (pp. 316-321).

Chapter IV
Stratified Constraint Satisfaction Networks in Synergetic Multi–Agent Simulations of Language Evolution

Alexander Mehler
Bielefeld University, Germany

ABSTRACT

We describe a simulation model of language evolution which integrates synergetic linguistics with multi-agent modelling. On the one hand, this enables the utilization of knowledge about the distribution of the parameter values of system variables as a touch stone of simulation validity. On the other hand, it accounts for synergetic interdependencies of microscopic system variables and macroscopic order parameters. This approach goes beyond the classical setting of synergetic linguistics by grounding processes of self-regulation and self-organization in mechanisms of (dialogically aligned) language learning. Consequently, the simulation model includes four layers, (i) the level of single information processing agents which are (ii) dialogically aligned in communication processes enslaved (iii) by the social system in which the agents participate and whose countless communication events shape (iv) the corresponding language system. In summary, the present chapter is basically conceptual. It outlines a simulation model which bridges between different levels of language modelling kept apart in contemporary simulation models. This model relates to artificial cognition systems in the sense that it may be implemented to endow an artificial agent community in order to perform distributed processes of meaning constitution.

INTRODUCTION

Computer-based simulation of sign processes is a much considered topic in cognitive linguistics, computer science and related disciplines. Starting from the insight that a biological agent's capacity to survive correlates with its ability to process linguistic signs, a lot of simulation models of the evolution of sign systems have been elaborated (Batali, 1998; Cangelosi & Parisi, 2002b; Kirby,

2002; Steels, 1996, 1998, 2000; Turner, 2002). According to these approaches, neither rule-based nor statistical models alone account for the dynamics of sign systems as an outcome of countless events in which agents make use of signs to serve their communication needs (Andersen, 2000). Rather, the evolution of sign systems—which natural agents use in order to collectively survive—is simulated by means of computer-based *multi-agent systems* (Christiansen & Kirby, 2003).

The paradigm of multi-agent modelling opposes any approach to the simulation of intelligent behaviour by means of *single* artificial agents operating (and thus processing language) in isolation. Rather, intelligent behaviour is seen to emerge from the cooperation of many cognitive systems without being reducible to any single one of them. This is what Hollan et al. (2000) call *distributed cognition*—cf. Maturana and Varela (1980) for a more philosophical grounding of this approach. According to this view, a full *semiotic* (i.e., sign processing) *agent* is seen to be definable only against the background of a community of structurally coupled agents. That is, a single agent is not supposed to re-use a pre-established language, but to cooperatively acquire a sign system as a means of representing and mastering his or her environment (Maturana & Varela, 1980; Rieger, 2002). This is tantamount to a reconstruction of the *grounding problem* (Ziemke, 1999; Riegler et al., 1999) in terms of distributed, social intelligence (Hollan et al., 2000; Steels, 2002). In methodological terms, this means to abandon the approach of strong *artificial intelligence* (Searle, 1980) and artificial life (Pattee, 1988)—insofar as they aim at *realizing* intelligent behaviour by means of artificial agents—in favour of computer-based *simulations* of language evolution.[1]

Approaches to simulation models of language evolution are well documented in the volume of Cangelosi and Parisi (2002b)—see also Kirby (2002) for a comprehensive overview of this field of research.[2] These approaches have in common that they utilize *multi-agent* computer-simulations

(Cangelosi & Parisi, 2002a; Gilbert & Troitzsch, 1999) in order to model aspects of phylo, onto or glossogenetic evolution of language (Christiansen & Kirby, 2003).[3] The *iterated learning model* (Kirby, 2002) can be referred to as an architectural simulation model which addresses the bottleneck problem, according to which a language is transmitted from generation to generation via agents who evidently do not have access to the totality of knowledge characterizing the language to be learned. Consequently, language change—subject to the pressure of varying speaker and hearer needs—is inescapable. Generally speaking, in this and related models language learning is tackled with respect to referential semantics and symbolic grounding in a multi-agent setting (Cangelosi et al., 2002; Steels, 1996, 2002), the learning of lexical knowledge (regarding the articulation of content and expression plane) (Hashimoto, 2002; Hutchins & Hazlehurst, 2002; Kirby & Hurford, 2002), the learning of syntax formation (Hashimoto, 2002; Kirby & Hurford, 2002) and the interrelation of lexico-grammar and semantics (as regards, for example, the emergence of compositionality) (Kirby & Hurford, 2002). All these approaches apply machine learning techniques (e.g., classification, grammar induction, etc.) in order to model language learning of individual agents and thus relate—from a methodological point of view—to *computational linguistics*. Moreover, Kirby and Hurford (2002) demonstrate the usability of frequency distributions as they are studied in quantitative linguistics. Generally speaking, knowledge about the validity of such distributions can be utilized in two respects: First, this knowledge can be used to constrain the model itself. That is, simulations can be endowed by the experimenter with probability distributions restricting the actualization of meanings as represented in semantic space.[4] The semantic space model is a reference model for mapping a certain meaning aspect in cognitive linguistics.

Second, they can be seen as specifying necessary conditions for the validity of the outcome of simulation experiments. In this chapter, we will refer to both of these readings, thereby describing a layered synergetic network of such constraints.

The chapter is organized around four questions:

- **What are relevant levels of linguistic dynamics to be mapped?** One of the central claims of simulation approaches is that they better account for the manifold dynamics of sign processing and thus allow tackling the grounding problem and related issues without the need to pre-establish artificial agents with sign knowledge. Although this chapter does not deal with grounding of meaning representations, it nevertheless identifies various levels of the dynamics of language evolution. This starts with the most elementary level of single sign processing systems and goes up to the level of the language as a whole.

- **What kind of machine learning can be applied in order to implement language learning by the simulation model under consideration?** Simulation models of language evolution necessarily realize a sort of unsupervised learning (though there are also approaches to utilizing the paradigm of supervised learning in language evolution simulation (cf. Turner, 2002)). Amongst other things, this relates to grounding developmental stages of the simulation in terms of corresponding stages (classes) of the social semiotic system(s) being modelled. This holds especially for agent learning as a model of learning as performed by real speakers. In order to shed light on this question, the apparatus of inductive learning is referred to with respect to lexical and schematic knowledge.

- **What are reliable sources of evaluating these simulation models?** As simulation models perform a kind of *unsupervised, distributed learning*, an answer to this question

is even harder to determine. However, there are several starting points of falsification: on the level of single agents, of interpersonal learning and of the speech community as a whole. The chapter contributes to this question too.

- **What are semiotic constraints of sign processing in multi-agent systems?** A central aim of the chapter is to describe *system variables* and *order parameters* which describe and control the unfolding of language acquisition in multi-agent systems, respectively. This is done regarding three operative levels: the level of *individual* sign processing systems, the level of dialogically communicating agents and the system of social networking structuring and stratifying the corresponding speech community. According to cognitive science (Rickheit & Strohner, 1992), any of these levels can be described in terms of its structural/functional integrity, its stability and its creativity to invent new systems. We will likewise outline constraints regarding the evolvement of sign system on these levels.

The chapter is organized as follows: we first integrate several paradigms of machine learning and language modelling utilizing the paradigms of synergetic linguistics and multi-agent simulation. Synergetic linguistics is not left unaffected by this integration. Rather, we reconstruct macroscopic order parameters and microscopic system variables in terms of social networks and agent communication, respectively, and thus dissolve the synergetic abstraction of system needs and speakers/hearers which, in synergetic linguistics, are conceived as, so to speak, idealized interlocutors. Next the four layer-model of language simulation is presented in more detail. That is, the simulated (class of) language system(s) is identified as an epiphenomenal system which is aggregated on grounds of countless communication events performed by information processing agents whose communication is enslaved by the encompassing social system (of social groups, social norms, etc.). We then take up this four-level model and sheds light on constraints interlinking these levels in more detail. Finally, we give a conclusion and prospective on future work. In summary, the chapter concentrates on conceptual modelling, leaving out its implementation to future work.

STRATIFICATION IN LANGUAGE SIMULATIONS

The model to be presented in the following sections is based on five paradigms of language modelling and machine learning: *constraint satisfaction, synergetic linguistics, inductive learning, distributed cognition* and *alignment in communication*. We refer to these paradigms as offering building blocks to be integrated into a simulation of language evolution which models processes of inductive learning on the level of single agents, groups of agents and social networks. A main contribution of the present chapter is an outline of how these strata interact, where their interaction is mainly specified in terms of synergetic constraint satisfaction of order parameters enslaving system variables on the level of individual text processing and dialogical communication.

Constraint Satisfaction

Communication in general, and language comprehension/production in particular, can be described in terms of *constraint satisfaction processes* providing or preventing *coherence* of the focal system (Smolensky, 1995a,b).[5] Thagard (2000) gives a general account of *parallel* constraint satisfaction in the context of optimizing a system's coherence. In this model, coherence maximization is understood as maximizing the degree to which the operative positive/negative constraints are met. More specifically, coherence relations are described as *soft constraints* (Zadeh,

1997). That is, optimizing coherence does not necessarily mean satisfying all, but as many of the most prioritized constraints as possible. The paradigm of constraint satisfaction is related to specifying fitness functions in agent-based simulations of language evolution in terms of genetic algorithms (Turner, 2002), where—instead of directly defining a target function of the system to be simulated—constraints are specified which any candidate solution has to satisfy. The general architecture of Thagard's model looks as follows:

1. **Constituents:** Let E be a finite set of elements $\{e_i \mid i \in I\}$ and $C \subseteq E \times E$ a set of binary constraints, e.g., $(e_i, e_j) \in C$, where C is divided into the set of positive and negative constraints C^+ and C^-, respectively.[6] Further, each constraint is assigned a number w representing its weight.

2. **Optimization:** The coherence problem defined by C on E is solved by partitioning E into two sets A and R (of accepted and refused elements, respectively) so that compliance with the following conditions is maximized:
   - $\forall (e_i, e_j) \in C^+ : e_i \in A \Leftrightarrow e_j \in A$ (a positive constraint is satisfied, if both its elements belong to A).
   - $\forall (e_i, e_j) \in C^- : e_i \in A \Leftrightarrow e_j \in R$ (a negative constraint is satisfied, if its elements are distributed among A and R).

3. **Quantification:** Against this background, "coherence maximization" means that E is partitioned into A and R so that the sum W of weights of positive and negative constraints satisfied by A and R, respectively, is maximized.

In order to instantiate this type of model, several parameters have to be set: "To show that a given problem is a coherence problem ... it is necessary to specify the elements and constraints, provide an interpretation of acceptance and rejection and show that solutions to the given problem do in fact involve satisfaction of the specified constraints" (Thagard, 2000, 20). Following the general idea of Thagard's approach of indirect, pattern-based specifications of fitness functions, we depart from his focus on *parallel* constraint satisfaction by describing constraint satisfaction as evolving in a *stratified* network of synergetic order parameters. Moreover, we do not concentrate on integration processes, but also account for construction in actual, onto-, and glossogenetic learning.

Synergetic Linguistics

A second methodological, but also epistemological, basis of the model to be presented is given by *synergetic linguistics* (Köhler, 1987). It is based on *synergetics* as the theory of spontaneous emergence and development of structures by means of self-organization and regulation (Haken, 1998). Synergetic linguistics describes languages as self-organizing systems whose evolvement is controlled by *order parameters* which constrain or "enslave" the dynamics of the focal system components. As macroscopic units, order parameters (e.g., system needs or groups of interlocutors) do not belong to the level of microscopic units they enslave. The idea is that their dynamics destabilize the language system and thus produce an adaptation pressure which the system answers by evoking mechanisms of self-organization and regulation in order to restore an equilibrium meeting the constraints induced by the operative order parameters. Because of permanently changing order parameters, languages do not reach stable states of equilibrium, but are in a constant state of flux on their own.

According to Köhler (1987), this process evolves by analogy with evolutionary processes based on selection and mutation. Regarding mutation, this can be outlined as follows: Random variants of system properties emerging according to countless fluctuating communication events are subject to a competition in which only those

variants survive which best meet the prevalent system needs. These mechanisms are manifested by microscopic processes (i.e., by processes internal to the system being enslaved) which adapt the affected language units in order to meet the operative system needs. The systematization of macroscopic needs and the clarification of their functional impact on various microscopic variables is an invaluable contribution of synergetic linguistics (Köhler, 1993). This holds, amongst others, for the *need of encoding* (Cod), i.e., the need for linguistic means of encoding meanings and its relation to functional equivalents meeting it (e.g., morphological, lexical, syntactical and prosodical means) (Köhler, 1999).

As will be shown, it is the synergetic perspective on the cooperation and competition of order parameters which allows for an understanding of system variables to span a *constraint network* which Köhler (1993) models, for example, as a system of equations. This conception of a macroscopic constraint network restricting a corresponding microscopic network of constraints enables one to go beyond any simple integration of Zipfian constraints[7] into the framework of simulating language evolution, since it necessarily focuses on the interrelation of order parameters and system variables to be integrated.

The synergetic conception of order parameters allows for the integration of Thagard's constraint satisfaction model: Elements are defined as order parameters or as system variables, whereas acceptance and rejection occur to the degree that the parameter value (or distribution) of a system variable meets the needs restricting it. As far as this integration is alternatively done in the framework of multi-agent-based simulations of language evolution, the level of abstraction of synergetic linguistics has to be replaced in favour of a model of finer resolution. This relates to the structures as well as processes involved. For the time being, synergetic linguistics accounts for the functional relation of order parameters (e.g., minimization of production effort or minimization of memory effort and inventory size) and enslaved variables of the language system (e.g., word length, frequency and lexicon size) on a rather abstract level. This leaves unspecified the learning and acquisition of *specific* linguistic units and their *specific* relations (e.g., of words and their sense relations) as a result of communication between *specific* agents in a multi-agent simulation setting. But from the point of view of agent-based simulations, these learning processes have to be made an object of modelling on their own. This also demands extending the class of models of linguistic dynamics which, for the time being, is modelled—beyond synergetic systems of equations—by means of steady state models and stochastic processes (Altmann & Köhler, 1996):

- *Steady state* models start from assumptions about boundary conditions of the focal language processes in equilibrium in order to derive, for example, probability distributions whose validity is the object of subsequent empirical studies. This kind of modelling does not deny the process view of language, but abstracts from the operative processes by focusing on their summary outputs.
- *Process models* incorporate discrete or continuous time variables in order to describe stochastic processes proceeding from state to state, where each state is described as a system of qualitative/quantitative variables (e.g., construction length, vocabulary size, etc.). Other than steady state models, this allows direct observation of changes of the focal system variables dependent on state alternation (Brainerd, 1976).

The present chapter complements these classes by a (type of) model which is based on a reconstruction of multi-agent-based language simulations in the framework of synergetic linguistics. This approach goes beyond any simple intersection of both modelling paradigms which can be explained as follows:

- *Other than in classical approaches to multi-agent-based simulations*, constraints regarding the values and distributions of the focal system variables are seen to be *systematically interrelated as constituents of a stratified constraint network.*
- *Other than in classical approaches to synergetic modelling*, processes of agent-based language learning are not abstracted away, but modelled with a resolution down to their input/output in the form of *concrete linguistic units, their relations and cognitive processes operating on them.*

It is the latter extension which demands specifying processes of language learning as they are actually performed by social networks and their constitutive agents. In order to do this, single agent learning has to be distinguished from distributed learning performed by groups of agents. We first consider inductive learning of single agents, leaving out deductive and abductive learning in order to keep the model simple.

Inductive Learning and Routinization

Dealing with learning lexico-grammatical knowledge of single agents, at least three questions have to be dealt with:

- How does an agent acquire knowledge about lexical items, their denotations and interrelating sense relations as they are relevant for him to successfully communicate with other agents of the same speech community?
- How does an agent learn references of utterances, that is, how is their interpretation in concrete communication situations finally grounded in sensory perceptions, collaboration with other agents and other kinds of (distributional) cognition?
- How does an agent acquire syntactical and textual knowledge which allows him to produce/comprehend an infinite number of

complex expressions on the basis of finite inventories of linguistic units and encoding means?

These questions refer to learning aspects of structural and referential meaning as well as to the semantic compositionality of complex signs. The following subsections outline first answers in the framework of machine learning and computational linguistics.

Structural Meaning

Latent semantic analysis (LSA) has been proposed as an approach to automatically learning unsystematic sense relations (i.e., contiguity and similarity associations) of lexical units. In the area of lexical ontology learning, this model (or some variant of it) is adapted to derive systematic sense relations (e.g., hyperonymy, synonymy, etc.). Thus, LSA can be seen as a partial answer to the first question. Based on single value decomposition, it proposes a formal mathematical framework for simulating the acquisition of lexical knowledge. More concretely, Landauer and Dumais (1997) propose it as a solution to the knowledge acquisition problem which they describe as follows:

One of the deepest, most persistent mysteries of cognition is how people acquire as much knowledge as they do on the basis of as little information as they get. (Landauer & Dumais, 1997, 212)

The solution Landauer and Dumais (1997) propose is based on the hypothesis that similarity relations of cognitive units result from a *two-level process of inductive learning* starting from the units' contiguity relations. In case of lexical items, these contiguity relations are equated with co-occurrence relations. More specifically, the learning of similarity relations of signs is described as a process of dimensionality reduction, as a result of which similarities of items can be detected even if they do not, or only rarely, co-occur. That

is, similarity associations of linguistic items are described as functions of their contiguity associations. According to this model, inductive learning of similarity relations of linguistic items results from exploiting the similarities of their usage contexts.

This and related approaches follow (some variant of) the so-called *weak contextual hypothesis* (Miller & Charles, 1991). It says that the similarity of the contextual representations of words contributes to their semantic similarity. The weak contextual hypothesis can be traced back to Harris' (1954, 156) distributional hypothesis which states that "... difference in meaning correlates with difference of distribution." Likewise following this line of argumentation is Rieger (2002). But instead of conceptualizing the two-stage process of learning in terms of associationism, he refers to the structuralist opposition of syntagmatic and paradigmatic relations. As these relations can be traced back to a cognitive reinterpretation of contiguity and similarity relations (cf. Jakobson, 1971), Rieger's approach coincides with LSA. Nevertheless, there are two differences which support its preference over LSA: First, his model does not amalgamate contiguity and similarity learning in a single step, but rather keeps both steps apart. Second, he endows a single artificial agent with his two-stage induction algorithm in order to let him learn reference relations. Thus, he tackles the first two questions, even if his model leaves out the collaborative learning of reference relations as claimed by answering the second question.

Referential Meaning

An answer to this second question would serve as a solution of the grounding problem (Ziemke, 1999) which is tackled, for example, in the work of Steels (2002, 2004). It will be disregarded in the present chapter; hence we abstract from the referential meaning of linguistic units. Furthermore, we do not model the agents' environments in terms of a model of physical environment. Rather, we restrict the notion of environment to communication systems and social networking, that is, the environment of an agent at a certain space-time location is seen to include those agents with which it participates in the same communication event at this location. In more general terms, environment is seen to be restricted by a social network which thereby also restricts agent interaction and thus communication. Whether it is possible to disregard grounding (as it is tackled in Steels' approach) and to still speak of a valuable simulation is an open question—for a related discussion in the area of artificial life, compare Pattee (1988). The present model also leaves unspecified social behaviour beyond communication and more elaborate cognitive processes as, for example, strategic planning and cooperative interaction in a simulated environment. How to grasp the dynamics of communication as based on environmental dynamics and the latter kind of processes is an open question too, which will need to be answered in order to make simulation models more realistic.[8]

Compositionality

A general contribution to the third question is given by the *principle of compositionality* (CP). It says that the meaning of a complex expression is a function of the meanings of its parts and the way they are combined (Janssen, 1997). In more general terms, a *compositionality theory* is a formal approach describing a family of properties $\{P_i \mid i \in I\}$ belonging to entities of the focal object area as a function of the same or related properties of these entities' constituents and the way they are combined (Kamp & Partee, 1995). The importance of the CP for simulating the acquisition of linguistic knowledge can be justified on grounds of its *empirical* interpretation in cognitive science. More specifically, Fodor and Pylyshyn (1988) ascribe to compositionality

the role of a precondition of three fundamental properties of cognitive representations as part of a "language of thought." According to the supposed homomorphism of the language of thought and natural languages (Fodor & McLaughlin, 1995), these properties can be reformulated in terms of natural language sentences:

- **Productivity:** Natural languages allow producing/comprehending an infinite number of complex expressions on the basis of finite inventories of elementary morphological, lexical, syntactical and prosodical inventories.
- **Systematicity:** (The meanings of) natural language sentences are systematically related (on the basis of their constituents and their systematic meanings).[9]
- **Inferrability:** Certain sentences are systematically related with certain systematically reproducible inferences.

According to Fodor and Pylyshyn (1988), these properties presuppose compositionality of the language of thought. Davidson (1994) and Partee (1995) likewise view compositionality as a precondition of the learnability of natural languages, an argumentation which can be traced back to Frege (1966). Hintikka and Kulas (1983) contradict these and related argumentations. They state that compositionality can play the role demanded only in conjunction with context-freeness of sign meaning—a demand which is obviously in contradiction to empirical observations. This contradiction is cleared when reformulating the CP in terms of situation semantics (Barwise & Perry, 1983). In order to do this, the principle's parameters need to be generalized accordingly. Replacing, amongst others, *function* by *relation*, one gets the following reformulation of it, henceforth called CP2 (cf. Mehler, 2005):

The meaning of a linguistic item x is a relation over:

- *its usage-regularities;*
- *its usage contexts as systems of (syntactic dependency and) cohesion and coherence relations to which it participates;*
- *the meanings of its components, the way they are combined; and*
- *described situations.*[10]

The interpretation of x in a given context is the situation it describes subject to concrete values of the latter parameters.

Starting from the relational concept of meaning as defined in situation semantics (Barwise & Perry, 1983), this informal specification introduces two extensions: First, *coherence relations* are additionally referred to as determinants of interpretation. Second, it refers to *usage regularities* according to which the interpretation of lexical items can change their usage conditions and thus their interpretation in subsequent communication situations. In this sense, the CP2 introduces a kind of dynamics which relates to *learning* linguistic knowledge (e.g., routinization, schematization, etc.) and which is left out in the classical reading of the CP.

The present version of the CP2 is underspecified in the sense that it contains several innumerable parameters. Usage regularities, for example, are dynamic entities which cannot be enumerated as lexicon entries. In order to tackle their dynamics, the CP2 needs to be redefined by including *procedural models of cognitive processes* which allow computing parameter values subject to the operative contexts:

The meaning of a linguistic item x is a procedure P generating its interpretation based on its usage regularities, the contexts of its usage, the meanings of its components and the way they are combined.

In order to guarantee interpretability of the measurement operation performed by P, it is required that not only its input and output have modelling function with respect to cognitive

entities, but also P with respect to cognitive processes.

In Mehler (2005) the criterion of procedural interpretability is met on grounds of the *constructions-integration* (CI) *theory* of Kintsch (1998). In this model, construction leads to the rather (though not completely) unconstrained generation of possibly incoherent candidate interpretations which are selected in subsequent integration processes in order to derive the most coherent interpretation. Thus, text interpretation is conceived as a process of alternating construction and integration processes, starting with elementary text components and finally integrating—if successful—the input text as a whole.

Comparable to its classical predecessor, the CP2 contains several parameters. This relates to the notion of *context, meaning, linguistic items,* their *components*, the way they are *combined* and the *usage regularities* of elementary items. In Mehler (2005), an instantiation of the CP2 is proposed in terms of a numerical semantics which extends the weak contextual hypothesis of Miller and Charles (1991) to discourse units and thus takes inductive learning of the structural meanings of lexical units into consideration. Moreover, it integrates usage regularities of elementary constituents as an additional parameter and thus accounts for the context-sensitive acquisition of lexical knowledge. Finally, it reconstructs—other than Thagard (2000)—compositionality in the framework of constraint satisfaction by taking integration *and* construction processes into account. This is done by means of operations on semantic spaces, resulting from the two-stage process of inductive learning described above (for details, see Mehler, 2005).

Syntactic Patterns

What is missed in this approach so far is an account of learning syntagmatic patterns (Stubbs, 2001), syntactic patterns and even more complex textual schemata (van Dijk & Kintsch, 1983) which constrain production and comprehension of complex expressions up to whole texts. Although Landauer and Dumais apply their model to learning lexical associations and text similarities only, it is evident how to extend it for learning higher level syntactic patterns. Examples of how this is done are given by Schütze (1997) and Ruge (1995) who apply LSA and related models of similarity associations in order to learn, for example, predicate argument structures and to disambiguate prepositional phrase (PP) attachment. In the present chapter we utilize the framework of Solan et al. (2003). The reason is that it directly builds on Harris's distributional hypothesis in order to develop an algorithm of grammar induction. This algorithm recursively applies the distributional hypothesis that units occurring in the same (or alike) contexts belong to the same category. The algorithm of Solan et al., automatically learns distributional categories and their relations on the basis of a stream of input sentences. Because of its general nature, it is directly applicable to higher level units and thus allows looking forward at learning other than by only syntactical relations (e.g., sentence, text and discourse schemata). This generality makes it suitable for the kind of grammar induction needed in the framework of language learning.

An approach which likewise integrates learning of lexical semantics and grammatical patterns is described by Hashimoto (2002). It can be seen as a reference approach which allows comparative evaluations of newly developed approaches using, for example, different procedural models of learning lexical semantics.

Synthesis

Endowing a single agent with these learning mechanisms, a foundation is laid for his or her solipsistic text comprehension and production. This raises the question of how inductive learning is interrelated with compositional text interpretation.

In other words: How are processes of construction and integration interrelated with processes of knowledge activation and expectation-driven information filtering, and how do these processes together interact with learning lexical, syntactical and textual knowledge by a single text processing system? In order to outline an answer, we utilize the text comprehension model of Schnotz (1994) (cf., Figure 1) who distinguishes the text base, the previous knowledge and the mental model (integrating the latter) as subsystems of text comprehension.[11] According to this approach, bottom-up operating processes of knowledge activation have two functions:

- They serve to transfer information (e.g., about previously unknown and unexpected linguistic/thematic/schematic units) from the stream of text comprehension into the long term memory. This transfer results in a modification of memory composition.
- Second, they concern modifications of the memory structure as a result of activation processes which, in the present model, are seen to be implemented by priming processes.[12] This relates to the priming of linguistic knowledge (as induced by the focal text base) and thematic/schematic knowledge (as induced by the active mental model).

These processes of information transfer and knowledge (pre)activation destabilize the system of previous knowledge which compensates perturbations by means of processes of inductive learning which finally result in modifications of this knowledge base. This affects lexical knowledge as well as syntactical and textual patterns. Beyond that, priming also affects the build-up of mental models. That is, text bases do not only provide informational input for the integration of mental models, but also prime *cotext* (i.e., *linguistic context*) adequate components of them.

Figure 1. The modified diagram of Schnotz (1994) added by pictograms of short and long-term cognitive processes

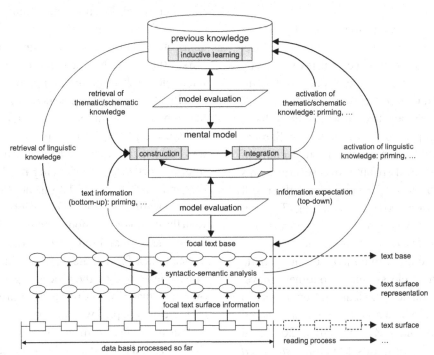

Top-down operating processes of knowledge retrieval have equally two functions:

- They provide linguistic, thematic and schematic knowledge as input for the generation of text bases and mental models, respectively.
- Beyond that, knowledge retrieval also provides expectation-driven constraints of text interpretation on both levels.

Following this line of argumentation, *construction* and *integration* occur on the level of the actual-genetic generation of text bases and mental models: Top-down operating retrieval processes provide, together with bottom-up operating priming processes, construction alternatives, where the former also retrieve integration constraints. Successfully integrated units are themselves the starting point of activation and information transfer (from the text base level to the level of mental models, and from there to the knowledge level). On the other hand, inductive learning occurs on the level of onto-genetic knowledge acquisition and maintenance. A central idea of the chapter is that the cooperation/competition of priming, construction and integration is described in summary by the CP2 , whereas inductive learning evolves according to the two-stage process of syntagmatic and paradigmatic learning—*on all levels of linguistic resolution*. Of course, this is a simplification regarding the variety of learning. It is indispensable in order to have, firstly, a sufficiently complex learning system which, secondly, allows simulating language learning *without the need to presuppose knowledge on any of these levels and thus without the need to supervise learning.*

Distributed Cognition and Alignment in Communication

The inductive learning model presented so far focuses on single learning agents which produce/process a stream of monological texts, thereby building-up a linguistic knowledge system (including, for example, lexical units, sense relations, syntactic patterns and textual schemata). What is missed in this approach is an account of collaborative, distributive learning, that is, an account of inductive learning distributed over several agents which is both the very condition and the result of their structural, cognitive coupling. To put it in other words: An approach to *organizational, glossogenetic learning* of linguistic structures is needed in addition to a model of ontogenetic learning of a single system as outlined above. Learning linguistic knowledge is now object to the acquisition of a shared lexicon and a shared grammar (Hutchins & Hazlehurst, 2002). In cognitive linguistics, this kind of *distributed learning* can be studied, as far as it is based on dialogical communication in terms of *alignment in communication* (Pickering & Garrod, 2004; Rickheit 2005).

Pickering and Garrod's alignment model describes dialogical communication as a process of mutual structural coupling of interlocutors on various levels of cognitive-linguistic representation. Other than approaches to coordination-by-negotiation, this approach to coordination-by-alignment hypothesizes a great part of structural coupling to be done automatically by means of short-term priming and long-term routinization mechanisms. More specifically, "data transmissions" of interlocutors via a restricted multi-model channel are seen to evoke, maintain and stabilize (if successful) a process of increasing structural coupling, possibly leading to a recurrent coupling of situation models and the generation of dialogue routines. A central advantage of this model is that it does not rely on a notion of strategically, intentionally controlled alignment, but focuses on

the emergence of aligned (though not necessarily shared) representations and processing/production routines of different interlocutors.

The alignment model can be utilized as an elementary *interaction model* (Hutchins & Hazlehurst, 2002, 281) which accounts for *collaborative* language production and comprehension. More specifically, it *couples* production and comprehension processes in the sense that, as Pickering and Garrod (2004, 176) put it, the "... interlocutors build up utterances as a joint activity ..., with interlocutors often interleaving production and comprehension tightly." This is the starting point for integrating the dialogical alignment model with the monological model of compositional text comprehension and inductive learning. It has to be accounted for that the input text in Figure 1 is in part generated by the processing agent on his own and that his text production/processing is dialogically coupled with at least one other agent so that inter-agent priming occurs according to Pickering and Garrod's model. If successful, this inter-agent priming invokes an actual-genetic coupling of the interlocutors' mental models, which may result in an ontogenetic coupling of their knowledge bases as it is confirmed by subsequent interactions. Figure 2 demonstrates this situation by example of two agents. The interlocking of their text productions simplifies the interleaving of production and comprehension processes. This asks for a quantitative, distributional model of turn-taking as an order parameter of dialogical alignment (see below) which obviously needs to be embedded into a model of group formation and social networking, allowing the derivation a respective turn-taking distribution for any group of interlocutors.

So far, the interaction model only describes immediate, dialogical communication of agents, which is seen to be further constrained by synergetic order parameters (see Figure 5). These constraints result from its embedding into a model of *distributed interaction* of possibly nested, overlapping groups of agents (see Figure

Figure 2. Dialogical alignment of two interlocutors

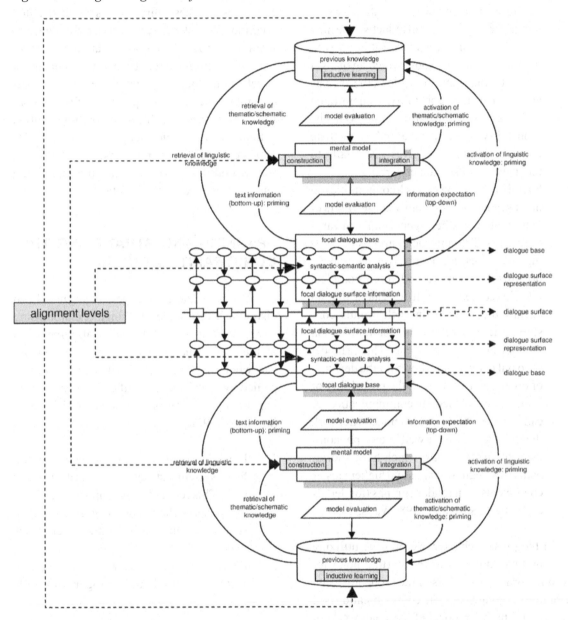

6). This embedding of the elementary dialogical model of linguistic interaction allows accounting for two related processes (left out in many other approaches to computer-based simulation of language evolution):

- **Mediate learning:** Speech communities with a literary language to allow for the

dispensing of the spatiotemporal continuity of text production and reception (Rieger, 2002). That is, interlocutors have the opportunity to learn *mediately* from other agents of the same community, even if they are not physically present in the communication situation, by reading their textual output, whether the writers are still alive or not. In the present framework, this situation is easily integrated by processes of inductive learning embodied by single agents. But in order to do this, we have to know which agents get which textual input by which other agents and with which probability. Generalizing this question, we need to know both: the probability of immediate and of mediate communication. This gives rise finally to the question of social networking.

- **Social networking:** Speech communities do not just consist of randomly chosen pairs of interlocutors. Rather, agents join—in varying roles—different social groups of varying size which are themselves recursively organized into more and more complex, interlinked networks. It is evident that an agent's membership in such groups constrains the probability of his communication with (groups of) other agents. Thus, a model of social networking allows for the deriving of order parameters with the probability of immediate and mediate communication. A candidate model comes from social network theory. It relates to the well known phenomenon of *small worlds*, which have shorter paths than regular graphs and higher cluster coefficients than random graphs (for details cf. Watts & Strogatz, 1998; Watts, 1999).

In the present chapter, we propose utilizing the small world theory as the starting point for deriving order parameters of the probability distribution of groupwise agent communication (see Figure 6). That is, a model of the small world of social networking is seen to allow for specifying the probability by which agents communicate with each other in certain roles.

So far, the synergetic multi-agent model accounts for language learning on three different strata: on the level of single agents, on the level of dialogical systems and on the level of social networks as a whole. The basic idea of the syn-

ergetic multi-agent model is to integrate learning processes on these three levels of distributed cognition: as enslaved system variables, as mechanisms of self-regulation/organization or as order parameters in a synergetic network of constraint satisfaction. Thus, an instantiation of this model specifies which input/output units of which cognitive processes of self-regulation/organization actually serve as microscopic system variables which enslave order parameters.[13] The following section outlines such a separation into explaining and explained variables in detail.

SPANNING AND STRATIFYING THE CONSTRAINT NETWORK

So far, three strata of language learning have been distinguished, on the level of single text processing systems, of systems of dialogical alignment and on the level of the corresponding social network as a whole. This vertical stratification is accompanied by a horizontal stratification distinguishing three perspectives on systems (Rickheit & Strohner, 1992):

1. From the point of view of *tectonics*, the focal system's structural integrity is dealt with. This relates to its composition, i.e., its components, their relations and the system's functional embedding into its environment.

2. From the point of view of *dynamics*, a system's (actual and ontogenetic) self-

Table 1. Representation levels of simulation models of language evolution

	Tectonics	Dynamics	Genetics
Text System	table (4)	table(4)	table (4)
Dialogue System	table (5)	table (5)	table (5)
Text Network	table(6)	table (6)	table (6)
Social Network	table(6)	table(6)	table (6)
Language System	table (7)	table (7)	table (7)

Figure 3. Comparison of the agent-abstracting model of synergetic linguistics and the agent-including model of synergetic simulation of language evolution

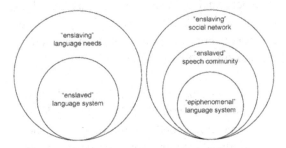

regulation is dealt with. This relates, more specifically, to processes of compensating perturbations from the system environment, which evoke destabilizing changes of system state. This perspective necessarily concerns the actual-genetic *process view* on a system's information processing.[14]

3. From the point of view of *genetics*, systems are described in terms of (onto- and phylogenetic) self-organization. This also includes the generation of new (sub) systems which are describable regarding their tectonics, dynamics and genetics on their own.[15]

As Rickheit and Strohner (1992) demonstrate, text processing, communication and language systems as a whole can be described along these perspectives. This gives a 3×3 matrix of views on language simulation. We extend this matrix in two respects (see Table 1):

•   First, a layer of text and social networking is introduced. The reason is twofold: First, dialogically manifested immediate learning operates as a process of self-organization on system variables whose dynamics are partly controlled by the small world of the encompassing social network which constrains, for example, the probability of verbal interaction. This dependence is reflected by introducing the

layer of social networking in Table 1. Secondly, textually manifested mediate learning likewise affects system variables, whose dynamics are partly controlled by the small world of the encompassing text network which constrains, for example, the probability of text linkage (e.g., by means of citation relations). This dependence is reflected by introducing the layer of text networking in matrix (1). Consequently, these two types of networks are likewise specified with respect to their tectonics, dynamics and genetics (see Table 4).

•   The second further development concerns the specification of each cell of Table 1, not only with respect to its support system (e.g., text, dialogue or language system), but in particular with respect to system variables (modelled, for example, as summary indices or distributions) and cognitive processes operating on them, which serve as candidate order parameters and enslaved system variables, respectively.

These preliminaries allow specifying a stratified synergetic constraint satisfaction process as the procedural kernel of simulations of language evolution: As far as language evolution is concerned, variables of the focal language system (e.g., the composition of its lexicon, the system of its text types, etc.—cf. Table 5) serve as "enslaved" units, whose parameter values are controlled by the dynamics of environmental order parameters. In accordance with Altmann (1985), this environment is seen to be spanned by the speakers/hearers of the corresponding speech community. But other than Altmann, we view it being stratified in the sense of Table 1. That is, we consider it to consist of a system of interlocutors whose (dialogical) text production is controlled by the social network to which they belong. In this sense, the language environment is seen to consist of agents and their mono- and dialogical output, whose environment is, in turn, spanned by the corresponding social network and its textual manifestation in the form of a text network. This has important consequences regarding the status of the language system to be simulated: Other than Köhler (1987, 1993), we do not consider it to be directly affected by environmental system needs whose procedural organization is— just as their corresponding language internal mechanisms of self-organization—abstracted away. Rather, the social network is (together with its textual manifestation) seen as enslaving the distributed system of speakers/hearers of the corresponding speech community. Consequently, parameter values of the focal language system are seen to be epiphenomenal with respect to these dynamics. At the same time, this conception allows specifying all processes of self-regulation and organization in terms of concrete cognitive processes which the enslaved systems invoke in order to compensate perturbations from their environment.[16] In other words: In the present framework, models of self-regulation and organization are introduced as models of agent internal cognitive processes (of language processing and learning), whereas social network internal processes are conceived as procedural order parameters. Finally, language internal processes, as described for example by Ricœur (1976), are seen as epiphenomenal abstractions of these latter processes.

But how do co-enslaving constraints interact in this model? And how do we know whether the simulation is valid? It is now that synergetic linguistics comes into play again. According to its terminology, we have to distinguish (i) system internal processes adapting (ii) system variables according to the dynamics of (iii) certain order parameters which may be given by system variables or processes on their own.[17] In this scenario, the role of synergetic constraints can be explained as follows: System variables span constraint networks restricting each other's parameter values. The smaller the inventory of phonemes of a language, for example, the longer the average length of its words. Interrelations of this kind can be seen to be mediated by the impact of system needs. In the present example, the need for mini-

mizing the effort of language production and of memorizing signs ask for shorter words (Köhler, 1986). A central insight of synergetic linguistics is that such interrelationships are common and thus span dense networks of constraints on the values of system variables (e.g., lexicon size, polylexy or polytexty). From the point of view of evaluation, this has important consequences:

- If a system variable *is not included* into the simulation, that is, if there is no order parameter included into the simulator, whose (im)mediate impact on this variable is simulated (or if its values are not pre-established by the modeller), the value taken by this variable as a result of simulation runs can be compared with the observed/expected value of the corresponding variable in the simulated (class of) system(s), provided that the initial conditions of the simulator and its simulation time measure a certain state of the (class of) simulated system(s) and a certain period of its lifetime, respectively. In this case, a correspondence, but not necessarily a similarity as claimed by Gilbert and Troitzsch (1999), between the *uncontrolled* and the *simulated* variable is a touchstone of simulation validity. That is, knowledge about a language subsystem behaving in a certain way and a simulation of this behaviour in which certain parameter values *emerge* as valuable measurements of certain simulated variables can be used as an indicator of simulation quality: If the correspondence is missed, the simulation is *falsified*, otherwise it is *not falsified*, but nothing more. According to synergetics, emergence means, amongst other things, that the parameter value of the corresponding system variable is neither predetermined by the modeller, nor determined by the operative order parameters. A prominent example is the emergence of compositionality in the experiments of Kirby and Hurford (2002).

Table 2 . Views on single text processing systems and their textual input/output

SYSTEM LEVEL	TECTONICS	DYNAMICS	GENETICS
Support System	a mental model resulting / underlying text processing / production	a text comprehension or production process of a single agent	the cognitive learning apparatus of a single agent
Microscopic System Variables:			
Attributes and Indices	**expression plane:** • text vocabulary size • segment length • text length and Zipfian number • Markov order of text structuring • ... **content plane:** • genre and register affiliation (w.r.t field, tenor and mode) • number of topics • readability, activity... • ...	• short term memory size • balance between compositionality and contextuality • processing time • cognitive capacity / cognitive load • Markov order of text processing / production • ...	• long term memory size (lexicon size, etc.) • balance between analytic / synthetic and idiomatic means of encoding • learner age / learning capacity / duration / transfer rate / etc. • learning periodicity • learnable "grammar" type • ...
Distributions	• frequency structure or spectrum of text units • length distribution of text units • preference ordering of topics ... • ...	• Markov processes on various language levels • vocabulary growth • periodicity (repetition / clustering / aggregation of identical / alike elements) • ...	• parameterization and transition between distributions • ...
Mechanisms of Self-Regulation (Dynamics) and -Organization (Genetics):			
Processes	• procedural organization of the operative mechanisms • ...	• construction and integration • evaluation and reparation • lexical, syntactic, semantical and textual priming • information percolation between different processing levels • ...	• memorization, inventarization, superization, idiomatization, routinization (as the long-term correspondent of priming) and schematization • (two-level) inductive learning of lexico-grammatical patterns (e.g., grammar and text schema induction) • synergetic balancing between functional equivalents of encoding • diversification, unification • ...

• If instead, the impact of competing/cooperating order parameters on the focal variable is part of the simulation, that is, if the modeller specifies the way they (in)directly affect its parameter values, three constellations of constraint satisfaction can be distinguished: on the level of interrelations of microscopic system variables, on the level of macroscopic order parameters and on the level of interrelations of these two levels. Köhler (1987) models these interrelations as functions in order to derive the controlled variables' values by means of value insertions. Grounding instead models of self-regulation and organization in models of cognitive processes of short-term priming and of long-term routinization, of text comprehension/production and of alignment, we propose to run simulations of the competition/cooperation of order parameters which derive *simulated data* regarding the composition of the lexico-grammatical system of the simulated (class of) language, which finally allows deriving summary indices as, for example, "lexicon size" and "polylexy." In this case, the pre-established parameter values and distributions serve as constraints on simulation runs.

In both scenarios, an evaluation of a simulation model also means an evaluation of the implementations of the cognitive processes included. But, as synergetic linguistics teaches, observing system variables in isolation does not suffice to evaluate a system. Consequently, the next modelling step concerns the specification of system variables, order parameters *and their interrelations*.[18] Quantitative linguistics and soft computing offer a great variety of choices for modelling them as univariate, bivariate or multivariate indices, as distributions and feature spaces or as systems of fuzzy rules and related systems of structure modelling (Mehler, 2004). If, for example, word length is considered as a system variable, it may be modelled by means of a statistical moment of a certain distribution or by the distribution itself. The Tables 2-5 make these distinctions on the levels of indices, distributions and multidimensional feature spaces, and map them onto the respective strata and system perspectives as distinguished in Table 1.

These considerations allow us to finally specify: A *synergetic multi-agent simulation model* is a four level multi-agent simulation model whose runs produce simulated data fitting a system of indices, distributions, etc. which independently characterizes the class of natural languages. Independently means that the validity of this system is confirmed by independent linguistic investigations on the synergetic nature of natural languages. A synergetic multi-agent simulation model thus includes (i) the microscopic level

of single information processing (i.e., text and dialogue processing/producing) agents (Table 2) which are (ii) dialogically aligned in communication processes (Table 3) enslaved (iii) by the macroscopic social system in which the agents participate (Table 4) and whose countless communication acts shape (iv) their language as an epiphenomenal system whose attributes aggregate the corresponding attributes of the single agents (Table 5).

CONSTRAINT NETWORKING IN A ZIPFIAN PERSPECTIVE

In the last section, social networks were described as providing order parameters with respect to the strata of monological and dialogical text processing. It was further argued that constraint networks operate on these three strata. Polytexty, for example, interrelates with polylexy which, on its part, interrelates with lexicon size (Köhler, 1986). This section sheds more light on this kind of constraint networking on the level of order parameters and microscopic system variables. This is done by focusing on lexical meaning, that is, on lexical relations of the content and expression plane.

According to Tuldava (1998), distributions of semiotic units tend to follow a preference ordering along decreasing importance. He refers to Zipf's first law (Zipf, 1972) as an example of this more general law of *semiotic preference order*. It describes a topological invariant which seems to play a comparative role in quantitative descriptions of social systems as the Gaussian distribution with respect to natural systems. Zipf-like distributions also play an invaluable role in constraining and evaluating simulations of language systems. Consequently, Table 5 mentions Zipf's law (on the relationship of rank and frequency) and (the law of) semantic diversification on a certain relation of expression and content plane. As Zipf's consideration on linguistic frequency

Table 3. Views on alignment systems and their dialogical manifestations

SYSTEM LEVEL	TECTONICS	DYNAMICS	GENETICS
Support System	an alignment model of a conversation of at least two interlocutors	an alignment process implemented by at least two interlocutors	a distributed cognitive system of at least two interlocutors
Microscopic System Variables			
Attributes and Indices	**field:** • number of topics communicated • ... **tenor:** • number, roles and relations of interlocutors • number of turns • ... **mode:** • modes and media • direct / indirect communication • ...	• Markov order of turn taking • inter-interlocutor latency, duration of priming • duration of communication • ...	• long term memory size (latency of models of interlocutors) • ...
Distributions	**field:** • topic distribution • ... **tenor:** • distribution of roles • distribution of turns • length distribution of turns • ... **mode:** • distribution of modes and media • ...	• Markov process of turn taking • periodicity (repetition, clustering and aggregation of like elements) across turn taking • ...	• parameterization and transition between distributions • ...
Mechanisms of Self-Regulation (Dynamics) and -Organization (Genetics):			
Processes	• procedural organization of the operative mechanisms • ...	• interpersonal alignment • cooperative evaluation and reparation • interpersonal lexical, syntactic and semantic priming between interlocutors • information percolation between alignment levels • ...	• cooperative memorization, inventarization, superization, idiomatization, routinization (as the long-term correspondent of priming) and schematization • interpersonal learning of dialogue routines, ... • synergetic balancing between functional equivalent modes in a multi-modal setting • ...

Table 4. Views on social networks and their textual/dialogical manifestations

SYSTEM LEVEL	TECTONICS	DYNAMICS	GENETICS
Support System	a cognitively distributed model of a text network	a short-term networking process of a speech community	the long-term learning apparatus of a speech community
Macroscopic Order Parameters			
Attributes and Indices	**expression plane (text network):** • number of nodes, hubs, edges, components, … • cluster coefficient, compactness • average path length, diameter • … **content plane (genre and register level):** • number of genres, registers, text types • …	• network latency • flow rate and velocity of topical, thematic propagation • Markov order of text chain and cluster formation • growth rate of text chains (of registers (thematic fields) and genres) • social permeability, openness,	• size of long-term cultural memory (capacity to invent different genres, registers and their relations) • birth- and mortality rate of registers (thematic fields) and genres • …
Distributions	**expression plane:** • distribution of component size, text chain length, node connectivity, clustering, centrality and prestige, of path length, … • distribution of main- and borderlines, branch points, … • … **content plane:** • preference order of genres / registers, • stratification, nesting of genres / registers • …	• Markov processes on text chain continuation, … • temporal organization of text chains • distribution of the growth rate • periodicity of thematization / topicalization (repetition, clustering, aggregation of alike text network components) • …	• distribution of birth, growth maturity, decay of genres, registers, text types, … • …
Mechanisms of Self-Regulation (Dynamics) and -Organization (Genetics):			
Processes	• procedural organization of the operative mechanisms • …	• initiation, continuation, combination, parallelization, …, termination of text chains • inserting, replacing, deleting, rewiring, linking, clustering, … of textual/dialogical units … • …	• conventionalization • inductive learning of types of single texts, of text chains, clusters, of (sub-) network types, … • synergetic balancing of the system of genres, registers and text types • …

Table 5. Views on language systems

SYSTEM LEVEL	TECTONICS	DYNAMICS	GENETICS
Support System	language system	language use	language change
Simulated, Epiphenomenal Microscopic System Variables			
Indices	• lexicon size • average unit (word, phrase, sentence, text ...) and length • average polylexy • average polytexty • rate of neologisms • rate of idiomatization • degree of compositionality • number of genres, registers and text types • ...	• polytexty rate of change • order of Markov processes of the genre- / register-sensitive usage of linguistic items • ...	• Polylexy rate of change invention / durability / shrinking rate of linguistic items, attributes and categories ... • velocity of propagation and propagation rate of new linguistic items, attributes and categories ... • rate of change of the fractions of morphological, lexical, syntactical and prosodical encoding means • ...
Distributions	• Zipf's laws • length distributions • semantic and formal diversification / unification • distribution of the fractions of morphological, lexical, syntactical and prosodical encoding means • distribution of linguistic units and pattern units over special languages • ...	• distribution of general and genre-/register-specific lexical units • Markov processes of the genre-/register-sensitive usage of linguistic items • distribution of the changes of polytexty • ...	• age distribution of linguistic units • distribution of the polytexty changes • word formation and loaning (Piotrowski's law) • time distribution of the fractions of morphological, lexical, syntactical and prosodical encoding means • ...
Structures and Processes	• kernel vocabulary, technical terminologies and special languages and lexical fields • lexico-grammar • text types • ...	• percolation of items between different word fields • ...	• invention of new lexico-grammatical and textual categories, patterns and schemata • invention, termination, fusion and splitting of lexical fields • ...

distributions have already been utilized for constraining the initial conditions of simulations of language evolution (Kirby & Hurford, 2002), we now place emphasis on the integration of preference orderings into the framework of synergetic constraint satisfaction. This is done with respect to *semantic diversification* (Altmann, 1991) on the level of single linguistic items and on the level of the lexical system as a whole.

Altmann (1996) explains the process of semantic diversification as follows: At the time of their emergence, lexical items are in a state of semantic

unification, that is, they have only one meaning. As their frequency of usage in ever-changing communication situations increases, they tend to adopt additional meanings in order to meet the speakers' need for minimizing encoding effort. If this process evolved without restraint, it would result in a system-wide semantic diversification in which as few lexical items as possible manifest as many meanings as are needed to encode. In this case, the polysemy of lexical items would increase on average. But diversification is opposed by unification processes which tend to decrease polysemy in order to meet the hearers' need for minimizing decoding effort. As a consequence of an unrestricted evolvement of unification, more and more items would carry less and less meanings. It is assumed that the competition of these opposing needs results in a dynamic equilibrium which is characterized by rank frequency distributions where—from the point of view of a single item—the empirically most frequent (theoretically most probable) meaning has the first rank, and the most infrequent meanings take up the lowest ranks. Distributions of this sort model a characteristic decrease in probability which guarantees that in cases of a decoding error (if the first option of highest rank fails) the proximate choice still has the same degree of differentiability compared to the remaining options. In other words, probability distributions are assumed which keep constant a high "recall rate" in case of successive decoding errors along the ranked meanings. From the point of view of the hearer, such distributions decrease the effort of decoding compared to rectangular distributions characterizing highly polysemous units. From the point of view of the speaker, such distributions decrease the effort of encoding compared to unambiguous items.

As theses processes are distributed over all communication situations in which speakers/ hearers of the corresponding speech community participate, they distinguish two perspectives: Whereas Altmann (1991) focuses on the semantic diversification of single units in isolation, it is the distribution of meanings over all lexical units which is studied by Krylov's *law of polysemy*. According to Krylov (1982), the distribution of the number f_x of lexical items with exactly x meanings, $x = 1, 2, ...$, shows concentration and dispersion effects as they are characteristic of diversification processes. Krylov hypothesizes that the number of polysemous words decreases according to a geometric progression with their number of meanings so that the set of unambiguous items covers 50 percent of the lexicon, the set of items with exactly two meanings 25 percent and so on

till the set of most polysemous words is reached covering only a tiny fraction of the lexicon. This relationship is described by the formula:

$$P_x = 2^{-x} \tag{1}$$

where P_x is the probability of randomly choosing a lexical item with exactly x meanings from the lexicon of the focal language. According to this model, Krylov hypothesizes that natural language words have on average two meanings.

Semantic diversification of single units and of the lexical system as a whole is complemented by inverse processes of synonym formation—on the level of single meanings and the meaning system as a whole (Altmann, 1996).[19] Whereas hypotheses on semantic diversification have already been confirmed in many empirical studies, their counterparts regarding formal diversification have not.

Now the question arises how polysemy and synonymy on a system level interact with semantic and formal diversification on the level of system components. That is, we ask how regularities on these different levels *constrain each other*. In order to keep things simple, we abstract away from the stratification of the lexicon according to common and genre/register specific vocabularies. This allows reformulating the latter question by

Table 6. A two-dimensional distribution of units of content and expression plane

	M_1	M_2	M_3	$\ldots$	M_n
x_1	f_{11}	$\ldots$			f_{1n}
x_2	$\vdots$	$\ddots$			
x_3					
$\vdots$					
x_m	f_{m1}				f_{mn}

means of Table 6 which opposes lexical units x_1, ..., x_m by meanings M_1, ..., M_n, abstracting from any concrete definition of what meaning is as well as from meaning relations as they are demanded by the purpose of getting a simplified picture of the whole landscape.

Next, we hypothesize that x_i is the ith most frequently used lexical item and M_j the jth most frequently coded meaning of the focal language L. Consequently, x_1 is the most frequently used item and M_1 the most frequently encoded meaning in L. In other words, it is hypothesized that—as predicted by the impact of diversification and unification *on the expression and content plane* of L—the most "important" meaning of a language is encoded by its most frequent word which, according to Köhler (1987), is also supposed to be (one of) the shortest items in the lexicon. Moreover, following the considerations on semantic diversification of single lexical units, it is implied that rows of matrix (2) tend by the majority to manifest a monotonously falling rank frequency distribution (supposing that those cells are disregarded for which $f_{ij} = 0, i \in \{1, ..., m\}, j \in \{1, ..., n\}$).[20] The same kind of consideration also relates to the content plane, and thus to the expectation of monotonously decreasing frequency distributions manifested by the columns of matrix (2). Further, we can assume that the marginal distribution of lexical items x_1, ..., x_m follows a variant of Zipf's law and that the marginal distribution of meaning units M_1, ..., M_n analogously follows a frequency distribution. Moreover, if we apply a function to any cell of matrix (2) which decides for any frequency f_{ij} whether item x_i should count as having meaning M_j, it is evident that this matrix also derives a distribution whose fitting with formula (1) can be tested. As far as all these assumed distributions are valid, an interrelation of semantic diversification on the level of single units and the law of polysemy can be stated too. These considerations finally raise the question for the kind of two-dimensional distribution of the total system of lexical units and lexically coded meanings of

L. That is, we can ask whether interdependencies of all diversification and unification processes are integrated by a single two-dimensional distribution. In order to make this model more realistic, the stratification of both planes according to the operative system of genres and registers (and their linguistic manifestations in the form of text types) has to be considered too. That is, we expect not a single two-dimensional distribution, but a system of them according to the distribution of language over these genres and registers, respectively. Nevertheless, each of these subsystem-specific distributions is expected to show the same kind of regularities and interdependencies as described so far. Thus, the evolvement of the genre/register system has to be considered a further level of synergetic constraint networking.[21]

These considerations show a remarkable interweaving of constraints regarding the distribution of lexical units and their meanings, which have to be reproduced by language simulations as far as these distributional hypotheses are empirically and sufficiently confirmed. As explained above, this includes semantic and formal diversification of single lexical items and meaning units as well as diversification on the level of the lexicon as a whole. This also includes the Zipfian gestalt of the frequency distribution of lexical units, its analogue on content plane and Krylov's considerations on the distribution of polysemy. It additionally includes Köhler's study on the relation of item frequency and item length and thus indirectly relates formal and semantic attributes. Following the line of argumentation of the last section, any specific simulation experiment has to decide *ex ante* which of these variables is controlled by which order parameters and which of them are left out as touchstones for a subsequent evaluation. The key point now is that whatever decision is made, synergetic linguistics places emphasis on a further level of evaluation: Although a simulation may result in simulated data which obey these distributions separately, it may nevertheless be the case that their interdependencies are not met—in contradiction to what is known about these interdependencies. In other words, obeying a distributional constraint is only a necessary, but not a sufficient, condition as long as their synergetic interdependencies are not taken into consideration.

These considerations motivate a sequence of stages of evaluation:

1. In this sequence, the lowest level of validity is reached if the simulated data only fit a single (probability) distribution in the sense that the differences of the simulated distribution and the one derived from theoretical and confirmed by empirical investigations (independently from the simulation) are statistically insignificant.[22]
2. This validity is augmented to the rate that more and more distribution models of the latter kind are fitted.
3. As long as the distributions are met independently form each other, a further level of validity is still missed which relates to the synergetic interdependencies of the distributions restricting their specific parameters.[23]

According to the varying numbers of distributions and their possible synergetic constraints, which are included as variables into the second and third stage of this sequence, this coarse-grained graduation can be further subdivided. Evidently, the system of indices and distributions characterizing the epiphenomenal language system layer is a valuable candidate for such evaluations.

CONCLUSION

This chapter presented a first attempt in systematizing the strata, order parameters and system variables of a simulation model of language evolution which finally grounds mechanisms of self-organization and regulation in cognitive processes

of inductive learning—*on the level of single agents and on the level of alignment in communication.* Following this line of argumentation, Section (4) exemplified a network of lexical-semantic system variables. It shows that the values they take by simulation runs cannot serve as a touchstone for the validity of the simulation model *as long as they are analyzed in isolation*, nor can they—for the very same reason—constrain the simulation separately if they are included as order parameters. Rather, system variables are synergetically interlinked and thus need to be observed in accordance with this network. This can be seen as making a speech for a cooperation of research in synergetic linguistics and machine learning in order to implement this new kind of simulation model of language evolution. As such, simulations indispensably include models of inductive learning of linguistic knowledge; they do not need to presuppose this knowledge and thus can perform without supervised learning. Such a simulation model prospectively integrates synergetic and fuzzy linguistics in order to reconstruct synergetic order parameters and their impact on system variables by means of fuzzy constraints.

ACKNOWLEDGMENT

Many thanks go to Reinhard Köhler and Burghard Rieger for their support on thinking about opening synergetic linguistics and fuzzy linguistics to computer-based simulations in the framework of *multi*-agent modelling and to the anonymous reviewers for their useful hints and comments to the present work.

REFERENCES

Altmann, G. (1985). On the dynamic approach to language. In T.T. Ballmer (Ed.), *Linguistic dynamics. Discourses, procedures and evolution* (pp. 181-189). Berlin-New York: de Gruyter.

Altmann, G. (1991). Modelling diversification phenomena in language. In U. Rothe (Ed.), *Diversification processes in language: Grammar* (pp. 33-46). Medienverlag, Hagen, The Netherlands: Margit Rottmann.

Altmann, G. (1996). Diversification processes of the word. In *Glottometrika 15* (pp. 102-111). WVT: Trier.

Altmann, G., & Köhler, R. (1996). "Language forces" and synergetic modelling of language phenomena. In *Glottometrika 15* (pp. 62-76). Bochum: Brockmeyer,.

Andersen, P. B. (2000). Genres as self-organising systems. In P.B. Andersen, C. Emmeche, N.O. Finnemann, & P.V. Christiansen (Eds.), *Downward causation: Minds, bodies and matter* (pp. 214-260). Aarhus: Aarhus University Press.

Barwise, J., & Perry, J. (1983). *Situations and attitudes.* Cambridge, MA: MIT Press.

Batali, J. (1998). Computational simulations of the emergence of grammar. In J. R. Hurford, M. Studdert-Kennedy, & C. Knight (Eds.), *Approaches to the evolution of language* (pp. 405-426). Cambridge: Cambridge University Press.

Brainerd, B. (1976). On the Markov nature of the text. *Linguistics, 176*, 5-30.

Cangelosi, A., Greco, A., & Harnad, S. (2002). Symbol grounding and the symbolic theft hypothesis. In A. Cangelosi & D. Parisi (Eds.), *Simulating the evolution of language* (pp. 191-210). London: Springer Verlag.

Cangelosi, A., & Parisi, D. (2002a). Computer simulation: A new scientific approach to the study of language evolution. In A. Cangelosi & D. Parisi (Eds.), *Simulating the evolution of language* (pp. 3-28). London: Springer.

Cangelosi, A., & Parisi, D. (Eds.). (2002b). *Simulating the evolution of language.* London: Springer.

Christiansen, M. H., & Kirby, S. (2003). Language evolution: Consensus and controversies. *Trends in Cognitive Sciences, 7*(7), 300-307.

Davidson, D. (1994). *Wahrheit und Interpretation.* Frankfurt am Main, Germany: Suhrkamp.

Ferrer i Chancho, R., Riordan, O., & Bollobas, B. (2005). The consequences of Zipf's law for syntax and symbolic reference. *Proceedings of the Royal Society, 272*, 561-565.

Fodor, J. A., & McLaughlin, B. P. (1995). Connectionism and the problem of systematicity: Smolensky's solution doesn't work. In C. MacDonald & G. MacDonald (Eds.), *Connectionism: Debates on psychological explanation* (pp. 199-222). Blackwell.

Fodor, J. A., & Pylyshyn, Z.W. (1988). Connectionism and cognitive architecture: A critical analysis. *Cognition, 28*(1-2), 3-71.

Frege, G. (1966). *Logische Untersuchungen.* Göttingen: Vandenhoeck & Ruprecht.

Gilbert, N., & Troitzsch, K. G. (1999). *Simulation for the social scientist.* Buckingham: Open University Press.

Haken, H. (1998). Can we apply synergetics to the human sciences? In G. Altmann & W.A. Koch (Eds.), *Systems: New paradigms for human sciences.* Berlin; New York: de Gruyter.

Harris, Z. S. (1954). Distributional structure. *Word, 10*, 146-162.

Hashimoto, T. (2002). The constructive approach to the dynamical view of language. In A. Cangelosi & D. Parisi, D. (Eds.), *Simulating the evolution of language* (pp. 307-324). London: Springer Verlag.

Hintikka, J., & Kulas, J. (1983). *The game of language.* Dordrecht: Reidel.

Hollan, J., Hutchins, E., & Kirsh, D. (2000). Distributed cognition: Toward a new foundation for human-computer interaction research. *ACM Transaction on Computer-Human Interaction, 7*(2), 174-196.

Hutchins, E., & Hazlehurst, B. (2002). Auto-organization and emergence of shared language structure. In A. Cangelosi & D. Parisi (Eds.), *Simulating the evolution of language* (pp. 279-306). London: Springer Verlag.

Jakobson, R. (1971). *Selected writings II: Word and language*. The Hague: Mouton.

Janssen, T. M. V. (1997). Compositionality (with an appendix by Barbara H. Partee). In J. van Benthem & A. ter Meulen (Eds.), *Handbook of logic and language* (pp. 417-473). Amsterdam: Elsevier.

Kamp, H., & Partee, B. (1995). Prototype theory and compositionality. *Cognition, 57*(2), 129-191.

Kintsch, W. (1998). *Comprehension: A paradigm for cognition.* Cambridge: Cambridge University Press.

Kintsch, W. (2001). Predication. *Cognitive Science, 25,* 173-202.

Kirby, S. (2002). Natural language from artificial life. *Artificial Life, 8*(2), 185-215.

Kirby, S., & Hurford, J. R. (2002). The emergence of linguistic structure: An overview of the iterated learning model. In A. Cangelosi & D. Parisi (Eds.), *Simulating the evolution of language* (pp. 121-148). London: Springer Verlag.

Köhler, R. (1986). *Zur linguistischen synerge-tik: Struktur und Dynamik der Lexik.* Bochum: Brockmeyer.

Köhler, R. (1987). Systems theoretical linguistics. *Theoretical Linguistics, 14*(2, 3), 241-257.

Köhler, R. (1993). Synergetic linguistics. In R. Köhler & B.B. Rieger (Eds.), *Contributions to quantitative linguistics* (pp. 41-51). Dordrecht: Kluwer.

Köhler, R. (1999). Syntactic structures: Properties and interrelations. *Journal of Quantitative Linguistics, 6,* 46-57.

Krylov, J. K. (1982). Eine Untersuchung statistischer Gesetzmäßigkeiten auf der paradigmatischen Ebene der Lexik natürlicher Sprachen. In H. Guiter & M.V. Arapov (Eds.), *Studies on Zipf 's law* (pp. 234-262). Bochum: Brockmeyer.

Landauer, T. K., & Dumais, S. T. (1997). A solution to Plato's problem: The latent semantic analysis theory of acquisition, induction, and representation of knowledge. *Psychological Review, 104*(2), 211-240.

Maturana, H. R., & Varela, F. J. (1980). *Autopoiesis and Cognition: The realization of the living.* Dordrecht: Reidel.

Mehler, A. (2004). Quantitative methoden. In H. Lobin & L. Lemnitzer (Eds.), *Texttechnologie: Perspektiven und Anwendungen* (pp. 83-107). Tübingen: Stauffenburg.

Mehler, A. (2005). Compositionality in numerical text semantics. In A. Mehler & R. Köhler (Eds.), *Aspects of automatic text analysis: Studies in fuzziness and soft computing.* Berlin: Springer.

Miller, G. A., & Charles, W. G. (1991). Contextual correlates of semantic similarity. *Language and Cognitive Processes, 6*(1), 1-28.

Partee, B. H. (1995). Lexical semantics and compositionality. In L.R. Gleitman & M. Liberman (Eds.), *Language: An invitation to cognitive science* (vol. 1, pp. 311-360). Cambridge: MIT Press.

Pattee, H. H. (1988). Simulations, realizations, and theories of life. In C.G. Langton (Ed.), *Artificial life: SFI studies in the sciences of complexity* (pp. 63-77). Redwood: Addison-Wesley.

Pickering, M. J., & Garrod, S. (2004). Toward a mechanistic psychology of dialogue. *Behavioral and Brain Sciences, 27,* 169-226.

Rickheit, G. (2005). Alignment und Aushandlung im Dialog. *Zeitschrift für Psychologie, 213*(3), 159-166.

Rickheit, G., & Strohner, H. (1992). Towards a cognitive theory of linguistic coherence. *Theoretical Linguistics, 18,* 209-237.

Ricœur, P. (1976*). Interpretation theory: Discourse and the surplus of meaning.* Fort Worth: The Texas Christian University Press.

Rieger, B. B. (1989). *Unscharfe Semantik: Die empirische Analyse, quantitative Beschreibung, formale Repräsentation und prozedurale Modellierung vager Wortbedeutungen in Texten.* Frankfurt am Main: Peter Lang.

Rieger, B. B. (2001). Computing granular word meanings: A fuzzy linguistic approach in computational semiotics. In P. Wang (Ed.), *Computing with words* (pp. 147-208). New York: John Wiley & Sons.

Rieger, B. B. (2002). Semiotic cognitive information processing: Learning to understand discourse. A systemic model of meaning constitution. In R. Kühn, R. Menzel, W. Menzel, U. Ratsch, M.M. Richter, & I.O. Stamatescu (Eds.), *Perspectives on adaptivity and learning* (pp. 47-403). Berlin: Springer.

Riegler, A., Peschl, M., & von Stein, A. (Eds.). (1999). *Understanding representation in the cognitive sciences: Does representation need reality?* New York; Boston; Dordrecht: Kluwer-Plenum.

Ruge, G. (1995). *Wortbedeutung und Termassoziation: Methoden zur automatischen semantischen Klassifikation.* Hildesheim: Olms.

Schnotz, W. (1994). *Aufbau von Wissensstrukturen: Untersuchungen zur Kohärenzbildung beim Wissenserwerb mit Texten.* Weinheim, Germany: Beltz.

Schütze, H. (1997). *Ambiguity resolution in language learning: Computational and cognitive*

models, Vol. 71, CSLI Lecture Notes. Stanford: CSLI Publications.

Searle, J. R. (1980). Minds, brains, and programs. *The Behavioral and Brain Sciences, 3,* 417-457.

Smolensky, P. (1995a). On the proper treatment of connectionism. In M. Donald & G. MacDonald (Eds.), *Connectionism: Debates on psychological explanation* (vol. 2, pp. 28-89). Oxford: Blackwell.

Smolensky, P. (1995b). Connectionism, constituency and the language of thought. In M. Donald & G. MacDonald (Eds.), *Connectionism: Debates on psychological explanation* (vol. 2, pp. 164-198). Oxford: Blackwell.

Solan, Z., Ruppin, E., Horn, D., & Edelman, S. (2003). Automatic acquisition and efficient representation of syntactic structures. In S. Thrun (Ed.), *Advances in neural information processing* (vol. 15). Cambridge: MIT Press.

Steels, L. (1996). Self-organising vocabularies. In C. Langton & T. Shimohara (Eds.), *Proceedings of Artificial Life V.* Japan: Nara.

Steels, L. (1998). Synthesizing the origins of language and meaning using coevolution, self-organization and level formation. In J.R. Hurford, M. Studdert-Kennedy, & C. Knight (Eds.), *Approaches to the evolution of language* (pp. 384-404). Cambridge: Cambridge University Press.

Steels, L. (2000). The puzzle of language evolution. *Kognitionswissenschaft, 8,*143-150.

Steels, L. (2002). Grounding symbols through evolutionary language games. In A. Cangelosi & D. Parisi (Eds.), *Simulating the evolution of language* (pp. 211-226). London: Springer Verlag.

Steels, L. (2004, July 21-26). Constructivist development of grounded construction grammars. In W. Daelemans (Ed.), *Proceedings of the 42nd Annual Meeting of the Association for Computational Linguistics* (pp. 9-16). Barcelona, Spain.

Stubbs, M. (2001). On inference theories and code theories: Corpus evidence for semantic schemas. *Text, 21*(3),437-465.

Thagard, P. (2000). *Coherence in thought and action.* Cambridge, MA: MIT Press.

Tuldava, J. (1998). *Probleme und Methoden der quantitativ-systemischen Lexikologie.* Trier: WVT.

Turner, H. (2002). An introduction to methods for simulating the evolution of language. In A. Cangelosi & D. Parisi (Eds.), *Simulating the evolution of language* (pp. 29-50). London; Berlin: Springer.

van Dijk, T. A., & Kintsch, W. (1983). *Strategies of discourse comprehension.* New York: Academic Press.

Vogt, P. (2004). Minimum cost and the emergence of the Zipf-Mandelbrot law. In J. Pollack, M. Bedau, P. Husbands, T. Ikegami, & R.A. Watson (Eds.), *Artificial life IX: Proceedings of the ninth international conference on the simulation and synthesis of living systems.* Cambridge, MA: MIT Press.

Watts, D. J. (1999). *Small worlds: The dynamics of networks between order and randomness.* Princeton: Princeton University Press.

Watts, D. J., & Strogatz, S. H. (1998). Collective dynamics of "small-world" networks. *Nature, 393,* 440-442.

Zadeh, L. A. (1997). Toward a theory of fuzzy information granulation and its centrality in human reasoning and fuzzy logic. *Fuzzy Sets and Systems, 90,* 111-127.

Ziemke, T. (1999). Rethinking grounding. In A. Riegler, M. Peschl, & A. von Stein (Eds.), *Understanding representation in the cognitive sciences: Does representation need reality?* (pp. 177-190). New York; Boston; Dordrecht: Kluwer-Plenum.

Zipf, G. K. (1972). *Human behavior and the principle of least effort: An introduction to human ecology.* New York: Hafner Publishing Company.

ENDNOTES

[1] The present chapter argues the possibility of computer-based realizations of natural language evolution. This means to refuse the view that the simulating system has essentially the same properties as the simulated one (instead of only having modelling function with respect to the latter). To put it in other terms: As a computer simulation of weather systems does not realize, but only simulates weather, we do not assume to realize natural languages.

[2] See also the "Language Evolution and Computation Bibliography" (http://www.isrl.uiuc.edu/~amag/langev/index.html) which collects relevant papers.

[3] That is, language evolution is described on at least three different time-scales (Kirby, 2002) so that simulation models face the problem of interrelating these different scales.

[4] The semantic space model is a refence model for mapping a certain meaning aspect in cognitive linguistics (Kintsch, 2001) and computational linguistics (Rieger, 2001, 2002). It will be explained in more detail next.

[5] Generally speaking, coherence means being connected. In cognitive linguistics (Kintsch, 1998) it is a well established term which is referred to, for example, in order to distinguish a random sequence of sentences from natural language texts.

[6] Since Thagard presupposes the order of elements in a constraint to be irrelevant, we represent these constraints as sets.

7   By the latter phrase we refer to ranked (e.g., frequency) distributions of linguistic units which are highly skewed and thus depart, for example, from normal distributions.

8   A method to integrate a sort of dynamics, which is otherwise left out, is to include, for example, probability functions introducing noise into the model according to the expected dynamics (Gilbert & Troitzsch, 1999).

9   This systematicity relates, for example, to logical relations and implicatures.

10 The notion of described situation (Barwise & Perry, 1983) denotes situations (modelled as systems of relations of varying arity) described by the focal sentence or text from the point of view of its content. It was proposed as an alternative to model theory in possible world semantics.

11 The terms text comprehension and interpretation stem from cognitive linguistics where they are well established—theoretically and empirically. For reference definitions see Kintsch (1998) and Schnotz (1994). In the present approach, they are not used metaphorically—as one may assume because we disregard referential semantics—but only dealt with in terms of a structural-cognitive semantics whose meaning units are purely conceptual. As proposed by LSA, these meaning units are derived on grounds of a learning model operating on linguistic units only. How this can be enlarged in order to model the meanings and interpretations of complex units was initially described by Kintsch (2001) and is extended in Mehler (2005).

12 Priming is a cognitive process in which a so-called prime systematically pre-activates certain (linguistic) knowledge from long-term memory in a way which increases the probability of primed (e.g., lexical) units to be produced or recognized, for example. In cognitive linguistics, there is much research on the sort of units having this priming func-

tion as, for example, isolated lexical units in contrast to the preceding text of a certain text position to be processed. See Kintsch (1998) for a prominent priming theory in cognitive linguistics.

13 In this chapter we refer to mechanisms of self-regulation if they result in changes of the focal system's structure (e.g., invention of lexical units). In contrast to this we speak of self-organization when changes of the system's organization, and thus of its function, are concerned (e.g., invention of a lexicon). In the following section, we will speak alternatively of a system's dynamics (self-regulation) and genetics (self-organization) in order to maintain this distinction.

14 In case of single cognitive information processing systems, this relates, more specifically, to short scale, reading/speaking time or position-dependent learning.

15 In case of cognitive information processing systems, this relates to learning (e.g., routinization and memorization) in long term memory.

16 This also prevents one from speaking of abstract mechanisms as, for example, the process of language internal "extension of the size of the lexicon" or the "invention of lexical coding means," etc.

17 It is common in synergetics to view the distinction of micro and macroscopic variables as a matter of modelling perspective in the sense that what is viewed as a microscopic variable in one experiment may be investigated as a macroscopic order parameter of certain enslaved system variables in another experiment.

18 Vogt (2004), for example, considers a Zipfian-ranked frequency distribution of category usage emerging from a multi-agent language game on grounds of the iterated learning model (ILM) (cf. Kirby, 2002). In this experiment, the assumed frequency distribution emerging in the simulation without being "directly" pre-established (e.g., by an appropriate signal-meaning mapping) serves as a criterion of simulation validity, that is, of the validity of the simulation model. In Vogt's model this relates, amongst others,

to the n-level multidimensional, though "hierarchicalized," category system. To what extent this "hierarchicalization" and the assumed procedure of category invention determine the resulting distribution in the framework of the ILM is an open question. This is a possible starting point for the present model as far as it proposes, for example, to restrict the build-up and maintenance of the category system by means of further "language laws" of the Zipfian nature. How such laws may interrelate is outlined in Section (4).

[19] These considerations presuppose countability of (forms and) meanings, a hypothesis which is disputed by fuzzy linguistics (Rieger, 2001). It gives rise to the introduction of fuzzy granules and distributed meaning representations and thus proposes to combine the apparatus of probability and fuzzy theory (Zadeh, 1997). Although this is a more realistic approach which coincides with models of inductive learning of lexical meanings, we will nevertheless retain Altmann's and Krylov's simplification.

[20] One may think that such a monotonously falling rank frequency distribution only arises if cells are appropriately re-ordered. But this is not expected to be necessary if this two-dimensional system is (almost) Zipfian as induced by the form and content-related Zipfian distributions supported on grounds of empirical investigations in quantitative linguistics.

[21] Another starting point for Zipf-like regularities of matrix (2) is proposed by Ferrer i Chancho et al. (2005) who describe a Zipfian law of node degree in a derived signal-signal matrix based on an analogue to (2). The idea of their approach is that the validity of such a distribution allows deriving (almost) connectedness (i.e., a large connected subgraph induced by the signal-signal matrix) as a precondition of syntax. Anyhow, this argumentation leaves out several prerequisites of syntactic structure. Amongst others, this relates to recursive structure.

[22] As the object being modelled by the simulations under consideration is not a specific language, this fitting does not relate to the factual values the fitted distribution takes for different values of the independent variable in any specific language.

[23] As an example, consider the parameters of models describing the vocabulary growth in texts which partly reflect the influence of genres, registers and their linguistic manifestations as text types (Altmann, 1991) whose evolvement can be described as a synergetic process on its own.

Chapter V
Soft–Constrained Linear Programming Support Vector Regression for Nonlinear Black–Box Systems Identification

Zhao Lu
Tuskegee University, USA

Jing Sun
University of Michigan, USA

ABSTRACT

As an innovative sparse kernel modeling method, support vector regression (SVR) has been regarded as the state-of-the-art technique for regression and approximation. In the support vector regression, Vapnik (2000) developed the ε-insensitive loss function as a trade-off between the robust loss function of Huber and one that enables sparsity within the support vectors. The use of support vector kernel expansion provides us a potential avenue to represent nonlinear dynamical systems and underpin advanced analysis. However, in the standard quadratic programming support vector regression (QP-SVR), its implementation is more computationally expensive and enough model sparsity can not be guaranteed. In an attempt to surmount these drawbacks, this chapter focuses on the application of soft-constrained linear programming support vector regression (LP-SVR) in nonlinear black-box systems identification, and the simulation results demonstrates that the LP-SVR is superior to QP-SVR in model sparsity and computational efficiency.

INTRODUCTION

Models of dynamical systems are of great importance in almost all fields of science and engineering and specifically in control, signal processing, and information science. A model is always only an approximation of a real phenomenon so that having an approximation theory which allows for the analysis of model quality is a substantial concern. A fundamental principle in system modeling is the Occam's razor arguing that the model should be no more complex than is required to capture the underlying systems dynamics. This concept, known as the parsimonious principle, which ensures the smallest possible model that explains the data, is particularly relevant in nonlinear model building because the size of a nonlinear model can easily become explosively large.

During the past decade, as an innovative sparse kernel modeling technique, support vector machine (SVM) has been gaining popularity in the field of machine learning and has been regarded as the state-of-the-art technique for regression and classification applications (Cristianini & Shawe-Taylor, 2000; Schölkopf & Smola, 2002; Vapnik, 2000). Essentially, SVM is a universal approach for solving the problems of multidimensional function estimation. Those approaches are all based on the Vapnik-Chervonenkis (VC) theory. Initially, it was designed to solve pattern recognition problem, where in order to find a decision rule with good generalization capability, a small subset of the training data, called the support vectors (SVs), are selected. Experiments showed that it is easy to recognize high-dimensional identities using a small basis constructed from the selected support vectors. Since the inception of this subject, the idea of support vector learning has also been applied to various fields, such as regression, density estimation, and linear operator equation, successfully. When SVM is employed to tackle the problems of function approximation and regression estimation, the approaches are often referred to as the support vector regression (SVR) (Smola & Schölkopf, 2004). The SVR type of function approximation is very effective, especially for the case of having a high-dimensional input space. Another important advantage for using SVR in function approximation is that the number of free parameters in the function approximation scheme is equal to the number of support vectors. Such a number can be obtained by defining the width

of a tolerance band, which can be implemented by using the ε-insensitive loss function. Thus, the selection of the number of free parameters can be directly related to the approximation accuracy and does not have to depend on the dimensionality of the input space or other factors as that in the case of multilayer feedforward neural networks.

The ε-insensitive loss function is attractive because unlike the quadratic and Huber cost functions, where all the data points will be support vectors, the SV solution can be sparse. In the realm of data modeling, the sparsity plays a crucial role in improving the generalization performance and computational efficiency. It has been shown that sparse data representations reduce the generalization error as long as the representation is not too sparse, which is consistent with the principle of parsimony (Ancona, Maglietta, & Stella, 2004; Chen, 2006).

For the purpose of modeling complex nonlinear dynamical systems by sparse representation, SVR was used in the context of nonlinear black-box system identification very recently (Chan, Chan, Cheung, & Harris, 2001; Drezet & Harrison, 1998; Gretton, Doucet, Herbrich, Rayner, & Schölkopf, 2001; Rojo-Alvarez, Martinez-Ramon, Prado-Cumplido, Artes-Rodriguez, & Figueiras-Vidal, 2006). Although it is believed that the formulation of SVM embodies the structural risk minimization principle, thus combining excellent generalization properties with a sparse model representation, data modeling practicians have begun to realize that the capability for the standard quadratic programming SVR (QP-SVR) method to produce sparse models has perhaps been overstated. For example, it has been shown that the standard SVM technique is not always able to construct parsimonious models in system identification (Drezet & Harrison, 1998). A recent study (Lee & Billings, 2002) has compared the standard SVM and uniformly regularized orthogonal least squares (UROLS) algorithms using time series prediction problems, and has found that both methods have similar excellent generalization performance but the resulting model from SVM is not sparse enough. It is explained that the number of support vectors found by a quadratic programming algorithm in a SVM is only an upper bound on the number of necessary and sufficient (optimal) support vectors, and the reasons for this effect are linear dependencies between support vectors in feature space.

On the other hand, due to the distinct mechanism for selecting support vectors from the QP-SVR, the linear programming support vector regression (LP-SVR) is advantageous over QP-SVR in model sparsity, ability to use more general kernel functions, and fast learning based on linear programming (Kecman, 2001; Hadzic & Kecman, 2000). The idea of linear programming support vector machines is to use the kernel expansion as an ansatz for the solution, but to use a different regularizer, namely the ℓ_1 norm of the coefficient vector. In other words, for LP-SVR, the nonlinear regression problem is treated as a linear one in the kernel space, rather than in the feature space as in the case of QP-SVR. In this chapter, we investigate the potential of LP-SVR in constructing sparse support vector model for the nonlinear dynamical systems identification. The rest of this chapter is organized as follows. In the next section, the soft-constrained LP-SVR, including details of the algorithm and its implementation, are introduced. We then compare and discuss the performance of LP-SVR and QP-SVR in robust function approximation and nonlinear dynamical systems identification through simulations. A conclusion and future works are given in the final section.

SOFT-CONSTRAINED LINEAR PROGRAMMING SVR

Conceptually, there are some similarities between the LP-SVR and QP-SVR. Both algorithms adopt the ε-insensitive loss function, and use kernel functions in feature space.

Consider regression in the following set of functions:

$$f(x) = w^T \varphi(x) + b \qquad (1)$$

with given training data, $\{(x_1, y_1), ..., (x_\ell, y_\ell)\}$ where ℓ denotes the total number of exemplars, $x_i \in R^n$ are the input, and $y_i \in R$ are the target output data. The nonlinear mapping $\varphi: R^n \rightarrow R^m (m > n)$ maps the input data into a so-called high dimensional feature space (which can be infinite dimensional) and $w \in R^m$, $b \in R$. In ε–SV regression, the goal is to find a function $f(x)$ that has at most ε deviation from the actually obtained targets y_i for all the training data, and at the same time, is as flat as possible. In the support vector method one aims at minimizing the empirical risk subject to elements of the structure

$$minimize \quad \frac{1}{2}\|w\|^2 + C\sum_{i=1}^{\ell}(\xi_i + \xi_i^*)$$

$$subject\ to \quad \begin{cases} y_i - \langle w, \varphi(x_i) \rangle - b \leq \varepsilon + \xi_i \\ \langle w, \varphi(x_i) \rangle + b - y_i \leq \varepsilon + \xi_i^* \\ \xi_i, \xi_i^* \geq 0 \end{cases} \quad (2)$$

where the ξ_i and ξ_i^* are the slack variables, corresponding to the size of the excess deviation for positive and negative deviation respectively. This is a classic quadratic optimization problem with inequality constraints, and the optimization criterion penalizes data points whose y–values differ from $f(x)$ by more than ε. The constant $C > 0$ determines the trade-off between the flatness of f and the amount up to which deviations larger than ε are tolerated. By defining the loss function,

$$L(y_i - f(x_i)) = \begin{cases} 0, & if\ |y_i - f(x_i)| \leq \varepsilon \\ |y_i - f(x_i)| - \varepsilon, & otherwise \end{cases} \quad (3)$$

The optimization problem (2) is equivalent to the following regularization problem,

$$minimize\ R_{reg}[f] = \sum_{i=1}^{\ell} L(y_i - f(x_i)) + \lambda \|w\|^2 \quad (4)$$

where $f(x)$ is in the form of (1) and $\lambda \|w\|^2$ is the regularization term. According to the well-known Representer Theorem (Schölkopf & Smola, 2002), the solution to the regularization problem (4) can be written as the SV kernel expansion

$$f(x) = \sum_{i=1}^{\ell} \beta_i k(x_i, x) \quad (5)$$

where $k(x_i, x)$ is the kernel function. Three commonly-used kernel functions in literature are:

- Gaussian radial basis function (GRBF) kernel:

$$k(x, x') = exp\left(\frac{-\|x - x'\|^2}{\sigma^2}\right)$$

- Polynomial kernel:

$$k(x, x') = (1 + \langle x, x' \rangle)^q$$

- Sigmoid kernel:

$$k(x, x') = tanh(\alpha \langle x, x' \rangle + \beta)$$

where σ, q, α, β are the adjustable parameters of the above kernel functions. The kernel function provides an elegant way of working in the feature space avoiding all the troubles and difficulties inherent in high dimensions, and this method is applicable whenever an algorithm can be cast in terms of dot products. Defining

$$\beta = [\beta_1\ \beta_2\ \cdots\ \beta_\ell]^T,$$

LP-SVR replaces (4) by

$$minimize\ R_{reg}[f] = \sum_{i=1}^{\ell} L(y_i - f(x_i)) + \lambda \|\beta\|_1 \quad (6)$$

where $f(x)$ is in the form of (5) and $\|\beta\|_1$ denotes the ℓ_1 norm in coefficient space. This regularization

problem is equivalent to the following constrained optimization problem

$$minimize\quad \frac{1}{2}\|\beta\|_1 + C\sum_{i=1}^{\ell}(\xi_i + \xi_i^*)$$

$$subject\ to\ \begin{cases} y_i - \sum_{j=1}^{\ell}\beta_j k(x_j, x_i) \le \varepsilon + \xi_i \\ \sum_{j=1}^{\ell}\beta_j k(x_j, x_i) - y_i \le \varepsilon + \xi_i^* \\ \xi_i, \xi_i^* \ge 0 \end{cases} \quad (7)$$

From the geometric perspective, it can be followed that $\xi_i \xi_i^* = 0$ in SV regression. Therefore, it is sufficient to just introduce slack ξ_i in the constrained optimization problem (7). Thus, we arrive at the following formulation of SV regression with fewer slack variables

$$minimize\quad \frac{1}{2}\|\beta\|_1 + 2C\sum_{i=1}^{\ell}\xi_i$$

$$subject\ to\ \begin{cases} y_i - \sum_{j=1}^{\ell}\beta_j k(x_j, x_i) \le \varepsilon + \xi_i \\ \sum_{j=1}^{\ell}\beta_j k(x_j, x_i) - y_i \le \varepsilon + \xi_i \\ \xi_i \ge 0 \end{cases} \quad (8)$$

In an attempt to convert the optimization problem above into a linear programming problem, we decompose β_i and $|\beta_i|$ as follows

$$\beta_i = \alpha_i^+ - \alpha_i^- \qquad |\beta_i| = \alpha_i^+ + \alpha_i^- \quad (9)$$

where α_i^+, $\alpha_i^- \ge 0$. It is worth noting that the decompositions in (9) are unique, that is, for a given β_i there is only one pair (α_i^+, α_i^-) which fulfils both equations. Furthermore, both variables can not be larger than zero at the same time, that is, $\alpha_i^+ \cdot \alpha_i^- = 0$. In this way, the ℓ_1 norm of β can be written as

$$\|\beta\|_1 = \left(\underbrace{1, 1, \cdots, 1}_{\ell}, \underbrace{1, 1, \cdots, 1}_{\ell} \right) \begin{pmatrix} \alpha^+ \\ \alpha^- \end{pmatrix} \qquad (10)$$

where $\alpha^+ = (\alpha_1^+, \alpha_2^+, ..., \alpha_\ell^+)^T$ and $\alpha^- = (\alpha_1^-, \alpha_2^-, ..., \alpha_\ell^-)^T$. Furthermore, the constraints in the formulation (8) can also be written in the following vector form

$$\begin{pmatrix} K & -K & -I \\ -K & K & -I \end{pmatrix} \cdot \begin{pmatrix} \alpha^+ \\ \alpha^- \\ \xi \end{pmatrix} \le \begin{pmatrix} y + \varepsilon \\ \varepsilon - y \end{pmatrix} \qquad (11)$$

where $K_{ij} = k(x_i, x_j)$, $\xi = (\xi_1, \xi_2, ..., \xi_\ell)^T$ and I is $\ell \times \ell$ identity matrix. Thus, the constrained optimization problem (8) can be implemented by the following linear programming problem with the variables α^+, α^-, ξ

$$minimize \quad c^T \begin{pmatrix} \alpha^+ \\ \alpha^- \\ \xi \end{pmatrix}$$

$$subject\ to \quad \begin{pmatrix} K & -K & -I \\ -K & K & -I \end{pmatrix} \cdot \begin{pmatrix} \alpha^+ \\ \alpha^- \\ \xi \end{pmatrix} \le \begin{pmatrix} y + \varepsilon \\ \varepsilon - y \end{pmatrix} \qquad (12)$$

where

$$c = \left(\underbrace{1, 1, \cdots, 1}_{\ell}, \underbrace{1, 1, \cdots, 1}_{\ell}, \underbrace{2C, 2C, \cdots, 2C}_{\ell} \right)^T.$$

In the QP-SVR case, the set of points not inside the tube coincides with the set of SVs. While, in the LP context, this is no longer true—although the solution is still sparse, any point could be an SV, even if it is inside the tube (Smola, Schölkopf, & Ratsch, 1999). Actually, the sparse solution still can be obtained in LP-SVR even though the size of the insensitive tube was set to zero (Drezet & Harrison, 2001) due to the soft constraints used; however, usually a sparser solution can be obtained by using non-zero ε.

*Figure 1. Approximation of Hermitian function by LP-SVR (**circled points:** SVs; **solid line:** model from LP-SVR; **dotted line:** tolerance band)*

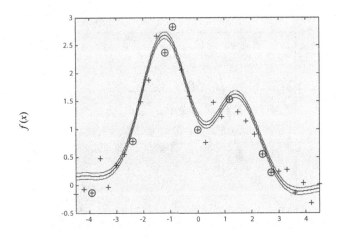

SIMULATIONS

In this section, the soft-constrained LP-SVR method is applied on the robust nonlinear function approximation and nonlinear black-box systems identification respectively. The experimental results are compared with those acquired from QP-SVR method in terms of robustness, sparsity, and prediction accuracy.

Example 1. An approximation of nonlinear Hermitian function.

$$f(x) = 1.1(1 - x + 2x^2)\, e^{-05x^2}$$

In this example, the soft-constrained LP-SVR and QP-SVR methods are employed in approximating the Hermitian function respectively by using the data polluted with 20% Gaussian zero-mean noise. The number of training pairs is 31. For the sake of comparison, the same kernel and learning parameters for LP-SVR and QP-SVR are used in our simulation: kernel—Gaussian radial basis function (RBF) kernel; kernel width parameter—1; C (bound)—100; ε (tolerance)—0.06. Figure 1 demonstrates the LP-SVR approxima-

tion result, where the ratio of SVs to the training vectors is 25.8%. Figure 2 illustrates the QP-SVR approximation result, in which the ratio of SVs to training vectors is 87.1%. The generalization capability and accuracy of regression algorithms could be evaluated by making use of the root mean square (RMS) error:

$$E_{RMS} = \sqrt{\frac{1}{N} \sum_{i=0}^{N} \left[\hat{f}(x_i) - f(x_i) \right]^2}$$

where $\hat{f}(x_i)$ is the estimated value at point x_i from the SVR model. In our experiment, the RMS errors are computed on 1000 equidistant points, and the RMS error for LP-SVR and QP-SVR is 0.1213 and 0.0888, respectively. For this example, the LP-SVR is around two times faster than QP-SVR in training. Obviously, LP-SVR enables us to obtain a much sparser approximation model with less computation time at the slight cost of accuracy.

Example 2. Nonlinear black-box systems identification of hydraulic robot arm. This is a

Figure 2. Approximation of Hermitian function by QP-SVR (circled points: SVs; solid line: model from QP-SVR; dotted line: tolerance band)

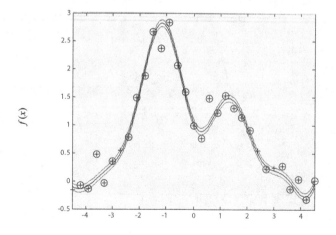

Figure 3. Identification of hydraulic robot arm dynamics by LP-SVR on the training set (solid line: observation; dotted line: model from LP-SVR)

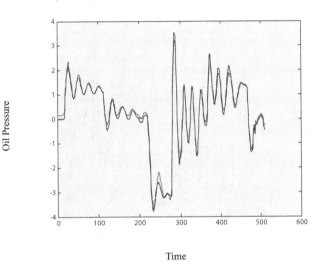

Time

benchmark problem in nonlinear systems identification, and it has been used widely for testing the various identification methods (Gretton et al., 2001; Sjöberg et al., 1995). In this nonlinear black-box dynamical system, the input $u(t)$ represents the size of the valve through which oil flow into the actuator, and the output $y(t)$ is a measure of oil pressure which determines the robot arm position. For the purpose of comparison, we use the same regressor,

$$X(t) = [y(t-1)\, y(t-2)\, y(t-3)\, u(t-1)\, u(t-2)]^{T}$$

as that in Drezet and Harrison (2001) and Gretton et al. (2001). We also used half of the data set containing 511 training data pairs for training, and half as validation data, again following the procedure in Gretton et al. (2001) and Sjöberg et al. (1995). In our simulation, the soft-constrained LP-SVR and QP-SVR are applied to model the dynamic behavior of a hydraulic robot arm respectively. Analogous to Example 1, the same kernel and learning parameters for LP-SVR and QP-SVR are used: kernel—Gaussian radial basis function (RBF) kernel; kernel width parameter—1; C

(bound)—100; ε (tolerance)—0.03. The identification results by LP-SVR are illustrated in Figures 3 and 4, where the RMS error on validation data is 0.1959 and the ratio of SVs to the training vectors is 6.5%. Figures 5-6 visualize the identification results by QP-SVR, where the RMS error on validation set is 0.1597 and the ratio of SVs to the training vectors is 39.7%. In this example, the prediction accuracy from LP-SVR is comparable with that from QP-SVR, and the LP-SVR is around 25 times faster than QP-SVR for training, which means that the computing resources required by QP-SVR may be prohibitively-expensive with the increase of the size of training set.

In Gretton et al. (2001) and Sjöberg et al. (1995), the RMS error on validation set acquired by using other identification algorithms are reported, such as 0.579 from wavelet networks, 0.467 from one-hidden-layer sigmoid neural networks with 10 hidden nodes, and 0.280 from ν-support vector regression. Evidently, higher prediction accuracy was obtained by using the soft-constrained LP-SVR and QP-SVR. Particularly, the model from LP-SVR is much sparser than that from QP-SVR.

Figure 4. Identification of hydraulic robot arm dynamics by LP-SVR on the validation set (solid line: observation; dotted line: model from LP-SVR)

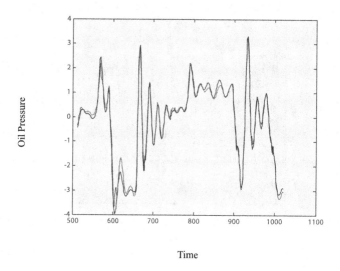

Figure 5. Identification of hydraulic robot arm dynamics by QP-SVR on the training set (solid line: observation; dotted line: model from QP-SVR)

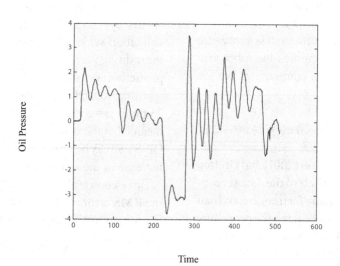

Figure 6. Identification of hydraulic robot arm dynamics by QP-SVR on the validation set (solid line: observation; dotted line: model from QP-SVR)

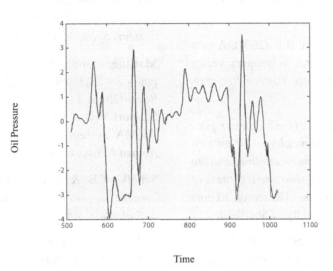

CONCLUSIONS AND FUTURE WORKS

In this chapter, we placed the emphasis on the sparsity in data representation, and it has been shown that the LP-SVR is very potential in modeling nonlinear dynamical systems and outperforms QP-SVR in model sparsity and computational efficiency. It is also believed that the sparsity can be improved further by the reduced-set method (Frieβ & Harrison, 1998).

Future research will be conducted in two different directions. The first project concentrates on the analysis of the mechanism of support vectors selection in LP-SVR, such that the online version of LP-SVR algorithm can be developed. Inspired by the ability to use more general kernels in LP-SVR, the other research project will investigate the roles of different kernel functions in LP-SVR.

REFERENCES

Ancona, N., Maglietta, R., & Stella, E. (2004). Data representation in kernel based learning machines. In *Proceedings of IASTED Int. Conf. on Artificial Intelligence and Soft Computing* (pp. 241-245).

Chan, W.C., Chan, C.W., Cheung, K.C., & Harris, C.J. (2001). On the modeling of nonlinear dynamic systems using support vector neural networks. *Engineering Applications of Artificial Intelligence, 14,* 105-113.

Chen, S. (2006). Local regularization assisted orthogonal least squares regression. *Neurocomputing, 69,* 559-585.

Cristianini, N., & Shawe-Taylor, J. (2000). *An introduction to support vector machines and other kernel-based learning methods.* Cambridge University Press.

Drezet, P.M.L., & Harrison, R.F. (1998). Support vector machines for system identification. In *UKACC International Conference on Control* (pp. 688-692).

Drezet, P.M.L., & Harrison, R.F. (2001). A new method for sparsity control in support vector classification and regression. *Pattern Recognition, 34*, 111-125.

Frieß, T.T., & Harrison, R., (1998). *Linear programming support vector machines for pattern classification and regression estimation; and the SR algorithm: Improving speed and tightness of VC bounds in SV algorithms* (Research Report No. 706). Sheffield: University of Sheffield.

Gretton, A., Doucet, A., Herbrich, R., Rayner, P.J.W., & Schölkopf, B. (2001). Support vector regression for black-box system identification. In *Proceedings of the 11th IEEE Workshop on Statistical Signal Processing* (pp. 341-344).

Hadzic, I., & Kecman, V. (2000) Support vector machines trained by linear programming: Theory and application in image compression and data classification. In *IEEE 5th Seminar on Neural Network Applications in Electrical Engineering* (pp. 18-23).

Kecman, V. (2001). *Learning and soft computing: Support vector machines, neural networks, and fuzzy logic models*. MIT Press.

Lee, K.L., & Billings, S.A. (2002). Time series prediction using support vector machines, the orthogonal and the regularized orthogonal least-squares algorithms. *International Journal of Systems Science, 33*(10), 811-821.

Martínez-Ramón, M., Rojo-Álvarez, J.L., Campus-Valls, G., Muñoz-Marí, J., Navia-Vázquez, Á., Soria-Olivas, E., & Figueiras-Vidal, A. R. (2006). Support Vector Machines for Nonlinear Kernel ARMA System Identification, *IEEE Trans. on Neural Networks, 17*(6), 1617-1622.

Schölkopf, B., & Smola, AJ. (2002). *Learning with kernels: Support vector machines, regularization, optimization, and beyond*. MIT Press.

Sjöberg, J., Zhang, Q., Ljung, L., Berveniste, A., Delyon, B., Glorennec, P., et al. (1995). Nonlinear black-box modeling in system identification: A unified overview. *Automatica, 31*(12), 1691-1724.

Smola, A.J., & Schölkopf, B. (2004). A tutorial on support vector regression. *Statistics and Computing, 14*, 199-222.

Smola, A., Schölkopf, B., & Ratsch, G. (1999). Linear programs for automatic accuracy control in regression. In *Proceeding of the International Conference on Artificial Neural Networks* (pp. 575-580), Berlin.

Vapnik, V.N. (2000). The nature of statistical learning theory (2nd ed.). Springer-Verlag.

Section III
Machine Learning

Chapter VI
Reinforcement Learning and Automated Planning:
A Survey

Ioannis Partalas
Aristotle University of Thessaloniki, Greece

Dimitris Vrakas
Aristotle University of Thessaloniki, Greece

Ioannis Vlahavas
Aristotle University of Thessaloniki, Greece

ABSTRACT

This chapter presents a detailed survey on Artificial Intelligent approaches that combine Reinforcement Learning and Automated Planning. There is a close relationship between those two areas, as they both deal with the process of guiding an agent, situated in a dynamic environment, in order to achieve a set of predefined goals. Therefore, it is straightforward to integrate learning and planning in a single guiding mechanism and there have been many approaches in this direction during the past years. The approaches are organized and presented according to various characteristics, as the used planning mechanism or the reinforcement learning algorithm.

INTRODUCTION

Reinforcement Learning and Automated Planning are two approaches in Artificial Intelligence that solve problems by searching in a state space. Reinforcement Learning is a subcategory of the Machine's Learning field, an area of Artificial Intelligence concerned with the computer systems design that improves through experience. Automated Planning is one of the most important areas of Artificial Intelligence; it deals with the design and implementation of systems (planners) that automatically produce plans (i.e., sequences of actions) which lead the world from its current state to another one that satisfies a set of predefined goals.

Machine Learning has been widely used to support planning systems in many ways. A detailed survey can be found in Zimmerman and Kambhambati (2003), where the authors describe numerous ways of how learning can assist planning. Furthermore, the existing techniques over the past three decades are categorized with respect to both the underlying planning and the learning component. More specifically, the techniques are organized according to: (a) the planning approach (state space search, plan space search), (b) the planning-learning goal (speed up planning, improve plan quality, learn or improve domain theory), (c) the learning phase (before planning, during planning process, during plan execution), and (d) the type of learning (analytic, inductive, multistrategy).

In Vrakas, Tsoumakas, Bassilliades, and Vlahavas (2005), a compact review of planning systems that utilize machine learning methods is presented, as well as background information on the learning methodologies that have been mostly used to support planning systems. Especially, this work concerns with the problem of the automatical configuring of a planning system's parameters, and how this problem is solved through machine learning techniques. In addition, it presents two different adaptive systems that set the planning parameters of a highly adjustable planner, based on the measurable characteristics of the problem instance.

Recently, Bonet and Geffner (2006) introduced a unified view of Planning and Dynamic Programming methods. More specifically, they combined the benefits of a general dynamic programming formulation with the power of heuristic-search techniques for developing an algorithmic framework.

In this chapter, we review methods that combine techniques from both Reinforcement Learning and Planning. The chapter is structured as follows: we provide the basic theory of Automated Planning and Reinforcement Learning, respectively. The following section reviews surveys that have been presented in the bibliography, about the research work related to the combination of Machine Learning and Planning. Then, the related articles are reviewed and they are categorized according to certain criteria; also their main aspects are presented. Finally, we discuss the findings of the survey and conclude the chapter.

BACKGROUND

Planning

Planning is the process of finding a sequence of actions (steps), which, if executed by an agent (biological, software, or robotic), result in the achievement of a set of predefined goals. The sequence of actions mentioned above is also referred to as a plan.

The actions in a plan may be either specifically ordered and their execution should follow the defined sequence (linear plan) or the agent is free to decide the order of executions as long as a set of ordering constraints are met. For example, if someone whishes to travel by plane, there are three main actions that have to be taken: (a) buy a ticket, (b) go to the airport, and (c) board the plane. A plan for traveling by plane could contain the above actions in a strict sequence as the one defined above (first do action a, then b, and finally c), or it could just define that action c (board the plane) should be executed after the first two actions. In the second case the agent would be able to choose which plan to execute, since both a→b→c, and b→a→c sequences would be valid.

The process of planning is extremely useful when the agent acts in a dynamic environment (or world) which is continuously altered in an unpredictable way. For instance, the auto pilot of a plane should be capable of planning the trajectory that leads the plane to the desired location, but also be able to alter it in case of an unexpected event, like an intense storm.

The software systems that automatically (or semi-automatically) produce plans are referred to as Planners or Planning Systems. The task of drawing a plan is extremely complex and it requires sophisticated reasoning capabilities which should be simulated by the software system. Therefore, Planning Systems make extensive use of Artificial Intelligence (AI) techniques and there is a dedicated area of AI called Automated Planning.

Automated Planning has been an active research topic for almost 40 years and during this period a great number of papers describing new methods, techniques, and systems have been presented that mainly focus on ways to improve the efficiency of planning systems. This can be done either by introducing new definition languages that offer more expressive power or by developing algorithms and methodologies that produce better solutions in less time.

Problem Representation

Planning Systems usually adopt the STRIPS (Stanford Research Institute Planning System) notation for representing problems (Fikes & Nilsson, 1971). A planning problem in STRIPS is a tuple $<I,A,G>$ where I is the Initial state, A is a set of available actions, and G is a set of goals.

States are represented as sets of atomic facts. All the aspects of the initial state of the world, which are of interest to the problem, must be explicitly defined in I. State I contains both static and dynamic information. For example, I may declare that object John is a truck driver and there is a road connecting cities A and B (static information) and also specify that John is initially located in city A (dynamic information). State G, on the other hand, is not necessarily complete. G may not specify the final state of all problem objects either because these are implied by the context or because they are of no interest to the specific problem. For example, in the logistics domain the final location of means of transportation is

usually omitted, since the only objective is to have the packages transported. Therefore, there are usually many states that contain the goals, so, in general, G represents a set of states rather than a simple state.

Set A contains all the actions that can be used to modify states. Each action A_i has three lists of facts containing:

a. The preconditions of A_i (noted as $prec(A_i)$),
b. The facts that are added to the state (noted as $add(A_i)$), and
c. The facts that are deleted from the state (noted as $del(A_i)$).

The following formulae hold for the states in the STRIPS notation:

- An action A_i is applicable to a state S if $prec(A_i) \subseteq S$.
- If A_i is applied to S, the successor state S' is calculated as: $S' = S \setminus del(A_i) \cup add(A_i)$
- The solution to such a problem is a sequence of actions, which if applied to I leads to a state S' such as $S' \supseteq G$.

Usually, in the description of domains, action schemas (also called operators) are used instead of actions. Action schemas contain variables that can be instantiated using the available objects and this makes the encoding of the domain easier.

The choice of the language in which the planning problem will be represented strongly affects the solving process. On one hand, there are languages that enable planning systems to solve the problems easier, but they make the encoding harder and pose many representation constraints. For example, propositional logic and first order predicate logic do not support complex aspects such as time or uncertainty. On the other hand there are more expressive languages, such as natural language, but it is quite difficult to enhance planning systems with support for them.

The PDDL Definition Language

PDDL stands for Planning Domain Definition Language. PDDL focuses on expressing the physical properties of the domain that we consider in each planning problem, such as the predicates and actions that exist. There are no structures to provide the planner with *advice*, that is, guidelines about how to search the solution space, although extended notation may be used, depending on the planner. The features of the language have been divided into subsets referred to as requirements, and each domain definition has to declare which requirements will put into effect.

After having defined a planning domain, one can define problems with respect to it. A problem definition in PDDL must specify an initial situation and a final situation, referred to as goal. The initial situation can be specified either by name, or as a list of literals assumed to be true, or both. In the last case, literals are treated as effects, therefore they are added to the initial situation stated by name. The goal can be either a goal description, using function-free first order predicate logic, including nested quantifiers, or an expansion of actions, or both. The solution given to a problem is a sequence of actions which can be applied to the initial situation, eventually producing the situation stated by the goal description and satisfying the expansion, if there is one.

The initial version of PDDL has been enhanced through continuous extensions. In version 2.1 (Fox & Long, 2003), the language is enhanced with capabilities for expressing temporal and numeric properties of planning domains. Moreover the language supports durative actions and a new optional field in the problem specification that allowed the definition of alternative plan metrics to estimate the value of a plan. PDDL 2.2 (Edelkamp & Hoffmann, 2004) added derived predicates, timed initial literals, which are facts that become true or false at certain time points known to the planner beforehand. In PDDL 3.0 (Gerevini & Long, 2005), the language was enhanced with constructs that increase its expressive power regarding the plan quality specification. These constructs mainly include strong and soft constraints and nesting of modal operators and preferences inside them.

Planning Methods

The roots of automated planning can be traced back in the early 1960s with the General Problem Solver (Newell & Simon, 1963) being the first planning system. Since then a great number of planning systems have been published that can be divided into two main categories: (a) classical and (b) neoclassical planning.

Classical Planning

The first approaches for solving planning problems included planning in state-spaces, planning is plan-spaces and hierarchical planning.

In state-space planning a planning problem is formulated as a search problem and then heuristic search algorithms, like Hill-Climbing or A* are used for solving it. The search in state-space planning can be forward (move from the initial state towards the goals), backward (start from the goals and move backward towards the goals), or bidirectional. Examples of this approach include the STRIPS planner among with some older systems such as GPS.

Plan-space differs from state-space planning in that the search algorithms do not deal with states but with incomplete plans. The algorithms in this category start with an empty plan and continually improve it by adding steps and correcting flaws until a complete plan is produced. A famous technique that is used by plan-space planners is the *Least Commitment Principle*, according to which the system postpones all the commitments (e.g., variable grounding) as long as it can. Such systems are the SNLP (McAllester & Rosenblitt, 1991) and UCPOP (Penberthy & Weld, 1992).

Hierarchical Planning is mainly an add-on to either state-space planning according to which the problem is divided into various levels of abstraction. This division requires extra knowledge provided by a domain expert, but the total time needed for solving the problem can be significantly reduced. The most representative examples of hierarchical planners are the ABSTRIPS (Sacerdoti, 1974) and the ABTWEAK (Yang & Tenenberg, 1990) systems.

Neoclassical Planning

The second era in planning techniques, called neoclassical planning, embodies planning methodologies and systems that are based on planning graphs, SAT encodings, CSPs, Model Checking and MDPs, and Automatic Heuristic Extraction.

Planning graphs are structures that encode information about the structure of the planning problems. They contain nodes (facts), arrows (operators), and mutexes (mutual exclusion relations) and are used in order to narrow the search for solution in a smaller part of the search space. The first planner in this category was the famous GRAPHPLAN (Blum and Furst 1995) and it was followed by many others such as IPP (Koehler, Nebel, Hoffmann, & Dimopoulos, 1997) and STAN (Long & Fox, 1998).

Another neoclassical approach for planning is to encode the planning problem in a propositional satisfiability problem, which is a set of logic propositions containing variables. The goal in such problems is to prove the truth of the set by assigning Boolean values to the referenced variables. The most representative systems based on satisfiability encodings are the SATPLAN (Kautz & Selman, 1992) and BLACKBOX (Kautz & Selman, 1998).

Transforming the planning problem in a constraint satisfaction problem is another neoclassical technique, able to handle problems with resources (e.g., time). By encoding the planning problem in a CSP one can utilize a number of efficient solving techniques and therefore obtain a good solution very fast. There are many systems and architectures based on this model such as OMP (Cesta,

Fratini, & Oddi, 2004) and CTP (Tsamardinos, Pollack, & Vidal, 2003).

Encoding the planning problem as a Model Checking or Markov Decision problem are two neoclassical approaches, able to support uncertainty in planning problems. Uncertainty is a key factor especially when planning in dynamic real word situations, as the environment of a robot. These two neoclassical techniques have proven to be quite efficient for uncertain environments with partial observability capabilities (Boutilier, Reiter, & Price, 2001; Giunchiglia & Traverso, 1999).

The last neoclassical methodology is to perform domain analysis techniques on the structure of the problem in order to extract knowledge that is then embedded in heuristic functions. The first system towards this direction was McDermott's UNPOP (McDermott, 1996) which used the means-end-analysis in order to analyze the problem and create a heuristic mechanism that was then used by a state-space heuristic search algorithm. The example of UNPOP was followed by a large number of systems, with the most important of them being HSP (Bonet & Geffner, 2001), FF (Hoffmann & Nebel, 2001), and AltAlt (Nguyen, Kamphambati, & Nigenda, 2000). The reader should consider Ghalab, Nau, and Traverso (2004) for a more comprehensive view of Automated Planning.

Reinforcement Learning

Introduction in Reinforcement Learning

Reinforcement learning (RL) addresses the problem of how an agent can learn a behaviour through trial and error interactions with a dynamic environment (Kaelbling, Littman, & Moore, 1996; Sutton & Barto, 1999). RL is inspired by the reward and punishment process encountered in the learning model of most living creatures. The main idea is that the agent (biological, software, or robotic) is evaluated through a scaled quantity, called reinforcement (or reward), which is received from the environment as an assessment of the agent's performance. The goal of the agent is to maximize a function of the reinforcement in the next iteration (greedy approach). The agent is not told which actions to take, as in most forms of Machine Learning, but instead it must discover which actions yield the most reward by trying them.

RL tasks are framed as Markov decision processes (MDP), where an MDP is defined by a set of states, a set of actions and the dynamics of the environment, a transition function, and a reward function. Given a state s and an action a the transition probability of each possible successor state s' is $P^a_{ss'} = \Pr\{s_{t+1} = s' \mid s_t = s, a_t = a\}$ and the expected value of the reward is $R^a_{ss'} = E\{r_{t+1} \mid s_t = s, a_t = a, s_{t+1} = s'\}$. Each MDP satisfies the Markov property which states that the environment's response at t+1 depends only on the state and actions representations at t, in which case the environment's dynamics can be defined by specifying only $\Pr\{s_{t+1} = s', r_{t+1} = r \mid s_t, a_t\}$, for all s', at, $r_t, ..., r_1, s_0, a_0$. Based on this property we can predict the next state and the expected next reward given the current state and action.

Reinforcement Learning Framework

In an RL task the agent, at each time step, senses the environment's state, $s_t \in S$, where S is the finite set of possible states, and selects an action $a_t \in A(s_t)$ to execute, where $A(S_t)$ is the finite set of possible actions in state S_t. The agent receives a reward, $r_{t+1} \in \Re$, and moves to a new state S_{t+1}. Figure 1 shows the agent-environment interaction. The objective of the agent is to maximize the cumulative reward received over time. More specifically, the agent selects actions that maximize the expected discounted return:

$$R_t = r_{t+1} + \gamma r_{t+2} + \gamma^2 r_{t+3} + \ldots = \sum_{k=0}^{\infty} \gamma^k r_{t+k+1},$$

where γ, $0 \leq \gamma < 1$, is the discount factor and expresses the importance of future rewards.

Figure 1.

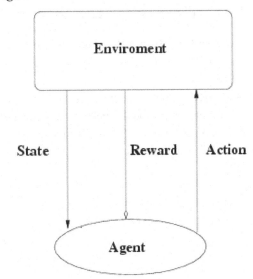

The agent learns a *policy* π, a mapping from states to probabilities of taking each available action, which specifies that in state s the probability of taking action a is $\pi(s,a)$. The above procedure is in real time (online) through the interaction of the agent and the environment. The agent has no prior knowledge about the behavior of the environment (the transition function) and the way that the reward is computed. The only way to discover the environment's behavior is through trial-and-error interactions and therefore the agent must be capable of exploring the state space to discover the actions which will yield the maximum returns. In RL problems, a crucial task is how to trade off exploration and exploitation, namely the need of exploiting quickly the knowledge that the agent acquired and the need of exploring the environment in order to discover new states and bear in a lot of reward over the long run.

Optimal Value Functions

For any policy π, the value of state s, $V^\pi(s)$, denotes the expected discounted return, if the agent starts from s and follows policy π thereafter. The value $V^\pi(s)$ of s under π is defined as:

$$V^{\pi}(s) = E_{\pi}\left\{R_t \mid s_t = s\right\} = E_{\pi}\left\{\sum_{k=0}^{\infty} \gamma^k r_{t+k+1} \mid s_t = s\right\},$$

where s_t and r_{t+1} denote the state at time t and the reward received after acting at time t, respectively.

Similarly the *action-value function*, $Q^{\pi}(s, a)$, under a policy π can be defined as the expected discounted return for executing a in state s and thereafter following policy π:

$$Q^{\pi}(s,a) = E_{\pi}\left\{R_t \mid s_t = s, a_t = a\right\} =$$

$$E_{\pi}\left\{\sum_{k=0}^{\infty} \gamma^k r_{t+k+1} \mid s_t = s, a_t = a\right\}.$$

The agent tries to find a policy that maximizes the expected discounted return received over time. Such a policy is called an *optimal* policy and is denoted as π^*. The optimal policies may be more than one and they share the same value functions. The optimal state-value function is denoted as:

$$V^*(s) = \max_a \sum_{s'} P_{ss'}^a \left[R_{ss'}^a + \gamma V^*(s') \right]$$

and the optimal action-value function as:

$$Q^*(s,a) = \sum_{s'} P_{ss'}^a \left[R_{ss'}^a + \gamma \max_{a'} Q^*(s',a') \right].$$

The last two equations are also known as the *Bellman optimality equations*. A way to solve these equations and find an optimal policy is the use of dynamic programming methods such as *value iteration* and *policy iteration*. These methods assume a perfect model of the environment in order to compute the above value functions. In real world problems, the model of the environment is often unknown and the agent must interact with its environment directly to obtain information which will help it to produce an optimal policy. There are two approaches to learn an optimal policy. The first approach is called *model-free* where the

agent learns a policy without learning a model of the environment. A well known algorithm of these approaches is Q-learning which is based on value iteration algorithm. The second approach is called *model-based* where the agent learns a model of the environment and uses it to derive an optimal policy. Dyna is a typical algorithm of model-based approaches. These techniques will be presented in detail in the following sections as well as the way that planning techniques are integrated with them.

Learning and Planning

Machine learning algorithms have been extensively exploited in the past to support planning systems in many ways. Learning can assist planning systems in three ways (Vrakas et al., 2005; Zimmerman & Kambhambati, 2003):

- **Learning to speed up planning:** In most of the problems a planner searches a space in order to construct a solution and many times it is forced to perform backtracking procedures. The goal of learning is to bias the search in directions that is possible to lead to high-quality plans and thus to speed up the planning process.
- **Improving domain knowledge:** Domain knowledge is utilized by planners in pre-processing phases in order to either modify the description of the problem in a way that it will make easier for solving or make the appropriate adjustments to the planner to best attack the problem so there are obvious advantages to a planner that evolves its domain knowledge by learning.
- **Learn optimization knowledge:** Optimization knowledge is utilized after the generation of an initial plan, in order to transform it in a new one that optimizes certain criteria, that is, the number of steps or usage of resources.

Reinforcement Learning and Planning

The planning approaches used by deliberative agents rely on the existence of a global model which simulates the environment (agent's world) during time. For example, if a state and an action are given, the model predicts the next state and can produce entire sequences of states and actions. The actions which the agent executes specify the plan, which can be considered as a policy. Planning methods involve computing utility functions (value functions) that represent goals, in order to guide the agent in selecting the next action (i.e., policy). Reinforcement learning methods are also based on the estimation of utility functions in order to improve the agent's policy. This common structure led researchers to integrate planning and reinforcement learning methods in order to improve their efficiency.

In reinforcement learning methods, the aim of the agent is to maximize the expected sum of the rewards received over time, while acting in a dynamic environment. This process is often very slow; in fact in real situations, where the complexity is very high, it is very hard to find an optimal policy. A method that can speed up process of learning is the use of planning algorithms; through this we can achieve a good policy with fewer environmental interactions, as they can improve the policy using the model of the environment.

Moreover, in planning under uncertain and partial observability, where the state of the environment is only partially visible at run-time, there is an impervious need to find ways to overcome the problems that arise in such environments. A solution is to model the problem of planning under the reinforcement learning framework and then to use the appropriate techniques in order to solve it.

APPROACHES COMBINING PLANNING WITH RL

We shall organize the various methodologies that combine planning and RL in two major categories: (a) Planning for Reinforcement Learning and (b) Reinforcement Learning for Planning. These categories will be further divided according to the RL and the planning methods that are used in the various approaches.

Planning for Reinforcement Learning

In this section we present the main aspects of the methods that combine RL and Planning techniques in order to accelerate the learning process. The methods presented in the following section are based on two architectures that integrate planning and reinforcement learning, called Dyna, originally proposed by Sutton (1990), and Prioritized Sweeping (Moore & Atkenson, 1993). The various methodologies are organized in the two following categories: (a) Dyna-based Methods and (b) Prioritized Sweeping-based Methods. There are also methods that do not fall

Figure 2. The Dyna framework

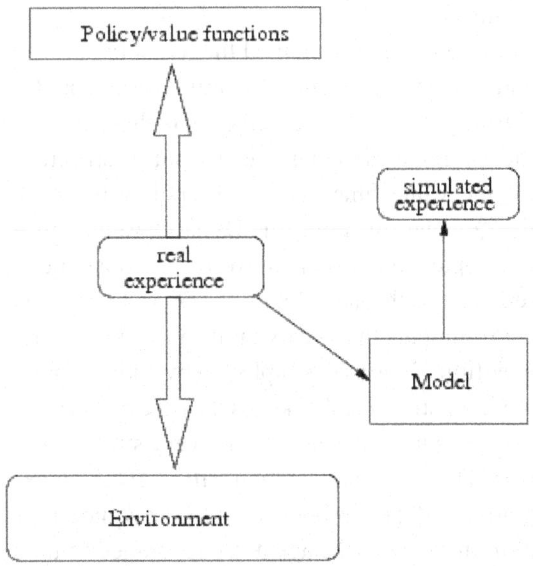

in these categories and will be presented in the Other Methods section.

Dyna Architecture

The most common and often used solution to speed up the learning procedure in RL is the Dyna framework (Sutton 1990, 1991). The basic idea of Dyna is that it uses the acquired experience in order to construct a model of the environment and then use this model for updating the value function without having to interact with the environment. Figure 2 shows the Dyna framework (Sutton & Barto, 1999).

Dyna-Based Methods

The dyna architecture forms as the basis of other techniques for combining reinforcement learning and planning. Sutton (1990) proposed a method that engages Dyna and Q-learning while Peng and Ronald (1993) presented a prioritized version of Dyna. Lin (1992) extended the Adaptive Heuristic Critic and Q-learning with the internalization of Dyna. Finally, Zhao, Tatsumi, and Sun (1999) extended the queue-Dyna algorithm by adding a component called exploration planning.

Dyna-Q

In Sutton (1990), a method that combines Dyna and Q-learning (Watkins, 1989) is proposed. Q-learning is a model free method, which means that there is no need to maintain a separate structure for the value function and the policy but only the Q-value function. The Dyna-Q architecture is simpler, as two data structures have been replaced with one. Moreover, Dyna-Q handles environments that are dynamic and may change over time. This is accomplished by adding a new memory structure that keeps the time steps n that elapsed since the last visit of every state-action pair. Then each state-action pair is given an exploration degree proportional to the square root of n. In this way the agent is encouraged to take

actions that have not been chosen for a long time and thus to explore the state space.

Queue-Dyna

Peng and Ronald (1993) introduced queue-Dyna, a version of Dyna in which not all the state action pairs are considered to be useful and thus there is no need to be updated. In this way the algorithm is focused on places that may require updating through the planning process. The basic idea is that the values of the states are prioritized according to a criterion and only those having the highest priority are updated at each time step. A critical procedure of the proposed algorithm is the identification of the *update candidates*, that is, places where the value function may require updating. The algorithm uses the Q-learning as the RL mechanism for updating the values for the state-action pairs. In order to determine the priority, the authors defined the *prediction difference* as the difference of the Q-value between the present state-action pair and the successor state. If this difference exhibits a predefined threshold the update candidate is placed in to the queue for updating. After this step the planning process is performed. The first update candidate from the queue is extracted and updated. Then the predecessors of the state updated are examined if their prediction differences are significant, and if they are then the states become update candidates and placed in to the queue. We must mention here that the priority which is assigned at the update candidates is based on the magnitude of the prediction difference which means that large differences get high priorities. The experimental results showed that the proposed method improves not only the computational effort of Dyna (Sutton 1990, 1991) but also the performance of the agent.

AHC-Relaxation Planning & Q-Relaxation Planning

In Lin (1992), two extensions of the Adaptive Heuristic Critic (AHC) (Barto, Sutton, & Anderson, 1983) and Q-learning are presented.

Adaptive heuristic critic architecture consists of two components: a method that learns a value function for a fixed policy and a method that uses the learned value function to adjust the policy in order to maximize the value function. Lin (1992) proposes a framework that combines AHC and a variation of relaxation planning (Sutton, 1990). The proposed planning algorithm addresses some problems of relaxation planning such as the effort that is spend in hypothetical situations that will not appear in the real world by executing actions from states actually visited and not from randomly generated states. The disadvantage of this approach is that the number of the hypothetical experiences that can be generated is limited by the number of states visited. Additionally, the planning steps are performed selectively, that is, when the agent is very decisive about the best action the planning process is omitted while on the other hand when the agent cannot decide accurately about the best action the planning process is performed. At the beginning of learning, the planning process is performed frequently as the actions are been chosen with equal probability. As the agent acquires knowledge the planning steps are performed less often. The author also proposed a similar algorithm which combines Q-learning and relaxation planning. We must mention here that the above approaches adopt function approximation methods in order to tackle the problem of the large state space. The value functions are represented using neural networks and learned using a combination of temporal difference methods (Sutton, 1988) and the back-propagation algorithm.

Exploration Planning

In Zhao et al. (1999), the authors proposed an extension of the queue-Dyna architecture by adding a module called *exploration planning*. This module helps the agent to search for actions that have not been executed in the visited states in order to accelerate the learning rate. This is achieved by defining state-action pairs as *subgoals*

according to a metric similar to that of prediction difference that is used in queue-Dyna. When the agent detects a subgoal, the path from the initial state is drawn. Then, starting from the subgoal the Q values of each state-action pair in the path are updated in a backward form.

Prioritized Sweeping-Based Methods

This section reviews methods that make use of the Prioritized Sweeping algorithm originally proposed by Moore and Atkenson (1993). Andre, Friedman, and Ronald (1998) presented an extension that scales up to complex environments. Dearden (2001) proposed a structured version of prioritized sweeping that utilizes Dynamic Bayesian Networks.

Prioritized Sweeping

The idea behind prioritized sweeping (Moore & Atkenson, 1993) is that instead of selecting randomly the state-action pairs that will be updated during the planning process is more efficient to focus in state-action pairs that are likely to be useful. This observation is similar but has been developed independently, as in queue-Dyna where some state-action pairs are more urgent to be updated. At the beginning of the learning process the agent has not yet acquired enough knowledge in order to construct an accurate model of the environment and thus planning is not efficient and spends time in making wasteful backups. This problem becomes noticeable in large domains where the planning process with randomly generated state-action pairs would be extremely inefficient.

The prioritized sweeping algorithm tries to determine which updates are likely to be interesting. It is assumed that the states belong in two disjoint subsets, the nonterminal and the terminal states. When the agent visits a terminal state it can not left it. An update is interesting when there is a large change between the values of the state and the terminal states. The algorithm uses a queue where it stores the interesting states according to the change. When a real world observation (state) is interesting then all its predecessors are placed near to the top of the queue in order to be updated. In this way the agent focuses in a particular area but when the states are not interesting, it looks for other areas in the state-space.

Experiments on discrete state problems shown that there was a large improvement in the computational effort that needed other methods like Dyna or Q-learning. But a question that arises at this point is how prioritized sweeping would behave in more complex and nondiscrete environments. In this case there is the need to alter the representation of the value functions and utilize more compact methods like neural networks instead of the common tabular approach.

Generalized Prioritized Sweeping

Andre, Friedman, and Parr (1998) presented an extension of prioritized sweeping in order to address the problems that arise in complex environments and to deal with more compact representations of the value function. In order to scale-up to complex domains they make use of the *Dynamic Bayesian Networks* (Dean & Kanazawa, 1990) to approximate the value functions as they were used with success in previous works. The proposed method is called Generalized Prioritized Sweeping (GenPs) and the main idea is that the candidate states for been updated are the states where the value function change the most.

Structured Prioritized Sweeping

In Dearden (2001), the *structured policy iteration* (SPI) algorithm applied in a structured version of prioritized sweeping. SPI (Boutilier, Dearden, & Goldszmidt, 1995) is used in decision-theoretic planning and is a structured version of policy iteration. In order to describe a problem (which is formalized as an MDP), it uses DBNs and conditional probability trees. The output of the algorithm is a tree-structured representation of a value function and a policy. The main component of the SPI algorithm is a regression operator over a value function and an action that produces a new value function before the action is performed. This is similar to planning that takes a goal and an action and determines the desired state before the action is performed. The regression operator is computed in a structured way where the value function is represented as a tree and the results is another tree in which each leaf corresponds to a region of the state space.

Structured prioritized sweeping is based on generalized prioritized sweeping (Andre et al., 1998). The main difference is that in the proposed method the value function is represented in a structured way as described in to the previous paragraph. Additionally, another major change is that the updates are performed for specific actions whereas in prioritized sweeping for each state that is been updated all the values of the actions in that state must be recomputed. This feature gives a great improvement in the computational effort as only the necessary updates are performed. The structured prioritized sweeping algorithm provides a more compact representation that helps the speed up of the learning process.

Other Methods

Several other methods have been proposed in order to combine Reinforcement Learning with Planning. Grounds and Kudenko (2005) presented a method that couples a Q-learner with a STRIPS planner. Ryan and Pendrith (1998) proposed a hybrid system that combines teleoreactive planning and reinforcement learning techniques while Ryan (2002) used planning to automatically construct hierarchies for hierarchical reinforcement learning. Finally, Kwee, Marcus, and Schmidhuber (2001) introduced a learning method that uses a gradient-based technique that plans ahead and improves the policy before acting.

PLANQ-learning

Grounds and Kudenko (2005) introduced a novel method in reinforcement learning in order to improve the efficiency in large-scale problems. This approach utilizes the prior knowledge of the structure of the MDP and uses symbolic planning to exploit this knowledge. The method, called *PLANQ-learning*, consists of two components: a STRIPS planner that is used to define the behavior that must be learned (high-level behavior) and a reinforcement learning component that learns a low level behavior. The high-level agent has multiple Q-learning agents to learn each STRIPS operator. Additionally, there is a low-level interface from where the low level percepts can be read in order to construct a low-level reinforcement learning state. Then this state can be transformed to a high-level state that can be used from the planner. At each time step the planner takes a representation of the state according to the previous interface and returns a sequence of actions which solves the problem. Then the corresponding Q-learner is activated and it receives a reward for performing the learning procedure. Experiments showed that the method constrains the number of steps required by the algorithm to converge.

Reinforcement Learned-TOPs

In this work, reinforcement learning is combined with teleoreactive planning to build behavior hierarchies to solve a problem like robot navigation. Teleoreactive planning (Nilsson, 1994) is based on teleo-operators (TOPs), where each of them is an action that can be a simple primitive action or a complex behavior. Teleoreactive plans are represented as trees which each node is a state, and the root is the goal state. The actions are represented as connections between the nodes and when an action is performed in a node then the conditions of the parent node are achieved. In the proposed method the reinforcement learnt behaviors are represented as a list of TOPs and then a TeleoReactive planner is used to construct a plan in the form of a tree. An action is then

selected to be executed and the result is used to determine the reinforcement reward to feed the learner and the process repeats by selecting the following actions until the goal is achieved. In this way, behavior hierarchies are constructed automatically and there is no need to predefine these hierarchies. Additionally, an advantage of the proposed architecture is that the low-level TOPs that are constructed in an experiment can be used as the basis of solving another problem. This feature is important as the system does not spend further time in the reconstruction of new TOPs.

Teleo-Reactive Q-learning

Ryan (2003) proposed a hybrid system that combines planning and hierarchical reinforcement learning. Planning generates hierarchies to be used by an RL agent. The agent learns a policy for choosing optimal paths in the plan that produced from the planner. The combination of planning and learning is done through the Reinforcement Learning Teleo-operator (Ryan & Pendrith, 1998) as described in to the previous section.

Reinforcement Learning for Planning

This section presents approaches that utilize reinforcement learning to support planning systems. Baldassarre (2003) presented a planner that uses RL to speed up the planning process. Sun and Sessions (1998), Sun (2000), and Sun, Peterson, and Sessions (2001) proposed a system that extract the knowledge from reinforcement learners and then uses it to produce plans. Finally, Cao, Xi, and Smith (2003) use RL to solve a production planning problem.

Forward and Bidirectional Planning based on Reinforcement Learning

Baldassarre (2003) proposed two reinforcement learning based planners that are capable of generating plans that can be used for reaching a goal state. So far planning was used for speed up learning like in Dyna. In this work reinforcement learning and planning are coordinated to solve problems with low cost by balancing between acting and planning. Specifically, the system consists of three main components: (a) the learner, (b) the forward planner, and (c) the backward planner. The learner is based on the Dyna-PI (Sutton, 1990) and uses a neural implementation of AHC. The neural network is used as a function approximator in order to anticipate the state space explosion. The forward planner comprises a number of experts that correspond to the available actions, and an action-planning controller. The experts take as input a representation of the current state and output a prediction of the next state. The action-planning controller is a hand-designed algorithm that is used to decide if the system will plan or act. Additionally, the forward planner is responsible for producing chains of predictions where a chain is defined as a sequence of predicted actions and states.

The experiments that contacted showed that bidirectional planning is superior to the forward planning. This was a presumable result as the bidirectional planner has two main advantages. The first is that the updates of the value function is done near the goal state and leads the system to find the way to the goal faster. The second advantage is that the same values are used to update the values of other states. This feature can be found in Lin (1992).

Extraction of Planning Knowledge from Reinforcement Learners

Sun and Sessions (1998), Sun (2000), and Sun et al. (2001) presented a process for extracting plans after performing a reinforcement learning algorithm to acquire a policy. The method is concerned with the ability to plan in an uncertain environment where usually knowledge about the domain is required. Sometimes is difficult to acquire this knowledge, it may impractical or

costly and thus an alternative way is necessary to overcome this problem. The authors proposed a two-layered approach where the first layer performs plain Q-learning and then the corresponding Q values along with the policy are used to extract a plan. The plan extractor starts form an initial state and computes for each action the transition probabilities to next states. Then for each action the probabilities of reaching the goal state by performing the specific action are computed and the action with the highest probability is been chosen. The same procedure is repeated for successor states until a predefined number of steps are reached. Roughly speaking, the method estimates the probabilities of the paths which lead to the goal state and produces a plan by selecting a path greedily.

From the view of reinforcement learning, the method is quite flexible because it allows the use of any RL-algorithm and thus one can apply the algorithm that is appropriate for the problem in hand. Additionally, the cost of sensing the environment continuously is reduced considerably as planning needs little sensing from the environment. In Sun (2000), the aforementioned idea was extended with the insertion of an extra component for extracting rules when applying reinforcement learning in order to improve the efficiency of the learning algorithm.

A Reinforcement Learning Approach to Production Planning

Cao et al. (2003) designed a system that solves a production planning problem. Production planning is concerned with the effective utilization of limited resources and the management of material flow through these resources, so as to satisfy customer demands and create profits. For a medium sized production planning problem is required to set thousands of control parameters which leads to a computational overhead. In order to make the problem tractable the authors modeled it as an MDP and used a Reinforcement

Learning based approach to solve it. In details, RL, and more specifically Q-learning, is applied to learn a policy that adjusts the parameters of the system. To improve the efficiency of learning, two phases of learning are used. In the first phase, the goal is to find the values of the parameters that are likely to lead to a near-optimal solution. In the second phase, these values are used to produce a plan.

DISCUSSION

This chapter deals with two research areas of Artificial Intelligence that aim at guiding an agent in order to fulfill his goals. These areas, namely Automated Planning and Reinforcement Learning attack the same problem from different perspectives, but at the bottom line share similar techniques and methodologies. The goal of both areas is to provide the agent with a set of guidelines for choosing the most appropriate action in each intermediate state between its initial position and the goal state.

Planning has been traditionally seen as a hierarchical paradigm for agent autonomy. In hierarchical models the agent senses the environment, constructs a model of it, searches for a plan achieving the problem goals, and then starts acting in the real world. In order for the produced plan to be useful, two conditions must be met: (a) the model of the world must be well defined and informative and (b) the world must not deviate from the maintained model at any time point. In other words, the agent must either assume that the world is static and it can only change by its own actions, or it should periodically sense the world and use a sophisticated algorithm for incorporating the perceived changes in the model and updating the plan accordingly.

On the other hand, Reinforcement Learning is closer to the reactive paradigm of agent autonomy since it is based on continuous interactions with the real world. The model is not purely reactive since the exploration process can be guided by the acquired experience, but it does not involve complex reasoning on a model. RL is very efficient for dynamic worlds that may change in an unpredictable way and it eliminates the need for storing an informative and yet compact model of the world (frame problem). However, in complex problems the reactions with the environment are expensive and the search space may become intractable for exploration.

The systems surveyed in the chapter combine the two approaches in a manner similar to the hybrid paradigm of autonomy in order to provide faster and better guidance to the agent. The key idea is to equip the agent with two modules, a planner, and a learner that cooperate either in a sequential or in a concurrent way. From this point view, there are three different approaches in combining planning and reinforcement learning:

a) **First Plan then Learn:** Planning is used to construct macro-operators, fixed sequences of actions, that can facilitate the value propagation and therefore speed-up the learning process. These macro-operators can be used in various forms: the simplest way is to pre-compile compound actions from simple ones. This can be either done manually or automatically using a planning process. This sort of hierarchical solving may rely on region based decomposition of MDPs (Dietterich, 2000; Hauskrecht et al., 1998; Szita, Takacs, & Lorincz, 2003) or on the idea of Teleo Reactive Planning (Nilsson, 1994) that solves the problem by producing abstract plans in the form of action trees (Grounds & Kudenko, 2005; Ryan, 2002; Ryan & Pendrith, 1998).

b) **First Learn then Plan:** Planning is combined with Reinforcement Learning in a two-step algorithm. In the first step a Reinforcement Learning algorithm is used in order to estimate the value function for each problem state. In the second phase, a planning algorithm is deployed in order to produce a plan according to the traditional formulation of AI planning. The plan that is produced is a complete control policy consisting of an explicit sequence of actions that requires minimal or zero environmental feedback during execution. The advantage of this approach is to improve the usability of the results. RL produces closed-loop policies that rely on moment-to-moment sensing, while the sequences of actions are very useful in situations where continuous sensing is difficult, unreliable or undesirable.

A representative example of this approach is the work by Sun, Sessions, and Peterson (Sun, 2000; Sun & Sessions, 1998; Sun & Sessions, 2000; Sun et al., 2001). The algorithm they use is a simple heuristic search starting from the initial state and moving forward. At each step the planning algorithm examines concurrently a constant number of promising states and thus performs a beam search on the space of states.

c) **Interchange Learning and Planning:** The last way to combine Planning with Reinforcement Learning is to maintain an internal model of the world and update the value function estimates by simulating transitions on the world model. This works concurrently with an actual reinforcement learning algorithm (e.g., Q-learning) that updates the same value functions by real interactions with the agents world. The values found by the two models are accumulated in the global policy and value function. This helps the value function to converge faster since the simulation of the interactions (performed by the Planning module) is done much faster than the actual interactions. Examples of this category include the DYNA family (Sutton, 1990, 1991; Szita, Takacs & Lorincz, 2003) and the Prioritized Sweeping (Andre et al., 1998; Dearden, 2001; Moore & Atkenson, 1993).

REFERENCES

Andre, D., Friedman N., & Parr, R. (1998). *Generalized prioritized sweeping. Advances in neural information processing systems* (pp. 1001-1007). MIT Press.

Baldassarre, G. (2003). Forward and bidirectional planning on reinforcement learning and neural networks in a simulated robot. In M. Butz, O. Sigaud & P. Gerard (Eds.), *Adaptive behaviour in anticipatory learning systems* (pp. 179-200). Springer-Verlag.

Barto, A.G., Sutton, R.S., & Anderson, C.W. (1983). Neuronlike adaptive elements that can solve difficult learning control problems. *IEEE Transactions on Systems, Man, and Cybernetics, 13*(5), 834-846.

Blum, A., & Furst, M. (1995). Fast planning through planning graph analysis. In *Proceedings of the 14th International Conference on Artificial Intelligence*, Berlin, Germany (pp.636-642).

Bonet, B., & Geffner, H. (2001). Planning as heuristic search [Special issue on heuristic search]. *Artificial Intelligence, 129*(1-2), 5-33.

Bonet, B., & Geffner, H. (2006). Learning depth-first search: A unified approach to heuristic search in deterministic and non-deterministic settings, and its application to MDPs. In *Proceedings of the 16th International Conference on Automated Planning and Scheduling (ICAPS-06)* (pp. 142-151).

Boutilier, C., Dearden, R., & Goldszmidt, M. (1995). Exploiting structure in policy construction. In *Fourteenth International Joint Conference on Artificial Intelligence* (pp. 1104-1111).

Boutilier, C., Reiter, R., & Price, B. (2001). Symbolic dynamic programming for first-order MDPs. In *Proceedings of the 17th Joint Conference on Artificial Intelligence* (pp. 690-700).

Cao, H., Xi, H., Smith, S., F. (2003). A reinforcement learning approach to production planning in the fabrication fulfillment manufacturing process. In *Winter Simulation Conference 2* (pp. 1417-1423).

Cesta, A., Fratini, S., & Oddi, A. (2004). Planning with concurrency, time and resources, a CSP-based approach. In I. Vlahavas & D. Vrakas (Eds.), *Intelligent techniques for planning* (pp. 259-295). Idea Group, Inc.

Dean T., & Kanazawa, K. (1990). A model for reasoning about persistence and causation. *Computational Intelligence, 5*(3), 142-150.

Dearden, R. (2001). Structured prioritized sweeping. In *International Conference on Machine Learning* (pp. 82-89).

Dietterich, T. (2000). An overview of MAXQ hierarchical reinforcement learning. In *Proceedings of the 4th International Symposium on Abstraction, Reformulation, and Approximation* (pp. 26-44).

Edelkamp, S. & Hoffmann, J. (2004). PDDL 2.1: The language for the classical part of IPC-4. In *Proceedings of the International Planning Competition. International Conference on Automated Planning and Scheduling* (pp., 1-7). Whistler.

Fikes, R.E., & Nilsson, N.J. (1974). STRIPS: A new approach to theorem proving in problem solving. *Artificial Intelligence, 2,* 189-208.

Fox, M. and Long, D., (2003). PDDL2.1: An extension to PDDL for expressing temporal planning domains. *Journal of Artificial Intelligence Research, 20,* 61-124. Retrieved from http://www.dur.ac.uk/d.p.long/pddl2.ps.gz

Gerevini, A. and Long, D. (2005). *Plan constraints and preferences in PDDL3,* (Tech Rep No. R.T. 2005-08-47), Dipartimento di Elettronica per l'Automazione, Università degli Studi di Brescia, Italy.

Ghallab, M., Nau, D., & Traverso, P. (2004). Automated planning: Theory and practice. Morgan Kaufmann Publishers.

Giunchiglia, F., & Traverso, P. (1999). Planning as model checking. In *Proceedings of the 5th European Conference on Planning*, Durham, UK (pp. 1-20).

Grounds, M., & Kudenko, D. (2005). Combining reinforcement learning with symbolic planning. In *Fifth European Workshop on Adaptive Agents and Multi-Agent Systems*, Paris.

Hoffmann, J., & Nebel, B. (2001). The FF planning system: Fast plan generation through heuristic search. *Journal of Artificial Intelligence Research, 14,* 253-302.

Kaelbling, L., Littman, M., & Moore, A. (1996). Reinforcement learning: A survey. *Journal of Artificial Intelligence Research, 4,* 237-285.

Kautz, H., & Selman, B. (1992). Planning as satisfiability. In *Proceedings of the 10th European Conference on Artificial Intelligence,* Vienna, Austria (pp. 359-363).

Kautz, H., & Selman, B. (1998). BLACKBOX: A new approach to the application of theorem proving to problem solving. In *Proceedings of the AIPS-98 Workshop on Planning as Combinatorial Search*, Pittsburgh, PA (pp. 58-60).

Koehler, J., Nebel, B., Hoffmann, J., & Dimopoulos, Y. (1997). Extending planning graphs to an ADL subset. In *Proceedings of the 4th European Conference on Planning*, Toulouse, France (pp. 273-285).

Kwee, I., Marcus, H., & Schmidhuber, J. (2001). Gradient-based reinforcement planning in policy-search methods. In *Fifth European Workshop on Reinforcement Learning* (pp. 27-29).

Lin, L.-J. (1992). Self-improving reactive agents based on reinforcement learning, planning and teaching. *Machine Learning, 8,* 293-321.

Long, D., & Fox, M. (1998). Efficient implementation of the plan graph in STAN. *Journal of Artificial Intelligence Research, 10,* 87-115.

McAllester, D. & Rosenblitt, D. (1991). Systematic nonlinear planning. In *Proceedings of the Ninth National Conference on Artificial Intelligence (AAAI-91)* (pp. 634-639).

McDermott, D. (1996). A heuristic estimator for means-end analysis in planning. In *Proceedings of the 3rd International Conference on Artificial Intelligence Planning Systems,* Edinburgh, UK (pp. 142-149).

Moore, A.W., & Atkenson, C.G. (1993). Prioritized sweeping: Reinforcement learning with less data and less real time. *Machine Learning, 13,* 103-130.

Newell, A., & Simon, H.A. (1963). GPS, a program that simulates human thought. In Feigenbaum & Feldman (Eds.), *Computers and thought* (pp. 279-293). New York: McGraw-Hill.

Nguyen, X., Kambhampati, S., & Nigenda, R. (2000). AltAlt: Combining the advantages of graphplan and heuristics state search. In *Proceedings of the 2000 International Conference on Knowledge-based Computer Systems,* Bombay, India.

Nilsson, N.J. (1994). Teleo-reactive programs for agent control. *Journal of Artificial Intelligence Research, 1,* 139-158.

Penberthy, J. & Weld, D. (1992). UCPOP: A sound and complete, partial order planner for ADL. In *Proceedings of the Third International Conference on Principles of Knowledge Representation and Reasoning* (pp. 103-114). Toulouse, France.

Peng, J., & Ronald J.W. (1993). Efficient learning and planning within the dyna framework. *Adaptive Behavior, 1*(4), 437-454.

Ryan, M.R.K. (2002). Using abstract models of behaviours to automatically generate reinforcement learning hierarchies. In *19th International Conference on Machine Learning* (pp. 522-529).

Ryan, M.R.K, & Pendrith, M.D. (1998). RL-TOPs: An architecture for modularity and re-use in reinforcement learning. In *15th International Conference of Machine Learning* (pp. 481-487).

Sacerdoti, E. (1974). Planning in a hierarchy of abstraction spaces. *Artificial Intelligence, 5,* 115-135.

Sun, R. (2000). Beyond simple rule extraction: The extraction of planning knowledge from reinforcement learners. In *International Joint Conference on Neural Networks* (p. 2105). Como, Italy. IEEE Press.

Sun, R., Peterson, T., & Sessions, C. (2001). Beyond simple rule extraction: Acquiring planning knowledge from neural networks.

Sun, R., & Sessions, C. (1998). Extracting plans from reinforcement learners. In *International Symposium on Intelligent Data Engineering and Learning* (pp. 243-248). Springer-Verlag.

Sun, R., & Sessions, C. (2000). Learning plans without a priori knowledge. *Adaptive Behavior, 18*(3), 225-253.

Sutton, R.S. (1988). Learning to predict by the methods of temporal differences. *Machine Learning, 3,* 9-44.

Sutton, R.S. (1990). Integrated architectures for learning, planning and reacting. In *Proceedings of the Seventh International Conference on Machine Learning,* (pp. 216-224).

Sutton, R.S. (1991). Planning by incremental dynamic programming. In *Proceedings of the Eighth International Workshop on Machine Learning* (pp. 353-357).

Sutton, R.S., & Barto, A.G. (1999). Reinforcement learning, an introduction. MIT Press.

Szita, I, Takacs, B, & Lorincz, A. (2003). ε-mdps: learning in varying environments. *Journal of Machine Learning Research, 3*, 145-174.

Tsamardinos, I., Vidal, T., & Pollack, M. (2003). CTP: A new constraint-based formalism for conditional, temporal planning [Special issue on planning]. *Consraints 8*(4), 365-388.

Vrakas, D., Tsoumakas, G., Bassilliades, N., & Vlahavas, I. (2005). Machine learning for adaptive planning. In I. Vlahavas & D. Vrakas (Eds.), *Intelligent techniques for planning* (pp. 90-120). Idea Group Publishing.

Watkins, C.J.J.H. (1989). *Learning with delayed rewards*. Unpublished Ph.D. thesis, Cambridge University Psychology Department.

Yang, Q., & Tenenberg, J. (1990). AbTWEAK: Abstracting a nonlinear least commitment planner. In *Proceedings of the 8th National Conference on Artificial Intelligence*, Boston, MA (pp. 204-209).

Zhao, G., Tatsumi, S., & Sun, R. (1999). RTP-Q: A reinforcement learning system with time constraints exploration planning for accelerating the learning rate. *IEICE Transactions on Fundamentals of Eloctronics, Communications and Computer Sciences, E82-A,* 2266-2273.

Zimmerman, T., & Kambhambati, S. (2003). Learning-assisted automated planning: Looking back, taking stock, going forward. *AI Magazine, 24*(2), 73-96.

Chapter VII
Induction as a Search Procedure

Stasinos Konstantopoulos
NCSR 'Demokritos', Greece

Rui Camacho
Universidade do Porto, Portugal

Nuno A. Fonseca
Universidade do Porto, Portugal

Vítor Santos Costa
Universidade Federal do Rio de Janeiro, Brasil

ABSTRACT

This chapter introduces inductive logic programming (ILP) from the perspective of search algorithms in computer science. It first briefly considers the version spaces approach to induction, and then focuses on inductive logic programming: from its formal definition and main techniques and strategies, to priors used to restrict the search space and optimized sequential, parallel, and stochastic algorithms. The authors hope that this presentation of the theory and applications of inductive logic programming will help the reader understand the theoretical underpinnings of ILP, and also provide a helpful overview of the State-of-the-Art in the domain.

INTRODUCTION

Induction is a very important operation in the process of scientific discovery, which has been studied from different perspectives in different disciplines. Induction, or inductive logic, is the process of forming conclusions that reach beyond the data (facts and rules), i.e., beyond the current boundaries of knowledge. At the core of inductive thinking is the 'inductive leap', the stretch of imagination that draws a reasonable inference from the available information. Therefore, inductive conclusions are only probable, they may turn out to be false or improbable when given more data.

In this chapter we address the study of induction from an artificial intelligence (AI) perspective and, more specifically, from a machine learning perspective, which aims at automating the inductive inference process. As is often the case in AI, this translates to mapping the 'inductive leap' onto a search procedure. Search, therefore, becomes a central element of the automation of the inductive inference process.

We consider two different approaches to the problem of induction as a search procedure: version spaces is an informal approach, more in line with traditional machine learning approaches; by contrast, search-based algorithms for inductive logic programming (ILP) rely on a formal definition of the search space. We compare the two approaches under several dimensions, namely, expressiveness of the hypothesis language underlying the space, completeness of the search, space traversal techniques, implemented systems and applications thereof.

Next, the chapter focuses on the issues related to a more principled approach to induction as a search. Given a formal definition and characterization of the search space, we describe the main techniques employed for its traversal: strategies and heuristics, priors used to restrict its size, optimized sequential search algorithms, as well as stochastic and parallel ones.

The theoretical issues presented and exposed are complemented by descriptions of and references to implemented and applied systems, as well as real-world application domains where ILP systems have been successful.

A PRAGMATIC APPROACH: VERSION SPACES

This section is structured into three parts. A first part presents a set of definitions and concepts that lay the foundations for the search procedure into which induction is mapped. In a second part we mention briefly alternative approaches that have been taken to induction as a search procedure and finally in a third part we present the *version spaces* as a general methodology to implement induction as a search procedure.

A Historical Road Map

Concept learning is a research area of machine learning that addresses the automation of the process of finding (inducing) a description of a concept (called the 'target concept' or hypothesis) given a set of instances of such concept. Concepts and instances have to be expressed in a *concept description language* or *hypothesis language*. Given a set of instances of some concept it is usually a rather difficult problem to (automatically) induce the 'target concept'. The major difficulty is that there may be a lot, if not an infinite, number of plausible conjectures (hypotheses) that are 'consistent' with the given instances. Automating the induction process involves the generation of the candidate concept descriptions (hypotheses), their evaluation, and the choice of 'the best one' according to some criteria. The concept learning problem is often mapped into a search problem, that looks for a concept description that explains the given instances and lies within the concept description language.

An important step towards the automation of the learning process is the structuring of the elements of the hypothesis language in a manner that makes it possible to perform systematic searches, to justifiably discard some 'uninteresting' regions of candidate descriptions, and to have a compact description of the search space.

For this purpose, machine learning borrows from mathematics the concept of a *lattice*, a partially ordered set with the property that all of its non-empty finite subsets have both a supremum (called join) and an infimum (called meet). A *semilattice* has either only a join or only a meet. The partial order can be any reflexive, anti-symmetric, and transitive binary relation. In machine learning a lattice is usually defined as follows:

Definition 1: *A lattice is a partially ordered set in which every pair of elements a,b has a greatest lower bound (glb, $a \sqcap b$) and least upper bound (lub, $a \sqcup b$).*

and the partial ordering is based of the concept of generality, which places clauses along general–specific axes. Such a partial ordering is called a *generalization ordering* or a *generalization model*, and has the advantage of imposing a structure that is convenient for systematically searching for general theories and for focusing on parts of the structure that are known to be interesting.

Different generalization models have been proposed in the Concept Learning literature; Mitchell (1997, p. 24), for example, defines generalization for a domain where instances (x) belong to a domain (X) of feature vectors and the target concept is encoded as a boolean-valued function (h):

Definition 2: *Let h_j and h_k be boolean-valued functions defined over X. Then h_j is more general than or equal to h_k (we write $h_j >_g h_k$) if and only if $(\forall x \in X)[h_k(x) = 1 \rightarrow h_j(x) = 1]$.*

Another popular definition of generality is based on the logical concept of semantic entailment:

Definition 3: *Given two clauses C_1 and C_2, we shall call C_1 more general (more specific) than C_2, and write $C_1 >_g C_2$ ($C_1 <_g C_2$), if and only if C_1 entails C_2 (C_2 entails C_1).*

with various syntactic logical operators suggested for the purpose of inferring entailment. We shall revisit this point in the context of inductive logic programming in the following section. This suggestion that induction may be automated by carrying a search through an order space was independently suggested by Popplestone (1970) and Plotkin (1970).

The search space of the alternative concept descriptions may be traversed using any of the traditional AI search strategies. In 1970 Winston (1970) describes a concept learning system using a depth-first search. In Winston's system one example at a time is analysed and a single concept description is maintained as the current best hypothesis to describe the target concept. The current best hypothesis is tested against a new example and modified to become consistent with the example while maintaining consistency with all previously seen examples. An alternative search strategy, breadth-first search, was used in concept learning by Plotkin (1970), Michalski (1973), Hayes-Roth (1974) and Vere (1975). These algorithms already take advantage of the order in the search space. Plotkin's work is revisited later, as it forms the basis for several developments in inductive logic programming.

Introducing Version Spaces

We now focus our attention on a general approach to concept learning, proposed by Mitchell (1978), called *version spaces*. A *version space* is the set of all hypotheses consistent with a set of training examples. In most applications the number of candidate hypotheses consistent with the examples is very large or even infinite. It is therefore impractical—or even infeasible—to store an enumeration of such candidates. The version space uses a compact and elegant representation of the set of candidate hypotheses. The representation takes advantage of the order imposed over such hypotheses and stores only the most general and most specific set of descriptions that limit the version space.

In order to make a more formal presentation of the version spaces approach to concept learning let us introduce some useful definitions. Assume that the function $tg(e)$ gives the 'correct' value of the target concept for each instance e. A hypothesis $h(e)$ is said to be consistent with a set of instances (examples) E **iff** it produces the same value of $tg(e)$ for each example e in E. That is:

$$\text{Consistent}(h, E) \equiv \forall e \in E, h(e) = tg(e) \quad (1)$$

Figure 1. The candidate-elimination algorithm

Candidate-Elimination
Input: Examples (E) – positive (E^+) and negative (E^-).
Output: The sets G and S.

```
1.    G = set of maximally general hypotheses in H
2.    S = set of maximally specific hypotheses in H
3.    for all e ∈ E
4.      if e ∈ E⁺ then
5.        remove from G any hypothesis inconsistent with e
6.          for all s ∈ S
7.            if s inconsistent with e then
8.              remove s from S
9.              add to S all minimal generalizations of h of s such that
10.                h is consistent with e and ∃g∈G g <g h
11.              remove any s ∈ S such that ∃s'∈S s <g s'
12.            endif
13.          end for all
14.      endif
15.      else (e ∈ E⁻)
16.        remove from S any hypothesis inconsistent with e
17.          for all g ∈ G
18.            if g inconsistent with e then
19.              remove g from G
20.              add to G all minimal specialisations h of g such that
21.                h is consistent with e and ∃s∈S h <g s
22.              remove any g ∈ G such that ∃g'∈G g' <g g
23.            endif
24.          end for all
25.    end for all
26.    return S and G
```

Examples are of two kinds: positive and negative. Positive examples are instances of the target concept whereas negative examples are not.

Let hypothesis space H be the set of all hypotheses that are part of hypothesis language L. Version space $VS_{H,E}$ with respect to hypothesis space H and training set E, is the subset of H consistent with E.

$$VS_{H,E} \equiv \left\{ h \in H \mid \text{Consistent}(h, E) \right\} \quad (2)$$

Since the set represented by the version space may be very large, a compact and efficient way of describing such set is needed. To fully characterize the version space Mitchell proposes to represent the most general and more specific elements, i.e., a version space is represented by the upper and lower boundaries of the ordered search space. Mitchell proposes also the CANDIDATE-ELIMINATION algorithm to efficiently traverse the hypothesis space.

In the CANDIDATE-ELIMINATION algorithm the boundaries of the version space are the only elements stored. The upper boundary is called G, the set of the most general elements of the space, and the lower boundary S, the set of the most specific hypotheses of the version space.

The upper (more general) boundary G, with respect to hypothesis space H and examples E, is the set of the maximally general members of H consistent with E. (See Box 1)

The CANDIDATE-ELIMINATION algorithm is outlined in Figure 1. The algorithm proceeds incrementally, by analysing one example at a time. It starts with the most general set G containing all hypotheses from L consistent with the first example and with the most specific set

Box 1. Formulas 3 and 4

$$G \equiv \left\{ g \in H \mid \text{Consistent}\left(g, E\right) \wedge \neg \left(\exists g' >_g g\right) \wedge \text{Consistent}\left(g', E\right) \right\} \qquad (3)$$

where $>_g$ denotes the 'more general than' relation. The lower (more specific) boundary S, with respect to hypothesis space H and training set E, is the set of maximally specific members of H consistent with E.

$$S \equiv \left\{ s \in H \mid \text{Consistent}\left(s, E\right) \wedge \neg \left(\exists s >_g s'\right) \wedge \text{Consistent}\left(s', E\right) \right\} \qquad (4)$$

S of hypotheses from L consistent with the first example (the set with the first example only). As each new example is presented, G gets specialized and S generalized, thus reducing the version space they represent. Positive examples lead to the generalization of S, whenever S is not consistent with a positive example. Negative examples prevent over-generalization by specializing G, whenever G is inconsistent with the a negative example. When specializing elements of G, only specializations that are maximally general and generalizations of some element of S are admitted. Symmetrically, when generalizing elements of S, only generalizations that are maximally specific and specializations of some element of G are admitted. When all examples are processed, the hypotheses consistent with the presented data are the set of hypotheses from L within the G and S boundaries.

Some advantages of the version space approach with the CANDIDATE-ELIMINATION algorithm is that partial descriptions of the concepts may be used to classify new instances, and that each example is examined only once and there is no need for backtracking. The algorithm is complete, i.e., if there is a hypothesis in L consistent with the data it will be found.

Version spaces and the CANDIDATE-ELIMINATION algorithm have been applied to several problems such as learning regularities in chemical mass spectroscopy (Mitchell, 1978) and control

rules for heuristic search (Mitchell et al., 1983). The algorithm was initially applied to induce rules for the DENDRAL knowledge-based system that suggested plausible chemical structure of molecules based on the analysis of information of the molecule chemical mass spectroscope data. Finally, Mitchell et al. (1983) uses the technique to acquire problem-solving heuristics for the LEX system in the domain of symbolic integration.

A Simple Example

The technique of version spaces is independent of the hypothesis representation language. According to the application, the hypothesis language used may be as simple as an attribute-value language or as powerful as First Order Logic. For illustrative purposes only (*proof-of-concept*) we present a very simple example using an attribute-value hypothesis language. We show an example of the CANDIDATE-ELIMINATION algorithm to induce a concept of a bird using five training examples of animals.

The hypothesis language will be the set of 4-tuples encoding the attributes *eats*, *has feathers*, *has claws* and *flies*. The domains of such attributes are: eats={meat, seeds, insects}, has feathers={yes, no}, has claws={yes, no} and flies={yes, no}. The representation of an animal that eats meat, has feathers, does not have claws and flies is the 4-tuple: <meat, yes, no, yes>. We

Figure 2. Simple example of the CANDIDATE-ELIMINATION algorithm sequence for learning the concept of bird.

training instances	version space	
	S set	G set
< meat, yes, yes, yes > (positive – an eagle)		
	{ < meat, yes, yes, yes > }	{ < _, _, _, _ > }
< meat, no, yes, no > (negative – a wolf)		
	{ < meat, yes, yes, yes > }	{ < _, yes, _, _ >, < _, _, _, yes > }
< seeds, yes, no, yes> (positive – a dove)		
	{ < _, yes, _, yes > }	{ < _, yes, _, _ >, < _, _, _, yes > }
< insects, no, no, yes > (negative — a bet)		
	{ < _, yes, _, yes > }	{ < _, yes, _, _ > }
< seeds, yes, no, no> (positive – an ostrich)		
	{ < _, yes, _, _ > }	{ < _, yes, _, _ > }

use the symbol _ (underscore) to indicate that any value is acceptable. We say that a hypothesis h_i matches an example if every feature value of the example is either equal for the corresponding value in h_i or h_i has the symbol "_" for that feature (meaning "any value" is acceptable). Let us consider that a hypothesis h_1 is more general than hypothesis h_2 if h_1 matches all the instances that h_2 matches but the reverse is not true. Figure 2 shows the sequence of values of the sets S and G after the analysis of five examples, one at a time. The first example is a positive example, an eagle (<meat, yes, yes, yes>), and is used to initialize the S set. The G set is initialized with the most general hypothesis of the language, the hypothesis that matches all the examples: <_, _, _, _>. The second example is negative and is a description of a wolf (<meat, no, yes, no>). The second example is not matched by the element of S and therefore S is unchanged. However the hypothesis in the G set covers the negative example and has to be minimally specialized. Minimal specializations of <_, _, _, _> that avoid covering the working example are: <seed, _, _, _>, <insects, _, _, _>,

<_, yes, _, _>, <_, _, no, _>, <_, _, _, yes>. Among these five specializations only the third and the fifth are retained since they are the only ones that cover the element of S. Analysing the third example (a dove – a positive example) leads the algorithm to minimally generalize the element of S since it does not cover that positive example. The minimal generalization of S's hypothesis is <_, yes, _, yes> that covers all seen positive and is a specialization of at least one hypothesis in G. The forth example is negative and is a description of a bet (<insects, no, no, yes>). This example forces a specialization of G. Finally the last example is a positive one (an ostrich – <seeds, yes, no, no>) that results in a minimal generalization of S. The final version space (delimited by the final S and G) defines bird as any animal that has a beak.

INDUCTIVE LOGIC PROGRAMMING THEORY

Inductive logic programming (ILP) is the machine learning discipline that deals with the induction of First-Order Predicate Logic programs. Related research appears as early as the late 1960's, but it is only in the early 1990's that ILP research starts making rapid advances and the term itself was coined.[1]

In this section we first present a formal setting for inductive logic programming and highlight the mapping of this theoretical setting into a search procedure. The formal definitions of the elements of the search and the inter-dependencies between these elements are explained, while at same time the concrete systems that implement them are presented.

It should be noted at this point that we focus on the, so to speak, mainstream line of ILP research, that most directly relates to ILP's original inception and formulation. And that, even within this scope, it is not possible to describe in depth all ILP systems and variations, so some will only receive a passing reference. With respect to systems, in particular, we generally present in more detail systems were a concept or technique was originally introduced, and try to make reference to as many subsequent implementations as possible.

The Task of ILP

inductive logic programming systems generalize from individual instances in the presence of background knowledge, conjecturing patterns about yet unseen data. inductive logic programming, therefore, deals with learning concepts given some *background knowledge* and *examples*[2]. Examples, background knowledge, and the newly learnt concepts are represented as logic programs.

Given this common ground, the learning process in ILP can be approached in two different ways. In *descriptive* induction one aims at describing regularities or patterns in the data. In *predictive* induction one aims at learning theories that solve classification/prediction tasks.

More precisely, let us assume there is some background knowledge B, some examples E, and

a hypothesis language $\mathcal{L}$. We define *background knowledge* to be a set of axioms about the current task that are independent of specific examples. We define the set of *examples*, or *instances*, or *observations* as the data we want to generalize from. Often, but not always, examples are divided into *positive examples*, or E^+, and *negative examples*, or E^-, such that $E = E^+ \cup E^-$.

The task of *descriptive ILP* is finding a theory that explains the examples in the presence of the background. More formally, descriptive ILP is defined as follows:

Definition 4: *Given background knowledge B, examples E, and hypothesis language $\mathcal{L}$, if the following prior condition holds:*
(Prior Necessity) *B does not explain E*
then the task of descriptive ILP is to find a maximally specific hypothesis H in $\mathcal{L}$, such that:
(Posterior Sufficiency) *H explains $B \wedge E$*
if such a hypothesis exists.

Definition 5: *Given background knowledge B, positive training data E^+, negative training data E^-, and hypothesis language $\mathcal{L}$, if the following prior conditions hold:*
(Prior Satisfiability) *B does not explain E^-*
(Prior Necessity) *B does not explain E^+*
then the task of predictive ILP is to find a hypothesis H in $\mathcal{L}$ with the following properties:
(Posterior Satisfiability) *$B \wedge H$ does not explain E^-*
(Posterior Sufficiency) *$B \wedge H$ explains E^+*
if such a hypothesis exists.

Informally, this definition states that first of all the negative data must be consistent with the background, since otherwise no consistent hypothesis can ever be constructed; and that a hypothesis must be necessary because the background is not a viable hypothesis on its own. Given that, predictive ILP augments existing (background) knowledge with a hypothesis, so that the combined result covers (predicts) the data.

Explanation Semantics

At the core of the ILP task definition is the concept of *explaining* observations by hypothesis, or, in other words, of hypotheses being *models* or *explanations*. There are two major *explanation semantics* for ILP, which substantiate this concept in different ways: *learning from interpretations* and *learning from entailment*.

Under learning from interpretations, a logic program covers a set of ground atoms which is a Herbrand interpretation of the program, if the set is a model of the program. That is, the interpretation is a valid grounding of the program's variables. Under learning from entailment, a program covers a set of ground atoms, if the program entails the ground atoms, that is, if the ground atoms are included in all models of the program. As De Raedt (1997) notes, learning from interpretations reduces to learning from entailment. This means that learning from entailment is a stronger explanation model, and solutions found by learning from interpretations can also be found by learning from entailment, but not vice versa.

From a practical point of view, in learning from interpretations each example is a separate Prolog program, consisting of multiple ground facts representing known properties of the example. A hypothesis covers the example when the latter is a model of the former, i.e., the example provides a valid grounding for the hypothesis. In learning from entailment, on the other hand, each example is a single fact. A hypothesis covers the example when the hypothesis entails the example.

A third explanation semantics that has been proposed is *learning from satisfiability* (De Raedt & Dehaspe, 1997), where examples and hypotheses are both logic programs, and a hypothesis covers an example if the conjunction of the hypothesis and the example is satisfiable. Learning from satisfiability is stronger than both learning from entailment and learning from interpretations.

ILP Settings

A *setting* of ILP is a complete specification of the task and the explanation semantics, optionally complemented with further restrictions on the hypothesis language and the examples representation.

Although in theory all combinations are possible, descriptive ILP is most suitable to learning from interpretations, since under this semantics, the data is organized in a way that is convenient for tackling the descriptive ILP task. Symmetrically, predictive ILP typically operates under learning from entailment semantics. In fact, this coupling is so strong, that almost all ILP systems operate in either the *non-monotonic* or the *normal setting*.

In the *non-monotonic setting* (De Raedt, 1997), descriptive ILP operates under learning from interpretations. The non-monotonic setting has been successfully applied to several problems, including learning association rules (Dehaspe & Toironen, 2000) and subgroup discovery (Wrobel, 1997). To perform subgroup discovery, the notion of explanation is relaxed to admit hypotheses that satisfy 'softer' acceptance criteria like, for example, similarity or associativity.

An interesting line of research is pursued by Blockeel & De Raedt (1998) who break the coupling we just described and propose TILDE, and ILP system that tackles the predictive ILP task under learning from interpretations. TILDE is used to induce *logical decision trees*, the first-order counter-part of decision trees.

A more surprising development is the application of ILP methodology to clustering, an unsupervised task where unlabeled examples are organized to clusters of examples with similar attributes. The underlying idea is based on Langley's (1996) view of decision trees as concept-hierarchies inducers where each node of the tree is associated with a concept. For this task, De Raedt & Blockeel (1997) build upon TILDE to propose C 0.5, a first-order clustering system that instead of class information to guide the

Figure 3. The Buendia family

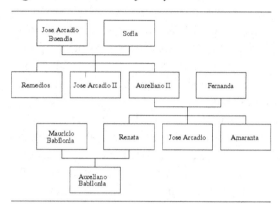

search, borrows the concept of distance metrics from *instance based learning*.

In the *normal setting* (Muggleton, 1991), also called *explanatory ILP* or *strong ILP*, predictive ILP operates under learning from entailment semantics. Most ILP systems operate in this setting, or rather a specialization of the normal setting called the *example setting* of the *definite semantics* (Muggleton & De Raedt, 1994). This setting

imposes the restrictions that the examples are ground instances of the target and the background and hypothesis are formulated as definite clause programs. As noted by Muggleton & De Raedt (1994, pp. 635-636), the restriction to definite semantics greatly simplifies the ILP task, since for every definite program T there is a model $\mathcal{M}^+(T)$ (its *minimal Herbrand model*) in which all formulae are decidable and the Closed World Assumption holds. In this example, definite setting, the task of normal ILP is defined as follows:

Definition 6: *Given background knowledge B, positive training data E^+, and negative training data E^-, a definite ILP algorithm operating within the example setting constructs a hypothesis H with the following properties:*

(Prior Satisfiability) All $e \in E^-$ are false in $\mathcal{M}^+(B)$
(Prior Necessity) Some $e \in E^+$ are false in $\mathcal{M}^+(B)$
(Posterior Satisfiability) All $e \in E^-$ are false in $\mathcal{M}^+(B \wedge H)$
(Posterior Sufficiency) All $e \in E^+$ are true in $\mathcal{M}^+(B \wedge H)$

Box 2. Equation 5

$$B = \begin{cases} father(X,Y) \leftarrow parent(X,Y) \wedge male(X) \\ sibling(X,Y) \leftarrow parent(Z,X) \wedge parent(Z,Y) \wedge X \neq Y \\ male(jArcadioBD) \qquad\qquad female(remedios) \\ male(aurelianoII) \qquad\qquad female(renata) \\ parent(jArcadioBD, remedios) \\ parent(sofia, remedios) \end{cases} \qquad (5)$$

Box 3. Formula 6

$$E^+ = \begin{cases} grandfather(jArcadioBD, jArcadio), grandfather(jArcadioBD, renata), \\ grandfather(aurelianoII, aureliano) \end{cases}$$
$$E^- = \{grandfather(sofia, jArcadio), grandfather(aurelianoII, renata)\} \qquad (6)$$

Box 4. Formulas 7, 8, and 9

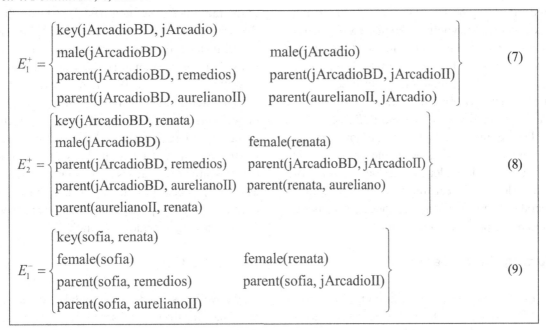

$$E_1^+ = \left\{ \begin{array}{ll} \text{key(jArcadioBD, jArcadio)} & \\ \text{male(jArcadioBD)} & \text{male(jArcadio)} \\ \text{parent(jArcadioBD, remedios)} & \text{parent(jArcadioBD, jArcadioII)} \\ \text{parent(jArcadioBD, aurelianoII)} & \text{parent(aurelianoII, jArcadio)} \end{array} \right\} \qquad (7)$$

$$E_2^+ = \left\{ \begin{array}{ll} \text{key(jArcadioBD, renata)} & \\ \text{male(jArcadioBD)} & \text{female(renata)} \\ \text{parent(jArcadioBD, remedios)} & \text{parent(jArcadioBD, jArcadioII)} \\ \text{parent(jArcadioBD, aurelianoII)} & \text{parent(renata, aureliano)} \\ \text{parent(aurelianoII, renata)} & \end{array} \right\} \qquad (8)$$

$$E_1^- = \left\{ \begin{array}{ll} \text{key(sofia, renata)} & \\ \text{female(sofia)} & \text{female(renata)} \\ \text{parent(sofia, remedios)} & \text{parent(sofia, jArcadioII)} \\ \text{parent(sofia, aurelianoII)} & \end{array} \right\} \qquad (9)$$

A Simple Example

To make the difference between ILP settings more concrete, let us consider as an example the task of learning the grandfather relation based on the family shown in Figure 3.

In the definite setting, the background theory includes abstract definitions as well as ground facts. Abstract definitions provide potentially useful background predicates (like 'father' and 'sibling' in our example) that represent general prior knowledge about family relations. Ground facts (like parent(jArcadioBD,remedios) in our example) substantiate the basic predicates that are the 'primitives' from which more complex relations are built, and represent concrete knowledge about this particular family (see Box 2).

We only show a fragment of the full background knowledge here, but the learning task needs that all relevant information in Figure 3 is included. Next, an ILP algorithm will receive the following example, (see Box 3), and construct a hypothesis regarding the intensional definition of the grandfather/2 predicate, so that it covers the positives without covering any of the negatives. Ideally, the learnt definition should *generalize* to unseen examples such as grandfather(jArcadio BD,amaranta).

In the non-monotonic setting, on the other hand, examples are organized as sets of ground terms, describing an object and the relations that it, or its sub-objects, take part in. Since we are interested in constructing the grandfather predicate, our objects are relationships between individuals, called *keys*. (See Box 4)

Each example contains facts related to two individuals. Note that facts may be repeated across examples: e.g., the first two examples share facts about jArcadioBD. From these examples an ILP algorithm will construct a hypothesis such that interpretations E_1^+ and E_2^+ are models for it, whereas E_1^- is not.

Note, however, that in our example the generation that is the 'link' between grandfathers and grandchildren is present in the examples, since the members of this intermediate generation are connected to the terms in the key via the parent/2 predicate. Imagine, however, that we were trying to to formulate a hypothesis about a more general ancestor/2 predicate, by including *key(jArcadioB D,aureliano)* as a positive example. The properties of the key's arguments fail to include the *two* intermediate generations necessary to make the link between *jArcadioBD* and *aureliano*.

This demonstrates the limitations of the non-monotonic setting when the data exhibits long-distance dependencies: the locality assumption under which learning from interpretations operates, keeps such long-distance dependencies from being present in the examples.

Setting Up the Search

As mentioned earlier, the definition of the task of ILP is agnostic as to how to search for good hypotheses and even as to how to verify entailment.[3] Leaving aside the issue of mechanizing entailment for the moment, we discuss first how to choose candidate hypotheses among the members of the hypothesis language.

The simplest, naïve way to traverse this space of possible hypotheses would be to use a generate-and-test algorithm that first, lexicographically enumerates all possible hypotheses, and second,

evaluates each hypothesis' quality. This approach is impractical for any non-trivial problem, due the large (possibly infinite) size of the hypothesis space. Instead, inductive machine learning systems (both propositional rule learning systems as well as first-order ILP systems) structure the search space in order to allow for the application of well-tested and established AI search techniques and optimizations. This structure must be such that, first, it accommodates a heuristics-driven search that reaches promising candidates as directly as possible; and, second, it allows for uninteresting sub-spaces to be efficiently pruned without having to wade through them.

Sequential Cover

Predictive ILP systems typically take advantage of the fact that the hypotheses are logic programs (and therefore sets of clauses) to use a strategy called *sequential cover* or *cover removal*, a greedy separate-and-conquer strategy that breaks the

Figure 4. The sequential cover strategy. The LearnOneRule() procedure returns the best rule found that explains a subset of the positive examples E⁺. Coverage() returns the subset of E⁺ covered by R.

```
covering(E)
Input: Positive and negative examples E⁺, E⁻.
Output: A set of consistent rules.

1.    Rules_Learned = ∅
2.    while E⁺ ≠ ∅ do
3.        R = LEARNONERULE (E, START_RULE)
4.        Rules_Learned = Rules_Learned ∪ R
5.        E⁺ = E⁺ \ COVERAGE(R, E⁺)
6.    end while
7.    return Rules_Learned
```

Figure 5. A procedure which returns the best rule found that explains a subset of the positive examples in E. The starting point of the search R0 is one of the extremities of the lattice, RefineRule() is the lattice traversal operator, and PickRules() combines the search strategy, the heuristics, and prior constraints of valid rules to generate an ordered subset of the NewRules set

```
learnOneRule (E, R₀)
Input: Examples E, used for evaluation. Initial rule R₀.
Output: A rule R.

1.    BestRule = R = R₀
2.    while stopping criteria not satisfied do
3.        NewRules = REFINERULE(R)
4.        GoodRules = PICKRULES(E, NewRules)
5.        for r ∈ GoodRules
6.            NewR = LEARNONERULE(E, r)
7.            if NewR better than BestRule
8.                BestRule = NewR
9.            endif
10.       end for
11.   end while
12.   return BestRule
```

problem of learning a set of clauses into iterations of the problem of learning a single clause.

The iterative algorithm relies on a pool of *active* examples, that is, of examples which have not been covered yet. Initially, the pool is set to all the positive examples. Each iteration first calls a lower-level algorithm to search for a single clause of the target predicate. After finding a clause, all positive examples that are covered by the clause are removed from the pool, so that the next iteration is guaranteed to find a different clause. Note that in this algorithm, as iterations proceed, clauses are evaluated on how well they cover the active examples, not the total set of positive examples. The process continues until all the examples are covered or some other termination criterion is met, e.g., a constraint on execution time or the maximum number of clauses. This procedure is also shown in Figure 4.

Most predictive ILP systems use some variant of this general strategy, and implement a variety of different algorithms to perform the clausal search that identifies the best clause to append to the theory at each iteration (step 4 in Figure 4).

Clause Generalization Search

In ILP, the search for individual rules is simplified by structuring the rule search space as a lattice or a semi-lattice, where a generality partial order is semantically defined using the concept of logical entailment, in the same way that we have discussed in the context of version spaces in the previous section.

Again, various generalization models have been proposed in the ILP literature, each based on different inference mechanisms for inferring entailment. Each of these defines a different *traversal operator* which maps conjunctions of clauses into generalizations (or, depending on the direction of the search, specializations) thereof.

Based on the above, the the *LearnOneRule*() procedure of Figure 4 works as shown in Figure 5, performing a lattice search by recursively transforming an initial clause into a series of hypotheses. The initial clause is one of the extremities of the lattice, and the search is either *open-ended* (for semi-lattices) or bound by the other extremity.

Regarding the extremities of the lattice, the maximally general clause (the *top clause*) of the generalization lattice is □, the empty clause. The construction of the maximally specific clause varies with different ILP algorithms and generalization models, and can be *saturation* or *least general generalization*, or simply a ground example. Which one of the maximally general and the maximally specific assumes the rôle of the join and which of the meet depends on the direction of the search along the general–specific dimension.

The Elements of the Search

We have identified the elements of the ILP search lattice, the mathematical construct that defines a search problem equivalent to the ILP task, as logically formulated before. With these elements in place, we can proceed to apply a lattice search strategy, a methodology for traversing the search space looking for a solution. Search strategies are typically driven not only by the shape of the search space, but also by a heuristics, which evaluates each node of the lattice and estimates its 'distance' from a solution.

To recapitulate, in order to perform an ILP run, the following elements must be substantiated:

- The hypothesis language, which is the set of eligible hypothesis clauses. The elements of this set are also the elements that form the lattice.
- A traversal operator that in-order visits the search space, following either the general-to-specific or the specific-to-general direction.
- The top and bottom clause, the extremities of the lattice. The top clause is the empty-

bodied clause that accepts all examples, and the bottom clause is a maximally specific clause that accepts a single example. The bottom clause is constructed by a process called *saturation.*

- The search strategy applied to the lattice defined by the three elements above.
- The heuristics that drive the search, an estimator of a node's 'distance' from a solution. Due to the monotonic nature of the definite programs, this distance can be reasonably estimated by an evaluation function that assigns a value to each clause related to its 'quality' as a solution.

We now proceed to describe how various ILP algorithms and systems realize these five elements, and show the impact of each design decision on the system's performance. The focus will be on the clause-level search performed by sequential-cover predictive ILP systems, but it should be noted that the same general methodology is followed by theory-level predictive ILP and (to a lesser extend) descriptive ILP algorithms as well.

Hypothesis Language

One of the strongest, and most widely advertised, points in favour of ILP is the usage of prior knowledge to specify the hypothesis language within which the search for a solution is to be contained. ILP systems offer a variety of tools for specifying the exact boundaries of the search space, which modify the space defined by the *background theory,* the clausal theory that represents the concrete facts and the abstract, first-order generalizations that are known to hold in the domain of application.

In more practical terms, the *background predicates,* the predicates defined in the background theory, are the building blocks from which hypothesis clauses are constructed. The background predicates should, therefore, represent all the relevant facts known about the domain of

the concept being learnt; the ILP algorithm's task is to sort though them and identify the ones that, connected in an appropriate manner, encode the target concept. Even ILP algorithms that go one step further and revise the background theory, rely on the original background to use as a starting point.

Prior knowledge in ILP is not, however, restricted to the set of predefined concepts available to the ILP algorithm, but extends to include a set of syntactic and semantic restrictions imposed on the set of admissible clauses, effectively restricting the search space. Such restrictions cannot be encoded in the background theory program of Definitions 5 and 5, but ILP systems provide external mechanisms in order to enforce them.[4] These mechanisms should be thought of as filters that reject or accept clauses—and, in some cases, whole areas of the search space—based on syntactic or semantic pre-conditions.

Hypothesis Checking

As explained before, managing the ILP search space often depends on having filters that reject uninteresting clauses. The simplest, but crudest approach, is to include or omit background predicates. By contract, some ILP systems, e.g., ALEPH (Srinivasan, 2004), allow users to build themselves filters that verify whether the clause is eligible for consideration or whether it should be immediately dropped. Such a *hypothesis checking* mechanism allows the finest level of control over the hypothesis language, but is highly demanding on the user and should be complemented with tools or mechanisms that facilitate the user's task.

Hypothesis checking mechanisms can be seen as a way to bias the search language, and therefore usually known as the *bias language.* One very powerful such example are declarative languages such as *antecedent description grammars,* definite-clause grammars that describe acceptable clauses (Cohen, 1994; Jorge & Brazdil, 1995), or the DLAB language of clause templates (Dehaspe

& De Raedt, 1996) used in CLAUDIEN (De Raedt & Dehaspe, 1996), one of the earliest descriptive ILP systems. As Cohen notes, however, such grammars may become very large and cumbersome to formulate and maintain; newer implementations of the CLAUDIEN algorithm (CLASSICCL, Stolle et al. 2005) also abandon DLAB and replace it with type and mode declarations (see below).

Finally, note that hypothesis checking mechanisms can verify a variety of parameters, both syntactic and semantic. As an example of semantic parameter, it is common for ILP systems to discard clauses with very low coverage, as such clauses often do not generalize well.

Determinacy

A further means of controlling the hypothesis language is through the concept of *determinacy*, introduced in this context by Muggleton & Feng (1990). Determinacy is a property of the variables of a clause and, in a way, specifies how 'far' they are from being bound to ground terms: a variable in a term is *j*-determinate if there are up to *j* variables in the same term. Furthermore, a variable is *ij*-determinate if it is *j*-determinate and its *depth* is up to *i*. A clause is *ij*-determinate is all the variables appearing in the clause are *ij*-determinate.

The depth of a variable appearing in a clause is recursively defined as follows :

Definition 7: *For clause C and variable v appearing in C, the depth of v, d(v), is*

$$d(v) = \begin{cases} 0 & \text{if } v \text{ is in the head of } C \\ 1 + \min_{w \in \text{var}(C,v)} d(w) & \text{otherwise} \end{cases}$$

where var(C,v) are all the variables appearing in those atoms of the body of C where v also appears.

The intuition behind this definition is that depth increases by 1 each time a body literal is needed to 'link' two variables, so that a variable's depth is the number of such links in the 'chain' of body literals that connects the variable with a variable of the head.[5] Simply requiring that the hypothesis language only include determinate clause, i.e., clauses with arbitrarily large but finite determinacy parameters, has a dramatic effect in difficulty of the definite ILP task, as it renders definite hypotheses PAC-learnable (De Raedt & Džeroski, 1994). Naturally, specifying smaller values for the determinacy parameters tightens the boundaries of the search space. Consider, for example, the formula in Box 5 as a possible solution for our grandfather-learning example.

This clause perfectly classifies the instances of our example (Figure 3) and is 2, 2-determinate.[6] Although this clause satisfies the posterior requirements for a hypothesis, a domain expert might have very good reasons to believe that the grandfather relation is a more direct one, and that solutions should be restricted to 1, 2-determinate clauses. Imposing this prior requirement would force a learning algorithm to reject clause *C* (equation (10)) as a hypothesis and formulate a more direct one, for example Box 6.

Box 5. Formula 10

$$C = \text{grandfather}(X,Y) \leftarrow \text{father}(X,U) \wedge \text{father}(U,V) \wedge \text{mother}(W,V) \wedge \text{mother}(W,Y) \quad (10)$$

Box 6. Formula 11

$$D = \text{grandfather}(X,Y) \leftarrow \text{father}(X,U) \wedge \text{parent}(U,Y) \quad (11)$$

Type and Mode Declarations

Type and *mode declarations* are further bias mechanisms that provide ILP algorithms with prior information regarding the semantic properties of the background predicates as well as the target concept. Type and mode declarations were introduced in PROGOL (Muggleton, 1995) and have since appeared in many modern ILP systems, most notably including the CLASSICCL (Stolle et al., 2005) re-implementation of CLAUDIEN, where they replace the declarative bias language used in the original implementation.

Mode declarations state that some literal's variables must be bound at call time (input, +) or not (output, -) and thus restrict the ways that literals can combine to form clauses. Mode declaration also specify the places where constants may appear (constant, #). For example, with the following mode declarations in the background:

$$B = \begin{cases} \text{mode}(\text{grandfather}(+,-)) \\ \text{mode}(\text{father}(+,+)) \\ \text{mode}(\text{parent}(+,+)) \end{cases} \qquad (12)$$

clause D (equation (11)) can not be formulated, as variable Y cannot be bound in the parent/2 literal if it is unbound in the head. The desired 'chain' effect of input/output variables may be achieved with the following background:

$$B = \begin{cases} \text{mode}(\text{grandfather}(+,-)) \\ \text{mode}(\text{father}(+,-)) \\ \text{mode}(\text{parent}(+,-)) \end{cases} \qquad (13)$$

achieves the desired 'chain' effect of input/output variables: X is bound in the head, so that father/2 can be applied to bind the unbound variable U, which in its turn can serve as input to parent/2. Modes are usually combined with *recall bounds* that restrict the number of possible instantiations

Box 7. Formula 14

$$B = \begin{cases} \text{mode}(1, \text{grandfather}(+,+)) \lor \text{mode}(2, \text{grandfather}(+,-)) \\ \text{mode}(1, \text{father}(+,+)) \lor \text{mode}(3, \text{father}(+,-)) \\ \text{mode}(1, \text{parent}(+,+)) \lor \text{mode}(3, \text{parent}(+,-)) \\ \text{mode}(1, \text{female}(+)) \lor \text{mode}(5, \text{female}(-)) \end{cases} \qquad (14)$$

Box 8. Formula 15

$$E = \text{grandfather}(X, Y) \leftarrow \text{father}(X, U) \land \text{parent}(U, Y) \land \text{female}(Y) \quad (15)$$

Box 9. Formula 16

$$B = \begin{cases} \text{mode}(2, \text{grandfather}(+M, -M)) \lor \text{mode}(2, \text{grandfather}(+F, -F)) \\ \text{mode}(2, \text{father}(+M, -M)) \lor \text{mode}(2, \text{father}(+M, -F)) \\ \text{mode}(2, \text{parent}(+M, -M)) \lor \text{mode}(2, \text{parent}(+M, -F)) \lor \\ \text{mode}(2, \text{parent}(+F, -M)) \lor \text{mode}(2, \text{parent}(+F, -F)) \\ \text{mode}(1, \text{female}(+F)) \lor \text{mode}(5, \text{female}(-F)) \\ \text{mode}(1, \text{male}(+M)) \lor \text{mode}(5, \text{male}(-M)) \end{cases} \qquad (16)$$

180

of a literal's variables for each mode of application (see Box 7).

This background restricts the second mode of *grandfather*/2 to two possible instantiations, so that hypothesis D (equation (11)) becomes unattainable and a different solution has to be identified. Consider Box 8.

Clause E focuses on grandfathers of granddaughters, and so satisfies the requirements of equation (14).

Finally, mode declarations are extended with a rudimentary type system, such that different modes apply to different instances. To demonstrate, the following background knowledge (see Box 9), admits hypotheses like D (equation (11)) which cover up to two grandchildren of each gender. Note, however, that types in ILP systems are most often flat tags; they do not support the supertype–subtype hierarchy that is so fundamental to modern type systems. As a result, it is not, for example, possible to express the fact that that although the *parent*/2 predicate can be instantiated for up to 2 children of each gender, it can be instantiated for up to 3 children of either gender, as this would require the definition of a *person* supertype for the M and F types.

Hypothesis Space Traversal

As already seen above, the elements of the hypothesis language are organized in a lattice by a partial-ordering operator. In theory, it would suffice to have an operator that simply evaluates the relation between two given clause as 'more general than', 'less general than', or neither. This would, however, be impractical since it would require that the whole search space is generated

and the relationship between all pairs of search nodes is evaluated before the search starts.

Instead, ILP systems use generative operators which map a given clause into a set of clauses that succeed the original clause according to the partial ordering.[7] Using such a *traversal operator* only the fragment of the search space that is actually visited is generated as the search proceeds. There are three main desiderata for the traversal operator:

- It should *only* generate clauses that are in the search space,
- It should generate *all* the clauses that are in the search space,
- It should be *efficient* and generate the most interesting candidate hypotheses first.

Satisfying these points does not only involve the traversal operator, but also its interaction with the other elements of the search. Prior knowledge, in particular, defines the hypothesis language and thus the elements of the search space and operates on the assumption of a monotonic entailment structure of the search space: whenever $C <_g D$, it must be that $C \vDash D$ (Definition 3). This places the requirement that the traversal operator is a syntactic inference operator that mechanizes the process of validating semantic entailment. Deductive inference operators that deduce D from C *only* when $C \vDash D$ are called *sound* and those that deduce D from C for *all* C,D where $C \vDash D$ are called *complete*.

A variety of sound first-order deductive inference operators have been proposed in the logic programming literature, each with their own advantages and limitations with respect to

Box 10. Formula 17

$$C = \text{mother}\,(X,Y) \leftarrow \text{parent}\,(X,Y) \wedge \text{female}\,(X)$$
$$D = \text{mother}\,(sofia,Y) \leftarrow \text{parent}\,(sofia,Y) \wedge \text{female}\,(sofia) \wedge \text{female}\,(Y) \tag{17}$$

completeness and efficiency. ILP borrows the deductive operators from the logic programming community for searching in the general-to-specific direction and derives their inductive inversions for the specific-to-general direction.

Subsumption

The earliest approaches to first-order induction were based on θ-subsumption (Plotkin, 1970), a sound deductive operator which deduces clause B from clause A if the antecedents of A are a subset of the antecedents of B, up to variable substitution:

Definition 8: *If there is a substitution θ such that $A\theta \subseteq B$, then A θ-subsumes B ($A \preceq B$).*

So, for example, given the clauses C and D (see Box 10), it is the case that $C \preceq D$, since $C\theta \subseteq D$ for $\theta = \{X/sofia\}$. And, indeed, it is also the case that C entails D since the mothers of daughters are a subset of mothers of children of either gender.

In practice, θ-subsumption is a purely syntactic operator: using θ-subsumption to make a clause more specific amounts to either adding a literal or binding a variable in a literal to a term. Inversely, generalization is done by dropping literals, replacing ground terms with variables, or introducing a new variable in the place of an existing one that occurs more than once in the same literal. When searching in either direction (specific-to-general or general-to-specific) between a (typically very specific) clause $\{H, \neg B_1, \neg B_2, ..., \neg B_n\}$ and the most general clause $\{H\}$ (where H contains no ground terms and all variables are different), the search space is confined within the power-set of $\{\neg B_i\}$

The FOIL algorithm (Quinlan, 1990) used

$$E_1 = \text{grandfather } (jArcadioBD, renata)$$
$$E_2 = \text{grandfather } (jArcadioBD, amaranta) \qquad (18)$$
$$\text{lgg } (E_1, E_2) = \text{grandfather } (jArcadioBD, X)$$

θ-subsumption to perform open-ended search. FOIL is the natural extension of the propositional rule-learning system CN2 (Clark & Niblett, 1989) to first order. it employs the same open-ended search strategy starting with an empty-bodied top clause and specializing it by adding literals. FOIL searches using a best-first strategy, where each step consists of adding all possible literals to the current clause, evaluating their quality, and then advancing to the next 'layer' of literals once the best clause at the current clause length has been identified. The list of candidate-literals at each layer consists of all background predicates with all possible arguments according to the current language, that is, new variables, variables already appearing in the body so far, and all constants and function symbols. FOIL allows some bias to constraint the search space. First, each new literal must have at least one variable that already appears in the current clause. Second, FOIL supports a simple type system that restricts the number of constants, functions and variables that can be placed as arguments.

Relative Least General Generalization

The direct approach of performing an open-ended θ-subsumption can generate search spaces with a very high branching factor. The problem is that whenever we expand a clause with a new literal

Box 12. Formula 19

$$\text{rlgg}\left(\{E_i\}, \{B_i\}\right) = \text{grandfather } (X, Y) \leftarrow \text{father } (X, Z) \wedge \text{parent } (X, Z) \wedge$$
$$\text{parent } (Z, Y) \wedge \text{sibling } (U, Z) \wedge \text{female } (U)... \qquad (19)$$

we need to consider *every* literal allowed by the language, that is, every literal in the language for which we have input variables bound. This is especially problematic if the new literal can have constants as arguments: in this case, we always need to consider every constant in the (typed) language when we expand a clause with a literal.

In order to achieve more informed search-coming, Muggleton & Feng (1990) introduced the concept of the *bottom clause*, the minimal generalization of a set of clauses. The process of achieving this idea is somewhat involved, but the original idea was based on Plotkin's (1970) work on inductive operators and, more specifically, work on defining the *least general generalization* (LGG) of two given terms as the most specific term that θ-subsumes them. Essentially, the LGG inverts unification by introducing variables that replace ground atoms in the original terms. See, as an example, Box 11, the clauses and their LGG.

LGG generalizes two (or more, by repeated application) terms in the absence of any background predicates that can be used to restrict the variables introduced. Plotkin (1971a) proceeds to define the *relative least general generalization* (RLGG) of a set of terms relative a set of background terms. RLGG generalizes the set of terms into a single ungrounded term and uses the background knowledge to restrict the possible bindings of the variables introduced. Plotkin's original idea was to induce theories by applying the RLGG to a set of examples relative to the background, (see Box 12), where the E_i are the positive examples in equation (6) and the B_i are the ground facts and all extensions of the intensionally defined predicates in equation (5). We only show a fragment

of the full RLGG here; the full clause contains all possible ways to relate the argument X with the argument Y, but even the fragment shown here is already overly specific and—correct as this theory might be according to the data—a shorter theory can be identified that accurately classifies the examples. In general, Plotkin (1971a) notes that the RLGG can be very long even for ground clauses, and potentially infinite when ungrounded clauses are involved, prohibiting its practical application.

Muggleton & Feng (1990) observe that the RLGG of the examples is an accurate but unnecessarily specific theory: thus, it should be considered a starting point to be further refined by searching in the space of clauses that can be found in the θ-subsumption lattice bounded between the *RLGG bottom* and an empty-bodied *top clause*. As a second step, and in order to avoid infinite RLGG bottoms, the hypothesis language is further restricted to *ij-determinate* definite clauses. Under the *ij*-determinacy restriction, the RLGG of a set of ground clauses (examples) relative to a set of background clauses is unique and finite.

These ideas were originally implemented in GOLEM, an ILP system which alleviates Plotkin's problem of unnecessarily specific and long hypotheses while at the same time bounding the search into clauses that take into account the totality of the background and the examples. This was a moment of paramount importance in ILP research, as it marked the transition from open-ended searches in semi-lattices to full-lattice searches; a development which, although by no means sufficient to guarantee termination, at least voided one of the possible causes of non-termination.

Box 13. Formula 20

$$A = ancestor\,(X,Y) \leftarrow parent\,(X,Z) \wedge ancestor\,(Z,Y)$$
$$B = ancestor\,(X,Y) \leftarrow parent\,(X,Z) \wedge parent\,(Z,W) \wedge ancestor\,(W,Y)$$

(20)

Inverse Resolution

Although θ-subsumption search have been successfully used in the early days of ILP, it has been known that, as Plotkin (1971b) originally noted, θ-subsumption is not *complete*, or, in other words, it is not able to infer B from A in all cases where A entails B; it naturally follows that inverse θ-subsumption is also not complete. Consider, for example, the clauses in Box 13, where B represents a stricter form of 'ancestry' than A, so that all models of A are also models of B. But, although $A \vDash B$, there is no variable substitution θ such that $A\theta \subseteq B$.[8] This incompleteness naturally propagates to inverse θ-subsumption as well: clause B cannot be generalized into A by inverse θ-subsumption (effectively, literal dropping and variable substitution) although A is more general than B.

In order to close the gap between true implication and θ-subsumption, ILP research has turned to complete deductive inference operators, like Robinson's *resolution rule*. The Robinson resolution rule (1965) raises the propositional resolution rule to the first order, and is defined as follows:

Definition 9: *Clause R is resolved from clauses C_1 and C_2 if and only if there are literals $l_1 \in C_1$ and $l_2 \in C_2$ and substitution θ such that:*

$$l_1\theta = \neg\, l_2\theta$$
$$R = (C_1 - \{l_1\})\theta \cup (C_2 - \{l_2\})\theta$$

By algebraically solving the equation in Definition 9 for C_2, an *inverse resolution* operator can be defined which generalizes clause R, given background clause C_1:

$$C_2 = (R - (C_1 - \{l_1\})\theta_1)\theta_2^{-1} \cup \{\neg l_1\theta_1\theta_2^{-1}\} \quad (21)$$

where $l_1 \in C_1$ and $\theta_1\theta_2$ is a factorization of the unifying substitution θ from Definition 9, such that θ_i contains all and only substitutions involving variables from C_i. Such a factorization is always possible and unique, because C_1 and C_2 are distinct

clauses, hence the variables appearing in C_1 are separate from those appearing in C_2.

The above generalization operator was the basis of CIGOL (Muggleton & Buntine, 1988), one of the earliest successful ILP systems. CIGOL follows a sequential-covering strategy, with individual clause search proceeding in the specific-to-general direction. The starting point of the search is a ground positive example, randomly selected from the pool of uncovered positives, that is generalized by repeated application of inverse resolution. The advantage is that *all* and *only* consistent clauses are generated, allowing for a complete, yet focused search.

Mode-Directed Inverse Entailment

While inverted resolution is complete, it disregards the background (modulo a single background clause at each application), so it does not provide for a focused search. RLGG-based search, on the other hand, does take into account the whole of the background theory, but it relies on inverting θ-subsumption, so it performs an incomplete search that can potentially miss good solutions.

In order to combine completeness with the informedness of the minimal-generalization bottom, Muggleton (1995) explores implication between clauses and ways of reducing inverse implication to a θ-subsumption search without loss of completeness, and defines the *inverse entailment* operator, based on the following proposition:

Lemma 1: *Let C, D be definite, non-tautological clauses and S(D) be the sub-saturants of D. Then $C \vDash D$ if and only if there exists $C' \in S(D)$ such that $C \preceq C'$.*

where the sub-saturants of a clause D are, informally,[9] all ungrounded clauses that can be constructed from the symbols appearing in D *and* cannot prove the complement of D (i.e., do not resolve to any of the atoms in the Herbrand model of the complement of D).

Box 14. Formula 22

$$\bot_1 = \text{ancestor}(A,B) \leftarrow$$
$$\text{parent}(A,C) \wedge \text{parent}(A,D) \wedge \text{parent}(A,E) \wedge \text{ancestor}(A,C) \wedge$$
$$B = aureliano \wedge A = jArcadioBD \wedge \text{parent}(E, F) \wedge \text{parent}(E,G) \wedge$$
$$\text{parent}(E,H) \wedge \text{sibling}(E,D) \wedge \text{sibling}(E,C) \wedge \text{sibling}(D,E) \wedge$$
$$\text{sibling}(D,C) \wedge \text{sibling}(C,E) \wedge \text{sibling}(C,D) \wedge \text{ancestor}(E,B) \wedge \qquad (22)$$
$$\text{ancestor}(A,E) \wedge \text{ancestor}(A,D) \wedge \text{ancestor}(E, F) \wedge E = aurelianoII \wedge$$
$$D = jArcadioII \wedge C = remedios \wedge \text{parent}(G,B) \wedge \text{sibling}(H,G) \wedge$$
$$\text{sibling}(H, F) \wedge \text{sibling}(G,H) \wedge \text{sibling}(G, F) \wedge \text{sibling}(F,H) \wedge$$
$$\text{sibling}(F,G) \wedge \text{ancestor}(G,B) \wedge \text{ancestor}(E,H) \wedge \text{ancestor}(A,H) \wedge$$
$$\text{ancestor}(E,G) \wedge \text{ancestor}(A,G) \wedge \text{ancestor}(A, F) \wedge H = amaranta \wedge$$
$$G = renata \wedge F = jArcadio$$

Inverse entailment starts by *saturating* a ground positive example into a *bottom clause*, an ungrounded clause which can prove only one ground positive example and no other. Because of Lemma 1, any clause which entails the original example will also θ-subsume the bottom clause; it is now sufficient to perform a θ-subsumption search in the full lattice between the empty-bodied top clause and the bottom clause without loss of completeness.

Mode-directed inverse entailment (MDIE) is a further refinement of inverse entailment where the semantics of the background predicates are taken into consideration during saturation (see below). The search in MDIE is organized in the general-to-specific direction in the original PROGOL system (Muggleton, 1995), as well as in most other successful MDIE ILP systems, like, e.g., ALEPH (Srinivasan, 2004), INDLOG (Camacho, 2000), CILS (Anthony & Frisch, 1999), and APRIL (Fonseca, 2006) although the alternative direction has been explored as well (Ong et al., 2005).

Saturation

Saturation is the process of constructing a *bottom clause*[10] which constitutes the most-specific end of the search lattice in mode-directed inverse entailment. The most prominent characteristic

Box 15. Formula 23

$$\bot_1 = \text{ancestor}(A,B) \leftarrow \text{parent}(A,C) \wedge \text{ancestor}(A,C) \wedge$$
$$B = aureliano \wedge A = jArcadioBD \wedge C = remedios \qquad (23)$$

Box 16. Formula 24

$$\bot_1 = \text{ancestor}(A,B) \leftarrow \text{parent}(A,C) \wedge \text{parent}(A,D) \wedge \text{parent}(A,E) \wedge$$
$$\text{ancestor}(A,C) \wedge B = aureliano \wedge A = jArcadioBD \qquad (24)$$

of saturation is that it fills the 'gap' between θ-subsumption and entailment: the literals of the bottom clause are the sub-saturants of a clause C, hence identifying clauses that entail C amounts to identifying clauses that θ-subsume the bottom clause (Lemma 1).

Saturation is performed by repeated application of inverse resolution on a ground example, called the *seed*. This introduces variables in place of the ground terms in a 'safe' manner: the bottom clause is guaranteed to include all of and only the sub-saturants of the seed.

Let us revisit the clauses in equation (20), used to demonstrate the incompleteness of θ-subsumption. Given the example *ancestor(jArcadioBD, aureliano)* as a seed, saturation would yield the bottom clause shown in Box 14.

Notice that $\perp_1$ is θ-subsumed by *both* clauses of equation (20).[11] In general, for all clauses A,B that subsume the seed, if A entails B, a complete generalization operator would first inverse-resolve B and, later in the search, A. In cases where $A \not\preceq B$, the bottom clause will complete a θ-subsumption search by including enough body literals to be θ-subsumed by both A and B.

Besides completing θ-subsumption search, saturation is also designed to take type-mode and determinacy declarations into consideration, so that they do not need to be explicitly checked during the search: saturation guarantees a bottom clause that is θ-subsumed only by conforming clauses. Consider, for example, a background in which all predicates are required to be determinate. The bottom clause of *ancestor(jArcadioBD, aureliano)* is shown in Box 15, since the constraint that all predicate be determinate can only be satisfied in our example model (Figure 3) by the *ancestor(renata,aureliano)* term.

Similarly, restricting variable depth to 1 would yield the bottom clause shown in Box 16, which is the subset of the bottom clause in equation (22) where all variables are of depth 0 or 1. Notice that there are no ancestor/2 literals, as they amount to ancestor/2 literals when depth is restricted to 1.

Search Strategy

Given a search space with some structure, we can consider a strategy to traverse the search space. The most important components of the strategy are the *direction* of the search and the *method* used to achieve it.

The *direction* of the search can be either top-down or bottom-up, depending on the traversal operator used. In a top-down, general-to-specific search the initial rule is the top clause, which is incrementally specialized through the repeated application of downward traversal operators, until inconsistencies with negative examples have been removed. In a bottom-up, specific-to-general search, on the other hand, a most specific clause is generalized by applying upward traversal operators. The original, most specific clause can be either one or more ground examples or the bottom clause.

More recently, there has been interest on stochastic approaches to search that do not properly fall under either of these strategies. Examples of these approaches are Stochastic Clause Selection and Randomized Rapid Restarts algorithms. (Železný et al., 2003; Tamaddoni-Nezhad & Muggleton, 2003; Srinivasan, 2000).

A second component of the search is the search method used to find a hypothesis. As is generally the case with problem solving in artificial intelligence, search methods can be either uninformed or informed, and can rely on heuristics to estimate how 'promising' or close to a solution each node of the search space is.

Uninformed Search

Some of the most well-known uninformed search methods are breadth-first, depth-first, and iterative-deepening search. *Breadth-first* search is a simple method in which the root node is expanded first, then all direct successors of the root node are expanded, then all their successors, and so on. In general, all the nodes are expanded at a given depth

Table 1. Evaluation of three clauses (positive and negative coverage in parenthesis) by the information gain function and the Laplace accuracy function.

	Inf. Gain	Laplace Acc.
C_1 (980,20)	0.141	0.979
C_2 (98,2)	0.141	0.971
C_3 (1,0)	1.000	0.667

of the search before any nodes in the following level are expanded. The main advantage of this method is that it is guaranteed to find a solution if one exists. The main drawbacks are the high memory requirements leading to poor efficiency. Several ILP systems use this search method, e.g., MIS (Shapiro, 1983) and WARMR (Dehaspe & Toironen, 2000). An advantage is that it visits clauses near the top of the lattice first, favouring clauses that are shorter and more general.

By contrast, *depth-first* search expands the deepest node first. This search strategy has the advantage of having lower memory requirements, since a node can be removed from memory after being expanded as soon all its descendants have been fully explored. On the other hand, this strategy can get lost in infinite branches. A variant of depth-first search, called *depth-limit search* imposes a limit on the depth of the graph explored. Obviously, this search is incomplete if a solution is in a region deeper than this pre-set limit.

Iterative depth-first search (IDS) is a general strategy often used in combination with depth-first search, that finds the best depth limit. It does this by gradually increasing the depth limit (first 0, then 1, then 2, and so on) until a solution is found. The drawback of IDS is the wasteful repetition of the same computations. Iterative deepening search is used in ILP systems like ALEPH (Srinivasan, 2004) and INDLOG (Camacho, 2000).

Informed Search

Informed (heuristic) search methods can be used to find solutions more efficiently than uninformed but can only be applied if there is a measure to evaluate and discriminate the nodes. Several heuristics have been proposed for ILP.

A general approach to informed searching is best-first search. *Best-first* search is similar to breadth-first but with the difference that the node selected for expansion is the one with the least value of an evaluation function that estimates the 'distance' to the solution.

Note that the evaluation functions will return an *estimate* of the quality of a node. This estimate is given by a *heuristics*, a function that tries to predict the cost/distance to the solution from a given node.

Best-first search is used in many ILP systems, like FOIL, CIGOL, INDLOG, and ALEPH. A form of best-first search is *greedy best-first* search as it expands only the node estimated to be closer to the solution on the grounds that it would lead to a solution quickly. The most widely known form of best-first search is called *A* search*, which evaluates nodes by combining the cost to reach the node and the distance/cost to the solution. This algorithm is used by the PROGOL ILP system.

The search algorithms mentioned so far explore the search space systematically. Alternatively, *local search algorithms* is a class of algorithms commonly used for solving computationally hard problems involving very large candidate solution spaces. The basic principle underlying local search is to start from an initial candidate solution and then, iteratively, make moves from one candidate solution to another candidate solution *in its direct neighbourhood*. The moves are based on information local to the node, and continue until a termination condition is met. Local search algorithms, although not systematic, have the advantage of using little memory and can find reasonable solutions in large or infinite search spaces, where systematic algorithms are unsuitable.

Hill-climbing search (Russell & Norvig, 2003) is one example of a local search algorithm. The algorithm does not look ahead beyond the immediate successor nodes of the current node, and for this reason it is sometimes called *greedy* local search. Although it has the advantage of reaching a solution more rapidly, it has some potential problems. For instance, it is possible to reach a *foothill* (*local maxima* or *local minima*), a state that is better than all its neighbours but it is not better than some other states farther away. Foothills are potential traps for the algorithm. Hill-climbing is good for a limited class of problems where we have an evaluation function that fairly accurately predicts the actual distance to a solution. ILP systems like FOIL and FORTE (Richards & Mooney, 1995) use hill-climbing search algorithms.

Preference Bias and Search Heuristics

Prior knowledge representations described so far express strict constraints imposed on the hypothesized clauses, realized in the form of yes–no decisions on the acceptability of a clause. The previous section demonstrated the need for heuristics that identify the solution closest to the unknown target predicate, but, in the general case, there may be multiple solutions that satisfy the requirements of the problem; or we may have no solution but still want the best approximation. ILP algorithms therefore need to choose among partial solutions and provide justification for this choice besides consistency with the background and the examples. *Preference bias* does just that: it assigns a 'usefulness' rating to clauses which typically says how close we are to the best solution. In practice, the is translated into an *evaluation function* that tries to estimate how well a clause will perform when applied to data unseen during training.

The user may provide general preferences, for instance towards shorter clauses, or towards clauses that achieve wide coverage, or towards clauses with higher predictive accuracy on the training data, or any other problem-specific preference deemed useful. Preference bias also must navigate a balance between specificity and generality: a theory with low coverage may describe the data too tightly and may not generalize well (overfit). Indeed, at its extreme may it only accepts the positive examples it was constructed from and nothing else. On the other hand, a theory that makes unjustified generalizations can underfit, and at the extreme, accept everything as a positive.

Entropy and m-Probability

Evaluation functions will typically judge a clause semantically and so the most commonly used evaluation functions refer to a clause's coverage over positive and negative examples. Such functions include simple coverage, information gain (Clark & Niblett 1989, based on the concept of entropy as defined by Shannon 1948), *m*-probability estimate (Cestnik, 1990), and the Laplace expected accuracy:

$$\text{Coverage}(P, N) = P - N \qquad (25)$$

$$\text{InfGain}(P, N) = -P_{rel} \cdot \log_2 P_{rel} - N_{rel} \cdot \log_2 N_{rel} \qquad (26)$$

$$\text{MEst}_{m, P_0}(P, N) = (P + mP_0)/(P + N + m) \qquad (27)$$

$$\text{Laplace}(P, N) = (P + 1)/(P + N + 2) \qquad (28)$$

where P, N is the positive and negative coverage, $P_{rel} = P/(P + N)$, $N_{rel} = 1 - P_{rel}$ the relative positive and negative coverage, P_0 is the prior probability of positive examples (i.e., the probability that a random example is positive) and m a parameter that weighs the prior probability against the observed accuracy. It should be noted that the Laplace function is a specialization of the *m*-probability estimate for uniform prior distribution of positives and negatives ($P_0 = 0.5$) with the *m* parameter set to a value of 2, a value that balances between prior and observation.

The advantage that accuracy estimation offers over information gain is that it favours more general clauses, even at the expense of misclassifying a small number of training examples. This makes it more appropriate for real-world applications where the training data contains noise and inconsistencies, since it will generalize at the expense of outliers.

As an example, let us consider a situation where three possible clauses C_1, C_2 and C_3 meet the minimum accuracy constraint we have set, and a choice needs to be made according to preference bias. Let us assume that the examples covered by each clause are (980, 20), (98, 2) and (1, 0) respectively, where each pair represents the number of positive and negative examples covered by the clause. Knowing that we are dealing with noisy data, the intuitive choice would be C_1, since it performs as well as C_2, but seems to be making a much broader generalization. And we would argue that both are preferable to C_3, which is simply re-iterating a piece of the training data.

The evaluation of these three clauses by Information Gain and Laplace accuracy is shown in Table 1. Evaluation functions that focus on minimizing entropy assign absolute preference to perfectly 'pure' partitions (like the one imposed by C_3), even in the trivial cases of maximally-specific rules that cover exactly one example. But even assuming that such extreme situations are treated by, for example, minimum coverage filters, information gain is unable to distinguish between C_1 and C_2, since they have identical relative coverage (980/1000 and 98/100).

Accuracy estimation, on the other hand, balances between rewarding wide coverage and penalizing low accuracy on the training data,

the point of balance determined by the *m* parameter.

Bayesian Evaluation

Another approach to clause evaluation is derived from Bayes' Theorem (Bayes, 1763, Proposition 3), which provides a formula for calculating $Pr(A|B)$, the probability of event *A* given event *B*:

Theorem 2: *Given random variables A, B with probabilities Pr(A) and Pr(B), then the probability of A given B is*

$$\Pr(A|B) = \frac{\Pr(B|A) \cdot \Pr(A)}{\Pr(B)}$$

where $\Pr(B|A)$ *is the probability of B given A.*

Suppose we have a clause of the form $A \leftarrow B$, and $Pr(A)$, $Pr(B)$ are the probabilities that predicates *A* and *B* hold for some random example. We can now apply Bayes' Theorem to calculate the probability that, for some random example, if the clause's antecedents hold, then the subsequent holds. In a semantics sense, this is the probability that the clause accurately classifies the example. Probability $Pr(A|B)$ is called the *posterior distribution* of *A*, by contrast to *prior distribution* $Pr(A)$, the distribution of *A* before seeing the example.

Bayes (idem., Proposition 7) continues by using the empirical data to estimate an unknown prior distribution. This last result is transferred to ILP by Cussens (1993) as the pseudo-bayes[12] evaluation function:

$$Acc = P / (P + N)$$
$$K = Acc \cdot (1 - Acc) / (P_0 - Acc)^2 \qquad (29)$$
$$\text{PBayes} = (P + K \cdot P_0) / (P + N + K)$$

where P_0 is the positive distribution observed in the data, and *P* and *N* are the positive and nega-

Box 17. Formula 30

$$
\text{size}(T) = \begin{cases}
1, & \text{if } T \text{ is a variable} \\
2, & \text{if } T \text{ is a constant} \\
2 + \sum_{i=1}^{n} \text{size}(\arg_i(T)), & \text{if } T \text{ is a term of arity } n
\end{cases} \tag{30}
$$

tive coverage of the clause. A comparison of the pseudo-Bayes evaluation function with m-estimation (equation (27)) shows that one way of looking at pseudo-Bayes evaluation is as an empirically justified way of calculating the critical *m* parameter of m-estimation.

Syntactic Considerations

Some evaluation functions will also refer to syntactic aspects of the hypothesized clause, implementing (for example) preference bias towards shorter or simpler clauses, in accordance with the general principle of parsimony known as Ockham's Razor. Unfortunately, quantifying 'simplicity' is hard, and there is no universal answer to what a 'simple' hypothesis is. Most approaches are equating being the simplest to being the smallest, in accordance with Rissanen's (1978) *minimum description length* (MDL) principle that the most probable hypothesis is the one that can be most economically encoded.

Such evaluation functions range from simply counting the number of literals in a clause, to taking into account each literal's structural complexity. (See Box 17)

This quantification of clause complexity was used in the MDL evaluation function of the COCKTAIL system (Tang & Mooney, 2001).

On the other hand, Muggleton, Srinivasan, and Bain (1992) take a different approach and re-introduce a semantic element in the notion of logic program complexity: the *proof complex-*

ity C of a logic program given a dataset is the number of choice-points that SLDNF resolution goes though in order to derive the data from the program. The *proof encoding length* L_{proof} of the hypothesis for each example can be approximated by combining the proof complexity with coverage results which estimate the compression achieved by the hypothesis and with the total (positive and negative) coverage, which is taken as a measure of the generality of the clause (idem., Section 3):

$$
L_{proof} = (P+N) \cdot \left(C_{av} + \log \frac{1}{Acc^{Acc} \cdot (1-Acc)^{1-Acc}} \right)
$$

$$\tag{31}$$

where *Acc* is the observed accuracy $P/(P+N)$ and C_{av} the average proof complexity of the hypothesis over all the examples. It is easy to see that the logarithmic term (which represents the performance of the hypothesis) is dominated by the proof complexity term and the generality factor, so that it comes into consideration when comparing hypotheses with similar (semantic) generality and (syntactic) complexity characteristics.

Positive-Only Evaluation

One other category of evaluation functions that should be particularly noted is those that facilitate learning in the absence of negative examples (positive examples only). Conventional semantic evaluation functions cannot be used because in this case, in the absence of negative examples, the trivial clause that accepts all examples will always score best.

For this reason, positive-only evaluation functions balance positive coverage against a clause's generality, to avoid favouring over-generalization. Generality can be estimated syntactically as well as semantically, as in the *posonly* function (Muggleton, 1996):

$$\text{PosOnly}_{C, R_{all}}(P, R, L) = \log P - C \log \frac{R+1}{R_{all}+2} - \frac{L}{P}$$

$$(32)$$

where $(R+1)/(R_{all}+2)$ is a Laplace-corrected estimation of the clause's generality. The estimation is made by randomly generating R_{all} examples and measuring the clause's coverage R over them. The formula is balancing between rewarding coverage (the first term) and penalizing generality (the second term), so as to avoid over-general clauses in the absence of negative data. The C parameter implements prior preference towards more general or more specific clauses and the third term implements syntactic bias towards shorter clauses, unless extended coverage compensates for the length penalty.

Other Approaches to ILP

We have so far focused ILP systems that perform a clause-level search on a pre-defined, static search space. Although these systems form the mainstream of ILP research, other options have been explored as well, namely searching at the theory level and searching in a dynamic space.

Theory-level Search

The sequential cover strategy has a profound impact on the size of the search space, as it restricts the search to the space of single clauses. It does so, however, at the risk of missing out on good solutions, since the concatenation of good clauses is not necessarily a good theory: the best clause, given a set of positives, might leave a positives pool that is not easily separable, whereas a (locally) worse clause might allow for a better overall theory.

This is especially true for systems that saturate examples to build the bottom clause, as the (random) choice of the seed is decisive for the search sub-space that will be explored. An unfortunate seed choice might 'trap' subsequent clausal searches with an unnecessarily difficult positives pool. In sequential-cover systems the problem can be somewhat alleviated by saturating multiple seeds; in the ALEPH system, to name one example, the user can specify the number of examples that must be saturated for each positives pool. After performing as many searches as there were bottom clauses constructed, the best clause is appended to the theory and the process re-iterates.

Such techniques can improve the quality of the constructed theories, but not completely solve the problem, which can only be tackled by evaluating the theory as a whole at each step for the search. In *theory-level searching* the search space is the lattice formed by the set all admissible *theories* (as opposed to clauses), structured into a lattice by a theory-level traversal operator. It is immediately obvious that not only does search space become dramatically larger, but the traversal operator also gains more degrees of indeterminism, making the search even harder: the traversal operator can (a) specify or generalize a clause, (b) delete a clause altogether, or (c) start a new (top or bottom) clause.

In order to handle the increase in the size and complexity of the search space ILP systems that support theory-level search, like ALEPH, exploit *randomized search methods* to improve efficiency. Randomized search methods and other efficiency optimizations used in ILP systems are further described.

Dynamically Changing Search Spaces

We end the section with an overview of algorithms that tackle dynamically changing search spaces, due to bias shift and background theory revision (background predicate invention and refinement).

Descriptive ILP systems readily offer themselves to predicate invention, since they are oriented towards discovering 'property clusters' in the data and multi-predicate learning. Systems like CLAUDIEN (De Raedt & Dehaspe, 1996) propose predicates that separate such clusters, and also re-use these predicates in the definitions of subsequently constructed predicate clauses.

Single-predicate learning, predictive ILP systems, on the other hand, typically assumed that the background predicates are both correct and sufficient to solve the problem, and no attempt is made to revise or supplement them. Some systems, however, do attempt background theory revision. SPECTRE (Boström, 1996), for example, attempts background theory refinement by examining the SLD proof-trees generated during hypothesis matching. When pruning a background predicate's proof-tree (effectively, specializing the predicate) eliminates negative coverage, the background predicate is amended accordingly.

The same idea was further explored in the MERLIN2.0 system (Boström, 1998), this time attempting *predicate invention*, which expands the background theory with new predicates deemed useful for constructing a theory. MERLIN2.0 unfolds the SLD proof-trees of background predicates, and identifies new sub-predicates (in the semantic sense of predicates achieving a subset of the original predicate's coverage) which improve accuracy when used to construct a theory.

Inverse resolution also offers an opportunity for predicate invention: Muggleton (1988) proposes a predicate invention algorithm which asserts a predicate when its presence allows an—otherwise unattainable—inverse resolution step to proceed, if the generalization performed by this step evaluates well on the data. This idea was implemented in CIGOL (Muggleton & Buntine, 1988), an inverse-resolution ILP system, but was later abandoned as predictive ILP research moved towards inverse entailment systems that use θ-subsumption as their traversal operator.

Statistical inductive logic programming

A new line of ILP research that is being actively pursued combines statistical machine learning with ILP. One such approach (Muggleton, 2003) combines a symbolic ILP step with a numerical step to learn a Stochastic Logic Program (SLP). The structure of the SLP is learnt without taking the numerical parameters into account, which are subsequently estimated to fit the program.

Another approach abandons the learning semantics discussed earlier in this section, and introduces *learning from proofs*. Under learning from proofs, the input is the proof trees of positive and negative derivations, which are used (in conjunction with a background theory) to build a statistical model of 'good' or 'applicable' derivations using. De Raedt et al. (2005) use a variant of Expectation Maximisation and Passerini et al. (2006) kernel-based methods to build the statistical model.

EFFICIENT INDUCTIVE LOGIC PROGRAMMING

A crucial point for the applicability of ILP is its efficiency in terms of computational resources needed to construct a theory. As has been experimentally verified Železný et al. (2003), ILP systems' run-times exhibit considerable variability, depending on the heuristics, the problem instance, and the choice of seed examples.

The total execution time of an ILP system can be roughly divided into three major components:

- time spent *generating* clauses, which can be a major concern for large real-world problems, and particularly in novel application domains where prior domain knowledge is fragmentary and the search space cannot be restricted without risking to exclude good solutions;
- time spent *evaluating* clauses, typically due to the size of the data, although Botta et al. (2003) have shown that there are circumstances under which evaluation can become extremely hard, even if model-spaces and datasets are quite small; and
- time spent *accessing* the data, as some datasets can be extremely large, e.g., biological databases arising from sequencing animal and plant genomes. Constructing models of such data requires an ILP system to be able to efficiently access millions of data items.

The relative weight of each component depends on the ILP system used, on the search algorithm, on the parameter settings, and on the data, but in most cases evaluating rule quality is responsible for most of the execution time.

In this section we describe methods for improving the efficiency of ILP systems directly related to the three concerns raised above (large search spaces, large datasets, evaluation). Some of these methods are improvements and optimizations of the sequential execution of ILP systems, whereas some are stochastic approaches to search or parallelisms of the search strategy.

Before proceeding, we provide a classification of the techniques regarding their correctness. In this context, a *correct technique* should be understood as yielding the same results as some reference algorithm that does not employ the technique. An *approximately correct technique* does not preserve correctness, but still gives results that are, with high probability, similar (in quality) to the results produced by the reference technique.

Reducing the Search Space

In the Hypothesis Language section above, we have discussed a variety of tools that ILP systems offer for controlling the search space. More specifically, we have discussed how the search space is initially defined by the vocabulary provided by the background theory and then further refined by language bias such as hypothesis checking and pruning, determinacy constrains, and type-mode declarations.

In the theoretic context of our previous discussion of these tools, they have been presented as a means of excluding potentially good solutions on grounds that the ILP algorithm cannot access through example-driven evaluation, like non-conformance with a theoretical framework. We shall here revisit the same tools in order to review them from a different perspective: instead of a means of excluding empirically good solutions that should be avoided on theoretical grounds, they are viewed as an optimization that excludes bad solutions before having to evaluate them in order to reject them.

Hypothesis Checking and Pruning

We have seen how hypothesis checking can be used to impose syntactic as well as as semantic constraints on the hypothesis language. In many situations it is possible to capitalize on the monotonicity of definite clause logic in order to direct the search away not from individual clauses, but from whole areas of the search space that are known to not contain any solutions.

Consider, for example, a clause containing in its body literals that are known to be inconsistent with each other, say $male(X)$ and $female(X)$. Not only is such a clause bound to not cover any examples, but all its specializations can also safely ignored. In systems that support *pruning*, prior knowledge can be provided which, once such a clause in encountered during the search, prunes away the whole sub-space subsumed by the clause.

Another method that takes advantage of prior expert knowledge to reduce the hypothesis language is *redundancy declarations*. Fonseca et al. (2004) propose a classification of redundancy in the hypothesis language and show how expert knowledge can be provided to an ILP system to in order reduce it. The technique is correct (if complete search is performed) and yields good results.

Two things must be noted at this point: first that useful as they might be, semantic hypothesis checking and pruning are bound to make a smaller difference with respect to efficiency that their syntactic counterparts since they require the—potentially expensive—coverage computations to be carried out whereas purely syntactic checking can discard a hypothesis beforehand. And, second, that the hypothesis checking, pruning, and redundancy declarations must be provided by the domain expert. This task that can be tedious and error-prone and has not been successfully automated.

Determinacy and Type-mode Declarations

Determinacy and type-mode declarations can also be used to state not a theoretical restriction, but an actual fact about the background theory. When used in this manner they are not excluding empirically possible—but otherwise unacceptable—solutions, but they are rather steering the search away from areas of the search that are known to be infertile.

Consider, for example, the declarations in equation (16) above. While the type-mode declarations for the *grandfather/2* predicate are, as we have already discussed, enforcing a genuine restriction, the rest are stating actual facts about the semantics of the background predicates. So, for instance, the *parent/2* declaration is prohibiting the consideration of hypotheses like the one shown in Box 18.

which only admits grand-fatherhood in the presence of three or more grand-sons. This clause is rejected because the background theory does not allow instantiations where three children are male. The clause can only succeed by unifying two of U,V,W and can be safely ignored: no ILP algorithm would have chosen this clause anyway, as the model of our example identical semantics can be achieved by a simpler clause.

In general, providing the smallest determinacy values that will not leave any solutions out of the hypothesis space is a correct optimization of the ILP search. Similarly for type declarations, where assigning incompatible types can help avoid evaluating obviously inconsistent clauses like the one shown in Box 19.

Prior knowledge of small, but safe, determinacy and type-mode parameters can significantly tighten the search space around the solutions. These semantic characteristics of the background theory are typically expected as user input, but

Box 18. Formula 33

$$C = \text{grandfather}\,(X,U) \leftarrow \text{father}\,(X,Y) \wedge \text{parent}\,(Y,U) \wedge \text{male}\,(U) \wedge$$
$$\text{parent}\,(Y,V) \wedge \text{male}\,(V) \wedge \text{parent}\,(Y,W) \wedge \text{male}\,(W) \tag{33}$$

Box 19. Formula 34

$$D = \text{grandfather}\,(X,Y) \leftarrow \text{female}\,(X) \wedge \text{father}\,(X,Z) \wedge \text{parent}\,(Z,Y) \tag{34}$$

research on their automatically extraction from the background has also been pursued (McCreath & Sharma, 1995).

Incremental Search

Another approach is to not restrict the hypothesis language, but to incrementally consider larger and larger subsets thereof. The whole hypothesis language will only be considered if we cannot find a model within one of these subsets. Srinivasan et al. (2003) propose a technique that explores human expertise to provide a relevance ordering on the set of background predicates. The technique follows a strategy of incrementally including sets of background knowledge predicates in decreasing order of relevance and has shown to yield good results.

Another technique that incrementally increases the hypothesis space is Incremental Language Level Search (ILLS) (Camacho, 2002). It uses an iterative search strategy to, starting from one, progressively increase the upper-bound on the number of occurrences of a predicate symbol in the generated hypotheses. This technique is correct if a complete search is performed and Camacho report substantial efficiency improvements on several ILP applications.

Efficient Evaluation

As described above, hypotheses are evaluated by metrics that make reference to their coverage over the training data. Coverage is calculated by matching (or testing) all examples against the hypothesis; this involves finding a substitution such that the body of one of the hypothesis' clauses is true given the example and background knowledge.

An often used approach in ILP to match hypotheses is to use logical querying. The logical querying approach to clause matching involves the use of a Prolog engine to evaluate the clause with the examples and background knowledge.

The execution time to evaluate a query depends on the number of examples, number of resolution steps, and on the execution time of individual literals. Thus, scalability problems may arise when dealing with a great number of examples or/and when the computational cost to evaluate a rule is high. Query execution using SLDNF resolution grows exponentially with the number of literals in the query (Struyf, 2004). Hence, evaluating a single example can take a long time.

Several techniques have been proposed to improve the efficiency of hypotheses evaluation. Firstly, the evaluation of a hypothesis can be optimized by transforming the hypothesis into an equivalent one that can be more efficiently executed (Santos Costa et al., 2000; Santos Costa, Srinivasan, et al., 2003). An important characteristic of these techniques is that the transformations between equivalent hypothesis are correct. The transformation can be done at the level of individual hypotheses (Santos Costa et al., 2000; Struyf & Blockeel, 2003) or at the level of sets of hypotheses (Tsur et al., 1998; Blockeel et al., 2002).

A different method to speedup evaluation explores the existing redundancy on the sets of hypotheses evaluated: similar hypotheses are generated and evaluated in batches, called *query packs* (Blockeel et al., 2002), thus avoiding the redundant repetition of the same proof steps in different, but similar, hypotheses.

Approximate evaluation is another well-studied way of reducing the execution time of hypothesis evaluation. Stochastic matching (Sebag & Rouveirol, 1997), or stochastic theorem proving, was tested with the PROGOL ILP system, and has yielded considerable efficiency improvements, without sacrificing predictive accuracy or comprehensibility. This approach was further pursued by Giordana et al. (2000), making the benefits of replacing deterministic matching with stochastic matching clearly visible. A variety of other approximate matching schemes (Srinivasan, 1999; Kijsirikul et al., 2001; DiMaio & Shavlik,

2004; Bockhorst & Ong, 2004) have also been successfully tried.

Another technique, called *lazy evaluation,*[13] of examples (Camacho, 2003) aims at speeding up the evaluation of hypotheses by avoiding the unnecessary use of examples in the coverage computations, yielding considerable reduction of the execution time. The rationale underlying lazy evaluation is the following: a hypothesis is allowed to cover a small number of negative examples (the *noise* level) or none. If a clause covers more than the allowed number of negative examples it must be specialized. *Lazy evaluation of negatives* can be used when we are interested in knowing if a hypothesis covers more than the allowed number of negative examples or not. Testing stops as soon as the number of negative examples covered exceeds the allowed noise level or when there are no more negative examples to be tested. Therefore, the number of negative examples effectively tested may be very small, since the noise level is quite often very close to zero. If the evaluation function used does not involve negative coverage in its calculations, then this produces exactly the same results (clauses and accuracy) as the non-lazy approach but with a reduction on the number of negative examples tested.

One may also allow positive coverage to be computed lazily (*lazy evaluation of positives*). A clause is either specialized (if it covers more positives than the best consistent clause found so far) or justifiably pruned away otherwise. When using lazy evaluation of positives it is only relevant to determine if a hypothesis covers more positives than the current best consistent hypothesis or not. We might then just evaluate the positive examples until we exceed the best cover so far. If the best cover is exceeded we retain the hypothesis (either accept it as final if it is consistent or refine it otherwise) or we may justifiably discard it. We need to evaluate its exact positive cover only when accepting a consistent hypothesis. In this latter case we don't need to restart the positive coverage computation from scratch, we may

simply continue the test from the point where we left it before.

Storing intermediate results during the evaluation for later use (i.e., by performing a kind of a cache) can be a solution to reduce the time spent in hypothesis evaluation. The techniques that follow this method are categorized as: improving the evaluation of the literals of a hypothesis (Rocha et al., 2005), or by reducing the number of examples tested (Cussens, 1996; Berardi et al., 2004). All these techniques are correct and attempt to improve time efficiency at the cost of increasing memory consumption.

Handling Large Datasets

The explanation semantics used to formulate the task at hand has a profound influence on how data is represented, stored, and manipulated and, subsequently, a great impact on the performance of an ILP system. Under learning from entailment, examples may relate to each other, so they cannot be handled independently. Therefore, there is no separation of either the examples (apart from being positive or negative) or the background knowledge.

Learning from interpretations, on the other hand, assumes that that the data exhibits a certain amount of locality and each example is represented as sub-database, i.e., a separate Prolog program, encoding its specific properties. This allows ILP techniques that operate under this semantics to scale up well (Blockeel et al., 1999). Naturally, this assumption makes learning from interpretations weaker than learning from entailment, but applications and purposes for which this semantics is sufficient, benefit from its inherent scalability.

Learning from subsets of data is another way of dealing with large datasets. For instance, *windowing* is a well known technique that learns from subsets of data. It tries to identify a subset of the original data from which a theory of sufficient quality can be learnt. It as been shown (Quinlan, 1993; Fürnkranz, 1998) that this technique increases the predictive accuracy and reduces the learning time. In ILP, studies shown that windowing reduces the execution time while preserving the quality of the models found (Srinivasan, 1999; Fürnkranz, 1997).

Search Algorithms

The hypothesis space determines the set of possible hypotheses that can be considered while searching for a good hypothesis. Several approaches to reduce the hypothesis space were described above. On the other hand, the search algorithm defines the order by which the hypotheses are considered and determines the search space (i.e., the hypotheses effectively considered during the search). The search algorithm used can have a great impact on efficiency, however, it can also have an impact on the quality of the hypothesis found.

A wide number of search techniques have been used in ILP systems, namely breadth-first search (in PROGOL), depth-first search (in ALEPH), beam-search (Džeroski, 1993; Srinivasan, 2004), heuristic-guided hill-climbing variants (Quinlan, 1990; Srinivasan, 2004), and simulated annealing (Srinivasan, 2004; Serrurier et al., 2004), just to mention a few. The choice of one in detriment of another has several effects (Russell & Norvig, 2003), namely on memory consumption, execution time, and completeness.

More advanced search techniques have been exploited in ILP systems. A genetic search algorithm was proposed in (Tamaddoni-Nezhad & Muggleton, 2000) but the impact on efficiency was not reported.

Probabilistically searching large hypothesis space (Srinivasan, 2000) restricts the search space by sacrificing optimality. It consists in randomly selecting a fixed-size sample of clauses from the search space which, with high probability, contains a good clause. The evaluation of the technique on three real world applications showed reductions in the execution time without significantly affecting the quality of the hypothesis found. However, this approach has difficulties with 'needle in a haystack' problems, where very few good hypotheses exist.

Randomized rapid restarts (Železný et al., 2003) combines (local) complete search with the probabilistic search. It performs an exhaustive search up to a certain point (time constrained) and then, if a solution is not found, restarts into randomly selected location of the search space, The application of the RRR technique in two applications yielded a drastic reduction of the search time at the cost of a small loss in predictive accuracy (Železný et al., 2003).

Parallelism

Parallelism provides an attractive solution for improving efficiency. ILP systems may profit from exploiting parallelism by decreasing learning time, handling larger datasets, and improving the quality of the induced models. The exploitation of parallelism introduces several challenges. Designing and validating a parallel algorithm is often harder than designing and validating sequential algorithms. Performance issues are complex: splitting work into too many tasks may introduce significant overheads, whereas using fewer tasks may result in load imbalance and bad speedups.

There are three main strategies to exploit parallelism in ILP systems are (Fonseca et al., 2005): parallel exploration of the search space (Dehaspe & De Raedt, 1995; Ohwada et al., 2000; Ohwada & Mizoguchi, 1999; Wielemaker, 2003); parallel hypothesis evaluation (Matsui et al., 1998; Konstantopoulos, 2003); and parallel execution of an ILP system over a partition of the data (Ohwada & Mizoguchi, 1999; Graham et al., 2003). A survey on exploiting parallelism in ILP is presented in (Fonseca et al., 2005). An evaluation of several parallel ILP algorithms showed that a good approach to parallelize ILP systems is one of the simplest to implement: divide the set of examples by the computers/processors available;

run the ILP system in parallel on each subset; in the end, combine the theories found into a single one (Fonseca et al., 2005; Fonseca, 2006). This approach not only reduced the execution time but also improved predictive accuracy.

APPLICATIONS

In this section we briefly outline and provide references to various real-world applications of ILP, from medicine and biology, to language technology where ILP systems have made significant contributions to the discovery of new scientific knowledge.

Although we discuss in more detail applications in the three main areas of Life Sciences, Language Processing, and Engineering, ILP has been used in a variety of other domains. Examples of important applications of ILP must, at the very least, include domains such as music (Pompe et al., 1996; Tobudic & Widmer, 2003), the environment (Džeroski et al., 1995; Blockeel et al., 2004), intelligence analysis (Davis, Dutra, et al., 2005), and mathematical discovery (Colton & Muggleton, 2003; Todorovski et al., 2004).

Life Sciences

Inductive logic programming has been applied in a wide variety of domains of the Life Sciences, ranging over domains as diverse as Medical Support Systems (Carrault et al., 2003) and Computational Biochemistry (Srinivasan et al., 1994; Page & Craven, 2003).

Clinical data is one of the major sources of challenging datasets for ILP. To cite but a few example applications we will mention successful work on the characterization of cardiac arrhythmias (Quiniou et al., 2001), intensive care monitoring (Morik et al., 1999), diagnosis support systems for rheumatic diseases (Zupan & Džeroski, 1998) or breast cancer (Davis, Burnside, et al., 2005).

One of the major applications of inductive logic programming so far has been in the area of Structure-Activity Relationships (SAR), the task of predicting the activity of drug molecules based on their structure. Early examples of this work include detecting mutagenic (Srinivasan et al., 1994) and carcinogenic (Srinivasan et al., 1997) properties in compounds. In the continuation, researchers have used ILP for 3D-SAR, where one uses a 3D description of the main elements in the compound to find *pharmacophores* that explain drug activity (Finn et al., 1998). Among the successful examples of ILP applications one can mention pharmacophores for dopamine agonists, ACE inhibitors, Thermolysin inhibitors, and antibacterial peptides (Enot & King, 2003). A related application with a different approach is the work in Diterpene structure elucidation by Džeroski et al. (1996).

ILP has also made significant contributions to the expanding area of Bio-informatics and Computational Biology. One major interest in this area has been in explaining protein structure, including secondary structure (Muggleton, King, & Sternberg, 1992; Mozetic, 1998) and fold prediction (Turcotte et al., 2001). Another very exciting area of ILP research is helping understand cell machinery; the work of Bryant et al. (2001) should be mentioned as the seminal work on understanding metabolic pathways of yeast. Finally, in genetics, recent work has also achieved promising results on using ILP to predict the functional class of genes (King, 2004) and to understand the combination of gene expression data with structure and/or function gene data (Struyf et al., 2005).

Recent studies on automating the scientific discovery process King et al. (2004) embed ILP systems in the cycle of scientific experimentation. The cycle includes the automatic generation of hypotheses to explain observations, the devising of experiments to evaluate the hypotheses, physically run the experiments using a laboratory robot, interprets the results to falsify hypotheses inconsistent with the data and then repeats the cycle.

Language Technology

The ability to take advantage of explicit background knowledge and bias constitutes one of the strongest points in favour of applying ILP to language technology tasks, as it provides a means of directly exploiting a very long and rich tradition of theoretical linguistics research.

More specifically, syntactic bias allows for the restriction of the hypothesis space within the limits of a meta-theory or theoretical framework. Except for the theoretical merit it carries on its own, this ability also offers the opportunity to capitalize on linguistic knowledge in order to reduce the computational cost of searching the hypothesis space, whereas many alternative learning schemes cannot make such explicit use of existing knowledge.

Language technology experimentation with ILP runs through the whole range of fields of the study of language, from phonology and morphology all the way to syntax, semantics and discourse analysis: we will mention work on prediction of past tenses (Muggleton & Bain, 1999), nominal paradigms (Džeroski & Erjavec, 1997), part-of-speech tagging (Dehaspe & De Raedt, 1997; Cussens, 1997), learning transfer rules (Boström, 2000), and focus on parsing and phonotactics (below).

Another exciting application of ILP is in the area of Information Extraction (IE). This includes work on document analysis and understanding (Esposito et al., 1993) and work on web page characterization that has had a profound practical impact (Craven & Slattery, 2001). Interesting results have been achieved when using ILP for performing IE over scientific literature (Califf & Mooney, 1999; Goadrich et al., 2004; Malerba et al., 2003).

Parser Construction

The syntax of an utterance is the way in which words combine to form grammatical phrases and sentences and the way in which the semantics of the individual words combine to give rise to the semantics of phrases and sentences. It is, in other words, the structure hidden behind the (flat) utterance heard and seen on the surface.

Since the seminal work of Chomsky (1957), it is the fundamental assumption of linguistics that this structure has the form of a tree, where the terminal symbols are the actual word-forms and the non-terminal symbols abstractions of words or multi-word phrases. It is the task of a *computational grammar* to describe the mapping between syntactic trees structures and flat utterances. Computational grammars are typically Definite Clause Grammars,[14] which describe syntactic structures in terms of derivations. Such grammars are used to control a *parser*, the piece of computational machinery that builds the *parse tree* of the phrase from the derivations necessary to successfully recognise the phrase.

Definite Clause Grammars can be naturally represented as Definite Clause Programs and their derivations map directly to Definite Logic Programming proofs. This does not, however, mean that grammar construction can be trivially formulated as an ILP task: this is for various reasons, but most importantly because ILP algorithms will typically perform single-predicate learning without attempting background knowledge revision.

Because of these difficulties, the alternative of refining an incomplete original grammar has been explored. In this approach learning is broken down in an abductive example generation and an inductive example generalization step. In the first step, examples are generated from a linguistic corpus as follows: the incomplete parser is applied to the corpus and, each time a parse fails, the most specific missing piece of the proof tree is identified. In other words, for all sentences that fail to parse, a ground, phrase-specific rule is identified that—if incorporated in the grammar—would have allowed that phrase's parse to succeed.

For the inductive step the parsing mechanism and the original grammar are included in the background knowledge and an ILP algorithm generalizes the phrase-specific rule examples into general rules that are appended to the original grammar to yield a complete grammar of the language of the corpus.

This abductive-inductive methodology has been successfully applied to Definite Clause grammars of English in two different parsing frameworks: (Cussens & Pulman, 2000) uses it to to extend the coverage of a chart parser (Pereira & Warren, 1983) by learning chart-licensing rules and Zelle & Mooney (1996) to restrict the coverage of an overly general shift-reduce parser (Tomita, 1986) by learning control rules for the parser's shift and reduce operators.

Phonotactic Modelling

The *Phonotactics* of a given language is the set of rules that identifies what sequences of phonemes constitute a possible word in that language. The problem can be broken down to the *syllable structure* (i.e. what sequences of phonemes constitute a possible syllable) and the processes that take place at the syllable boundaries (e.g. assimilation). Phonotactic models assist in many Information Extraction tasks, like optical character recognition and speech recognition, as they can be applied to catch recognition errors or limit the space of possibilities that the main recognition algorithm has to consider.

Phonotactic modelling tasks have been tackled by various machine learning methodologies and in various languages. Just to mention learning the syllable structure of the Dutch language from the CELEX (Burnage, 1990) lexical corpus, we find symbolic methods, like abduction (Tjong Kim Sang & Nerbonne, 2000) and ILP (Nerbonne &

Konstantopoulos, 2004), as well as stochastic and distributed models, like Hidden Markov Models (Tjong Kim Sang, 1998) and Simple Recurrent Networks (Stoianov et al., 1998).

Nerbonne & Konstantopoulos (2004) compare the results of all these approaches, and identify the relative advantages and disadvantages of ILP. In short, ILP and abduction achieve similar accuracy, but ILP constructs a first-order syllabic theory which is formulated in about one fifth of the number of rules used by abduction to formulate a propositional syllabic theory.

Furthermore, it should be noted that the background knowledge in these experiments is both language-neutral and unrelated to the problem at hand. In a second series of experiments, both ILP and abduction are fortified with a background theory that transfers results from phonology theory. ILP was given access to background encoding a hierarchical feature-class description of Dutch phonetic material (Booij, 1995), a theory which is language-specific but not related to the problem at hand. Abduction was biased toward a general theory of syllable structure (Cairns & Feinstein, 1982), which is language-neutral but does constitute a step towards solving the problem at hand. In these second series of experiments, the first-order ILP solution is expressed in one tenth of the clauses of the propositional one.[15] These results leave ample space for further experimentation, since the backgrounds provided to the two algorithms are not directly comparable, but do show a very clear tendency of ILP to take very good advantage of sophisticated background knowledge when such is provided.

Engineering

ILP has been applied to a wide variety of engineering applications. One classical application of ILP is in finite element mesh design for structure analysis ("Finite element mesh design: an engineering domain for ILP applications",

1994; Dolšak et al., 1997). This is a difficult task that depends on body geometry, type of edges, boundary conditions and loading.

Camacho (1998, 2000) has used ILP to automatically construct an autopilot for a flight simulator. The approach used was based on a reverse engineering technique called *behavioural cloning*. The basic idea is to have a human expert pilot flying the flight simulator and collect state and control variables of the plane during the flight manoeuvres conducted by the human pilot. In a second step the collected traces of the flights are pre-processed and taken as examples for a machine learning (ILP in our case) algorithm. The learning algorithm produces a model of the human pilot for each of the flight manoeuvres. These models are put together and an auto-pilot is assembled.

Further examples include traffic control (Džeroski et al., 1998), spatial data mining (Pope-linsky, 1998), and intrusion detection in computer networks (Gunetti & Ruffo, 1999; Ko, 2000)

CONCLUSION

In this chapter we have described inductive logic programming and demonstrated how it builds upon artificial intelligence strategies for searching in lattices. ILP relies on the vast body of research on search strategies that has been developed within AI. On the other hand, ILP fortifies lattice searching with powerful tools for expressing prior knowledge to control the search space, which constitutes a significant theoretical and computational contribution. We argue, therefore, that ILP is of significant interest to AI research on search.

ILP systems are very versatile tools, that have been adapted to an extensive domain of applications. As these applications expand to range over more sophisticated and complex domains, ILP has needed to tackle larger searcher spaces. Indeed, Page & Srinivasan (2003) argue that improvements

in search are one of the critical areas where ILP research should focus on. This chapter shows a number of recent works on improving search in ILP, through techniques such as stochastic search and parallelism. We expect that this research will continue and we believe that major contributions will be of interest to the whole AI community. In the end, ILP is not the silver bullet that will tackle all AI problems, but a sound understanding of its strengths and weaknesses can yield fruitful results in many domains.

The Limitations of ILP

ILP inherits from its logical foundations the difficulties of symbolic (as opposed to numerical) computation: it is computationally demanding and difficult to scale up, and does not handle numerical data well.

With respect to the computational demands of ILP, it should be noted that most often cost is dominated by hypothesis matching, which relies on performing unification and symbolic manipulation on a large scale. Although many important optimizations have been proposed, as discussed earlier, the elementary search step in ILP is very inefficient when compared to other machine learning and pattern recognition methodologies. On a more optimistic note, the inefficiency of the elementary search step is counter-balanced by the fact that fewer such steps need to be taken to reach a solution, as ILP is particularly good at capitalizing on prior domain knowledge to restrict the search space and perform a more focused search.

Scalability issues pertaining to the volume of the data that needs to be processed are also difficult to tackle, but considerable ground has been covered in that direction as well. First of all, learning from interpretations takes advantage of localities in the data and scales up well. But under the stronger model of learning from entailment, where no such data locality assumptions are made, stochastic evaluation and parallelization techniques allow ILP systems to handle large volumes of data, as discussed.

A second limitation is that handling numerical data is difficult and cumbersome in ILP, as is usually the case with symbolic manipulation systems. In fact, it is only very recently that hybrid modelling languages like Stochastic Logic Programming (Cussens, 2000) and Bayesian Logic Programming (Kersting & Raedt, 2001) combine first-order inference with probability calculus. Searching in this combined hypothesis language is a very promising and exciting new sub-discipline of ILP (Muggleton, 2003; Kersting & Raedt, 2002; Santos Costa, Page, et al., 2003).

The Argument for Prior Knowledge

The explicit control over the exact boundaries of the hypothesis language that ILP systems offer, constitutes one of the strongest advantages of ILP. This is of relevance to theoretical as well as computational aspects of Artificial Intelligence.

From a *theoretical* point of view, it provides a means of restricting the search space within the limits of a meta-theory or theoretical framework. Such a framework might be justified by theoretical grounds and not necessarily relate to (or be derivable from) the empirical evaluation of hypotheses, hence purely empirical machine learning algorithms will not necessarily propose conforming hypotheses.

From a *computational* point of view, it is generally accepted in the Computer Science literature and practice that one of the most important aspects of setting up a search task properly is tightly delineating the search space so that it contains the solution, but as little more than that as possible. Explicit control over the hypothesis language offers an opportunity to capitalize on prior domain knowledge in order to reduce the computational cost of searching the hypothesis space, by encoding known qualities that good hypotheses possess, so that the search for a solution focuses on clauses where these qualities are present.

This is, of course, not to argue that control over the feature set, constraint satisfaction and bias cannot be implemented in statistical or distributed-computation approaches to machine learning. But the qualitative difference that ILP makes, is the ability to express those in Definite Horn clauses, an explicit and symbolic formalism that is considered—for reasons independent from its being at the foundations of ILP—to be particularly suitable for knowledge representation.

The Versatility of ILP

We have seen how several different evaluation measures have been proposed that estimate the quality of a hypothesis, reviewed here and also by Lavrač et al. (1999) and Fürnkranz & Flach (2003). This diversity a consequence of the variety of learning tasks and applications that ILP has been applied to, and different evaluation methods have been designed for different kinds of problems.

One point that should made here is the flexibility that this wide range of evaluation functions gives to ILP. In particular the ability to take advantage of explicit negative examples should be noted, by allowing the distinction between explicit negative examples (propositions that should not be covered) and non-positives examples (propositions that are not in the set of proposition that should be covered, propositions that are not interesting.)

At the same time, the ability to exploit negatives does not imply a reliance on their existence or their reliability. Restrictions on maximum negative coverage can be relaxed to accommodate noisy domains and some evaluation functions, like the the *m*-probability estimate, also provide parameters for applying a preference bias towards stricter or more liberal clauses. Finally, in the total absence of explicit negatives, positive-only evaluation is employed. This last approach most closely resembles some regression-based machine learning disciplines in that they are both trying to guess a concept's boundaries by interpolating between positive data-points, rather than by looking for a separating line between the positive and the negative points.

Future Directions of ILP

As more and more data is stored in more powerful computers, ILP systems face a number of challenges. Page & Srinivasan propose five areas as critical to the future of ILP: the ability to process and reason with uncertain information, leading to the use of probabilities; improvements in search; the ability to take best advantages of progress in computing power, and namely of parallel computing; and, last not least, improvements in user interaction that will facilitate using ILP across a wider community. This is but a simplification. Current research shows a number of other exciting directions such as progress in database interfacing, better usage of propositional learners, learning second order extensions such as aggregated functions, and even a recent revival of areas such as predicate invention. Most important, ILP is now being applied on larger, and more complex datasets than some would believe was possible a few years ago, with exciting results. Ultimately, we believe it is the fact that ILP is indeed useful for practical applications that will drive its growth, and that will guarantee its contribution to the wider Computer Science community.

REFERENCES

Anthony, S., & Frisch, A. M. (1999, January). Cautious induction: An alternative to clause-at-a-time induction in inductive logic programming. *New Generation Computing, 17*(1), 25-52.

Bayes, T. (1763). An essay towards solving a problem in the doctrine of chances. *Philosophical Transactions of the Royal Society of London, 53*, 370-418.

Berardi, M., Varlaro, A., & Malerba, D. (2004). On the effect of caching in recursive theory learning. In *Proceedings of the 14th international conference on inductive logic programming* (pp. 44-62). Berlin: Springer-Verlag.

Blockeel, H., Dehaspe, L., Demoen, B., Janssens, G., Ramon, J., & Vandecasteele, H. (2002). Improving the efficiency of inductive logic programming through the use of query packs. *Journal of machine learning Research, 16*, 135-166.

Blockeel, H., & De Raedt, L. (1998). Top-down induction of first-order logical decision trees. *Artificial Intelligence, 101*(1-2), 285-297.

Blockeel, H., Džeroski, S., Kompare, B., Kramer, S., Pfahringer, B., & Laer, W. V. (2004). Experiments in predicting biodegradability. *Applied Artificial Intelligence, 18*(2), 157-181.

Blockeel, H., Raedt, L. D., Jacobs, N., & Demoen, B. (1999). Scaling up inductive logic programming by learning from interpretations. *Data Mining and Knowledge Discovery, 3*(1), 59-93.

Bockhorst, J., & Ong, I. M. (2004). FOIL-D: Efficiently scaling FOIL for multi-relational data mining of large datasets. In *Proceedings of the 14th International Conference on Inductive Logic Programming* (pp. 63-79).

Booij, G. (1995). *The phonology of Dutch.* Oxford: Clarendon Press.

Boström, H. (1996). Theory-guided induction of logic programs by inference of regular languages. In *Proceedings of the 13th International Conference on Machine Learning* (pp. 46-53). San Francisco: Morgan Kaufmann.

Boström, H. (1998). Predicate invention and learning from positive examples only. In *Proceedings of the Tenth European Conference on MachineLearning* (pp. 226-237). Berlin: Springer Verlag.

Boström, H. (2000, June). Induction of recursive transfer rules. In J. Cussens & S. Džeroski (Eds.), *Lecture notes in computer science: Vol. 1925. Learning Language in Logic* (pp. 237-246). Berlin: Springer-Verlag.

Botta, M., Giordana, A., Saitta, L., & Sebag, M. (2003). Relational learning as search in a critical region. *Journal of Machine Learning Research, 4*, 431-463.

Bryant, C., Muggleton, S., Oliver, S., Kell, D., Reiser, P., & King, R. (2001). Combining Inductive Logic programming, Active Learning and robotics to discover the function of genes. *Electronic Transactions on Artificial Intelligence, 5*(B1), 1-36.

Burnage, G. (1990). *CELEX: A guide for users.*

Cairns, C., & Feinstein, M. (1982). Markedness and the theory of syllable structure. *Linguistic Inquiry, 13.*

Califf, M. E., & Mooney, R. J. (1999, July). Relational learning of pattern-match rules for information extraction. In *Proceedings of the 17th National Conference on Artificial Intelligence.* Orlando, FL.

Camacho, R. (1998). Inducing models of human control skills. In C. Nedellec & C. Rouveirol (Eds.), *Lecture notes in computer science: Vol. 1398. ECML* (pp. 107-118). Berlin: Springer-Verlag.

Camacho, R. (2000). *Inducing models of human control skills using machine learning algorithms.* Unpublished doctoral dissertation, Department of Electrical Engineering and Computation, Universidade do Porto.

Camacho, R. (2002). Improving the efficiency of ILP systems using an incremental language level search. In *Annual Machine Learning Conference of Belgium and the Netherlands.*

Camacho, R. (2003). As lazy as it can be. In P. Doherty, B. Tassen, P. Ala-Siuru, & B. Mayoh (Eds.), *The Eighth Scandinavian Conference on Artificial Intelligence (SCAI '03), Bergen, Norway, November 2003* (pp. 47-58).

Carrault, G., Cordier, M., Quiniou, R., & Wang, F. (2003, July). Temporal abstraction and inductive logic programming for arrhythmia recognition from electrocardiograms. *Artificial Intelligence in Medicine, 28*(3), 231-63.

Cestnik, B. (1990). Estimating probabilities: A crucial task in machine learning. In *European conference on artificial intelligence* (pp. 147-149).

Chomsky, N. (1957). *Syntactic structures.* The Hague: Mouton. (first mention of trees and such).

Clark, P., & Niblett, T. (1989). The CN2 induction algorithm. *Machine Learning, 3*(4), 261-83.

Cohen, W. W. (1994). Grammatically biased learning: Learning logic programs using an explicit antecedent description language. *Artificial Intelligence, 68*, 303-366.

Colton, S., & Muggleton, S. (2003). ILP for mathematical discovery. In T. Horváth (Ed.), *Lecture Notes in Computer Science: Vol. 2835. ILP* (pp. 93-111). Berlin: Springer-Verlag.

Craven, M., & Slattery, S. (2001, April). Relational learning with statistical predicate invention: Better models for hypertext. *Machine Learning, 43*(1/2), 97-119.

Cussens, J. (1993). Bayes and pseudo-Bayes estimates of conditional probabilities and their reliability. In *Proceedings of the European Conference on Machine Learning (ecml93)* (pp. 136-152). Berlin: Springer Verlag.

Cussens, J. (1996). *Part-of-speech disambiguation using ILP* (Tech. Rep. No. PRG-TR-25-96). Oxford University Computing Laboratory.

Cussens, J. (1997). Part-of-speech tagging using progol. In S. Džeroski & N. Lavrač (Eds.), *Lecture notes in artificial intelligence: Vol. 1297.*

Proceedings of the 7th International Workshop on Inductive Logic Programming (pp. 93-108). Berlin: Springer-Verlag.

Cussens, J. (2000). Stochastic logic programs: Sampling, inference and applications. In C. Boutilier & M. Goldszmidt (Eds.), *Proceedings of the 16th Annual Conference on Uncertainty in Artificial Intelligence*. Morgan Kaufmann.

Cussens, J., & Džeroski, S. (Eds.). (2000). *Learning language in logic*. Berlin: Springer-Verlag.

Cussens, J., & Pulman, S. (2000). Experiments in inductive chart parsing. In J. Cussens & S. Džeroski (Eds.), *Lecture notes in artificial intelligence: Vol. 1925. Learning Language in Logic*. Berlin: Springer-Verlag.

Davis, J., Burnside, E. S., Dutra, I. d. C., David, P. C., & Santos Costa, V. (2005). Knowledge discovery from structured mammography reports using inductive logic programming. In *American Medical Informatics Association 2005 Annual symposium*.

Davis, J., Dutra, I. d. C., Page, C. D., & Santos Costa, V. (2005). Establishing identity equivalence in multi-relational domains. In *Proceedings of the 2005 International Conference on Intelligence Analysis*.

Dehaspe, L., & De Raedt, L. (1995). Parallel inductive logic programming. In *Proceedings of the MLnet Familiarization Workshop on Statistics, Machine Learning and Knowledge Discovery in Databases*.

Dehaspe, L., & De Raedt, L. (1996, July). DLAB: *a declarative language bias for concept learning and knowledge discovery engines* (Tech. Rep. No. CW 214). Leuven: Department of Computing Science, K.U.Leuven.

Dehaspe, L., & De Raedt, L. (1997). Mining association rules in multiple relations. In S. Džeroski & N. Lavrač (Eds.), *Lecture notes in artificial intelligence: Vol. 1297. Proceedings of the 7th International Workshop on Inductive Logic Programming* (pp. 125-132). Berlin: Springer-Verlag.

Dehaspe, L., & Toironen, H. (2000). *Relational data mining*. In (pp. 189-208). Berlin: Springer-Verlag.

De Raedt, L. (1997). Logical settings for concept-learning. *Artificial Intelligence, 95*(1), 187-201.

De Raedt, L., & Blockeel, H. (1997). Using logical decision trees for clustering. In *Proceedings of the 7th International Workshop on Inductive Logic Programming* (pp. 133-140). Springer-Verlag.

De Raedt, L., & Dehaspe, L. (1996). *Clausal discovery* (Tech. Rep. No. CW 238). Leuven: Department of Computing Science, K.U.Leuven.

De Raedt, L., & Dehaspe, L. (1997). Learning from satisfiability. In *Proceedings of the Ninth Dutch Conference on Artificial Intelligence (NAIC'97)* (pp. 303-312).

De Raedt, L., & Džeroski, S. (1994). First-order jk-clausal theories are pac-learnable. *Artificial Intelligence, 70*(1-2), 375-392.

De Raedt, L., Kersting, K., & Torge, S. (2005). Towards learning stochastic logic programs from proof-banks. In *Proceedings of the 23th National Conference on Artificial Intelligence, (AAAI 2005)* (pp. 752-757).

DiMaio, F., & Shavlik, J. W. (2004). Learning an approximation to inductive logic programming clause evaluation. In *Proceedings of the 14th International Conference on Inductive Logic Programming* (pp. 80-97).

Dolšak, B., Bratko, I., & Jezernik, A. (1997). Application of machine learning in finite element computation. In R. Michalski, I. Bratko, & M. Kubat (Eds.), *Machine learning, data mining and knowledge discovery: Methods and applications*. John Wiley and Sons.

Džeroski, S. (1993). Handling imperfect data in inductive logic programming. In *Proceedings of the 4th Scandinavian Conference on Artificial Intelligence* (pp. 111-125). IOS Press.

Džeroski, S., Dehaspe, L., Ruck, B., & Walley, W. (1995). Classification of river water quality data using machine learning. In *Proceedings of the 5th International Conference on the Development and Application of Computer Techniques to Environmental Studies.*

Džeroski, S., & Erjavec, T. (1997). Induction of Slovene nominal paradigms. In N. Lavrac & S. Džeroski (Eds.), *Lecture notes in computer science: Vol. 1297. ILP* (pp. 141–148). Berlin: Springer-Verlag.

Džeroski, S., Jacobs, N., Molina, M., & Moure, C. (1998). ILP experiments in detecting traffic problems. In C. Nedellec & C. Rouveirol (Eds.), *Lecture Notes in Computer Science: Vol. 1398. ECML* (pp. 61-66). Berlin: Springer-Verlag.

Džeroski, S., Schulze-Kremer, S., Heidtke, K., Siems, K., & Wettschereck, D. (1996). Applying ILP to diterpene structure elucidation from ^{13}C NMR spectra. In *Proceedings of the MLnet Familiarization Workshop on Data Mining with Inductive Logic Programing* (pp. 12-24).

Enot, D. P., & King, R. D. (2003). Application of inductive logic programming to structure-based drug design. In N. Lavrac, D. Gamberger, H. Blockeel, & L. Todorovski (Eds.), *Lecture notes in computer science: Vol. 2838. Proceedings of the 7th European Conference on Principles of Data Mining and Knowledge Discovery* (pp. 156-167). Berlin: Springer-Verlag.

Esposito, F., Malerba, D., & Semeraro, G. (1993). Automated acquisition of rules for document understanding. In *Proceedings of the 2nd International Conference on Document Analysis and Recognition* (pp. 650-654).

Finite element mesh design: an engineering domain for ILP applications. (1994). In *Proceedings of the 4th International Workshop on Inductive Logic Programming (ILP-94), Bad Honnef/Bonn, Germany, September 12-14.*

Finn, P. W., Muggleton, S. H., Page, C. D., & Srinivasan, A. (1998). Pharmacophore discovery using the inductive logic programming system PROGOL. *Machine Learning, 30*(2-3), 241-270.

Fonseca, N. A. (2006). *Parallelism in inductive logic programming systems.* Unpublished doctoral dissertation, University of Porto.

Fonseca, N. A., Santos Costa, V., Camacho, R., & Silva, F. (2004). On avoiding redundancy in inductive logic programming. In R. Camacho, R. D. King, & A. Srinivasan (Eds.), *Lecture notes in artificial intelligence: Vol. 3194. Proceedings of the 14th International Conference on inductive logic programming, Porto, Portugal, September 2004* (pp. 132-146). Berlin: Springer-Verlag.

Fonseca, N. A., Silva, F., Santos Costa, V., & Camacho, R. (2005). Strategies to paralilize ILP systems. In *Lecture notes in ai. 15th International Conference on Inductive Logic Programming (ILP 2005), Bonn, August 2005* (pp. 136-153). Berlin: Springer-Verlag. (Best paper ILP 2005)

Fürnkranz, J. (1997, August). Dimensionality reduction in ILP: a call to arms. In L. De Raedt & S. H. Muggleton (Eds.), *Proceedings of the IJCAI-97 Workshop on Frontiers of Inductive Logic Programming* (pp. 81-86). Nagoya, Japan.

Fürnkranz, J. (1998). Integrative windowing. *Journal of Machine Learning Research, 8*, 129-164.

Fürnkranz, J., & Flach, P. (2003). An analysis of rule evaluation metrics. In *Proceedings of the 20th International Conference on Machine Learning (icml-03).* San Francisco: Morgan Kaufmann.

Giordana, A., Saitta, L., Sebag, M., & Botta, M. (2000). Analyzing relational learning in the phase transition framework. In *Proceedings of the 17th International Conference on Machine*

Learning (pp. 311-318). San Francisco: Morgan Kaufmann.

Goadrich, M., Oliphant, L., & Shavlik, J. W. (2004). Learning ensembles of first-order clauses for recall-precision curves: A case study in biomedical information extraction. In R. Camacho, R. D. King, & A. Srinivasan (Eds.), *Lecture notes in computer science: Vol. 3194. ILP* (pp. 98–115). Berlin: Springer-Verlag.

Graham, J., Page, C. D., & Kamal, A. (2003). Accelerating the drug design process through parallel inductive logic programming data mining. In *Proceeding of the Computational Systems Bioinformatics (csb'03)*. IEEE.

Gunetti, D., & Ruffo, G. (1999). Intrusion detection through behavioral data. In S. Wrobel (Ed.), *Lecture notes in computer science. Proceedings of The Third Symposium on Intelligent Data Analysis*. Berlin: Springer-Verlag.

Hayes-Roth, F. (1974). Schematic classification problems and their solution. *Pattern Recognition*, *6*(2), 105-113.

Horváth, T. (Ed.). (2003). *Inductive logic programming: Proceeding of the 13th International Conference, ILP 2003, Szeged, Hungary, September 29–October 1, 2003*. Berlin: Springer-Verlag.

Jorge, A., & Brazdil, P. (1995). Architecture for iterative learning of recursive definitions. In L. De Raedt (Ed.), *Proceedings of the 5th International Workshop on Inductive Logic Programming* (pp. 95-108). Department of Computer Science, Katholieke Universiteit Leuven.

Kersting, K., & Raedt, L. D. (2001, November). *Bayesian logic programs* (Tech. Rep. No. 151). Georges-Koehler-Allee, D-77110, Freiburg: Institute for Computer Science, University of Freiburg.

Kersting, K., & Raedt, L. D. (2002). *Basic principles of learning bayesian logic progras* (Tech.

Rep. No. 174). Georges-Koehler-Allee, D-77110, Freiburg: Institute for Computer Science, University of Freiburg.

Kijsirikul, B., Sinthupinyo, S., & Chongkasemwongse, K. (2001). Approximate match of rules using backpropagation neural networks. *Machine Learning*, *44*(3), 273-299.

King, R. D. (2004). Applying inductive logic programming to predicting gene function. *AI Magazine*, *25*(1), 57-68.

King, R. D., Whelan, K. E., Jones, F. M., Reiser, P. G., Bryant, C. H., Muggleton, S. H., et al. (2004, January). Functional genomic hypothesis generation and experimentation by a robot scientist. *Nature*, *427*(6971), 247-252.

Ko, C. (2000). Logic induction of valid behavior specifications for intrusion detection. In *SP 2000: Proceedings of the 2000 IEEE Symposium on Security and Privacy*. Washington, D.C., USA: IEEE Computer Society.

Konstantopoulos, S. (2003, September). A data-parallel version of Aleph. In *Proceedings of the Workshop on Parallel and Distributed Computing for Machine Learning, co-located with ECML/ PKDD'2003*. Dubrovnik, Croatia.

Langley, P. (1996). *Elements of Machine Learning*. Morgan-Kaufmann.

Lavrac, N., & Džeroski, S. (Eds.). (1997). In *Proceedings of the 7th International Workshop on Inductive Logic Programming (ILP-97), Prague, Czech Republic, September 17-20, 1997*. Berlin: Springer-Verlag.

Lavrač, N., Flach, P., & Zupan, B. (1999, June). Rule evaluation measures: A unifying view. In S. Džeroski & P. Flach (Eds.), *Lecture notes in artificial intelligence: Vol. 1634. Proceedings of the 9th International Workshop on Inductive Logic Programming* (pp. 174–185). Berlin: Springer-Verlag.

Lloyd, J. W. (1997). *Foundations of logic programming* (2nd ed.). Berlin: Springer-Verlag.

Malerba, D., Esposito, F., Altamura, O., Ceci, M., & Berardi, M. (2003). Correcting the document layout: A machine learning approach. *IEEE Computer Society*, p. 97.

Matsui, T., Inuzuka, N., Seki, H., & Itoh, H. (1998). Comparison of three parallel implementations of an induction algorithm. In *Proceedings of the 8th International Parallel Computing Eorkshop* (pp. 181-188). Singapore.

Matwin, S., & Sammut, C. (Eds.). (2003). In *Proceedings of the 12th International Workshop on Inductive Logic Programming (ilp 2002)*. Berlin: Springer Verlag.

McCreath, E., & Sharma, A. (1995, November). Extraction of meta-knowledge to restrict the hypothesis space for ILP systems. In X. Yao (Ed.), *Proceedings of the eighth Australian Joint Conference on Artificial Intelligence* (pp. 75-82). World Scientific.

Michalski, R. S. (1973). Aqval/1-computer implementation of a variable-valued logic system vl1 and examples of its application to pattern recognition. In *Proceeding of the First International Joint Conference on Pattern Recognition* (p. 3-17).

Mitchell, T. M. (1978). *Version spaces: An approach to concept learning.* Unpublished doctoral dissertation, Stanford University.

Mitchell, T. M. (1997). *Machine learning* (Second ed.). McGraw Hill.

Mitchell, T. M., Utgoff, P., & Banerji, R. (1983). Learning by experimentation: Acquiring and refining problem-solving heuristics. In R. Michalski, J. Carbonnel, & T. Mitchell (Eds.), *Machine learning: An artificial intelligence approach*. Palo Alto, CA: Tioga.

Morik, K., Brockhausen, P., & Joachims, T. (1999). Combining statistical learning with a knowledge-based approach — A case study in intensive care monitoring. In I. Bratko & S. Džeroski (Eds.), *Icml* (pp. 268–277). San Francisco: Morgan Kaufmann.

Mozetic, I. (1998, December). Secondary structure prediction by inductive logic programming. In *Third meeting on the critical assessment of techniques for protein structure prediction, casp3* (pp. 38-38). Asilomar, CA: CASP3 organizers.

Muggleton, S. H. (1988). A strategy for constructing new predicates in first order logic. In D. Sleeman (Ed.), *Proceedings of the 3rd European Working Session on Learning* (pp. 123–130). Pitman.

Muggleton, S. H. (1991). Inductive logic programming. *New Generation Computing, 8*(4), 295–317.

Muggleton, S. H. (1995). Inverse entailment and Progol. *New Generation Computing, Special Issue on Inductive Logic Programming, 13*(3-4), 245-286.

Muggleton, S. H. (1996). Learning from positive data. In *Proceedings of the Sixth International Workshop on Inductive Logic Programming, lnai 1314* (pp. 358-376). Berlin: Springer-Verlag.

Muggleton, S. H. (2003). Learning structure and parameters of stochastic logic programs. In S. Matwin & C. Sammut (Eds.), *Lecture notes in artificial intelligence: Vol. 2583. Proceedings of the 12th International Workshop on Inductive Logic Programming (ILP 2002)* (pp. 198-–206). Berlin: Springer Verlag.

Muggleton, S. H., & Bain, M. (1999). Analogical prediction. In S. Džeroski & P. A. Flach (Eds.), *Lecture Notes in Computer Science: Vol. 1634. ILP* (pp. 234-244). Berlin: Springer-Verlag.

Muggleton, S. H., & Buntine, W. (1988). Machine invention of first-order predicates by inverting resolution. In *Proceedings of the 5th International*

Conference on Machine Learning (pp. 339-352). Kaufmann.

Muggleton, S. H., & De Raedt, L. (1994). inductive logic programming: Theory and methods. *Journal of Logic Programming, 19*(20), 629-679. (Updated version of technical report CW 178, May 1993, Department of Computing Science, K.U. Leuven)

Muggleton, S. H., & Feng, C. (1990). Efficient induction of logic programs. In *Proceedings of the 1st Conference on Algorithmic Learning Theory* (pp. 368-381). Tokyo: Ohmsha.

Muggleton, S. H., King, R. D., & Sternberg, M. J. E. (1992). Protein secondary structure prediction using logic. In S. H. Muggleton (Ed.), *Report ICOT TM-1182. Proceedings of the 2nd International Workshop on Inductive Logic Programming* (pp. 228–259).

Muggleton, S. H., Srinivasan, A., & Bain, M. (1992). Compression, significance and accuracy. In D. Sleeman & P. Edwards (Eds.), *Proceedings of the 9th International Workshop on Machine Learning* (pp. 338-347). San Francisco: Morgan Kaufmann.

Nedellec, C., & Rouveirol, C. (Eds.). (1998). In *Proceedings of the 10th European Conference on Machine Learning (ECML 1998), Chemnitz, Germany, April 21-23*. Berlin: Springer-Verlag.

Nerbonne, J., & Konstantopoulos, S. (2004, May). Phonotactics in inductive logic programming. In M. Klopotek, S. Wierzchon, & K. Trojanowski (Eds.), *Advances in soft computing. Intelligent Information Processing and Web Mining. Proceedings of the International IIS: IIPWM'04 Conference, Zakopane, Poland, May 17-20, 2004* (pp. 493-502). Berlin: Springer-Verlag.

Ohwada, H., & Mizoguchi, F. (1999). Parallel execution for speeding up inductive logic programming systems. In *Lecture notes in artificial intelligence. Proceedings of the 9th International Workshop on Inductive Logic Programming* (pp. 277-286). Springer-Verlag.

Ohwada, H., Nishiyama, H., & Mizoguchi, F. (2000). Concurrent execution of optimal hypothesis search for inverse entailment. In J. Cussens & A. Frisch (Eds.), *Lecture notes in artificial intelligence: Vol. 1866. Proceedings of the 10th International Conference on Inductive Logic Programming* (pp. 165-173). Berlin: Springer-Verlag.

Ong, I. M., Dutra, I. d. C., Page, C. D., & Santos Costa, V. (2005). Mode directed path finding. In *Lecture notes in computer science: Vol. 3720. Proceedings of the 16th European Conference on Machine Learning* (pp. 673-681).

Page, C. D., & Craven, M. (2003). Biological applications of multi-relational data mining. *SIGKDD Explor. Newsl., 5*(1), 69-79.

Page, C. D., & Srinivasan, A. (2003, August). ILP: A short look back and a longer look forward. *Journal of Machine Learning Research*(4), 415-430.

Passerini, A., Frasconi, P., & De Raedt, L. (2006). Kernels on prolog proof trees: Statistical learning in the ILP setting. In *Probabilistic, logical and relational learning. Towards a synthesis. 30 Jan - 4 Febr 2005* (pp. 307-342). Internationales Begegnungs- und Forschungszentrum für Informatik (IBFI), Schloss Dagstuhl, Germany.

Pereira, F., & Warren, D. S. (1983). Parsing as deduction. In dunno (Ed.), *Proceedings of the 21st Conference of the acl* (pp. 137-44).

Plotkin, G. D. (1970). A note on inductive generalization. In B. Meltzer & D. Michie (Eds.), *Machine Intelligence, 5*, 153-163. Edinburgh University Press.

Plotkin, G. D. (1971a). *Automatic methods of inductive inferrence*. Unpublished doctoral dissertation, University of Edinburgh.

Plotkin, G. D. (1971b). A further note on inductive generalization. In D. Michie, N. L. Collins, & E. Dale (Eds.), *Machine Intelligence, 6,* 101-124. Edinburgh University Press.

Pompe, U., Kononenko, I., & Makše, T. (1996). An application of ILP in a musical database: Learning to compose the two-voice counterpoint. In *Proceedings of the MLnet Familiarization Workshop on Data Mining with Inductive Logic Programing* (pp. 1-11).

Popelinsky, L. (1998, September). Knowledge discovery in spatial data by means of ILP. In J. M. Zytkow & M. Quafafou (Eds.), *Lecture notes in computer science: Vol. 1510. Principles of Data Mining and Knowledge Discovery. PKDD'98 Nantes France.* (pp. 271-279). Berlin: Springer Verlag.

Popplestone, R. J. (1970). An experiment in automatic induction. In *Machine Intelligence, 5,* 204-215. Edinburgh University Press.

Quiniou, R., Cordier, M.-O., Carrault, G., & Wang, F. (2001). Application of ILP to cardiac arrhythmia characterization for chronicle recognition. In C. Rouveirol & M. Sebag (Eds.), *Lecture notes in computer science: Vol. 2157. ILP* (pp. 220-227). Berlin: Springer-Verlag.

Quinlan, J. R. (1990). Learning logical definitions from relations. *Machine Learning, 5,* 239-266.

Quinlan, J. R. (1993). *C4.5: programs for machine learning.* San Francisco: Morgan Kaufmann Publishers Inc.

Richards, B. L., & Mooney, R. J. (1995). Automated refinement of first-order horn-clause domain theories. *Machine Learning, 19*(2), 95-131.

Rissanen, J. (1978). Modeling by shortest data description. *Automatica, 14,* 465-471.

Robinson, J. A. (1965). A machine-oriented logic based on the resolution principle. *Journal of the ACM, 12*(1), 23-41.

Rocha, R., Fonseca, N. A., & Costa, V. S. (2005). On Applying Tabling to inductive logic programming. In *Lecture notes in artificial intelligence: Vol. 3720. Proceedings of the 16th European Conference on Machine Learning, ECML-05, Porto, Portugal, October 2005* (pp. 707-714). Berlin: Springer-Verlag.

Russell, S., & Norvig, P. (2003). *Artificial intelligence: A modern approach* (2nd ed.). Prentice-Hall, Englewood Cliffs, NJ.

Santos Costa, V., Page, C. D., Qazi, M., & Cussens, J. (2003, August). CLP(BN): Constraint logic programming for probabilistic knowledge. In *Proceedings of the 19th Conference on Uncertainty in Artificial Intelligence (UAI03), Acapulco, Mexico* (pp. 517-524).

Santos Costa, V., Srinivasan, A., & Camacho, R. (2000). A note on two simple transformations for improving the efficiency of an ILP system. In *Proceedings of the 10th International Conference on Inductive Logic Programming* (pp. 225-242).

Santos Costa, V., Srinivasan, A., Camacho, R., Blockeel, H., Demoen, B., Janssens, G., et al. (2003). Query transformations for improving the efficiency of ILP systems. *Journal of Machine Learning Research, 4,* 465-491.

Sebag, M., & Rouveirol, C. (1997). Tractable induction and classification in first order logic via stochastic matching. In *Proceedings of the 15th International Joint Conference on Artificial Intelligence* (pp. 888-893). San Francisco: Morgan Kaufmann.

Serrurier, M., Prade, H., & Richard, G. (2004). A simulated annealing framework for ILP. In *Proceedings of the 14th International Conference on Inductive Logic Programming* (pp. 288-304).

Shannon, C. E. (1948, July, October). The mathematical theory of communication. *Bell Systems Technical Journal, 27,* 379-423, 623-656.

Shapiro, E. (1983). *Algorithmic program debugging*. The MIT Press.

Srinivasan, A. (1999). A study of two sampling methods for analysing large datasets with ILP. *Data Mining and Knowledge Discovery*, 3(1), 95-123.

Srinivasan, A. (2000). *A study of two probabilistic methods for searching large spaces with ILP* (Tech. Rep. No. PRG-TR-16-00). Oxford University Computing Laboratory.

Srinivasan, A. (2004). *The Aleph manual*. (Available at http://www.comlab.ox.ac.uk/oucl/research/areas/machlearn/Aleph/)

Srinivasan, A., King, R. D., & Bain, M. E. (2003). An empirical study of the use of relevance information in inductive logic programming. *Journal of Machine Learning Research*.

Srinivasan, A., King, R. D., Muggleton, S., & Sternberg, M. J. E. (1997). Carcinogenesis predictions using ILP. In N. Lavrac & S. Džeroski (Eds.), *Lecture notes in computer science: Vol. 1297. inductive logic programming* (pp. 273-287). Berlin: Springer-Verlag.

Srinivasan, A., Muggleton, S., King, R. D., & Sternberg, M. J. E. (1994). ILP experiments in a non-determinate biological domain. In S. Wrobel (Ed.), *Gmd-studien. Proceedings of the Fourth International ILP Workshop* (pp. 217-232). Gesellschaft für Mathematik und Datenverarbeitung MBH.

Stoianov, I., Nerbonne, J., & Bouma, H. (1998). Modelling the phonotactic structure of natural language words with Simple Recurrent Networks. In *Proceedings of the 8th Conference on Computational Linguistics in the Netherlands (CLIN 98)*.

Stolle, C., Karwath, A., & De Raedt, L. (2005). CLASSIC'CL: an integrated ILP system. In *Lecture notes in artificial intelligence: Vol. 3735. Proceedings of the 8th International Conference of Discovery Science, DS 2005* (pp. 354-362). Berlin: Springer-Verlag.

Struyf, J. (2004). *Techniques for improving the efficiency of inductive logic programming in the context of data mining*. Unpublished doctoral dissertation, Katholieke Universiteit Leuven Department of Computer Science.

Struyf, J., & Blockeel, H. (2003). Query optimization in inductive logic programming by reordering literals. In *Proceedings of the 13th International Conference on Inductive Logic Programming* (pp. 329-346).

Struyf, J., Džeroski, S., Blockeel, H., & Clare, A. (2005). Hierarchical multi-classification with predictive clustering trees in functional genomics. In C. Bento, A. Cardoso, & G. Dias (Eds.), *Lecture notes in computer science: Vol. 3808. Progress in Artificial Intelligence, 12th Portuguese Conference on Artificial Intelligence, EPIA 2005, Covilhã, Portugal, December 5-8, 2005, Proceedings* (pp. 272-283). Berlin: Springer-Verlag.

Tamaddoni-Nezhad, A., & Muggleton, S. (2000). Searching the subsumption lattice by a genetic algorithm. In J. Cussens & A. Frisch (Eds.), *Lecture notes in artificial intelligence: Vol. 1866. Proceedings of the 10th International Conference on Inductive Logic Programming* (pp. 243-252). Springer-Verlag.

Tamaddoni-Nezhad, A., & Muggleton, S. (2003). A genetic algorithm approach to ILP. In S. Matwin & C. Sammut (Eds.), *Lecture notes in artificial intelligence: Vol. 2583. Proceedings of the 12th International Conference on Inductive Logic Programming* (pp. 285-300). Berlin: Springer-Verlag.

Tang, L. R., & Mooney, R. J. (2001). Using multiple clause constructors in inductive logic programming for semantic parsing. In *Lecture notes in computer science: Vol. 2167. Proceedings of the 12th European Conference on Machine Learning (ECML-2001)*. Berlin: Springer Verlag.

Tjong Kim Sang, E. F. (1998). Machine learning of phonotactics (Doctoral dissertation, Rijksuniversiteit Groningen). *Groningen Dissertations in Linguistics Series.*

Tjong Kim Sang, E. F., & Nerbonne, J. (2000). Learning the logic of simple phonotactics. In J. Cussens & S. Džeroski (Eds.), *Lecture notes in artificial intelligence: Vol. 1925. Learning Language in Logic.* Berlin: Springer-Verlag.

Tobudic, A., & Widmer, G. (2003). Relational ibl in music with a new structural similarity measure. In T. Horváth (Ed.), *Lecture notes in computer science: Vol. 2835. ILP* (pp. 365-382). Berlin: Springer-Verlag.

Todorovski, L., Ljubic, P., & Džeroski, S. (2004). Inducing polynomial equations for regression. In J.-F. Boulicaut, F. Esposito, F. Giannotti, & D. Pedreschi (Eds.), *Lecture notes in computer science: Vol. 3201. Proceedings of the 15th European Conference on Machine Learning* (pp. 441-452). Berlin: Springer-Verlag.

Tomita, M. (1986). *Efficient parsing for natural language.* Boston: Kluwer Academic Publishers.

Tsur, D., Ullman, J. D., Abiteboul, S., Clifton, C., Motwani, R., Nestorov, S., et al. (1998). Query flocks: a generalization of association-rule mining. In *SIGMOD '98: Proceedings of the 1998 ACM SIGMOD International Conference On Management Of Data* (pp. 1-12). New York, USA: ACM Press.

Turcotte, M., Muggleton, S. H., & Sternberg, M. J. E. (2001, April). The effect of relational background knowledge on learning of protein three-dimensional fold signatures. *Machine Learning, 43*(1/2), 81-95.

Vere, S. A. (1975). Induction of concepts in the predicate calculus. In *Proceedings of the 4th International Joint Conference on Artificial Intelligence* (p. 281-287).

Železný, F., Srinivasan, A., & Page, C. D. (2003). Lattice-search runtime distributions may be heavy-tailed. In S. Matwin & C. Sammut (Eds.), *Lecture notes in artificial intelligence: Vol. 2583. Proceedings of the 12th International Workshop on Inductive Logic Programming (ILP 2002)* (pp. 333–345). Berlin: Springer Verlag.

Wielemaker, J. (2003). Native preemptive threads in SWI-Prolog. In C. Palamidessi (Ed.), *Lecture notes in artificial intelligence: Vol. 2916. Proceedings of the 19th International Conference on Logic Programming* (pp. 331–345). Springer-Verlag.

Winston, P. H. (1970). *Learning structural descriptions from examples.* Unpublished doctoral dissertation, MIT.

Wrobel, S. (1997). An algorithm for multi-relational discovery of subgroups. In *Proceedings of the First European Symposium on Principles of data mining and knowledge discovery* (pp. 78-87). Springer-Verlag.

Zelle, J. M., & Mooney, R. J. (1996). Learning to parse database queries using inductive logic programming. In dunno (Ed.), *Proceedings of the 13th National Conference on Artificial Intelligence, Portland, USA.*

Zupan, B., & Džeroski, S. (1998). Acquiring background knowledge for machine learning using function decomposition: a case study in rheumatology. *Artificial Intelligence in Medicine, 14*(1-2), 101-117.

ENDNOTES

[1]   To the best of our knowledge, Muggleton was the first to use the term as the title of his invited talk at the first conference on Algorithmic Learning Theory (Tokyo, 1990). It is noteworthy that Muggleton & Feng presented a research paper on the ILP system GOLEM at the same conference where the

term does not appear at all. The term ILP was formally introduced by Muggleton one year later at his landmark publication with the New Generation Computing journal (Muggleton, 1991).

2   Arguably, this definition may nowadays be somewhat narrow. The representation and learning strategies used in ILP are germane to work such as relational instance based learning (**??**) and Analogical Prediction (Muggleton & Bain, 1999). ILP is also a key influence in the development of statistical relational learning, that often combines logical and statistical modelling.

3   Inferring entailment is necessary for validating a hypothesis under learning from entailment semantics. Similarly, learning under interpretations requires a procedure for inferring whether an example is a model of a hypothesis.

4   Only a second-order background theory would be able to represent such restrictions, and handling such a background theory would be far beyond the scope of current ILP. The external mechanisms currently used, effectively amount to 'mildly' second-order expressivity, that allows for certain kinds of restrictions to be represented and extra-logically tested. It might, in theory, be possible to identify a logic which captures only and all of these restrictions and thus incorporate them into the background theory. Such a line of research has not, however, been pursued by the ILP community which builds upon Logic Programming and first-order SLDNF resolution engines.

5   Variable depth is defined as the shortest link path to a head variable in various of Muggleton's publications, including the original definition (Muggleton & Feng, 1990, p. 8) and the Journal of Logic Programming article about the theory of ILP (Muggleton & De Raedt, 1994, p. 657). There is one notable exception, however, as Muggleton (1995, p

11) defines depth to be the longest path to the variable in his PROGOL article. The authors tested current ILP implementations, and found them conforming to the original definition.

6   Variables X and Y have depth 0; variables U and W have depth 1; variable V has depth 2.

7   Strictly speaking, traversal operators map conjunctions of clauses to sets of conjunctions of clauses. However, we typically focus on a single clause and perceive this mapping as being applied to one of the clauses in the conjunction in the presence of a background.

8   Z/W is forced in order to unify the **ancestor/2** literals, but then **parent(W,Y)** cannot unify with either **parent(Z,Y)** or **parent(W,Z)** unless we further substitute X/Z, which would render the heads ununifiable.

9   Muggleton (1995, Section 6) offers a formal and complete exposition of this reduction of implication to a θ-subsumption search and its logical foundations.

10   Not to be confused with what is usually called bottom in logic programming, namely the empty predicate. There is an analogy, however, in that in the sense used here, the bottom is also the 'most specific' clause.

11   For $\theta1 = \{X/A, Y/B, Z/E, W/G\}$ we get $A\theta \subseteq \perp1$ and $B\theta \subseteq \perp1$.

12   'Pseudo' in the sense that a true posterior probability can only be derived from a true prior probability, whereas here we only have an empirical approximation of the true prior.

13   The term is used in the sense of making the minimal computation to obtain useful information.

14   Many grammatical formalisms of greater computational complexity, for example, Head Phrase-driven Structure Grammar (HPSG), have also been proposed in the literature and gained wide acceptance. It

is, however, the general consensus that grammatical formalisms beyond DCGs are justified on grounds of linguistic-theoretical conformance and compression on the grammar and that definite-clause grammars are powerful enough to capture most of the actual linguistic phenomena.

15   The propositional theory describes syllable structure with 674 prevocalic and 456 postvocalic clauses. The first-order theory comprises 13 and 93 clauses, resp. When no language-specific prior phonological knowledge is used, the exact numbers are: for the propositional theory 577 clauses for the prevocalic and 577 clauses for the postvocalic material, and for the first-order theory 145 and 36 clauses, resp.

APPENDIX: LOGIC PROGRAMMING

This chapter assumes that the reader is familiar with Logic Programming terminology. We provide here a very short and incomplete introduction to Logic Programming for ease of reference, but for a more complete treatment the reader is referred to Logic Programming textbooks like the one by Lloyd (1997).

A *term* of *arity N* is a *functor symbol* followed by an *N*-tuple of terms. A *variable* is also a term. Thus, *f* is a term of arity 0 and $g(h(a,b,c),X)$ is a term of arity 2 with sub-terms $g(a,b,c)$ (arity 3) and variable *X*. An atom is a *predicate symbol* of arity *N* followed by a *N*-tuple of terms. If *A* is an atom, then *A* is a *positive literal* and $\neg A$ is a *negative literal*.

A *clause* is a disjunction of literals. All the variables in a clause are implicitly universally quantified. The empty clause and the logical constant *false* are represented by □. A *Horn clause* is a disjunction of any number of negated literals and up to one non-negated literal, for example:

$$h \vee \neg l_1 \vee \neg l_2 \ldots \vee \neg l_n$$
$$\neg l_1 \vee \neg l_2 \ldots \vee \neg l_n$$
$$h$$

The positive literal is called the *head* of the clause and the negative literals (if any) are collectively known as the *body*. Horn clauses can be equivalently represented as sets of literals that are meant to be logically or'ed together or as Prolog clauses:

$$\{h, \neg l_1, \neg l_2, \ldots \neg l_n\} \qquad \texttt{h} \leftarrow \texttt{l}_1, \texttt{l}_2, \ldots \texttt{l}_n.$$
$$\{\neg l_1, \neg l_2, \ldots \neg l_n\} \Leftrightarrow \bot \leftarrow \texttt{l}_1, \texttt{l}_2, \ldots \texttt{l}_n.$$
$$\{h\} \qquad\qquad\quad \texttt{h.}$$

A *definite Horn clause* is a Horn clause with *exactly* one positive literal, for example:

$$h \vee \neg l_1 \vee \neg l_2 \ldots \vee \neg l_n$$
$$h$$

A *substitution* is a function that maps a set of variables to a set of terms or variables. We apply a substitution to a term by replacing all variables in the term with the terms or variables indicated by the mapping. We usually denote a substitution as a set of from/to pairs and we write $A\theta$ to denote the result of applying substitution θ to term *A*. For example, if $\theta = \{X/Z, Y/\text{aureliano}\}$ and $A = \text{parent}(X,Y)$ then $A\theta = \text{parent}(Z, \text{aureliano})$.

Related to substitution is the concept of *unification*. Unification is the operation of making two terms identical by substitution. Such substitutions are called *unifiers* of the terms. The *most general unifier* is the unifier which minimally instantiates the two terms.

A *predicate* is a disjunction of definite Horn clauses where (a) no pair of clauses shares a common variable and (b) the heads of the clauses are the same up to substitution, i.e. they are terms with the same functor and arity. A *program* is a conjunction of predicates where no pair of predicates shares a common variable. The empty program and the logical constant *true* are represented by ■.

The *Herbrand base* of a clause, predicate, or program is the set of all ground (variable-free) atoms composed from symbols found in the clause, predicate, or program. An *interpretation* is a total function from ground atoms to {true,false}. A *Herbrand interpretation* for program P is an interpretation for *all* the atomic symbols in the Herbrand base of P. The valuation of a non-atomic clauses, predicates, and programs can be derived from the definitions of the logical connectives (conjunction, disjunction, negation, implication, existential and universal quantification) used to construct them from atoms. The logical connectives are set-theoretically defined in the usual manner (intersection, union, complement, etc) which we shall not re-iterate here.

We shall use the term interpretation to mean Herbrand interpretation. An interpretation M for P is a *model* of P if and only if P is *true* under M. Every program P has a unique *minimal Herbrand model* $\mathcal{M}^+(P)$ such that every atom a in P is true under $\mathcal{M}^+(P)$ if and only if a is true under all models of P.

Let P and Q be programs. We say that P entails Q ($P \vDash Q$) if and only if every model of P is also a model of Q. A clause, predicate, or program is *satisfiable* if and only if there exists a model for it. Equivalently, P is satisfiable if and only if $P \nvDash \Box$ and *unsatisfiable* if and only if $P \vDash \Box$.

A query is a conjunction of positive literals. Posing a query Q to a program P amounts to asking about the satisfiability of $P \vDash Q$; if the program $P \vDash Q$ is satisfiable then the query gets an affirmative answer. Computational algorithms for answering first-order logical queries rely on deductive methods which can infer semantic entailment by syntactic manipulation of the programs involved. Deductive inference that deduces D from C *only* when $C \vDash D$ (according to the set-theoretic, semantic definitions of the logical symbols and connectives) is called *sound* and deductive inference that deduces D from C for *all* C,D where $C \vDash D$ is called *complete*. *Tableaux methods* and *resolution* and sound and complete deductive methodologies.

Selection linear definite resolution (SLD resolution) is an algorithm for resolving define clause programs. SLD *negation-as-failure* resolution (SLDNF resolution) extends SLD resolution to normal clause programs, which admit negative literals as premises, but only under the *closed world assumption* (CWA). CWA is the assumption that statements that cannot be proved true, are not true. Prolog is a resolution engine that operates under the CWA to perform SLDNF resolution. Almost all ILP systems (and especially predictive ILP systems) rely on a Prolog implementation for inferring entailment relationships.

Chapter VIII
Single- and Multi-Order Neurons for Recursive Unsupervised Learning

Kiruthika Ramanathan
National University of Singapore, Singapore

Sheng Uei Guan
Brunel University, UK

ABSTRACT

In this chapter we present a recursive approach to unsupervised learning. The algorithm proposed, while similar to ensemble clustering, does not need to execute several clustering algorithms and find consensus between them. On the contrary, grouping is done between two subsets of data at one time, thereby saving training time. Also, only two kinds of clustering algorithms are used in creating the recursive clustering ensemble, as opposed to the multitude of clusterers required by ensemble clusterers. In this chapter a recursive clusterer is proposed for both single and multi order neural networks. Empirical results show as much as 50% improvement in clustering accuracy when compared to benchmark clustering algorithms.

INTRODUCTION

The key idea of recursive unsupervised learning is to decompose a given problem and find several partitions of data, such that they can be grouped together to result in a system with higher correlation to ground truth information. The algorithm achieves this by using a combination of global and local search, implementing a repetitive sequence of global search, data splitting, local search, and recombination to solve the problem. Further, global search is conducted using genetic algorithm based self organizing and higher order neurons, ensuring that arbitrary cluster shapes can be found in the process.

Data clustering is an important problem, but is extremely difficult, due to the absence of pattern labels. The objective of clustering is to partition a set of unlabelled patterns into homogeneous clusters. A number of applications use clustering techniques to organize data. Some applications of clustering include data mining (Judd, McKinley, & Jain, 1997), information retrieval (Bhatia, 1998), and machine learning. However, in real world problems, clusters can take on arbitrary shapes, sizes, and degrees of separation. Clustering techniques require us to define a similarity measure between patterns, which is not easy due to the varying shapes of information present in data.

Self organizing maps (SOMs) (Kohonen, 1997) represent a type of neural network proposed for clustering purposes. They assign a synaptic weight (denoted by the column vector $\mathbf{w}^{(j)}$) to each neuron. The winning neuron j(x) is the neuron that has the highest correlation with the input x, it is the neuron for which $\mathbf{w}^{(j)T}\mathbf{x}$ is the largest, that is,

$$\mathbf{j}(\mathbf{x}) = \mathbf{arg}_j\mathbf{max}\|\mathbf{w}^{(j)T}\mathbf{x}\| \qquad (1)$$

where the operator $\|\cdot\|$ represents the Euclidean norm of the vector. The idea behind equation (1) is to select the neuron which exhibits maximum correlation with the input. Often used instead of equation (1) is the minimum Euclidean distance matching criterion (Kohonen, 1997)

$$\mathbf{j}(\mathbf{x}) = \mathbf{arg}_j\mathbf{min}\|\mathbf{w}^{(j)}\text{-}\mathbf{x}\| \qquad (2)$$

However, the use of the highest correlation or the minimum distance matching criterion implies that (a) the features of the input domain are spherical, that is, deviations are equal in all dimensions and (b) the distance between features must be larger than the distance between points in a feature. These two implications of the data can be summarized in the equations below:

$$\forall m, n \in D, m \neq n, \lambda_m(\Sigma_I) \approx \lambda_n(\Sigma_I) \qquad (3)$$

$$\forall x, y \in \mathbf{I}, \|x^T y\| \text{ if } (j(x) = j(y)) > \| x^T y \| \text{ if } (j(x) \neq j(y)) \qquad (4)$$

In the above equations, the Σ_I operator represents the covariance of the data matrix $\mathbf{I}$, λ_m is

the mth eigenvalue, D is the dimension of the input domain, x and y are arbitrary data vectors.

For an arbitrary set of data to fulfill these conditions could be difficult, especially in cases where such distributions of data are difficult to visualize and detect due to the high dimensionality of the problem. Even when the distribution of the data is detected through visualization, when the conditions described in equations (3) and (4) are not satisfied, there is no guarantee that the use of an SOM will solve the problem.

Consider, for example, the arrangements of two data clusters in two dimensions as shown in

Figure 1. Artificially generated two-dimensional two class clusters illustrating the weakness of SOMs

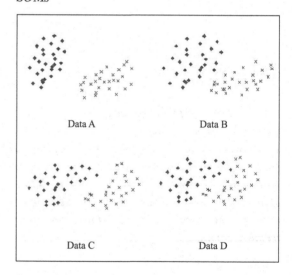

Table 1. Summary of the properties of the data in Figure 1

Data Name	Spherical clusters (Satisfies equation 3)?	Clusters are sufficiently far apart (Satisfies equation 4)?
Data A	Yes	Yes
Data B	Yes	No
Data C	No	Yes
Data D	No	No

Figure 1. Table 1 summarizes the properties of these datasets in terms of their ability to satisfy equations (3) and (4). Due to the nature of the data there is no guarantee that the SOM will be able to cluster correctly the sets of data other than Data A.

Several methods have been proposed to overcome this problem. Second order curves, with the use of inverse covariance matrix, are often used to capture ellipsoidal properties (Lipson, Hod, & Siegelmann, 1998). The concept of second order curves was expanded in several cases to include second order shells. Kohonen discussed the use of weighted Euclidean distance (Kohonen, 1997) that captures different variances in the components of input signals. The use of the Mahlanobhis distance (Mao & Jain, 1996) was also considered.

On the other hand, nonparametric techniques such as agglomeration (Blatt, Wiseman, & Domany, 1996) attempt to find arbitrary shapes in the clusters. However, their performance also depends on the ability of the cluster to satisfy equation (4).

Lipson and Siegelmann (2000) proposed the generalized higher order neuron (HON) structure, which extended second order surfaces to arbitrary order hyper surfaces. These neurons had the capability of detecting arbitrarily shaped clusters and were therefore desirable over spherical or ellipsoidal detecting of clusters. HON could also, in a correctly prescribed order, yield results similar to non parametric clustering techniques.

On the other end of the clustering spectrum are the ensemble approaches. Ensemble learning, which is highly popular in the supervised learning domain (Meir & Ratsch, 2003), has just begun to take root in the domain of unsupervised learning.

While there are many ensemble approaches to supervised classifications, combination of clustering partitions is a more challenging task than combining partitions of labeled data. In the absence of labels, labeling clusters in different parts of the ensemble becomes a problem. A common approach to resolving this problem is consensus clustering (Fred & Jain, 2002, 2005; Strehl & Ghosh, 2005).

The other problem associated with ensemble clustering methods is the generation of partitions. Several methods are used to create partitions for clustering ensembles. Some choices of partition generation include the use of different regular clustering algorithms, different initializations, parameters values, and so forth, to induce randomness into a specific clustering algorithm, the use of weak clustering algorithms (Jain & Dubes, 1998). All these methods generate independent partitions, and an ensemble is created based on the similarity between the data in each partitioning algorithm.

While the ensemble clustering approach combines the strengths of different clustering approaches, the optimal number of partitions is unknown. Strehl and Ghosh (2005) showed consensus clustering applied to some benchmark datasets using as many as 25 to 150 partitions.

Inspired by our earlier work on recursive supervised learning (Guan & Ramanathan, 2004), we propose here a recursive divide-and-conquer approach to clustering, which applies an evolutionary clustering algorithm to the data. We then use a neighborhood measure to remove from the data those patterns which are clustered with high confidence. Their centroids are then shifted (using a local algorithm) to better represent these clusters. The patterns that were clustered earlier with low confidence are now focused upon and reclustered.

In a way, we can look at recursive clustering as a situation where a child learns to distinguish between two sets of photographs, one taken in the jungle and another in the desert. There are also photographs in the set which show different degrees of jungle/desert combination. One would want to cluster them according to the percentage of jungle in them (>50% jungle: cluster 1; <50% jungle: cluster 2). However, instead of distinguishing the photos all at once, it makes more sense to first distinguish between the all jungle and all desert photos. The next level would be to distinguish between the jungle-predominant and desert-predominant photos. The jungle-predominant photos will then be associated with the jungle photos and the desert-predominant ones with the desert photos and so on. The advantage of this approach, compared to ensemble clustering, are as follows:

1. The approach does not need to execute several clustering algorithms and find consensus between them, as grouping is done between two subsets of data at one time. This is expected to save the training time.
2. We hypothesize that only two clustering algorithms (one global and one local in nature) are needed, as opposed to the multitude of algorithms required by the ensemble methods.

The rest of the chapter is organized as follows: The next section reviews the higher order neurons (HONs) (Lipson & Siegelmann, 2000) and evolutionary self organizing maps (Painho & Bacao, 2000) and proposes the evolutionary higher order neurons (eHONs) used to conduct global search. We then present the Recursive Unsupervised Learning algorithm based on the eHON and the HON structures. Experimental results on both synthetic and real data illustrate the robustness of the proposed method as opposed to the clustering methods produced by well known algorithms and compared to the ensemble clustering methods.

RELATED THEORY

In this section we present the tools used in the development of the recursive unsupervised learning algorithm. As the recursive unsupervised learning algorithm is a hybrid approach, genetic algorithm based global clustering techniques are given high importance and their development, with respect to the scope of this chapter is outlined in this section.

Higher Order Neurons (HONs)

The Higher order neuron structure (Lipson & Siegelmann, 2000) generalizes the spherical and ellipsoidal scheme that is proposed by the self organizing maps and second order structures. The use of the higher order neuron structure gives rise to a continuum of cluster shapes between the classic spherical-ellipsoidal clustering systems and the fully parametric approach. Clusters of data in the real world are usually in arbitrary shapes. The "shape" of a cluster is referred to as the order of the neuron representing it.

The spherical restriction of ordinary neurons is relaxed by replacing the weight vector with a general higher order tensor. This tensor captures multilinear correlations among the signals associated with the neurons. It also permits capturing shapes with holes or detached areas. In their work, Lipson and Siegelmann (2000) have shown that higher order neurons exhibit stability and good training performance with Hebbian learning.

The higher order unsupervised learning algorithm proposed by Lipson and Siegelmann (2000) is performed as follows:

1. Select the number of clusters (or number of neurons) K, and the order of the neurons (m) for a given problem.
2. The neurons are initialized with $Z_H = \sum_{i=1}^{n} x_i^{2(m-1)}$. Z_H is the covariance tensor of the data, initialized to a midpoint value. In the case of a second order problem, the covariance tensor is simply the correlation matrix $Z_H = \sum_{i=1}^{n} x_i^{T} x_i$. For higher order tensors, this value is calculated by writing

down $x_H{}^{m-1}$ as a vector with all the mth degree permutations of $\{x_1, x_2, ..., x_d, 1\}$ and finding Z_H as the matrix summing the outer product of all these vectors. The value of the inverse of the tensor is found and normalized using its determinant f to obtain Z_H^{-1}/f.

3. The winning neuron for a given pattern is computed using $j = \arg_j \min \|Z_H^{-1}/f \otimes x^{(m-1)}\|$. Here, $\otimes$ denotes tensor multiplication.

4. The winning neuron is now updated using $Z_{H,new} = Z_{H,old} + \eta x_i^{2(m-1)}$, where η is the learning rate. The new values of Z_H and Z_H^{-1}/f are stored.

5. Steps 3 and 4 are repeated.

Evolutionary Self Organizing Maps

Evolutionary algorithms have been used to find global solutions in many applications, including neural network applications for supervised learning (Yao, 1993). Inspired by this, in Painho and Bacao (2000), the authors apply genetic algorithms to clustering problems with good effect. The genetic algorithm applied is simple and retains the form of SOMs, but with evolutionary representation of the weights.

More simply, since the objective is to maximize the value $\|\mathbf{w}^{(k)\mathsf{T}}\mathbf{x}\|$ for each pattern $\mathbf{x}$, a population of real coded chromosomes encode $\mathbf{w}^{(k)}$, for each cluster k. Each chromosome therefore consists of K*d elements, where K is the number of clusters and d is the dimension of the input data. The chromosomes are evaluated in batch mode, such as to maximize:

$$\sum_{k=1}^{K} \sum_{x \in C_k} \|\mathbf{w}^{(k)\mathsf{T}}\mathbf{x}\| \qquad (5)$$

Crossover and mutation are performed and a new generation of chromosomes is produced. The process is continued until the system stagnates or until a maximum number of epochs is reached.

EVOLUTIONARY HIGHER ORDER NEURONS (EHONS)

We propose the evolutionary higher order neurons as an extension of the Higher Order Neuron Structure and the Evolutionary Self Organizing map. The idea of evolutionary higher order neurons is motivated by the following reasoning: Lipson's Higher Order Neurons are shown to exhibit improved performance. However, some of our simulations (presented later) showed that the order of the neuron plays an important part in the meaning of the clusters formed. A higher order neuron does not necessarily perform better than a lower order neuron. In the HONs, the order of the neuron is prespecified by the user.

Moreover, for a given dataset, only a single order of neuron is used to represent all the clusters in their work. We feel that this is a limitation to the algorithm. Data is usually distributed irregularly, with some classes taking on spherical forms, some with elliptical or banana forms or even higher order forms.

We propose in this chapter a Messy Evolutionary Algorithm (Goldberg, Deb, & Korb, 1991) based on multi-order HONs. The algorithm is outlined below.

Batch Version of HONs

A batch version of HONs is implemented to facilitate their use with evolutionary algorithms. The batch algorithm is similar to the online algorithm proposed by Lipson and Siegelmann (2000). However, instead of choosing a winning neuron by using $j = \arg_j \min \left\| Z_H^{-1}/f \otimes x^{(m-1)} \right\|$, we implemented a batch minimization criterion such as the one used in equation (5) of the evolutionary SOMs. The algorithm focuses on minimizing equation (6),

$$\sum_{k=1}^{K} \sum_{x \in C_k} \left\| \left(Z_H^k\right)^{-1}/f_k \otimes x^{(m-1)} \right\| \qquad (6)$$

Chromosome Initialization

The initialization of chromosomes is done as outlined by the following steps:

1. Each data point is randomly assigned to one of the K clusters.
2. The covariance tensor of order m, Z^k_{IP}, for the cluster $k \in K$ is initialized as

$$Z^k_{II} = \sum_{x \in C_k} x^{2(m-1)} \qquad (7)$$

Chromosome Structure

Each chromosome is coded as an array of structures, each consisting of two components: the order of a chromosome and the value of the tensor:

```
struct chromosome
{
    neuron NEURON[K];
};
struct neuron
{
    int order ;
    int tensor[][] ;
} ;
```

A tensor, regardless of the neuron order, is flattened out into a two-dimensional kronecker matrix (Graham, 1981) in a similar form as used by Lipson.

Global Search Properties

As in the recursive supervised learning application (Guan & Ramanathan, 2004), global search is simulated by large range mutation. There are two criteria for large range mutation:

1. A random element in a tensor is mutated with a probability p_1.

2. The order of the tensor is changed with a probability p_2. The tensor is now reinitialized using equation (7).

Fitness Function

The fitness function is the optimization of the expression in equation (6). The expression is minimized so as to maximize the cluster tightness.

RECURSIVE CLUSTERING ALGORITHMS

Two sets of recursive clustering algorithms are presented in this chapter. The single order recursive unsupervised learning uses a combination of self organizing maps and eSOMs to create clustering ensembles, illustrating the effectiveness of the recursive partitioning algorithm.

The Multi Order Recursive unsupervised leaning algorithm combines the eHONs and the HON algorithms. The implementation of the recursive algorithm on top of the HON structure shows that the recursive algorithm improves the results of the base clustering algorithm.

Notation Used

Overview of Producing Recursive Clustering Ensembles

Both the Single-order and the Multi-order recursive clustering algorithm produce a clustering ensemble $\mathbf{P} = \{P_1, P_2, ..., P_n\}$ as described. The ensembles P_1 to P_n are created as shown in Table 3.

In order to better understand how the RUL algorithm works, we present the hypothetical distribution of data as shown in Figure 2, where each of the steps in Table 3 is illustrated for two recursions.

Table 2. Explanation of notation used in this chapter

Input:

n—number of patterns N—number of recursions K—number of clusters required

x—input pattern $X = \{x_1, x_2, ..., x_n\}$—set of n input patterns

Process parameters:

$P = \{P^1, P^2, ..., P^N\}$—clustering ensemble

P^i—k_i clusters, each with n^i_j patterns, such that $\sum_{i=1}^{N}\sum_{j=1}^{k_i} n^i_j = n$, $k_i \leq K$

m—neuron order Z_H—covariance tensor of Higher order neuron

w—weight vector of SOM neuron

f—Normalization factor: determinant of Z_H^{-1}

Output:

P^{opt}—Combined data partition into K clusters

Table 3. Creating the data ensemble P

Terms:

Global Clustering: Clustering using either eSOMs or eHONs
Local Clustering: Clustering using either SOMs or HONs

Initialization: Number of Recursions n Re c = 1, *Data* = X
1. while n Re c < max Re c do
1.1. Global clustering *Data*
1.2. [*wellClustered, illClustered*] = split(*Data*)
1.3. P^{nRec} = Local clustering *wellClustered*
1.4. if n Re c > 1 do
      1.4.1. P^{opt} = combine(P^{opt}, P^{nRec})
    else do
      1.4.2. $P^{opt} = P^{nRec}$
1.5. *Data* = illClustered, n Re c ++;

Splitting the Data

Step 1.2 of each recursion involves splitting the data into well clustered and ill clustered patterns. The splitting process involves two steps: (a) Sorting using the minmin rule and (b) choosing well-clustered data.

Sorting the Data

For a given recursion r, after step 1.1, a partition $P^r = \{C^r_1, C^r_2, ..., C^r_{k_r}\}$, is created. The data is now sorted based on the clusters formed using a minmin rule, as given by expression (8).

$$\min (\min (Dist (x_i, x_j))), \forall x_i \in C_i, x_j \in C_j, C_i \neq C_j, i, j \in k_r \tag{8}$$

Here, $Dist(x_i, x_j)$, refers to a measure of distance between two patterns, x_i and x_j. In the case of first order neurons, it simply translates to a Euclidean distance. In the case of higher order neurons, $Dist(x_i, x_j)$ is evaluated as given in (9)

$$Dist (x_i, x_j) = x_i^{(m_i-1)} \otimes x_j^{(m_j-1)} \tag{9}$$

Effectively, expression (8) means that the patterns are sorted such that patterns from a cluster i which are closest to patterns in cluster j, $i \neq j$ (i.e., patterns nearest to the cluster boundary in part (a) of Figure 2), can be isolated. These are the patterns which are clustered with the most uncertainty.

Choosing Well-Clustered Data

The patterns with the most uncertainty, that is, the patterns which best satisfy expression (8) are isolated. We motivate this by referring to equation (4), which is rewritten as:

$$\forall x_i, x_j \in Data, \| x_i^T x_j \| \text{ if } (C_i = C_j) > \| x^T y \| \text{ if } (C_i \neq C_j) \tag{10}$$

Removing the uncertain data set will ensure more patterns are present in the resulting subset which satisfy equation (10). Equation (10) represents the agreement of the clusters formed by the unsupervised learning algorithm with the ground truth information.

Figure 2. Illustration of RUL for two recursions on a hypothetical data set

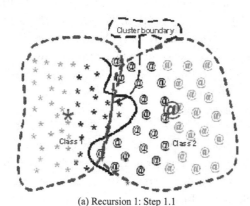

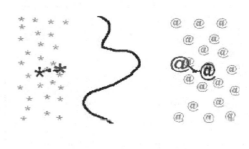

(a) Recursion 1: Step 1.1

* and @ denote the neurons representing the clusters found. - - - represents the cluster boundary while ___ represents the true class boundary. Patterns close to the cluster boundary are defined as ill clustered

(b) Recursion 1: Steps 1.2, 1.3, 1.4

The well clustered patterns are now removed and isolated. A local clustering algorithm (SOM/HON) is applied to shift the neurons as indicated by the arrows.

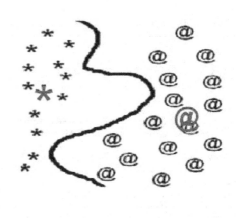

(c) Recursion 2: Step 1.5, 1.1

Ill clustered patterns from the previous recursion re clustered. Cluster boundaries represented by - - -

(d) Recursion 2: Steps 1.2, 1.3

The well clustered patterns are isolated and the means shifted

(e) Recursion 2: Step 1.4

Neurons of each recursion are associated with nearest neurons of previous recursions. New associated clusters formed

Heuristically, we have set the number of patterns isolated as 50% of the data in that recursion, that is, *wellClustered = sizeof (Data)/2*

The Single-Order Recursive Unsupervised Learning Algorithm

The single-order recursive clustering algorithm aims at identifying irregularly shaped clusters. Using the spherical property of the SOM recursively to cluster and decompose the dataset, the algorithm aims to find boundaries that are closer to the ground truth information. Figure 3 describes the single-order recursive clustering algorithm

Figure 3. Flowchart describing the single-order recursive learning algorithm

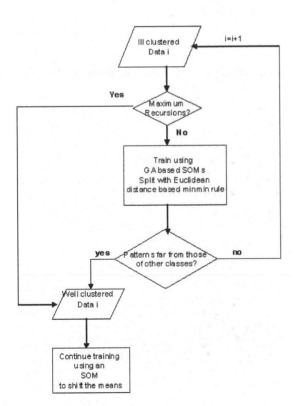

The algorithm is Figure 3 is similar to that in Table 3 with the addition of the stopping process. During the last recursion, all the remaining ill clustered patterns are taken as well clustered and clustered to the best possible extent.

The Multi-Order Recursive Unsupervised Learning Algorithm

The development of the multi-order recursive clustering algorithm arose due to the following factors:

1. Different classes of the same data could have different orders of clusters, that is, the ground truth of one class may be of a different order from the ground truth of another class
2. Different parts of the same class may have different orders, that is, a class of patterns may be partly spherical and partly "banana shaped" necessitating the use of a combination of first and third order neurons to cluster the class properly.

Due to these concerns, especially the second one, it seems to us that representing a K class data with K clusters of the same order, as done by Lipson, or even with K clusters of different orders, as in the case of eHONs, may not be an adequate representation.

However, the eHONs deal with the first problem by forming clusters of different orders. The recursive Multi Order Neurons aim to solve the second problem of irregularly shaped clusters without resorting to arbitrarily high orders.

The multi order recursive learning algorithm is similar to the single order recursive learning algorithm, except for the following differences:

1. The multi order recursive clustering algorithm makes use of the eHONs
2. The minmin rule for checking the uncertainty of clustering is based on the higher

order of the neurons instead of the Euclidean distance.

3. The local clustering to shift the means is based on the order that was found by the global clustering phase

4. To simplify the computation, we implement the system such that the maximum order that a neuron can take increases with the number of recursions. This follows from the fact that the complexity of the border increases as we increase the number of recursions. The implementation is such that the first recursion only implements first and second order neuron, the second recursion implements second and third order neurons and so on.. The multi order structure of each recursion aims to select the best natural clusters for the data present.

EXPERIMENTAL RESULTS

Results on Hypothetical Data

In this section we consider the four different datasets presented in Figure 1. These datasets represent different combinations under which equations (3) and (4) are satisfied. With these datasets, we illustrate the use of single order recursive clustering to create the clustering ensemble **P**, and in creating the final data partition P^{opt}.

Figure 4 shows the clusters obtained by using SOMs on each of the datasets in Figure 1 and the number of misassigned patterns in each case.

In order to illustrate the effect of recursion, we apply the Single-Order Recursive clusterer on these datasets. The data partitions P^1 to P^N that form the clustering ensemble **P** are shown, as well as their integration to form P^{opt} are shown in the figures below.

Figure 4. Clusters obtained by implementing SOMS on the data in Figure 1 and the number of misassigned patterns in each case

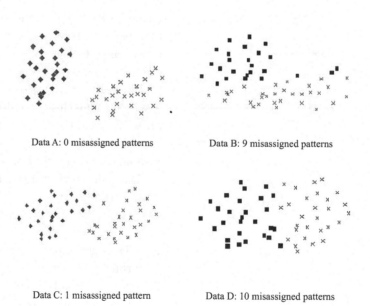

Data A: 0 misassigned patterns

Data B: 9 misassigned patterns

Data C: 1 misassigned pattern

Data D: 10 misassigned patterns

Figure 5. P¹, P² and Pᵒᵖᵗ for dataset A: 0 misclustered patterns for the recursive single-order algorithm. Dots in Pᵒᵖᵗ indicate the representing single-order neurons

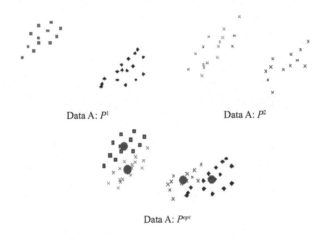

Data A: P^1 Data A: P^2

Data A: P^{opt}

Figure 6. P¹, P² and Pᵒᵖᵗ for dataset B: 3 misclustered patterns for the recursive single-order algorithm. Dots in Pᵒᵖᵗ indicate the representing single-order neurons

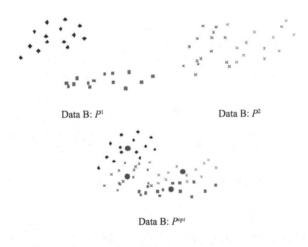

Data B: P^1 Data B: P^2

Data B: P^{opt}

From the figures, it is observed that the use of recursion to decompose and recluster data improves significantly the clustering accuracy, that is, the number of misassigned patterns is significantly reduced. This is especially true in the case of datasets B and D, which do not satisfy equation (10).

RESULTS ON REAL WORLD DATA

Data and Algorithm Descriptions

This chapter effectively proposes three new algorithms:

Figure 7. P^1, P^2, P^3 and P^{opt} for dataset B: 1 misclustered pattern for the recursive single-order algorithm. Dots in P^{opt} indicate the representing single-order neurons

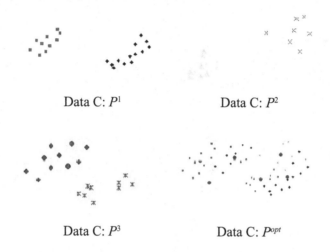

Data C: P^1 Data C: P^2

Data C: P^3 Data C: P^{opt}

Figure 8. P^1, P^2, P^3 and P^{opt} for dataset D: 0 misclustered patterns for the recursive single-order algorithm. Dots in P^{opt} indicate the representing single-order neurons

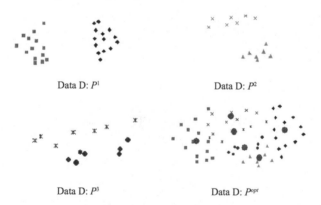

Data D: P^1 Data D: P^2

Data D: P^3 Data D: P^{opt}

1. **eHONs:** Higher order self organizing neurons with evolutionary capabilities which identify the best possible order for a chromosome based on a population generated with various multi-order chromosomes.

2. **Recursive SOMs:** This algorithm operated using the system design given in section 4.4. Recursive clustering is done with purely single-order neurons

3. **Recursive multi-order clustering:** The algorithm is operated using the system

design given in section 4.5. Recursion is performed using multi-order neurons and the eHON structure.

For comparison, we further implement the following algorithms:

4. **HON:** The higher-order neuron structure proposed by Lipson and Siegelmann (2000). Simulations are run with order 2 and order 3. Order 2 detects elliptical, oval and, to a

Figure 9. Distribution of data in (a) IRIS (3 clusters), (b) WINE (3 clusters), and (c) GLASS (6 clusters) datasets

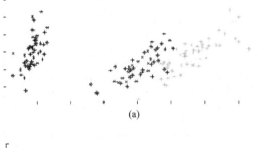

(a)

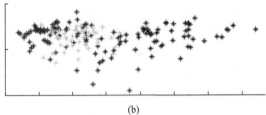

(b)

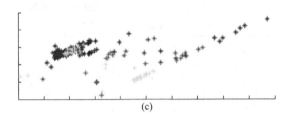

(c)

certain extent, banana shapes, while order 3 detects other higher-order shapes to some extent

5. **SOM:** The self organizing map or HON of order 1 (Kohonen, 1997). This algorithm detects spherical clusters and, to an extent, oval shaped clusters.

6. **Consensus clustering:** We also compared results of some of our experiments to those of consensus clustering as reported in Fred and Jain (2002) and Jain and Dubes (1998). Consensus clustering is also an ensemble approach using the agreement of weak learners to create the optimal partitioning.

The algorithms 1 to 5 will be applied to the following benchmark datasets:

1. Iris dataset (4 dimensional, 150 patterns)
2. Wine dataset (13 dimensional, 178 patterns)
3. Glass dataset (9 dimensions, 214 patterns)

Figure 9 shows the two-dimensional Principal component projections of these datasets.

Table 4. Results of the IRIS data

Algorithm	Mean number of misassigned patterns	Standard deviation	Number of partitions in the data ensemble
HON *(Higher Order Neuron), order=2*	4	0.0	1
HON *(Higher Order Neuron), order=3*	7	0.0	1
SOM *(Self Organising map) HON order =1*	23	0.0	1
Ensemble clustering	4.5 (lowest error obtained)	N.A	100
eSOMs *(Evolutionary evolved SOMs)*	16	3.38	1
eHONs *(to find the optimal order for a given class)*	3.5	0.99	1
Recursive SOMs *(Single-order recursive unsupervised learning)*	8	0.57	3
Recursive HONs *(multi-order recursive unsupervised learning)*	2	0.57	3

Table 5. Results of the WINE data

Algorithm	Mean number of mis-assigned patterns	Standard deviation	Number of partitions in the data ensemble
HON *(Higher Order Neuron), order=2*	60	0.0	1
HON *(Higher Order Neuron), order=3*	70	0.0	1
SOM *(Self Organising map) HON order =1*	72	0.0	1
Ensemble clustering	30 (lowest error obtained)	N.A	25
eSOMs *(Evolutionary evolved SOMs)*	57	2.45	1
eHONs *(to find the optimal order for a given class)*	49	1.84	1
Recursive SOMs *(Single-order recursive unsupervised learning)*	51	0.66	4
Recursive HONs *(multi-order recursive unsupervised learning)*	30	0.43	4

Table 6. Results of the GLASS data

Algorithm	Mean number of misassigned patterns	Standard deviation	Number of partitions in the data ensemble
HON *(Higher Order Neuron), order=2*	176	0.0	1
HON *(Higher Order Neuron), order=3*	157	0.0	1
SOM *(Self Organising map) HON order =1*	115	0.0	1
eSOMs *(Evolutionary evolved SOMs)*	115	2.59	1
eHONs *(to find the optimal order for a given class)*	110	1.32	1
Recursive SOMs *(Single order recursive unsupervised learning)*	111	0.73	6
Recursive HONs *(Multi-order recursive unsupervised learning)*	104	0.48	6

Correlation with Ground Truth Information in Real World Data

In this section we present the correlation with ground truth information (the available class labels), for the IRIS, WINE, and GLASS datasets. The tables below present the average number of misassigned patterns, the standard deviation across 20 runs, as well as the number of partitions in the data ensemble **P** for each of the algorithms described in section 5.3.1. Training was carried out, in each problem, for a total of 300 epochs, or until stagnation. Stagnation for 10 epochs or more during recursive training was used as a criterion for splitting the data into well clustered and ill clustered patterns.

DISCUSSIONS

The above results show that the recursive approach generally improves the performance of the underlying clustering algorithm. For all the results reported, with the same number of partitions in the ensemble, the recursive single-order clustering improves the results of the SOMs and the eSOMs, while the use of the recursive multi-order clustering improves the results obtained by the HONs and the eHONs. The number of misassigned patterns for the IRIS and the WINE datasets are better than or comparable to those of ensemble clustering, albeit requiring a fewer number of partitions.

CONCLUSION

In this chapter, we have introduced the concept of recursive clustering, an ensemble approach to unsupervised learning. Unlike other ensemble approaches, which are based on the consensus between several weak clusterers, the recursive clustering approach creates ensembles by recursive decomposition of data, thereby focusing more and more on the cluster boundary, and thus making it better correlated with ground truth information.

In addition to the recursive approach, we have also introduced the idea of evolutionary Higher Order Neurons. The eHONs work by identifying the best order a cluster can take, thereby identifying the complexity of each cluster.

The combination of the eHONs and recursive clustering appears to work well on the real world data presented in this chapter, with the number of misassigned patterns reduced by as much as 50% on the wine dataset. We also saw empirically that the performance is better than or comparable to ensemble clustering approaches, though with a significantly smaller number of partitions.

Although the recursive approach to clustering is an effective one, it has only been targeted for irregular clusters, but not for overlapping clusters. Overlapping clusters, however, occur commonly in the real world and future work on the recursive approach will be needed to handle overlapping clusters.

REFERENCES

Bhatia, S.K., & Deogun, J.S. (1998). Conceptual clustering in information retreival. *IEEE Trans System, Man and Cybernetics, 28*(3), 427-536.

Blatt, M., Wiseman, S., & Domany, E. (1996). Supermagnetic clustering of data. *Physical Review Letters, 76*(18), 3251-3254

Fred, A., & Jain, A.K. (2002). Data clustering using evidence accumulation. In *Procedings of the 16th International Conference on Pattern Recognition* (pp. 276-280).

Fred, A., & Jain, A.K. (2005). Combining multiple clustering using evidence accumulation. *IEEE Transactions on Pattern Analysis and Machine Intelligence, 27*(6), 835-850.

Goldberg, D.E., Deb, K., & Korb, B. (1991). Don't worry, be messy. In R. Belew & L. Booker (Eds.), *Proceedings of the Fourth International Conference in Genetic Algorithms and Their Applications* (pp. 24-30).

Graham, A. (1981). *Kronecker products and matrix calculus: With applications.* New York: Wiley.

Guan, S.U., & Ramanathan, K. (2004). Recursive percentage based hybrid pattern training for curve fitting. *IEEE conference on Cybernetics and Intelligent systems, 1,* 445-450.

Jain, A.K., & Dubes, R.C. (1998). *Algorithms for clustering data.* Prentice Hall.

Judd, D., McKinley, P., & Jain, A.K. (1997). Large scale parallel data clustering. *IEEE Trans Pattern Analysis and Machine Intelligence, 19*(2), 153-158.

Kohonen, T. (1997). *Self organizing maps.* Berlin, Germany: Springer-Verlag.

Lipson, H., Hod, Y., & Siegelmann, H.T. (1998). Higher order clustering metrics for competitive learning neural networks. In *Proceedings of the*

Isreal-Korea Bi National Conference on New Themes in Computer Aided Geometric Modeling, Tel-Aviv, Israel.

Lipson, H., & Siegelmann (2000). Clustering irregular shapes using higher order neurons. *Neural Computation, 12,* 2331-2353.

Mao, J., & Jain, A. (1996). A self organizing network for hyper ellipsoidal clustering (HEC). *IEEE Transactions on Neural Networks, 7,* 16-39.

Meir, R., & Rätsch, G. (2003). An introduction to boosting and leveraging. In S. Mendelson & A. Smola (Eds.), *Advanced Lectures on Machine Learning* (LNCS, pp. 119-184). Springer.

Painho, M., & Bacao, R. (2000). Using genetic algorithms in clustering problems. *Geocomputation 2000.* Retrieved August 20, 2007, from http://www.geocomputation.org/2000/GC015/Gc015.htm

Strehl, A., & Ghosh, J. (2005). Cluster ensembles—a knowledge reuse framework for combining multiple partitions. *Journal of Machine Learning Research, 3,* 583-617.

The UCI Machine Learning Repository. Retrieved August 20, 2007, from http://www.ics.uci.edu/~mlearn/MLRepository.html

Yao, X. (1993). A review of evolutionary artificial neural networks. *International Journal of Intelligent Systems, 8*(4), 539-567.

Section IV
Optimization

Chapter IX
Optimising Object Classification:
Uncertain Reasoning–Based Analysis Using CaRBS Systematic Research Algorithms

Malcolm J. Beynon
Cardiff University, U.K.

ABSTRACT

This chapter investigates the effectiveness of a number of objective functions used in conjunction with a novel technique to optimise the classification of objects based on a number of characteristic values, which may or may not be missing. The classification and ranking belief simplex (CaRBS) technique is based on Dempster-Shafer theory and, hence, operates in the presence of ignorance. The objective functions considered minimise the level of ambiguity and/or ignorance in the classification of companies to being either failed or not-failed. Further results are found when an incomplete version of the original data set is considered. The findings in this chapter demonstrate how techniques such as CaRBS, which operate in an uncertain reasoning based environment, offer a novel approach to object classification problem solving.

INTRODUCTION

The classification and ranking belief simplex (CaRBS) is a nascent technique for object classification and ranking, introduced in Beynon (2005a, 2005b). With its rudiments based on Dempster-Shafer theory (DST) (Dempster, 1967; Shafer, 1976), it is closely associated with the notion of uncertain reasoning. The applications of CaRBS have included credit rating classification (Beynon,

2005b), ranking long term systems (Beynon & Kitchener, 2005), and bird gender classification (Beynon & Buchanan, 2004). From these applications it is seen both classification and ranking analyses are able to be performed when employing CaRBS. In this chapter the CaRBS technique is used as a classification tool.

The utilisation of CaRBS here is to classify objects to a given hypothesis, its complement, and also a level of concomitant ignorance. This third classification, ignorance, is a direct consequence of its operational reliance on DST, and is separate to the common issue of ambiguity that is often present in an object's classification. In an application with a number of objects having known classes, the solving of the classification problem using CaRBS is structured as a constrained optimisation problem. That is, the optimisation is through the systematic assigning of values to internal control variables that appropriately configure a CaRBS system.

The effectiveness of any optimisation driven classification technique is the suitability of the objective function utilised to quantify the prevalent classification. With the allowed presence of ignorance in the classification of objects when using CaRBS, the structure of an associated objective function is a pertinent issue. The central theme of this chapter is a comparative investigation of three objective functions used to effectively classify objects when using CaRBS. In summary, these objective functions prioritise different aspects of the classification process, essentially whether ambiguity and/or ignorance should be minimised within each object's final classification.

An additional issue discussed here, through the use of the CaRBS technique, is the ability to analyse incomplete data without the need for any inhibiting external management of the missing values present (Little, 1988; Schafer & Graham, 2002). That is, within CaRBS, a missing value is considered an ignorant value and retained in the data set. Further, the use of the CaRBS technique allows the fullest visualisation of the results, able through the depiction of the classification evidence from characteristics describing each object as a simplex coordinate in a simplex plot domain.

The well known corporate failure problem is used throughout this chapter. Moreover, a small data set is considered made up of known failed and not-failed companies, each described by financial and nonfinancial characteristics. The data set enables the clear demonstration of the effectiveness of the different objective functions

employed with CaRBS, as well as the effects of the presence of missing values. On the latter issue, comparisons are further made between when purposely imposed missing values are retained and when they are replaced through the use of mean imputation (Huisman, 2000).

It is hoped that this chapter offers the interested reader the clearest discussion on issues such as ambiguity, ignorance, and incompleteness in the area of optimising object classification, which, while present in the applied world, have rarely been fully accommodated for in the more traditional classification techniques. Moreover, it offers a new dimension to classification based problem solving, through the positive inclusion of ignorance in such analysis.

BACKGROUND

The background in this chapter includes the description of the general methodology Dempster-Shafer theory (DST) and the CaRBS technique which operates using DST.

DST (Dempster, 1967; Shafer, 1976) is a general methodology closely associated with the notion of uncertain reasoning (Chen, 2001). In summary, DST provides a non-Bayesian attitude to quantify evidence of a subjective nature, in contrast to the more frequentist approach exhibited with the Bayesian orientation. The rudiments of DST are to formulate the evidential support for propositions involving uncertainty/ignorance and to represent the degree of the support through terms called *mass values*. Srivastava and Liu (2003) describe three reasons for the recent surge in the utilisation of DST, using the concomitant term of belief functions, namely:

1. The ease with which belief functions map uncertainties present in the real world,
2. The theoretical developments in local computations for propagating belief functions in a network, and

3. Availability of friendly software incorporating the local computations such as "Auditor's Assistant" (see Shafer, Shenoy, & Srivastava, 1988).

These reasons exemplify the encompassing attitude a DST-based approach invigorates. Following this brief synopsis of the origination of DST, it has itself been developed in the form of the transferable belief model (see Smets, 1990).

To demonstrate the advantage of DST in representing ignorance, let us consider the classic example of nonadditive probabilities (adapted from Hacking, 1975). A fragment of newspaper predicts a blizzard (b), which is regarded as infallible. There is a 75% certainty that the newspaper is today's. Therefore, there is 75% surety of an upcoming blizzard, giving a belief mass value of $m(\{b\}) = 0.75$. However, if the newspaper is not today's, anything can happen since the newspaper carries no information on future weather. Accordingly, the remaining belief mass value of 0.25 is allocated to both "blizzard" and "no blizzard ($\neg b$)" as a whole, that is, $m(\{b, \neg b\}) = 0.25$ viewed as ignorance here. With DST it is unnecessary, and insensible in this case, to divide the belief mass value of 0.25 and assign partial beliefs to b and $\neg b$ because there exists no evidence in support of such a re-allocation. The DST methodology undermines the operational structure of the CaRBS technique, next described.

The classification and ranking belief simplex (CaRBS), introduced in Beynon (2005a, 2005b), is a novel object classification and ranking technique, where each object o_j is described by a series of characteristics $c_1, ..., c_n$, which individually contribute evidence to whether the classification of the object is to a given hypothesis ($\{x\}$), its complement ($\{\neg x\}$), and a level of concomitant ignorance ($\{x, \neg x\}$). With DST, the basis for the operation of the CaRBS technique is termed around the formation of bodies of evidence (BOEs) made up of mass values representing the levels of exact belief (mass values) in the focal elements; the hypothesis, its complement, and concomitant ignorance.

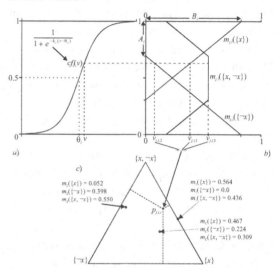

More formally, within CaRBS, the evidence from a characteristic c_i, for the object o_j, is defined in a characteristic BOE, termed $m_{j,i}(\cdot)$, made up of a triplet of mass values; $m_{j,i}(\{x\})$, $m_{j,i}(\{x, \neg x\})$ and $m_{j,i}(\{\neg x\})$, where $\{x\}$, $\{\neg x\}$ and $\{x, \neg x\}$ are the focal elements previously discussed. The rudiments of the CaRBS technique can then be best described by reference to Figure 1, where the construction of a characteristic BOE is shown.

The construction process reported in Figure 1 can be broken down into three stages. Stage (a) shows the transformation of a characteristic value v (j^{th} object, i^{th} characteristic) into a confidence value $cf_i(v)$, using a sigmoid function, with control variables k_i and θ_i.

Stage (b) transforms a $cf_i(v)$ into a characteristic BOE $m_{j,i}(\cdot)$, made up of the three mass values, $m_{j,i}(\{x\})$, $m_{j,i}(\{\neg x\})$ and $m_{j,i}(\{x, \neg x\})$, defined by:

$$m_{j,i}(\{x\}) = \max\left(0, \frac{B_i}{1 - A_i} cf_i(v) - \frac{A_i B_i}{1 - A_i}\right),$$

$$m_{j,i}(\{\neg x\}) = \max\left(0, \frac{-B_i}{1 - A_i} cf_i(v) + B_i\right),$$

and $m_{j,i}(\{x, \neg x\}) = 1 - m_{j,i}(\{x\}) - m_{j,i}(\{\neg x\})$,

where A_i and B_i are two further control variables.

Stage *(c)* shows a BOE $m_{j,i}(\cdot)$; $m_{j,i}(\{x\}) = v_{j,i,1}$, $m_{j,i}(\{\neg x\}) = v_{j,i,2}$ and $m_{j,i}(\{x, \neg x\}) = v_{j,i,3}$, can be represented as a simplex coordinate $(p_{j,i,v})$ in a simplex plot (equilateral triangle). More formally, the simplex coordinate $p_{j,i,v}$ exists such that the least distance to each of the sides of the equilateral triangle are in the same proportion (ratio) to the values $v_{j,i,1}$, $v_{j,i,2}$ and $v_{j,i,3}$. With an equilateral triangle of unit side with vertex coordinates $(1, 0)$, $(0, 0)$ and $(0.5, \sqrt{3}/2)$, then the associated values in the simplex coordinate (x, y) are given by $x = v_{j,i,2} + (1/2)v_{j,i,3}$ and $y = (\sqrt{3}/2)v_{j,i,3}$. The notion of simplex plots, also called ternary diagrams, has been used in a plethora of studies, including Flemming (2000) and Canongia Lopes (2004), which offer alternative descriptions of their utilisation.

Within DST, Dempster's (1967) rule of combination is used to combine a series of characteristic BOEs to produce an *object* BOE associated with an object and their level of classification to $\{x\}$, $\{\neg x\}$ and $\{x, \neg x\}$. The combination of two BOEs, $m_{j,i}(\cdot)$ and $m_{j,k}(\cdot)$, defined $(m_{j,i} \oplus m_{j,k})(\cdot)$, results in a combined BOE whose mass values are given by equations (1), (2) and (3).

This process of combining two BOEs, $m_{1,1}(\cdot)$ and $m_{1,2}(\cdot)$, to produce a further BOE $m_C(\cdot)$ is demonstrated in Figure 1, and next described. The two BOEs, $m_{1,1}(\cdot)$ and $m_{1,2}(\cdot)$ have mass values in the vector form $[m_{j,i}(\{x\}), m_{j,i}(\{\neg x\}), m_{j,i}(\{x, \neg x\})]$, as [0.564, 0.000, 0.436] and [0.052, 0.398, 0.550], respectively. The combination of $m_{1,1}(\cdot)$ and $m_{1,2}(\cdot)$, using the above expressions, is evaluated to be [0.467, 0.224, 0.309] ($= m_C(\cdot)$). In Figure 1, the simplex coordinates of the BOEs, $m_{1,1}(\cdot)$ and $m_{1,2}(\cdot)$, are shown along with that of the resultant combined BOE $m_C(\cdot)$. This example illustrates the clarity in the interpretation of the interaction between BOEs and their combination that the simplex plot representation allows.

This example highlights one further point, namely that the resultant BOE has less ignorance associated with it than either of its constituent BOEs. The desribed combination process can then be used iteratively to combine the n characteristic BOEs describing each object into an *object* BOE. It is noted, the CaRBS system is appropriate for a problem where each related characteristic has a noticeable level of concomitant ignorance associated with it and its contribution to the problem (Gerig, Welti, Guttman, Colchester, & Szekely, 2000).

The effectiveness of the CaRBS system is governed by the values systematically assigned to the incumbent control variables, k_i, θ_i, A_i and B_i ($i = 1, ..., n$). This necessary configuration is considered as a constrained optimisation prob-

Equation 1.

$$(m_{j,i} \oplus m_{j,k})(\{x\}) = \frac{m_{j,i}(\{x\})m_{j,k}(\{x\}) + m_{j,k}(\{x\})m_{j,i}(\{x, \neg x\}) + m_{j,i}(\{x\})m_{j,k}(\{x, \neg x\})}{1 - (m_{j,i}(\{\neg x\})m_{j,k}(\{x\}) + m_{j,i}(\{x\})m_{j,k}(\{\neg x\}))}$$

Equation 2.

$$(m_{j,i} \oplus m_{j,k})(\{\neg x\}) = \frac{m_{j,i}(\{\neg x\})m_{j,k}(\{\neg x\}) + m_{j,k}(\{x, \neg x\})m_{j,i}(\{\neg x\}) + m_{j,k}(\{\neg x\})m_{j,i}(\{x, \neg x\})}{1 - (m_{j,i}(\{\neg x\})m_{j,k}(\{x\}) + m_{j,i}(\{x\})m_{j,k}(\{\neg x\}))}$$

Equation 3.

$$(m_{j,i} \oplus m_{j,k})(\{x, \neg x\}) = 1 - (m_{j,i} \oplus m_{j,k})(\{x\}) - (m_{j,i} \oplus m_{j,k})(\{\neg x\})$$

lem, solved here using trigonometric differential evolution (TDE) (Fan & Lampinen, 2003; Storn & Price, 1997). When the classification of a number of objects is known, the effectiveness of a configured CaRBS system can be measured by a defined objective function (OB). Three objective functions are considered here, each based around the optimization of the final object BOEs, but taken into account differently the presence of ambiguity and ignorance.

Beynon (2005a) included an objective function which maximised the certainty in each object's final classification (minimising ambiguity and ignorance). This first OB considered, defined OB1, uses the mean simplex coordinates of the final object BOEs of objects known to be classified to $\{x\}$ or $\{\neg x\}$, the sets of objects are termed equivalence classes ($E(\cdot)$), defined $E(x)$ and $E(\neg x)$. Then the mean simplex coordinate of an equivalence class $E(\cdot)$ is $\left(\dfrac{1}{|E(\cdot)|} \sum_{o_j \in E(\cdot)} x_j, \dfrac{1}{|E(\cdot)|} \sum_{o_j \in E(\cdot)} y_j \right)$,

where (x_j, y_j) is the simplex coordinate of the object BOE associated with the object o_j and $|E(\cdot)|$ is the number of objects in the respective equivalence class. An objective function traditionally uses a

best fitness of zero. It follows the OB1 is given by equation (4).

where (x_H, y_H) and (x_N, y_N) are the simplex coordinates of the $\{x\}$ and $\{\neg x\}$ vertices in the domain of the simplex plot, respectively. In general, the OB1 has range $0 \leq OB1 \leq \sqrt{(x_N - x_H)^2 + (y_N - y_H)^2}$. For a simplex plot with vertex coordinates (1, 0), (0, 0) and (0.5, $\sqrt{3}/2$), it is an equilateral triangle with unit side, then $0 \leq OB1 \leq 1$.

The second objective function considered here was constructed in Beynon (2005b), which in contrast to OB1, considers optimisation through the minimisation of only the ambiguity in the classification of the set of objects. For objects in the equivalence classes, $E(x)$ and $E(\neg x)$, the optimum solution is to maximise the difference values $(m_j(\{x\}) - m_j(\{\neg x\}))$ and $(m_j(\{\neg x\}) - m_j(\{x\}))$, respectively. This objective function, defined OB2, where optimisation is minimisation with a lower limit of zero, is given by equation (5).

In the limit, each of the difference values, $(m_j(\{x\}) - m_j(\{\neg x\}))$ and $(m_j(\{\neg x\}) - m_j(\{x\}))$, has domain [–1, 1], then $0 \leq OB2 \leq 1$. It is noted, maximising a difference value such as $(m_j(\{x\}) - m_j(\{\neg x\}))$, only indirectly affects the associated ignorance $(m_j(\{x, \neg x\}))$ rather than making it a direct issue, as with OB1.

Equation 4.

$$OB1 = \frac{1}{2}\left(\sqrt{\left(x_H - \frac{1}{|E(x)|}\sum_{o_j \in E(x)} x_j \right)^2 + \left(y_H - \frac{1}{|E(x)|}\sum_{o_j \in E(x)} y_j \right)^2} \right.$$
$$\left. + \sqrt{\left(x_N - \frac{1}{|E(\neg x)|}\sum_{o_j \in E(\neg x)} x_j \right)^2 + \left(y_N - \frac{1}{|E(\neg x)|}\sum_{o_j \in E(\neg x)} y_j \right)^2} \right),$$

Equation 5.

$$OB2 = \frac{1}{4}\left(\frac{1}{|E(x)|}\sum_{o_j \in E(x)} (1 - m_j(\{x\}) + m_j(\{\neg x\})) + \frac{1}{|E(\neg x)|}\sum_{o_j \in E(\neg x)} (1 + m_j(\{x\}) - m_j(\{\neg x\})) \right).$$

Equation 6.

$$OB3 = \frac{1}{2}\left(\frac{1}{|E(x)|} \sum_{o_j \in E(x)} \frac{1}{1 + \exp(-4(m_j(\{x\}) - m_j(\{\neg x\})))} \right.$$
$$\left. + \frac{1}{|E(\neg x)|} \sum_{o_j \in E(\neg x)} \frac{1}{1 + \exp(-4(m_j(\{\neg x\}) - m_j(\{x\})))} \right).$$

The third, and final, objective function introduced here is a development on OB2 with more attempt to remove close ambiguity from the classification of objects. That is, it is a weighted version of OB2, whereby there is a larger penalty for when $(m_j(\{x\}) - m_j(\{\neg x\}))$ and $(m_j(\{\neg x\}) - m_j(\{x\}))$ are near zero than when they are away from zero. More formally, this objective function, defined OB3, where optimisation is minimisation with a lower limit of zero, is given by equation (6).

In the limit, each of the constituent parts of a summation has domain [0, 1], then $0 \le OB3 \le 1$. The value 4 is a simple choice of any positive value, in the constituent parts it dictates the level of change in the induced penalty depending on how ambiguous the evidence currently is in an object BOE. This value can be changed depending on the desired level of penalty, the higher the value the more draconian the penalty changes.

There is one final feature of the CaRBS technique that separates it from the majority of other classification techniques, namely on how it models the presence of missing values. Moreover, with CaRBS, if a characteristic value is missing its respective characteristic BOE supports only ignorance, namely $m_{j,i}(\{x, \neg x\}) = 1$ (with $m_{j,i}(\{x\}) = 0$ and $m_{j,i}(\{\neg x\}) = 0$). That is, a missing value is considered an ignorant value and so offers no evidence in the subsequent classification of an object. This means that the missing values can be retained in the analysis rather than having to be imputed or managed in any way, which would change the data set considered.

The objective functions defined here acknowledge the presence of missing values differently, with OB2 and OB3 more positive about their presence, whereas OB1 directly attempts to minimise its presence (along with ambiguity). The visual interpretation to this variation in the acknowledgment of ignorance in the classification of objects is that within a simplex plot, results from using OB2 and OB3 may be spread over all of the simplex plot domain, whereas when using OB1, their may be more concentration of results near the base of the simplex plot, associated with lesser ignorance, as intended by the objective function.

CaRBS ANALYSES USING DIFFERENT OBJECTIVE FUNCTIONS

The main thrust of this chapter employs the CaRBS technique on a relatively small corporate failure data set, where a number of companies, each described by a series of financial and non-financial characteristics, are known to be either failed (F) or not-failed (N). The corporate failure problem is a well established classification issue, with a number of traditional techniques regularly employed in its analysis (Lennox, 1999). This problem was first used to introduce the CaRBS technique (Beynon, 2005a); hence, the contrast in the results here are indicative of the developments in its original presentation. Throughout the remainder of this chapter, when using CaRBS, the hypothesis is defined as being a failed company $(x = F)$, and its complement is not-failed $(\neg x = N)$, with concomitant ignorance $(\{x, \neg x\} = \{F, N\})$.

The data utilised in this corporate failure problem were obtained from the Financial Analysis Made Easy CD-ROM UK corporate database (FAME, 1995). The database covers all medium-sized and large firms, together with a large sample of smaller firms (in excess of 200,000 British companies). The selection of a sample of companies was considered carefully (Taffler, 1984) to reduce the influence of structural differences within companies, as a consequence only manufacturing firms were used, for which a common fiscal year was chosen (latest available). The firms excluded are defined as those with total assets not exceeding £1.0m and with sales less than £20m (FAME, 1995).

Here, 80 companies are analysed without loss of generality, equally split between being known to be failed (F) and not-failed (N). Due to the disproportionate numbers of failed and not-failed companies to choose from, the 40 failed companies were identified first then the 40 not-failed companies randomly selected from the available population. This population was purposely restricted to companies with characteristic variables within the respective domains constructed from the failed companies. The reasons for this restriction is two-fold; firstly it means that there are no obvious differences in the companies considered, failed and not-failed, on the individual characteristics; second it suggests there will be ambiguity in the classification of the 80 companies. This latter restriction is purposely included here so that it allows the fullest opportunity to see how the different objective functions affect the final classification results.

In this study there are five financial and non-financial characteristics that are used to describe each company (see Table 1).

From Table 1, it is seen the five characteristics embody key attributes associated with corporate failure analysis (see Beynon & Peel, 2001; Peel, 1990; Taffler, 1984), and the references contained therein. The two descriptive measures are the mean and standard deviation of the characteristic values describing the 80 companies considered (used later).

When using the CaRBS technique, the descriptive characteristics are considered low level measurements. That is, no characteristic on its own offers certainty in the final classification of a company to being failed or not-failed. To assure this, and reacting to previous findings (including Beynon, 2005b), the control variables B_i, $i = 1, ...,$ 5 are fixed as 0.5, signifying each characteristic could have an associated "ignorance" mass value not less than 0.5 ($m_{j,i}(\{F, N\}) \geq 0.5$ in a characteristic BOE).

With the intention of assigning domains to the control variables inherent in CaRBS, the series of characteristic values were standardised so they are described with a zero mean and unit standard deviation. This allows the standardisation of the bounds on certain control variables present in CaRBS (k_i, θ_i and A_i), set as: $-3 \leq k_i \leq 3$, $-2 \leq \theta_i \leq 2$, $0 \leq A_i < 1$. It is suggested that values outside these bounds would have a limited marginal effect on results.

Table 1. Description of corporate failure characteristics

Variable	Description	Mean	Std dev
SALES	Annual sales figure (£1,000s)	6583.155	4735.162
ROCE	Ratio of profit before tax to capital employed (%)	−8.964	73.314
GEAR	Gearing ratio (%)	468.103	1253.245
LIQD	Liquidity ratio (ratio)	0.885	0.388
AGE	Age of company (years)	22.563	17.463

To utilise the TDE method to configure a CaRBS system, a number of parameters are required. Following Fan and Lampinen (2003), amplification control $F = 0.99$, crossover constant $CR = 0.85$, trigonometric mutation probability $M_t = 0.05$, number of parameter vectors $NP = 10 \times$ number of control variables = 150. The TDE method was then employed, with the different objective functions, to systematically assign values to the control variables next described.

CaRBS Analysis with Objective Function OB1

The utilisation of the objective function OB1 in the configuration of the CaRBS system is to directly minimize the levels of ambiguity and ignorance present in the classification of companies to being either failed or not-failed. The TDE method was employed based on the previously defined parameters and run five times, each time converging to an optimum value, the best out of the five runs being OB1 = 0.441. A reason for this value being away from its lower bound of zero is related to the implicit minimum levels of ignorance associated with each characteristic (fixing of B_i control variables), possibly also due to the presence of conflicting evidence from the characteristics. The resultant control variables found from the best TDE run are reported in Table 2.

A brief inspection of these results shows the near uniformity in the k_i and A_i control variables. With all but one of the k_i variables taking either of the values –3 or 3, this exhibits the attempt to

Table 2. Control variable values associated with company characteristics, using OB1

Characteristic	SALES	ROCE	GEAR	LIQD	AGE
k_i	3.000	–3.000	0.577	–3.000	–3.000
θ_i	0.108	–0.065	1.390	–0.057	1.543
A_i	0.164	0.225	0.000	0.203	0.122

offer most discernment between the hypothesis and its complement, for each set of characteristics values (see Figure 1). The assignment of values near to 0.000 for each A_i value is informative and a consequence of the utilisation of OB1. That is, from Figure 1, a value of A_i near 0.000 is allowing noticeable ambiguity, but minimises the concomitant ignorance with the evidence from each characteristic.

The role of these defined control variables is to allow the construction of characteristic BOEs and their subsequent combination to formulate a series of company BOEs for the 80 companies considered. The construction of a characteristic BOE is next demonstrated, considering the company o_{23} and the financial characteristic LIQD. Starting with the evaluation of the confidence factor $cf_{LIQD}(\cdot)$ (see Figure 1a), for the company o_{23}, from Table 8, LIQD = 0.827, when standardised, it is $v = -0.152$ (see Table 3) then:

$$cf_{LIQD}(-0.152) = \frac{1}{1 + e^{-2.000(-0.152 + 0.057)}}$$

$$= \frac{1}{1 + 0.752} = 0.571,$$

using the control variables in Table 2. This confidence value is used in the expressions making up the mass values in the characteristic BOE $m_{23,LIQD}(\cdot)$, namely; $m_{23,LIQD}(\{F\})$, $m_{23,LIQD}(\{N\})$ and $m_{23,LIQD}(\{F, N\})$, found to be:

$$m_{23,LIQD}(\{F\}) =$$

$$\max\left(0, \frac{0.5}{1 - 0.203} 0.571 - \frac{0.203 \times 0.5}{1 - 0.203}\right) =$$

$$\max(0, 0.358 - 0.127) = 0.231,$$

$$m_{23,LIQD}(\{N\}) =$$

$$\max\left(0, \frac{-0.5}{1 - 0.203} 0.571 + 0.5\right) =$$

$$\max(0, -0.358 + 0.5) = 0.142,$$

$$m_{23,LIQD}(\{F, N\}) = 1 - 0.231 - 0.142 = 0.627.$$

Table 3. Characteristic and company BOEs for the companies, o_{23} and o_{71}

BOE	SALES	ROCE	GEAR	LIQD	AGE	Company BOE
o_{23}	−0.543	0.344	−0.256	−0.152	−0.719	
$m_{23,i}(\{F\})$	0.000	0.000	0.140	0.231	0.499	0.305
$m_{23,i}(\{N\})$	0.426	0.354	0.360	0.142	0.000	0.573
$m_{23,i}(\{F, N\})$	0.574	0.646	0.500	0.627	0.501	0.122
o_{71}	−0.847	−0.120	−0.244	1.036	0.311	
$m_{71,i}(\{F\})$	0.000	0.204	0.140	0.000	0.486	0.230
$m_{71,i}(\{N\})$	0.468	0.151	0.360	0.477	0.000	0.669
$m_{71,i}(\{F, N\})$	0.532	0.646	0.500	0.523	0.514	0.101

For the company o_{23}, this characteristic BOE is representative of the characteristic BOEs $m_{23,i}(\cdot)$, presented in Table 3 (using standardised characteristic values), along with those for the company o_{71}. These characteristic BOEs describe the evidential support from all the financial and non-financial characteristics to a company's failed or not-failed classification (from Table 8 in Appendix A, o_{23} and o_{71}, are known to be not-failed and failed, respectively).

In Table 3, for the company o_{23}, to support correct classification, it would be expected the $m_{23,i}(\{N\})$ mass values to be larger than their respective $m_{23,i}(\{F\})$ mass values, which is the case for the characteristics, SALES, ROCE, and GEAR. The large $m_{23,i}(\{F, N\})$ mass values are a direct consequence of the imposed values on the B_i control variables. The majority of characteristic BOEs supporting correct classification is reflected in the final company BOE $m_{23}(\cdot)$ produced (through their combination), which suggests, with $m_{23}(\{N\})$ = 0.573 > 0.305 = $m_{23}(\{F\})$, it is a not-failed company, which is the correct classification.

For the company o_{71}, the evidence from the characteristics is further conflicting (some suggesting failed and some not-failed classification), their combination produces a company BOE $m_{71}(\cdot)$, which indicates not-failed, which is incorrect in this case. For further interpretation of the characteristic and company BOEs associated with companies, o_{23} and o_{71}, their representation as simplex coordinates in a simplex plot are reported in Figure 2.

Figure 2. Simplex coordinates of characteristic and company BOEs for o_{23} and o_{71}, using OB1

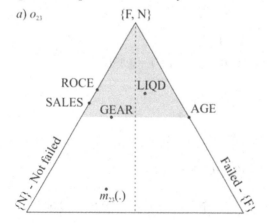
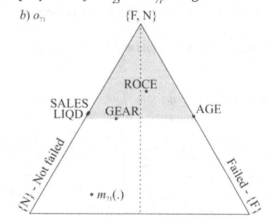

Figure 3. Simplex plot representation of final company BOEs when classification optimised using OB1

a) Not-failed

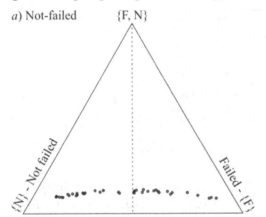

b) Failed

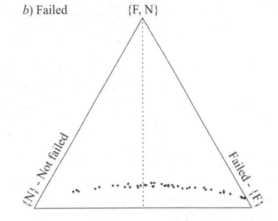

Figure 2 offers a visual representation of the evidence from the five characteristics to the classification of the companies, o_{23} and o_{71}, as to whether they are failed or not-failed. In each simplex plot the dashed vertical line partitions the regions where either of the mass values assigned to {N} (to the left) and {F} (to the right) is the larger in a BOE. In both simplex plots, the simplex coordinates of the final company BOEs, $m_{23}(\cdot)$ and $m_{71}(\cdot)$, are nearer their base lines than those of the characteristic BOEs. This is solely due to the reduction of ignorance from the combination of evidence present in the characteristic BOEs (see also Table 3). The positions of the simplex coordinates of the characteristic BOEs allow their possibly conflicting support for correct (or incorrect) classification of the companies to be identified.

The process of positioning the classification of a company in a simplex plot can be undertaken for each of the 80 companies considered (see Figure 3).

Figures 3 partitions the presentation of the companies' company BOEs between those associated with being not-failed (3*a*) and failed (3*b*), where each company BOE is labelled with a circle and cross, respectively. The consistent distances away from the base line of the simplex plots indicates similar levels of concomitant ignorance still present in each company BOE. The

relative nearness to the base line is a consequence of the objective function used here (OB1), which directly attempts to minimise ignorance along with ambiguity in the final classification of the companies (within their company BOE).

Based on their company BOE positions, either side of the vertical dashed lines in the simplex plots in Figure 3, it was found that 28 out of 40 (70.000%) and 24 out of 40 (60.000%) companies were correctly classified as not-failed (N) and failed (F), respectively. This combines to a total 65.000% classification accuracy. Inspection of this value shows it to be low, not far away from that found from a random choice approach, a feature of the data set considered which, with intention, may exhibit a noticeable level of ambiguity.

CaRBS Analyses Using Objective Functions OB2 and OB3

This section briefly describes further CaRBS analyses of the corporate failure data set (see Appendix A), this time using the two other objective functions described in the background section, namely, OB2 and OB3. From their description previously given, both of these objective functions are more tolerant of ignorance in the final classification of companies than in the case of OB1.

When both objective functions were used, the TDE based optimal configuration of the CaRBS

Table 4. Control variable values for company characteristics, using OB2 and OB3

	Characteristic	SALES	ROCE	GEAR	LIQD	AGE
OB2	k_i	−3.000	−3.000	3.000	−3.000	−3.000
	θ_i	0.215	0.008	0.750	−0.082	−0.003
	A_i	0.907	0.336	0.952	0.354	0.953
	Characteristic	SALES	ROCE	GEAR	LIQD	AGE
OB3	k_i	−3.000	−3.000	3.000	−3.000	−3.000
	θ_i	−0.065	−0.102	0.841	−0.594	1.527
	A_i	0.955	0.269	0.963	0.620	0.170

technique produced different sets of optimum control variables (from their series of runs), as reported in Table 4.

The variations in the values assigned to the control variables in Table 4 (and Table 2) are indicative of the influence of the objective functions utilised. Indeed, there is consistency in the k_i values shown between the two sets of control variables shown in Table 4 (for OB2 and OB3), but a number of the A_i control variables are away from the 0.000 value, not the case when using OB1. Amongst the noticeable differences are those associated with the evidence of the AGE characteristic, with respect to the θ_i and A_i control variables.

The effects of the sets of control variables identified are again shown through the construction of certain characteristic and company BOEs. The sets of characteristic BOEs, associated with the company o_{23}, from using the two different objective functions, OB2 and OB3, are reported in Table 5.

The results in Table 5 show similarity in the evidential support in the characteristic BOEs, when using the different objective functions. One exception is with the AGE characteristic, where with OB2 it offers total ignorance, whereas with OB3, there is considerable evidential belief in its (o_{23}) classification to being a failed company. This being a consequence of the noticeable differences in the θ_i and A_i control variables for the AGE characteristic, when using OB2 and OB3, see Table 4 and the accompanying discussion. Further comparison of the differences in the evidence and final classifications of the companies, o_{23} and o_{71}, are shown in Figure 4, through their simplex plot based representation.

The simplex plots in Figure 4 show the classification of the companies o_{23} (4a and 4c) and o_{71} (4b and 4d), for when the objective functions OB2 (4a and 4b) and OB3 (4c and 4d) are employed. Concentrating only on the different final classifications of the companies, for o_{23}, when

Table 5. Characteristic and company BOEs for the company o_{23}, when using OB2 and OB3

	BOE	SALES	ROCE	GEAR	LIQD	AGE	Company BOE
OB2	$m_{23,i}(\{F\})$	0.000	0.000	0.000	0.153	0.000	0.111
	$m_{23,i}(\{N\})$	0.000	0.299	0.017	0.073	0.000	0.329
	$m_{23,i}(\{F, N\})$	1.000	0.701	0.983	0.774	1.000	0.560
OB3	$m_{23,i}(\{F\})$	0.000	0.000	0.000	0.000	0.499	0.328
	$m_{23,i}(\{N\})$	0.000	0.358	0.017	0.224	0.000	0.343
	$m_{23,i}(\{F, N\})$	1.000	0.642	0.983	0.776	0.501	0.329

Figure 4. Simplex coordinates of characteristic and company BOEs for o_{23} (a and c) and o_{71} (b and d), when using OB2 (a and b) and OB3 (c and d)

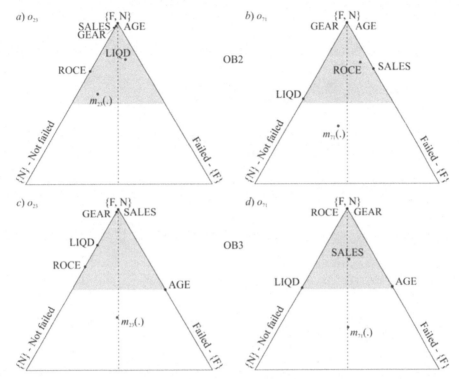

using OB2 and OB3, it is consistently correctly classified but with increasing ambiguity and decreasing ignorance, respectively, whereas for o_{71}, when using OB2 and OB3, it is incorrectly and correctly classified, respectively.

Next shown are the final company BOEs for all the 80 companies considered, when using the control variables found from the separate employment of objective functions, OB2 and OB3 (see Figure 5).

The results in Figure 5 are conspicuously different to those from using the objective function OB1 (see Figure 3). Moreover, the simplex coordinates representing the company BOEs are further up the simplex plots presented, indicating more ignorance is associated with many of the companies' final classification to being failed or not-failed. This is clearly a consequence of the objective functions OB2 and OB3 being more

tolerant of ignorance in the final classification of companies, more interested in minimising the ambiguity in their classification.

With respect to the classification accuracy when using the objective functions OB2 and OB3, for OB2 there is a total of 70.000% classification accuracy (29 not-failed and 27 failed companies correctly classified), and for OB3 there is a total of 72.500% classification accuracy (28 not-failed and 30 failed companies correctly classified). These classification results are an improvement on those found when using the objective function OB1, indicating that a more tolerant attitude to the presence of ignorance can aid in the minimising of the ambiguity in the classification, so improving overall accuracy.

The results presented so far demonstrate how the classification problem is dynamic, in that here the issues of ambiguity and ignorance are consid-

Figure 5. Simplex plot representation of final company BOEs when classification optimised using OB2 and OB3

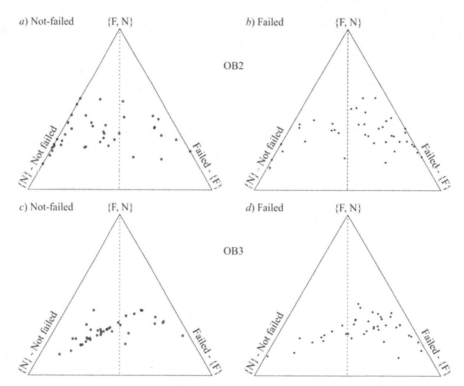

ered separate from each other. The appropriateness of this dynamism is application dependent to a point, when ignorance is inherent through the presence of missing values its appropriateness, if further endorsed.

CaRBS Aalyses on Incomplete Company Data Set Using Objective Functions OB2

This subsection undertakes two further CaRBS analyses, to demonstrate the advantageous feature of CaRBS to be able to analyse incomplete data. Moreover, the CaRBS technique does not need to manage the missing values that may be present in a data set, instead they are retained and simply considered as offering total ignorance in terms of evidence towards the classification of companies on their failure risk (see background section).

To demonstrate the effect of managing or not managing the presence of missing values, the original complete company data set is purposely transformed to create an incomplete data set to further analyse. That is, 50% of the present values in the data set were removed and termed missing (see Appendix A for further details). This level of missingness would be considered critical for the practical analysis of a data set (see Carriere, 1999).

When confronted by the presence of missing values in a data set, the expected solution is to manage their presence (Schafer & Graham, 2002). One common approach is the replacement of the missing values with surrogates, often referred to as imputation (Lakshminarayan, Harp, & Samad, 1999). In this study, mean imputation is employed, whereby over an individual characteristic, each missing value is replaced by the mean of the present

Table 6. Control variable values for company characteristics when missing values are retained and mean imputed, using OB2

	Characteristic	SALES	ROCE	GEAR	LIQD	AGE
missing	k_i	−3.000	−3.000	3.000	−3.000	−3.000
values	θ_i	−0.181	−0.833	−0.398	−0.270	0.638
retained	A_i	0.977	0.841	0.349	0.303	0.937
missing	k_i	−3.000	−3.000	3.000	−3.000	−3.000
values	θ_i	−0.572	0.107	0.625	0.086	0.215
imputed	A_i	0.993	0.421	0.920	0.436	0.982

Table 7. Characteristic and company BOEs for the company o_{23}, using OB2, when missing values are retained and mean imputed

	BOE	SALES	ROCE	GEAR	LIQD	AGE	Company BOE
Missing values retained	o_{23}	−0.535	-	-	−0.258	-	
	$m_{23,i}(\{F\})$	0.000	0.000	0.000	0.135	0.000	0.135
	$m_{23,i}(\{N\})$	0.000	0.000	0.000	0.147	0.000	0.147
	$m_{23,i}(\{F, N\})$	1.000	1.000	1.000	0.718	1.000	0.718
Missing values imputed	o_{23}	−0.535	0.000	0.000	−0.258	0.000	
	$m_{23,i}(\{F\})$	0.000	0.137	0.000	0.267	0.000	0.368
	$m_{23,i}(\{N\})$	0.000	0.000	0.000	0.000	0.000	0.000
	$m_{23,i}(\{F, N\})$	1.000	0.863	1.000	0.733	1.000	0.632

values for that characteristic (Huisman, 2000).

Two CaRBS analyses are undertaken here, when the missing values in the incomplete version of the company data set are retained and when they are managed using mean imputation. In these analyses, the objective function OB2 is consistently employed. The TDE approach to the optimal configuration of the CaRBS technique was employed and produced two optimal sets of concomitant control variables (see Table 6).

There is little variation in a number of the control variables identified through the best TDE runs on the two new versions of the company data set; two exceptions are the ROCE and GEAR characteristics, which have noticeably different θ_i and A_i control variables.

The effects of the sets of control variables are shown through the construction of certain char-

acteristic and company BOEs. The sets of BOEs, associated with the company o_{23}, from when the missing values are retained and managed, are reported in Table 7.

An important feature of the data presented in Table 7 are the dashed lines representing certain standardised characteristic values of the company o_{23}, which denote that they are missing (only SALES and LIQD remain). Further down the table, when the missing values are mean imputed, their standardised values are now 0.000 in each case (since standardised values have mean zero). This description demonstrates the different ways missing values can be represented in a data set.

Concentrating on the ROCE characteristic, when the missing values are retained it offers only total ignorance in its concomitant characteristic BOE, whereas when this missing value is imputed,

Figure 6. Simplex coordinates of characteristic and company BOEs for o_{23} and o_{71}, using OB2, when missing values retained and mean imputed

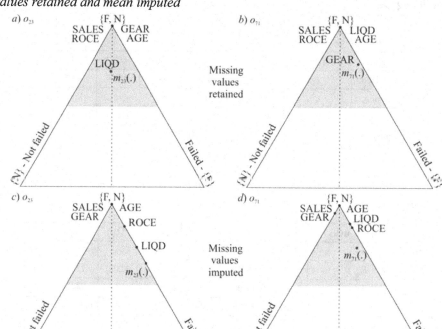

Figure 7. Example of final company BOEs when classification optimised using OB2

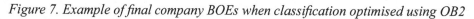

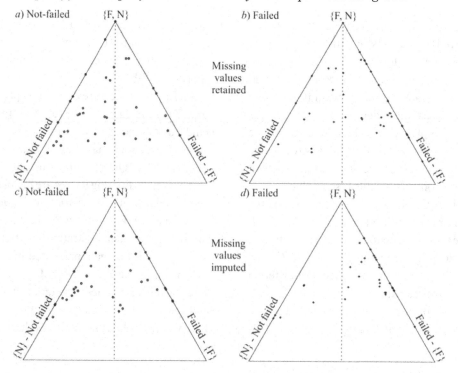

the characteristic BOE offers some evidence to the company being failed ($m_{23,\text{ROCE}}(\{F\}) = 0.137$). This finding is clear evidence of the impact of imputing missing values, since any evidence apart from ignorance is false evidence whether it supports or does not support correct classification.

Further elucidation of the variation in the classification of the companies, o_{23} and o_{71}, depending on whether missing values were retained or mean imputed, is given through their representation in simplex plots (see Figure 6).

Considering the final classification of the company o_{23}, when the missing values were retained (Figure 6, section a), it has correct classification (marginally, see also Table 7), but when the missing values are mean imputed (Figure 6, section c), it is noticeably incorrectly classified. For the company o_{71}, it is consistently correctly classified (Figure 6, sections b and d). The variations in the evidence from the characteristics, for the same company, depending on how the missing values are managed are indicative of the impact of varying the treatment of missing values.

Next shown are the final company BOEs for all 80 companies considered when using the control variables found from the separate employment of the objective function OB2, when the missing values are retained and mean imputed (see Figure 5).

Amongst the results in Figure 7 are the simplex coordinates representing companies BOEs at the {F, N} vertex in Figure 7, sections a and b. For these companies, there is total ignorance in their classification due to two reasons: first that a large number of their characteristics are now missing so contribute only ignorance towards their classification and second that those characteristic values that are still present are deemed to offer only ignorance themselves.

With respect to the classification accuracy when the missing values are retained or imputed, when retained there is a total of 71.250% classification accuracy (28 not-failed and 29 failed companies correctly classified), when imputed

there is a total of 68.750% classification accuracy (21 not-failed and 34 failed companies correctly classified).

CONCLUSION

Within an object classification context, problem solving means the *a priori* training of a system with the future intention to predict the classification of previously unconsidered objects. The CaRBS technique is one technique that enables such a classification of objects to a given hypothesis ($\{x\}$) and not the hypothesis ($\{\neg x\}$), based on a number of descriptive characteristics. The pertinence of the CaRBS technique is in its analysis in the presence of ignorance ($\{x, \neg x\}$), a facet of the general philosophy of uncertain reasoning.

In this chapter, the CaRBS technique, accompanied by a series of different objective functions used to quantify the undertaken classification, clearly demonstrates the effect of the acknowledgment of ambiguity and ignorance in such analyses. The objective functions described and utilised in the analysis, through the definition of CaRBS with Dempster-Shafer theory, show how ambiguity and ignorance can be differently quantified.

This chapter offers a further important insight into problem solving in an uncertain environment through the CaRBS approach to handling missing values in analysed data sets and the allowance for the retention of missing values, rather than their external management.

REFERENCES

Beynon, M.J. (2005a). A novel technique of object ranking and classification under ignorance: An application to the corporate failure risk problem. *European Journal of Operational Research, 167*, 493-517.

Beynon, M.J. (2005b). A novel approach to the credit rating problem: Object classification under ignorance. *International Journal of Intelligent Systems in Accounting, Finance and Management, 13,* 113-130.

Beynon, M.J., & Buchanan, K. (2004). Object classification under ignorance using CaRBS: The case of the European barn swallow. *Expert Systems with Applications, 27*(3), 403-415.

Beynon, M.J., & Kitchener, M. (2005). Ranking the balance of state long-term care systems: A comparative exposition of the SMARTER and CaRBS techniques. *Health Care Management Science, 8,* 157-166.

Beynon, M., & Peel, M. (2001). Variable precision rough set theory and data discretisation: An application to corporate failure prediction. *OMEGA - International Journal of Management Science, 29*(6), 561-576.

Canongia Lopes, J.N. (2004) On the classification and representation of ternary phase diagrams: The yin and yang of a T–x approach. *Phys. Chem. Chem. Phys., 6,* 2314-2319.

Carriere, K.C. (1999). Methods for repeated measures data analysis with missing values. *Journal of Statistical Planning and Inference, 77,* 221-236.

Chen, Z. (2001). *Data mining and uncertain reasoning: An integrated approach.* New York: John Wiley.

Dempster, A.P. (1967). Upper and lower probabilities induced by a multiple valued mapping. *Ann. Math. Statistics, 38,* 325-339.

FAME. (1995). *FAME for Windows user guide.* London: Bureau Van Dijk Electronic Publishing Limited.

Fan, H.-Y., & Lampinen, J.A. (2003). Trigonometric mutation operation to differential evolution. *Journal of Global Optimization, 27,* 105-129.

Flemming, B.W. (2000) A revised textural classification of gravel-free muddy sediments on the basis of ternary diagrams. *Continental Shelf Research, 20,* 1125-1137.

Gerig, G., Welti, D., Guttman, C.R.G, Colchester, A.C.F., & Szekely G. (2000). Exploring the discrimination power of the time domain for segmentation and characterisation of active lesions in serial MR data. *Medical Image Analysis, 4,* 31-42.

Hacking, I. (1975) *The emergence of probability.* New York, Cambridge University Press.

Huisman, M. (2000). Imputation of missing item responses: Some simple techniques. *Quality & Quantity, 34,* 331-351.

Lakshminarayan, K., Harp, S.A., & Samad, T. (1999). Imputation of missing data in industrial databases. *Applied Intelligence, 11,* 259-275.

Lennox, C. (1999). Identifying failing companies: A re-evaluation of the logit, probit and DA approaches. *Journal of Economics and Business, 51,* 347-364.

Little, R.J.A. (1988). Missing-data adjustments in large surveys. *Journal of Business & Economic Statistics, 6,* 287-296.

Peel, M. (1990). *The liquidation/merger alternative.* Avebury: Aldershot.

Schafer, J.L., & Graham, J.W. (2002). Missing data: Our view of the state of the art. *Psychological Methods, 7*(2), 147-177.

Shafer, G.A. (1976). *Mathematical theory of evidence.* Princeton: Princeton University Press.

Shafer, G., Shenoy, P.P., & Srivastava, R.P. (1988) Auditor's assistant: A knowledge engineering tool for audit decisions. In *Proceedings of 1988 Touche Ross University of Kansas Symposium on Auditing Problems* (pp. 61-84).

Smets, P. (1990) The combination of evidence in the transferable belief model. *IEEE Transactions on Pattern Analysis and Machine Intelligence, 12*(5), 447-458.

Srivastava, R.P., & Liu, L. (2003) Applications of belief functions in business decisions: A review. *Information Systems Frontiers, 5*(4), 359-378.

Storn, R., & Price, K. (1997). Differential evolution—a simple and efficient heuristic for global optimization over continuous spaces. *Journal of Global Optimisation, 11*, 341-59.

Taffler, R. (1984). Empirical models for the monitoring of UK corporations. *Journal of Banking and Finance, 8*, 199-227.

APPENDIX

This Appendix presents the characteristic details of the 80 companies considered throughout the chapter, along with their known classification to being failed (F) or not-failed(N) (see Table 8).

Beyond the characteristic values and classification presented in Table 1, those characteristic values underlined were considered missing when analysing the incomplete data set.

Table 8. Characteristic and classification details of companies

Comp	SALES	ROCE	GEAR	LIQD	AGE	Class	Comp	SALES	ROCE	GEAR	LIQD	AGE	Class
o_1	3519	23.207	23.988	1.459	19	N	o_{33}	7859	19.292	1194.475	0.931	5	N
o_2	4297	21.172	30.201	1.315	41	N	o_{34}	15273	29.243	83.520	1.409	36	N
o_3	1474	−25.377	784.247	0.411	21	N	o_{35}	6285	72.214	10.728	1.127	11	N
o_4	15731	−2.338	70.397	0.410	23	N	o_{36}	4056	30.441	121.041	0.927	17	N
o_5	6822	3.506	96.69	0.736	28	N	o_{37}	14648	−1.920	1510.445	0.653	3	N
o_6	4525	−9.309	154.827	0.522	9	N	o_{38}	1065	2.487	129.509	0.485	63	N
o_7	4283	3.729	23.894	1.490	45	N	o_{39}	14251	2.547	31.632	1.211	29	N
o_8	1336	12.545	44.296	1.401	36	N	o_{40}	4985	4.621	101.306	0.578	50	N
o_9	4190	0.600	120.454	0.501	3	N	o_{41}	9638	−617.629	939.051	0.774	27	F
o_{10}	4512	9.437	650.072	0.943	7	N	o_{42}	2288	−23.315	140.562	0.537	15	F
o_{11}	2306	1.124	416.101	0.898	17	N	o_{43}	1348	36.313	129.217	0.638	8	F
o_{12}	3160	33.75	131.091	0.898	8	N	o_{44}	8450	−48.734	132.447	1.826	37	F
o_{13}	2699	−109.133	605.054	0.636	61	N	o_{45}	10251	−15.286	840.370	1.260	27	F
o_{14}	11905	5.838	16.934	1.830	14	N	o_{46}	2794	−24.984	95.862	0.828	7	F
o_{15}	6329	24.392	110.682	1.488	30	N	o_{47}	12496	−5.273	145.814	0.323	21	F
o_{16}	1967	7.936	1203.368	1.005	7	N	o_{48}	12215	−2.075	71.784	1.869	106	F
o_{17}	1945	−9.224	64.333	0.961	46	N	o_{49}	16681	−10.152	9801.852	0.376	6	F
o_{18}	10693	6.189	15.579	1.047	23	N	o_{50}	2295	−36.599	128.685	0.347	16	F
o_{19}	3717	15.491	21.621	1.130	27	N	o_{51}	1734	−1.688	285.398	0.559	5	F
o_{20}	13259	14.225	190.704	0.598	5	N	o_{52}	13692	21.692	65.545	1.388	10	F
o_{21}	1506	14.088	1279.092	1.034	28	N	o_{53}	9664	4.459	448.607	0.470	3	F
o_{22}	11875	21.637	198.981	0.837	33	N	o_{54}	10614	24.272	34.229	1.624	17	F
o_{23}	4010	16.289	147.596	0.827	10	N	o_{55}	7562	6.027	36.662	0.435	28	F
o_{24}	13352	2.628	100.161	0.766	37	N	o_{56}	3162	−3.246	199.779	0.877	25	F
o_{25}	2631	−19.744	100.363	0.565	7	N	o_{57}	6026	−4.926	85.098	1.352	48	F
o_{26}	1372	10.422	16.076	1.515	25	N	o_{58}	5740	2.146	117.621	0.626	40	F
o_{27}	5569	4.260	127.225	1.251	4	N	o_{59}	12483	−4.215	96.075	0.970	21	F
o_{28}	15575	3.366	96.175	0.900	28	N	o_{60}	9962	−23.109	104.097	0.848	14	F
o_{29}	1938	6.711	402.578	0.602	5	N	o_{61}	4287	−13.158	420.350	0.752	34	F
o_{30}	4659	−5.030	160.010	0.559	18	N	o_{62}	1793	−35.594	168.415	1.092	33	F
o_{31}	2752	5.539	345.843	0.627	13	N	o_{63}	7192	5.330	1129.588	0.811	2	F
o_{32}	15836	−22.908	791.917	0.701	10	N	o_{64}	2077	5.274	116.950	0.718	36	F

continued on following page

Table 8. continued

Comp	SALES	ROCE	GEAR	LIQD	AGE	Class
o_{65}	16569	−50.122	84.825	0.523	46	F
o_{66}	11191	−26.574	5527.778	0.534	5	F
o_{67}	7844	44.088	50.253	0.882	22	F
o_{68}	2524	0.374	324.783	0.536	14	F
o_{69}	10335	−66.614	1311.225	0.827	38	F
o_{70}	2702	2.403	158.505	0.652	3	F
o_{71}	2570	−17.770	162.857	1.287	28	F
o_{72}	2107	−43.857	75.314	0.753	24	F

Comp	SALES	ROCE	GEAR	LIQD	AGE	Class
o_{73}	3320	27.488	90.469	0.876	2	F
o_{74}	2609	17.823	202.800	1.888	9	F
o_{75}	2339	−21.999	1119.882	0.420	13	F
o_{76}	2544	−21.482	276.498	0.686	34	F
o_{77}	11100	19.179	94.463	0.465	19	F
o_{78}	12042	24.381	267.148	0.732	4	F
o_{79}	3122	−67.370	214.942	0.638	47	F
o_{80}	1097	3.414	29.252	0.648	9	F

Chapter X
Application of Fuzzy Optimization in Forecasting and Planning of Construction Industry

P. Vasant
Universiti Teknologi Petronas, Malaysia

N. Barsoum
Curtin University of Technology, Malaysia

C. Kahraman
Istanbul Technical University, Turkey

G. M. Dimirovski
Dogus University, Turkey

ABSTRACT

This chapter proposes a new method to obtain optimal solution using satisfactory approach in uncertain environments. The optimal solution is obtained by using possibilistic linear programming approach and intelligent computing by MATLAB®. The optimal solution for profit function, index quality, and worker satisfaction index in the construction industry is considered. Decision makers and implementers tabulate the final possibilistic and realistic outcome for objective functions with respect to level of satisfaction and vagueness for forecasting and planning. When the decision maker finds the optimum parameters with acceptable degrees of satisfaction, the decision makes can apply the confidence of gaining much profit in terms of helping the public with high quality and low cost products. The proposed fuzzy membership function allows the implementer to find a better arrangement for the equipments in the production line to fulfill the wanted products in an optimum way.

INTRODUCTION

In this chapter, a methodology for possibilistic linear programming (PLP) is discussed and a formulation of a new modified s-curve membership function is investigated (Vasant, 2004, 2006; Vasant & Barsoum, 2006). This modified S-curve membership function is a modified form of logistic membership function (Watada, 1997). It is ensured that this proposed S-curve membership function is flexible in applying to construction industry problems (Petrovic-Lazarevic & Abraham, 2003). It was found that the proposed S-curve membership function is one among useful membership functions such as linear, exponential, hyperbolic, and hyperbolic inverse (Watada, 1997). This S-curve membership function will be used in this chapter to represent the possible objective function, the technical coefficient, and the resource variable occurring in PLP problems. Since these parameters represent profit, index quality, worker satisfaction index, capacity of the concrete plant, and man hours, the S-curve membership function is very much suitable to apply in construction industry problem in manufacturing plant.

As mentioned by Watada (1997), trapezoidal membership function will have some difficulties such as degeneration while solving linear programming problems. In order to solve the issue of degeneration, we should employ a nonlinear logistic function such as a tangent hyperbolic, which has asymptotes at 1 and 0 (Leberling, 1981).

Possibilistic programming models are robust and flexible. Decision makers and implementers consider the existing preferences under given uncertain constraints, but also develop new preferences by considering all possible outcomes (Lai & Hwang, 1993).

The transitional step towards possibilistic criteria models is a model that has some possible value. Some of these models are a linear mathematical formulation of multiple objective decision making presented by mainly crisp and some possible values. Many authors studied such models (Bellman & Zadeh, 1970; Inuiguchi & Ramik, 2000). Bellman and Zadeh (1970) and Zimmermann (1978, 1991) offered most powerful methodology for possibilistic programming models in an uncertain environment.

The membership functions can be any nondecreasing functions for maximization objectives and nonincreasing functions for maximizing objectives such as linear, exponential, and hyperbolic. Lai and Hwang (1993) and Petrovic-Lazarevic and Abraham (2003) assume linear membership functions since the other nonlinear membership functions can be transformed into linear forms. Triangular function (Varela, 2003) is for the simple reasons. According to Watada (1997), it is possible that the nonlinear membership functions change shape according to the parameter values. A decision maker is then able to apply his strategy to a possibilistic programming problems using these parameters. Therefore, the nonlinear membership function is much more convenient and flexible than the linear ones. Carlsson and Korhonen (1986) used the exponential form of membership function which is not as restrictive as the linear form but flexible enough to describe the vagueness in the parameter. Therefore in this chapter the modified S-curve membership is used to capture the vagueness in the possible parameter of resource variables.

The main goal of a possibilistic solution approach is to find the solution or the alternative decision that better satisfies and suites a situation that occurs in an uncertain environment. This is an attractive technique because it allows a finding near optimal solutions without high computational effort, and it is relatively simple to implement and manipulate its parameters. Here the focus is on the construction of modified S-curve membership function and solving possibilistic optimization problems.

Business decisions relate to future events. They influence the future business success of an organization. Business decisions must be continuously revised. The model of multiple objective decision making, based on fuzzy optimization, seems to apply when continuous business decision making revisions are used. The linear mathematical formulation of multiple objective decision making of Petroviv-Lazarevic and Abraham (2003) might be implemented in a decision making process in the construction industry. That is the fuzzy parameters of linear programming are modeled by preference-based membership functions. These functions represent subjective degrees of satisfaction or degrees of optimalities or feasibilities within a given tolerance. The membership functions are similar to utility functions. They are determined by subjective judgment. This chapter deals with Petrovic-Lazarevic and Abharam's (2003) model of multiple objective decision-makings. The first part of the chapter explains the modified version of the model itself in construction industry circumstances by using a fuzzy satisfactory approach. The second part gives an example that illustrates the improvement of business decision-making when it is supported by computational intelligent technology. The chapter ends with conclusions and future research directions.

MODIFIED S-CURVE MEMBERSHIP FUNCTION

The S-curve membership function is a particular case of the logistic function with specific values of B, C, and α, as in equation (1). These values are found in Vasant (2006) and Bhattacharya and Vasant (2007). This logistic function is indicated as S-shaped membership function by Gonguen (1969) and Zadeh (1971).

The modified S-curve membership function was defined as follows:

$$\mu(x) = \begin{cases} 1 & x < x^a \\ 0.999 & x = x^a \\ \dfrac{B}{1 + Ce^{\alpha\left(\frac{x-x^a}{x^b-x^a}\right)}} & x^a < x < x^b \\ 0.001 & x = x^b \\ 0 & x > x^b \end{cases} \quad (1)$$

where μ is the degree of membership function. The values for B = 1, C = 001001001, and α = 13.8135.

PROPOSED SYSTEM MODEL

A possibilistic linear program can be stated as:

$$Maximize \quad \sum_{j=1}^{n} c_j x_j \quad (2)$$

$$subject\ to \quad \sum_{i=1}^{m}\sum_{j=1}^{n} a_{ij} x_j \le \hat{b}_i$$

where, $\hat{b}_i$ be uncertain with possibilistic membership function (Jamison & Lodwick, 2002). The index n represents number of variables and m the number of constraints.

Since b_i is the possible resource variable, it is denoted by $\hat{b}_i$. Equation (3) is derived in Vasant and Bhattacharya (2007). Therefore

$$\hat{b}_i\Big|_{\mu=\varpi_{b_i}} = b_i^a + \left(\frac{b_i^b - b_i^a}{\alpha}\right)\ln\frac{1}{C}\left(\frac{B}{\mu_{b_i}}-1\right) \quad (3)$$

Equation (3) substituted in to equation (2) to form an equivalent parametric programming, while $\mu \in [0, 1]$ is a parameter (Vasant, 2003). Thus, the possibilistic linear programming problem given by equation (2) can be equivalent to a crisp parametric linear programming problem. It is noted that for each μ, one can have an optimal solution, so the solution with μ grade of membership is actually possible value. Thus with transformation of another parameter $\phi = 1 - \mu$ which represents a level of satisfaction, one can provide the decision-maker a solution table with different ϕ in [0, 1]. The level of satisfaction ϕ is also provided in the form of percentage (%).

Using equations (1) and (2) the formulation (2) is made equivalent to:

$$Max \quad \sum_{j=1}^{n} c_j \, x_j$$

Subject to

$$\sum_{i=1}^{m} a_{ij} x_j \leq b_i^a + \left[\frac{b_i^b - b_i^a}{\alpha} \right] \ln \frac{1}{C} \left[\frac{B}{\mu_{b_i}} - 1 \right]$$

$$where \quad \hat{x}_j \geq 0, \quad j = 1, 2, 3, \ldots, n, \quad 0 < \mu_{b_i} < 1, \quad \alpha = 13.8135.$$

(4)

SOLVING POSSIBILISTIC OPTIMIZATION PROBLEMS

In general, the process of solving a possibilistic optimization problem consists of the following steps.

1. Depend on the problem type, formulate it in the form of a linear programming problem or in the form of a multi-objective problem or even as a nonlinear programming problem.
2. If we intend to optimize the objectives function, define their objectives and formulate the mathematical model for the problems.
3. Select the membership function to represent the possibilistic of any parameter and coefficients such as, triangular, sinusoidal, trapezoidal, or others.
4. Define the membership functions with the necessary parameters for the preference value and tolerances.
5. Define thresholds for the allowable degree of the deviation (violation) in the constraints satisfaction.
6. Solve the problem with an approach algo-

rithm and method (Linear Programming with MATLAB® Tool Box Optimization and Parametric Programming).

7. Provide the solution in the form of Figures and Tables to the decision makers for implementation of solutions.

Formulation of Problem Statement

The operations of a concrete manufacturing plant, which produces and transports concrete to buildings sites, have been analyzed (Petrovic-Lazarevic & Abraham, 2003). Fresh concrete is produced at a central concrete plant and transported by seven transit mixers over the distance of between 1500-3000 m (depending on the location of the construction site) to the three construction sites. Three concrete pumps and eleven interior vibrators are used for delivering, placing and consolidating the concrete at each construction site. Table 1 illustrates the manufacturing capacities of the plant, operational capacity of the concrete mixer, interior vibrator, pumps, and manpower requirement at the three construction sites. A quick analysis will reveal the complexity of the variables and constraints of this concrete production plant and delivery system. The plant decision maker's task is to optimize the profit by utilizing the maximum plant capacity while meeting the three construction site's concrete and other resource requirement through flexible schedule.

Multi Objective Formulations

The best possible outcome of any decision model will directly depend on the formulation of the objective function, taking into account all the influential factors. The final objective functions have been modeled taking into account three independent factors: (1) profit expressed as $/m^3, (2) index of work quality (performance), and (3) worker satisfaction.

Table 1. Concrete plant capacity and construction site's resource demands

	Concrete plant	Site A	Site B	Site C	Remarks
Plant capacity	60m³/h 2520m³ (weekly)				200 m³ (tolerance)
Transit mixers (total=7)		8.45 m³/h	9.26 m³/h	7.26 m³/h	Operated by 7 workers
Concrete pumps (total=3)		16 m³/h	22 m³/h	26 m³/h	Operated by 6 workers
Interior vibrators (total=11)		4.0m³/h			
Worker requirement	5	6	7	9	
Minimal concrete requirement (tolerance)		14.0 m³/h 588 m³/week (47m³)	18.0 m³/h 756 m³/week (60 m³)	21.5 m³/h 903 m³/week (72 m³)	
	Weekly values are based on 42 working hours/week				

Table 2. Modeling profit as an objective

	Site A	Site B	Site C
Expected profit(AU$/m³)	12	10	11

Profit: *The expressed profit as related to the volume of concrete to be manufactured is modeled as the first objective and is shown in Table 2. The minimal expected profit as a possible value is z_1 = AU$ 27,000 per week with tolerance, p_1 = AU$ 2,100.*

Index of Quality

Equal to, or sometimes more important than, the profit, quality plays an important role in every industry. The model for the index quality at construction sites given as the second objective. The index is ranged from 5 points/m³ (bad) quality to 10 points/m³ (excellent) quality and

Table 3. Modeling index of quality as an objective

	Site A	Site B	Site C
Index of quality	9	10	7.5

Table 4. Modeling worker satisfaction as an objective

	Site A	Site B	Site C
Worker satisfaction index	8	7	9

the assigned values are shown in Table 3. The minimal expected total weekly number of points for quality, as possible value, is z_2 = 21400 with tolerance, p_2 = 1700 points.

Worker Satisfaction Index

The index of worker satisfaction is modeled as the third objective and is ranged from 5 to 10 points per m³ of produced, transported, and placed concrete. The assigned values are depicted in Table 4. The minimal expected total weekly number of points as a possible value is z_3 = 18000 with tolerance, p_3 = 1400.

Optimization of Objective Function

The main purpose of this chapter is to find the optimal value for the objective function respect to vagueness and level of satisfaction. The second purpose is to obtain the actual quantities of concrete which have to be delivered to Site A, B, and C respectively. Third is to utilize the idle resource variables in the labor hour manpower of the concrete plant. According to problem requirements and available data (Petrovic-Lazarevic & Abraham, 2003), the objective functions can be modeled as follows (Parra, Tero, & Rodrfguez Una, 1999):

Max $z_1 = 12x_1 + 10x_2 + 11x_3$ with tolerance, $p_1 = 2100$ (profit)

Max $z_2 = 9x_1 + 10x_2 + 7.5x_3$ with tolerance, $p_2 = 1700$ (index of quality)

Max $z_3 = 8x_1 + 7x_2 + 9x_3$ with tolerance, $p_3 = 1400$ (worker satisfaction index)

$x_1 + x_2 + x_3$ $(\leq, \wedge)$ 2520 with tolerance $d_1 = 200$ (weekly capacity of the concrete plant)

$0.12x_1 + 0.11x_2 + 0.14x_3 (\leq, \wedge)$ 7x42=294 h, tolerance $d_2 = 23$ h (weekly engagement of 7 transit mixers, taking into account of their working capacity)

$0.06x_1 + 0.05x_2 + 0.04x_3$ $(\leq, \wedge)$ 3x42=126 h, tolerance $d_3 = 10$ h (weekly engagement of 3 concrete pumps)

$6x_1 + 7x_2 + 9x_3$ $(\leq, \wedge)$ 22x42=924, tolerance $d_4 = 74$. (weekly engagement of 22 workers for interior delivering, placing and consolidating concrete at sites A, B and C)

Minimal weekly requests for concrete from three construction sites:

Site A, $x_1 \geq 588$ m^3, tolerance $d_5 = 47$m^3
Site B, $x_2 \geq 756$ m^3, tolerance $d_6 = 60$m^3
Site C, $x_3 \geq 903$ m^3, tolerance $d_7 = 72$ m^3

These constraints written in full as:

$x_1 + x_2 + x_3$ $(<, \wedge)$ 2520
$0.12x_1 + 0.11x_2 + 0.14x_3$ $(<, \wedge)$ 294
$0.06x_1 + 0.05x_2 + 0.04x_3$ $(<, \wedge)$ 126
$0.10x_1 + 0.117x_2 + 0.15x_3$ $(<, \wedge)$ 924
$x_1 (>, \wedge) 588$ $\quad x_2 (>, \wedge)$ 756 $\quad x_3 (>, \wedge)$ 903

The symbols p_1, p_2, and p_3 are to represent the minimum and maximum range for the objective function z_1, z_2, and z_3 in equation (2) and (4). The symbol d_1, d_2, d_3, and d_4 are to represent the lowest and largest value for the b_i variable in equation (2). Furthermore d_5, d_6, and d_7 are to represent the lowest and largest value for the $\hat{x}_j$ of decision variables in equation (4). The symbol $(<, \wedge)$ is to represent the less than inequality and the possible values for the minimum and maximum respectively.

By using the parametric linear programming technique, we will be able to solve the above equations using MATLAB® optimization computational toolbox. We implemented the problem in MATLAB® and executed it in a Windows 2000, Pentium II Machine. The obtained results are summarized in Tables and Figures in 2D and 3D.

COMPUTATIONAL RESULTS

The result in Table 5, 6, 7, and 8 are obtained for the modified s-curve membership function with $\alpha = 13.8135$.

Membership value μ, level of satisfaction ϕ, z_1 expected profit, z_2 total index of quality, and z_3 total worker satisfaction index.

The outcome of optimal solution for profit function z_1 is given in Table 5 for the modified S-curve membership with $\alpha = 13.8135$. The profit z_1 values are decreasing as membership values increase. The total index of quality z_2 and the total worker satisfaction index z_3 are decreasing as membership value μ increases.

The result for the actual use of weekly capacity of the concrete plant b_1, weekly engagement

Table 5. Optimal value of z_1, z_2 and z_3

μ	φ	z_1	z_2	z_3
0.10	99.90	26301	21048	19567
5.09	94.91	25753	20608	19151
10.08	89.92	25651	20527	19074
15.07	84.93	25588	20476	19026
20.06	79.94	25540	20438	18990
25.05	74.95	25501	20406	18960
30.04	69.96	25466	20379	18933
35.03	64.97	25435	20353	18910
40.02	59.98	25405	20330	18887
45.01	54.99	25377	20307	18866
50.00	50.00	25350	20285	18845
54.99	45.01	25322	20263	18824
59.98	40.02	25294	20240	18803
64.97	35.03	25265	20217	18780
69.96	30.04	25233	20192	18757
74.95	25.05	25199	20164	18730
79.94	20.06	25159	20132	18700
84.93	15.07	25112	20094	18664
89.92	10.08	25048	20043	18616
94.91	5.09	24947	19962	18539
99.99	0.10	24399	19522	18123

μ *and* φ *are given in terms of percentage*

Table 6. Actual b_i used

μ %	b_1	b_2	b_3	b_4
0.10	2407	296	113	302
5.09	2357	290	111	296
10.08	2348	289	110	295
15.07	2342	288	110	294
20.06	2338	287	110	294
25.05	2334	287	110	293
30.04	2331	287	109	293
35.03	2328	286	109	293
40.02	2325	286	109	292
45.01	2323	286	109	292
50.00	2320	285	109	292
54.99	2318	285	109	291
59.98	2315	285	109	291
64.97	2313	284	109	291
69.96	2310	284	108	290
74.95	2307	284	108	290
79.94	2303	283	108	289
84.93	2299	283	108	289
89.92	2293	282	108	288
94.91	2284	281	107	287
99.99	2233	275	105	281

of seven transit mixers b_2, weekly engagement of three concrete pumps b_3, and weekly engagement of 22 workers for interior delivering, placing, and consolidating concrete b_4 are displayed in the Table 6. The actual quantities of concrete (x_1, x_2, x_3) used is given in Table 7. These results are very useful in making the system become a high productive system in decision making and planning.

Membership value μ % = degree of possibility and it's given in terms of percentage.

Membership value μ %, b_1 actual weekly capacity of the concrete plant, b_2 actual weekly engagement of seven transit mixers, b_3 actual weekly engagement of three concrete pumps, and b_4 actual weekly engagement of 22 workers for interior delivering, placing, and consolidating concrete.

Membership value μ % = degree of possibility and it's given in terms of percentage.

The optimal solution for profit function with respect to vagueness and level of satisfaction is provided in Table 8. In Table 8, we analyze the profit function for selected vagueness and level of satisfaction. The result shows that the profit function z_1 increases as α and φ increases. It is possible to compute the realistic possible outcome for the profit function using the expected value and the definition in the probability theory (Heshmaty & Kandel, 1985; Sudkamp, 1992). The computed results are shown in the Table 8. Moreover it is also possible to find the crisp value for the profit function z_1 and the range for vagueness α and level of satisfaction φ respectively. The precise value for α and φ can be obtained by the decision

Table 7. Actual quantities of concrete used

μ	x_1	x_2	x_3
0.10	635	816	975
5.09	621	799	954
10.08	619	796	950
15.07	617	794	948
20.06	616	792	946
25.05	615	791	945
30.04	614	790	943
35.03	614	789	942
40.02	613	788	941
45.01	612	787	940
50.00	612	786	939
54.99	611	785	938
59.98	610	784	937
64.97	609	783	936
69.96	609	782	935
74.95	608	781	933
79.94	607	780	932
84.93	606	778	930
89.92	604	776	928
94.91	602	773	924
99.99	588	756	903

Figure 1. Optimal z_1^* for various α

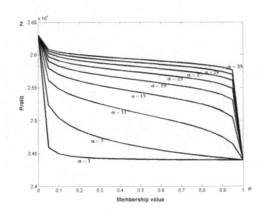

maker through heuristically and experientially. $z_{i\ poss}^*$ = Optimal possible crisp value. The possible crisp outcome for profit value is $z_{1\ poss}^* = 25488.71$. The range for the possible vagueness and level of satisfaction are $15 \leq \alpha_{poss} \leq 19$ and $40\% \leq \phi_{poss} \leq 50\%$, respectively. The above result is possible realistic outcomes in the uncertain environment where vagueness parameter α determines the influential factors in the given model. This result is compared with Petrovic-Lazarevic and Abraham (2003). The optimal profit z_1 obtained by Petrovic-Lazarevic and Abraham (2003) is 26,199 at coefficient of satisfaction 0.996.

Level of satisfaction ϕ %, vagueness α, profit z_1^*, α_{poss} = possible vagueness and ϕ_{poss} = possible level of satisfaction. Expected value of $z_1^* = E(z_1^*)$

$$= \sum_{i=1}^{10} z_i \Pr(z_i) = 24400\,(0.0958) + 24464\,(0.0960) +$$

$24967\,(0.0980) + 25374\,(0.0996) + 25609\,(0.1005)$
$+ 25763\,(0.1011) + 25874\,(0.1016) + 25962\,(0.1019)$
$+ 26044\,(0.1022) + 26301\,(\ 0.1032) = 25488.71$

The possible crisp outcome for total index of quality is $z_{2\ poss}^* = 20435.7$. The range for the possible vagueness and level of satisfaction are $15 \leq \alpha_{poss} \leq 19$ and $40\% \leq \phi_{poss} \leq 50\%$ respectively. This solution is comparable with Petrovic-Lazarevic and Abraham (2003), 21,130 at $\phi = 0.996$.

The possible crisp outcome for total worker satisfaction index is $z_{3\ poss}^* = 18949.72$. The range for the possible vagueness and level of satisfaction are $15 \leq \alpha_{poss} \leq 19$ and $40\ \% \leq \phi_{poss} \leq 50\ \%$ respectively. This solution is comparable with Petrovic-Lazarevic and Abraham (2003) 19,259 at $\phi = 0.998$.

DISCUSSION AND SUMMARY

The developed algorithm will also help the decision maker to vary the values of the coefficients ϕ in the interval [0, 1] and to obtain the corresponding optimal values of profit with corresponding values of possibility. After through analysis of the optimal values of the objective functions

Table 8. Profit for various vagueness and level of satisfaction

z_1^*	Vagueness α									
$\phi\%$	3	7	11	15	19	23	27	31	35	39
0.10	24399	24399	24399	24399	24399	24399	24399	24399	24399	24397
5.09	24399	24414	24645	25052	25315	25486	25607	25696	25765	25820
10.08	24400	24430	24751	25147	25389	25548	25659	25742	25806	25857
15.07	24401	24447	24822	25205	25436	25586	25692	25771	25831	25879
20.06	24402	24464	24878	25249	25471	25615	25717	25792	25850	25896
25.05	24403	24483	24925	25286	25499	25639	25737	25810	25866	25910
30.04	24404	24503	24967	25318	25525	25660	25755	25825	25879	25923
35.03	24405	24525	25005	25347	25547	25678	25771	25839	25892	25934
40.02	24407	24548	25041	25374	25569	25696	25786	25852	25903	25944
45.01	24408	24573	25075	25400	25589	25713	25800	25865	25915	25954
50.00	24411	24600	25109	25425	25609	25730	25814	25877	25925	25964
54.99	24413	24630	25143	25450	25629	25746	25828	25889	25936	25974
59.98	24417	24663	25178	25476	25650	25763	25843	25902	25947	25984
64.97	24421	24700	25215	25503	25671	25781	25858	25915	25959	25994
69.96	24426	24743	25254	25532	25694	25800	25874	25929	25971	26005
74.95	24434	24794	25297	25564	25719	25820	25891	25944	25985	26017
79.94	24445	24855	25346	25600	25748	25844	25912	25962	26001	26031
84.93	24463	24934	25406	25644	25783	25873	25936	25983	26019	26048
89.92	24498	25045	25485	25703	25828	25911	25968	26011	26044	26071
94.91	24592	25232	25613	25796	25902	25972	26020	26057	26085	26107
99.99	26301	26301	26301	26301	26301	26301	26301	26301	26301	26301

Level of satisfaction $\phi\%$ and z_1^* (Profit); the ϕ is given in terms of percentage.

Table 9. z_1^*, z_2^*, z_3^* for selected α and $\phi\%$

$\phi\%$	α	z_1^*	z_2^*	z_3^*
10.08	3	24400	19523	18125
20.06	7	24464	19575	18173
30.04	11	24967	19978	18554
40.02	15	25374	20304	18863
50.00	19	25609	20493	19042
59.98	23	25763	20617	19159
69.96	27	25874	20706	19243
79.94	31	25962	20776	19310
89.92	35	26044	20843	19372
99.99	39	26301	21043	19567

The ϕ given in terms of percentage.

Table 10. Possible optimal profit z_1^*

z_1^*	$Pr(z_1^*)$	$z_1^* \, Pr(z_1^*)$
24400	0.0958	2337.52
24464	0.0960	2348.54
24967	0.0980	2446.77
25374	0.0996	2527.25
25609	0.1005	2573.70
25763	0.1011	2604.64
25874	0.1016	2628.80
25962	0.1019	2645.53
26044	0.1022	2661.70
26301	0.1032	2714.26
254758	$E(z_1^*) = 25488.71$	

Table 11. Possible optimal value z_2^*

z_2^*	$Pr(z_2^*)$	$z_2^* Pr(z_2^*)$
19523	0.0958	1870.30
19574	0.0980	1918.25
19978	0.0980	1957.84
20304	0.0996	2022.28
20493	0.1005	2059.55
20617	0.1011	2084.38
20706	0.1016	2103.73
20776	0.1019	2117.07
20843	0.1022	2130.15
21048	0.1032	2172.15
203862	$E(z_2^*) = 20435.7$	

Table 12. Possible optimal value z_3^*

z_3^*	$Pr(z_3^*)$	$z_3^* Pr(z_3^*)$
18125	0.0957	1734.56
18173	0.0960	1744.61
18554	0.0980	1818.29
18863	0.0996	1878.75
19042	0.1005	1913.72
19159	0.1012	1938.89
19243	0.1016	1955.09
19310	0.1020	1969.62
19343	0.1021	1974.92
19567	0.1033	2021.27
189379	$E(z_3^*) = 18949.72$	

Table 13. Range of φ_{poss} and α_{poss} for z_{iposs}^*

i	z_i^*	α_i	$\phi_i\%$
1	25488.71	[15,19]	[40,50]
2	20435.70	[15,19]	[40,50]
3	18949.72	[15,19]	[40,50]

ϕ_{poss} *is given in terms of percentage.*

and the various constraints, very often expert problem domain knowledge and experience will be required to understand the possibility of the achieved results.

Table 13 provides the possible range for ϕ_{poss} and α_{poss} with respect to possible realistic outcome for z_i^*.

CONCLUSION AND FUTURE WORK

Forecasting and planning processes that support organizing industrial activities, being subject to uncertain data and heuristic judgments, can be explained by the possibilistic approach of the multiple objective criteria models. The analysis and modeling of the construction industry problem discussed in this chapter is based on both linear objective functions and constraints in the form of nonlinear membership functions. The results clearly indicate the superiority of the possiblistic approach in terms of best realistic solution for the objective function with respect to vagueness and level of satisfaction. This solution is comparable with the solution of Petrovic-Lazarevic and Abraham (2003). Future research will be on interactive flexible computation techniques using the modified S-curve membership function and dynamic membership function in industry activities other than construction. When the decision maker finds the optimum parameters with acceptable degrees of satisfaction, he can apply the confidence of gaining much profit in terms of helping the public achieve high quality, low cost products. The proposed fuzzy membership function allows the implementer to find a better arrangement for the equipments in the line of production to fulfill the wanted products in an optimum way.

ACKNOWLEDGMENT

The authors would like to sincerely thank the referees for their valuable and constructive comments and suggestions for the improvement of the quality of the chapter.

REFERENCES

Bellman, R.E., & Zadeh, L.A. (1970). Decision making in a fuzzy environment. *Management Science, 17,* 141-164.

Bhattacharya, A., & Vasant, P. (2007). Soft-sensing of level of satisfaction in TOC product-mix decision heuristic using robust fuzzy-LP. *European Journal of Operational Research. 177,* 55-70.

Carlsson, C., & Korhonen, P.A. (1986). Parametric approach to fuzzy linear programming. *Fuzzy Sets and Systems, 20,* 17-30.

Goguen, J.A. (1969). The logic of inexact concepts. *Syntheses, 19,* 325-373.

Heshmaty, B., & Kandel, A. (1985). Fuzzy linear regression and its application to forecasting in uncertain environment. *Fuzzy Sets and Systems, 15,* 159-191.

Inuiguchi, M., & Ramik, J. (2000). Possiblilistic linear programming: A brief review of fuzzy mathematical programming and comparison with stochastic programming in portfolio selection problem. *Fuzzy Sets and Systems, 111,* 3-28.

Jamison, K.D., & Lodwick, W.A. (2002). The construction of consistent possibility and necessity measures. *Fuzzy Sets and Systems, 132,* 1-10.

Lai, T.Y., & Hwang, C.L. (1993). Possibilistic linear programming for managing interest rate risk. *Fuzzy Sets aAnd Systems, 54,* 135-146.

Leberling, H. (1981). On finding compromise solutions in multicriteria problems using the fuzzy min-operator. *Fuzzy Sets and Systems, 6,* 105-118.

Parra, M.A., Terol, A.B., & Rodrfguez Una, M.V. (1999). Theory and methodology solving the multi-objective possiblistic linear programming problem. *European Journal of Operational Research, 117,* 175-182.

Petrovic-Lazarevic, S., & Abraham, A. (2003). Hybrid fuzzy-linear programming approach for multicriteria decision making problems. *International Journal of Neural, Parallel, and Scientific Computations, 11,* 53-68.

Sudkamp, T. (1992). On probability-possibility transformations. *Fuzzy Sets and Systems, 51,* 73-81.

Varela, L.R., & Ribeiro, R.A. (2003). Evaluation of simulated annealing to solve fuzzy optimization problems. *Journal of Intelligent and Fuzzy Systems, 14,* 59-71.

Vasant, P. (2003). Application of fuzzy linear programming in production planning. *Fuzzy Optimization and Decision Making, 3,* 229-241.

Vasant, P. (2004). Industrial production planning using interactive fuzzy linear programming. *International Journal of Computational Intelligence and Applications, 4,* 13-26.

Vasant, P. (2006). Fuzzy decision making of profit function in production planning using s-curve membership function. *Computers & Industrial Engineering, 51,* 715-725.

Vasant, P., & Barsoum, N.N. (2006). Fuzzy optimization of units products in mix-products selection problem using FLP approach. *Soft Computing - A Fusions of Foundation, Methodologies, and Applications, 10,* 140-143.

Vasant, P., & Bhattacharya, A. (2007). Sensing degree of fuzziness in MCDM model using modified flexible s-curve MF. *International Journal of Systems Science, 38,* 279-291.

Watada, J. (1997). Fuzzy portfolio selection and its applications to decision making. *Tatra Mountains Mathematics Publication, 13,* 219-248.

Zadeh, L.A. (1971). Similarity relations and fuzzy orderings. *Information Science, 3,* 177-206.

Zimmermann, H.J. (1978). Fuzzy programming and linear programming with several objective functions. *Fuzzy Sets and Systems, 1,* 45-55.

Zimmermann, H.J. (1991). Fuzzy set theory and its application. Kluwer Academic Publishers.

Chapter XI
Rank Improvement Optimization Using PROMETHEE and Trigonometric Differential Evolution

Malcolm J. Beynon
Cardiff University, UK

ABSTRACT

This chapter investigates the modelling of the ability to improve the rank position of an alternative in relation to those of its competitors. PROMETHEE is one such technique for ranking alternatives based on their criteria values. In conjunction with the evolutionary algorithm trigonometric differential evolution, the minimum changes necessary to the criteria values of an alternative are investigated to allow it to achieve an improved rank position. This investigation is compounded with a comparison of the differing effects of two considered objective functions that measure the previously mentioned minimization. Two data sets are considered. The first concerns the ranking of environmental projects and the second concerns the ranking of brands of a food product. The notion of modelling preference ranks of alternatives and the subsequent improvement of alternative's rank positions is the realism of a stakeholders' appreciation of their alternative in relation to that of their competitors.

INTRODUCTION

In a competitive environment, a stakeholder needs to be aware of the relative position of the alternative (for example, projects or products) in relation to those of their competitors, often accomplished through a comparison of alternatives. To demonstrate, a company knowing the chances of success of its proposed environmental project (Lahdelma, Salminen, & Hokkanen, 2000) and

a manufacturer knowing its product preference ranking in the market place (Lee & O'Mahony, 2005). This ranking is often modelled through a rank ordering of alternatives based on values over a number of different criteria. Regularly considered as a multicriteria decision making problem, a number of techniques facilitating ranking analysis exist. These include ELECTRE (Benayoun, Roy, & Sussmann, 1966; Roy, 1991), TOPSIS (Abo-Sinna & Amer, 2005; Hwang & Yoon, 1981), and

PROMETHEE (Beynon & Wells, 2008; Brans, Mareschal, & Vincke, 1984).

Concentrating in this chapter on the PROMETHEE technique (without loss of generality), it was introduced specifically to rank alternatives as described previously, with the case of the ranking of powerstation projects used in its introduction (Brans, Vincke, & Mareschal, 1986). Further examples of its application include environmental projects (Simon, Brüggemann, & Pudenz, 2004), chemometric performances (Ni, Huang, & Kokot, 2004), and stock trading choices (Albadvi, Chaharsooghi, & Esfahanipour, 2006). In reality, the ranking process identifies winners and losers, namely those stakeholders associated with the alternatives near the top and bottom rank positions. For a stakeholder, PROMETHEE and techniques like it can prepare stakeholders for the ranking results, or, more pertinently here, the findings used to plan ahead to improve their alternative's future rank position.

This notion of pre-emptive planning, using PROMETHEE, is modelled here as a constrained optimisation problem, with the minimum changes found to the criteria values of an alternative to achieve its desired improved rank position (Hyde & Maier, 2006). That is, if the PROMETHEE technique is adopted as an appropriate model for the preferencing of alternatives, these minimum changes are the least necessary to improve an alternative's rank position. Previous applications that consider the uncertainty of rank order and rank improvement of alternatives include water management projects (Hyde & Maier, 2006; Hyde, Maier, & Colby, 2003) and motor vehicles based on chemical emissions (Beynon & Wells, 2008).

The constrained optimisation problem is a regularly researched area (see, for example, Michalewicz, Logan, & Swaminathan, 1994) with the constrained domain, in this case the known ranges of the considered criteria by which the alternatives are described. Here, the identification of the minimum changes in the criteria values of a comparatively lower ranked alternative to

improve its rank position is solved using the evolutionary algorithm, trigonometric differential evolution (TDE) (Fan & Lampinen, 2003). TDE is itself a development on the original differential evolution, which obtains a solution through the augmentation of an interim solution with the difference between two other interim solutions (Storn & Price, 1997).

The appropriateness of the use of TDE is dictated by the objective function employed. In this case two objective functions are considered, taken from Hyde and Maier (2006), namely, Euclidean distance and Manhattan distance. Further, how improving the rank position of an alternative affects the other alternatives considered means further constraints may need to be included within the optimization process beyond a simple minimum distance remit. The employment of TDE here also demonstrates how artificial intelligence can be employed in conjunction with more traditional techniques, such as PROMETHEE, to develop their domain of problem solving.

Underlying this chapter is the general problem of the desire of a stakeholder (project manager, food manufacturer, and so forth), to improve the rank position of alternatives against those of their competitors. Indeed, the requirement for ranking and subsequently rank improvement is present throughout society, including within government, environment, business, and commercial areas, and so forth. The techniques employed here, PROMETHEE and TDE, are without loss of generality to the use of other techniques and issues surrounding ranking and rank improvement. Moreover, it is hoped that this chapter offers a clear benchmark as to how rank position planning can be undertaken and how this can be done optimally.

BACKGROUND

The background described in this chapter is made up of the two contributing techniques that contribute to the ranking and subsequent pre-emptive planning of stakeholders to improve the ranking of their alternative, namely PROMETHEE and trigonometric differential evolution.

The PROMETHEE Technique

PROMETHEE (**P**reference **R**anking **O**rganization **METH**od for **E**nrichment **E**valuation) was introduced in Brans et al. (1984) and Brans et al. (1986) to preference rank a set of decision alternatives based on their values over a number of different criteria. Its introduction was to offer a means of multicriteria decision support characterized by simplicity and clearness to the decision maker (Brans et al., 1986), also considered as having a transparent computational procedure (Georgopoulou, Sarafidis, & Diakoulaki, 1998). Put simply, a ranking of alternatives is established based on the accumulative preference comparisons of pairs of alternatives' values over the different criteria.

More formally, to express the preference structure of alternatives and to withdraw the scaling effects of the K criteria considered ($c_1, ..., c_K$), with PROMETHEE, generalized criterion preference functions are defined $P_k(\cdot, \cdot)$ ($k = 1, ..., K$). Each is a function of the difference between criterion values of pairs of alternatives (from $a_1, ..., a_N$), where $P_k(a_i, a_j) \in [0, 1]$, confers the directed intensity of the preference of alternative a_i over a_j, with respect to a single criterion c_k. The often exposited limiting qualitative interpretations to the $P_k(a_i, a_j)$ values are, according to Brans et al. (1986):

$P_k(a_i, a_j) = 0 \Leftrightarrow a_i$ is not better than a_j with respect to criterion c_k,

$P_k(a_i, a_j) = 1 \Leftrightarrow a_i$ is 'strictly' better than a_j with respect to criterion c_k.

This qualitative interpretation highlights that at least one of the values, $P_k(a_i, a_j)$ and $P_k(a_j, a_i)$,

will be zero, depending on whether a_i or a_j is the more preferred between them. Expressing the $P_k(a_i, a_j)$ by

$$P_k(a_i, a_j) = \begin{cases} \mathrm{H}(d) & a_i - a_j > 0, \\ 0 & a_i - a_j \leq 0, \end{cases}$$

where $a_i - a_j > 0$ and $a_i - a_j \leq 0$ refer to whether a_i or a_j is the more preferred of that criterion (taking into account the direction of preferment of the criterion values), and $d = v(a_i) - v(a_j)$ is the specific difference between the criterion values of a_i and a_j. The extant research studies have worked on the utilization of six types of generalized preference functions for H(d). Their names, labels (also required parameters), and graphical representations are given as (Brans *et al.*, 1986):

I: Usual (-)

II: Quasi (q)

III: Linear preference (p)

IV: Level (p, q)

V: Linear preference and indifference (p, q)

VI: Gaussian (σ)

The graphical representations shown for the generalized preference functions highlight an important point, namely that some of them are continuous (III, V, and VI) and the others not continuous (I, II, and IV), with respect to the $P_k(a_i, a_j)$ value over the $v(a_i) - v(a_j)$ domain. The noncontinuous feature means that small changes to criteria values may mean a dramatic change in the associated preference function values (see later).

The augmentation of the numerical preference values throughout the operation of PROMETHEE is described through the notion of flows. A *criterion flow* $\phi_k(a_i)$ value for an alternative a_i from a criterion c_k can be defined by

$$\phi_k(a_i) = \sum_{a_j \in A} \{P_k(a_i, a_j) - P_k(a_j, a_i)\},$$

where A is the set of N alternatives, a_1, ..., a_N, considered, it follows $-(N-1) \le \phi_k(a_i) \le N-1$ and $\sum_{a_i \in A} \phi_k(a_i) = 0$ (the bounds are due to not normalizing by $(N-1)$ in each case). In words, a criterion flow represents the preference of an alternative over the other $(N-1)$ alternatives, with respect to a single criterion. A subsequent *net flow* $\phi(a_i)$ value is defined by

$$\phi(a_i) = \sum_{k=1}^{K} w_k \phi_k(a_i),$$

where w_k, $k = 1, ..., K$ denote the relative importance of the criterion c_k (the criteria importance weights). The conditions $-(N-1) \le \phi(a_i) \le N-1$ and $\sum_{a_i \in A} \phi(a_i) = 0$ similarly hold for the net flow values (when w_k are normalized so they sum to one). Example calculations of the above expressions are given in Appendix A. The magnitudes of the net flow values subsequently exposit the relevant rank order of the N alternatives considered. The larger an alternative's net flow value, the higher its rank position.

An associated issue recently considered is the uncertainty in this ranking (Hyde et al., 2003), redefined here as the consideration of the rank improvement of those alternatives ranked below the top rank position (Hyde & Maier, 2006). They investigated the possibility of changes to the criteria values of an alternative and the concomitant criteria importance weights, which reversed the ranks of two alternatives. Considering only changes to criteria values and concentrating on the rank improvement of an alternative

a_{r_1}, it is necessary for a change of the r_1^{th} ranked alternative's criteria values so its net flow value is larger than or equal to that of the r_2^{th} ranked, $\phi(a_{r_1}) \ge \phi(a_{r_2})$.

The minimum changes necessary to achieve this is evaluated by minimizing some distance function (d_{r_1,r_2}) between the original and proposed criteria values of the considered alternative. Hyde and Maier (2006) described three such distance functions, two of which are called:

Euclidean distance: $d_{r_1,r_2}^E = \sqrt{\sum_{k=1}^{K} \left(v_{r_1,k}^i - v_{r_1,k}^o\right)^2}$

Manhattan distance: $d_{r_1,r_2}^M = \sum_{k=1}^{K} \left| v_{r_1,k}^i - v_{r_1,k}^o \right|,$

where $v_{r_1,k}^i$ and $v_{r_1,k}^o$ are the initial and optimized criteria values. The changes to the criteria values of the r_1^{th} ranked alternative are kept within known domains, given by $LL_{v,k} \le v_{r_1,k}^o \le UL_{v,k}$, where $[LL_{v,k}, UL_{v,k}]$ is the allowed interval domain of the kth criterion value. With the presence of noncontinuous preference functions, the requirement for $\phi(a_{r_1}) \ge \phi(a_{r_2})$ may not be strong enough. That is, small changes in the proposed criteria values may cause disproportionate changes in the resultant net flow value, so other alternatives may take the desired rank position (since $\sum_{a_i \in A} \phi(a_i)$ =0). A stronger condition is simply that the new $\phi(a_{r_1})$ value affords the desired rank position for the considered alternative.

Trigonometric Differential Evolution

The constrained optimisation problem formulated within the rank improvement analysis using PROMETHEE is solved here using trigonometric differential evolution (TDE) (Fan & Lampinen, 2003; Storn & Price, 1997). The domain of TDE is the continuous space made up of the K criteria domains. For an alternative, its series of criteria values are represented as a point in this continuous space (parameter/target vector). In TDE, a population of NP parameter vectors, $\vec{y_i^G}$, $i = 1$, ..., NP, is considered at each generation G of the progression to an optimum solution, measured through a defined objective function (OB).

Starting with an initial population, TDE generates new parameter vectors by adding to a third member the difference between two other members (this change subject to a crossover operator). If the resulting vector yields a lower OB value then a predetermined population member, it takes its place. More formally, a parameter vector $\vec{y_i^G}$ is made up of the values $y_{i,j}^U, j = 1, ..., K$ in the Gth generation. In the next generation, the possible change in a value $y_{i,j}^G$ to a mutant vector value $z_{i,j}$ is given by

$$z_{i,j} = y_{r_1,j}^G + F(y_{r_2,j}^G - y_{r_3,j}^G), \qquad (1)$$

where $r_1, r_2, r_3 \in [1, NP]$, are integer and mutually different, with $F > 0$ and controls the amplification of the differential variation. This construction of a trial vector $\vec{z_i}$ is elucidated in Figure 1, where an example of two dimensional (X_1, X_2) case is presented.

In Figure 1, the effect of the "vector" difference between $y_{r_2}^G$ and $y_{r_3}^G$ on the constructed mutant vector $\vec{z_i}$ from $y_{r_1}^G$ is elucidated. A further operation takes into account the OB values associated with the three vectors $\vec{y_{r_1}^G}$, $\vec{y_{r_2}^G}$ and $\vec{y_{r_3}^G}$ chosen,

used to perturb the trial vector according to the following formulation;

$$z_{i,j} = (y_{r_1,j}^G + y_{r_2,j}^G + y_{r_3,j}^G)/3 + (p_2 - p_1)(y_{r_1,j}^G - y_{r_2,j}^G)$$
$$+ (p_3 - p_2)(y_{r_2,j}^G - y_{r_3,j}^G) + (p_1 - p_3)(y_{r_3,j}^G - y_{r_1,j}^G),$$

where $p_1 = \text{OB}(\vec{y_{r_1}^G})/p_T$, $p_2 = \text{OB}(\vec{y_{r_2}^G})/p_T$ and $p_3 = \text{OB}(\vec{y_{r_3}^G})/p_T$ with $p_T = \text{OB}(\vec{y_{r_1}^G}) + \text{OB}(\vec{y_{r_2}^G}) + \text{OB}(\vec{y_{r_3}^G})$. This trigonometric operation, on occasions, takes the place of the original mutation, for example, see (1), using a "trigonometric mutation probability" parameter M_t, where a random value less than M_t implies the use of the trigonometric mutation. A crossover operator then combines the mutant vector $z_i = [z_{i,1}, z_{i,2}, ..., z_{i,4n_C}]$ with the target (old) vector $\vec{y_i^G} = [y_{1,j}^G, y_{2,j}^G, ..., y_{i,4n_C}^G]$ into a trial vector $\vec{y_i^T} = [y_{1,j}^T, y_{2,j}^T, ..., y_{i,4n_C}^T]$ according to

$$y_{i,j}^T = \begin{cases} z_{i,j} & \text{If rand}(j) \leq CR, \\ y_{i,j}^G & \text{If rand}(j) > CR, \end{cases}$$

where rand$(j) \in [0, 1]$ is a random value and CR is the defined crossover constant. It follows, if $\text{OB}(\vec{y_i^T}) < \text{OB}(\vec{y_i^G})$ then replacement takes place and the progression continues. The progression of the construction of new generations continues until a satisfactory OB value is achieved. This may mean a required level has been attained or a zero decrease in the OB value is identified (over a number of generations).

MAIN THRUST

The main thrust of this chapter centres on the rank improvement investigations of two real world problems, which illustrate the diverse areas that ranking can be associated with, and the modelling of perceived rank improvement. The first application was presented in Brans et al. (1986), during the introduction of PROMETHEE, and concerns

Figure 1. Example of an OB with contour lines and process for generation of the new vector $\vec{z_i}$

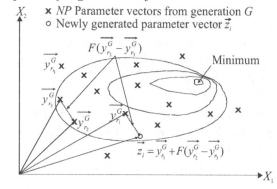

ranking powerstation projects, the second is considered with a general tin food product, namely macaroni cheese, with brand ranking the issue.

Powerstation Data Set

The powerstation data set considered concerns the ranking of six proposed hydroelectric powerstation projects $(a_1, a_2, ..., a_6)$ using the different criteria: c_1 - manpower, c_2 - power (MW), c_3 - construction cost (10^9 \$), c_4 - maintenance cost (10^6 \$), c_5 - number of villages to extract, and c_6 - security level (see Table 1). Since this data set was used to introduce PROMETHEE, it allows the concomitant literature to be used as a benchmark for the results presented here.

The information in Table 1 reports the criteria values for each alternative (project), as well as the necessary parameters for the specific generalized preference function used for each criterion (I, II, etc.), and the associated direction of improved preference (Min. or Max.). Furthermore, without loss of generality, all of the six criteria were considered of equal importance ($w_i = 1/6$, $i = 1$, ..., 6). The functions and parameters are factors pertinent to PROMETHEE. Importantly these include continuous and noncontinuous functions (certain step functions in the case of the latter), which infer the possibility of dramatic changes to the preference of one alternative over another through small differences in the respective criterion values.

Employing PROMETHEE on the powerstation data set, the criterion flow values over the different criteria and subsequent net flow values for each alternative can be evaluated (see Table 2).

Table 2 reports the necessary criterion and net flow values used to rank the six powersta-

Table 1. Details of powerstation data set (Brans et al., 1986)

Criteria	Min. or Max.	Alternatives						Function	Parameters
		a_1	a_2	a_3	a_4	a_5	a_6		
c_1	Min.	80	65	83	40	52	94	II	$q = 10$
c_2	Max.	90	58	60	80	72	96	III	$p = 30$
c_3	Min.	6	2	4	10	6	7	V	$p = 5, q = 0.5$
c_4	Min.	5.4	9.7	7.2	7.5	2.0	3.6	IV	$p = 6, q = 1$
c_5	Min.	8	1	4	7	3	5	I	-
c_6	Max.	5	1	7	10	5	6	VI	$\sigma = 5$

Table 2. Criterion and net flow values for powerstation project alternatives

Criterion flow	a_1	a_2	a_3	a_4	a_5	a_6
$\phi_1(a_i)$	−2.0000	1.0000	−2.0000	5.0000	3.0000	−5.0000
$\phi_2(a_i)$	2.7333	−3.2667	−3.0000	0.8000	−0.8000	3.5333
$\phi_3(a_i)$	−0.2222	3.8889	1.8889	−4.1111	−0.2222	−1.2222
$\phi_4(a_i)$	0.5000	−3.5000	−1.0000	−1.0000	3.0000	2.0000
$\phi_5(a_i)$	−5.0000	5.0000	1.0000	−3.0000	3.0000	−1.0000
$\phi_6(a_i)$	−0.3810	−2.6074	0.4254	1.7110	0.8092	0.0427
$\phi(a_i)$	−0.7283	0.0858	−0.4476	−0.1000	1.4645	−0.2744
Rank	6	2	5	3	1	4

tion project alternatives (see Appendix A, for a demonstration of the construction of criterion flow values). The evaluated net flow values ($\phi(a_i)$) are the same as presented in Brans et al. (1986), with the subsequently identified rank order also shown in Table 2, which identifies the projects a_5 and a_1 as top (1st) and bottom (6th) ranked, respectively.

If these results were a provisional comparison of the projects, the stakeholder associated with the top ranked project a_5 would be content, but the other projects' stakeholders would need to consider how, if possible/allowed, they could improve their project's rank position. Considering the bottom (6th) ranked project a_1, its potential for rank improvement could be to any of the five higher rank positions (5th to 1st). It follows, five different sets of proposed minimum changes to its criteria values are needed to be identified that will purport the desired rank improvements (similar changes could be identified to improve the other non-top ranked projects). The identified changes would then form the focus for the planned rank improvement of this project.

To identify a set of minimum changes to the criteria values, the TDE-based optimisation is run, using the parameters, amplification control $F = 0.99$, crossover constant $CR = 0.85$, trigonometric mutation probability $M_t = 0.05$, and number of parameter vectors $NP = 50$. The two sets of results presented are dependent on which of the distance-based objective functions are utilized to quantify the achieved optimizations.

Euclidean Distance

Using the Euclidean distance ($d^E_{r1,r2}$)-based objective function, the technical details of the progressive improvement of the bottom placed project a_1 are reported. This commences with a presentation of the net flow values of the six projects, while the rank position of the a_1 project is improved (see Figure 2).

The results in Figure 2 show the progressive changes in the net flow values associated with the six projects due to the successive rank improvement of the project a_1 (originally bottom placed 6th). On the left hand side, the first column of values is a graphical representation of the original net flow values reported in Table 2, this graph shows the relative positions of the projects in the rank order also presented in Table 2. That is, the top ranked project a_5 is considerably away from the other projects based on their net flow values. This information clearly illustrates the lost reality when presented solely with a rank order, rather than any actual values used to identify such a ranking.

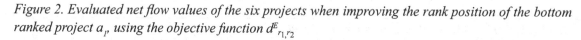

Figure 2. Evaluated net flow values of the six projects when improving the rank position of the bottom ranked project a_1, using the objective function $d^E_{r1,r2}$

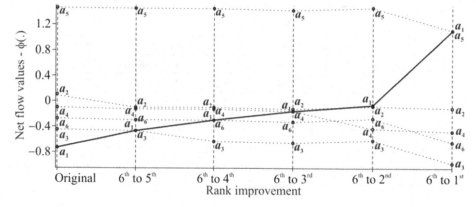

Table 3. Proposed changes to criteria values of project a_1 to achieve improved rank positions

Criterion flow	c1	c2	c3	c4	c5	c6
6th	80.000	90.000	6.000	5.400	8.000	5.000
6th = 5th	75.000	91.053	5.577	5.400	8.000	5.213
6th = 4th	73.000	91.478	5.606	5.400	8.000	5.187
6th = 3rd	73.000	92.828	5.043	5.400	8.000	5.412
6th = 2nd	73.000	90.000	6.000	5.400	7.000	5.000
6th = 1st	73.000	92.328	5.324	5.400	3.000	5.314

In Figure 2, from left to right, the positions of the circles representing the net flow values of the project a_1 progressively show it moving up in rank order. To complement this increase in the net flow values of the project a_1, the respective net flow values of certain projects are moving down, a consequence of the sum of net flow values required to equal zero ($\sum_{a_i \in A} \phi(a_i) = 0$ constraint shown in the background section). One issue is the consistency of the changes of the other projects. To demonstrate, for the movement of the project a_1 from 3rd to 2nd rank positions, it suggests a dramatic change solely in the position of the project a_4, in terms of its net flow value.

These changes in the net flow values have come about from changes to the criteria values

of the considered project a_1. Moreover, for each rank improvement it is the minimum changes in the criteria value that were necessary to be made, found using TDE (minimising $d^E_{r_1, r_2}$ in this case). The relevant changes that allowed the proposed rank improvements of the a_1 project are reported in Table 3 and Figure 3.

Describing the values reported in Table 3, the criterion c_4 is shown to never have to be changed. Among those criteria consistently showing proposed changes, for each rank improvement, the c_6 criterion uses the type VI (Gaussian) preference function, which is continuous over its domain, inferring small changes to criteria values produce small changes to the concomitant net flow value. The c_5 criterion is noticeable here since it uses type I (Usual) preference function which contributes 0 or 1 depending on whether the project a_1's criterion value is less than or greater than it comparator. The first change to this criterion value is to achieve 2nd place, it is no coincidence that this is when there is a noticeable change in the net flow value of the a_4 project, which would have the same value as this proposed value for a_1. This now offers no preference to a_4 over a_1 anymore, hence the noticeable decrease in its final net flow value (see Figure 2).

In Figure 3, the x-axis lists the six criteria and the y-axis identifies their level of change, mea-

Figure 3. Progressive changes of the criteria values of the 6th ranked project a_1 when achieving the specific rank improvements

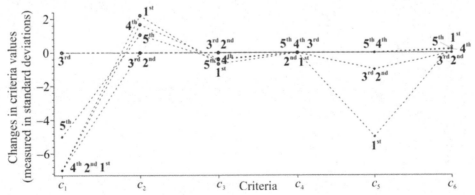

sured in standard deviations from their original values, so the relative sizes of the changes to the criteria values of the project a_1 can be exposited. The zero line of the graph represents the original criteria values of a_1. Each series of circles connected by dashed lines are the proposed values of the criteria whose collective movement would improve the project's rank position (lines are labeled with the rank position the project a_1 would attain). The identified decrease and increase in criteria values are a direct result of the difference in the directions of preference associated with the criteria (see Table 1).

Manhattan Distance

This subsection briefly exposits the rank improvement results on the 6th ranked a_1 project to attain the higher rank positions, this time with the Manhattan distance objective function (d_{r_1,r_2}^{M}) used to quantify the effect of the proposed changes to its criteria values. The first results presented report the changes in the net flow values of the projects that purport the project a_1's achievement of the required improved rank positions (see Figure 4).

The results in Figure 4 are comparable with those reported in Figure 2 which employed the Euclidean distance measure. The similarities are

Figure 4. Evaluated net flow values of the six projects when improving the rank position of the bottom ranked project a_1, using the objective function d_{r_1,r_2}^{M}

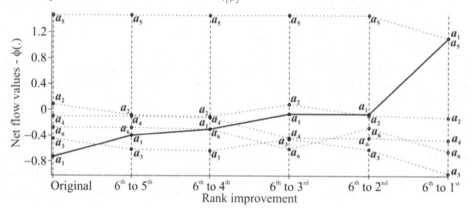

Figure 5. Proposed minimum changes of the criteria values of the originally bottom ranked project a_1 to achieve rank positions 5th to 1st

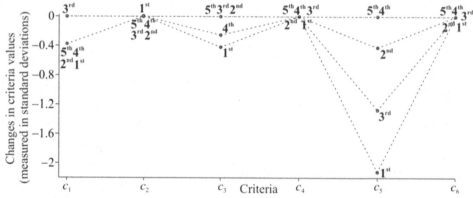

noticeable, pertinently including the dramatic decrease in the net flow values of the project a_4 (and a_3 and a_5), when the project a_1 achieves the 3rd rank position (and others). The nonconsistent decrease of the net flow values of projects to compensate the increase in the net flow of the project a_1 is again due to the variation in the preference function types used in the powerstation project data set (see Table 1). The proposed minimum changes in the criteria values of the project a_1 that results in the net flow values that progressively improve its rank position are reported in Figure 5.

When compared with the results using the Euclidean distance shown in Figure 3, the proposed minimum changes of the criteria values of the project a_1 exposited in Figure 5 are similar. The differences include that there are now no required changes to the c_2 and c_6 criteria, but there are more changes to the c_5 criterion, which supports the dramatic changes in the net flow values of certain projects previously described in Figure 4.

Food Product Data Set

A second example data set is next investigated, while similar in details to the powerstation data set, it considers the possible ranking of different brands of a certain food product by a consumer or manufacturer. Support for the preference ranking of food brands is that it is simple for consumers to perform (Lee & O'Mahony, 2005). As a consequence, manufacturers can use a technique such as PROMETHEE to preference rank the food brands

to identify the relative level of preference of its product. The planning issue in this case is then that of the manufacturers of the brands to move their product up the preference rank order.

The data set considered here is a consequence of a series of mini surveys undertaken by the U.K.'s Foods Standard Agency (2004) on the levels of nutrients, including salt, fat, and sugar, in a variety of baked beans and tinned pasta food products. In this study a selection of tinned "macaroni cheese" brands are considered, each described by the levels of five nutrients shown on their packaging. The seven tinned macaroni cheese brands considered are: a_1 is Heinz, a_2 is Tesco, a_3 is Sainsbury's, a_4 is Asda, a_5 is Asda Smart Price, a_6 is Safeway, and a_7 is Morrisons. Further, the nutrient-based criteria considered are: c_1 is energy (kcal), c_2 is protein (g), c_3 is sugars (g), c_4 is fat (g), and c_5 is salt (g). The full details of these brands are reported in Table 4.

The information in Table 4 reports the criteria values for each brand, as well as the necessary parameters for the generalized preference functions used for the criteria (type VI in each case), and the direction of improved preference (Min. or Max.). Furthermore, all the five criteria were considered of equal importance ($w_i = 1/5$, $i = 1, \ldots,$ 5). The consistent use of the type VI (Gaussian) preference function shown in Table 4 is an attempt to model the gradual (continuous) change in the preferences of a consumer towards one brand over another. The parameter σ used in each preference function is assigned the standard deviation value

Table 4. Details of macaroni cheese data set

Criteria	Min. or Max.	Alternatives							Function	Parameters
		a_1	a_2	a_3	a_4	a_5	a_6	a_7		
c_1	Min.	95	133	133	120	126	116	116	VI	σ = 13.63
c_2	Max.	3.4	4.5	5.1	4.4	5.0	4.4	4.4	VI	σ = 1.091
c_3	Min.	1.1	0.7	1.8	1.6	1.1	1.6	1.6	VI	σ = 0.845
c_4	Min.	4.7	6.3	7.1	6.0	6.0	5.8	5.8	VI	σ = 1.029
c_5	Min.	1.0	1.3	1.3	1.3	1.0	1.3	1.3	VI	σ = 0.155

Table 5. Criterion and net flow values for macaroni cheese brands

Criterion flow	a_1	a_2	a_3	a_4	a_5	a_6	a_7
$\phi_1(a_i)$	5.3796	−2.8327	−2.8327	0.0023	−1.3460	0.8148	0.8148
$\phi_2(a_i)$	−5.4422	0.0816	3.3316	−0.2708	2.8414	−0.2708	−0.2708
$\phi_3(a_i)$	2.2104	4.7431	−3.0846	−2.0265	2.2104	−2.0265	−2.0265
$\phi_4(a_i)$	5.1559	−1.1209	−4.7286	−0.0974	−0.0974	0.4442	0.4442
$\phi_5(a_i)$	4.5685	−1.8274	−1.8274	−1.8274	4.5685	−1.8274	−1.8274
$\phi(a_i)$	1.9787	−0.1594	−1.5236	−0.7033	1.3628	−0.4776	−0.4776
Rank	1	3	7	6	2	=5	=5

associated with a criterion, so taking into account the spread of the criterion values, when taking into account the difference between them.

It should also be noticed in Table 4 that the a_6 (Safeway) and a_7 (Morrisons) brands have exactly the same criteria values, so it is expected that they should have the same final net flow values and the same rank positioned. Using PROMETHEE on the details in Table 4, the associated net flow values for each brand can be evaluated (see Table 5).

Table 5 reports the necessary criterion and net flow values used to rank the seven brands of the macaroni cheese tin food brands. Based on the net flow values evaluated the identified rank order of these brands is also presented in Table 5, which shows the brands, a_3 and a_1, as top and bottom ranked, respectively. As expected, the brands a_6 and a_7 are equally ranked 5th, since they have the same criteria values (no 1th rank position shown). The next results outline the proposed minimum changes of criteria values of the bottom ranked brand a_3 that would improve it rank position, using either of the Euclidean ($d^E_{r_1,r_2}$) or Manhattan ($d^M_{r_1,r_2}$) distance-based objective functions.

Euclidean Distance

Using the Euclidean distance ($d^E_{r_1,r_2}$)-based objective function, the technical details of the progressive improvement of the bottom place brand (a_3) are first reported, starting with the net flow values of the seven brands, while the rank position of the a_3 brand is improved (see Figure 6).

In Figure 6, the bold solid line shows the successive increase in the net flow value associated with the originally bottom ranked brand a_3, to

Figure 6. Evaluated net flow values of the seven brands when improving the rank position of the bottom ranked brand a_3, using the objective function $d^E_{r_1,r_2}$

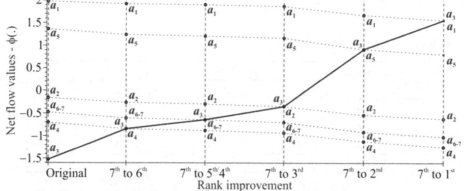

Table 6. Proposed changes to criteria values of brand a_3 to achieve improved rank positions

Criterion flow	c_1	c_2	c_3	c_4	c_5
7th	133.00	5.10	1.80	7.10	1.30
7th = 6th	127.135	5.100	1.679	6.730	1.222
7th = 5th/4th	126.293	5.100	1.670	6.651	1.193
7th = 3rd	124.136	5.100	1.655	6.570	1.155
7th = 2nd	116.115	5.100	1.190	6.243	1.076
7th = 1st	103.615	5.100	1.126	6.152	1.055

each of the higher rank positions. The exception here being the improvement to the 5th rank position is the same as achieving the 4th rank position (abbreviated to 5th/4th) due to the equally 5th ranked brands a_6 and a_7, labeled a_{6-7} in Figure 6 (see Table 5).

The subsequent decreases in the net flow values of the other brands to accommodate the successive increases in the net flow values of the brand a_3 are shown to be nearly equally spread over the other brands. These findings are in contrast to those found when analyzing the powerstation data set, which showed dramatic variations in the changes to the net flow values of the nonimproving projects. The reason for these sets of consistent decreasing of the other brands' net flow values is due to the consistent use of the continuous Type VI (Gaussian) preference function for all criteria.

The proposed minimum changes to the criteria values of the brand a_3 that allowed its perceived rank improvements are reported in Table 6 and Figure 7.

The proposed minimum changes to criteria values of the brand a_3 given in Table 6, to achieve improved rank positions show one important feature: they are consistent in terms of the rank improvement achieved. That is, the four criteria on which changes are suggested, c_1, c_3, c_4, and c_5, all have increased preference through reducing their values (Min. in Table 4), so to successively improve its rank position there are progressive decreases in each of these criteria values. In Figure 7, the progressive changes to the criteria values are clearly shown all to be monotonically decreasing when attempting to improve the rank position of the brand a_3.

Figure 7. Proposed minimum changes of the criteria values of the originally bottom ranked brand a_3 to achieve rank positions 6th to 1st

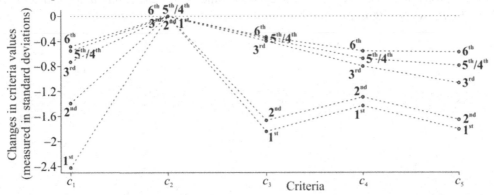

Manhattan Distance

This subsection briefly exposits the rank improvement results on the 7th ranked brand a_3 to attain the higher rank positions, when employing the Manhattan distance objective function ($d^M_{r_1,r_2}$). The first results presented report the changes in the net flow values of all the brands as the brand a_3 achieves improved rank positions (see Figure 8).

The results on the net flows of the seven brands are noticeably similar to those found when the Euclidean distance measure was employed (see Figure 6). This similarity includes the regular decrease in the net flow values of the compared to

brands, enforcing the implication when comprehensively using the Type VI preference function on all the criteria. The relevant minimum changes to the criteria values that allowed the proposed rank improvements of the a_3 brand are reported in Figure 9.

The proposed changes to the criteria values of the brand a_3 in Figure 9 are more inconsistent than when the Euclidean distance measure was employed (compare with Figure 7). This is interesting because the resultant net flow values evaluated were similar. These findings indicate the underlying variation in how the two objective functions quantify the minimisation of the changes in a brand's criteria values to improve its rank position among other brands.

Figure 8. Evaluated net flow values of the seven brands when improving the rank position of the bottom ranked brand a_3, using the objective function $d^M_{r_1,r_2}$

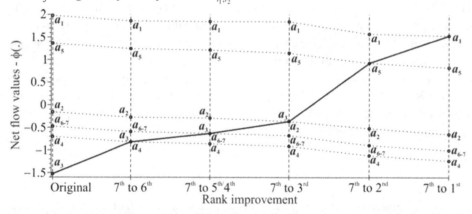

Figure 9. Proposed minimum changes of the criteria values of the originally bottom ranked brand a_3 to achieve rank positions 6th to 1st

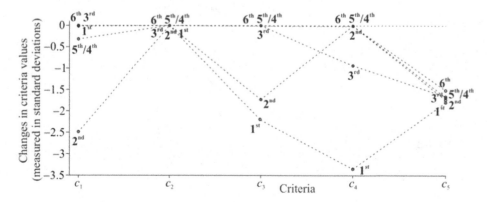

CONCLUSION

The conclusions surrounding this chapter are a consequence of the fact that stakeholders are keen to identify how their alternative compares against their identified competitors, elucidated through their ranking. However, this consequence means that such investigation should not just stop there but should go on to evaluate the associated uncertainty, and subsequent ability for the rank improvement of certain alternatives. Techniques such as PROMETHEE attempt to model such ranking through the preference comparison of alternatives over different criteria. The diversity of situations where ranking takes place means that this issue will always be prevalent in societies around the world.

Optimisation techniques importantly contribute to solve the further issues of rank uncertainty and improvement, in this case the employment of trigonometric differential evolution. Here they offer practical results that outline planning advice, so stakeholders benefit from their utilisation. That is, they enable the identification of the minimum changes of the criteria values describing an alternative that would enable its desired rank improvement.

If future planning-based research, using rank improvement analysis is considered through the costs involved in such criteria value changes, then identifying the most cost efficient "minimum" changes offers a practical benefit to the stakeholder, and may dictate the future planning options. Further, with respect to the rank improvement analysis shown, only considering the changes to one alternative's criteria values, so assuming that that stakeholder's competitors' alternatives are not altered is an assumption, that perhaps should be loosened in future research.

With respect to the PROMETHEE ranking technique, there is a clear influence in the types of preference functions, defined on the different criteria, used to quantify the comparative preference between pairs of alternatives' criteria values.

This technical issue is pertinent since it highlights the importance of appropriately modelling the preference of one alternative over another.

REFERENCES

Abo-Sinna, M.A., & Amer, A.H. (2005). Extensions of TOPSIS for multi-objective large-scale nonlinear programming problems. *Applied Mathematics and Computation, 162,* 243-256.

Albadvi, A., Chaharsooghi, S.K., & Esfahanipour, A. (2006). Decision making in stock trading: An application of PROMETHEE. *European Journal of Operational Research, 177*(2), 673-683.

Benayoun, R., Roy, B., & Sussmann, B. (1966). Manuel de réference du programme ELECTRE. Nothe de synthèse, formation n°. 25, Direction scientifique SEMA, Paris.

Beynon, M.J., & Wells, P. (2008). The lean improvement of the chemical emissions of motor vehicles based on preference ranking: A PROMETHEE uncertainty analysis. *OMEGA - International Journal of Management Science, 36,* 384-394.

Brans, J.P., Mareschal, B., & Vincke, P.H. (1984). PROMETHEE: A new family of outranking methods in MCDM. In *IFORS 84*, North Holland (pp. 470-490).

Brans, J.P., Vincke, P.H., & Mareschal, B. (1986). How to select and how to rank projects: The PROMETHEE method. *European Journal of Operational Research, 24,* 228-238.

Fan, H-Y., & Lampinen, J.A. (2003). Trigonometric mutation operation to differential evolution. *Journal of Global Optimisation, 27,* 105-129.

Food Standards Agency. (2004). *Survey of baked beans and canned pasta* (Information Sheet 57/04). Retrieved August 21, 2007, from http://www.food.gov.uk/science/surveillance/fsis2004/branch/fsis5704

Georgopoulou, E., Sarafidis, Y., & Diakoulaki, D. (1998). Design and implementation of a group DSS for sustaining renewable energies exploitation. *European Journal of Operational Research, 109,* 483-500.

Hwang, C.L., & Yoon, K. (1981). *Multiple attributes decision making methods and applications.* Berlin, Heidelberg, Germany: Springer.

Hyde, K.M., & Maier, H.R. (2006). Distance-based and stochastic uncertainty analysis for multi-criteria decision analysis in Excel using visual basic for applications. *Environmental Modelling & Software, 21*(12), 1695-1710.

Hyde, K.M., Maier, H.R., & Colby, C.B. (2003). Incorporating uncertainty in the PROMETHEE MCDA method. *Journal of Multi-Criteria Decisions Analysis, 12,* 245-259.

Lahdelma, R., Salminen, P., & Hokkanen, J. (2000). Using multicriteria methods in environmental planning and management. *Environmental Management, 26*(6), 595-605.

Lee, H.-S., & O'Mahony, M. (2005). Sensory evaluation and marketing: Measurement of a consumer concept. *Food Quality and Preference, 16,* 227-235.

Michalewicz, Z., Logan, T.D., & Swaminathan, S. (1994). Evolutionary operators for continuous convex parameter spaces. In *Proceedings of the 3rd Annual Conference on Evolutionary Programming,* World Scientific (pp. 84-96).

Ni, Y., Huang, C., & Kokot, S. (2004). Application of multivariate calibration and artificial neural networks to simultaneous kinetic-spectrophotometric determination of carbamate pesticides. *Chemometrics and Intelligent Laboratory Systems, 71,* 177-193.

Roy, B. (1991). The outranking approach and the foundations of ELECTRE methods. *Theory and Decision, 31*(1), 49-73.

Simon, U., Brüggemann, R., & Pudenz, S. (2004). Aspects of decision support in water management—example Berlin and Potsdam (Germany) I—spatially differentiated evaluation. *Water Research, 38,* 1809-1816.

Storn, R., & Price, K. (1997). Differential evolution—a simple and efficient heuristic for global optimisation over continuous spaces. *Journal of Global Optimisation, 11,* 341-59.

KEY TERMS

Alternative: Abstract or real objects, or actions, which can be chosen. Here, one of a number of objects/options considered for preference ranking, each described by values over a series of criteria.

Criterion: A feature or standard on which alternatives are preferenced that has a known direction of improving preference.

Evolutionary Algorithm: An algorithm that incorporates mechanism inspired by biological evolution, including reproduction, mutation, recombination, natural selection, and survival of the fittest.

Flow Values: Within PROMETHEE, totals of preference function values on alternatives, including criterion, outgoing, incoming, and net.

Objective Function: A positive function of the difference between predictions and data estimates that are chosen so as to optimize the function or criterion.

Preference Function: A function to standardize (remove scale effects) the difference between two alternative's values over a single criterion.

PROMETHEE: The multicriteria decision making technique **P**reference **R**anking **O**rganization **METH**od for **E**nrichment **E**valuation.

Ranking: An ordering of alternatives with respect to some preface.

Trigonometric Differential Evolution: The evolutionary algorithm trigonometric differential evolution (TDE), which belongs to the class of evolution strategy optimizers. The central idea behind TDE-type algorithms is to add the weighted difference between two population vectors to a third vector within the optimisation process.

APPENDIX

In this appendix the evaluation of the criterion flow values is demonstrated. Using the powerstation data set, the case of when the project, a_1, is considered for rank improvement (see Table 7), where the $P_k(a_i, a_j)$ and $P_k(a_j, a_i)$ values are calculated over the c_2 criterion.

In Table 7, the final column cell of the $P_2(a_1, a_j) - P_2(a_j, a_1)$ row is the criterion flow value $\phi_2(a_1)$ (shown in Table 2). To demonstrate, the construction of the $P_2(a_1, a_4) - P_2(a_4, a_1)$ value is considered, which in Table 7 has value 0.333. First, for c_2 from Table 1, since $a_1 = 90 > 80 = a_4$ then $P_2(a_4, a_1) = 0$. However, with c_2 based on the type III preference function (linear preference), the general form for $P_k(a_i, a_j)$ is given by:

$$P_k(a_i, a_j) = \begin{cases} d/p & \text{if } -p \le d \le p \\ 1 & \text{if } d < -p \text{ or } d > p \end{cases}$$

where p is the threshold parameter and d is the difference between criteria values. Here, $p = 30$ and $d = 90 - 80 = 10$, then $P_2(a_1, a_4) = 10/30 = 0.333$, as given in Table 7.

Table 7. Preference value functions for comparison of the project a_1 with the others

$P_k(a_i, a_j)$	a_1	a_2	a_3	a_4	a_5	a_6	Sum
$P_2(a_1, a_j)$	-	1.000	1.000	0.333	18/30	0.000	2.933
$P_2(a_j, a_1)$	-	0.000	0.000	0.000	0.000	0.200	0.200
$P_2(a_1, a_j) - P_2(a_j, a_1)$	-	1.000	1.000	0.333	0.600	−0.200	2.733

Section V
Genetic Algorithms and Programming

Chapter XII
Parallelizing Genetic Algorithms:
A Case Study

Iker Gondra
St. Francis Xavier University, Canada

ABSTRACT

Genetic Algorithms (GA), which are based on the idea of optimizing by simulating the natural processes of evolution, have proven successful in solving complex problems that are not easily solved through conventional methods. This chapter introduces their major steps, operators, theoretical foundations, and problems. A parallel GA is an extension of the classical GA that takes advantage of a GA's inherent parallelism to improve its time performance and reduce the likelihood of premature convergence. An overview of different models for parallelizing GAs is presented along with a discussion of their main advantages and disadvantages. A case study: A parallel GA for finding Ramsey Numbers is then presented. According to Ramsey Theory, a sufficiently large system (no matter how random) will always contain highly organized subsystems. The role of Ramsey numbers is to quantify some of these existential theorems. Finding Ramsey numbers has proven to be a very difficult task that has led researchers to experiment with different methods of accomplishing this task. The objective of the case study is both to illustrate the typical process of GA development and to verify the superior performance of parallel GAs in solving some of the problems (e.g., premature convergence) of traditional GAs.

INTRODUCTION

Evolutionary Algorithms

Nature has always served as a source of inspiration in engineering and science. When looking for the best problem solvers known in nature, two candidates stand out: the human brain and the evolutionary mechanism that created the human brain. Attempting to design artificial models of those two problem solvers leads to the fields of neurocomputing and evolutionary computing, respectively. The fundamental metaphor of evolutionary algorithms, or evolutionary computing, relates natural evolution to problem solving in a trial-and-error approach (Eiben & Smith, 2003). In natural evolution, a population of individuals exists in an environment with limited resources. Competition for those resources results in the selection of fitter individuals (i.e., individuals that are better adapted to the environment). Then, those individuals act as seeds for the new generation of individuals through the processes of recombination and mutation. The fitness of the new individuals is evaluated and they compete (possibly also with their parents) for survival. Over time, this natural selection process results in a rise in the fitness of the population (Eiben & Smith, 2003).

There are many different variations of evolutionary algorithms but the underlying idea is the same: given a population of individuals, environmental pressure results in natural selection, which results in a rise in the overall fitness of the entire population. It is easy to think of such process as optimization. That is, given an objective function that is to be maximized, an initial population of randomly generated solutions is obtained. Then, a fitness (evaluation) function that represents the requirements that the population should adapt to is used to assign a single real-valued fitness to each individual in the population. The selection mechanism, which is based on the fitness value, is stochastic. That is, the probability that a particular individual is selected to act as a seed for the next generation is based on the individual's fitness. Thus, high-quality solutions are more likely to be selected than low-quality solutions but this is not guaranteed and even the worst solution in the population usually has a nonzero probability of being selected. This stochastic nature can aid in escaping from local optima. Recombination is a binary variation operator that merges information from parents (i.e., selected solutions) into offspring (i.e., new solutions). The choice of what information to merge is also usually stochastic. The hope is that, by combining good solutions, better solutions may be obtained. This principle has been used for millennia by breeders of plants and livestock. Mutation is a unary variation operator that randomly modifies one solution to deliver another. Thus, recombination allows us to perform exploitation by optimizing promising areas of the

search space whereas, by creating random small diversions, mutation is explorative. The variation operators (i.e., recombination and mutation) generate the necessary diversity whereas selection acts as a force pushing quality. It is this combination of variation and selection that generally leads to improvements in the overall fitness value of successive generations. The whole field of evolutionary computing, or evolutionary algorithms, includes evolutionary programming, evolution strategies, genetic algorithms, and genetic programming as subareas (Eiben & Smith, 2003).

Genetic Algorithms

Genetic algorithms (GA) are adaptive methods that can be used to solve search and optimization problems. They are based on the mechanics of natural selection and genetic processes of living organisms. From one generation to another, populations evolve according to the principles of natural selection and the survival of the fittest individuals (Darwin, 1859). By imitation of the natural process, GAs are capable of developing solutions to real problems.

The basic principles of GAs were established by Holland (1975). Holland's insight was to be able to represent the fundamental biological mechanisms that permit system adaptation into an abstract form that could be simulated on a computer for a wide range of problems. He introduced bit strings to represent feasible solutions (or individuals) in some problem space. GAs are analogous to the natural behavior of living organisms. Individuals in a population compete for resources. Those individuals that are better adapted survive and have a higher probability of mating and generating descendants; therefore, the genes of stronger individuals will increase in successive generations.

A GA works with a population of individuals, each representing a feasible solution to a given problem. During each iteration step, called a generation, the individuals in the current population are evaluated and given a fitness value, which is proportional to the "goodness" of the solution in solving the problem. Individuals are represented with strings of parameters or genes known as chromosomes. The phenotype, the chromosome, contains the information that is required to construct an individual (i.e., a solution to the problem). The phenotype is used by the fitness function to determine the genotype, which denotes the level of adaptation of the chromosome to the particular problem. To form a new population, individuals are selected with a probability proportional to their relative fitness. This ensures that well-adapted individuals (i.e., good solutions) have a greater chance of reproducing. Once two parents have been selected, their chromosomes are combined and the traditional operators of crossover and mutation (Holland, 1975) are applied to generate new individuals (i.e., new search points). In its simplest form, crossover consists of selecting random points in a string and swapping the substrings of the parents (Figure 1).

The mutation operator is applied by changing at random the value of a bit in a string with a certain probability called the *mutation rate*. This operator is used to prevent premature convergence to local optima by introducing new genetic material (i.e., new points in the search space). Algorithm A shows a standard or simple GA (SGA).

In Algorithm A, the termination criteria may be triggered when either an acceptable solution has been found or when a problem-specific maximum number of generations has been reached.

GAs have been successful in solving complex problems that are not easily solved through conventional methods for several reasons. They start

Algorithm A. Standard genetic algorithm (SGA)

```
BEGIN SGA
    Randomly Create an initial population
    WHILE NOT termination criteria DO
        BEGIN
            Assign a fitness value to each individual
            Select individuals for reproduction
            Produce new individuals
            Mutate some individuals
            Generate new population by replacing bad
            individuals with some new good individuals
    END
END SGA
```

with a population of points rather than a single point; therefore, many portions of the domain are searched simultaneously and, as a result, they are less prone to settling at local optima during the search. GAs work with an encoding of the parameter set, not the parameters themselves. Because they do not depend on domain knowledge in performing the search, inconsistent or noisy domain data are less likely to affect them as is common with hill-climbing or domain specific heuristics (Stracuzzi, 1998).

Why They Work: The Schemata Theorem

Holland (1975) presents the theoretical foundations explaining the robustness of GAs as a search technique. The key to finding an optimal solution for a given problem is to be able to identify and exploit useful properties in a large search space S. Each chromosome (or solution) $C_i \in S$ is represented by a set of genes (attributes or bits). For example, the chromosome 011100101011101 could represent a solution to a particular problem. If "*" is used as a "don't care" symbol, then this chromosome can also be represented by the string 011**********01. Strings containing one or more "don't care" symbols are referred to as schemata. A string corresponds to a particular schemata if we can obtain the string by substituting the "don't care" symbols with the corresponding bit value. For example, the string 100110 corresponds to the schemata 10***0 but not to 00***0.

Figure 1. Simple crossover operator

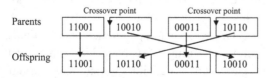

	Crossover point		Crossover point	
Parents	11001	10010	00011	10110
Offspring	11001	10110	00011	10010

Holland (1975) makes the important observation that every string (i.e., chromosome or solution) corresponds to $2^m - 1$ different schemata, where m is the length of the string. To show this, observe that there are m positions in a string of length m and each position can contain either a bit value or the "don't care" symbol "*". A one is subtracted because the string of all "*" symbols represents the search space S itself, not an schemata (or partition of S). As a result, each time a string (i.e., chromosome or solution) is evaluated, many (i.e., $2^m - 1$) different schemata (or partitions of S) are sampled. Consequently, every time a population is explicitly evaluated, a number of schemata much greater than the population size is implicitly sampled. This is what is meant when referring to a GA's implicit parallelism. From one generation to the next, the representation of a particular schemata in the population will increase or decrease according to the relative fitnesses of the strings that correspond to that schemata (Holland, 1975). For example, if a particular schemata is sampled by N strings at generation g, it will be sampled by $N * (\mathrm{fv}(N) / \mathrm{fv})$ strings at generation $g+1$, where $\mathrm{fv}(N)$ is the average fitness value of the N strings and fv is the average population fitness value.

Holland (1975) discusses many other important details and observations related to the Schemata Theorem which are beyond the scope of this chapter. One of the most important observations he makes is that crossover disrupts schemata, so an offspring may not contribute to the representation of its parents' schemata. Therefore, after crossover is performed, a given schemata will both gain and lose strings in a way that is independent of the fitness of its current strings. After taking several factors into consideration, he establishes the Schemata Theorem (Holland, 1975): Schemata sampled by a set of strings with an average fitness that is larger than the population's average fitness value will receive an exponential increase of sampling strings in successive generations. This establishes the validity of GAs as a sound search technique.

Premature Convergence

Premature convergence is a common problem of any SGA. It occurs when the individuals in the population are selected proportionally according to their relative fitness. Some individuals may have a very high fitness value and, as the algorithm continues executing, they may dominate the entire population. Once a suboptimal solution dominates the population, selection will keep it there and prevent any further adaptation to the problem. When crossover occurs, no new patterns will be created, causing the search to stop. In other words, the search may stop after converging to a (local) maximum of the search space. Previous research has focused on two general approaches to address this problem (Goodman, Lin, & Punch, 1994). The first approach affects the selection phase and focuses on lowering the convergence speed so the algorithm can do a more thorough search before converging. The second approach attempts to keep high population diversity by modifying traditional replacement and mating operators. Some proposed methods for avoiding premature convergence are discussed next.

Goldberg and Richardson (1987) proposed a method to increase population diversity by modifying the fitness value of every individual. The basic idea is to lower the fitness value of individuals that are similar to one another and to increase the fitness value of solutions that are isolated or different from the rest of the population. In this manner, individuals that are close to one another (i.e., similar) will reduce their chances of being selected for crossover, thus increasing the probability of selecting isolated individuals. For example, if $d(I_j, I_i)$ denotes the Hamming distance between individuals I_j and I_i, and k is a positive real parameter, we can define the following function h:

$$h(d(I_j, I_i)) = \begin{cases} k - d(I_j, I_i) & \text{if } d(I_j, I_i) < k \\ 0 & \text{if } d(I_j, I_i) \geq k \end{cases}$$

Now, for each individual I_j, σ^j is defined as the summation of $h(d(I_j, I_i))$ for all individuals I_i where $i \neq j$. The value of σ^j is then used to modify the fitness function of each individual I_j. If $g(I_j)$ gives the fitness value of solution I_j, the new value would be $g(I_j) / \sigma^j$ (Goldberg & Richardson, 1987). In other words, we determine how similar each individual is to all the other solutions in the population and modify its fitness value accordingly.

Another possible improvement over the traditional method of proportional selection is to set a limit on the number of times that an individual can be selected for reproduction. For each individual i, we could use a counter initialized to $fv_i / fv_{average}$ where fv_i is the fitness value of solution i and $fv_{average}$ is the average fitness value of the entire population. In this manner, we allow a good individual to be chosen more times but only up to a certain limit (i.e., until the value of the counter reaches 0).

Another commonly used method for dealing with premature convergence is tournament selection. It consists of randomly choosing k individuals out of the entire population to form a tournament. The best individual in the tournament is then selected for reproduction. In this way, the selection of individuals which are not necessarily the best solutions in the population is permitted.

De Jong (1975) introduced the concept of a crowding scheme. The approach consists of randomly choosing a subpopulation of individuals. Hamming's distance is used to determine a value for each individual according to its similarity with other individuals in the subpopulation. An offspring then replaces one of the individuals with a high "similarity value." Therefore, similar solutions in a subpopulation will compete with one another and the speed at which convergence occurs is reduced. Another approach for maintaining diversity is to allow the insertion of an offspring into the population only if it is different enough from all other individuals (Mouldin, 1984).

PARALLEL GENETIC ALGORITHMS

Introduction

Consider the problem of delaying premature convergence on an SGA. We can take either of two approaches. If we maintain a very large population of individuals on each generation, it will take longer for good individuals to dominate. However, the high computational cost associated with the evaluation of the fitness of each individual in a big population makes the algorithm very inefficient. Another approach is to use a small population and maintain diversity by using some of the previously discussed methods; however, the similarity comparisons on which those methods are based are also computationally expensive. The fact that GAs search numerous points in the problem domain simultaneously makes them ideal candidates for parallelization. A parallel genetic algorithm (PGA) is an extension of the classical GA that takes advantage of this property to improve its time performance and reduce the likelihood of premature convergence. Following nature's parallel model, these algorithms maintain multiple, independent populations that each focus on a different part of the problem (i.e., different regions of the search space). The occasional interchange of solutions between these populations introduces diversity and allows for combinations that often result in a global optimum. The following section presents a common classification of PGAs based on their level of parallelism.

Classification of Parallel Genetic Algorithms

We can distinguish four different models for implementing a PGA according to the desired level of parallelism: Micro-Grain GA, Fine-Grain GA, Coarse-Grain GA, and Massively Distributed Parallel GA. These models are briefly described.

Micro-Grain GA(mgGA)

This model is different from other parallel approaches in that a single population is maintained. Also known as a global GA, it is the simplest model and it is equivalent to an SGA. The parallelism of this model comes from the use of multiple processors for evaluating individual fitnesses (Goodman et al., 1994). A master process maintains a single population and performs classical genetic operators while assigning the task of fitness evaluations to the slave processes (Figure 2). Maximum speedup can be attained if every slave process receives an equal amount of work. This model is useful when the fitness evaluation is the most expensive operation. However, mgGAs do not address the problem of premature convergence (Stracuzzi, 1998).

Fine-Grain GA (fgGA)

This model is a compromise between the mgGA and models with fully separated individual populations (Stracuzzi, 1998). The algorithm maintains a single population and allows two individuals to mate only if they are close to one another (neighbors). The entire population can be viewed as a set of small overlapping subpopulations (Figure 3). When selection is performed, only individuals within the same subpopulation may mate. Because some individuals are members of several subpopu-lations, genetic material is transferred from one population to another (Stracuzzi, 1998).

The purpose of an fgGA is to delay the spread of genetic information among the subpopulations while still allowing some migration. The main issue affecting this model deals with the connectivity between neighbors. High connectivity makes subpopulations susceptible to premature convergence. On the other hand, low connectivity limits individual interactions and can result in a slowdown of the algorithm (Stracuzzi, 1998).

Coarse-Grain GA (cgGA)

A cgGA is based upon the theory of punctuated equilibria. Cohoon, Hedge, Martin, and Richards, (1991) describe this theory as follows:

Punctuated equilibria is based on two principles: allopatric speciation and stasis. Allopatric speciation involves the rapid evolution of new species after a small set of members of a species, peripheral isolates, becomes segregated into a new environment. Stasis, or stability, of a species is simply the notion of lack of change. It implies that after equilibria is reached in an environment, there is very little drift away from the genetic composition of the species. Ideally, a species would persist until its environment changes (or the species would drift very little). Punctuated equilibria stresses that a powerful method for generating new species is to thrust an old species

Figure 2. A Micro-grain GA (mgGA)

Figure 3. A fine-grain GA (fgGA). The individuals located on the boundaries between populations can mate. Thus, genetic material is transferred among populations

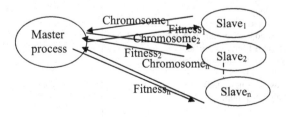

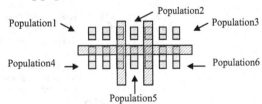

into a new environment, where change is beneficial and rewarded. For this reason, we should expect a genetic algorithm approach based on punctuated equilibria to perform better than the typical single environment scheme.

The implication of this theory upon the structure of a GA is that given a single large population in which the environment is unchanging, equilibrium will be rapidly attained as the population converges. The offspring produced will be very similar to each other and to their parents, causing the population to stabilize on a local optimum. Allopatric speciation indicates that evolution can continue by the introduction of stabilized species into different subpopulations (Cohoon et al., 1991).

Papadopoulos (1994) indicated the effectiveness of the cgGA in solving many "GA-hard" problems which other GAs are not able to solve. He outlines a common implementation of a

cgGA. A set of n individuals can be assigned to a dedicated processor. Given that N processors are available, the size of the total population is $n \times N$. During a major iteration or epoch, every processor works in parallel, yet independently, evolving its individuals (Papadopoulos, 1994). In theory, a processor should continue evolving its individuals until it reaches equilibrium. However, because there is no known adequate equilibrium stopping criteria, an epoch consists of a fixed number of generations, which greatly simplifies the task of synchronizing the processors (Cohoon et al., 1991). When the processors stop, chromosomes are interchanged between subpopulations. This migration of individuals has the effect of introducing new genetic material into populations that may have slowed down their evolution due to equilibrium (Papadopoulos, 1994). Algorithm B is a generalized cgGA.

The efficiency of a cgGA depends on the choices of several new parameters:

Algorithm B. A generalized cgGA

```
Global Data
graph           migration_topology;

Local Data
population       my_pop, my_new_pop, migrant_pop;
float           p_cross, p_mutation,
                migration_rate;    /* percent of pop moved during each migration */
int             N,                 /* population size */
                N_migrants;        /* n_migrants = N * migration_rate */

 1.   for all processing nodes
 2.       my_pop = new random individual(s)
 3.       evaluate(my_pop)
 4.       while termination criteria not satisfied
 5.           if migration criteria satisfied
 6.               if using dynamic network connection
 7.                   update(migration_topology)
 8.               migrant_pop = select(N_migrants, my_pop)
 9.               send migrant_pop to another node according to migration_topology
10.               migrant_pop = receive migrants from another node
11.               add migrant_pop to my_pop and maintain population size N
12.           my_new_pop = select(N, my_pop)
13.           my_pop = crossover(p_cross, my_new_pop)
14.           my_pop = mutate(p_mutation, my_pop)
15.           evaluate(my_pop)
16.       end while
17.   end forall
```

Migration Policy

The following parameters define the migration mechanism (Rebaudergo & Sonza Reorda, 1992): *Migration Frequency* determines the number of generations between two migrations (i.e., the size of an epoch). Frequent communications are useless because similar individuals are transmitted on each migration. Less frequent migrations increase the running time of the algorithm. *Migration Size* determines the number of individuals composing each migration. Sending too many individuals will result in a decrease of the average fitness. On the other hand, if only a few individuals are transmitted, they may be quickly eliminated if the receiving subpopulation has a much higher average fitness value. *Migrant Selection* determines which immigrants are chosen within the source subpopulation. The individuals with the highest fitness could be chosen or they could be selected at random (Rebaudergo & Sonza Reorda, 1992). The most common method is to choose an individual with probability proportional to its fitness value. In this manner, diversity increases as it is not only the good individuals that migrate. Whether the communication between processing nodes is done in a synchronous or an asynchronous manner, is another issue to be considered.

Connection Schemes

There are two widely used connection schemes: *static connection scheme* and *dynamic connection scheme*. In a *static connection scheme*, the connections between processors are established at the beginning and not modified during execution. There are several different topologies: rings, lines, n-cubes, and so forth (Goodman et al., 1994). In a *dynamic connection scheme*, the network topology is allowed to change during run time.

Node Structure

There are two different approaches depending on the similarity of the SGAs running on each processor: *homogeneous island GA*, and *heterogeneous island GA*. In a *homogeneous island GA*, every processor uses the same parameters (i.e., crossover rate, mutation rate, population size, etc.). A *heterogeneous island GA* allows subpopulations with different parameters to evolve. This will increase the chance of finding an ideal set of parameters (Goodman et al., 1994).

Massively Distributed Parallel GA (mdpGA)

In a mdpGA, every processor is assigned a small subpopulation (e.g., 10 individuals). Because of the small population size, selection must be done carefully.

CASE STUDY

Ramsey Theory

"Complete disorder is impossible."
—T. S. Motzkin

Ramsey (1930), proved that complete disorder is an impossibility. Ramsey theory studies the existence of highly regular patterns within a large object or set of randomly selected points or numbers. The role of Ramsey numbers is to quantify some of the general existential theorems in Ramsey theory.

The party puzzle is a classical problem used to introduce the theory. What is the minimum number of guests that must be invited to a party so that either a group of at least three people will know one another or at least three guests will not mutually know each other? The answer to this problem, which equals 6, is called the Ramsey number R(3,3). Stated in a mathematical way, given 6 points or vertices, we draw a line segment between every pair of vertices to obtain a complete graph of order 6 (denoted by K_6). If the symmetric relationship of knowing/not knowing between 2 points in the graph is represented by the color of the edge connecting the two vertices, then the claim is that every one of the possible 32,768 colorings will yield a monochromatic K_3 (i.e., a complete graph of order 3 in which every edge has the same color). The special notation $K_6 \rightarrow K_3$ is used to record this result. In general, $K_n \rightarrow K_m$ states that every two coloring of the edges of K_n yields a monochromatic K_m.

Generalizing these observations, suppose that a and b are integers with $a, b \geq 2$, then a possible integer N has the (a,b) Ramsey property if the following holds: Given any set S of N elements, if we divide the 2-element subsets of S into two classes A and B, then either:

1. There is an a-element subset of S all of whose 2-element subsets are in A, or
2. There is a b-element subset of S all of whose 2-element subsets are in B.

The smallest integer N that has the (a,b) Ramsey property is called a Ramsey number and is denoted by $R(a,b)$ (Erickson, 1996). Thus, 6 has the $(3,3)$ Ramsey property and $R(3,3) = 6$. As the following theorem shows, Ramsey's theory is generalized to graphs with an arbitrary number of edge colors.

For any integer $c \geq 2$, and integers $A_1, A_2, ...,$ $A_c \geq 2$, there exists a least integer $R(A_1, A_2, ...,$ $A_c)$ with the following property: If the edges of the complete graph on $R(A_1, A_2, ..., A_c)$ vertices are partitioned into color classes $A_1, A_2, ..., A_c$, then for some i there exists a complete graph on A_i vertices all of whose edges are color A_i. (Erickson, 1996)

The only known value for a multicolor classical Ramsey number is $R(3,3,3) = 17$. The interpretation of this is the following: Every coloring of the edges of a complete graph with 17 vertices in 3 colors will give rise to a triangle that is monochromatic in one of the 3 colors. Ramsey's theorem is also extended to hypergraphs.

Let integer $c \geq 2$ and integers $A_1, A_2, ..., A_c \geq t \geq 2$. There exists a least integer $R(A_1, ..., A_c; t)$ with the following property: Every c-coloring of

the complete t-uniform hypergraph $[R(A_1, A_2, ..., A_c; t)]^t$ with colors $A_1, A_2, ..., A_c$ yields a complete t-uniform hypergraph on A_i vertices in color A_i, for some i. (Erickson, 1996)

If in the notation $R(G_1, G_2, ..., G_m; s)$ s is not specified, a 2-uniform hypergraph (i.e., a conventional graph) is assumed. Thus $R(3,3) = R(3,3;2)$ and $R(3,3,3) = R(3,3,3;2)$. In order to find a Ramsey number, say $R(G_1, G_2, ..., G_k)$, we need to find the largest number N such that a k-colored complete graph K_N does not contain a monochromatic subgraph G_i in color i for $1 \leq i \leq k$. Once such an N is found, then $(N + 1)$ is $R(G_1, G_2, ..., G_k)$. For example, to deduce that $R(3,3) = 6$, we would have to show that 5 is the largest N such that a complete graph on N vertices does not necessarily contain a monochromatic triangle of either of 2 colors. Unfortunately, attempting to find Ramsey numbers is an arduous task that is too often unfruitful. Only a handful of specific numbers are known. Erdo's anecdote captures the difficulty of finding even the comparatively simple diagonal Ramsey numbers (i.e., $R(a,a)$),

Aliens invade the earth and threaten to obliterate it in a year's time unless human beings can find the Ramsey number for red five and blue five. We could marshal the world's best minds and fastest computers, and within a year we could probably calculate the value. If the aliens demanded the Ramsey number for red six and blue six, however, we would have no choice but to launch a preemptive attack. (Graham & Spencer, 1990)

This state of limited knowledge is exasperating because Ramsey numbers are intimately connected with other numbers and functions such as the Stirling numbers. It is well known that any new Ramsey number would be very valuable (Erickson, 1996). If complete disorder is an impossibility, what order is there in apparent disorder? The case study presented in this chapter is based on an earlier work (Gondra & Samadzadeh, 2003) that investigates and compares the performance of SGAs and PGAS in improving the bounds of Ramsey numbers which attempt to quantify this "order."

Approach and Representation

Given the problem of finding a Ramsey number, say $R(G_1, G_2, ..., G_k)$, we need to find the largest number N such that a k-colored complete graph K_N does not contain a monochromatic subgraph G_i in color i for $1 \leq i \leq k$. Once such an N is found, then $(N+1)$ is $R(G_1, G_2, ..., G_k)$. For example, it is known that $43 \leq R(5,5) \leq 49$; therefore, to improve the lower bound of $R(5,5)$, the first step would be to find a 2-colored graph of order 43 with no monochromatic subgraph of order 5. Then we could conclude that $44 \leq R(5,5) \leq 49$. We would then repeat the same process, each time increasing the lower bound by one, until the largest possible N can be found.

The first step in developing a GA that will solve a given problem is to define the following two mechanisms:

1. A way of encoding solutions to the problem in terms of chromosomes.
2. An evaluation function that returns a measurement of the fitness of a chromosome in solving the given problem.

These two steps are discussed in the following two subsections. The third subsection explains the need to use permutation-respecting crossover operators when using an order-based solution encoding.

Solution Encoding

A solution to the problem will be a complete graph of order N with a number X of monochromatic subgraphs of order K. In the optimal solution, $X=0$. There are several ways of representing a graph as a chromosome. An entry (i,j) in an NxN adjacency matrix can store the color of the edge (i,j). The lower or upper triangle of the adjacency matrix can then be mapped into a single dimensional array (a chromosome). A better approach is to use an order-based representation in which

each chromosome is a permutation of edges. A "decoder" is then used to color the edges of a permutation (Eiben & van der Hauw, 1998). The results of numerous experiments (Eiben & van der Hauw, 1998) conducted on a graph coloring problem have showed that other representations are inferior to the order-based representation.

Evaluation Function

As the decoder encounters the edges in the order that they occur in a certain chromosome, it assigns the smallest possible color from the set of k colors. If each of the k colors leads to a constraint violation (i.e., the formation of a monochromatic subgraph), the edge is left uncolored (Eiben & van der Hauw, 1998). The fitness of a chromosome is then equal to the sum of the uncolored edges; thus a chromosome with a fitness value of 5 is more fit than one with a fitness value of 10. The evaluation function to be minimized is defined as:

$$f(x) = \sum_{i=1}^{n} W_i * \chi(x,i)$$

where n is the number of edges in the chromosome x, W_i is the local penalty (or weight) assigned to edge x_i, and

$$\chi(x,i) = \begin{cases} 1 \text{ if edge } x_i \text{ is left uncolored} \\ 0 \text{ otherwise} \end{cases}$$

If we simply count the uncolored edges, then $W_i \equiv 1$. However, not every edge is equally hard to color. For example, coloring the first edge that appears in a chromosome is an easy task; the decoder may choose any of the k possible colors. On the other hand, coloring the edges at the end of the chromosome may be very difficult as the number of colors that do not result in a constraint violation may be heavily reduced. A better approach would then be to give "hard" edges (i.e., the edges that are colored last) a high weight since this gives the evaluation function a high reward when satisfying them, thus concentrating on these edges (Eiben & van der Hauw, 1998).

In this chapter, we use a modified version of the evaluation function in which all edges are colored. The evaluation function to be maximized is defined as:

$$f(x) = n - \sum_{i=1}^{n} W_i * \chi(x,i)$$

where *n* is the number of edges in the chromosome *x*, W_i is the local penalty (or weight) assigned to edge x_i, and

$$\chi(x,i) = \begin{cases} 1 \text{ if all } k \text{ colorings of edge } x_i \text{ create subgraph(s)} \\ 0 \text{ otherwise} \end{cases}$$

The local penalty W_i is equal to the number of monochromatic subgraphs that are created after coloring the edge with the color that minimizes the resulting number of monochromatic subgraphs. Because edges near the end of the chromosome result in more monochromatic subgraphs, this function gives a higher weight to those edges.

Crossover

Ordinary crossover and mutation operators cause problems for order-based representations. The reason for this is that offspring generated by means of ordinary operators may not be valid solutions for the problem being solved anymore. For example, suppose we have a complete graph of order 4 as shown in Figure 4.

Also, suppose two chromosomes are selected for crossover (Figure 5).

Figure 4. A complete graph of order 4

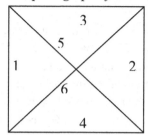

Figure 5. Creation of invalid permutations with traditional crossover operator

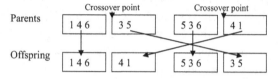

As can be observed, the offspring are not valid permutations anymore (i.e., for the first offspring, and analogously for the second offspring, the decoder would try to color edges 4 and 1 twice and never try to color edges 3 and 5). The way in which the ordinary mutation operator can produce invalid chromosomes is obvious. Several solutions have been suggested to deal with this problem (Poon & Carter, 1995). An invalid chromosome could simply be disqualified, it could also be repaired. The approach that is followed in this chapter consists of using specialized permutation-respecting operators instead of creating invalid chromosomes (Ugoluk, 1997).

Experiments

We compared the performance of a traditional GA with that of a cgGA with several parameter values, when applied to the problem of finding R(3,3,3). R(3,3,3), which is equal to 17, is the only known multicolor Ramsey Number. It is used to observe and compare the rate of premature convergence as well as the performance of the traditional GA and the cgGA. Because the value of R(3,3,3) is known, the global optimum for a particular run is also known, so we can detect when the algorithm converges to a local optimum.

Simulated cgGA

We implemented a tool that uses JAVA threads to simulate the operation of a cgGA. The interface allows the user to input the problem, define the parameters, and run either a simple GA or the simulated parallel version and view the results. The main window (Figure 6) is divided into five parts: problem construction, control buttons, global statistics, log window, and local statistics.

In Figure 6, the problem construction part is used to enter the problem and define the GA parameters. The *Number of Populations* parameter determines whether a simple GA or the simulated cgGA is to be run. For a simple GA, the user only needs to assign the value 1 to *Number of Populations* and a value greater than 2 to run the simulated cgGA. *Population Size* determines the number of permutations that will evolve in each subpopula-

tion. Choosing a larger value for this parameter does not necessarily lead to a better solution since it will slow down the execution. *Number of Colors* specifies the number of colors that will be used to color the edges of the particular complete graph with *Number of Vertices* vertices. For instance, in order to test whether R(3,3,3,3) > 51, the user would set *Number of Colors* to 4 and *Number of Vertices* to 51. *Selection Strategy* and *Migrant Selection* identify the strategies that will be used to choose the permutations that will mate and migrate to different subpopulation respectively. *Crossover Strategy* and *Crossover Rate* indicate the permutation-respecting operator that will be used and the percent of permutations that will be involved in crossover respectively. *Mutation Rate* identifies the probability that a particular permutation will undergo swap mutation. *Migration Frequency* and *Migration Size* indicate the number of generation between two migrations and the number of permutations composing each migration, respectively. *Migration Topology*

Figure 6. Graphical user interface of simulated cgGA tool

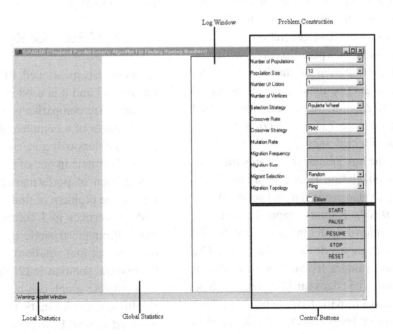

Figure 7. Snapshot of simulated cgGA tool

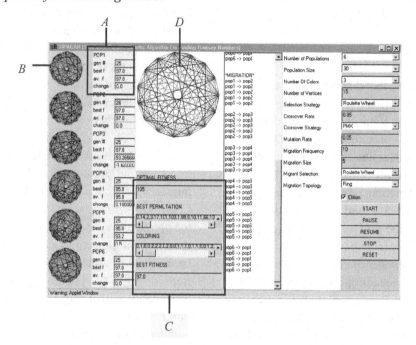

determines the way in which the subpopulations will share information. If the *Elitism* option is checked, a permutation with the highest fitness value in a given generation is guaranteed to be a member of the successive generation.

The global statistics part displays an enlarged graphical representation of the best permutation among all subpopulations as well as global statistical information (e.g., best fitness, best permutation). Figure 7 is a snapshot of this tool when executed with 6 subpopulations.

In Figure 7, the box labeled *A* contains the local statistics for population 1. At generation 25, the highest fitness value in population 1 was 97.0. The K_{15} labeled *B* is the Ramsey graph of a permutation in population 1 with fitness value 97.0. The global statistics are inside the box labeled *C*. The optimal fitness value is 105 and corresponds to a K_{15} all of whose 105 edges can be colored with no resulting monochromatic triangle in any of the 3 colors (the optimal permutation). The K_{15} labeled

D is an enlarged display of the Ramsey graph of a permutation with highest fitness value among the 6 populations.

Results of Runs for R(3,3,3)

As previously mentioned, R(3,3,3) is known to be equal to 17 and it is used in this experiment for performance comparisons only. Every coloring of the edges of a complete graph with 17 vertices in 3 colors will give rise to a triangle that is monochromatic in one of the 3 colors. To do the comparison of performance mentioned above, we use the problem of finding a complete graph with 16 vertices in 3 colors and containing no monochromatic triangle in any of the 3 colors (i.e., the optimal solution). The fitness value of the optimal solution is 120 (i.e., all the edges of the complete graph can be colored without any resulting monochromatic triangle). The problem was first run on the traditional GA option of the simulated cgGA tool with the following parameter values:

Number of Populations: 1
Population Size: 20
Number of Colors: 3
Number of Vertices: 16
Selection Strategy: Roulette-Wheel
Crossover Rate: 0.85
Crossover Strategy: Partially Matched Crossover
Mutation Rate: 0.05
Migration Frequency: N/A (Not Applicable)
Migration Size: N/A (Not Applicable)
Migrant Selection: N/A (Not Applicable)
Migration Topology: N/A (Not Applicable)
Elitism: True

Figure 8 shows a snapshot of this run when stopped at generation 107,199.

In order to observe the relationship between population size and the rate of premature convergence, the same problem was run on the traditional GA with population sizes of 40, 60, 80, and 100 with the values for all the other parameters kept

unchanged. Figure 9 shows the effect of population size on premature convergence.

As Figure 9 illustrates, increasing the population size results in a solution that is nearer to the optimal solution. It also delays premature convergence to local optima. In a small population, a permutation with a relatively high fitness value will be selected very often and its descendants will quickly dominate the population. This will result in reduced genetic diversity and the search will quickly stop after converging on a local optimum. On the other hand, as the population size increases, many permutations are evaluated at each generation and premature convergence is discouraged. This results in more paths being searched and thus an increase in the fitness of the solution. However, in our implementation, the time it takes the decoder to evaluate the fitness of a permutation dominates the execution time; therefore, a very large population can be very expensive in terms of time, so a smaller population is desirable. A cgGA is capable of maintaining the time performance of a small population while maintaining a high genetic diversity and thus do-

Figure 8. Snapshot of first run

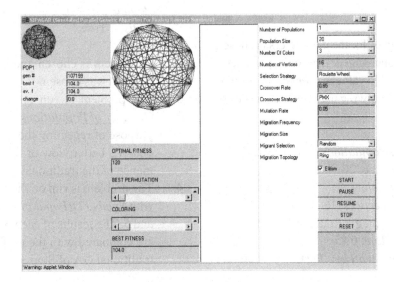

Figure 9. Effect of population size on premature convergence

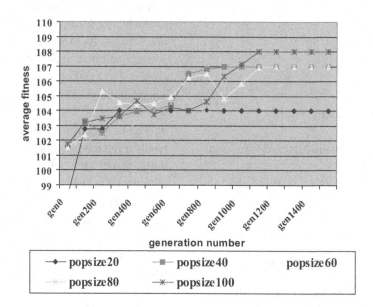

ing a more complete search of the problem space. The remaining part of this section consists of outlines of the experiments that were conducted to validate the previous statement.

In order to compare the performance of a traditional GA with that of a cgGA, an experiment consisting of the following parts was conducted:

1. A set of values for the parameters is chosen and kept unchanged. The only parameter with a variable value is *Number of Populations*. The following parameter values were chosen:

    Number of Populations: VARIABLE
    Population Size: 20
    Number of Colors: 3
    Number of Vertices: 16
    Selection Strategy: Roulette-Wheel
    Crossover Rate: 0.85
    Crossover Strategy: Partially Matched Crossover

    Mutation Rate: 0.05
    Migration Frequency: 20 (if *Number Of Populations* > 1)
    Migration Size: 3 (if *Number Of Populations* > 1)
    Migrant Selection: Roulette-Wheel (if *Number Of Populations* > 1)
    Migration Topology: Ring (if *Number Of Populations* > 1)
    Elitism: True

2. A problem is chosen and kept unchanged. R(3,3,3) was chosen.

3. The problem is run on a traditional GA (*Number of Populations* = 1) 10 times. The purpose of repeating the run 10 times is to obtain a better view of the average performance of the traditional GA.

4. The problem is run on the simulated cgGA with *Number Of Populations* equal to 2,3,4,5, and 5. The results of each one of these runs are compared with the performance of the traditional GA of Step 3 above.

A summary of the results of Step 3 is shown in Table 1. Figure 10 shows the change in the average fitness value of the populations in each one of the 10 runs.

As Figure 10 shows, there is no improvement after at most 600 generations and the search stagnates. Many runs were performed for each of the choices of *Population Size* and similar results were obtained. As shown in Figure 9, the larger the value of *Population Size*, the longer it took the population to converge to a local optimum and thus the search to stagnate. However, regardless of the value of *Population Size*, the traditional GA was never able to find a fitness value better than 108. After converging to a local optimum, the search stagnated even when allowed to run for hundreds of thousands of generations. Continuing with the experiment, the problem was run on the simulated cgGA with *Population Size* = 2 and 3. Tables 2 and 3 are a summary of the results obtained.

Comparing Figure 11 with Figure 10, it is seen that the average fitness values of the two populations take about twice as many generations to converge to a suboptimal solution. A comparison between Figures 11 and 12 shows a lack of improvement when increasing the number of populations from 2 to 3. The fitness values of the globally best permutations were identical in both cases. Furthermore, the populations in the run with 3 populations converged more rapidly than those in the run with 2 populations. This may be due to the fact that the local optimum (a permutation with fitness value equal to 107) was present in generation 0 of the run with 3 populations. The early appearance of a permutation with a relatively high fitness value may have triggered these results. Table 4 summarizes the results obtained when the problem was run with 4 populations. Figure 13 shows the change in the average fitness value of each one of the four populations.

As can be observed, a permutation with fitness value equal to 108 is found when a run with 4 populations is performed. This is the highest fitness value that was achieved when multiple runs of the traditional GA with population sizes equal to 40, 60, 80, or 100 were done. This result is very significant from the point of view of computing time. As previously discussed, the time it takes the decoder to evaluate the fitness of a permutation dominates the execution time thus a very large population can be very expensive in terms of time. However, the simulated cgGA with 4 populations and a small population size of 20 was able to find a permutation with a fitness value equal to the one found by a traditional GA with a large population size. This suggests that if several processors are available and a truly parallel cgGA is implemented, a great improvement in execution time would be obtained. Table 5 summarizes the results obtained when the problem was run with 5 populations. Figure 14 shows the change in the average fitness value of each one of the 5 populations.

When several runs of the traditional GA with population size equal to 100 were performed, no permutation with fitness value higher than 108 was found; thus, the results obtained indicate that a cgGA is capable of finding permutations with higher fitness values than those found with a traditional GA. In the case of a truly parallel cgGA, one would expect it to do this in a shorter time. Table 6 summarizes the results obtained when the problem was run with 6 populations. Figure 15 shows the change in the average fitness value of each one of the 6 populations.

From the above results we can observe that increasing the number of populations in a cgGA does not necessarily result in better performance. The optimal number of populations in a cgGA is a research question that is beyond the scope of this chapter.

CONCLUSION

This chapter presented an overview of Genetic Algorithms as a search technique. Parallel GAs were introduced as an extension of traditional

Table 1. Statistics for 10 runs of R(3,3,3) (number of populations = 1; population size = 20)

	Run 1	Run 2	Run 3	Run 4	Run5	Run 1	Run 2	Run 3	Run 4	Run5
Generation	**Best Fitness**					**Average Fitness**				
0	107.00	107.00	104.00	106.00	105.00	101.25	101.55	100.55	101.75	101.60
50	107.00	107.00	106.00	106.00	105.00	104.50	104.00	102.65	102.45	101.70
100	107.00	107.00	106.00	106.00	105.00	105.75	104.60	101.60	100.80	101.60
150	107.00	107.00	106.00	106.00	105.00	106.40	103.70	103.20	101.00	102.95
200	107.00	107.00	106.00	106.00	105.00	105.80	105.20	103.60	100.90	102.95
250	107.00	107.00	106.00	106.00	105.00	106.00	105.20	106.00	102.60	104.45
300	107.00	107.00	106.00	106.00	105.00	107.00	104.00	106.00	104.80	104.85
350	107.00	107.00	106.00	106.00	105.00	107.00	107.00	106.00	103.60	104.50
450	107.00	107.00	106.00	106.00	105.00	107.00	107.00	106.00	106.00	105.00
500	107.00	107.00	106.00	106.00	105.00	107.00	107.00	106.00	106.00	105.00
550	107.00	107.00	106.00	106.00	105.00	107.00	107.00	106.00	106.00	105.00
600	107.00	107.00	106.00	106.00	105.00	107.00	107.00	106.00	106.00	105.00
	Run 6	**Run 7**	**Run 8**	**Run 9**	**Run10**	**Run 6**	**Run 7**	**Run 8**	**Run 9**	**Run10**
Generation	**Best Fitness**					**Average Fitness**				
0	104.00	105.00	105.00	105.00	106.00	101.05	100.75	101.60	100.80	101.35
50	105.00	106.00	107.00	105.00	106.00	102.65	102.10	103.45	102.00	100.85
100	105.00	106.00	107.00	105.00	106.00	102.15	101.20	105.50	102.15	102.05
150	105.00	106.00	107.00	105.00	106.00	101.85	102.70	105.10	103.05	105.70
200	105.00	106.00	107.00	105.00	106.00	102.60	104.20	104.20	103.50	106.00
250	105.00	106.00	107.00	105.00	106.00	102.00	105.40	103.95	103.95	106.00
300	105.00	106.00	107.00	105.00	106.00	101.55	106.00	104.00	105.00	106.00
350	105.00	106.00	107.00	105.00	106.00	102.00	106.00	105.00	105.00	106.00
450	105.00	106.00	107.00	105.00	106.00	104.10	106.00	104.80	105.00	106.00
500	105.00	106.00	107.00	105.00	106.00	104.55	106.00	105.00	105.00	106.00
550	105.00	106.00	107.00	105.00	106.00	103.95	106.00	106.60	105.00	106.00
600	105.00	106.00	107.00	105.00	106.00	105.00	106.00	107.00	105.00	106.00

Figure 10. Average fitness in 10 runs (number of populations = 1; population size = 20)

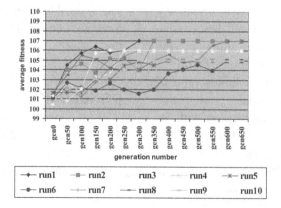

300

Table 2. Statistics for R(3,3,3) (number of populations = 2; population size = 20)

	Population 1	Population2	Population1	Population2
Generation	Best Fitness		Average Fitness	
0	105.00	106.00	101.85	101.55
50	107.00	107.00	102.90	102.80
100	107.00	107.00	103.75	102.80
150	107.00	107.00	103.95	100.25
200	107.00	107.00	105.80	102.85
250	107.00	107.00	101.05	105.80
300	107.00	107.00	103.80	106.80
350	107.00	107.00	106.60	106.30
400	107.00	107.00	106.90	107.00
450	107.00	107.00	106.60	106.60
500	107.00	107.00	106.60	106.80
550	107.00	107.00	105.90	105.60
600	107.00	107.00	105.60	106.30
650	107.00	107.00	106.80	106.70
700	107.00	107.00	106.80	107.00
750	107.00	107.00	106.10	106.80
800	107.00	107.00	106.40	106.40
850	107.00	107.00	106.60	106.20
900	107.00	107.00	106.80	105.60
950	107.00	107.00	106.70	105.40
1000	107.00	107.00	106.50	105.80
1050	107.00	107.00	106.20	106.30
1100	107.00	107.00	106.40	106.90
1150	107.00	107.00	107.00	106.90
1200	107.00	107.00	107.00	107.00

Figure 11. Average fitness vs. generation number (number of populations = 2; population size = 20)

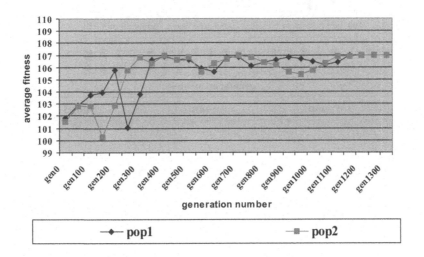

Table 3. Statistics for R(3,3,3) (number of populations = 3; population size = 20)

	Pop1	Pop2	Pop3	Pop1	Pop2	Pop3
Generation	BestFitness			AverageFitness		
0	105.00	106.00	107.00	101.65	102.65	101.05
50	107.00	107.00	107.00	102.65	103.85	101.95
100	107.00	107.00	107.00	104.40	103.50	104.45
150	107.00	107.00	107.00	103.40	101.50	104.20
200	107.00	107.00	107.00	105.50	102.20	104.90
250	107.00	107.00	107.00	104.30	104.90	103.40
300	107.00	107.00	107.00	104.00	103.70	104.30
350	107.00	107.00	107.00	107.00	103.70	102.50
400	107.00	107.00	107.00	105.50	104.90	102.80
450	107.00	107.00	107.00	103.10	107.00	104.00
500	107.00	107.00	107.00	105.80	104.30	106.40
550	107.00	107.00	107.00	106.70	106.10	106.70
600	107.00	107.00	107.00	106.40	106.40	107.00
650	107.00	107.00	107.00	107.00	106.40	107.00
700	107.00	107.00	107.00	107.00	107.00	107.00
750	107.00	107.00	107.00	107.00	107.00	107.00

Figure 12. Average fitness vs. generation number (number of populations = 3; population size = 20)

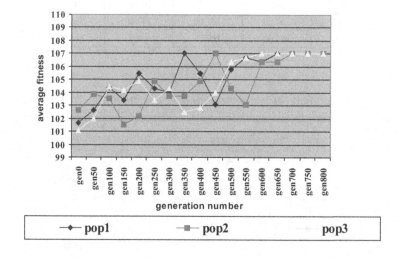

Table 4. Statistics for R(3,3,3) (number of populations = 4; population size = 20)

	Pop1	Pop2	Pop3	Pop4	Pop1	Pop2	Pop3	Pop4
Generation	BestFitness				AverageFitness			
0	105.00	106.00	106.00	106.00	100.85	101.60	102.40	101.70
50	105.00	106.00	106.00	106.00	101.50	102.45	102.70	102.35
100	106.00	106.00	106.00	106.00	102.60	103.45	103.25	102.35
150	106.00	106.00	106.00	106.00	102.90	103.30	103.95	105.60
200	108.00	106.00	108.00	108.00	103.25	105.35	103.55	105.60
250	108.00	108.00	108.00	108.00	106.00	104.05	105.80	103.30
300	108.00	108.00	108.00	108.00	104.40	104.30	104.10	107.30
350	108.00	108.00	108.00	108.00	105.00	104.85	105.35	106.50
400	108.00	108.00	108.00	108.00	104.00	105.40	105.00	107.85
450	108.00	108.00	108.00	108.00	106.00	103.20	105.40	107.50
500	108.00	108.00	108.00	108.00	105.40	103.85	105.80	106.55
550	108.00	108.00	108.00	108.00	104.65	104.00	106.00	105.80
600	108.00	108.00	108.00	108.00	106.60	106.00	107.20	107.40
650	108.00	108.00	108.00	108.00	108.00	104.80	107.60	107.60
700	108.00	108.00	108.00	108.00	108.00	105.80	107.80	107.80
750	108.00	108.00	108.00	108.00	107.20	106.00	107.80	108.00
800	108.00	108.00	108.00	108.00	108.00	107.80	108.00	108.00
850	108.00	108.00	108.00	108.00	108.00	108.00	108.00	108.00
900	108.00	108.00	108.00	108.00	108.00	108.00	108.00	108.00

Figure 13. Average fitness vs. generation number (number of populations = 4; population size = 20)

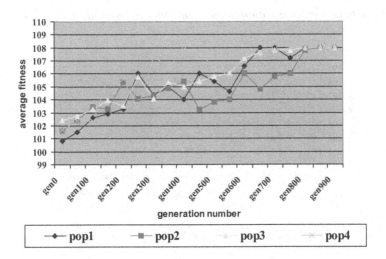

Table 5. Statistics for R(3,3,3) (number of populations = 5; population size = 20)

	Pop1	Pop2	Pop3	Pop4	Pop5	Pop1	Pop2	Pop3	Pop4	Pop5
Generation	BestFitness					AverageFitness				
0	105.00	104.00	106.00	105.00	107.00	102.35	100.75	101.75	101.65	101.70
50	107.00	107.00	106.00	105.00	108.00	102.80	104.40	102.50	102.30	102.40
100	106.00	105.00	107.00	107.00	108.00	103.25	103.95	103.85	103.50	104.90
150	106.00	108.00	107.00	107.00	108.00	105.05	105.25	104.35	105.50	106.00
200	108.00	108.00	107.00	108.00	108.00	104.50	106.05	105.75	105.95	106.30
250	110.00	108.00	108.00	108.00	108.00	106.20	105.45	106.70	104.75	103.60
300	110.00	110.00	110.00	108.00	108.00	104.85	106.75	106.90	106.85	106.45
350	110.00	110.00	110.00	108.00	108.00	107.25	105.65	108.00	105.90	105.95
400	110.00	110.00	110.00	110.00	110.00	106.15	107.50	107.50	106.35	104.80
450	110.00	110.00	110.00	110.00	110.00	107.10	105.15	107.75	107.75	107.40
500	110.00	110.00	110.00	110.00	110.00	107.50	106.00	107.25	106.95	106.45
550	110.00	110.00	110.00	110.00	110.00	107.00	108.00	104.25	105.25	107.10
600	110.00	110.00	110.00	110.00	110.00	108.50	104.75	107.75	107.85	107.00
650	110.00	110.00	110.00	110.00	110.00	107.75	108.00	105.00	107.75	107.55
700	110.00	110.00	110.00	110.00	110.00	108.75	110.00	106.75	107.00	108.00
750	110.00	110.00	110.00	110.00	110.00	109.50	107.50	109.75	108.00	107.25
800	110.00	110.00	110.00	110.00	110.00	110.00	109.00	110.00	108.00	109.75
850	110.00	110.00	110.00	110.00	110.00	110.00	110.00	110.00	110.00	110.00
900	110.00	110.00	110.00	110.00	110.00	110.00	110.00	110.00	110.00	110.00

Figure 14. Average fitness vs. generation number (number of populations = 5; population size = 20)

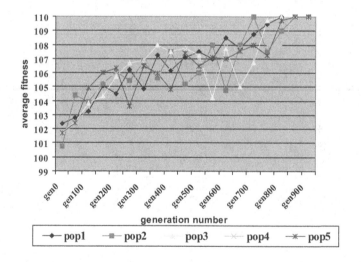

Table 6. Statistics for R(3,3,3) (number of populations = 6; population size = 20)

	Pop1	Pop2	Pop3	Pop4	Pop5	Pop6	Pop1	Pop2	Pop3	Pop4	Pop5	Pop6
Generation			**BestFitness**						**AverageFitness**			
0	104.00	103.00	106.00	105.00	106.00	107.00	101.35	101.80	101.70	102.25	101.90	101.50
50	103.00	106.00	107.00	106.00	105.00	105.00	102.10	102.45	103.60	106.00	101.90	100.20
100	107.00	109.00	107.00	105.00	106.00	106.00	104.15	103.40	102.95	103.25	103.50	103.50
150	107.00	109.00	109.00	109.00	107.00	106.00	100.35	102.45	103.80	102.85	104.60	104.50
200	107.00	109.00	100.00	109.00	109.00	107.00	104.70	103.50	103.10	104.95	104.00	103.35
250	107.00	109.00	100.00	109.00	107.00	109.00	103.70	105.95	105.20	104.60	106.10	103.85
300	109.00	109.00	109.00	109.00	108.00	109.00	104.70	105.65	106.10	105.30	106.00	106.75
350	109.00	109.00	109.00	109.00	109.00	109.00	106.90	106.10	106.85	104.55	106.90	107.00
400	109.00	109.00	109.00	109.00	109.00	109.00	105.30	106.10	107.00	105.20	106.80	106.80
450	109.00	109.00	109.00	109.00	109.00	109.00	106.20	105.80	106.50	107.00	106.80	107.00
500	109.00	109.00	109.00	109.00	109.00	109.00	106.80	106.70	107.00	107.00	107.00	106.20
550	109.00	109.00	109.00	109.00	109.00	109.00	106.80	107.00	106.60	106.80	107.00	107.00
600	109.00	109.00	109.00	109.00	109.00	109.00	105.80	107.60	106.50	107.00	107.00	106.60
650	109.00	109.00	109.00	109.00	109.00	109.00	109.00	107.80	108.00	109.00	106.90	108.90
700	109.00	109.00	109.00	109.00	109.00	109.00	108.80	109.00	109.00	109.00	109.00	109.00
750	109.00	109.00	109.00	109.00	109.00	109.00	109.00	109.00	109.00	109.00	109.00	109.00

Figure 15. Average fitness vs. generation number (number of populations = 6; population size = 20)

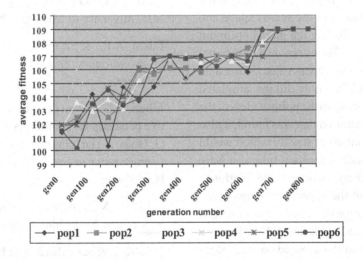

GAs that is capable of improving the time performance and of reducing the likelihood of premature convergence. CgGAs were presented as a type of PGA that maintain a number of independent populations and allow for the occasional interchange of individuals. It was discussed how, in this manner, cgGAs increase the diversity of search paths and thus have a better chance of finding an optimal solution. As a case study, a cgGA for solving one of the most interesting and difficult problems in combinatorics, finding Ramsey Numbers, was proposed. In order to verify and validate the superior performance of cgGAs over traditional GAs in finding Ramsey Numbers, a simulated cgGA was developed. According to the experimental results, increasing the number of populations in a cgGA does not help in reducing the rate of premature convergence; however, the difference between the fitness value of the permutations found with the traditional GA and with the simulated cgGA is evident. The reason for the superior performance of the cgGA is that it maintains multiple populations that evolve independently. In this manner, each population explores different parts of the search space and thus the chances of finding the global optimum increase. When R(3,3,3) was run on a traditional GA, no permutation with fitness value greater than 108 was ever found. Not only did the simulated cgGA perform better from the point of view of the quality of the permutation that was found, it also used a small population of size 20 which would result in a much faster execution time if it were to be implemented on a truly parallel platform. Thus, the results of the experiments conducted lead us to the conclusion that cgGA-based attempts to improve the bounds of Ramsey Numbers are more promising than those based on traditional GA's, and, hence, lead us to look with increased confidence in these directions.

There is ample opportunity for future work on this problem. We will investigate finding the ideal values for the following parameters: Crossover Rate, Mutation Rate, Migration Frequency, and Migration Size. A comparative study of the effects of these parameters can give greater insight into their optimal values. It will also be very interesting to experiment with different Crossover Selection, Crossover, and Migrant Selection strategies as well as with different Migration topologies. Probably the most important work that we plan to carry out in the future is to implement the cgGA proposed in this chapter on a truly parallel platform.

REFERENCES

Cohoon, J.P., Hedge, S.U., Martin, W.N., & Richards, D.S. (1991). Distributed genetic algorithms for the floorplan design problem. *IEEE Transactions on Computer-Aided Design of Integrated Circuits and Systems, 10*(4), 483-492.

Darwin, C. (1859). *On the origin of species by means of natural selection.* London: J. Murray Press.

De Jong, K. (1975). *An analysis of the behavior of a class of genetic adaptive systems.* Ann Arbor, MI: University of Michigan Press.

Eiben, A.E., & Smith, J.E. (2003). *Introduction to evolutionary computing.* Berlin, Germany: Springer.

Eiben, A.E., & van der Hauw, J.K. (1998). Adaptive penalties for evolutionary graph coloring. In G. Goos, J. Hartmanis & J. van Leeuwen (Eds.), *Lecture notes in computer science* (pp. 95-106). Heidelberg, Germany: Springer.

Erickson, M.J. (1996). *Introduction to combinatorics.* New York: John Wiley & Sons.

Gondra, I., & Samadzadeh, M.H. (2003). A coarse-grain parallel genetic algorithm for finding ramsey numbers. In *Proceedings of the Annual ACM Symposium on Applied Computing* (pp. 2-8).

Goodman, E.D., Lin, S., & Punch, W.F. (1994). Coarse-grain parallel genetic algorithms: Categorization and new approach. In *Proceedings of the IEEE Symposium on Parallel and Distributed Processing* (pp. 28-37).

Goldberg D.E., & Richardson, J.T. (1987). Genetic algorithms with sharing for multi-modal function optimization. In *Proceedings of the International Conference on Genetic Algorithms and Their Applications* (pp. 41-49).

Graham, R.L., & Spencer, J.H. (1990). Ramsey theory. *Scientific American, 263*(1), 112-117.

Holland, J. (1975). *Adaptation in natural and artificial systems.* Ann Arbor, MI: University of Michigan Press.

Mouldin, M. (1984). Maintaining diversity in genetic search. In *Proceedings of the National Conference on Artificial Intelligence* (pp. 247-250).

Papadopoulos, C.V. (1994). On the parallel execution of combinatorial heuristics. In *Proceedings of the International Conference on Massively Parallel Computing Systems* (pp. 423-427).

Poon, P.W., & Carter, J.N. (1995). Genetic algorithm crossover operators for ordering applications. *Computers and Operations Research, 22*(1), 135-147.

Ramsey, F.P. (1930). On a problem of formal logic. *London Mathematical Society, 30*, 264-286.

Rebaudergo, M., & Sonza Reorda, M. (1992). An experimental analysis of the effects of migration in parallel genetic algorithms. In *Proceedings of the Euromicro Workshop on Parallel and Distributed Processing* (pp. 232-238).

Stracuzzi, D.J. (1998). *Some methods for the parallelization of genetic algorithms.* Retrieved August 22, 2007, from http://ml-www.cs.umass.edu/~stracudj/genetic/dga.html

Ugoluk, G. (1997). A method for chromosome handling of r-permutations of n-element sets in genetic algorithms. In *Proceedings of the IEEE International Conference on Evolutionary Computation* (pp. 55-58).

Chapter XIII
Using Genetic Programming to Extract Knowledge from Artificial Neural Networks

Daniel Rivero
University of A Coruña, Spain

Miguel Varela
University of A Coruña, Spain

Javier Pereira
University of A Coruña, Spain

ABSTRACT

A technique is described in this chapter that makes it possible to extract the knowledge held by previously trained artificial neural networks. This makes it possible for them to be used in a number of areas (such as medicine) where it is necessary to know how they work, as well as having a network that functions. This chapter explains how to carry out this process to extract knowledge, defined as rules. Special emphasis is placed on extracting knowledge from recurrent neural networks, in particular when applied in predicting time series.

INTRODUCTION

Through the use of artificial neural networks (ANN), satisfactory results have been obtained in the most diverse fields of application, including the classification of examples, the identification of images, and processing of natural language.

However, in some fields there is still some reticence toward their use, mainly as a result of

one single issue: the fact that they do not justify their answer. An ANN extracts information from a training series (formed by input-output pairs, or simply input if unsupervised training is used). Based on the information obtained, it will be able to offer output for input not previously seen during the learning process. Even if the answer provided is correct, the ANN does not provide any information about why one particular solution has been chosen: it behaves like a "black box". This is unacceptable in certain fields. For example, any system used in medical diagnosis must not only reach the correct conclusions, but also be able to justify on what it has based its decision. For this reason, expert systems are commonly used in medicine.

Expert systems (ES) are able to explain the solution or response achieved, which is their main core and also their guarantee of success. Therefore, this chapter attempts to develop a system that carries out an automatic extraction of rules from previously trained ANN, thereby obtaining the knowledge that an ANN obtains from the problem it solves.

Different rule-extraction techniques using ANN have been used to date, always applied to multi-layer ANN, as they are easier to handle. These networks also have a limited capacity with regard to the knowledge that can be distributed among their connections.

As may be inferred, the extraction of rules and expressions from recurrent ANN is more complicated, due to the fact that past states intervene in neural activation, and that their distributed knowledge capacity is considerably higher than that of multi-layer ANN, as there are no restrictions to neural connectivity. Also, if recurrent ANNs are used in dynamic problems where certain time characteristics such as the prediction of time series intervene, the task of extracting using the methods developed so far becomes harder, if not impossible for most of them.

However, if ANN provides good results, why reject them? It would be enough to find a method that justifies the output offered by ANN based on the input values. This method would have to be able to be applied to networks of any type, meaning that they would have to comply with the following characteristics (Tickle, 1998):

- **Independence of the architecture:** The method for extracting rules should be able to be applied independently from the ar-

chitecture of the ANN, including recurrent architectures.

- **Independence of the training algorithm:** The extraction of rules cannot depend on the algorithm used for the ANN's learning process.
- **Correction:** Many methods for extracting rules only create approximations of the functioning of the ANN, instead of creating rules as precisely as possible.
- **Eloquence:** The language used to describe the rules extracted must represent the knowledge obtained from the ANN as eloquently as possible.

STATE OF THE ART

Genetic Programming

Some believe that Cramer (1985) and Fujiki (1987), who published on evolving programs in 1985 and 1987 at the very first ICGA conference, are the pioneers of genetic programming (GP). However, others think that Friedberg, who from 1958 to 1959 evolved machine language programs (Friedberg, 1958, Friedberg, 1959), is really the pioneer.

John Koza (1992) devised the term used as the title of his book *Genetic Programming*. This book formally establishes the basis of GP used nowadays. Later, the same author published *Genetic Programming I* (Koza, 1994), and, recently, *Genetic Programming III* (Koza, 1999). Both explore the new possibilities of GP.

Different fields are derived from GP. One of the most promising with regard to knowledge discovery (KD) is that of "fuzzy rules" (Fayaad, 1996; Bonarini, 1996). This field derives from the union between fuzzy logic and systems based on rules (SBR). Fuzzy rules can be obtained through evolutionary computation (EC) with the technique known as automatically defined functions (ADF) (Koza, 1994), an evolution of the concept known as "classical genetic programming."

GP works through the evolution of a population. In this population, each individual is a solution to the problem we are trying to solve. This evolution occurs by selecting the best individuals (although the worst also have a small probability of being selected) and combining them to create new solutions. This process is carried out using selection, mutation, and crossover algorithms. After some generations, the population is expected to contain a good enough solution to the problem.

In GP, the codification of solutions is carried out in the shape of "trees." As a result, the user must specify which terminals ("leaves") and functions can be used by the algorithm. With them, complex expressions can be produced that are either mathematical (i.e., involving arithmetical operators), logical (involving Boolean or relational operators), or even more complex.

ANN Rule Extraction

The extraction of rules representing the knowledge stored in an ANN is an NP-complete problem. However, this has not been an obstacle to the development of a large number of systems that carry out this task, more or less successfully (Rabuñal, 2004).

Andrews (1995, 1996) identifies three techniques for discovering rules: "decompositional," "pedagogical," and "eclectic." The first refers to discovery at neural level, focusing on dealing with each of the ANN's neurons, particularly those in the hidden and output layers. Therefore, rules are extracted from each neuron and its relation to the other neurons. This makes the methods related to this technique totally dependent on the architecture of the ANN to be dealt with, meaning their applicability is generically limited. The second treats the ANN as a "black box," where by applying inputs, only the relations between these inputs and the ANN outputs are analysed. The main goal of this technique is to obtain the function that is computed by the ANN. The third technique uses the ANN's architecture and the input-output pairs as a complement to a symbolic training algorithm. This technique combines elements from the first two.

"Decompositional" and "pedagogical" rule-extraction techniques may be combined. An example is DEDEC (Tickle, 1996), which uses trained ANN to create examples from which the underlying rules may be extracted. However, an important difference is that it extracts additional information from the trained ANN by subjecting the resultant weight vectors to further analysis (a "partial" decompositional approach). This information is then used to direct the strategy for generating a (minimal) set of examples for the learning phase. It also uses an efficient algorithm for the rule extraction phase.

Rabuñal (2004) contains an introduction to the most important techniques for extracting rules from neuronal networks. Rabuñal (2004) discusses methods such as the following: those described in Jang (1992), Buckley (1993), and Benítez (1997), which use diffuse rules; Towell (1994) who analysed the network's connections; using lineal programming as in Thrun (1995); GA as in Keedwell (2000); other algorithms such as RULENEG (Pop, 1994) and TREPAN (Craven, 1996a, 1996b), and others based on them (Chalup, 1998; Visser, 1996).

One of the most remarkable aspects in every discovery process is the optimization of the rules obtained from the analysis of the ANN. It should be noted that the rules discovered may have redundant conditions; many specific rules may be contained in general ones, and many of the logical expressions that have been discovered may be simplified if they are written another way. Therefore, rule optimization consists of the simplification and elaboration of symbolic operations with the rules. Depending on the discovery method and the type of rules that have been obtained, various optimization techniques may be applied. Therefore, they may be classified into two main groups: *a posteriori* methods and implied optimization methods. The first group usually consists of a syntactic analysis algorithm which is applied to the rules discovered in order to simplify them. For instance, Duch (2001) uses Prolog as programming language in order to carry out a post-processing of the rules obtained. In this way, optimal linguistic variables are achieved, which help to discover simplified rules which use these variables. Implied optimization methods are techniques used in rule-discovery algorithms that intrinsically cause the algorithm to produce better and better rules.

KNOWLEDGE EXTRACTION SYSTEMS

Development Premises

When faced with the design of a discovery algorithm, the most important task is that of deciding its modus operandi. As previously explained, discovery techniques may be classified into three main groups: "decompositional," "pedagogical," and "eclectic."

In the pedagogical method, the rules are created based on an empirical analysis of the pairs (input, output) presented to the ANN. This is an approximation based on the "black box," as it completely ignores the internal functioning of the ANN. The basic idea consists of seeing the rule extraction process as a learning task in which the concept sought is the function calculated by the ANN, and the input characteristics are the inputs of the ANN. Techniques of this kind will attempt to extract rules that directly transform these inputs into the outputs.

On the contrary, in the decompositional method, the rules are determined by inspecting the "weight" of each of the ANN neurones and the relationship between one neurone and the rest. This technique has several inconveniences. First, by independently analysing the nodes, the results wholly depend on the architecture of the ANN analysed. Second, the complexity of the rule

extraction grows exponentially as the size of the ANN increases, meaning that techniques of this kind are not valid for use with complex ANN.

The third "eclectic" method blends together elements from the first two. In this category, techniques may be classified that use knowledge of the internal architecture or the vectors of ANN weights to complement a learning algorithm.

The combination of CE techniques with traditional inductive algorithms has shown to be capable of offering better results than by applying the previous techniques on an individual basis.

However, the individual application of developmental algorithms reduces the complexity of the method of rule extraction, and produces results equally as good as those that would be obtained in combination with other methods. An example of this is the GABIL system, which carries out an incremental search for a group of classification rules represented by a sequence of fixed-length bits.

The application of CE techniques is to some extent similar to applying an ANN to solving problems. Both are based on the translation of biological processes to computing. They are highly recommendable techniques when working on problems that grow exponentially as the number of variables have to be considered increase. In these situations, which make it unviable to apply deterministic search processes, they behave with tremendous efficiency.

Amongst the CE techniques, opting for the GA as a rule-extracting algorithm presents a series of difficulties. The most important of these is that in order to store the rules extracted in the chromosome, it is necessary to use a GA with variable length individuals, as it is not possible to previously establish the number of rules that will be extracted, which considerably increases the complexity involved. Furthermore, codifying the problem of rule extraction as an easily understood and interpretable chain of values is a highly complex task.

A large number of these inconveniences are solved with GP. Firstly, the codification of solutions as a tree does not predetermine a fixed size for the solution, or a specific number of rules. Furthermore, the tree is the traditional method of representation used by lexical and syntactical analysers that have always been used for analysing programmes, which may be seen as a generalisation of the rules extracted from an ANN. For these reasons GP was chosen for use as the inductive algorithm for rule extraction.

In this article, GP is used as an algorithm for constructing syntactic trees that represent rules. To do so, a process of symbolic regression has been used, applied to input-output patterns. The input patterns are the input sequences applied to the ANN and the outputs desired are those produced by the ANN. Therefore, the rules returned by GP will imitate the functioning of the ANN. This type of technique may be considered as "pedagogical," in which the ANN is treated as a "black box." The advantage of this is that it is not necessary to know anything about the internal functioning of the ANN. However, it may be desirable to some knowledge of the internal structure and functioning of the ANN with the aim of largely reducing the search area of the rules. Systems of this type, for which there is some information about how they function, are known as "grey boxes." By using GP, it is possible to enter information about the ANN through the configuration of the GP algorithm for the task designated for the ANN. For example, if it is known that the ANN carries out classification tasks, the type of rules wished

to be obtained may be limited to Boolean values, avoiding floating point values. This eliminates a large number of mathematical expressions in which to carry out the search, meaning that the system will be more efficient. If a certain level of knowledge of the ANN is used in the system, the technique may be considered as "eclectic" instead of "pedagogical."

System Description

A pedagogical methodology was chosen for use, with the aim of obtaining the greatest independence of the ANN architecture and the learning algorithm used. In this way, the ANN is considered as a system capable of abstracting the peculiarities of a problem, from which it provides outputs to the input patterns used. When extracting rules that explain the functioning of the ANN, it will be of interest that these capture the generality of the resolution process, and not the individual contribution of each of the elements of the network. Therefore, as mentioned previously, the ANN may be treated as if it were a black box or a function—albeit complex—that transforms input patterns into output patterns.

As mentioned previously, the process to be carried out consists of discovering the ANN's rules based on input-output patterns. Inputs are applied to the ANN and, by using the outputs produced, the "inputs_training_set - outputs_ANN" patterns are built. The inductive algorithm (GP) will use these patterns in order to quantify the adjustment achieved by the rules obtained (fitness)

Figure 1. Rule extraction process of ANN

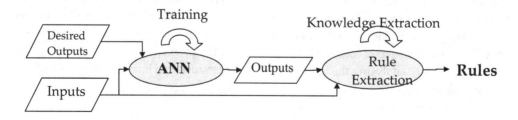

Figure 2. Rule extraction process

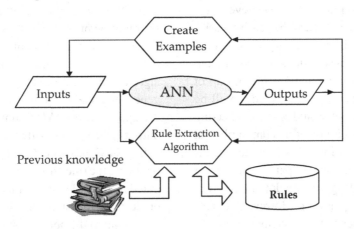

with the pair "outputs (ANN) - outputs_obtained (rules)" (Rabuñal, 2004).

Once the ANNs have been designed and trained, the same training and test values may be used in order to generate a second data pattern which will be used to search for the rules that the ANN has acquired during the training process. Figure 1 shows a general chart of what the process would be like.

This previous knowledge would include the information about the type of data used by the ANN, or the type of problem trying to be solved. For example, if it is known that the ANN is working exclusively on Boolean values, it may be possible to prevent the extraction algorithm attempting to seek out rules that include continuous operators or variables. In this way, it is possible to reduce the search area that the algorithm has to explore, with the subsequent improvement in efficiency, depending on the quantity of knowledge held about the network and the type of problem being dealt with.

Figure 2 shows the discovery process diagram followed for the development of the rule discovery system.

Discovering the Generalization Capacity

Another aspect to be taken into account when designing the discovery mechanism is that it may be expanded in order to determine an important feature presented by ANNs, which has been one of the main reasons for their success: the generalisation capacity. The purpose is to extract the knowledge which the ANN obtains from the training patterns and from test cases that have not been provided during the learning process.

For this purpose, we must design an algorithm to create new test cases which are going to be applied to the ANN, allowing its behaviour to be analysed when faced with new situations, and also to discover its functional limitations. This aspect is of particular relevance when applying ANNs to certain fields with a high practical risk, such as monitoring nuclear power plants and diagnosing certain medical conditions, and it has not been clearly used in the scientific literature about ANNs and rule discovery until now.

The ideal situation to be able to extract knowledge about the generalisation ability of the ANN would be to analyse the results produced by the ANN when faced with all of the possible combinations of input values. However, this becomes unviable as the search area increases, meaning that it will be necessary to provide a mechanism that makes selections depending from which input-output combinations (the group of examples) the extraction of knowledge will be made. One alternative would involve selecting a subgroup of these combinations randomly and in a uniform distribution. This leads to obtaining a relatively low number of patterns, meaning that the rule extracting process does not require excessive computing power. However, it docs have the inconvenience that it is not possible to guarantee that all of the combinations have been selected, making it possible to extract all of the generalisation capacity of the ANN.

As regards discovering the generalisation capacity, an algorithm known as the "algorithm for the creation of new patterns" has been designed. New test cases may be created using this algorithm, making it possible to discover rules and expressions of those parts of the ANN's internal functioning which have not been explored by the learning patterns. We are not sure if the behaviour of the ANN matches the behaviour of the external reality; we only hope so. The use of new test cases has the sole purpose to better mimic the model of the ANN; it cannot necessarily be extended to the point that the rule set will better mimic the problem being considered. For this purpose, we start with the learning patterns, applying to them the rule-discovery algorithm that has been previously used through GP. The solution used is based on the premise that all ANNs obtain the capacity for generalisation from the implicit knowledge of the training files. This means that the example-creating algorithm will have to make use of these files. Additionally, it will be provided with a new set of input combinations, selected at random and based on the inputs of the previous files.

Having determined the existence of this group of new inputs, its size will have to be established. If it is small, its influence will barely be notice-

able in the final result. On the contrary, if it is too high, it will make the solutions tend toward the information provided by these new inputs, minimizing the contribution of the original training patterns. Once a good adjustment is obtained, the algorithm for creating new patterns is applied, thus generating a series of new input patterns which are applied to the ANN, obtaining the relevant outputs. These new patterns "new_inputs - outputs_ANN" are added to the training patterns, renewing the rule-discovery process. It should be noted that in order to continue with the discovery process, the first step is to reassess each and every individual in the population in order to calculate its new adjustment. Once this has been done, the discovery process may continue.

As the rule extraction process advances, it is possible to eliminate the examples that the rules obtained so far have captured from the group of new inputs. When there is a new test case in which the ANN's output coincides with that produced by the best combination of rules obtained, then that test case is eliminated, as it is considered that the rules obtained have acquired the knowledge represented by that test case. It is possible to add new examples at the same time, making it possible to explore new regions of the search space. The examples provided by the training files will stay constant throughout the process, meaning they will always be presented to the rule extraction algorithm.

Therefore, the process is carried out in an iterative manner: A number of generations or simulations of the rule-discovery algorithm are simulated, new test cases are generated once it is finished, and those whose result coincides with that of the ANN are eliminated. Once all the relevant test cases have been eliminated, new cases are created in order to fill in the gaps left by those that have been deleted. Each new case is compared with the existing ones in order to determine if it is already present in the test cases. In this case, it is eliminated and a new one created in the same way. Then the process starts again, running the discovery algorithm N generations, once again repeating the elimination and creation of test cases. This process will be complete when the user determines that the rules obtained are those desired.

The parameters used by the algorithm for the creation of new patterns are described in detail in Rabuñal (2004), together with a more formal description of the algorithm.

In order to generate a new input pattern from those already existing, a number of different alternatives may be applied: creating all of the new values randomly, or, starting out with some of the original patterns, modifying them in some way in order to generate a new entry. Using the first method, it is possible to generate patterns that vary greatly from each other, and which do not correspond to the areas of the search space in which the ANN work, which may reduce the validity of the rules obtained. However, this may be interesting in the event of wishing to check how the ANN responds in extreme situations. In the case of the second alternative, one of the training patterns is chosen at random, and by slightly modifying its values, a new example case is constructed. In this way, inputs are generated that are not too far apart in the search space of the training cases. Therefore, the tendency will be to produce new input sequences from which all of the possible output cases are generated for which the ANN has been trained.

Although the algorithm for generating examples is totally independent from the architecture of the ANN, the fact of working with a feedforward or recurrent network means that the algorithm is totally different.

When working with recurrent networks, it is not enough to compare the output offered by the RANN with that offered by the rules for an input pattern to determine if the rules have captured the correct knowledge or not. This is due to the fact that the functioning of an RANN is not based on individual input patterns, but instead on sequences of inputs. This means that

the behaviour of the RANN can only be said to have been captured when the rules offer the same outputs as the RANN itself for all of the values of a sequence of entries.

The solution adopted in the particular case of the RANN uses the training files as its initial base, in order to generate a new starting sequence which, when applied as input to the ANN, will produce the subsequent input-output combinations. For example, if an RANN is used for predicting a short-term time series, it will work as a feedback system: The value is given at moment t and the network predicts the value at the moment $t+1$, and this value at moment $t+1$ is provided as input to predict the value at moment $t+2$, and so on.

A sequence of inputs will be eliminated when the rules simulate the behaviour of all of the values of the series with an error below a pre-established threshold — when the sequence of output values for the ANN obtained from the new value created coincides with the sequence obtained applying the rules extracted about this value. When this occurs, a new input value must be created, from which a new sequence of inputs will be generated so that the rule extraction process can start again.

In the case of working with RANN, the system will have a series of additional parameters. In total, it will have the following parameters:

- **Percentage of new patterns**. How many new patterns will be used apart from the training patterns. In the case of not working with time series, these new patterns are checked so that they are different from the training patterns. If working with a time series, these new random patterns are added at the end of the series used for training.
- **Probability of change**. The process for creating new test cases focuses on generating new sequences from the training data. A sequence of inputs is chosen at random from the training file. For each input, the same value is maintained or a new one is generated at random, following a certain

Figure 3. Initial process for crating examples in cases of RANN and Temporary ANN

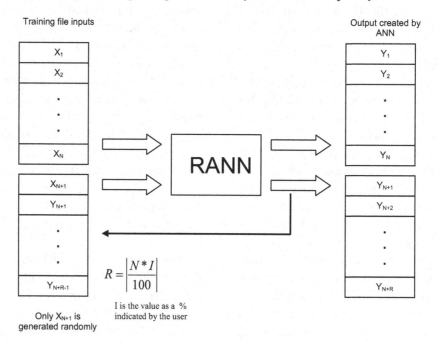

probability. This technique is similar to the EC mutation process.

- **Minimum error for survival**. Once the process has started to extract rules, and as these are generated, they reflect the patterns with which they are being trained. Once the rules extracted sufficiently reflect the behaviour of the ANN with a given pattern, this pattern is no longer necessary, and so it is discarded and a new one created. This parameter indicates when a pattern should be discarded, when the error value obtained for the rules in this specific pattern is below a certain threshold.

- **Number of feedback outputs**. When working with recurrent networks, the aim is also to study the behaviour of the network by taking the outputs it returns and using them as inputs. This parameter indicates the number of patterns (the group of patterns whose size is indicated by the parameter "percentage of

new patterns") that will not be generated at random, but which instead will be the result of simulating the network, taking each input as the output in the previous moment.

Figure 3 is a graphic representation of the idea. The way of eliminating the sequence of examples also will vary. In this case, only a random value is created, and this is what creates all of the following cases. The criteria for elimination will be when the *R* new sequences created have a comparison error with those produced by the RANN of zero, or when the rules assimilate the knowledge that exists in all of the subseries of new cases. As a result, all of them will be eliminated. The next step will be to create a new random value, use it to construct the new subseries, and start the extraction process again until the adjustment is achieved, and so on.

As may be seen in Figure 3, an overlapping occurs in the sequence of inputs created between the inputs (X) and the outputs, as a result of the first randomly generated value. In this way, it is possible to analyse the behaviour of the RANN faced with a multitude of possible future sequences, and to abstract the generalisation knowledge resident in its recurrent connections.

Here, it is important to note that in order to obtain an output, the RANN not only takes into account the input value at the actual moment, but that the outputs from previous moments also have an influence. This means it makes use of the ability for *internal memory* provided by the feedback, and therefore that every effort should be made to ensure that this information stored in the ANN does not affect the outputs associated with the new patterns created by feedback. To do so, before generating a new example sequence, a series of randomly generated values are entered into the ANN so that the internal memory is not determined by previous examples.

Rule Extraction with RANNs for Time Series Forecasts

When working with temporary RANN to predict series, the data used during the training process are usually values or measurements taken from a real process. For example, in the prediction of sunspots, the quantity of sunspots produced each year are represented, and these values are cannot be altered. In this and other similar cases, the unknowns are the future values and the behaviour of the ANN in order to predict these values.

In the case of short-term prediction, the aim will be for the ANN, or otherwise the rules extracted from its behaviour, to predict the output value at the moment t – $Y(t)$ — using the input values $X(t)$ and the outputs of the previous moments $Y(t-1)$, …, $Y(t-n)$.

The process is slightly different for long-term prediction. In this case, the input values are known up to moment t – $X(1)$, …, $X(t)$ — and the aim is to predict the output value at a future moment, for example at $t=N$. In this case, the outputs provided by the ANN in a given moment will be re-entered as inputs in the following cycle. This means that the value of $Y(N)$ may be obtained from the values $X(1)$, …, $X(t)$, $Y(t)$, $Y(t+1)$, …, $Y(N-1)$.

Rule extraction will be the same in both cases; what will vary is adapting these rules depending on whether greater importance is to be given to prediction in the short or long term. This adaptation will be determined by comparing the output values provided by the ANN and the rules themselves. The difference lies in how the output for the rules is obtained in the case of the examples created by feedback (patterns $X(i+1)$, …, $X(i+n)$ in Figure 3).

This means that in order to check how the rules adjust the behaviour of the ANN, it is necessary to compare, from a given moment $t=i$, the output provided by the ANN– $Y\_ANN_{t=I}$ — with that obtained using the rule — $Y\_Rule_{=i}$. In the case of short-term prediction, in the following cycles the rule will use that provided by the ANN in the previous moment as the input:

$$X\_Rule_{t=i+1} = Y\_ANN_{t=i}$$

Here the aim is to favour rules that best adjust the behaviour of the ANN at a given moment, only using information from the previous outputs of the ANN.

On the contrary, in case of long-term prediction, the rule will use as an entry value at moment $i+1$ the feedback output from the rule at the moment immediately beforehand. In this way, the output from the moment $t+n$ (long-term prediction) will be a direct consequence of the outputs provided by the rules, not by the ANN, from moment i.

$$X\_Rule_{t=i+1} = Y\_Rule_{t=i}$$

Optimization of Rules Obtained

Whatever the methodology chosen to extract the rules, one of the most important steps involves the optimization or post-processing of the rules obtained. This optimization is necessary for several reasons:

- Multiple specific rules may be summarized in a single, more general rule.
- Redundancies may appear amongst the rules obtained.
- Many rules may be simplified just by rewriting them in a different way.

Also, the optimization process includes the simplification and/or creation of symbolic operations between the rules.

Various optimization techniques may be applied, depending on the extraction method used and the type of rules obtained. These techniques may be divided into two groups: a posteriori methods and implicit optimization methods.

The first group is generally formed by syntactic analysis algorithms. One example is the use of the Prolog language to carry out the simplification and validation of the new rules obtained. To do so, a series of linguistic variables are generated, which are then used to find the simplified rules that use these variables the implicit optimization methods are formed by a group of techniques used in rule discovery algorithms, which intrinsically lead to the algorithm discovering improved rules.

As mentioned, GP was chosen as the rule extraction algorithm. One of the classic configuration parameters of GP, parsimony or penalisation for profundity, may be used in the process of optimizing the rules extracted.

In conceptual terms, when the level of adaptation of a genetic individual is evaluated — in this case each individual or tree will be the representation of a rule — its "goodness" value is reduced by a certain amount depending on the number of terminal and non-terminal nodes it presents. The larger the number of nodes, the greater the amount by which its goodness value is reduced. This method is used to benefit the creation of simpler rules which are therefore easier to interpret.

Table 1. Possible GP parameters and their values

Parameter	Options
Population creation algorithm	Full
	Partial
	Ramped Half&Half
Selection algorithm	Tournament
	Roulette
	Stochastic remainder
	Stochastic universal
	Deterministic sample
Mutation algorithm	Subtree
	Punctual
Elitist strategy	YES-NO
Crossover rate	0-100 %
Mutation rate	0-100 %
Non-terminal selection probability	0-100 %
Population size	Number of individuals
Parsimony level	Penalty value

Table 2. Possible elements of groups of terminals and functions

Parameter	Options
Logical Operators	AND
	OR
	NOT
Relational Operators	$>, <, =, <>, >=, <=$
Arithmetic Functions	+, -, *, % (protected division)
Decision Functions	IF–THEN– ELSE over real values
IF–THEN– ELSE over Boolean values	
Constants	Random rank selection or manually established (indicating rank or one by one)
Input Variables	Determining one by one whether it is real or Boolean
Type of Outputs	Real
	Boolean
	Turning Real into Boolean (specifying the threshold)

GP PARAMETER CONFIGURATION

The next step in discovering rules is the numeric calculation of the parameters involved in the algorithm.

Experimentation is used to adjust the GP-related parameters. These are the implemented parameters:

When specifying terminal and non-terminal operators, a type must be specified: Each node will have a type, and non-terminal nodes will demand a particular type from their offspring (Montana, 1995). This guarantees that the trees generated in this way satisfy the grammar specified by the user. Also, both sets of specified operators must fulfill two requirements: closure and sufficiency; it must be possible to build correct trees with the specified operators, and to express the solution to the problem (the expression we are searching for) using these operators.

An empirical analysis must be carried out in order to adjust the ideal parameters, trying different combinations in order to adjust the various values progressively until the best results are achieved.

The following parameter adjustment is related to the terminal and non-terminal nodes that will take part in the execution of the algorithm. The knowledge we already possess about the ANN, together with the types of problems for which it was designed, will be of consequence in this case.

These are the parameters to be selected:

As may be seen, a wide range of configurations is possible. The more information we have about the ANN, the easier it is to establish the values of the parameters detailed above. Otherwise, experimentation is required in order to determine which are the best for each ANN.

RESULTS

Redes Feedforward for Classification

Rabuñal (2004) provides an extensive description of how to apply ANNs in different types of problems, as well as the subsequent extraction of rules from the networks obtained using the technique described in this article. The problems resolved in this case are the classification of iris flowers (Fisher, 1936) and poisonous mushrooms (Blake, 1998) and the diagnosis of breast cancer, hepatitis, and appendicitis (Blake, 1998). The results obtained in solving these problems using genetic programming and ANN, as well as their comparison against other techniques, may be found in Rabuñal (2004).

Having trained the network for each problem, the rule extraction algorithm is applied only using the training patterns as inputs, and using the algorithm for creating new patterns. Table 3 shows a comparison of the adjustments obtained by using only the learning patterns, and those achieved

Table 3. Adjustment values obtained in the process of extracting rules, using only training patterns and the algorithm for creating new examples

Method	Problem						
	Iris Flower			Breast Cancer	Hepatitis	Poisonous Mushrooms	Appendicitis
	Iris setosa	Iris versicolor	Iris virginica				
Without dynamic creation	63.34%	56.97%	57.23%	64.56 %	59.95 %	77.44 %	78.93 %
With dynamic creation	95.45%	88.81%	77.88%	71.91 %	73.34 %	82.51 %	85.97 %

by using the algorithm for creating new patterns. In order to create this table, an analysis file was built with all of the possible values for the input variables, taking regular intervals (normalized inputs). By using these intervals, it is possible to analyse the whole possible range of classifications that the rules carry out. Table 3 shows the adjustment values produced by the rules obtained with both methods when the analysis file patterns are evaluated.

Time Series Forecast

RANN architectures must be used for the prediction of time series and for modeling problems of this type. In this section we will show that the system proposed in this chapter can also successfully perform knowledge extraction from RANNs. The extraction of rules from ANNs with recurrent architecture presents an additional hurdle, as these ANN are characterised by their immense capacity for representation and distributed knowledge among their connections. This can be specifically applied to time and dynamic problems. The problem to be solved will be the prediction of a classic chaotic laboratory time series: the Mackey-Glass series (Mackey, 1977). The following results show that the rules to be obtained from this ANN should incorporate

Figure 4. RANN that emulate the Mackey-Glass function

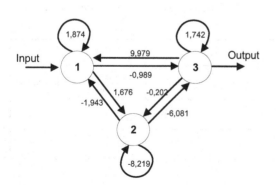

mechanisms for treating time values. Therefore, non-terminal nodes representing mathematical and trigonometrical operations will be used, together with input variables at previous n moments (X_n). Most of these time series cases are structures with a single input and a single output. The input corresponds to a number value at the moment t, while the system's output is the prediction of the number value at t+1. The Mackey-Glass equation is an ordinary differential delay equation:

$$\frac{dx}{dt} = \frac{ax(t-\tau)}{1+x^c(t-\tau)} - bx(t) \tag{3}$$

Choosing $\tau = 30$, the equation becomes chaotic, and only short-term predictions are feasible. Integrating the equation (3) in the rank [t, t + τ t] we obtain:

$$x(t+\Delta t) = \frac{2-b\Delta t}{2+b\Delta t}x(t) + \frac{\alpha\Delta t}{2+b\Delta t}\left[\frac{x(t+\Delta t-\tau)}{1+x^c(t+\Delta t-\tau)} + \frac{x(t-\tau)}{1+x(t-\tau)}\right] \tag{4}$$

The first step is to obtain an RANN which emulates the behaviour of the time series. The RANN we used has three neurons with tangent hyperbolic activation function with total interconnection. The training files used correspond to the first 200 values of the time series (Figure 5). The RANN resulting from the training process which yielded the least mean square error (MSE=0.000072) is shown in Figure 4.

Once we obtained the RANN, we attempted to obtain the rules and the expressions which direct its functioning by using symbolic regression. In this case, we used a test file containing the first 1,000 values of the time series. These 1,000 values were transferred to the RANN, obtaining the corresponding outputs. Using the input-output file, we ran the GP algorithm.

Different combinations of terminal and function elements and GP parameters were tried, and the following used:

Figure 5. Comparison between the RANN forecast and the function forecast (4)

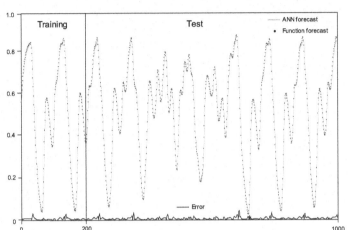

Figure 6. Mackey-Glass series: Adjustment obtained with 200 feedbacks

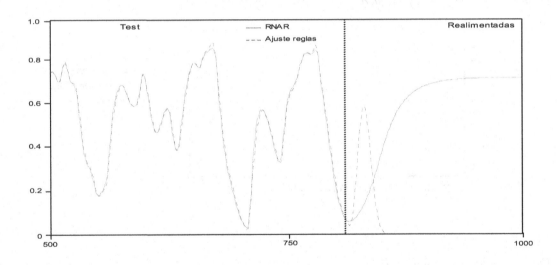

- *Arithmetic functions*: +, -, *, % (protected division)
- *Constants*: 10 random values in [0,1]
  Variables: X_n, X_{n-1}, X_{n-2}, X_{n-3}
- *Selection algorithm*: Tournament
  Population size: 1,000 individuals
- *Crossover rate*: 95%
  Mutation rate: 4%
- *Parsimony level*: 0.0001

Also, the elitist strategy was used, not permitting the loss of the best individual. The rule expressed as a mathematical function is as follows:

$$((X_n * (((((X_n * (X_n * X_{n-2})) \% X_{n-2}) * ((((0.9834 * (((((X_n * (X_{n-2} \% X_{n-3})) * X_{n-3}) * X_{n-3}) \% X_{n-3}) \% (X_n \% X_{n-3}))) \% X_{n-3}) \% ((X_{n-2} * X_{n-2}) \% X_{n-3})) \% X_{n-3}) * X_{n-2}) \% X_{n-2})) \% ((X_n * X_{n-2}) \% X_{n-3}) * 0.9834))$$

Figure 7. Mackey-Glass series: Adjustment obtained with 150 feedbacks

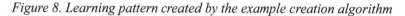

Figure 8. Learning pattern created by the example creation algorithm

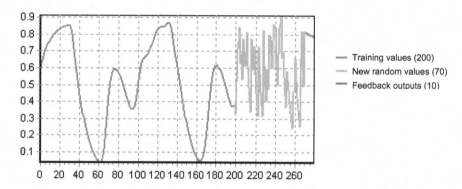

Figure 9. Adjustment obtained

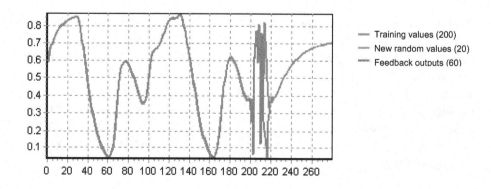

Figure 10. Mackey-Glass series: Adjustment obtained with extraction of generalisation

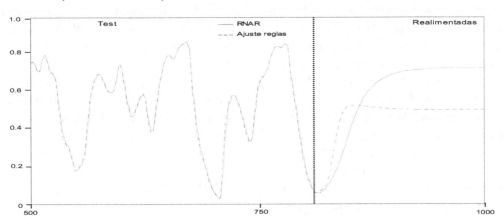

This function obtains a fitness value (normalised) on the 1,000 values produced by the RANN of 0.0029. Figure 5 compares the values produced by the function forecast (4) and the RANN forecast.

Considering Figure 5, it may be concluded that the rules adjust the short-term prediction of the ANN in a satisfactory manner. But what happens in the case of long-term prediction? To verify this, it is necessary to introduce the feedback of the outputs obtained in the immediately previous moment as input values to the rule.

The results show how the behaviour of the rule clearly differs from that of the ANN. While the ANN normally tends toward the middle values of the series, the outputs of the rules will tend toward one value or another, depending on the previous tendency — meaning if the series is on an ascending or descending slope at the moment when the feedback of the outputs begins. If the slope is descending (see Figure 6) the values provided by the rules tend toward 0 or $-\infty$, whereas if the slope is ascending (see Figure 7) the values tend toward 1 or $+\infty$.

Here it is possible to see how the output provided by the rules starts to grow in an undefined manner (specifically, at moment 1,000 it has a value of $1.94 * 10^{10}$).

Therefore, it seems apparent that the rule extracted has not apprehended the generalization capacity of the RANN as successfully as required. In order to solve this problem, the rule extracting process must be carried out again, this time with the improvement referred to. In this case the suitability of a rule will be obtained based on the feedback of its outputs, and not on the real values of the series itself or the outputs provided by the RANN. The scheme used to configure the rule extraction process includes the first 200 values from the series, 20 random values (to wipe the internal memory of the RANN) and 60 feedback entries, using the following parameter configuration:

- *Percentage of new patterns:*
  40% (Total of 200 + 80 patterns)
- *Probability of change:*
  20%
- *Minimum error for survival:*
  0.01
- *N° of feedback outputs:*
  between 10 and 60

At first, 10 values were used for this last parameter, and while the algorithm was being executed it was modified until it ended with 60 values. The reason for doing it this way is that if the process starts with a high value, the behaviour of the RANN tends toward the average of the last former values, and as a result the extraction process becomes stuck in a local minimum situated in the rule: Output = X_n (the output is the entry value → $X_{n+1} = X_n$). Therefore, in order to prevent this from happening, the random creation of new values is favoured over feedback outputs, and once the local minimum is exceeded, feedback outputs are favoured. This must be done manually, as the algorithm does not know if it has fallen in a local minimum or not, and by observing the type of rules obtained, the online parameters are readjusted.

In the case of the parameters for the extraction algorithm, the same were used as in the previous case, as the type of problem is the same, and also the expressions obtained and the results they produce may be compared more significantly in the same case scenarios.

Figure 8 shows an example for the creation of the initial values obtained by the algorithm for the dynamic creation of examples.

After one day and four hours of execution the following equation was obtained as a result of the extraction process:

$$((((((X_{n-1} - X_{n-3})*(-((X_n * X_n) - 0.7554)))*(-2.3241))*(-0.2474))+X_n) - ((((X_{n-1}*(-((X_n * X_n) - 0.7554)))*(-2.3241))*(-0.2474))*((((X_n - (-0.2457)) - X_{n-2})*(X_{n-3} + ((X_n * X_n)-0.7554))) \% ((X_{n-3} - (0.2979 * X_{n-4})) \% 0.0752))))$$

Figure 9 shows the adjustment obtained from the previous equation with the learning patterns configured as 200 training values, 20 random values, and 60 feedback inputs. It shows in greater detail the behaviour of the RANN when faced with the feedback of its outputs.

In Figure 9, it is possible to start to see how this rule behaves for long-term prediction. Here we may see how the outputs of the expression

are profiled within the range [0.1], the same presented by the original signal. Furthermore, as may be seen in Figure 10, the behaviour of the output provided by the rules is very similar to that provided by the RANN with an initial zone with rising values that are then stabilized toward the midway values of the signal, and with a highly satisfactory prediction in the initial moments in which there is output feedback.

CONCLUSION

As mentioned in the introduction to this chapter, any system that attempts to extract rules from knowledge stored in an ANN has to comply with a series of features: It must be independent from the architecture of the network, independent from the learning algorithm used, have a suitable level of correction, and generate highly expressive rules.

Thanks to the proposal presented here it is possible to treat the ANN as if it were a "black box," using an EC technique like GP, by only considering the inputs and outputs produced by the ANN. In this way, it is possible to comply with the requirements that the architecture and learning algorithm are independent.

Also, the rules generated approximate the functioning of the ANN in the same way as the adjustment value produced by the extraction algorithm (GP), meaning that correction is guaranteed. Furthermore, these rules provide the semantic value of the trees of expressions with which the genetic individuals of the extraction algorithm are codified.

Therefore, it may be said that extraction algorithms based on EC techniques meet the requirements demanded of algorithms of this type, as well as producing similar, if not superior results to those provided by methods that are more specific and dependent on the problem.

The results of the tests carried out are presented in support of these ideas. The example chosen (the Mackey Glass series) is frequently included and studied in the literature from different scientific areas (mathematics, statistics, etc.) and is sufficiently complex in order to determine if the extraction algorithms are efficient at carrying out their task. A detailed study of these results reveals how the rules obtained by the algorithm proposed obtain results that are as good as, if not better than, several of the other methods specifically designed for each of the problems proposed.

Moreover, we may conclude from the results obtained from discovering the generalisation capacity, that a rather accurate simulation of the ANN's behaviour has been achieved with regard to the possible combinations of values that may occur in the inputs. Therefore, we obtained a high fidelity of ANN behaviour, seen in the high success rate of rule extraction from the ANNs. We may also state that the knowledge treasured by the ANN was obtained in an explicit and comprehensible way from a human's point of view. It was also possible to express the ANN's generalisation capacity using a symbolic rule.

FUTURE STUDIES

A future development will be the analysis of the different parameters that intervene in the correct functioning of the algorithm, depending on the type of problem solved by the ANN. The ANN should be treated not as a "black box," but as a "grey box," in which, for instance, the activation function of the ANN is known, being incorporated as one of the mathematical operators of GP, and analysing which rules are extracted by this operator.

In order to accelerate the rule-extraction process, a network may be used with several computers so that the search is conducted in a distributed and concurrent manner, exchanging rules (sub-trees) between each.

REFERENCES

Andrews, R., Cable, R., Diederich, J., Geva, S., Golea, M., Hayward, R., Ho-Stuart, C., & Tickle A.B. (1996). *An evaluation and comparison of techniques for extracting and refining rules from artificial neural networks*. Queensland University of Technology, Neurocomputing Research Centre. QUT NRC Technical report.

Andrews, R., Diederich, J., & Tickle, A. (1995). A survey and critique of techniques for extracting rules from trained artificial neural networks. *Knowledge Based Systems, 8*, 373-389.

Andrews, R., & Geva, S. (1994). Rule extraction from a constrained error backpropagation MLP. *Proceedings of the Australian Conference on Neural Networks,* Brisbane, Queensland (pp. 9-12).

Benítez, J.M., Castro, J.L., & Requena, I. (1997). Are artificial neural networks black boxes? *IEEE Transactions on Neural Networks,* 8(5), 1156-1164.

Blake, C.L., & Mertz ,C.J. (1998). *UCI repository of machine learning databases*. University of California, Department of Information and Computer Science. Retrieved from www-old.ics.uci.edu/pub/machine-learning-databases

Bonarini, A. (1996). Evolutionary learning of fuzzy rules: Competition and cooperation. In W. Pedrycz (Ed.), *Fuzzy modelling: Paradigms and practice*. Norwell, MA: Kluwer Academic Press.

Browne, C., Düntsch, I., & Gediga, G. (1998). IRIS revisited: A comparison of discriminant and enhanced rough set data analysis. In *Rough sets in knowledge discovery* (vol. 2, pp. 345-368). Heidelberg: Physica Verlag.

Buckley, J.J., Hayashi, Y., & Czogala, E. (1993). On the equivalence of neural nets and fuzzy expert systems. *Fuzzy Sets Systems, 53,* 29-134.

Chalup, S., Hayward, R., & Diedrich, J. (1998). *Rule extraction from artificial neural networks trained on elementary number classification task.* Queensland University of Technology, Neurocomputing Research Centre. QUT NRC Technical report.

Cramer, N.L. (1985). A representation for the adaptive generation of simple sequential programs. *Grefenstette: Proceedings of First International Conference on Genetic Algorithms.*

Craven, M.W. (1996). *Extracting comprehensible models from trained neural networks.* Ph.D. thesis, University of Wisconsin, Madison.

Craven, M.W., & Shavlik, J.W. (1996). Extracting tree-structured representations of trained networks. *Advances in neural information processing systems* (vol. 8). Cambridge, MA: MIT Press.

Duch, W., Adamczak, R., & Grbczewski, K. (2001). A new methodology of extraction, optimisation and application of crisp and fuzzy logical rules. *IEEE Transactions on Neural Networks, 12,* 277-306.

Engelbrecht, A.P., Rouwhorst, S.E., & Schoeman, L. (2001). A building block approach to genetic programming for rule discovery. In R. Abbass & C. Newton (Eds.), *Data mining: A heuristic approach.* Hershey, PA: Idea Group Publishing.

Fayyad, U., Piatetsky-Shapiro, G., Smyth, P., & Uthurusamy, R. (1996). *Advances in knowledge discovery and data mining.* AAAI/MIT Press.

Fisher, R.A. (1936). The use of multiple measurements in taxonomic problems. *Annals of Eugenics, 7,* 179-188.

Friedberg, R.M. (1958). A learning machine: Part I. *IBM Journal of Research and Development, 2*(1), 2-13.

Friedberg, R.M., Dunham, B., & North, J.H. (1959). A learning machine: Part II. *IBM Journal of Research and Development, 3*(3), 282-287.

Fujiki, C. (1987). Using the genetic algorithm to generate lisp source code to solve the prisoner's dilemma. *International Conf on Gas,* 236-240.

Halgamuge, S.K., & Glesner, M. (1994) Neural networks in designing fuzzy systems for real world applications. *Fuzzy Sets and Systems, 65,* 1-12.

Jagielska, I., Matthews, C., & Whitfort, T. (1996). The application of neural networks, fuzzy logic, genetic algorithms and rough sets to automated knowledge acquisition. *4th Int. Conf. on Soft Computing, IIZUKA'96,* Japan (vol. 2, pp. 565-569).

Jang, J., & Sun, C. (1992). Functional equivalence between radial basis function networks and fuzzy inference systems. *IEEE Transactions on Neural Networks, 4,* 156-158.

Jankowski, N., & Kadirkamanathan, V. (1997). Statistical control of RBF-like networks for classification. *7th International Conference on Artificial Neural Networks,* Lausanne, Switzerland (pp. 385-390).

Kasabov, N. (1996). *Foundations of neural networks, fuzzy systems and knowledge engineering.* Cambridge, MA: MIT Press.

Keedwell, E., Narayanan, A., & Savic, D. (2000). Creating rules from trained neural networks using genetic algorithms. *International Journal of Computers, Systems and Signals (IJCSS), 1*(1), 30-42.

Koza, J. (1992). *Genetic programming: On the programming of computers by means of natural selection.* Cambridge, MA: MIT Press.

Koza, J. (1994). *Genetic programming II: Automatic discovery of reusable programs (complex adaptive systems).* Cambridge, MA: The MIT Press.

Koza, J., Bennett, F.H., Andre, D., & Keane, M.A. (1999). *Genetic programming III: Darwinian invention and problem solving.* Morgan Kauffman.

Mackey, M., & Glass, L. (1977). Oscillation and chaos in physiological control systems. *Science, 197,* 287.

Martínez, A., & Goddard, J. (2001). Definición de una red neuronal para clasificación por medio de un programa evolutivo. *Revista Mexicana de Ingeniería Biomédica, 22*(1), 4-11.

Montana, D.J. (1995). Strongly typed genetic programming. In *Evolutionary computation* (pp. 199-200). Cambridge, MA: MIT Press.

Nauck, D., Nauck, U., & Kruse, R. (1996). Generating classification rules with the neuro-fuzzy system NEFCLASS. *Proceedings of Biennal Conference of the North American Fuzzy Information Processing Society (NAFIPS'96),* Berkeley, CA.

Pop, E., Hayward, R., & Diederich, J. (1994). *RULENEG: Extracting rules from a trained ANN by stepwise negation.* Queensland University of Technology, Neurocomputing Research Centre. QUT NRC Technical report.

Rabuñal, J.R. (1999). *Entrenamiento de Redes de Neuronas Artificiales mediante Algoritmos Genéticos.* Graduate thesis, Facultad de Informática, Universidade da Coruña.

Rabuñal, J.R., Dorado, J., Pazos, A., Pereira, J., & Rivero, D. (2004). A new approach to the extraction of ANN rules and to their generalization capacity through GP. *Neural Computation, 16*(7), 1483-1524.

Shang, N., & Breiman, L. (1996). Distribution based trees are more accurate. *International Conference on Neural Information Processing* (vol. 1, pp. 133-138). Hong Kong.

Ster, B., & Dobnikar, A. (1996). Neural networks in medical diagnosis: Comparaison with other methods. *Proceedings of the International Conference on Engineering Applications of Neural Networks, EANN'96* (pp. 427-430).

Thrun, S. (1995). Extracting rules from networks with distributed representations. In G. Tesauro, D. Touretzky, & T. Leens (Eds.), *Advances in neural information processing systems (NIPS)* (vol. 7). Cambridge, MA: MIT Press.

Tickle, A.B., Andrews, R., Golea, M., & Diederich, J. (1998). The truth will come to light: Directions and challenges in extracting the knowledge embedded within trained artificial neural networks. *IEEE Transaction on Neural Networks, 9*(6), 1057-1068.

Tickle, A.B., Orlowski, M., & Diedrich J. (1996). *DEDEC: A methodology for extracting rules from trained artificial neural networks.* Queensland University of Technology, Neurocomputing Research Centre. QUT NRC Technical report.

Towell, G., & Shavlik, J.W. (1994). Knowledge-based artificial neural networks. *Artificial Intelligence, 70,* 119-165.

Visser, U., Tickle, A., Hayward, R., & Andrews, R. (1996). Rule-extraction from trained neural networks: Different techniques for the determination of herbicides for the plant protection advisory system PRO_PLANT. *Proceedings of the rule extraction from trained artificial neural networks workshop,* Brighton, UK (pp. 133-139).

Weiss, S.M., & Kulikowski, C.A. (1990). *Computer systems that learn.* San Mateo, CA: Morgan Kauffman.

Wong, M.L., & Leung, K.S. (2000). *Data mining using grammar based genetic programming and applications.* Kluwer Academic Publishers.

Compilation of References

Abo-Sinna, M.A., & Amer, A.H. (2005). Extensions of TOPSIS for multi-objective large-scale nonlinear programming problems. *Applied Mathematics and Computation, 162,* 243-256.

Agosta, J.M., & Wilkins, D.E. (1996). Using SIPE-2 to plan emergency response to marine oil spills. *IEEE Expert, 11*(6), 6-8.

Agre, P.E., & Chapman, D. (1987). Pengi: An implementation of a theory of activity. In *Proceedings of the Sixth National Conference on Artificial intelligence* (pp. 268-272).

Alami, R., Chatila, R., Fleury, S., Ghallab, M., & Ingrand, F. (1998). An architecture for autonomy. *International Journal of Robotic Research, 17*(4), 315-337.

Alami, R., Ingrand, F., & Qutub, S. (1997). Planning coordination and execution in multirobots environement. In *Proceedings of the 8th International Conference on Advanced Robotics* (pp. 525-530).

Albadvi, A., Chaharsooghi, S.K., & Esfahanipour, A. (2006). Decision making in stock trading: An application of PROMETHEE. *European Journal of Operational Research, 177*(2), 673-683.

Allen, J. (1983). Maintaining knowledge about temporal intervals. *Communications of the ACM, 26*(11), 832-843.

Allen, J. (1991). Planning as temporal reasoning. In J. Allen, R. Fikes & E. Sandewall (Eds.), *Proceedings of the KR'91: Principles of Knowledge Representation and Reasoning* (pp. 3-14). Morgan Kaufmann.

Allo, B., Guettier, C., Legendre, V., Poncet, J.C., & Strady-Lecubin, N. (2002). Constraint model-based planning and scheduling with multiple resources and complex collaboration schema. In *Proceedings of the 6th International Conference on Artificial intelligence Planning and Scheduling* (pp. 284-293).

Altmann, G. (1985). On the dynamic approach to language. In T.T. Ballmer (Ed.), *Linguistic dynamics. Discourses, procedures and evolution* (pp. 181-189). Berlin-New York: de Gruyter.

Altmann, G. (1991). Modelling diversification phenomena in language. In U. Rothe (Ed.), *Diversification processes in language: Grammar* (pp. 33-46). Medienverlag, Hagen, The Netherlands: Margit Rottmann.

Altmann, G. (1996). Diversification processes of the word. In *Glottometrika 15* (pp. 102-111). WVT: Trier.

Altmann, G., & Köhler, R. (1996). "Language forces" and synergetic modelling of language phenomena. In *Glottometrika 15* (pp. 62-76). Bochum: Brockmeyer,.

Ancona, N., Maglietta, R., & Stella, E. (2004). Data representation in kernel based learning machines. In *Proceedings of IASTED Int. Conf. on Artificial Intelligence and Soft Computing* (pp. 241-245).

Andersen, P. B. (2000). Genres as self-organising systems. In P.B. Andersen, C. Emmeche, N.O. Finnemann, & P.V. Christiansen (Eds.), *Downward causation: Minds, bodies and matter* (pp. 214-260). Aarhus: Aarhus University Press.

Andre, D., Friedman N., & Parr, R. (1998). *Generalized prioritized sweeping. Advances in neural information processing systems* (pp. 1001-1007). MIT Press.

Andrews, R., & Geva, S. (1994). Rule extraction from a constrained error backpropagation MLP. *Proceedings of the Australian Conference on Neural Networks,* Brisbane, Queensland (pp. 9-12).

Andrews, R., Cable, R., Diederich, J., Geva, S., Golea, M., Hayward, R., Ho-Stuart, C., & Tickle A.B. (1996). *An evaluation and comparison of techniques for extracting and refining rules from artificial neural networks.* Queensland University of Technology, Neurocomputing Research Centre. QUT NRC Technical report.

Andrews, R., Diederich, J., & Tickle, A. (1995). A survey and critique of techniques for extracting rules from trained artificial neural networks. *Knowledge Based Systems, 8,* 373-389.

Anthony, S., & Frisch, A. M. (1999, January). Cautious induction: An alternative to clause-at-a-time induction in inductive logic programming. *New Generation Computing, 17*(1), 25–52.

Apt, K.R. (2003). *Principles of constraint programming.* Cambridge University Press.

Association for Constraint Programming. (2007). Retrieved August 17, 2007, from http://slash.math.unipd.it/acp/

Bacchus, F., & van Beek, P. (1998). On the conversion between non-binary and binary constraint satisfaction problems. In *Proceedings of the National Conference on Artificial Intelligence (AAAI-98)* (pp. 311-318). Madison, WI: AAAI Press.

Baldassarre, G. (2003). Forward and bidirectional planning on reinforcement learning and neural networks in a simulated robot. In M. Butz, O. Sigaud & P. Gerard (Eds.), *Adaptive behaviour in anticipatory learning systems* (pp. 179-200). Springer-Verlag.

Baptiste, P., Le Pape, C., & Nuijten, W. (2001). *Constraint-based scheduling: Applying constraints to scheduling problems.* Dordrecht: Kluwer Academic Publishers.

Barták, R. (1998). *Online guide to constraint programming.* Retrieved August 17, 2007, from http://kti.mff.cuni.cz/~bartak/constraints

Barták, R. (2002). Modelling soft constraints: A survey. *Neural Network World, 12*(5), 421-431.

Barták, R. (2002). Modelling resource transitions in constraint-based scheduling. In W.I. Grosky & F. Plášil (Eds.), *Proceedings of SOFSEM 2002: Theory and Practice of Informatics* (LNCS 2540, pp. 186-194). Springer Verlag.

Barták, R. (2004). Incomplete depth-first search techniques: A short survey. In *Proceedings of CPDC 2004,* Gliwice, Poland (pp. 7-14).

Barták, R. (2005). Effective modeling with constraints. In *Applications of declarative programming and knowledge management* (LNAI 3392, pp. 149-165). Springer Verlag.

Barto, A.G., Sutton, R.S., & Anderson, C.W. (1983). Neuronlike adaptive elements that can solve difficult learning control problems. *IEEE Transactions on Systems, Man, and Cybernetics, 13*(5), 834-846.

Barwise, J., & Perry, J. (1983). *Situations and attitudes.* Cambridge, MA: MIT Press.

Batali, J. (1998). Computational simulations of the emergence of grammar. In J. R. Hurford, M. Studdert-Kennedy, & C. Knight (Eds.), *Approaches to the evolution of language* (pp. 405-426). Cambridge: Cambridge University Press.

Bayes, T. (1763). An essay towards solving a problem in the doctrine of chances. *Philosophical Transactions of the Royal Society of London, 53,* 370–418.

Beard, R.W., McLain, T.W., Goodrich, M.A., & Anderson, E.P. (2002). Coordinated target assignment and intercept for unmanned air vehicles. *Institute of Electrical and Electronics Engineers Transactions on Robotics and Automation, 18*(6), 911-922.

Beck, J.C., & Perron, L. (2000). Discrepancy-bounded depth first search. In *Proceedings of CP-AI-OR* (pp. 7-17).

Beldiceanu, N., Bourreau, E., Chan, P., & Rivreau, D. (1997). Partial search strategy in CHIP. In *Proceedings of 2nd International Conference on Metaheuristics-MIC97.*

Beldiceanu, N., Carlsson, M., & Rampon, J.X. (2005). *Global constraint catalogue* (Tech. Rep. No. T2005-06, SICS).

Bellifemine, F., Poggi, A., & Rimassa, G. (1999). JADE–A FIPA-compliant agent framework. In *Proceedings of the Fourth International Conference on the Practical Application of Intelligent Agents and Multi-Agent Technology* (pp. 97-108).

Bellman, R.E. (1957). *Dynamic programming.* Princeton University Press.

Bellman, R.E., & Zadeh, L.A. (1970). Decision making in a fuzzy environment. *Management Science, 17,* 141-164.

Benayoun, R., Roy, B., & Sussmann, B. (1966). *Manuel de référence du programme ELECTRE. Nothe de synthèse, formation n°. 25,* Direction scientifique SEMA, Paris.

Benítez, J.M., Castro, J.L., & Requena, I. (1997). Are artificial neural networks black boxes? *IEEE Transactions on Neural Networks, 8*(5), 1156-1164.

Benson, S.S. (1995). *Learning action models for reactive autonomous agents.* Stanford: Stanford University.

Berardi, M., Varlaro, A., & Malerba, D. (2004). On the effect of caching in recursive theory learning. In *Proceedings of the 14th international conference on inductive logic programming* (pp. 44–62). Berlin: Springer-Verlag.

Berlandier, P. (1995). Improving domain filtering using restricted path consistency. In *Proceedings of the IEEE CAIA-95* (pp. 32-37). Los Angeles, CA.

Bessiere, C. & Régin, J.-Ch. (2001). Refining the basic constraint propagation algorithm. In *Proceedings of IJCAI-01* (pp. 309-315).

Bessiere, C. (1994). Arc-consistency and arc-consistency again. *Artificial Intelligence, 65,* 179-190.

Bessiere, C., & Régin, J.-Ch. (1996). MAC and combined heuristics: Two reasons for forsake FC (and CBJ?) on hard problems. In *Proceedings of the Second International Conference on Principles and Practice of Constraint programming (CP)* (LNCS 1118, pp. 61-75). Springer Verlag.

Bessiere, C., Freuder, E.C., & Régin, J.-R. (1999). Using constraint metaknowledge to reduce arc consistency computation. *Artificial Intelligence, 107,* 125-148.

Bessiere, C., Meseguer, P., Freuder, E.C., & Larrosa, J. (2002). On forward checking for non-binary constraint satisfaction. *Artificial Intelligence, 141,* 205-224.

Beynon, M., & Peel, M. (2001). Variable precision rough set theory and data discretisation: An application to corporate failure prediction. *OMEGA - International Journal of Management Science, 29*(6), 561-576.

Beynon, M.J. (2005). A novel technique of object ranking and classification under ignorance: An application to the corporate failure risk problem. *European Journal of Operational Research, 167,* 493-517.

Beynon, M.J. (2005). A novel approach to the credit rating problem: Object classification under ignorance. *International Journal of Intelligent Systems in Accounting, Finance and Management, 13,* 113-130.

Beynon, M.J., & Buchanan, K. (2004). Object classification under ignorance using CaRBS: The case of the European barn swallow. *Expert Systems with Applications, 27*(3), 403-415.

Beynon, M.J., & Kitchener, M. (2005). Ranking the balance of state long-term care systems: A comparative exposition of the SMARTER and CaRBS techniques. *Health Care Management Science, 8,* 157-166.

Beynon, M.J., & Wells, P. (2008). The lean improvement of the chemical emissions of motor vehicles based on preference ranking: A PROMETHEE uncertainty analysis. *OMEGA - International Journal of Management Science, 36,* 384-394.

Bhatia, S.K., & Deogun, J.S. (1998). Conceptual clustering in information retreival. *IEEE Trans System, Man and Cybernetics, 28*(3), 427-536.

Bhattacharya, A., & Vasant, P. (2007). Soft-sensing of level of satisfaction in TOC product-mix decision heuristic using robust fuzzy-LP. *European Journal of Operational Research. 177,* 55-70.

Bistarelli, S., Montanari, U., & Rossi, F. (1997). Semiring-based constraint satisfaction and optimization. *Journal of the ACM, 44*(2), 165-201.

Bitnerm, J.R., & Reingold, E.M. (1975). Backtracking programming techniques. *Communications of the ACM, 18*(11), 651-656.

Blake, C.L., & Mertz ,C.J. (1998). *UCI repository of machine learning databases.* University of California, Department of Information and Computer Science. Retrieved from www-old.ics.uci.edu/pub/machine-learning-databases

Blatt, M., Wiseman, S., & Domany, E. (1996). Supermagnetic clustering of data. *Physical Review Letters, 76*(18), 3251-3254

Blockeel, H., & De Raedt, L. (1998). Top-down induction of first-order logical decision trees. *Artificial Intelligence, 101*(1–2), 285–297.

Blockeel, H., Dehaspe, L., Demoen, B., Janssens, G., Ramon, J., & Vandecasteele, H. (2002). Improving the efficiency of inductive logic programming through the use of query packs. *Journal of machine learning Research, 16*, 135–166.

Blockeel, H., Džeroski, S., Kompare, B., Kramer, S., Pfahringer, B., & Laer, W. V. (2004). Experiments in predicting biodegradability. *Applied Artificial Intelligence, 18*(2), 157–181.

Blockeel, H., Raedt, L. D., Jacobs, N., & Demoen, B. (1999). Scaling up inductive logic programming by learning from interpretations. *Data Mining and Knowledge Discovery, 3*(1), 59–93.

Blum, A., & Furst, M. (1995). Fast planning through planning graph analysis. In *Proceedings of the 14th International Conference on Artificial Intelligence*, Berlin, Germany (pp.636-642).

Blum, A.L., & Furst, M.L. (1997). Fast planning through planning graph analysis. *Artificial Intelligence, 90*, 281-300.

Bockhorst, J., & Ong, I. M. (2004). FOIL-D: Efficiently scaling FOIL for multi-relational data mining of large datasets. In *Proceedings of the 14th international conference on inductive logic programming* (pp. 63–79).

Bonarini, A. (1996). Evolutionary learning of fuzzy rules: Competition and cooperation. In W. Pedrycz (Ed.), *Fuzzy modelling: Paradigms and practice.* Norwell, MA: Kluwer Academic Press.

Bonet, B., & Geffner, H. (1999). Planning as heuristic search: New results. In S. Biundo & M. Fox (Eds.), *Proceedings of the European Conference on Planning (ECP-99)* (pp. 360-372). Springer.

Bonet, B., & Geffner, H. (2001). Planning as heuristic search [Special issue on heuristic search]. *Artificial Intelligence, 129*(1-2), 5-33.

Bonet, B., & Geffner, H. (2006). Learning depth-first search: A unified approach to heuristic search in deterministic and non-deterministic settings, and its application to MDPs. In *Proceedings of the 16th International Conference on Automated Planning and Scheduling (ICAPS-06)* (pp. 142-151).

Booij, G. (1995). *The phonology of Dutch.* Oxford: Clarendon Press.

Borning, A. (1981). The programming language aspects of ThingLab, a constraint-oriented simulation laboratory. *ACM Transactions on Programming Languages and Systems, 3*(4), 252-387.

Boström, H. (1996). Theory-guided induction of logic programs by inference of regular languages. In *Proc. of the 13th international conference on machine learning* (pp. 46–53). San Francisco: Morgan Kaufmann.

Boström, H. (1998). Predicate invention and learning from positive examples only. In *Proceedings of the tenth european conference on machine learning* (pp. 226–237). Berlin: Springer Verlag.

Boström, H. (2000, June). Induction of recursive transfer rules. In J. Cussens & S. Džeroski (Eds.), *Lecture notes in computer science: Vol. 1925. Learning Language in Logic* (pp. 237–246). Berlin: Springer-Verlag.

Botta, M., Giordana, A., Saitta, L., & Sebag, M. (2003). Relational learning as search in a critical region. *Journal of machine learning Research, 4*, 431–463.

Boutilier, C., Dearden, R., & Goldszmidt, M. (1995). Exploiting structure in policy construction. In *Fourteenth International Joint Conference on Artificial Intelligence* (pp. 1104-1111).

Boutilier, C., Reiter, R., & Price, B. (2001). Symbolic dynamic programming for first-order MDPs. In *Proceedings of the 17th Joint Conference on Artificial Intelligence* (pp. 690-700).

Brainerd, B. (1976). On the Markov nature of the text. *Linguistics, 176,* 5-30.

Brans, J.P., Mareschal, B., & Vincke, P.H. (1984). PRO-METHEE: A new family of outranking methods in MCDM. In *IFORS 84,* North Holland (pp. 470-490).

Brans, J.P., Vincke, P.H., & Mareschal, B. (1986). How to select and how to rank projects: The PROMETHEE method. *European Journal of Operational Research, 24,* 228-238.

Brélaz, D. (1979). New methods to color the vertices of a graph. *Communications of the ACM, 22,* 251-256.

Bresina, J.L., & Drummond, M. (1990). Integrating planning and reaction. A preliminary report. In *Proceedings of the American Association of Artificial intelligence Spring Symposium on Planning in Uncertain, Unpredictable or Changing Environments* (pp. 24-28).

Bresina, J.L., & Washington, R. (2001). Robustness via run-time adaptation of contingent plans. In *Proceedings of the American Association of Artificial intelligence Spring Symposium on Robust Autonomy* (pp. 24-30).

Brooks, R. (1986). A robust layered control system for a mobile robot. *Institute of Electrical and Electronics Engineers Journal of Robotics and Automation, 2*(1), 14-23.

Browne, C., Düntsch, I., & Gediga, G. (1998). IRIS revisited: A comparison of discriminant and enhanced rough set data analysis. In *Rough sets in knowledge discovery* (vol. 2, pp. 345-368). Heidelberg: Physica Verlag.

Brumitt, B.L., & Stentz, A. (1998). GRAMMPS: A generalized mission planner for multiple mobile robots in unstructured environements. In *Proceedings of the Institute of Electrical and Electronics Engineers International Conference on Robotics and Automation* (vol. 3, pp. 2396-2401).

Bryant, C., Muggleton, S., Oliver, S., Kell, D., Reiser, P., & King, R. (2001). Combining Inductive Logic programming, Active Learning and robotics to discover the function of genes. *Electronic Transactions on Artificial Intelligence, 5*(B1), 1–36.

Buckley, J.J., Hayashi, Y., & Czogala, E. (1993). On the equivalence of neural nets and fuzzy expert systems. *Fuzzy Sets Systems, 53,* 29-134.

Burnage, G. (1990). *CELEX: A guide for users.*

Cairns, C., & Feinstein, M. (1982). Markedness and the theory of syllable structure. *Linguistic Inquiry, 13.*

Califf, M. E., & Mooney, R. J. (1999, July). Relational learning of pattern-match rules for information extraction. In *Proceedings of the 17th national conference on artificial intelligence.* Orlando, FL.

Camacho, R. (1998). Inducing models of human control skills. In C. Nedellec & C. Rouveirol (Eds.), *Lecture notes in computer science: Vol. 1398. ECML* (pp. 107–118). Berlin: Springer-Verlag.

Camacho, R. (2000). *Inducing models of human control skills using machine learning algorithms.* Unpublished doctoral dissertation, Department of Electrical Engineering and Computation, Universidade do Porto.

Camacho, R. (2002). Improving the efficiency of ILP systems using an incremental language level search. In *Annual machine learning conference of Belgium and the Netherlands.*

Camacho, R. (2003). As lazy as it can be. In P. Doherty, B. Tassen, P. Ala-Siuru, & B. Mayoh (Eds.), *The eighth Scandinavian conference on Artificial Intelligence (SCAI '03), Bergen, Norway, November 2003* (pp. 47–58).

Cangelosi, A., & Parisi, D. (2002). Computer simulation: A new scientific approach to the study of language evolution. In A. Cangelosi & D. Parisi (Eds.), *Simulating the evolution of language* (pp. 3-28). London: Springer.

Cangelosi, A., & Parisi, D. (Eds.). (2002). *Simulating the evolution of language*. London: Springer.

Cangelosi, A., Greco, A., & Harnad, S. (2002). Symbol grounding and the symbolic theft hypothesis. In A. Cangelosi & D. Parisi (Eds.), *Simulating the evolution of language* (pp. 191-210). London: Springer Verlag.

Canongia Lopes, J.N. (2004) On the classification and representation of ternary phase diagrams: The yin and yang of a T–x approach. *Phys. Chem. Chem. Phys., 6*, 2314-2319.

Cao, H., Xi, H., Smith, S., F. (2003). A reinforcement learning approach to production planning in the fabrication fulfillment manufacturing process. In *Winter Simulation Conference 2* (pp. 1417-1423).

Carlsson, C., & Korhonen, P.A. (1986). Parametric approach to fuzzy linear programming. *Fuzzy Sets and Systems, 20*, 17-30.

Carrault, G., Cordier, M., Quiniou, R., & Wang, F. (2003, July). Temporal abstraction and inductive logic programming for arrhythmia recognition from electrocardiograms. *Artificial Intelligence in Medicine, 28*(3), 231–63.

Carriere, K.C. (1999). Methods for repeated measures data analysis with missing values. *Journal of Statistical Planning and Inference, 77*, 221-236.

Cesta, A., Fratini, S., & Oddi, A. (2004). Planning with concurrency, time and resources, a CSP-based approach. In I. Vlahavas & D. Vrakas (Eds.), *Intelligent techniques for planning* (pp. 259-295). Idea Group, Inc.

Cestnik, B. (1990). Estimating probabilities: A crucial task in machine learning. In *European conference on artificial intelligence* (pp. 147–149).

Chalup, S., Hayward, R., & Diedrich, J. (1998). *Rule extraction from artificial neural networks trained on elementary number classification task*. Queensland University of Technology, Neurocomputing Research Centre. QUT NRC Technical report.

Chan, W.C., Chan, C.W., Cheung, K.C., & Harris, C.J. (2001). On the modeling of nonlinear dynamic systems using support vector neural networks. *Engineering Applications of Artificial Intelligence, 14*, 105-113.

Cheadle, A.M., Harvey, W., Sadler, A.J., Schimpf, J., Shen K., & Wallace, M.G. (2003). ECLiPSe: An introduction (Tech. Rep. No. IC-Parc-03-1). Imperial College London.

Chen, S. (2006). Local regularization assisted orthogonal least squares regression. *Neurocomputing, 69*, 559-585.

Chen, Y., Hsu, C.W., & Wah, B.W. (2004). SGPlan: Subgoal partitioning and resolution in planning. In *Proceedings of the International Conference on Automated Planning and Scheduling (ICAPS-2004) – International Planning Competition* (pp. 30-32).

Chen, Y.X., Wah, B.W., & Hsu, C.W. (2006). Temporal planning using subgoal partitioning and resolution in SGPlan. *Journal of Artificial Intelligence Research, 26*, 323-369.

Chen, Z. (2001). *Data mining and uncertain reasoning: An integrated approach*. New York: John Wiley.

Chien, S., Rabideau, G., Knight, R., Sherwood, R., Engelhardt, B., Mutz, D., et al. (2000). ASPEN—automating space mission operations using automated planning and scheduling. In *Proceedings of the SpaceOps 2000* (pp. 1-10).

Chomsky, N. (1957). *Syntactic structures*. The Hague: Mouton.

Christiansen, M. H., & Kirby, S. (2003). Language evolution: Consensus and controversies. *Trends in Cognitive Sciences, 7*(7), 300-307.

Clark, P., & Niblett, T. (1989). The CN2 induction algorithm. *machine learning, 3*(4), 261–83.

Cohen, W. W. (1994). Grammatically biased learning: Learning logic programs using an explicit antecedent description language. *Artificial Intelligence, 68*, 303–366.

Cohoon, J.P., Hedge, S.U., Martin, W.N., & Richards, D.S. (1991). Distributed genetic algorithms for the floorplan design problem. *IEEE Transactions on Computer-Aided Design of Integrated Circuits and Systems, 10*(4), 483-492.

Colton, S., & Muggleton, S. (2003). ILP for mathematical discovery. In T. Horváth (Ed.), *Lecture notes in computer science: Vol. 2835. ILP* (pp. 93–111). Berlin: Springer-Verlag.

Constraints archive. (2007). Retrieved August 17, 2007, from http://4c.ucc.ie/web/archive/

Corre, J. (2003). *Planification distribuée sous contrainte de communication.* Master of Science dissertation, ESIG-ELEC, UFR des sciences de Rouen, Rouen, France.

Cramer, N.L. (1985). A representation for the adaptive generation of simple sequential programs. *Grefenstette: Proceedings of First International Conference on Genetic Algorithms.*

Craven, M., & Slattery, S. (2001, April). Relational learning with statistical predicate invention: Better models for hypertext. *machine learning, 43*(1/2), 97–119.

Craven, M.W. (1996). *Extracting comprehensible models from trained neural networks.* Ph.D. thesis, University of Wisconsin, Madison.

Craven, M.W., & Shavlik, J.W. (1996). Extracting tree-structured representations of trained networks. *Advances in neural information processing systems* (vol. 8). Cambridge, MA: MIT Press.

Cristianini, N., & Shawe-Taylor, J. (2000). *An introduction to support vector machines and other kernel-based learning methods.* Cambridge University Press.

Currie, K., & Tate, A. (1991). O-plan: The open planning architecture. *Artificial Intelligence, 52*(1), 49-86.

Cussens, J. (1993). Bayes and pseudo-Bayes estimates of conditional probabilities and their reliability. In *Proceedings of the european conference on machine learning (ecml93)* (pp. 136–152). Berlin: Springer Verlag.

Cussens, J. (1996). *Part-of-speech disambiguation using ILP* (Tech. Rep. No. PRG-TR-25-96). Oxford University Computing Laboratory.

Cussens, J. (1997). Part-of-speech tagging using progol. In S. Džeroski & N. Lavrač (Eds.), *Lecture notes in artificial intelligence: Vol. 1297. Proceedings of the 7th International Workshop on inductive logic programming* (pp. 93–108). Berlin: Springer-Verlag.

Cussens, J. (2000). Stochastic logic programs: Sampling, inference and applications. In C. Boutilier & M. Goldszmidt (Eds.), *Proceedings of the 16th annual conference on uncertainty in artificial intelligence.* Morgan Kaufmann.

Cussens, J., & Džeroski, S. (Eds.). (2000). *Learning language in logic.* Berlin: Springer-Verlag.

Cussens, J., & Pulman, S. (2000). Experiments in inductive chart parsing. In J. Cussens & S. Džeroski (Eds.), *Lecture notes in artificial intelligence: Vol. 1925. Learning Language in Logic.* Berlin: Springer-Verlag.

Damiani, S., Verfaillie, G., & Charmeau, M.C. (2004). An anytime planning approach for the management of an Earth watching satellite. In *4th International Workshop on Planning and Scheduling for Space* (pp. 54-63). Darmstadt, Germany.

Darwin, C. (1859). *On the origin of species by means of natural selection.* London: J. Murray Press.

Davidson, D. (1994). *Wahrheit und Interpretation.* Frankfurt am Main, Germany: Suhrkamp.

Davis, J., Burnside, E. S., Dutra, I. d. C., David, P. C., & Santos Costa, V. (2005). Knowledge discovery from structured mammography reports using inductive logic programming. In *American medical informatics association 2005 annual symposium.*

Davis, J., Dutra, I. d. C., Page, C. D., & Santos Costa, V. (2005). Establishing identity equivalence in multi-relational domains. In *Proceedings of the 2005 International Conference on Intelligence Analysis.*

De Jong, K. (1975). *An analysis of the behavior of a class of genetic adaptive systems.* Ann Arbor, MI: University of Michigan Press.

De Raedt, L. (1997). Logical settings for concept-learning. *Artificial Intelligence, 95*(1), 187–201.

De Raedt, L., & Blockeel, H. (1997). Using logical decision trees for clustering. In *Proceedings of the 7th international workshop on inductive logic programming* (pp. 133–140). Springer-Verlag.

De Raedt, L., & Dehaspe, L. (1996). *Clausal discovery* (Tech. Rep. No. CW 238). Leuven: Department of Computing Science, K.U.Leuven.

De Raedt, L., & Dehaspe, L. (1997). Learning from satisfiability. In *Proceedings of the ninth dutch conference on artificial intelligence (NAIC'97)* (pp. 303–312).

De Raedt, L., & Džeroski, S. (1994). First-order jk-clausal theories are pac-learnable. *Artificial Intelligence, 70*(1-2), 375–392.

De Raedt, L., Kersting, K., & Torge, S. (2005). Towards learning stochastic logic programs from proof-banks. In *Proceedings of the 23th national conference on artificial intelligence, (AAAI 2005)* (pp. 752–757).

Dean T., & Kanazawa, K. (1990). A model for reasoning about persistence and causation. *Computational Intelligence, 5*(3), 142-150.

Dean, T.L., & McDermott, D.V. (1987). Temporal data base management. *Artificial Intelligence, 32,* 1-55.

Dean, T.L., Firby, R.J., & Miller, D. (1988). Hierarchical planning involving deadlines, travel time and resources. *Computational Intelligence, 4,* 381-398.

Dearden, R. (2001). Structured prioritized sweeping. In *International Conference on Machine Learning* (pp. 82-89).

Debruyne, R., & Bessiere, C. (1997). Some practicable filtering techniques for the constraint satisfaction problem. In *Proceedings of the 15th IJCAI* (pp. 412-417).

Dechter, R. (1990). Enhancement schemes for constraint processing: Backjumping, learning, and cutset decomposition. *Artificial Intelligence, 41,* 273-312.

Dechter, R. (1997). Bucket elimination: A unifying framework for processing hard and soft constraint. *Constraints: An International Journal, 2,* 51-55.

Dechter, R. (2003). *Constraint processing.* Morgan Kaufmann.

Dechter, R., & Frost, D. (1998). Backtracking algorithms for constraint satisfaction problems; a survey. Retrieved December 5, 2007, from citeseer.ist.psu.edu/dechter-98backtracking.html

Dechter, R., & Pearl, J. (1988). Network-based heuristics for constraint satisfaction problems. *Artificial Intelligence, 34,* 1-38.

Dechter, R., & Rish, I. (2003). Mini-buckets: A general scheme for approximating inference. *Journal of the ACM, 50*(2), 107-153.

Dechter, R., Meiri, I., & Pearl, J. (1991). Temporal constraint networks. *Artificial Intelligence, 49,* 61-95.

Dehaspe, L., & De Raedt, L. (1995). Parallel inductive logic programming. In *Proceedings of the MLnet familiarization workshop on statistics, machine learning and knowledge discovery in databases.*

Dehaspe, L., & De Raedt, L. (1996, July). DLAB: *a declarative language bias for concept learning and knowledge discovery engines* (Tech. Rep. No. CW 214). Leuven: Department of Computing Science, K.U.Leuven.

Dehaspe, L., & De Raedt, L. (1997). Mining association rules in multiple relations. In S. Džeroski & N. Lavrač (Eds.), *Lecture notes in artificial intelligence: Vol. 1297. Proceedings of the 7th International Workshop on inductive logic programming* (pp. 125–132). Berlin: Springer-Verlag.

Dehaspe, L., & Toironen, H. (2000). Relational data mining. In (pp. 189–208). Berlin: Springer-Verlag.

Dempster, A.P. (1967). Upper and lower probabilities induced by a multiple valued mapping. *Ann. Math. Statistics, 38,* 325-339.

Dietterich, T. (2000). An overview of MAXQ hierarchical reinforcement learning. In *Proceedings of the 4th International Symposium on Abstraction, Reformulation, and Approximation* (pp. 26-44).

Dijkstra, E.W. (1959). A note on two problems in connection with graphs. *Numerische Mathematik, 1,* 269-271.

DiMaio, F., & Shavlik, J. W. (2004). Learning an approximation to inductive logic programming clause evaluation. In *Proceedings of the 14th international conference on inductive logic programming* (pp. 80–97).

Do, M.B., & Kambhampati, S. (2001). SAPA: A domain-independent heuristic metric temporal planner. In A. Cesta & D. Borrajo (Eds.), *Proceedings of the European Conference on Planning (ECP-2001)* (pp. 109-120).

Do, M.B., & Kambhampati, S. (2003). SAPA: A multi-objective metric temporal planner. *Journal of Artificial Intelligence Research, 20,* 155-194.

Dolšak, B., Bratko, I., & Jezernik, A. (1997). Application of machine learning in finite element computation. In R. Michalski, I. Bratko, & M. Kubat (Eds.), *Machine learning, data mining and knowledge discovery: Methods and applications.* John Wiley and Sons.

Drabble, B., & Kirby, R. (1991). Associating AI planner entities with an underlying time point network. In *European Workshop on Planning (EWSP'91)* (LNCS 522, pp. 27-38). Springer-Verlag.

Drabble, B., & Tate, A. (1994). The use of optimistic and pessimistic resource profiles to inform search in an activity based planner. In *Proceedings of the 2nd Conference on Artificial Intelligence Planning Systems (AIPS-94)* (pp. 243-248).

Drezet, P.M.L., & Harrison, R.F. (1998). Support vector machines for system identification. In *UKACC International Conference on Control* (pp. 688-692).

Drezet, P.M.L., & Harrison, R.F. (2001). A new method for sparsity control in support vector classification and regression. *Pattern Recognition, 34,* 111-125.

Duch, W., Adamczak, R., & Grbczewski, K. (2001). A new methodology of extraction, optimisation and application of crisp and fuzzy logical rules. *IEEE Transactions on Neural Networks, 12,* 277-306.

Džeroski, S. (1993). Handling imperfect data in inductive logic programming. In *Proceedings of the 4th*

scandinavian conference on artificial intelligence (pp. 111–125). IOS Press.

Džeroski, S., & Erjavec, T. (1997). Induction of Slovene nominal paradigms. In N. Lavrac & S. Džeroski (Eds.), *Lecture notes in computer science: Vol. 1297. ILP* (pp. 141–148). Berlin: Springer-Verlag.

Džeroski, S., Dehaspe, L., Ruck, B., & Walley, W. (1995). Classification of river water quality data using machine learning. In *Proceedings of the 5th international conference on the development and application of computer techniques to environmental studies.*

Džeroski, S., Jacobs, N., Molina, M., & Moure, C. (1998). ILP experiments in detecting traffic problems. In C. Nedellec & C. Rouveirol (Eds.), *Lecture notes in computer science: Vol. 1398. ECML* (pp. 61–66). Berlin: Springer-Verlag.

Džeroski, S., Schulze-Kremer, S., Heidtke, K., Siems, K., & Wettschereck, D. (1996). Applying ILP to diterpene structure elucidation from CNMR spectra. In *Proceedings of the MLnet Familiarization Workshop on Data Mining with Inductive Logic Programing* (pp. 12–24).

Edelkamp, S. & Hoffmann, J. (2004). PDDL 2.1: The language for the classical part of IPC-4. In *Proceedings of the International Planning Competition. International Conference on Automated Planning and Scheduling* (pp., 1-7). Whistler.

Edelkamp, S. (2002). Mixed propositional and numeric planning in the model checking integrated planning system. In M. Fox & A. Coddington (Eds.), *Proceedings of the Workshop on Planning for Temporal Domains (AIPS-2002)* (pp. 47-55).

Edelkamp, S., & Hoffmann, J. (2004). PDDL2.2: The language for the classical part of IPC-4. In *Proceedings of the International Conference on Automated Planning and Scheduling (ICAPS-2004) – International Planning Competition* (pp. 2-6).

Edelkamp, S., Jabbar, S., & Nazih, M. (2006). Large-scale optimal PDDL3 planning with MIPS-XXL. In *Proceedings of the International Conference on Automated Planning and Scheduling (ICAPS-2006) – International Planning Competition* (pp. 28-30).

Eiben, A.E., & Smith, J.E. (2003). *Introduction to evolutionary computing*. Berlin, Germany: Springer.

Eiben, A.E., & van der Hauw, J.K. (1998). Adaptive penalties for evolutionary graph coloring. In G. Goos, J. Hartmanis & J. van Leeuwen (Eds.), *Lecture notes in computer science* (pp. 95-106). Heidelberg, Germany: Springer.

Engelbrecht, A.P., Rouwhorst, S.E., & Schoeman, L. (2001). A building block approach to genetic programming for rule discovery. In R. Abbass & C. Newton (Eds.), *Data mining: A heuristic approach*. Hershey, PA: Idea Group Publishing.

Enot, D. P., & King, R. D. (2003). Application of inductive logic programming to structure-based drug design. In N. Lavrac, D. Gamberger, H. Blockeel, & L. Todorovski (Eds.), *Lecture notes in computer science: Vol. 2838. Proceedings of the 7th European Conference on Principles of Data Mining and Knowledge Discovery* (pp. 156–167). Berlin: Springer-Verlag.

Erickson, M.J. (1996). *Introduction to combinatorics*. New York: John Wiley & Sons.

Esposito, F., Malerba, D., & Semeraro, G. (1993). Automated acquisition of rules for document understanding. In *Proceedings of the 2nd international conference on document analysis and recognition* (pp. 650–654).

Fabiani, P., Smith, P., Schulte, A., Ertl, C., Peeling, E., Lock, Z., et al. (2004). *Overview of candidate methods for the «autonomy for UAVs » design challenge problem*. Group for Aeronautical Research and Technology in EURope, Flight Mechanics Action Group 14 Report.

FAME. (1995). *FAME for Windows user guide*. London: Bureau Van Dijk Electronic Publishing Limited.

Fan, H.-Y., & Lampinen, J.A. (2003). Trigonometric mutation operation to differential evolution. *Journal of Global Optimization, 27,* 105-129.

Fayyad, U., Piatetsky-Shapiro, G., Smyth, P., & Uthurusamy, R. (1996). *Advances in knowledge discovery and data mining*. AAAI/MIT Press.

Ferrer i Chancho, R., Riordan, O., & Bollobas, B. (2005). The consequences of Zipf's law for syntax and symbolic reference. *Proceedings of the Royal Society, 272,* 561-565.

Fikes, R.E., & Nilsson, N.J. (1971). STRIPS: A new approach to the application of theorem proving to problem solving. *Artificial Intelligence, 2,* 189-208.

Finite element mesh design: an engineering domain for ILP applications. (1994). In *Proc. of the 4th international workshop on inductive logic programming (ILP-94), Bad Honnef/Bonn, Germany, September 12–14.*

Finn, P. W., Muggleton, S. H., Page, C. D., & Srinivasan, A. (1998). Pharmacophore discovery using the inductive logic programming system PROGOL. *machine learning, 30*(2-3), 241-270.

Flemming, B.W. (2000) A revised textural classification of gravel-free muddy sediments on the basis of ternary diagrams. *Continental Shelf Research, 20,* 1125-1137.

Fodor, J. A., & McLaughlin, B. P. (1995). Connectionism and the problem of systematicity: Smolensky's solution doesn't work. In C. MacDonald & G. MacDonald (Eds.), *Connectionism: Debates on psychological explanation* (pp. 199-222). Blackwell.

Fodor, J. A., & Pylyshyn, Z.W. (1988). Connectionism and cognitive architecture: A critical analysis. *Cognition, 28*(1-2), 3-71.

Fonseca, N. A. (2006). *Parallelism in inductive logic programming systems*. Unpublished doctoral dissertation, University of Porto.

Fonseca, N. A., Santos Costa, V., Camacho, R., & Silva, F. (2004). On avoiding redundancy in inductive logic programming. In R. Camacho, R. D. King, & A. Srinivasan (Eds.), *Lecture notes in artificial intelligence: Vol. 3194. Proceedings of the 14th International Conference on inductive logic programming, Porto, Portugal, September 2004* (pp. 132–146). Berlin: Springer-Verlag.

Fonseca, N. A., Silva, F., Santos Costa, V., & Camacho, R. (2005). Strategies to paralize ILP systems. In *Lecture notes in ai. 15th International Conference on inductive logic programming (ILP 2005), Bonn, August 2005* (pp. 136–153). Berlin: Springer-Verlag. (Best paper ILP 2005)

Food Standards Agency. (2004). *Survey of baked beans and canned pasta* (Information Sheet 57/04). Retrieved August 21, 2007, from http://www.food.gov.uk/science/surveillance/fsis2004/branch/fsis5704

Fox, M. and Long, D., (2003). PDDL2.1: An extension to PDDL for expressing temporal planning domains. *Journal of Artificial Intelligence Research, 20*, 61-124. Retrieved from http://www.dur.ac.uk/d.p.long/pddl2.ps.gz

Fox, M., & Long, D. (1999). Efficient implementation of the plan graph in STAN. *Journal of Artificial Intelligence Research, 10,* 87-115.

Fox, M., & Long, D. (2003). PDDL2.1: An extension to PDDL for expressing temporal planning domains. *Journal of Artificial Intelligence Research, 20,* 61-124.

Fred, A., & Jain, A.K. (2002). Data clustering using evidence accumulation. In *Proceedings of the 16th International Conference on Pattern Recognition* (pp. 276-280).

Fred, A., & Jain, A.K. (2005). Combining multiple clustering using evidence accumulation. *IEEE Transactions on Pattern Analysis and Machine Intelligence, 27*(6), 835-850.

Frege, G. (1966). *Logische Untersuchungen.* Göttingen: Vandenhoeck & Ruprecht.

Freuder, E.C. (1978). Synthesising constraint expressions. *Communications of the ACM, 21*(11), 958-966.

Freuder, E.C. (1982). A sufficient condition for backtrack-free search. *Journal of the ACM, 29,* 24-32.

Freuder, E.C. (1985). A sufficient condition for backtrack-bounded search. *Journal of the ACM, 32*(4), 755-761.

Freuder, E.C. (1992). Partial constraint satisfaction. *Artificial Intelligence, 50,* 510-530.

Freuder, E.C., & Elfe, C.D. (1996). Neighborhood inverse consistency preprocessing. In *Proceedings of the AAAI National Conference* (pp. 202-208). AAAI Press.

Freuder, E.C., & Quinn, M.J. (1985). Taking advantage of stable sets of variables in constraint satisfaction problems. In *Proceedings of the Ninth International Joint Conference on Artificial Intelligenc* (pp. 1076-1078).

Friedberg, R.M. (1958). A learning machine: Part I. *IBM Journal of Research and Development, 2*(1), 2-13.

Friedberg, R.M., Dunham, B., & North, J.H. (1959). A learning machine: Part II. *IBM Journal of Research and Development, 3*(3), 282-287.

Frieß, T.T., & Harrison, R., (1998). *Linear programming support vector machines for pattern classification and regression estimation; and the SR algorithm: Improving speed and tightness of VC bounds in SV algorithms* (Research Report No. 706). Sheffield: University of Sheffield.

Frost, D., & Dechter, R. (1995). Look-ahead value ordering for constraint satisfaction problems. In *Proceedings of the Fourteenth International Joint Conference on Artificial Intelligence* (pp. 572-578).

Frühwirth, T., & Abdennadher, S. (2003). *Essentials of constraint programming.* Springer.

Fujiki, C. (1987). Using the genetic algorithm to generate lisp source code to solve the prisoner's dilemma. *International Conf on Gas,* 236-240.

Fulkerson, D.R., Dantzig, G.B., & Johnson, S.M. (1954). Solution of a large scale travelling salesman problem. *Operations Research, 2,* 393-410.

Fürnkranz, J. (1997, August). Dimensionality reduction in ILP: a call to arms. In L. De Raedt & S. H. Muggleton (Eds.), *Proceedings of the IJCAI-97 workshop on frontiers of inductive logic programming* (pp. 81–86). Nagoya, Japan.

Fürnkranz, J. (1998). Integrative windowing. *Journal of machine learning Research, 8,* 129–164.

Fürnkranz, J., & Flach, P. (2003). An analysis of rule evaluation metrics. In *Proceedings of the 20th international conference on machine learning (icml-03).* San Francisco: Morgan Kaufmann.

Gallaire, H. (1985). Logic programming: Further developments. In *IEEE Symposium on Logic Programming* (pp. 88-96), Boston, MA. IEEE.

Garrido, A., & Long, D. (2004). Planning with numeric variables in multiobjective planning. In L. Saitta (Ed.), *Proceedings of the European Conference on AI (ECAI-2004)* (pp. 662-666). Amsterdam: IOS Press.

Garrido, A., & Onaindía, E. (2003). On the application of least-commitment and heuristic search in temporal planning. In *Proceedings of the International Joint Conference on AI (IJCAI-2003)* (pp. 942-947). Acapulco, Mexico: Morgan Kaufmann.

Garrido, A., & Onaindía, E. (2006). Interleaving planning and scheduling: A collaborative approach. In *Proceedings of the ICAPS Workshop on Constraint Satisfaction Techniques for Planning and Scheduling Problems* (pp. 31-38).

Garrido, A., Fox, M., & Long, D. (2002). A temporal planning system for durative actions of PDDL2.1. In F. Van Harmelen (Ed.), *Proceedings of the European Conference on AI (ECAI-2002)* (pp. 586-590). Amsterdam: IOS Press.

Garrido, A., Onaindía, E., & Arangu, M. (2006). Using constraint programming to model complex plans in an antegrated approach for planning and scheduling. In *Proceedings of the 25th UK Planning and Scheduling SIG Workshop* (pp. 137-144).

Gaschnig, J. (1974). A constraint satisfaction method for inference making. In *Proceedings of the 12th Annual Allerton Conference on Cirucit and System Theory* (pp. 866-874).

Gaschnig, J. (1979). Performance measurement and analysis of certain search algorithms. CMU-CS-79-124, Carnegie-Mellon University.

Gat, E. (1992). Integrating planning and reacting in a heterogeneous asynchronous architecture for controlling real-world mobile robots. In *Proceedings of the National Conference on Artificial intelligence* (pp. 809-815).

Geelen, P.A. (1992). Dual viewpoint heuristics for binary constraint satisfaction problems. In *Proceedings of the Tenth European Conference on Artificial Intelligence* (pp. 31-35).

Georgopoulou, E., Sarafidis, Y., & Diakoulaki, D. (1998). Design and implementation of a group DSS for sustaining renewable energies exploitation. *European Journal of Operational Research, 109,* 483-500.

Gerevini, A. and Long, D. (2005). *Plan constraints and preferences in PDDL3,* (Tech Rep No. R.T. 2005-08-47), Dipartimento di Elettronica per l'Automazione, Università degli Studi di Brescia, Italy.

Gerevini, A., Saetti, A., & Serina, I. (2003). Planning through stochastic local search and temporal action graphs in LPG. *Journal of Artificial Intelligence Research, 20,* 239-290.

Gerig, G., Welti, D., Guttman, C.R.G, Colchester, A.C.F., & Szekely G. (2000). Exploring the discrimination power of the time domain for segmentation and characterisation of active lesions in serial MR data. *Medical Image Analysis, 4,* 31-42.

Ghallab, M., & Laruelle, H. (1994). Representation and control in IxTeT, a temporal planner. In *Proceedings of the 2nd International Conference on AI Planning Systems* (pp. 61-67). Hammond.

Ghallab, M., Nau, D., & Traverso, P. (2004). *Automated planning: Theory and practice.* Morgan Kaufmann Publishers.

Gilbert, N., & Troitzsch, K. G. (1999). *Simulation for the social scientist.* Buckingham: Open University Press.

Ginsberg, M.L. (1993). Dynamic backtracking. *Journal of Artificial Intelligence Research, 1,* 25-46.

Ginsberg, M.L., & Harvey, W.D. (1990). Iterative broadening. In *Proceedings of Eighth National Conference on Artificial Intelligence (AAAI-90)* (pp. 216-220). AAAI Press.

Ginsberg, M.L., Frank, M., Halpin, M.P., & Torrance, M.C. (1990). Search lessons learned from crossword puzzles. In *Proceedings of the Eighth National Conference on Artificial Intelligence (AAAI)* (pp. 210-215). AAAI Press.

Giordana, A., Saitta, L., Sebag, M., & Botta, M. (2000). Analyzing relational learning in the phase transition framework. In *Proceedings of the 17th international conference on machine learning* (pp. 311–318). San Francisco: Morgan Kaufmann.

Giunchiglia, F., & Traverso, P. (1999). Planning as model checking. In *Proceedings of the 5th European Conference on Planning*, Durham, UK (pp. 1-20).

Goadrich, M., Oliphant, L., & Shavlik, J. W. (2004). Learning ensembles of first-order clauses for recall-precision curves: A case study in biomedical information extraction. In R. Camacho, R. D. King, & A. Srinivasan (Eds.), *Lecture notes in computer science: Vol. 3194. ILP* (pp. 98–115). Berlin: Springer-Verlag.

Goguen, J.A. (1969). The logic of inexact concepts. *Syntheses, 19*, 325-373.

Goldberg D.E., & Richardson, J.T. (1987). Genetic algorithms with sharing for multi-modal function optimization. In *Proceedings of the International Conference on Genetic Algorithms and Their Applications* (pp. 41-49).

Goldberg, D.E., Deb, K., & Korb, B. (1991). Don't worry, be messy. In R. Belew & L. Booker (Eds.), *Proceedings of the Fourth International Conference in Genetic Algorithms and Their Applications* (pp. 24-30).

Golomb, S., & Baumert, L. (1965). Backtrack programming. *Journal of the ACM, 12,* 516-524.

Gomes, C., Selman, B., & Kautz, H. (1998). Boosting combinatorial search through randomization. In *Proceedings of National Conference on Artificial Intelligence (AAAI)* (pp. 432-327). AAAI Press.

Gondra, I., & Samadzadeh, M.H. (2003). A coarse-grain parallel genetic algorithm for finding ramsey numbers. In *Proceedings of the Annual ACM Symposium on Applied Computing* (pp. 2-8).

Goodman, E.D., Lin, S., & Punch, W.F. (1994). Coarse-grain parallel genetic algorithms: Categorization and new approach. In *Proceedings of the IEEE Symposium on Parallel and Distributed Processing* (pp. 28-37).

Graham, A. (1981). *Kronecker products and matrix calculus: With applications.* New York: Wiley.

Graham, J., Page, C. D., & Kamal, A. (2003). Accelerating the drug design process through parallel inductive logic programming data mining. In *Proceeding of the computational systems bioinformatics (csb'03).* IEEE.

Graham, R.L., & Spencer, J.H. (1990). Ramsey theory. *Scientific American, 263*(1), 112-117.

Gretton, A., Doucet, A., Herbrich, R., Rayner, P.J.W., & Schölkopf, B. (2001). Support vector regression for black-box system identification. In *Proceedings of the 11th IEEE Workshop on Statistical Signal Processing* (pp. 341-344).

Grounds, M., & Kudenko, D. (2005). Combining reinforcement learning with symbolic planning. In *Fifth European Workshop on Adaptive Agents and Multi-Agent Systems*, Paris.

Guan, S.U., & Ramanathan, K. (2004). Recursive percentage based hybrid pattern training for curve fitting. *IEEE conference on Cybernetics and Intelligent systems, 1,* 445-450.

Gunetti, D., & Ruffo, G. (1999). Intrusion Detection through Behavioral Data. In S. Wrobel (Ed.), *Lecture notes in computer science. Proc. of The Third Symposium on Intelligent Data Analysis.* Berlin: Springer-Verlag.

Hacking, I. (1975) *The emergence of probability.* New York, Cambridge University Press.

Hadzic, I., & Kecman, V. (2000) Support vector machines trained by linear programming: Theory and application in image compression and data classification. In *IEEE 5th Seminar on Neural Network Applications in Electrical Engineering* (pp. 18-23).

Haken, H. (1998). Can we apply synergetics to the human sciences? In G. Altmann & W.A. Koch (Eds.), *Systems: New paradigms for human sciences.* Berlin; New York: de Gruyter.

Halgamuge, S.K., & Glesner, M. (1994) Neural networks in designing fuzzy systems for real world applications. *Fuzzy Sets and Systems, 65,* 1-12.

Han, C., & Lee, C. (1988). Comments on Mohr and Henderson's path consistency algorithm. *Artificial Intelligence, 36,* 125-130.

Haralick, R.M., & Elliot, G.L. (1980). Increasing tree search efficiency for constraint satisfaction problems. *Artificial Intelligence, 14,* 263-314.

Harmon, M.E., & Harmon, S.S. (1996). Reinforcement learning: A tutorial. Retrieved on August 14, 2007, from http://iridia.ulb.ac.be/~fvandenb/qlearning/rltutorial.pdf

Harris, Z. S. (1954). Distributional structure. *Word, 10,* 146-162.

Harvey, W.D. (1995). Nonsystematic backtracking search (Ph.D. thesis, Stanford University).

Harvey, W.D., & Ginsberg, M.L. (1995). Limited discrepancy search. In *Proceedings of the 14th International Joint Conference on Artificial Intelligence* (pp. 607-613).

Hashimoto, T. (2002). The constructive approach to the dynamical view of language. In A. Cangelosi & D. Parisi, D. (Eds.), *Simulating the evolution of language* (pp. 307-324). London: Springer Verlag.

Haslum, P. (2006). Improving heuristics through relaxed search–an analysis of TP4 and HSP$^*_a$ in the 2004 planning competition. *Journal of Artificial Intelligence Research, 25,* 233-267.

Haslum, P., & Geffner, H. (2001). Heuristic planning with time and resources. In A. Cesta & D. Borrajo (Eds.), *Proceedings of the European Conference on Planning (ECP-2001)* (pp. 121-132).

Hayes, A.T., & Dormiani-Tabatabaei, P. (2002). Self-organized flocking with agent failure: Off-line optimization and demonstration with real robots. In *Proceedings of the Institute of Electrical and Electronics Engineers International Conference on Robotics and Automation* (p. 4).

Hayes-Roth, B. (1993). *An architecture for adaptive intelligent systems.* Stanford University: Knowledge Systems Laboratory.

Hayes-Roth, B., Pfleger, K., Lalanda, P., & Morignot, P. (1995). A domain-specific software architecture for adaptive intelligent systems. *Institute of Electrical and Electronics Engineers Transactions on Software Engineering, 21*(4), 288-301.

Hayes-Roth, F. (1974). Schematic classification problems and their solution. *Pattern Recognition, 6*(2), 105-113.

Heshmaty, B., & Kandel, A. (1985). Fuzzy linear regression and its application to forecasting in uncertain environment. *Fuzzy Sets and Systems, 15,* 159-191.

Hintikka, J., & Kulas, J. (1983). *The game of language.* Dordrecht: Reidel.

Hoffmann, J., & Nebel, B. (2001). The FF planning system: Fast plan generation through heuristic search. *Journal of Artificial Intelligence Research, 14,* 253-302.

Hollan, J., Hutchins, E., & Kirsh, D. (2000). Distributed cognition: Toward a new foundation for human-computer interaction research. *ACM Transaction on Computer-Human Interaction, 7*(2), 174-196.

Holland, J. (1975). *Adaptation in natural and artificial systems.* Ann Arbor, MI: University of Michigan Press.

Horváth, T. (Ed.). (2003). *Inductive logic programming: Proceeding of the 13th international conference, ILP 2003, Szeged, Hungary, September 29–October 1, 2003.* Berlin: Springer-Verlag.

Hsu, C-W., Wah, B.W., Huang, R., & Chen, Y. (2006). New features in SGPlan for handling preferences and constraints in PDDL3.0. In *Proceedings of the International Conference on Automated Planning and Scheduling (ICAPS2006) – International Planning Competition* (pp. 39-41).

Huisman, M. (2000). Imputation of missing item responses: Some simple techniques. *Quality & Quantity, 34,* 331-351.

Hutchins, E., & Hazlehurst, B. (2002). Auto-organization and emergence of shared language structure. In A. Cangelosi & D. Parisi (Eds.), *Simulating the evolution of language* (pp. 279-306). London: Springer Verlag.

Hwang, C.L., & Yoon, K. (1981). *Multiple attributes decision making methods and applications*. Berlin, Heidelberg, Germany: Springer.

Hyde, K.M., & Maier, H.R. (2006). Distance-based and stochastic uncertainty analysis for multi-criteria decision analysis in Excel using visual basic for applications. *Environmental Modelling & Software, 21*(12), 1695-1710.

Hyde, K.M., Maier, H.R., & Colby, C.B. (2003). Incorporating uncertainty in the PROMETHEE MCDA method. *Journal of Multi-Criteria Decisions Analysis, 12*, 245-259.

Inuiguchi, M., & Ramik, J. (2000). Possiblilistic linear programming: A brief review of fuzzy mathematical programming and comparison with stochastic programming in portfolio selection problem. *Fuzzy Sets and Systems, 111,* 3-28.

Jaffar, J., & Lassez, J.L. (1987). Constraint logic programming. In *Proceedings of the ACM Symposium on Principles of Programming Languages* (pp. 111-119). ACM.

Jaffar, J., & Maher, M.J. (1996). Constraint logic programming—a survey. *Journal of Logic Programming, 19/20,* 503-581.

Jagielska, I., Matthews, C., & Whitfort, T. (1996). The application of neural networks, fuzzy logic, genetic algorithms and rough sets to automated knowledge acquisition. *4th Int. Conf. on Soft Computing, IIZUKA'96,* Japan (vol. 2, pp. 565-569).

Jain, A.K., & Dubes, R.C. (1998). *Algorithms for clustering data*. Prentice Hall.

Jakobson, R. (1971). *Selected writings II: Word and language*. The Hague: Mouton.

Jamison, K.D., & Lodwick, W.A. (2002). The construction of consistent possibility and necessity measures. *Fuzzy Sets and Systems, 132,* 1-10.

Jang, J., & Sun, C. (1992). Functional equivalence between radial basis function networks and fuzzy inference systems. *IEEE Transactions on Neural Networks, 4,* 156-158.

Jankowski, N., & Kadirkamanathan, V. (1997). Statistical control of RBF-like networks for classification. *7th International Conference on Artificial Neural Networks,* Lausanne, Switzerland (pp. 385-390).

Janssen, T. M. V. (1997). Compositionality (with an appendix by Barbara H. Partee). In J. van Benthem & A. ter Meulen (Eds.), *Handbook of logic and language* (pp. 417-473). Amsterdam: Elsevier.

Jonsson, A., Morris, P., Muscettola, N., Rajan, K., & Smith, B. (2000). Planning in interplanetary space: Theory and practice. In *Proceedings of the 5th International Conference on AI Planning Systems (AIPS-2000)* (pp. 177-186). AAAI Press.

Jorge, A., & Brazdil, P. (1995). Architecture for iterative learning of recursive definitions. In L. De Raedt (Ed.), *Proceedings of the 5th international workshop on inductive logic programming* (pp. 95–108). Department of Computer Science, Katholieke Universiteit Leuven.

Joslin, D., & Pollack, M.E. (1996). Is "early commitment" in plan generation ever a good idea? In *Proceedings of the 13th Nat. Conference on AI (AAAI-96)* (pp. 177-186).

Judd, D., McKinley, P., & Jain, A.K. (1997). Large scale parallel data clustering. *IEEE Trans Pattern Analysis and Machine Intelligence, 19*(2), 153-158.

Kaelbling, L., Littman, M., & Moore, A. (1996). Reinforcement learning: A survey. *Journal of Artificial Intelligence Research, 4,* 237-285.

Kamp, H., & Partee, B. (1995). Prototype theory and compositionality. *Cognition, 57*(2), 129-191.

Kasabov, N. (1996). *Foundations of neural networks, fuzzy systems and knowledge engineering*. Cambridge, MA: MIT Press.

Kautz, H., & Selman, B. (1992). Planning as satisfiability. In *Proceedings of the 10th European Conference on Artificial Intelligence,* Vienna, Austria (pp. 359-363).

Kautz, H., & Selman, B. (1998). BLACKBOX: A new approach to the application of theorem proving to problem solving. In *Proceedings of the AIPS-98 Workshop on Planning as Combinatorial Search*, Pittsburgh, PA (pp. 58-60).

Kecman, V. (2001). *Learning and soft computing: Support vector machines, neural networks, and fuzzy logic models*. MIT Press.

Keedwell, E., Narayanan, A., & Savic, D. (2000). Creating rules from trained neural networks using genetic algorithms. *International Journal of Computers, Systems and Signals (IJCSS), 1*(1), 30-42.

Kersting, K., & Raedt, L. D. (2001, November). *Bayesian logic programs* (Tech. Rep. No. 151). Georges-Koehler-Allee, D-77110, Freiburg: Institute for Computer Science, University of Freiburg.

Kersting, K., & Raedt, L. D. (2002). *Basic principles of learning bayesian logic progras* (Tech. Rep. No. 174). Georges-Koehler-Allee, D-77110, Freiburg: Institute for Computer Science, University of Freiburg.

Kijsirikul, B., Sinthupinyo, S., & Chongkasemwongse, K. (2001). Approximate match of rules using back-propagation neural networks. *machine learning, 44*(3), 273–299.

King, R. D. (2004). Applying inductive logic programming to predicting gene function. *AI Magazine, 25*(1), 57–68.

King, R. D., Whelan, K. E., Jones, F. M., Reiser, P. G., Bryant, C. H., Muggleton, S. H., et al. (2004, January). Functional genomic hypothesis generation and experimentation by a robot scientist. *Nature, 427*(6971), 247–252.

Kintsch, W. (1998). *Comprehension: A paradigm for cognition*. Cambridge: Cambridge University Press.

Kintsch, W. (2001). Predication. *Cognitive Science, 25*,173-202.

Kirby, S. (2002). Natural language from artificial life. *Artificial Life, 8*(2), 185-215.

Kirby, S., & Hurford, J. R. (2002). The emergence of linguistic structure: An overview of the iterated learning model. In A. Cangelosi & D. Parisi (Eds.), *Simulating the evolution of language* (pp. 121-148). London: Springer Verlag.

Knoblock, C.A. (1991). *Automatically generation abstractions for problem solving*. Unpublished doctoral dissertation, Carnegie Mellon University, School of Computer Science.

Ko, C. (2000). Logic induction of valid behavior specifications for intrusion detection. In *SP 2000: Proceedings of the 2000 IEEE symposium on security and privacy*. Washington, DC, USA: IEEE Computer Society.

Koehler, J., Nebel, B., Hoffmann, J., & Dimopoulos, Y. (1997). Extending planning graphs to an ADL subset. In *Proceedings of the 4th European Conference on Planning*, Toulouse, France (pp. 273-285).

Köhler, R. (1986). *Zur linguistischen synergetik: Struktur und Dynamik der Lexik*. Bochum: Brockmeyer.

Köhler, R. (1987). Systems theoretical linguistics. *Theoretical Linguistics, 14*(2, 3), 241-257.

Köhler, R. (1993). Synergetic linguistics. In R. Köhler & B.B. Rieger (Eds.), *Contributions to quantitative linguistics* (pp. 41-51). Dordrecht: Kluwer.

Köhler, R. (1999). Syntactic structures: Properties and interrelations. *Journal of Quantitative Linguistics, 6*, 46-57.

Kohonen, T. (1997). *Self organizing maps*. Berlin, Germany: Springer-Verlag.

Konstantopoulos, S. (2003, September). A data-parallel version of Aleph. In *Proceedings of the workshop on parallel and distributed computing for machine learning, co-located with ECML/PKDD'2003*. Dubrovnik, Croatia.

Korf, R. (1985). Depth-first iterative-deepening: an optimal admissible tree search. *Artificial Intelligence, 27*(1), 97-109.

Korf, R.E. (1996). Improved limited discrepancy search. In *Proceedings of National Conference on Artificial Intelligence (AAAI-96)* (pp. 286-291). AAAI Press.

Koza, J. (1992). *Genetic programming: On the programming of computers by means of natural selection*. Cambridge, MA: MIT Press.

Koza, J. (1994). *Genetic programming II: Automatic discovery of reusable programs (complex adaptive systems)*. Cambridge, MA: The MIT Press.

Koza, J., Bennett, F.H., Andre, D., & Keane, M.A. (1999). *Genetic programming III: Darwinian invention and problem solving*. Morgan Kauffman.

Krylov, J. K. (1982). Eine Untersuchung statistischer Gesetzmäßigkeiten auf der paradigmatischen Ebene der Lexik natürlicher Sprachen. In H. Guiter & M.V. Arapov (Eds.), *Studies on Zipf 's law* (pp. 234-262). Bochum: Brockmeyer.

Kumar, V. (1992). Algorithms for constraint satisfaction problems: A survey. *AI Magazine, 13*(1), 32-44.

Kuwata, Y. (2003). *Real-time trajectory design for unmanned aerial vehicles using receding horizon control*. Master of Science dissertation, Massachusetts Institute of Technology.

Kuwata, Y., & How, J.P. (2004). *Three dimentional receding horizon control for UAVs*. Paper presented at the American Institute of Aeronautics and Astronautics Guidance, Navigation, and Control Conference and Exhibit.

Kwee, I., Marcus, H., & Schmidhuber, J. (2001). Gradient-based reinforcement planning in policy-search methods. In *Fifth European Workshop on Reinforcement Learning* (pp. 27-29).

Laborie, P., & Ghallab, M. (1995). Planning with sharable resource constraints. In *Proceedings of the International Joint Conference on AI (IJCAI-95)* (pp. 1643-1647). Morgan Kaufmann.

Laburthe, F. (2000). CHOCO: Implementing a CP kernel. In *Proceedings of the Workshop on Techniques for Implementing Constraint Programming Systems,* Singapour (pp. 71-85).

Lahdelma, R., Salminen, P., & Hokkanen, J. (2000). Using multicriteria methods in environmental planning and management. *Environmental Management, 26*(6), 595-605.

Lai, T.Y., & Hwang, C.L. (1993). Possibilistic linear programming for managing interest rate risk. *Fuzzy Sets aAnd Systems, 54,* 135-146.

Lakshminarayan, K., Harp, S.A., & Samad, T. (1999). Imputation of missing data in industrial databases. *Applied Intelligence, 11,* 259-275.

Landauer, T. K., & Dumais, S. T. (1997). A solution to Plato's problem: The latent semantic analysis theory of acquisition, induction, and representation of knowledge. *Psychological Review, 104*(2), 211-240.

Langley, P. (1996). *Elements of machine learning*. Morgan-Kaufmann.

Lavrac, N., & Džeroski, S. (Eds.). (1997). *Proceedings of the 7th international workshop on inductive logic programming (ILP-97), Prague, Czech Republic, September 17-20, 1997*. Berlin: Springer-Verlag.

Lavrač, N., Flach, P., & Zupan, B. (1999, June). Rule evaluation measures: A unifying view. In S. Džeroski & P. Flach (Eds.), *Lecture notes in artificial intelligence: Vol. 1634. Proceedings of the 9th International Workshop on inductive logic programming* (pp. 174–185). Berlin: Springer-Verlag.

Leberling, H. (1981). On finding compromise solutions in multicriteria problems using the fuzzy min-operator. *Fuzzy Sets and Systems, 6,* 105-118.

Lee, H.-S., & O'Mahony, M. (2005). Sensory evaluation and marketing: Measurement of a consumer concept. *Food Quality and Preference, 16,* 227-235.

Lee, K.L., & Billings, S.A. (2002). Time series prediction using support vector machines, the orthogonal and the regularized orthogonal least-squares algorithms. *International Journal of Systems Science, 33*(10), 811-821.

Lee, T.J., & Wilkins, D.E. (1996). Using SIPE-2 to integrate planning for military air campaigns. *IEEE Expert, 11*(6), 11-12.

Lennox, C. (1999). Identifying failing companies: A re-evaluation of the logit, probit and DA approaches. *Journal of Economics and Business, 51,* 347-364.

Lhomme, O. (1993). Consistency techniques for numeric CSPs. In *Proceedings of the 13th International Joint Conference on Artificial Intelligence* (pp. 232-238).

Lin, L.-J. (1992). Self-improving reactive agents based on reinforcement learning, planning and teaching. *Machine Learning, 8,* 293-321.

Lipson, H., & Siegelmann (2000). Clustering irregular shapes using higher order neurons. *Neural Computation, 12,* 2331-2353.

Lipson, H., Hod, Y., & Siegelmann, H.T. (1998). Higher order clustering metrics for competitive learning neural networks. In *Proceedings of the Isreal-Korea Bi National Conference on New Themes in Computer Aided Geometric Modeling,* Tel-Aviv, Israel.

Little, R.J.A. (1988). Missing-data adjustments in large surveys. *Journal of Business & Economic Statistics, 6,* 287-296.

Lloyd, J. W. (1997). *Foundations of logic programming* (2nd ed.). Berlin: Springer-Verlag.

Long, D., & Fox, M. (1998). Efficient implementation of the plan graph in STAN. *Journal of Artificial Intelligence Research, 10,* 87-115.

Long, D., & Fox, M. (2001). Encoding temporal planning domains and validating temporal plans. In *Proceedings of the 20th UK Planning and Scheduling SIG Workshop* (pp. 167-180).

Long, D., & Fox, M. (2002). Progress in AI planning research and applications. *UPGRADE, The European Online Magazine for the IT Professional, 3*(5), 10-24.

Long, D., & Fox, M. (2003). Exploiting a graphplan framework in temporal planning. In *Proceedings of the International Conference on Automated Planning and Scheduling (ICAPS-2003)* (pp. 51-62).

Long, D., & Fox, M. (2003). Time in planning. In *Handbook of temporal reasoning in AI. Foundations of Artificial Intelligence*, vol. 1 (pp. 497-537). Elsevier Science.

Mackey, M., & Glass, L. (1977). Oscillation and chaos in physiological control systems. *Science, 197,* 287.

Mackworth, A.K. (1977). Consistency in networks of relations. *Artificial Intelligence, 8,* 99-118.

Mackworth, A.K. (1977). On reading sketch maps. In *Proceedings IJCAI 1977* (pp. 598-606).

Mackworth, A.K., & Freuder, E.C. (1985). The complexity of some polynomial network consistency algorithms for constraint satisfaction problems. *Artificial Intelligence, 25,* 65-74.

Malerba, D., Esposito, F., Altamura, O., Ceci, M., & Berardi, M. (2003). Correcting the document layout: A machine learning approach. In *Icdar* (p. 97-). IEEE Computer Society.

Mao, J., & Jain, A. (1996). A self organizing network for hyper ellipsoidal clustering (HEC). *IEEE Transactions on Neural Networks, 7,* 16-39.

Marriott, K., & Stuckey, P.J. (1998). *Programming with constraints: An introduction.* The MIT Press.

Martínez, A., & Goddard, J. (2001). Definición de una red neuronal para clasificación por medio de un programa evolutivo. *Revista Mexicana de Ingeniería Biomédica, 22*(1), 4-11.

Martínez-Ramón, M., Rojo-Álvarez, J.L., Campus-Valls, G., Muñoz-Marí, J., Navia-Vázquez, Á., Soria-Olivas, E., & Figueiras-Vidal, A. R. (2006). Support Vector Machines for Nonlinear Kernel ARMA System Identification, *IEEE Trans. on Neural Networks, 17*(6), 1617-1622.

Matsui, T., Inuzuka, N., Seki, H., & Itoh, H. (1998). Comparison of three parallel implementations of an induction algorithm. In *8th int. parallel computing workshop* (pp. 181–188). Singapore.

Maturana, H. R., & Varela, F. J. (1980). *Autopoiesis and Cognition: The realization of the living.* Dordrecht: Reidel.

Matwin, S., & Sammut, C. (Eds.). (2003). *Proceedings of the 12th international workshop on inductive logic programming (ilp 2002).* Berlin: Springer Verlag.

McAllester, D. & Rosenblitt, D. (1991). Systematic non-linear planning. In *Proceedings of the Ninth National Conference on Artificial Intelligence* (AAAI-91) (pp. 634-639).

McCreath, E., & Sharma, A. (1995, November). Extraction of meta-knowledge to restrict the hypothesis space for ILP systems. In X. Yao (Ed.), *Proceedings of the eighth australian joint conference on artificial intelligence* (pp. 75–82). World Scientific.

McDermott, D. (1996). A heuristic estimator for means-end analysis in planning. In *Proceedings of the 3rd International Conference on Artificial Intelligence Planning Systems*, Eddinburgh, UK (pp. 142-149).

McGregor, J.J. (1979). Relational consistency algorithms and their application in finding subgraph and graph isomorphisms. *Information Science,19*(3), 229-250.

Mehler, A. (2004). Quantitative methoden. In H. Lobin & L. Lemnitzer (Eds.), *Texttechnologie: Perspektiven und Anwendungen* (pp. 83-107). Tübingen: Stauffenburg.

Mehler, A. (2005). Compositionality in numerical text semantics. In A. Mehler & R. Köhler (Eds.), *Aspects of automatic text analysis: Studies in fuzziness and soft computing*. Berlin: Springer.

Meir, R., & Rätsch, G. (2003). An introduction to boosting and leveraging. In S. Mendelson & A. Smola (Eds.), *Advanced Lectures on Machine Learning* (LNCS, pp. 119-184). Springer.

Meseguer, P. (1997). Interleaved depth-first search. In *Proceedings of 15th International Joint Conference on Artificial Intelligence* (pp. 1382-1387).

Michalewicz, Z., Logan, T.D., & Swaminathan, S. (1994). Evolutionary operators for continuous convex parameter spaces. In *Proceedings of the 3rd Annual Conference on Evolutionary Programming, World Scientific* (pp. 84-96).

Michalski, R. S. (1973). Aqval/1-computer implementation of a variable-valued logic system vl1 and examples of its application to pattern recognition. In *Proceeding of the first international joint conference on pattern recognition* (p. 3-17).

Miller, G. A., & Charles, W. G. (1991). Contextual correlates of semantic similarity. *Language and Cognitive Processes, 6*(1),1-28.

Mitchell, T. M. (1978). *Version spaces: An approach to concept learning.* Unpublished doctoral dissertation, Stanford University.

Mitchell, T. M. (1997). *Machine learning* (Second ed.). McGraw Hill.

Mitchell, T. M., Utgoff, P., & Banerji, R. (1983). Learning by experimentation: Acquiring and refining problem-solving heuristics. In R. Michalski, J. Carbonnel, & T. Mitchell (Eds.), *Machine learning: An artificial intelligence approach.* Palo Alto, CA: Tioga.

Mohr, R., & Henderson, T.C. (1986). Arc and path consistency revised. *Artificial Intelligence, 28,* 225-233.

Montana, D.J. (1995). Strongly typed genetic programming. In *Evolutionary computation* (pp. 199-200). Cambridge, MA: MIT Press.

Montanari, U. (1974). Networks of constraints fundamental properties and applications to picture processing. *Information Sciences, 7,* 95-132.

Moore, A.W., & Atkenson, C.G. (1993). Prioritized sweeping: Reinforcement learning with less data and less real time. *Machine Learning, 13,* 103-130.

Morik, K., Brockhausen, P., & Joachims, T. (1999). Combining statistical learning with a knowledge-based approach — a case study in intensive care monitoring. In I. Bratko & S. Džeroski (Eds.), *Icml* (pp. 268–277). San Francisco: Morgan Kaufmann.

Mouldin, M. (1984). Maintaining diversity in genetic search. In *Proceedings of the National Conference on Artificial Intelligence* (pp. 247-250).

Mozetic, I. (1998, December). Secondary structure prediction by inductive logic programming. In *Third meeting on the critical assessment of techniques for protein structure prediction, casp3* (pp. 38–38). Asilomar, CA: CASP3 organizers.

Muggleton, S. H. (1988). A strategy for constructing new predicates in first order logic. In D. Sleeman (Ed.), *Proceedings of the 3rd european working session on learning* (pp. 123–130). Pitman.

Muggleton, S. H. (1991). Inductive logic programming. *New Generation Computing, 8*(4), 295–317.

Muggleton, S. H. (1995). Inverse entailment and Progol. *New Generation Computing, Special issue on inductive logic programming, 13*(3–4), 245–286.

Muggleton, S. H. (1996). Learning from positive data. In *Proceedings of the sixth international workshop on inductive logic programming, lnai 1314* (pp. 358–376). Berlin: Springer-Verlag.

Muggleton, S. H. (2003). Learning structure and parameters of stochastic logic programs. In S. Matwin & C. Sammut (Eds.), *Lecture notes in artificial intelligence: Vol. 2583. Proceedings of the 12th International Workshop on inductive logic programming (ILP 2002)* (pp. 198–206). Berlin: Springer Verlag.

Muggleton, S. H., & Bain, M. (1999). Analogical prediction. In S. Džeroski & P. A. Flach (Eds.), *Lecture notes in computer science: Vol. 1634. ILP* (pp. 234–244). Berlin: Springer-Verlag.

Muggleton, S. H., & Buntine, W. (1988). Machine invention of first-order predicates by inverting resolution. In *Proceedings of the 5th international conference on machine learning* (pp. 339–352). Kaufmann.

Muggleton, S. H., & De Raedt, L. (1994). inductive logic programming: Theory and methods. *Journal of Logic Programming, 19*(20), 629–679. (Updated version of technical report CW 178, May 1993, Department of Computing Science, K.U. Leuven)

Muggleton, S. H., & Feng, C. (1990). Efficient induction of logic programs. In *Proceedings of the 1st conference on algorithmic learning theory* (pp. 368–381). Tokyo: Ohmsha.

Muggleton, S. H., King, R. D., & Sternberg, M. J. E. (1992). Protein secondary structure prediction using logic. In S. H. Muggleton (Ed.), *Report ICOT TM-1182.*

Proceedings of the 2nd International Workshop on inductive logic programming (pp. 228–259).

Muggleton, S. H., Srinivasan, A., & Bain, M. (1992). Compression, significance and accuracy. In D. Sleeman & P. Edwards (Eds.), *Proceedings of the 9th international workshop on machine learning* (pp. 338–347). San Francisco: Morgan Kaufmann.

Muscettola, N. (1994). HSTS: Integrating planning and scheduling. In M. Zweben & M.S. Fox (Eds.), *Intelligent Scheduling* (Vol 1, pp. 169-212). San Mateo, CA: Morgan Kaufmann.

Muscettola, N., Nayak, P.P., Pell, B., & Williams, B.C. (1998). Remote agent: To boldly go where no AI system has gone before. *Artificial intelligence, 103*(1/2), 5-47.

Nauck, D., Nauck, U., & Kruse, R. (1996). Generating classification rules with the neuro-fuzzy system NEFCLASS. *Proceedings of Biennal Conference of the North American Fuzzy Information Processing Society (NAFIPS'96),* Berkeley, CA.

Nedellec, C., & Rouveirol, C. (Eds.). (1998). *Proceedings of the 10th european conference on machine learning (ECML 1998), Chemnitz, Germany, April 21-23.* Berlin: Springer-Verlag.

Nerbonne, J., & Konstantopoulos, S. (2004, May). Phonotactics in inductive logic programming. In M. Klopotek, S. Wierzchon, & K. Trojanowski (Eds.), *Advances in soft computing. Intelligent Information Processing and Web Mining. Proceedings of the International IIS: IIPWM'04 Conference, Zakopane, Poland, May 17–20, 2004* (pp. 493–502). Berlin: Springer-Verlag.

Newell, A., & Simon, H.A. (1963). GPS, a program that simulates human thought. In Feigenbaum & Feldman (Eds.), *Computers and thought* (pp. 279-293). New York: McGraw-Hill.

Nguyen, X., Kambhampati, S., & Nigenda, R. (2000). AltAlt: Combining the advantages of graphplan and heuristics state search. In *Proceedings of the 2000 International Conference on Knowledge-based Computer Systems,* Bombay, India.

Nguyen, X., Kambhampati, S., & Nigenda, R.S. (2002). Planning graph as the basis for deriving heuristics for plan synthesis by state space and CSP search. *Artificial Intelligence, 135*, 73-123.

Ni, Y., Huang, C., & Kokot, S. (2004). Application of multivariate calibration and artificial neural networks to simultaneous kinetic-spectrophotometric determination of carbamate pesticides. *Chemometrics and Intelligent Laboratory Systems, 71*, 177-193.

Nilsson, N.J. (1994). Teleo-reactive programs for agent control. *Journal of Artificial Intelligence Research, 1*, 139-158.

Ohwada, H., & Mizoguchi, F. (1999). Parallel execution for speeding up inductive logic programming systems. In *Lecture notes in artificial intelligence. Proceedings of the 9th International Workshop on inductive logic programming* (pp. 277–286). Springer-Verlag.

Ohwada, H., Nishiyama, H., & Mizoguchi, F. (2000). Concurrent execution of optimal hypothesis search for inverse entailment. In J. Cussens & A. Frisch (Eds.), *Lecture notes in artificial intelligence: Vol. 1866. Proceedings of the 10th International Conference on inductive logic programming* (pp. 165–173). Berlin: Springer-Verlag.

Olfati-Saber, R., & Murray, R.M. (2003). Flocking with obstacle avoidance: Cooperation with limited information in mobile networks. In *Proceedings of the 42nd Institute of Electrical and Electronics Engineers Conference on Decision and Control* (pp. 2022-2028). Retrieved on August 14, 2007, from http://www.cds.caltech.edu/~olfati/papers/cdc03/cdc03b_ros_rmm.pdf

Ong, I. M., Dutra, I. d. C., Page, C. D., & Santos Costa, V. (2005). Mode directed path finding. In *Lecture notes in computer science: Vol. 3720. Proceedings of the 16th European Conference on machine learning* (pp. 673–681).

Page, C. D., & Craven, M. (2003). Biological applications of multi-relational data mining. *SIGKDD Explor. Newsl., 5*(1), 69–79.

Page, C. D., & Srinivasan, A. (2003, August). ILP: A short look back and a longer look forward. *Journal of machine learning Research*(4), 415–430.

Painho, M., & Bacao, R. (2000). Using genetic algorithms in clustering problems. *Geocomputation 2000*. Retrieved August 20, 2007, from http://www.geocomputation.org/2000/GC015/Gc015.htm

Papadopoulos, C.V. (1994). On the parallel execution of combinatorial heuristics. In *Proceedings of the International Conference on Massively Parallel Computing Systems* (pp. 423-427).

Parra, M.A., Terol, A.B., & Rodrfguez Una, M.V. (1999). Theory and methodology solving the multi-objective possiblistic linear programming problem. *European Journal of Operational Research, 117*, 175-182.

Partee, B. H. (1995). Lexical semantics and compositionality. In L.R. Gleitman & M. Liberman (Eds.), *Language: An invitation to cognitive science* (vol. 1, pp. 311-360). Cambridge: MIT Press.

Passerini, A., Frasconi, P., & De Raedt, L. (2006). Kernels on prolog proof trees: Statistical learning in the ILP setting. In *Probabilistic, logical and relational learning. Towards a synthesis. 30 Jan - 4 Febr 2005* (pp. 307–342). Internationales Begegnungs- und Forschungszentrum für Informatik (IBFI), Schloss Dagstuhl, Germany.

Pattee, H. H. (1988). Simulations, realizations, and theories of life. In C.G. Langton (Ed.), *Artificial life: SFI studies in the sciences of complexity* (pp. 63-77). Redwood: Addison-Wesley.

Peel, M. (1990). *The liquidation/merger alternative*. Avebury: Aldershot.

Penberthy, J. & Weld, D. (1992). UCPOP: A sound and complete, partial order planner for ADL. In *Proceedings of the Third International Conference on Principles of Knowledge Representation and Reasoning* (pp. 103-114). Toulouse, France.

Penberthy, J. (1993). Planning with continuous change. Technical Report Ph.D. dissertation 93-12-01, University of Washington, Department of Computer Science and Engineering.

Penberthy, J., & Weld, D. (1994). Temporal planning with continuous change. In *Proceedings of the 12th National Conference on AI* (pp. 1010-1015).

Penberthy, J., & Weld, D.S. (1992). UCPOP: A sound, complete, partial-order planner for ADL. In *Proceedings of the International Conference on Principles of Knowledge Representation and Reasoning* (pp. 103-114). Los Altos, CA: Kaufmann.

Peng, J., & Ronald J.W. (1993). Efficient learning and planning within the dyna framework. *Adaptive Behavior, 1*(4), 437-454.

Penix, J., Pecheur, C., & Havelund, K. (1998). Using model checking to validate AI planner domain models. In *Proceedings of the 23rd Annual Software Engineering Workshop* (pp. 356-364). NASA Goddard.

Pereira, F., & Warren, D. S. (1983). Parsing as deduction. In dunno (Ed.), *Proceedings of the 21st conference of the acl* (pp. 137–44).

Pesant, G. (2004). A regular language membership constraint for finite sequences of variables. In *Proceedings of the Tenth International Conference on Principles and Practice of Constraint Programming (CP)* (LNCS 3258, pp. 183-195). Springer Verlag.

Petrovic-Lazarevic, S., & Abraham, A. (2003). Hybrid fuzzy-linear programming approach for multicriteria decision making problems. *International Journal of Neural, Parallel, and Scientific Computations, 11*, 53-68.

Pickering, M. J., & Garrod, S. (2004). Toward a mechanistic psychology of dialogue. *Behavioral and Brain Sciences, 27*, 169-226.

Plotkin, G. D. (1970). A note on inductive generalization. In B. Meltzer & D. Michie (Eds.), *Machine intelligence* (Vol. 5, pp. 153–163). Edinburgh University Press.

Plotkin, G. D. (1971). *Automatic methods of inductive inferrence.* Unpublished doctoral dissertation, University of Edinburgh.

Plotkin, G. D. (1971). A further note on inductive generalization. In D. Michie, N. L. Collins, & E. Dale (Eds.), *Machine intelligence* (Vol. 6, pp. 101–124). Edinburgh University Press.

Pompe, U., Kononenko, I., & Makše, T. (1996). An application of ILP in a musical database: Learning to compose the two-voice counterpoint. In *Proceedings of the MLnet Familiarization Workshop on Data Mining with Inductive Logic Programing* (pp. 1–11).

Poon, P.W., & Carter, J.N. (1995). Genetic algorithm crossover operators for ordering applications. *Computers and Operations Research, 22*(1), 135-147.

Pop, E., Hayward, R., & Diederich, J. (1994). *RULENEG: Extracting rules from a trained ANN by stepwise negation.* Queensland University of Technology, Neurocomputing Research Centre. QUT NRC Technical report.

Popelinsky, L. (1998, September). Knowledge discovery in spatial data by means of ILP. In J. M. Zytkow & M. Quafafou (Eds.), *Lecture notes in computer science: Vol. 1510. Principles of Data Mining and Knowledge Discovery. PKDD'98 Nantes France.* (pp. 271–279). Berlin: Springer Verlag.

Popplestone, R. J. (1970). An experiment in automatic induction. In *Machine Intelligence* (Vol. 5, p. 204-215). Edinburgh University Press.

Prosser, P. (1993). Hybrid algorithms for constraint satisfaction problems. *Computational Intelligence, 9*(3), 268-299.

Prosser, P., Stergiou, K., & Walsh, T. (2000). Singleton consistencies. In *Proceedings, Principles and Practice of Constraint Programming (CP2000)* (LNCS 1894, pp. 353-368). Springer Verlag.

Puget, J. (1998). A fast algorithm for the bound consistency of Alldiff constraints. In *National Conference on Artificial Intelligence (AAAI)* (pp. 359-366). AAAI Press.

Quimper, C.-G., & Walsh, T. (2006). Global grammar constraints. In *12th International Conference on Principles and Practices of Constraint Programming (CP-2006)* (LNCS 4204, pp. 751-755). Springer Verlag.

Quiniou, R., Cordier, M.-O., Carrault, G., & Wang, F. (2001). Application of ILP to cardiac arrhythmia characterization for chronicle recognition. In C. Rouveirol & M. Sebag (Eds.), *Lecture notes in computer science: Vol. 2157. ILP* (pp. 220–227). Berlin: Springer-Verlag.

Quinlan, J. R. (1990). Learning logical definitions from relations. *machine learning, 5,* 239–266.

Quinlan, J. R. (1993). *C4.5: programs for machine learning.* San Francisco: Morgan Kaufmann Publishers Inc.

Rabuñal, J.R. (1999). *Entrenamiento de Redes de Neuronas Artificiales mediante Algoritmos Genéticos.* Graduate thesis, Facultad de Informática, Universidade da Coruña.

Rabuñal, J.R., Dorado, J., Pazos, A., Pereira, J., & Rivero, D. (2004). A new approach to the extraction of ANN rules and to their generalization capacity through GP. *Neural Computation, 16*(7), 1483-1524.

Ramsey, F.P. (1930). On a problem of formal logic. *London Mathematical Society, 30,* 264-286.

Rebaudergo, M., & Sonza Reorda, M. (1992). An experimental analysis of the effects of migration in parallel genetic algorithms. In *Proceedings of the Euromicro Workshop on Parallel and Distributed Processing* (pp. 232-238).

Refanidis, I. (2005). Stratified heuristic POCL temporal planning based on planning graphs and constraint programming. In *Proceedings of the ICAPS-2005 Workshop on Constraint Programming for Planning and Scheduling* (pp. 66-73).

Régin, J.-C. (1994). A filtering algorithm for constraints of difference in CSPs. In *Proceedings of the National Conference on Artificial Intelligence (AAAI-94)* (pp. 362-367). AAAI Press.

Régin, J.-C. (1996). Generalized arc consistency for global cardinality constraint. In *Proceedings of National Conference on Artificial Intelligence (AAAI-96)* (pp. 209-215). AAAI Press.

Régin, J.-C. (1999). Arc consistency for global cardinality constraints with costs. In *Proceedings of the Fifth International Conference on Principles and Practice of Constraint Programming (CP)* (LNCS 1713, pp. 390-404). Springer Verlag.

Richards, B. L., & Mooney, R. J. (1995). Automated refinement of first-order horn-clause domain theories. *machine learning, 19*(2), 95–131.

Rickheit, G. (2005). Alignment und Aushandlung im Dialog. *Zeitschrift für Psychologie, 213*(3), 159-166.

Rickheit, G., & Strohner, H. (1992). Towards a cognitive theory of linguistic coherence. *Theoretical Linguistics, 18,* 209-237.

Ricœur, P. (1976). *Interpretation theory: Discourse and the surplus of meaning.* Fort Worth: The Texas Christian University Press.

Rieger, B. B. (1989). *Unscharfe Semantik: Die empirische Analyse, quantitative Beschreibung, formale Repräsentation und prozedurale Modellierung vager Wortbedeutungen in Texten.* Frankfurt am Main: Peter Lang.

Rieger, B. B. (2001). Computing granular word meanings: A fuzzy linguistic approach in computational semiotics. In P. Wang (Ed.), *Computing with words* (pp. 147-208). New York: John Wiley & Sons.

Rieger, B. B. (2002). Semiotic cognitive information processing: Learning to understand discourse. A systemic model of meaning constitution. In R. Kühn, R. Menzel, W. Menzel, U. Ratsch, M.M. Richter, & I.O. Stamatescu (Eds.), *Perspectives on adaptivity and learning* (pp. 47-403). Berlin: Springer.

Riegler, A., Peschl, M., & von Stein, A. (Eds.). (1999). *Understanding representation in the cognitive sciences: Does representation need reality?* New York; Boston; Dordrecht: Kluwer-Plenum.

Rissanen, J. (1978). Modeling by shortest data description. *Automatica, 14,* 465–471.

Robinson, J. A. (1965). A machine-oriented logic based on the resolution principle. *Journal of the ACM, 12*(1), 23–41.

Rocha, R., Fonseca, N. A., & Costa, V. S. (2005). On Applying Tabling to inductive logic programming. In *Lecture notes in artificial intelligence: Vol. 3720. Proceedings of the 16th European Conference on machine learning, ECML-05, Porto, Portugal, October 2005* (pp. 707–714). Berlin: Springer-Verlag.

Rossi, F., Dahr V., & Petrie, C. (1990). On the equivalence of constraint satisfaction problems. In *Proceedings of the European Conference on Artificial Intelligence*

(ECAI-90) (pp. 550-556). Stockholm. MCC (Tech. Rep. No. ACT-AI-222-89).

Rossi, F., Van Beek, P., & Walsh, T. (2006). *Handbook of constraint programming.* Elsevier.

Roy, B. (1991). The outranking approach and the foundations of ELECTRE methods. *Theory and Decision, 31*(1), 49-73.

Ruge, G. (1995). *Wortbedeutung und Termassoziation: Methoden zur automatischen semantischen Klassifikation.* Hildesheim: Olms.

Russell, S., & Norvig, P. (2003). *Artificial intelligence: A modern approach.* Prentice Hall.

Rutten, E., & Hertzberg, J. (1993). Temporal planner=nonlinear planner+time map manager. *AI Communications, 6*(1), 18-26.

Ryan, M.R.K, & Pendrith, M.D. (1998). RL-TOPs: An architecture for modularity and re-use in reinforcement learning. In *15th International Conference of Machine Learning* (pp. 481-487).

Ryan, M.R.K. (2002). Using abstract models of behaviours to automatically generate reinforcement learning hierarchies. In *19th International Conference on Machine Learning* (pp. 522-529).

Sabin, D., & Freuder, E.C. (1994). Contradicting conventional wisdom in constraint satisfaction. In *Proceedings of ECAI* (pp. 125-129).

Sabin, D., & Freuder, E.C. (1997). Understanding and improving the MAC algorithm. In *Proceedings of the Third International Conference on Principles and Practice of Constraint Programming* (LNCS 1330, pp. 167-181). Springer Verlag.

Sacerdoti, E. (1974). Planning in a hierarchy of abstraction spaces. *Artificial Intelligence, 5,* 115-135.

Santos Costa, V., Page, C. D., Qazi, M., & Cussens, J. (2003, August). CLP(*BN*): Constraint logic programming for probabilistic knowledge. In *Proceedings of the 19th conference on uncertainty in artificial intelligence (UAI03), Acapulco, Mexico* (pp. 517–524).

Santos Costa, V., Srinivasan, A., & Camacho, R. (2000). A note on two simple transformations for improving the efficiency of an ILP system. In *Proceedings of the 10th international conference on inductive logic programming* (pp. 225–242).

Santos Costa, V., Srinivasan, A., Camacho, R., Blockeel, H., Demoen, B., Janssens, G., et al. (2003). Query transformations for improving the efficiency of ILP systems. *Journal of machine learning Research, 4,* 465–491.

Schafer, J.L., & Graham, J.W. (2002). Missing data: Our view of the state of the art. *Psychological Methods, 7*(2), 147-177.

Schnotz, W. (1994). *Aufbau von Wissensstrukturen: Untersuchungen zur Kohärenzbildung beim Wissenserwerb mit Texten.* Weinheim, Germany: Beltz.

Schölkopf, B., & Smola, AJ. (2002). *Learning with kernels: Support vector machines, regularization, optimization, and beyond.* MIT Press.

Schoppers, M. (1995). The use of dynamics in an intelligent controller for a space faring rescue robot. *Artificial intelligence, 73*(1/2), 175-230.

Schütze, H. (1997). *Ambiguity resolution in language learning: Computational and cognitive models, Vol. 71, CSLI Lecture Notes.* Stanford: CSLI Publications.

Searle, J. R. (1980). Minds, brains, and programs. *The Behavioral and Brain Sciences, 3,* 417-457.

Sebag, M., & Rouveirol, C. (1997). Tractable induction and classification in first order logic via stochastic matching. In *Proceedings of the 15th international joint conference on artificial intelligence* (pp. 888–893). San Francisco: Morgan Kaufmann.

Sellmann, M. (2006). The theory of grammar constraints. In *Proceedings of 12th International Conference on Principles and Practice of Constraint Programming (CP2006)* (LNCS 4204, pp. 530-544). Springer Verlag.

Serrurier, M., Prade, H., & Richard, G. (2004). A simulated annealing framework for ILP. In *Proceedings of the 14th international conference on inductive logic programming* (pp. 288–304).

Shafer, G., Shenoy, P.P., & Srivastava, R.P. (1988) Auditor's assistant: A knowledge engineering tool for audit decisions. In *Proceedings of 1988 Touche Ross University of Kansas Symposium on Auditing Problems* (pp. 61-84).

Shafer, G.A. (1976). *Mathematical theory of evidence.* Princeton: Princeton University Press.

Shang, N., & Breiman, L. (1996). Distribution based trees are more accurate. *International Conference on Neural Information Processing* (vol. 1, pp. 133-138). Hong Kong.

Shannon, C. E. (1948, July, October). The mathematical theory of communication. *Bell Systems Technical Journal, 27,* 379–423, 623–656.

Shapiro, E. (1983). *Algorithmic program debugging.* The MIT Press.

Simon, U., Brüggemann, R., & Pudenz, S. (2004). Aspects of decision support in water management—example Berlin and Potsdam (Germany) I—spatially differentiated evaluation. *Water Research, 38,* 1809-1816.

Singh, M. (1995). Path consistency revised. In *Proceedings of the 7th IEEE International Conference on Tolls with Artificial Intelligence* (pp. 318-325).

Sjöberg, J., Zhang, Q., Ljung, L., Berveniste, A., Delyon, B., Glorennec, P., et al. (1995). Nonlinear black-box modeling in system identification: A unified overview. *Automatica, 31*(12), 1691-1724.

Smets, P. (1990) The combination of evidence in the transferable belief model. *IEEE Transactions on Pattern Analysis and Machine Intelligence, 12*(5), 447-458.

Smith, B.M. (1995). A tutorial on constraint programming (Tech. Rep. No. 95.14). University of Leeds.

Smith, D.E., & Peot, M.A. (1992). A critical look at Knoblock's hierarchy mechanism. In *1ˢᵗ International Conference on Artificial intelligence Planning Systems* (pp. 307-308).

Smith, D.E., & Weld, D.S. (1999). Temporal planning with mutual exclusion reasoning. In *Proceedings of the 16th International Joint Conference on AI (IJCAI-99)* (pp. 326-337), Stockholm, Sweden.

Smith, D.E., Frank, J., & Jonsson, A.K. (2000). Bridging the gap between planning and scheduling. *Knowledge Engineering Review, 15*(1), 47-83.

Smola, A., Schölkopf, B., & Ratsch, G. (1999). Linear programs for automatic accuracy control in regression. In *Proceeding of the International Conference on Artificial Neural Networks* (pp. 575-580), Berlin.

Smola, A.J., & Schölkopf, B. (2004). A tutorial on support vector regression. *Statistics and Computing, 14,* 199-222.

Smolensky, P. (1995). On the proper treatment of connectionism. In M. Donald & G. MacDonald (Eds.), *Connectionism: Debates on psychological explanation* (vol. 2, pp. 28-89). Oxford: Blackwell.

Smolensky, P. (1995). Connectionism, constituency and the language of thought. In M. Donald & G. MacDonald (Eds.), *Connectionism: Debates on psychological explanation* (vol. 2, pp. 164-198). Oxford: Blackwell.

Solan, Z., Ruppin, E., Horn, D., & Edelman, S. (2003). Automatic acquisition and efficient representation of syntactic structures. In S.Thrun (Ed.), *Advances in neural information processing* (vol. 15). Cambridge: MIT Press.

Srinivasan, A. (1999). A study of two sampling methods for analysing large datasets with ILP. *Data Mining and Knowledge Discovery, 3*(1), 95–123.

Srinivasan, A. (2000). *A study of two probabilistic methods for searching large spaces with ILP* (Tech. Rep. No. PRG-TR-16-00). Oxford University Computing Laboratory.

Srinivasan, A. (2004). *The Aleph manual.* (Available at http://www.comlab.ox.ac.uk/oucl/research/areas/machlearn/Aleph/)

Srinivasan, A., King, R. D., & Bain, M. E. (2003). An empirical study of the use of relevance information in inductive logic programming. *Journal of machine learning Research.*

Srinivasan, A., King, R. D., Muggleton, S., & Sternberg, M. J. E. (1997). Carcinogenesis predictions using ILP. In N. Lavrac & S. Džeroski (Eds.), *Lecture notes in computer science: Vol. 1297. inductive logic programming* (pp. 273–287). Berlin: Springer-Verlag.

Srinivasan, A., Muggleton, S., King, R. D., & Sternberg, M. J. E. (1994). ILP experiments in a non-determinate biological domain. In S. Wrobel (Ed.), *Gmd-studien. Proceedings of the Fourth International ILP Workshop* (pp. 217–232). Gesellschaft für Mathematik und Datenverarbeitung MBH.

Srivastava, R.P., & Liu, L. (2003) Applications of belief functions in business decisions: A review. *Information Systems Frontiers, 5*(4), 359-378.

Steels, L. (1996). Self-organising vocabularies. In C. Langton & T. Shimohara (Eds.), *Proceedings of Artificial Life V.* Japan: Nara.

Steels, L. (1998). Synthesizing the origins of language and meaning using coevolution, self-organization and level formation. In J.R. Hurford, M. Studdert-Kennedy, & C. Knight (Eds.), *Approaches to the evolution of language* (pp. 384-404). Cambridge: Cambridge University Press.

Steels, L. (2000). The puzzle of language evolution. *Kognitionswissenschaft, 8,*143-150.

Steels, L. (2002). Grounding symbols through evolutionary language games. In A. Cangelosi & D. Parisi (Eds.), *Simulating the evolution of language* (pp. 211-226). London: Springer Verlag.

Steels, L. (2004, July 21-26). Constructivist development of grounded construction grammars. In W. Daelemans (Ed.), *Proceedings of the 42nd Annual Meeting of the Association for Computational Linguistics* (pp. 9-16). Barcelona, Spain.

Ster, B., & Dobnikar, A. (1996). Neural networks in medical diagnosis: Comparaison with other methods. *Proceedings of the International Conference on Engineering Applications of Neural Networks, EANN'96* (pp. 427-430).

Stergiou, K., & Walsh, T. (1999). Encodings of non-binary constraint satisfaction problems. In *Proceedings of the National Conference on Artificial Intelligence (AAAI-99)*, Orlando, FL (pp. 163-168). AAAI Press.

Stoianov, I., Nerbonne, J., & Bouma, H. (1998). Modelling the phonotactic structure of natural language words with Simple Recurrent Networks. In *Proceedings of the 8th conference on computational linguistics in the netherlands (CLIN 98)*.

Stolle, C., Karwath, A., & De Raedt, L. (2005). CLASSIC'CL: an integrated ILP system. In *Lecture notes in artificial intelligence: Vol. 3735. Proceedings of the 8th International Conference of Discovery Science, DS 2005* (pp. 354–362). Berlin: Springer-Verlag.

Storn, R., & Price, K. (1997). Differential evolution—a simple and efficient heuristic for global optimisation over continuous spaces. *Journal of Global Optimisation, 11,* 341-59.

Stracuzzi, D.J. (1998). *Some methods for the parallelization of genetic algorithms.* Retrieved August 22, 2007, from http://ml-www.cs.umass.edu/~stracudj/genetic/dga.html

Strady-Lécubin, N., & Poncet, J.C. (2003). Mission management system high level architecture, report 4.3. MISURE/TR/4-4.3/AX/01, EUCLID RTP 15.5.

Strehl, A., & Ghosh, J. (2005). Cluster ensembles—a knowledge reuse framework for combining multiple partitions. *Journal of Machine Learning Research, 3,* 583-617.

Struyf, J. (2004). *Techniques for improving the efficiency of inductive logic programming in the context of data mining.* Unpublished doctoral dissertation, Katholieke Universiteit Leuven Department of Computer Science.

Struyf, J., & Blockeel, H. (2003). Query optimization in inductive logic programming by reordering literals. In *Proceedings of the 13th international conference on inductive logic programming* (pp. 329–346).

Struyf, J., Džeroski, S., Blockeel, H., & Clare, A. (2005). Hierarchical multi-classification with predictive clustering trees in functional genomics. In C. Bento, A. Cardoso,

& G. Dias (Eds.), *Lecture notes in computer science: Vol. 3808. Progress in Artificial Intelligence, 12th Portuguese Conference on Artificial Intelligence, EPIA 2005, Covilhã, Portugal, December 5-8, 2005, Proceedings* (pp. 272–283). Berlin: Springer-Verlag.

Stubbs, M. (2001). On inference theories and code theories: Corpus evidence for semantic schemas. *Text, 21*(3),437-465.

Sudkamp, T. (1992). On probability-possibility transformations. *Fuzzy Sets and Systems, 51,* 73-81.

Sun, R. (2000). Beyond simple rule extraction: The extraction of planning knowledge from reinforcement learners. In *International Joint Conference on Neural Networks* (p. 2105). Como, Italy. IEEE Press.

Sun, R., & Sessions, C. (1998). Extracting plans from reinforcement learners. In *International Symposium on Intelligent Data Engineering and Learning* (pp. 243-248). Springer-Verlag.

Sun, R., & Sessions, C. (2000). Learning plans without a priori knowledge. *Adaptive Behavior, 18*(3), 225-253.

Sun, R., Peterson, T., & Sessions, C. (2001). Beyond simple rule extraction: Acquiring planning knowledge from neural networks.

Sutton, R.S. (1988). Learning to predict by the methods of temporal differences. *Machine Learning, 3,* 9-44.

Sutton, R.S. (1990). Integrated architectures for learning, planning and reacting. In *Proceedings of the Seventh International Conference on Machine Learning,* (pp. 216-224).

Sutton, R.S. (1991). Planning by incremental dynamic programming. In *Proceedings of the Eighth International Workshop on Machine Learning* (pp. 353-357).

Sutton, R.S., & Barto, A.G. (1999). Reinforcement learning, an introduction. MIT Press.

Szczerba, R.J., Galkowski, P., Glickstein, I.S., & Ternullo, N. (2000). Robust algorithm for real-time route planning. *Institute of Electrical and Electronics Engineers Transactions on Aerospace and Electronics Systems, 36*(3), 869-878.

Szita, I, Takacs, B, & Lorincz, A. (2003). ε-mdps: learning in varying environments. *Journal of Machine Learning Research, 3,* 145-174.

Taffler, R. (1984). Empirical models for the monitoring of UK corporations. *Journal of Banking and Finance, 8,* 199-227.

Tamaddoni-Nezhad, A., & Muggleton, S. (2000). Searching the subsumption lattice by a genetic algorithm. In J. Cussens & A. Frisch (Eds.), *Lecture notes in artificial intelligence: Vol. 1866. Proceedings of the 10th International Conference on inductive logic programming* (pp. 243–252). Springer-Verlag.

Tamaddoni-Nezhad, A., & Muggleton, S. (2003). A genetic algorithm approach to ILP. In S. Matwin & C. Sammut (Eds.), *Lecture notes in artificial intelligence: Vol. 2583. Proceedings of the 12th International Conference on inductive logic programming* (pp. 285–300). Berlin: Springer-Verlag.

Tang, L. R., & Mooney, R. J. (2001). Using multiple clause constructors in inductive logic programming for semantic parsing. In *Lecture notes in computer science: Vol. 2167. Proceedings of the 12th European Conference on machine learning (ECML-2001).* Berlin: Springer Verlag.

Tate, A., Dalton, J., & Levine, J. (2000). O-plan: A Web-based AI planning agent. In *Intelligent Systems Demonstrator, Proc. Nat. Conf. on Artificial Intelligence (AAAI-00)* (pp. 1131-1132).

Tavares, A.I., & Campos, M.F.M. (2004). Balancing coordination and synchronization cost in cooperative situated multi-agent systems with imperfect communication. In *Proceedings of the 16th European Conference on Artificial intelligence* (pp. 68-73).

Teichteil-Königsbuch, F., & Fabiani, P. (2006). Autonomous search and rescue rotorcraft mission stochastic planning with generic DBNs. In M. Bramer (Ed.), *International federation for information processing* (p. 217), *Artificial intelligence in theory and practice* (pp. 483-492). Boston, MA: Springer.

Thagard, P. (2000). *Coherence in thought and action.* Cambridge, MA: MIT Press.

The UCI Machine Learning Repository. (2007). Retrieved August 20, 2007, from http://www.ics.uci.edu/~mlearn/MLRepository.html

Thrun, S. (1995). Extracting rules from networks with distributed representations. In G. Tesauro, D. Touretzky, & T. Leens (Eds.), *Advances in neural information processing systems (NIPS)* (vol. 7). Cambridge, MA: MIT Press.

Tickle, A.B., Andrews, R., Golea, M., & Diederich, J. (1998). The truth will come to light: Directions and challenges in extracting the knowledge embedded within trained artificial neural networks. *IEEE Transaction on Neural Networks, 9*(6), 1057-1068.

Tickle, A.B., Orlowski, M., & Diedrich J. (1996). *DEDEC: A methodology for extracting rules from trained artificial neural networks.* Queensland University of Technology, Neurocomputing Research Centre. QUT NRC Technical report.

Tjong Kim Sang, E. F. (1998). Machine learning of phonotactics (Doctoral dissertation, Rijksuniversiteit Groningen). *Groningen Dissertations in Linguistics Series.*

Tjong Kim Sang, E. F., & Nerbonne, J. (2000). Learning the logic of simple phonotactics. In J. Cussens & S. Džeroski (Eds.), *Lecture notes in artificial intelligence: Vol. 1925. Learning Language in Logic.* Berlin: Springer-Verlag.

Tobudic, A., & Widmer, G. (2003). Relational ibl in music with a new structural similarity measure. In T. Horváth (Ed.), *Lecture notes in computer science: Vol. 2835. ILP* (pp. 365–382). Berlin: Springer-Verlag.

Todorovski, L., Ljubic, P., & Džeroski, S. (2004). Inducing polynomial equations for regression. In J.-F. Boulicaut, F. Esposito, F. Giannotti, & D. Pedreschi (Eds.), *Lecture notes in computer science: Vol. 3201. Proceedings of the 15th European Conference on machine learning* (pp. 441–452). Berlin: Springer-Verlag.

Tomita, M. (1986). *Efficient parsing for natural language.* Boston: Kluwer Academic Publishers.

Towell, G., & Shavlik, J.W. (1994). Knowledge-based artificial neural networks. *Artificial Intelligence, 70,* 119-165.

Tsamardinos, I., Vidal, T., & Pollack, M. (2003). CTP: A new constraint-based formalism for conditional, temporal planning [Special issue on planning]. *Consraints 8*(4), 365-388.

Tsang, E. (1993). *Foundations of constraint satisfaction.* Academic Press.

Tsur, D., Ullman, J. D., Abiteboul, S., Clifton, C., Motwani, R., Nestorov, S., et al. (1998). Query flocks: a generalization of association-rule mining. In *SIGMOD '98: Proceedings of the 1998 ACM SIGMOD international conference on management of data* (pp. 1–12). New York, NY, USA: ACM Press.

Tuldava, J. (1998). *Probleme und Methoden der quantitativ-systemischen Lexikologie.* Trier: WVT.

Turcotte, M., Muggleton, S. H., & Sternberg, M. J. E. (2001, April). The effect of relational background knowledge on learning of protein three-dimensional fold signatures. *machine learning, 43*(1/2), 81–95.

Turner, H. (2002). An introduction to methods for simulating the evolution of language. In A. Cangelosi & D. Parisi (Eds.), *Simulating the evolution of language* (pp. 29-50). London; Berlin: Springer.

Ugoluk, G. (1997). A method for chromosome handling of r-permutations of n-element sets in genetic algorithms. In *Proceedings of the IEEE International Conference on Evolutionary Computation* (pp. 55-58).

van Beek, P., & Chen, X. (1999). CPlan: A constraint programming approach to planning. In *Proceedings of American Association for Artificial intelligence* (pp. 585-590).

Van Beek, P., & Chen, X. (1999). CPlan: A constraint programming approach to planning. In *Proc. Nat. Conf. on Artificial Intelligence (AAAI-99)* (pp. 585-590).

van Dijk, T. A., & Kintsch, W. (1983). *Strategies of discourse comprehension.* New York: Academic Press.

Van Hentenryck, P. (1989). *Constraint satisfaction in logic programming*. The MIT Press.

Van Hentenryck, P., & Carillon, J.-P. (1988). Generality vs. specificity: An experience with AI and OR techniques. In *National Conference on Artificial Intelligence (AAAI)* (pp. 660-664). AAAI Press.

Van Hentenryck, P., & Michel, L. (2005). *Constraint-based local search*. The MIT Press.

Van Hentenryck, P., Deville, Y., & Teng, C.-M. (1992). A generic arc-consistency algorithm and its specializations. *Artificial Intelligence, 57*, 291-321.

Van Hoeve, W.-J. (2004). A hyper-arc consistency algorithm for the soft all different constraint. In *Proceedings of the Tenth International Conference on Principles and Practice of Constraint Programming (CP)* (LNCS 3258, pp. 679-689). Springer Verlag.

Vapnik, V.N. (2000). The nature of statistical learning theory (2nd ed.). Springer-Verlag.

Varela, L.R., & Ribeiro, R.A. (2003). Evaluation of simulated annealing to solve fuzzy optimization problems. *Journal of Intelligent and Fuzzy Systems, 14*, 59-71.

Vasant, P. (2003). Application of fuzzy linear programming in production planning. *Fuzzy Optimization and Decision Making, 3*, 229-241.

Vasant, P. (2004). Industrial production planning using interactive fuzzy linear programming. *International Journal of Computational Intelligence and Applications, 4*, 13-26.

Vasant, P. (2006). Fuzzy decision making of profit function in production planning using s-curve membership function. *Computers & Industrial Engineering, 51*, 715-725.

Vasant, P., & Barsoum, N.N. (2006). Fuzzy optimization of units products in mix-products selection problem using FLP approach. *Soft Computing - A Fusions of Foundation, Methodologies, and Applications, 10*, 140-143.

Vasant, P., & Bhattacharya, A. (2007). Sensing degree of fuzziness in MCDM model using modified flexible s-curve MF. *International Journal of Systems Science, 38*, 279-291.

Vere, S. (1983). Planning in time: Windows and durations for activities and goals. *IEEE Transactions on Pattern Analysis and Machine Intelligence, 5*, 246-267.

Vere, S. A. (1975). Induction of concepts in the predicate calculus. In *Proceedings of the 4th international joint conference on artificial intelligence* (p. 281-287).

Verfaillie, G., & Fabiani P. (2000). Planification dans l'incertain, planification en ligne. Presentation at Rencontres Nationales des Jeunes Chercheurs en Intelligence Artificielle.

Verfaillie, G., Lemaitre, M., & Schiex, T. (1996). Russian doll search for solving constraint optimization problems. In *Proceedings of AAAI National Conference* (pp. 181-187). AAAI Press.

Verfaillie, G., Martinez, D., & Bessiere, C. (1999). A generic customizable framework for inverse local consistency. In *Proceedings of the AAAI National Conference* (pp. 169-174). AAAI Press.

Vidal, V., & Geffner, H. (2004). Branching and pruning: An optimal temporal POCL planner based on constraint programming. In *Proc. Nat. Conf. on Artificial Intelligence (AAAI-04)* (pp. 570-577).

Vidal, V., & Geffner, H. (2006). Branching and pruning: An optimal temporal POCL planner based on constraint programming. *Artificial Intelligence, 170*, 298-335.

Visser, U., Tickle, A., Hayward, R., & Andrews, R. (1996). Rule-extraction from trained neural networks: Different techniques for the determination of herbicides for the plant protection advisory system PRO_PLANT. *Proceedings of the rule extraction from trained artificial neural networks workshop*, Brighton, UK (pp. 133-139).

Vogt, P. (2004). Minimum cost and the emergence of the Zipf-Mandelbrot law. In J. Pollack, M. Bedau, P. Husbands, T. Ikegami, & R.A. Watson (Eds.), *Artificial life IX: Proceedings of the ninth international conference on the simulation and synthesis of living systems*. Cambridge, MA: MIT Press.

Vossen, T., Ball, M., Lotem, A., & Nau, D. (1999). On the use of integer programming models in AI planning. In *Proceedings of the 16th International Joint Conference on Artificial intelligence* (pp. 304-309).

Vrakas, D., Tsoumakas, G., Bassilliades, N., & Vlahavas, I. (2005). Machine learning for adaptive planning. In I. Vlahavas & D. Vrakas (Eds.), *Intelligent techniques for planning* (pp. 90-120). Idea Group Publishing.

Walkers, T., Kudenko, D., & Strens, M. (2004). Algorithms for distributed exploration. In *Proceedings of the 16th European Conference on Artificial intelligence* (pp. 84-88).

Walsh, T. (1997). Depth-bounded discrepancy search. In *Proceedings of 15th International Joint Conference on Artificial Intelligence* (pp. 1388-1393).

Waltz, D.L. (1975). Understanding line drawings of scenes with shadows. In *Psychology of Computer Vision*. New York: McGraw-Hill.

Washington, R., Golden, K., Bresina, J., Smith, D.E., Anderson, C., & Smith, T. (1999). Autonomous rovers for Mars exploration. In *Proceedings of the Institute of Electrical and Electronics Engineers Aerospace Conference* (Vol. 1, pp. 237-251).

Watada, J. (1997). Fuzzy portfolio selection and its applications to decision making. *Tatra Mountains Mathematics Publication, 13,* 219-248.

Watkins, C.J.J.H. (1989). *Learning with delayed rewards*. Unpublished Ph.D. thesis, Cambridge University Psychology Department.

Watts, D. J. (1999). *Small worlds: The dynamics of networks between order and randomness*. Princeton: Princeton University Press.

Watts, D. J., & Strogatz, S. H. (1998). Collective dynamics of "small-world" networks. *Nature, 393,* 440-442.

Weiss, S.M., & Kulikowski, C.A. (1990). *Computer systems that learn*. San Mateo, CA: Morgan Kauffman.

Weld, D. (1994). An introduction to least commitment planning. *AI Magazine, 15*(4), 93-123.

Weld, D.S. (1999). Recent advances in AI planning. *AI Magazine, 20*(2), 93-123.

Wielemaker, J. (2003). Native preemptive threads in SWI-Prolog. In C. Palamidessi (Ed.), *Lecture notes in artificial intelligence: Vol. 2916. Proceedings of the 19th International Conference on Logic Programming* (pp. 331–345). Springer-Verlag.

Wilkins, D. (1988). *Practical planning: Extending the classical AI planning paradigm*. San Mateo, CA: Morgan Kaufmann.

Wilkins, D.E., & desJardins, M. (2001). A call for knowledge-based planning. *AI Magazine, 22*(1), 99-115.

Winston, P. H. (1970). *Learning structural descriptions from examples*. Unpublished doctoral dissertation, MIT.

Wong, M.L., & Leung, K.S. (2000). *Data mining using grammar based genetic programming and applications*. Kluwer Academic Publishers.

Wrobel, S. (1997). An algorithm for multi-relational discovery of subgroups. In *Proceedings of the first european symposium on principles of data mining and knowledge discovery* (pp. 78–87). Springer-Verlag.

Yang, Q., & Tenenberg, J. (1990). AbTWEAK: Abstracting a nonlinear least commitment planner. In *Proceedings of the 8th National Conference on Artificial Intelligence,* Boston, MA (pp. 204-209).

Yao, X. (1993). A review of evolutionary artificial neural networks. *International Journal of Intelligent Systems, 8*(4), 539-567.

Younes, H.L.S., & Simmons, R.G. (2003). VHPOP: Versatile heuristic partial order planner. *Journal of Artificial Intelligence Research, 20,* 405-430.

Zadeh, L. A. (1997). Toward a theory of fuzzy information granulation and its centrality in human reasoning and fuzzy logic. *Fuzzy Sets and Systems, 90,* 111-127.

Zadeh, L.A. (1971). Similarity relations and fuzzy orderings. *Information Science, 3,* 177-206.

Železný, F., Srinivasan, A., & Page, C. D. (2003). Lattice-search runtime distributions may be heavy-tailed. In S. Matwin & C. Sammut (Eds.), *Lecture notes in artificial intelligence: Vol. 2583. Proceedings of the 12th International Workshop on inductive logic programming (ILP 2002)* (pp. 333–345). Berlin: Springer Verlag.

Zelle, J. M., & Mooney, R. J. (1996). Learning to parse database queries using inductive logic programming. In dunno (Ed.), *Proceedings of the 13th national conference on artificial intelligence, Portland, USA.*

Zhang, Y., & Yap, R. (2001). Making AC-3 an optimal algorithm. In *Proceedings of IJCAI-01* (pp. 316-321).

Zhao, G., Tatsumi, S., & Sun, R. (1999). RTP-Q: A reinforcement learning system with time constraints exploration planning for accelerating the learning rate. *IEICE Transactions on Fundamentals of Eloctronics, Communications and Computer Sciences, E82-A,* 2266-2273.

Ziemke, T. (1999). Rethinking grounding. In A. Riegler, M. Peschl, & A. von Stein (Eds.), *Understanding representation in the cognitive sciences: Does representation need reality?* (pp. 177-190). New York; Boston; Dordrecht: Kluwer-Plenum.

Zilberstein, S. (1993). *Operational rationality through compilation of anytime algorithms.* Unpublished doctoral dissertation, Computer Science Division, University of California at Berkeley.

Zilberstein, S., & Russel, S.J. (1993). Anytime sensing, planning and action: A practical model for robot control. In *Proceedings of the 13th International Joint Conference on Artificial intelligence,* Chambery, France (pp. 1402-1407).

Zimmerman, T., & Kambhambati, S. (2003). Learning-assisted automated planning: Looking back, taking stock, going forward. *AI Magazine, 24*(2), 73-96.

Zimmermann, H.J. (1978). Fuzzy programming and linear programming with several objective functions. *Fuzzy Sets and Systems, 1,* 45-55.

Zimmermann, H.J. (1991). Fuzzy set theory and its application. Kluwer Academic Publishers.

Zipf, G. K. (1972). *Human behavior and the principle of least effort: An introduction to human ecology.* New York: Hafner Publishing Company.

Zupan, B., & Džeroski, S. (1998). Acquiring background knowledge for machine learning using function decomposition: a case study in rheumatology. *Artificial Intelligence in Medicine, 14*(1–2), 101-117.

About the Contributors

Dimitris Vrakas is a lecturer at the Department of Informatics at the Aristotle University of Thessaloniki, Greece (AUTH). He has worked as an adjunct lecturer at the above department and the Computer & Communication Engineering department of the University of Thessaly. He has also taught at post-graduate courses in the Aristotle University and the University of Macedonia. He specializes in automated planning, heuristic search, and problem solving and he has published more than 30 papers and co-authored 2 books in the above areas. More information can be found at http://lpis.csd.auth.gr/vrakas.

Ioannis Vlahavas is a professor at the Department of Informatics at the Aristotle University of Thessaloniki, Greece (AUTH). He received his PhD in logic programming systems from AUTH (1988). He was a visiting scholar at the Department of CS at Purdue University (1997). He specializes in logic programming, machine learning, automated planning, and knowledge-based and AI systems. He has published over 140 papers and 6 books and has been involved in more than 25 projects. He is leading the Programming Languages and Software Engineering Laboratory and the Logic Programming and Intelligent Systems Group (more information at www.csd.auth.gr/~vlahavas).

***

Johan Baltié graduated in 2002 from engineering school EPITA with a specialization in artificial intelligence. He started working as a trainee at Axlog Ingénierie studying multicriteria optimization problems applied to spacecraft and spacecraft swarms. Afterwards, he worked on rule-based system and linear optimization in a financial context. He started to work on domains related to autonomous aircrafts systems in 2003 under the direction of Jean-Clair Poncet and Philippe Morignot.

Nader Barsoum specializes in electric machines control and stability, power electronics, and speed drive systems. He has also extensive experience in teaching mathematics for engineers. He has published two books and over than 40 scientific research papers in these fields. Nader obtained his first degrees from Alexandria University. He holds a BEng with honor in electrical power engineering (1976), a BSc in pure and applied mathematics (1979), and an MSc in engineering mathematics (1983). Dr. Nader is an associate professor in the School of Engineering and Science, Curtin University of Technology, Sarawak Campus. He obtained a University Encouragement Award for Scientific Research (Silver Medal) from Alexandria University, Egypt (1992). After receiving his PhD from the University of Newcastle upon Tyne, England, U.K. (1989) he went back to Alexandria University, where he spent 3 years as a lecturer.

Roman Barták works as an associate professor and a researcher at Charles University, Prague (Czech Republic). He leads the Constraint and Logic Programming Research Group that is involved in activities of the ERCIM Working Group on Constraints, PLANET II, and CologNet. From 1999-2004, Doctor Barták led research activities of Visopt BV, a multinational company located in The Netherlands, Israel, Germany, and The Czech Republic. He was a main architect of the scheduling engine developed by this company. His work focuses on techniques of constraint satisfaction and their application to planning and scheduling. Since 1998 he has taught a course on constraint programming at Charles University. He had several tutorials on constraint processing at conferences and summer schools and he is an author of *The On-Line Guide to Constraint Programming* (the number one source for Constraint Programming in Google).

Eric Bensana, born in 1959, got a PhD on the use of artificial intelligence in job shop scheduling (1987) and then joined the Systems Control and Flight Dynamics Department at ONERA, Toulouse, France, as a research scientist. He mainly works in the field of problem solving algorithms for design, planning, and scheduling applications with a specific interest in discrete optimization and constraint (logic) programming approaches. He is also involved in projects dealing with autonomy for space systems and uninhabited aerial vehicle applications.

Malcolm J. Beynon is a reader in Cardiff Business Cardiff at Cardiff University (U.K.). He gained his BSc and PhD in pure mathematics and computational mathematics, respectively, at Cardiff University. His research areas include the theoretical and application of uncertain reasoning methodologies, including rough set theory, Dempster-Shafer theory, and fuzzy set theory and the introduction and development of multicriteria-based decision making and classification techniques, including the classification and ranking belief simplex. He has published over 100 research articles. He is a member of the International Rough Set Society, the International Operations Research Society, and the International Multicriteria Decision Making Society.

Rui Camacho holds a degree in engineering and computer science from the University of Porto, Portugal, an MSc in engineering and computer science from the Technical University of Lisbon, Portugal, and a PhD in engineering and computer science from the University of Porto, Portugal. During his PhD studies, he worked under the supervision of Stephen Muggleton at the Turing Institute and at the Oxford University Computing Laboratory and, also during his PhD studies, he developed the IndLog ILP system. Camacho participated in the April Portuguese project where the April ILP system was developed and where several techniques were developed to improve ILP systems execution and several techniques for the parallel execution of ILP systems were developed. He organised conferences such as the 14th International Conference on Inductive Logic Programming (ILP 2004), the 16th European Conference on Machine Learning (ECML 2005), and the 9th European Conference on Principles and Practice of Knowledge Discovery in Databases (PKDD 2005). Rui Camacho was one of the guest editors of the ILP 2004 special issue of the *Machine Learning Journal*.

Vítor Santos Costa holds a degree in engineering and computer science from the University of Porto, Portugal, and a PhD in computer science from the University of Bristol, U.K., where he graduated under Professor David H.D. Warren. He is a lecturer at the University of Rio de Janeiro, Brazil. Previously, he was a lecturer at the Universidade do Porto, Portugal. He was twice visiting professor at the

University of Wisconsin-Madison. Vítor Santos Costa's research has centered on the sequential and parallel execution of logic programs. He is the main developer for the YAP Prolog system, and he also contributed to several other systems, such as the and-or-parallel system Andorra-I. More recently, he has collaborated with researchers in the areas of inductive logic programming and in statistical relational learning. His work has been published on major venues in logic programming, parallel programming, and machine learning.

Georgi Marko Dimirovski was born in Greece, in the village of Nestorion/Nesram in Aegean Macedonia, in 1941. He is an emeritus professor of automation & systems engineering at SS Cyril & Methodius University of Skopje, Rep. of Macedonia, and Professor of Computer Science & Information Technologies at Dogus University of Istanbul, Turkey. Also, he is an invited professor at Istanbul Technical University on a part-time basis. He is a foreign member of the Academy of Engineering Sciences in Belgrade, Serbia. He held a postdoctoral position in 1979 and was a visiting professor at University of Bradford (1984 and 1986) and a senior fellow & visiting professor at Free University of Brussels, Belgium, (1994) and at Johannes Kepler University of Linz, Austria (2000). He has successfully supervised two postdoctoral, 15 PhD, and 27 MSc as well as more than 250 graduation students' projects, and published over 30 journal articles and 300 papers on IEEE and IFAC conferences. Currently, he is a member of the IFAC Technical Board and chairman of its Coordination Committee CC-9, and serves on the editorial board of two other international journals.

Patrick Fabiani is the director of the Systems Control and Flight Dynamics Department (DCSD) of ONERA. He has been the manager of the ReSSAC autonomous helicopter project since 2002. His research and teaching activity is related to models, methods, algorithms, and tools for sequential decision making and planning under uncertainty. His work is applied to autonomous aircraft mission management systems. Fabiani graduated from Ecole Polytechnique Paris (1990) and from SupAero in Toulouse (1992) with an MSc in automatic control. He completed his PhD in artificial intelligence (1996) at SupAero. He has been a research scientist at ONERA since 1993 in the Control and Decision Research Group. He was a visiting scholar in the Computer Science Department Robotics Laboratory at Stanford University between 1997 and 1999.

Jean-Loup Farges was born in 1956. He obtained a degree in electric engineering at ENSEEIHT (1978) and a PhD in control of urban traffic by dynamic programming and hierarchical methods at ENSAE (1983). Since 1983, he has been a research scientist at ONERA in the Control and Decision research unit of the Control and Flight Dynamics Department. He has written various publications and has taught at the Federal University of Santa Catarina (1978-1980), at ENST (1984-1991), at ENSEEIHT (since 1984), at the University of Corté (1990-1991), and at SUPAERO (1998).

Nuno Fonseca holds a degree in computer science from the University of Porto, Portugal, an MSc in artificial intelligence and computation, in Faculty of Engineering of the University of Porto, and is completing his PhD in computer science from the University of Porto. Fonseca has done considerable work on the implementation and performance of ILP systems. He implemented an ILP system that encompasses several algorithms and search strategies. He also worked on the parallelization of ILP systems, having several publications about the subject. His paper on "Strategies to Parallelize ILP Systems" was selected as the best student paper in the 15th International Conference in Inductive Logic

Programming. He currently collaborates with researchers in the areas of chemistry and structural and molecular biology.

Antonio Garrido is an associate professor for technical studies at the Technical University of Valencia (Spain), where he obtained his PhD in computer science (2003). His topics of research are related to domain-independent planning, temporal planning, heuristics, and integration of planning and scheduling. He has participated in several national and local projects (MCyT, MEC, and GVA), and he currently leads a research project founded by the Valencian government. He has been a reviewer for several international conferences (IJCAI, ICAPS, and ECAI) and has been (co)author of more than 20 papers related to AI planning and scheduling.

Iker Gondra received a BS, an MS, and a PhD in computer science from Oklahoma State University, OK, (1998, 2002, and 2005, respectively). Since 2005, he has been an assistant professor in the Department of Mathematics, Statistics, and Computer Science at St. Francis Xavier University, Antigonish, NS, Canada. His research interests include machine learning, content-based image retrieval, and evolutionary algorithms

Sheng Uei Guan received his MSc and PhD from the University of North Carolina at Chapel Hill. He joined La Trobe University with the Department of Computer Science and Computer Engineering where he helped to create a new multimedia systems stream. He joined the National University of Singapore in 1998, where he conducted extensive research work in computational intelligence, multimedia, mobile agents, electronic commerce and personalisation, and random number generation. He is currently working as the Chair in Intelligent Systems at Brunel University, U.K.

Cengiz Kahraman is a professor in the Department of Industrial Engineering of Istanbul Technical University (ITU). He received his a BSc, an MSc, and a PhD in industrial engineering from ITU (1988, 1990, and 1996, respectively). His research areas include engineering economics, statistical decision making, quality engineering and management, fuzzy sets, and applications. He is the editor of a Springer book entitled *Fuzzy Applications in Industrial Engineering* and the guest-editor of many international journals. He has published many papers in *Information Sciences, International Journal of Production Economics,* and *International Journal of Intelligent Systems.* He is now editing two Springer books on fuzzy multicriteria decision making and fuzzy engineering economics.

Stasinos Konstantopoulos holds a degree in computer science and engineering from the University of Patras, Greece, an MSc in artificial intelligence from the University of Edinburgh, U.K., and a PhD in computational linguistics from the Rijksuniversiteit Groningen, The Netherlands. During his PhD studies, he participated in the EU-funded project "Learning Computational Grammars," where he investigated the application of inductive logic programming to language technology tasks. He is currently affiliated with the National Centre for Scientific Research, Demokritos, Athens, Greece, where he investigates computational logic inference for the purposes of ontology representation and maintenance, in the framework of the EU-funded project "SHARE: Mobile Support for Rescue Forces."

Zhao Lu received an MS in control theory and engineering from Nankai University, Tianjin, China, (2000), and a PhD in electrical engineering from University of Houston, TX, (2004). From 2004 to 2006, he worked as a post-doctoral research fellow in the Department of Electrical and Computer Engineering at Wayne State University, Detroit, MI, and the Department of Naval Architecture and Marine Engineering at the University of Michigan, Ann Arbor, MI, respectively. In 2007, he joined the faculty of the Department of Electrical Engineering at Tuskegee University, Tuskegee, TN. His research interests mainly include nonlinear control theory, machine learning, and pattern recognition.

Stéphane Millet obtained his engineering diploma from ESIEA (Paris) and has been working for Dassault Aviation as a software engineer for 11 years. He began his career in charge of subcomponents of the RAFALE hybrid simulation and then supported the work done on simulation tools dedicated to operational studies. He now works in the advanced studies service where he develops and supports the different simulations needed to answer requests from different national and European research programs. These simulations are based upon the ATHENA platform that he is developing in parallel.

Philippe Morignot obtained a BSc in Ecole Centrale de Paris (Chatenay-Malabry, France) (1986). He then earned a master's in artificial intelligence at Paris 6 University. He obtained a PhD in artificial intelligence at Ecole Nationale Superieure des Telecommunications (Paris, France) (1991), entitled *Truth Criteria in Planning*. He then spent 5 years as a postdoctoral research fellow at Knowledge Systems Laboratory (Stanford University), LORIA (Nancy, France), Institute for Computer Science FORTH (Iraklio, Crete, Greece), and GMD (Bonn, Germany). He came back to France in 1997 and promotes artificial intelligence ideas and algorithms in parisian software houses.

Eva Onaindia is an associate professor of computer science at the Technical University of Valencia. She received her PhD in computer science from the same university (1997). She has worked on several projects in temporal models for knowledge-based systems, including the CEE ESPRIT project REAKT. She currently leads the group of planning and conducts research in temporal planning, development of techniques for integrating planning and scheduling, reactive planning, and planning under uncertainty. She has led national research projects (MCyT, MEC) as well as sat on various scientific committees in her field (IJCAI, ICAPS, ECAI, etc.) and recently served as PC vicechair of the Spanish Conference on AI (CAEPIA'05). She has published about 50 articles in specialized conferences and scientific journals related to topics of planning in AI.

Ioannis Partalas was born in Aiani-Kozanis, Greece, in 1980. He received a BSc in informatics from the University of Ioannina, Greece (April 2004), and an MSc in information systems from Aristotle University of Thessaloniki, Greece (September 2006). He is currently pursuing a PhD in the area of reinforcement learning under the supervision of Professor Ioannis Vlahavas at Aristotle University of Thessaloniki. His main interests include multiagent reinforcement learning, ensemble methods, and web crawling. He is a member of the Machine Learning and Knowledge Discovery Group (http://mlkd. csd.auth.gr) at the same institute.

Bruno Patin was born in 1961. He obtained his master's in theoretical physics from Paul Sabatier University (Toulouse) (1983) and his engineering diploma from ENSERG (Grenoble) (1986) and started at Dassault Aviation in 1987. He was in charge, for 10 years, of the Electromagnetic (RCS and Antenna) ground laboratory. Since 1998, he has worked on the high-level control algorithms for the UCAV and their applications to the civil field.

Gérald Petitjean is a senior optimization and software-engineering consultant at EURODECISION. He previously worked at AXLOG Ingénierie, participating in ARTEMIS project. He works on decision aiding systems and applications, using techniques from applied mathematics, operations research, combinatorial optimization, and artificial intelligence. He has designed and developed problem solving algorithms in the fields of autonomous vehicles, production planning, and scheduling, and railway transport.

Gauthier Pitois obtained a master's degree in theoretical and applied computer science in Le Havre University (2004). He specialized in artificial intelligence, then in multiagent systems and their suitability to complex distributed systems. More particularly, he was interested in multiagent systems related to bioinformatics. In 2005, he started to work at Axlog Ingénierie on autonomous aircraft systems participating in the Artemis project.

Jean-Clair Poncet was born in 1971. He obtained a high degree in artificial intelligence at the University Pierre et Marie Cury in Paris. He worked for a time at Biostat, a medical software company, and joined Axlog Engineering in 1998 as a software engineer. Between 2001 and 2006 he managed and worked on various projects related to autonomous systems, in space and aeronautics domains. Since December 2006 he has worked at Sophis Technology as a project manager in charge of software scalability and optimisation.

Kiruthika Ramanathan obtained her bachelor's degree in electrical and computer engineering at the National University of Singapore. She is currently working on her PhD in soft computing and is a research fellow at the Data Storage Institute, Singapore. Her research interests include artificial intelligence, neural networks, evolutionary algorithms, and cognitive computing.

Jing Sun received her PhD from University of Southern California (1989), and her BS and MS from University of Science and Technology of China (1982 and 1984, respectively). From 1989 until 1993, she was an assistant professor in the Electrical and Computer Engineering Department at Wayne State University. She joined Ford Research Laboratory in 1993 where she worked in the Powertrain Control Systems Department. After spending almost 10 years in the industry, she came back to academia and joined the faculty of the College of Engineering at University of Michigan (2003) as an associate professor. Her research interests include system and control theory and its applications to marine and automotive propulsion systems. She holds over 30 U.S. patents and has co-authored a textbook on robust adaptive control. She is an IEEE Fellow and one of the three recipients of the 2003 IEEE Control System Technology Award. She is also a subject editor for the *International Journal of Adaptive Control and Signal Processing*.

P. Vasant is a lecturer at University Teknologi Petronas in Malaysia. He graduated in 1986 from the University of Malaya in Kuala Lumpur, obtaining a BSc (Honours) in mathematics, and in 1988 obtained a diploma in English for Business from Cambridge Tutorial College, Cambridge, England. In the year 2002, he obtained his MSc in engineering mathematics (by research) from the School of Engineering & Information Technology of University of Malaysia Sabah, and currently he is pursuing a PhD at the University Putra Malaysia in Malaysia. He became senior lecturer of Engineering Mathematics in American Degree Program at Nilai International College, Malaysia. His main research interests are in the areas of optimization methods, applications to decision and soft computing, fuzzy optimization, computational intelligence, and industrial production planning. Vasant has published 40 over articles in national journals and international journals and book chapters, some of them under review, and more than 40 research papers in conference, seminar, and symposium proceedings. He has served on TC-9.3 of IFAC as a group initiator for Asia since September 2004. Currently he is a reviewer for reputed international journals and conference proceedings.

Index

A

action-value function 154
active mental model 116
alignment in communication 110, 118
a posteriori method 310
artificial agent 108
artificial agent, community 107
artificial intelligence (AI) 1, 2, 19, 21, 22, 63, 75,
    94, 102, 104, 105, 108, 166, 168, 176, 201,
    207, 329, 343, 344, 347, 351, 356
artificial neural networks 308
automated planning 151, 165, 358
automatically defined functions (ADF) 309

B

backjumping 63, 70, 71, 72, 73, 74, 90, 91
backmarking 63, 70, 72, 73, 74, 90, 91
backtracking (BT) 69, 70, 90, 91, 92
Bellman optimality equations 154
bodies of evidence (BOEs) 236, 237, 238, 241, 242,
    243, 244, 245, 246, 247, 248, 249
bottleneck problem 108
branch-and-bound (B&B) 98, 99, 100

C

classification and ranking belief simplex
 (CaRBS) 234, 235, 234, 235, 234, 235, 236, 249,
    235, 237, 238, 239, 240, 241, 243, 246, 247,
    249, 250
clustering, consensus 219, 229
clustering, recursive 217, 219, 222, 225, 226, 231
cluster partitions 217, 219, 226, 229, 230, 231, 232,
    353

co-occurrence 113
cognitive processes 112
coherence maximization 110
coherence relations 115
collaborative language 118
command and control (C2) center 2, 10, 18, 19
communication processes 107
components 115
compositionality 114
comprehension processes 118
computational linguistics 108, 113
computer-simulations 108
conceptual modelling 110
concern modifications 116
consistency 63, 67, 70, 73, 75, 76, 77, 78, 79, 80,
    81, 82, 83, 84, 85, 86, 87, 86, 87, 88, 89, 90,
    91, 92, 93, 94, 97, 102, 103, 104, 105, 330,
    338, 341, 345, 346, 349, 350, 352, 356
constituents 110
constrained optimisation problem 267, 269
constraint, definition of 64
constraint, satisfaction 63, 64, 65, 66, 74, 75, 88,
    89, 90, 94, 100, 101, 102, 103, 98, 103, 101,
    104, 105, 329, 330, 331, 335, 338, 339, 341,
    344, 345, 349, 350, 351, 353, 355
constraint network 111
constraint networking 124
constraint satisfaction 110, 121, 123, 127
constraint satisfaction problem (CSP) 63, 64, 65,
    73, 75, 76, 78, 79, 81, 83, 84, 85, 86, 87, 88,
    90, 96, 97, 98, 99, 101
constraint satisfaction problems (CSP) 23, 26, 41,
    42, 43, 46, 47, 50, 51, 56, 57, 60, 348
constraint satisfaction processes 110

construction 117
constructions-integration (CI) theory 115
context 115
CPT 26, 46, 50, 53, 54, 61
crossover 294, 295, 297, 298, 306

D

database layers, deliberative 1, 6, 7
database layers, reactive 1, 2, 5, 6, 7, 13, 18, 20, 330
data clustering 217, 218, 219, 220, 221, 222, 223, 224, 225, 226, 227, 228, 229, 230, 231, 232, 330, 331, 338, 342, 345, 348
data mining 218
decompositional rule extraction 310
Dempster-Shafer theory (DST) 234, 235, 236, 237
denotations 112
dialogical alignment 107, 118, 119
distance, Euclidean 267, 269, 272, 274, 275, 276, 278
distance, Manhattan 267, 269, 274, 278
distributed cognition 108, 110, 118
distributed interaction 118
distributed learning 109, 118
distribution 124
domain filtering 87, 102, 330
durative action 28, 36, 41
DYNA algorithm 162
dynamical systems 137, 138, 139, 145
dynamics 120, 121

E

elf-organization 130
empirical interpretation 114
encompassing social system 110
ensemble clustering 217, 219, 220, 231
enumeration 63, 101
epiphenomenal system 109
evolutionary algorithms 284, 285
evolutionary computing 284, 285, 306, 337
evolutionary higher order neurons (eHONs) 220, 221, 222, 223, 225, 228, 229, 230, 231
exact belief 236
exploration planning 156, 157, 165, 358

F

forward edge of battle area (FEBA) 3, 11, 18
four layer-model of language simulation 109
fuzzy constraints 130

fuzzy membership function 254, 263
fuzzy optimization 256, 264, 356
fuzzy parameters 256
fuzzy rules 124

G

genetic algorithms (GA) 289, 284, 307, 284, 287, 285, 286, 288, 285, 291, 289, 290, 293, 294, 295, 296, 297, 298, 299, 306, 307, 333, 340, 350, 353, 355
genetic programming 308
genetics 121
gent communication 109
global positioning system (GPS) 4
graphplan 59, 345
grounding problem 108, 113
group decision making 2

H

heuristic planning 36, 59, 341
heuristics 63, 65, 97, 98, 102, 103, 167, 170, 176, 177, 178, 186, 187, 188, 192, 208, 286, 307, 330, 335, 339, 346, 348
higher order neuron (HON) structure 219, 220, 222, 224, 228, 229, 230

I

implied optimization method 310
imputation 235, 246, 247
inductive algorithm 312
inductive learning 110, 112, 113
inductive logic programming (ILP) 166, 167, 171, 172, 173, 174, 175, 176, 177, 178, 179, 180, 181, 182, 183, 184, 185, 187, 188, 189, 191, 192, 193, 194, 195, 196, 197, 198, 199, 200, 201, 202, 203, 204, 206, 207, 208, 209, 210, 211, 212, 213, 216, 332, 334, 336, 337, 338, 340, 341, 344, 346, 347, 348, 349, 351, 352, 353, 354, 355, 357
inductive logic programming (ILP), descriptive 172, 173, 178, 179
inductive logic programming (ILP), predictive 172, 173, 174, 177, 178, 192, 216
inference operators 181, 184
inferrability 114
integration 117
interaction model 118
interlocutors 111
iterated learning model 108

K

kernel functions 139, 140, 145
knowledge 308
knowledge extraction 311
Koza, J. 309

L

language change 108
language evolution 107
language of thought 114
language simulations 110, 129
language system 107
latent semantic analysis (LSA) 113
law of polysemy 128
learning 115
learning machine (ML) 149
learning semantics 192
level of satisfaction 254, 257, 258, 259, 260, 261,
        262, 263, 264, 330
lexico-grammar 108
lexicon size 124
linear programming 137, 139, 140, 141, 146, 340
linear programming, support vector regression (LP-
        SVR) 139, 137, 141, 140, 141, 142, 143,
        144, 145
linguistic context 116
linguistic items 115
linguistic signs 107
logic programming 166, 167, 168, 171, 172, 181,
        182, 192, 198, 201, 203, 204, 205, 206, 207,
        208, 209, 210, 211, 212, 213, 329, 330, 331,
        333, 334, 335, 336, 337, 338, 340, 341, 342,
        343, 344, 345, 346, 347, 348, 350, 351, 352,
        353, 354, 357, 358
long term memory 116
look-ahead 92

M

machine learning 109, 113
machine learning perspective 166, 167, 171, 176,
        192, 200, 201, 202, 203, 204, 205, 206, 207,
        208, 209, 210, 211, 212, 331, 332, 333, 334,
        335, 336, 337, 338, 340, 343, 344, 345, 347,
        348, 350, 351, 352, 354, 355, 358
macroscopic order parameters 107
macroscopic units 111
Markov decision process (MDP) 153, 158, 159, 160
MATLAB® 257, 259
meaning 115

meaning constitution 107
Mediate learning 119
mission management system (MMS) 1, 2, 4, 10, 18
mission management system (MMS) architecture 1
mobile agents 5
model sparsity 137, 139, 145
multi-agent-based simulation 112
multi-agent modelling 107
multi-agent simulation model 124
multi-agent systems 108
mutation 285, 286, 290, 291, 294, 295

N

need of encoding 111
negative constraint 110
neural networks (NN) 217, 231, 232, 345, 357

O

objective function 235, 238, 239, 241, 243, 245,
        247, 249, 255, 257, 258, 259, 263, 267, 270,
        272, 274, 276, 278, 272, 274, 276, 278
optimal planners 53, 54
optimal solution 254, 256, 259, 260
optimization 110
order parameters 109, 111, 120, 121

P

parallel constraint satisfaction 110
parallel genetic algorithms 306, 307, 340, 350
partial-order causal-link (POCL) 23, 26, 30, 39, 40,
        41, 42, 44, 45, 43, 44, 45, 46, 49, 50, 51, 54,
        55, 56, 60, 350, 356
party puzzle 291
pedagogical rule extraction 310
planning-graph 23, 26, 30, 32, 35, 55
planning domain definition language (PDDL) 151
planning system 149, 151, 163
polylexy 124
polysemy 128
possibilistic linear programming (PLP) 255
preference function 268, 271, 273, 275, 277, 278,
        280, 282
preference ranking organization method for enrich-
        ment evaluation
(PROMETHEE) 266, 267, 268, 269, 270, 271, 275,
        276, 279, 280
premature convergence 284, 286, 287, 288, 289,
        294, 297, 298, 306
prepositional phrase (PP) attachment 116
principle of compositionality (CP) 114

prioritized sweeping 157, 158, 162, 163, 328, 335
procedural models of cognitive processes 115
processing agents 107
process models 112
productivity 114

Q

quadratic programming 137, 138, 139
quadratic programming support vector regression
    (QP-SVR) 137, 138, 139, 141, 142, 143,
    144, 145
quantification 110
quantitative linguistics 108

R

Ramsey numbers 284, 291, 292, 284, 306
Ramsey theory 284, 291, 307, 340
rank improvement 267, 269, 270, 272, 273, 274,
    277, 278, 279, 282
ranking 266, 267, 268, 269, 270, 271, 272, 275,
    279, 280
ranking, analysis 266
realizing 108
referential meaning 113
regularization 139, 140, 145, 146, 333, 351
reinforcement learning (RL) 152, 153, 155, 156,
    159, 160, 161, 162, 164, 351
relation 64
restriction 73, 75, 87
routinization 112, 115
rule extraction 310

S

S-curve membership function 255, 256, 263
schematic knowledge 116
schematization 115
Schnotz 117
search 63, 67, 68, 69, 72, 73, 74, 75, 79, 81, 87, 88,
    90, 91, 92, 93, 94, 95, 96, 97, 98, 100, 101,
    102, 103, 104, 105, 329, 338, 339, 340, 341,
    343, 346, 356, 357
search procedure 166, 167, 172, 167, 176, 177, 186,
    187, 188, 191, 192, 193, 195, 197
self-organization 107, 122
self-regulation 107
self organizing maps (SOMs) 218, 219, 221, 223,
    224, 225, 226, 228, 229, 230, 231
semantic diversification 127, 128
semantics 108
semantic similarity 113

semiotic 108
semiotic preference orde 124
sense relations 113
sign processing 108, 109
sign processing, systems 109
sign systems 107
simplex plot 235, 237, 238, 239, 242, 243, 244
simulated data 124
simulation 107
simulation model 107, 108, 109
simulation models of language evolution 120
simulation validity 107
single agents 112
small worlds 120
social networking 109, 120, 121, 122
soft constraints 110
speech community 121, 128
Stanford Research Institute planning system
    (STRIPS) 150, 151, 158, 159, 163
statistical moment 124
steady state 112
stratification 110
stratified constraint network 112
stratified constraint satisfaction network 107
structural meaning 113
structure modelling 124
suboptimal planners 53, 54, 55
support vector regression (SVR) 137, 140, 141,
    139, 138, 137, 138, 141, 139, 137, 142, 141,
    139, 141, 142, 143, 144, 145, 146, 352
suppression of enemy air defense (SEAD) mission
    2, 3, 17
synergetic linguistics 107, 110, 111
synergetic multi-agent simulation model 107, 124
synergetics 111
synonymy 128
syntactic dependency 115
syntactic patterns 115
syntax formation 108
synthesis 116
synthetic aperture radar (SAR) 4
systematically interrelated 112
systematicity 114
system components 111
systems identification 137, 139, 142, 143
system variables 107, 109

T

tectonics 120, 121
temporal planning 23, 25, 26, 28, 30, 32, 33, 34, 35,
    36, 37, 38, 39, 40, 41, 42, 44, 46, 51, 52, 54,

55, 56, 57, 58, 59, 60, 338, 339, 345, 350
text comprehension 123
text network 121, 122
text networking 121
TGP 26, 32, 34, 35, 36, 37, 44, 51
thematic knowledge 116
time series forecast 317
TPSYS 35, 45
trigonometric differential evolution (TDE) 266,
        267, 269, 270, 272, 273, 281, 266, 267, 268,
        269, 279, 281

U

unmanned combat air vehicles (UCAV) 1, 2, 3, 4, 5,
        8, 9, 10, 11, 12, 13, 14, 15, 16, 17, 18, 19
unsupervised learning 217, 219, 220, 222, 223, 229,
        230, 231
usage regularities 115

V

vagueness 254, 255, 258, 260, 261, 262, 263
validity 130
value, mass 236, 240
value, missing 235, 239, 246, 247, 248, 249, 250
version spaces 166, 167, 168, 170, 177

W

weak contextual hypothesis 113

Z

Zipf-like distributions 124
Zipfian perspective 124